LAWYER, SCHOLAR, TEACHER AND ACTIVIST
A *LIBER AMICORUM* IN HONOUR OF DEREK ROEBUCK

Also by Derek Roebuck
Published by HOLO Books: The Arbitration Press

Arbitration and Mediation in Seventeenth-Century England 2017
The Golden Age of Arbitration 2015
Mediation and Arbitration in the Middle Ages 2013
Disputes and Differences 2010
Early English Arbitration 2008
The Charitable Arbitrator 2002
Ancient Greek Arbitration 2001
A Miscellany of Disputes 2000

With Francis Calvert Boorman and Rhiannon Markless
English Arbitration and Mediation in the Long Eighteenth Century 2019

With Susanna Hoe
Women in Disputes 2018

With Bruno de Loynes de Fumichon
Roman Arbitration 2004

LAWYER, SCHOLAR, TEACHER AND ACTIVIST

A *LIBER AMICORUM* IN HONOUR OF DEREK ROEBUCK

EDITED BY
NEIL KAPLAN
ROBERT MORGAN

HOLO BOOKS
THE ARBITRATION PRESS
OXFORD
2021

First published 2021 by
HOLO Books: The Arbitration Press
Clarendon House
52 Cornmarket
Oxford OX1 3HJ

email: holobooks@yahoo.co.uk
www.holobooks.co.uk
and www.centralbooks.com

British Library Cataloguing in Publication Data
A catalogue record for this book is available from the British Library

ISBN 978-0-9572153-9-9

This book is printed on paper suitable for recycling and made from
fully managed and sustained forest sources. Logging, pulping and
manufacturing processes are expected to conform to the
environmental regulations of the country of origin.

Produced and typeset for HOLO Books: The Arbitration Press by
Stanford DTP Services, Northampton, England
Printed and bound by CPI Group (UK) Ltd

CONTENTS

PART FOUR:
SELECTED CHARTERED INSTITUTE OF ARBITRATORS
ROEBUCK LECTURES

PREFACE

It is an honour and a privilege for both of us to have edited and contributed to this *Liber Amicorum* for Derek Roebuck.

It is a strong indication that Derek was a very special man that so many of his friends and colleagues contributed so willingly and efficiently to this book. They were all placed under time constraints because we wanted to publish the book on or around 27 April 2021, the first anniversary of Derek's death.

Both of us knew Derek from his Hong Kong days (1987–1997). Once you met him, you knew that he was special. Bonds of friendship and fellowship with him were strong. He was personally kind and caring and his knowledge was phenomenal – indeed, polymathic. This much is clear from the contribution by Sir Stephen Sedley, who writes:

> Until Derek Roebuck set about it, nobody had attempted a panoptic history of arbitration. ...
>
> In the unsurprising absence of much other hard evidence of earlier dispute resolution, at least before the 11th century, Professor Roebuck's method is an engaging series of polymathic raids into the territory of geographers, ethnographers, linguists, lawyers, historians and archaeologists, fetching back the kind of data that reminds one there is no such thing as useless information, and assembling it into tentative shapes.

No less cogently, Lord Neuberger reminds us in his contribution that, as in his professional and academic lives, Derek was as interested in people as in processes:

> ... [L]ike all good writing which focuses on a limited aspect of life in the past, his books cast a fascinating shaft of light onto the way people lived over the period which he covered.

Derek's interest in people embraced both regular folk and the personalities involved in dispute resolution. As to the latter, see the contribution by Francis

Calvert Boorman and Rhiannon Markless and also the volume Derek co-authored with his wife and fellow historian, Susanna Hoe.[1]

We shall say no more here, because all of us have expressed our feelings for Derek in our own contributions, both scholarly and tributary. *Res ipsa loquitur.*

This book has four constituent parts.

First, there are several *In Memoriam* contributions from friends and colleagues, containing revealing and occasionally surprising reminiscences which help to build up a fully rounded picture of their subject. Also included in this section is the obituary that appeared in *Asian Dispute Review*, the journal published by the Hong Kong International Arbitration Centre, and (with slight differences in wording) in *Arbitration*, the Journal of the Chartered Institute of Arbitrators, as well as Susanna Hoe's touching and revealing contribution on her life with Derek, 'A Room Shared: My Late Husband as Feminist'.

Secondly, there are scholarly articles written by Derek himself. One of these is his introductory chapter, 'A short history of arbitration' (his first on the subject) which he kindly wrote for Kaplan, Spruce and Moser's *Hong Kong and China Arbitration: Cases and Materials*, published in 1994.[2] It is important to note that Derek wrote this chapter under heavy time constraints and without access to the materials to which he later had access. This chapter sparked his interest in the subject and the rest is truly history.

Also included in this section are two articles. The first (first published in 1998) concerns Captain Charles Elliot RN, who took Hong Kong for the British in 1841 and became its first administrator, evoking the response from Foreign Secretary Lord Palmerston, 'But it is a rock with barely a house on it'. Wouldn't it be nice to bring him back to show him what has been built upon that rock! The second of Derek's articles is much more recent (2016), on mediation and arbitration in colonial America.

The main section contains a number of scholarly contributions on a wide range of subjects. The roll call of topics and their contributors is as follows: (1) the rule of law (Sir Geoffrey Bindman); (2) aspects of historical arbitration, embracing (i) personalities in early modern English arbitration (Francis Calvert Boorman and Rhiannon Markless), (ii) the *Alabama* Arbitration 1871–1872 (Bruno de Loynes de Fumichon), (iii) Rembrandt and arbitration (Neil Kaplan), (iv) lessons from history for modern arbitration (William W Park), (v) a review of Derek's 2008 volume, *Early English Arbitration* (Sir Stephen Sedley), and (vi) who might attend a medieval arbitration between feuding lords and in what capacity (David J Seipp); (3) aspects of modern

1. Susanna Hoe and Derek Roebuck, *Women in Disputes: A History of European Women in Mediation and Arbitration* (2018, Oxford: HOLO Books: The Arbitration Press and The Women's History Press).
2. Hong Kong: Butterworths Asia/LexisNexis Hong Kong.

international arbitration, embracing (i) the right to arbitrate (Gary B Born), (ii) similarities and differences between the judicial and arbitral roles (Lord Neuberger), and (iii) transparency and efficiency in international commercial arbitration (Janet Walker and Doug Jones); (4) the binding effect of unilateral undertakings by States in investor-State dispute settlement (Jan Paulsson); (5) nurturing professionalism through clinical legal education (Mary Gold and Neil Gold); (6) transnational and comparative commercial law (Sir Roy Goode); (7) law modernisation in South-East Asia (Mary E Hiscock); (8) the role of modern mediation in resolving conflicts (Sir Bernard Rix); (9) a book review of Derek's final volume (co-written with Francis Calvert Boorman and Rhiannon Markless), *English Arbitration and Mediation in the Long Eighteenth Century* (Karyl Nairn); and (10) a literature review of Derek's histories (Robert Morgan).

The final section contains several of the Roebuck Lectures. After his many years as Editor of *Arbitration*, the Chartered Institute kindly inaugurated an annual lecture in Derek's honour. We have included not only his Inaugural Lecture but also those given by Cherie Blair QC, Stavros Brekoulakis (the current Editor-in-Chief of *Arbitration*), former Justice of Appeal Dame Elizabeth Gloster and Stephen Ruttle QC. All of the chosen lectures have the common denominator of having addressed themes particularly close to Derek's heart and interest, such as ethics, diversity, human rights and the historical development of dispute resolution processes.

No single volume can hope to do justice to Derek, who published fifty learned and authoritative books on a variety of subjects. He also introduced the world to a highly acclaimed series of volumes on the international history of arbitration and mediation which showed us that there is nothing new under the sun; they are widely cited in leading lectures and in legal and dispute resolution journals worldwide.[3] The titles in the history series are depicted in the image on the front cover. They are also listed on the reverse of the half-title page of this volume.

Derek influenced and touched the lives and careers of so many that this book cannot and does not intend to say it all. All of his friends, colleagues and admirers know that they have lost a dear friend and mentor. We hope that the sight of this volume on their bookshelves and, better still, its practical utility, will keep his memory alive and his erudition forever available.

Neil Kaplan CBE, QC
Robert Morgan JP, Barrister
Contributing Editors

---

3. See, for example, David W Rivkin, 'The Impact of International Arbitration on the Rule of Law: The 2012 Clayton Utz/University of Sydney International Arbitration Lecture' (2013) 29(3) *Arbitration International* 327–360.

ACKNOWLEDGEMENTS

We are exceedingly grateful to all contributors for making a sterling effort to contribute – in some cases, by providing new and thoughtful insights – which we hope will lead to the book being of wide and considerable interest. Much to our delight, which Derek would no doubt have shared, getting so many learned and eminent colleagues together so quickly was anything but akin to herding cats!

The Contributing Editors also wish to express their deepest gratitude for the similarly sterling efforts of several people without whose guidance and assistance this *Liber Amicorum* would not have seen the light of day.

Susanna Hoe, who throughout has provided us with information, guidance and support, as well as with contacts. As the now sole proprietor of our publisher HOLO Books: The Arbitration Press, she has given us wise counsel on publishing issues. As Derek's wife, she has provided invaluable comments on and insights to the draft contributions.

Susan Faircloth, who has edited so much of Derek's work down the years, in Hong Kong for OUP, for *Arbitration* and as Editorial Consultant to HOLO Books: The Arbitration Press. Susan has been nothing short of incredible in ensuring that editing and a myriad other tasks have been completed on time and, so far as possible, in accordance with HOLO Books' house style. Where contributions have been published previously, she has ensured that all permissions have been sought and obtained.

Dave Stanford has been part of the publication team of HOLO Books since its founding in 1999, initially responsible for typesetting. In recent years, the death of the original 'project manager' has meant increased responsibilities which have been so important in this publication, including the design of the cover.

A new member of the team for this publication is Max Bramley who, with great patience, produced the photograph of the image for the front cover.

Neil Kaplan's Hong Kong Associate, Joris Bertrand, has given him invaluable help in keeping up with the flow of emails and communicating with authors.

Finally, our thanks are also due to our wives Su Kaplan and Suzan Hellings-Morgan for their assistance, patience and support during the sometimes frantic editorial and production processes!

PART ONE

IN MEMORIAM

[Editorial note: These *In Memoriam* contributions to Derek begin with Susanna Hoe's moving tribute. This is followed by tributes from a number of friends and colleagues. These are in order of the authors' first meeting Derek.]

A ROOM SHARED: MY LATE HUSBAND AS FEMINIST

Susanna Hoe

I have this vague memory, reinforced by attempts to retrieve it, of discussing Virginia Woolf's 1928 essay 'A Room of One's Own'[1] with Derek beside the willow-fringed lake in the grounds of Peking University where we were staying.[2] Had one of us just read it? Perhaps I had earlier in the day, sitting by the lake while Derek was at his conference. I cannot think he had persevered with it because she takes what he would call 'a very long run up' to get to the point – a practice he favoured only when he was bowling.

There is a coincidence concerning the location in which this discussion took place: Virginia Woolf did her best mulling over her thesis – 'A woman must have money and a room of her own if she is to write fiction' – under a willow by the river in Oxford which, as it happens, is the city in which I am developing my reply – 'A Room Shared', underpinned by my writing partnership with my husband over our 41 years together.

I should perhaps say in parenthesis that I am not suggesting that Virginia Woolf's thesis should be ignored, though she did not have to heed her own advice: she tells us that her aunt's legacy 'unveiled the sky to me',[3] allowing her the luxury of being able to explore the fate of those less fortunate, both her contemporaries and historically, in her own room. Nor am I ignoring the fact that very many women today manage to write fiction, or anything else, with or without money or a room of their own. I merely suggest that it is possible, perhaps as a development of the work feminists and other women have done over the century since that essay appeared, to rejoice in the possibility of a room shared.

1. Virginia Woolf, *A Room of One's Own and Other Essays* (London: The Folio Society, 2000), originally published in 1929. It started as two lectures, then embellished, given at the women's colleges, Girton and Newnham, Cambridge, in 1928.
2. While much else concerning China's capital now calls it Beijing, the University has stuck to the earlier name. Its short name is, however, Beida.
3. Woolf, *ibid*, p 49.

Ironically, with the arrival of Covid-19, still very prevalent globally as I write, the advances made by women have, during lockdown, been noticeably set back: there is evidence to suggest that they take on rather more of the home management, childcare and home schooling than their partner. And I suspect that others in the family have priority in the available working space. More long term, there is evidence that women are bearing the economic brunt of the pandemic: mothers are more likely than fathers to lose their jobs.[4]

I should also say that what I write will be treating 'A Room Shared' as both literal, Derek and I writing together in one room, and even writing two books together, and metaphorical. I'm concerned, though, that the metaphorical, that is, including our personal relationship, our marriage, should not descend into over-sharing. But it is out of the personal that the literal was able to develop. I am aware that newspaper and magazine articles discussing committed relationships claim the importance of couples also having separate lives – interests and friends. That is not something that Derek and I felt the need of; indeed, I have been gratified by the many communications of condolence that have praised our obvious closeness. Typical are these:

> You had one of the best marriages I know. It always gave me a sudden rush of happiness when I thought of you both and how lucky you were to have met each other … We had both been rather awed by you two for your close and happy daily sharing.

And: 'What a fabulous partnership you made, a man both distinguished and made a joyous equal partnership with a woman.'[5] I chose those two because, as well as how moving they are, and the solace they brought me, they mention the words 'sharing' and 'equal partnership'.

If what follows seems to be as much about me as it is about Derek, that is because he, and our relationship, have enabled and encouraged me to flourish in a way that would otherwise have been unlikely. This was an inherent aspect of Derek's feminism. As well as highlighting his feminism, in what follows I also touch on his other attributes spelt out in the title of this *Liber Amicorum* – 'Lawyer, Scholar, Teacher and Activist' – which are further discussed in this *In Memoriam* section.

When Derek and I met in 1979, I had been a feminist since 1971 when I was invited by the Foreign Press Association to take part in a debate on

---

4. According to research from the Institute of Fiscal Studies and others, as reported in *The Observer*, 11 October 2020.

5. It was hard to choose; I have not felt able to leave this one out: 'I never told you, but I often thought that your couple was for me an example: it was nice to see you together, always taking care of one another. Your couple was intensely close, and that was very moving.'

the pros and cons of the subject which was then called Women's Liberation or Women's Lib. This followed the publication of my novel *Lady in the Chamber*[6] and a rather nice review in *Punch* by MP and writer of political novels Maurice Edelman.[7] The novel itself drew on my several years working in the House of Commons.

For the debate, I was to be junior to MP Joyce Butler in favour of women's liberation and, against, Sally Oppenheim MP and her junior (I ask her to forgive me for forgetting her name).[8] To be honest, I had not realised that by featuring a woman MP recently elected in a by election at the centre of my novel I displayed a feminist sensibility. But the preparation for the debate, and the debate itself, made it clear that I was, indeed, a feminist, and a proud one ever since. So, when I met Derek, one of his important attributes was that he was also a feminist, and had been since about the time that I realised I was.

Derek had arrived at the University of Tasmania's Law School at the end of 1968, at a time when, in the early 1970s, Tasmania was to become a hotbed of feminism. In her entry on feminism in *The Companion to Tasmanian History*,[9] Kate Murphy writes,

> Tasmanian feminists were active in the powerful so called 'second wave' of feminism. The Hobart Women's Action Group, founded in 1972, which had a counterpart in Launceston, was influential in the early Women's Liberation movement ...

One of Derek's first tasks as a burgeoning feminist was to help a lesbian couple with the surname they should adopt. Obviously, it could not be the father's name of either, and even their mothers' names were those of their fathers. Derek came up with the name 'Egg', which met with approval.

With apologies to the Governor of Tasmania, and still professor in the University Law School, Kate Warner, I would like to pre-empt, and cannibalise from, her contribution to this book:

> In the late 1960s and early 1970s, women had begun to enrol in law degrees in greater numbers. My year was the first to enrol more than one woman and, from then on, the proportion of women law students grew exponentially. This was a trend Derek supported. He strongly

6. Susanna Hoe, *Lady in the Chamber* (London: Collins, 1971).
7. Maurice Edelman, 1911–1975, MP 1945–1975, author of, among others, *Who Goes Home?* (1953).
8. Joyce Butler 1910–1992, MP, 1955–1979; Sally Oppenheim, 1928–, MP 1970–1987; now Baroness.
9. Alison Alexander, ed., *The Companion to Tasmanian History* (Hobart: Centre for Tasmanian Historical Studies, 2005).

encouraged the female students to take leadership roles in the Tasmanian University Law Society (TULS), participate in mooting competitions and embark on academic careers.

An extension of Derek's feminism was his involvement with the Women's International League for Peace and Freedom. While men cannot be members of the still-flourishing organisation, they could be supporters, and that Derek became. The organisation's added attraction was its internationality and its commitment to peace. It had been founded in 1915 specifically to campaign against the First World War.

These aspects, internationality and peace, were to send Derek's politics leftwards, a direction which had started while he was teaching at the Victoria University of Wellington in New Zealand. In the preface to an unpublished manuscript Derek has left, entitled, 'Rants: Occasional Outbursts 1951-2009', he wrote, 'I am surprised and a bit sad that nothing has survived from my other political activities: against the death penalty, the Vietnam War, colonialism in South Africa and as a feminist.'

From being a solicitor in his home town of Stalybridge, Derek had moved, in 1962, to New Zealand to teach law. There he became involved in the anti-apartheid movement and how it affected sport, particularly when the all-white Springbok team toured in 1965. This development in his thinking meant that, because of Australia's involvement in the Vietnam War, he became a leading figure in Tasmania's anti-war activities; indeed, he became both famous and notorious, once nearly arrested for sedition. One of the kinder epithets used for him was 'the Red Dean'. Lawyer, and later judge, Pierre Slicer, a comrade of Derek's, goes into more detail in his contribution to this book, as well as into their joint work on behalf of Aboriginal Tasmanians.

To be anti-war was not new to Derek; it dates from at least when he was 16 in the Classical Sixth at Manchester Grammar School when the class was asked to write a poem illustrating onomatopoeia about the dropping of the bomb on Hiroshima. The penultimate stanza of his 16-stanza poem reads:

With a merry throbbing, bobbing
Flies the homebound terror-plane,
Leaving widows, fathers sobbing
For the children death is robbing
From them, to be seen again
Never.

At the same time as his anti-Vietnam War activities, Derek had become a Tasmanian member of Amnesty International. How he came to the notice of Amnesty's International Secretariat may have been because he had been invited to be a member of a 47-strong international commission of enquiry on mercenaries and attended the trial held in Angola of mercenary soldiers who had been employed to overthrow the government and later suffered the death penalty. The death penalty was one of Amnesty's then three concerns.[10] However he was spotted, he became head-hunted to become head of Amnesty's Research Department.

His appointment was not universally well received: he was vilified in some parts of the international press for his politics, and the harm it would do to Amnesty International which prided itself on concentrating on certain narrowly defined human rights abuses, taking money from no government and owing no allegiance to any ideology. Even some members of the organisation whose preferred work was on behalf of Prisoners of Conscience in the Soviet Union spoke out against him. That is why, when newly appointed Derek, a key speaker, arrived late to the AGM of Amnesty's French Section in March 1979, I went up and said hello to him during the break for dinner. With his alleged reputation, based on a total misapprehension of reality, and as the only two English people in a potentially hostile forum, it seemed only right.

As a member of staff, Campaign Co-ordinator in the British Section since the day Amnesty won the Nobel Peace Prize in October 1977, I should not have been at the AGM at all. The day before I flew out to Nantes, the member of the British Section's executive committee who was slated to attend was too ill to do so. The director's secretary appeared in the doorway of my office and said, 'You speak French, don't you?' I agreed with some diffidence and was told which flight I was to catch. And, although I usually say that was when I first met Derek, it was not strictly true. When he took up his position in mid-January 1979, he was brought upstairs to the British Section to be introduced to us. Derek's reply when I said hello was 'Let's go and have dinner.'

It transpired that the reason for his late arrival was that floods along the banks of the Seine made the roads impassable. On his return as Head of Research from a meeting of the African Union in Addis Ababa, he had stayed the previous night with Wilfred and Vessa Burchett who lived just outside Paris. Wilfred had not only been at the trial in Angola as a journalist, but he and Derek, as a result of their meeting there, had jointly

10. Amnesty International's mandate has now spread much wider than those three concerns: against the death penalty, against torture, and working on behalf of 'Prisoners of Conscience' – an expansion, many issues of which are covered by other organisations, we felt was liable to make Amnesty less effective. We remained ordinary members, not to suggest approval of the changes, but because it was Amnesty that put human rights, and the violation of them, on the map.

written *Whores of War: Mercenaries Today*.[11] The ground for Derek's and
my 41-year partnership was prepared that evening, and cemented when we
both knew more about each other's beliefs, values, political proclivities,
and obsession with words.

At the time Derek and I met, I was in the process of buying a flat within
walking distance of Amnesty International, the International Secretariat
and the British Section, then just off the Strand. To do so would not have
been possible without my raised consciousness of my rights as a woman.
I had been saving the £2,000 then required by my chosen building society
to obtain a mortgage, and had succeeded even more than was necessary,
having been paid to leave the flat I then occupied. But, because I was
a woman, the building society demurred. Suffice it to say, they were
persuaded to change their mind.

This flat was to be vital in my forthcoming relationship with Derek
because it was a symbol of Virginia Woolf's precept, that a woman should
have money to write, or do whatever else she wanted. I was never to be
financially dependent; indeed, when Derek joined me in the flat, because
of the way his marriage broke up he came with only a suitcase. I not only
had a car as well but, because the British Section had a trade unionist on its
staff, who had negotiated on our behalf, I also earned £40 more a year than
Derek. Whatever I did in the future, wherever in the world we lived, that
flat, that capital, and the income it was able to generate when let, meant we
were an economic partnership, and I was free to study and write, though
I was not to need a room of my own because of the other aspects of our
marriage and partnership. Thenceforward, too, I was to be in charge of our
finances, particularly during our last 20 years together.

My only practical stipulations in our relationship were that I would
not iron shirts, nor type manuscripts. For the three years we lived in the
London flat, we cooked and cleaned together. The latter activity was not as
well performed as it might have been. When Derek's boss, the Secretary
General of the International Secretariat, came to dinner with his wife
and two young sons, the boys were left on our bed to amuse themselves.
This they did by rolling into a large, dirty pink ball the fluff accumulated
between the bed and the wall. We preferred to spend Saturdays trailing
round second-hand bookshops throughout London.

There was a nice link between me, the flat and Virginia Woolf's
membership of the Bloomsbury Group. The bush telegraph worked quickly
when Derek moved in with me: what emerged was the gossip that Derek

11. Wilfred Burchett and Derek Roebuck, *The Whores of War: Mercenaries Today* (London:
Penguin Books, 1977).

was 'Shacked up with a lady novelist in Bloomsbury'. I had had one more novel published since my first, as well as a biography.[12]

During those three years, I left Amnesty International, apart from staying as the volunteer anti-death penalty coordinator, and started a degree as a mature student at the nearby London School of Economics (LSE). Having been brought up traditionally for a girl at a time when only two girls in my class in Kenya went on to university, I had not done so earlier. Instead I had been sent for a year to a Swiss finishing school to improve my French, and to the University for Foreigners in Perugia for six months to learn Italian. I do not regret that: those languages have facilitated some of my writing. In 1980, not only was university education free, but then, still unmarried, I was paid a grant as well; this continued until we married. Neither of us had much time then for creative writing: I wrote rather unoriginal essays for my various courses, and had a room of my own during the day in which to write them; Derek was occupied with running his department and editing Amnesty's annual report. For both activities mutual moral support was called upon, and we could still walk or cycle to work and have lunch together. One of my first-year courses – anthropology – was to stand me in good stead in the next phase of our life.

We married in August 1981 at the Camden Registry Office, where we did not exchange wedding rings. When we went to get the marriage licence at the Town Hall, I insisted on paying for it; only, I didn't have enough cash on me and Derek had to chip in. On the day itself, at the reception at the Law Society, Mary Hiscock, friend and writing partner of some years who, with her husband David Allan, had travelled from Australia, gave the 'best person's' speech, while I, instead of Derek, responded.[13] That may be unexceptional today, but I'm not sure that it was then.

The reason for our marriage was so that I could accompany Derek to take up his new appointment in the law school of the University of Papua New Guinea, starting in June 1982. Only a spouse qualified for the necessary visa. One of the attractions of the island chain country not far from the northern tip of Australia, was that it was much nearer Derek's three children, the younger two, who had come to London on Derek's Amnesty appointment, were by then back in Hobart with their older brother and mother. With our move across the world they could come up to us and we could see them in Hobart more easily.[14] Derek and I had agreed not to

12. Susanna Hoe, *God Save the Tsar, A Novel* (London: Michael Joseph and New York: St Martin's Press, 1978); *The Man Who Gave His Company Away: A Biography of Ernest Bader, Founder of the Scott Bader Commonwealth* (London: Heinemann, 1978).
13. Mary's contribution details the trio's writing partnership.
14. Derek had three children with his first wife: Derek John, now a consultant and professor in Perth, Western Australia; Lucy, a GP married to a GP with two children studying medicine, and Paul, trained as a lawyer. Paul was to be particularly taken with Papua New Guinea and its artefacts; Dr Derek was to do his medical elective there. We were to enjoy the company

have children and it is difficult to know how different our lives might have been if we had not made that decision; would a room shared have been more difficult? Plenty of women today (pre-Covid-19 at least) manage to combine children and writing though, traditionally, many women writers, including Virginia Woolf, were without.

Derek had been to Papua New Guinea before, though only for a conference and, having spent 10 years in Australia, he knew a bit about it. I knew nothing, hardly even where it was. But the adventure sounded wonderful, and so it proved to be; we spent five years there, Derek renewing his contract after three years. There can be no other place that can expand the mind, horizons and understanding of the world more than this former UN protectorate under Australian administration, independent since 1975. Derek, soon professor and Dean, had a most original law school to run, and such a wealth of material to write up.

He wrote two books about Papua New Guinean law and one about Pacific contract law. Two of the books were written with two co-authors, one a Papua New Guinean colleague, the other Indian/Australian.[15] He also published for the first time a manuscript that he had earlier sketched out, *The Background of the Common Law*, a slim volume that students world-wide still find useful.[16] For once I renounced my stricture never to type a manuscript for Derek. The team had to pull together, as did those responsible for running the newly established University of Papua New Guinea Press. Once Derek didn't have a secretary, following our return to England, he was perfectly capable of doing his own typing, slow, but annoyingly accurate compared with my fast inaccuracy.

Typing that manuscript, rather than just reading it, confirmed what I had realised from the start. Quite apart from his 10 years' more experience of life than me, he was much cleverer, however generous he always was in praising my intellect. He was also much better educated: from a working class background and a little local school, though with a good reputation, he had gained a scholarship to Manchester Grammar School where, in spite of his attraction to the English stream, he was deemed too intelligent not to be in Classics. This allowed him to gain a place at Hertford College,

of Derek John during a stint he spent in a Hong Kong hospital, and the many years he was a consultant at London's Great Ormond Street Hospital for Children, and Paul as he transferred to law in Manchester, having previously studied architecture in Tasmania.

15. Derek Roebuck, DK Srivastava and John Nonggorr, *The Context of Contract in Papua New Guinea* (Port Moresby: The University of Papua New Guinea Press, 1984); Derek Roebuck, *The Modern Law: an introduction to the study of law in Papua New Guinea* (Port Moresby: UPNG Printery, 1986); Derek Roebuck, DK Srivastava and John Nonggorr, *Pacific Contract Law: a source book for the South Pacific* (Port Moresby: UPNG Press, 1986).

16. Derek Roebuck, *The Background of the Common Law* (Port Moresby: UPNG Press, 1983); (Hong Kong: Oxford University Press 2nd impression 1988); (Hong Kong: OUP, 2nd edn, 1990).

Oxford, and set him on his distinguished future career path. With every piece of his writing I was to read in the future, because he trusted my judgement and valued my approval, and every lecture I heard him give, I was to be brought up anew by how well his mind was ordered.

Derek's book on Pacific law was for the Pacific islanders for whom he set up distance learning; he would also spend a couple of weeks a year with the students in both Vanuatu and Fiji. I would hardly have been left behind; indeed, living on a Pacific island enabled us also to travel for pleasure, or on the way home on leave, even more widely in the Pacific – The Solomon Islands, Tonga, Western Samoa, the Cook Islands, Tahiti, Easter Island – stretching our minds still further, and allowing me to squirrel away women's lore to enrich future writing.

As well as his teaching and administration, Derek also practised as a barrister. His first case comprised two women who had hurled abuse at each other over the use, or misuse, of a stretch of their local stream. It was a criminal case and Derek, having done two years of Classics at Oxford, and then only two years of law, had not done criminal law. He learnt fast as a wily and locally experienced Australian barrister ran rings around him, but only once. When Derek appeared in court, I would not have missed going with him. His appearance in a magistrate's court in the Highlands, defending a young woman called Lucy who had replied '*appy noon*' to the greeting of a woman prisoner behind a wire fence, was the emotional highlight of that part of his career. He carried out the defence before a woman magistrate in the country's primary lingua franca *Tok Pisin*, before a packed courtroom hanging on his every word; what is more, he was successful. To see his newly minted barrister's mind at work was a joy. Royale Thompson describes another, equally fascinating, but very different case in her contribution to this book.

Although the LSE had given me two years' leave of absence with an option to return to finish my degree, I decided instead to do so at the University of Papua New Guinea, based in the history department. It was run by our large but soft-voiced Tongan neighbour on campus, Sione Latukefu, who introduced us to growing vegetables in that clime, in the most unlikely garden that went with the house from the University's stock. We were helped, or put upon, by Karman, one of his train of gardeners.

Sione soon licked my essay writing into shape – my published books he discounted; it was the bad habits I had acquired at the LSE that provoked a little lecture. In due course, in 1984, I won for him the University's Pacific History Prize, as well as the Tangi Hiroa Pacific History Prize of the Pacific Universities. In neither instance would he let me write about women. Together Derek and I did the linguistics course. When I had gained my degree I was appointed part-time tutor in the Department of Anthropology and Sociology. I was also commissioned to write a weekly column – 'International Bookshelf' – for *The Times* of Papua New Guinea, in which I recommended novels available in local libraries.

To get my degree I had to pass in a subject called 'Say it with figures' (otherwise known as 'Say it with fingers'). If it hadn't been for Derek being able to tell me that there were misprints in the textbook, there would have been a lot more rants of frustration ringing through the house. I had a room of my own, the only room with air conditioning, but I usually wrote at the dining room table because from there I could talk through the hatch to Margaret, our *haus meri*, working in the kitchen. She taught me *Tok Pisin*; I taught her to read and write in *Tok Pisin*, and some English. When I could persuade her to have lunch with us, she loved to make clear how much better Derek's *Tok Pisin* was than mine. In addition to language and teasing interchange, she kept me up to date on her life, watching carefully through the hatch to see that I had got it all down in my diary.

As a result of the interchange between house and garden, I later published *At Home in Paradise* which I dedicated to Margaret.[17] A manuscript – provisionally entitled 'More At Home in Paradise' – about Margaret's life more generally, including her 'too much husbands', as one of them ranted – still waits for me to get round to licking it into shape for publication. I've been held up by not being able to contact Margaret, as I was able to do with the first volume, to have it read to her, and discussed with her, for her approval. The story includes her extended family, her sister, her brother, the children of one of her 'husband's' other wives, which were also hers. Lending her sister money, looking after Margaret's, ministering to their various injuries and minor illnesses, or driving them to hospital when it was more serious, were part of our responsibility.

But my support for Margaret, and Derek's and my encouragement and legal advice enabling her finally to buy a home of her own, was only part of my involvement with women's issues, particularly the rights, or lack of them, of *haus meris*. I did learn, though, when I approached the authorities, that an expatriate was not the person to take that on. Some of the *haus meris* also came to me for help in finding them jobs on campus. I suppose you could say that our house was a women's refuge, though only for Margaret when she needed to escape from one or other of her two 'husbands'. At least once Derek had to drive out at night – never entirely safe, and increasingly less so during our stay – to pick her up from where she had escaped to. She arrived at our house cowed in a way most unlike her, with some wound, usually on her face.

Money, hers earned as a *haus meri* for several houses, was often the centre of the row that often led to violence fuelled by alcohol. With a mug

17. Susanna Hoe, *At Home in Paradise: A House and Garden in Papua New Guinea* (Oxford: HOLO Books: The Women's History Press, 2003).

of hot milk and a shortbread or two she soon revived. That night she slept in a proper bed with sheets that she had laundered, instead of on the floor. Though we did buy her a mattress when, after some years, responding to a question about her bad back, she told me that she usually slept straight on the floor. Usually she sofa-surfed, without the sofa, at the abode of a *wantok*. This could be an extended family member, or someone from the same place. She once said something to me that I particularly valued: almost in so many words she told me that I had taught her the importance of perseverance.

The University's hours were 8 to 4. Because we lived on campus, Derek could come home for lunch and at 4 pm we would go to the nearby Cathay Club, play tennis with friends, then swim in the pool and often eat afterwards in the Chinese restaurant. Often at the weekend, Derek's cricket team, with me as scorer, would compete against, for example, that of the (local) *The Times*. I came from a family with no interest in sport but, under Derek's enthusiasm and commitment, I took to it with ease, though only ever in a limited and partisan way. On Saturday morning, instead of trailing round London's second-hand bookshops, we haunted the market for fruit and vegetables we couldn't grow ourselves, or outlets of any sort where we might find artefacts to add to our collection. But this sybaritic life of heart, mind and body had to end. Five years was deemed a good time to stop taking essential anti-malaria tablets without them causing long-lasting adverse effects. Our last day before we flew to Hong Kong was horrible as we helped Margaret and family take many of the contents of our house, including our double mattress, to her brand new one, and said goodbye.

Our life in Papua New Guinea was unbelievably privileged compared with that of Margaret and most of her compatriots but, compared to that we were to lead in Hong Kong, it was rather rough and ready.

Derek had been appointed to set up a second law school at City Polytechnic, a year later City University, to join that of the long-established University of Hong Kong. A more than adequate salary and a spacious, subsidised flat in a luxury complex overlooking the harbour, with its own tennis courts, swimming pool, and paid annual leave home to England, went with the job. There was not only one writing room to share, but two, the study where we had two desks facing each other, and a work room where my electronic typewriter and filing cabinets and metal shelves lived (that was in addition to a spare bedroom). There was also a cheerless hutch beyond the kitchen designed for a live-in Filipina 'amah' which we did not use. We did, however, employ a part-time Chinese cleaner, two during our 10 years, about whom, inevitably, I was to write.[18]

18. Danny with whom I soon fell out, and Pet who sustained us for more than nine years and allowed me many insights into her culture, as Margaret had done in Papua New Guinea. She

Derek had a support staff of young women whom he mentored, encouraging them to progress in the University's administration; they have remained friends. He did the same with his teaching colleagues: he was determined that as well as high-class teaching in the law school, it should produce quality research and writing. To that end, he instituted Wednesdays for that. Thus we came, finally, to have a literal room shared, and worked in at the same time most Wednesdays and at weekends. I was to have three books published during the next 10 years, as well as to take back to England the material for two more, and two manuscripts, one of them jointly written with Derek. He was to publish six books, usually in collaboration with colleagues, and to be general editor of six volumes concerning Hong Kong law in collaboration with Peking University and published by them, as well as being fully responsible for one of them. That was in addition to articles and conference papers.[19]

The Peking University connection starts this account: that was to be the first of many visits together to Beijing. Both of us had been there before we met: Derek, on a delegation to and from North Korea in 1971; me in 1976, thanks to Ernest Bader whose biography I had written. Because he felt that he and his wife, Dora, were by then too old, he paid for me to go on a SACU (Society for Anglo-Chinese Understanding) tour of China. But now Derek's work was to take us to China probably four times a year. There he gave lectures both at Beida and Renda (People's University) and in due course Renda was to make him a visiting professor. He was also invited more than once to a university in Shanghai. His subject was usually English Common Law and Hong Kong law, given in English which students understood. I remember that one of those lectures was to magistrates of whom at least one was a ballerina. Not only did he give lectures, but the visits were often diplomatic and cemented the ties that were to lead not just to the joint volumes on Hong Kong law, but an attempt at mutual understanding. For me it was an eagerly seized opportunity to talk to and write about women, pieces which I plan one day will form part of a book.

As a result of my Hong Kong research and writing, I did establish a personal work connection in China. That led to my being invited in 1995 to give a paper – 'After Reading Xiao Hong: The Experience and Expression of Xiao Hong and Agnes Smedley' – at the 1st International Symposium, Women and Literature, at Peking University. Derek doubtless combined that visit with his own work there. The fine Harbin-born writer Xiao Hong had not only lived for a while in Hong Kong, but had died there during the

---

was quite clear that her visit to the temple to pray for Derek when he was seriously ill was the reason he pulled through.

19. It would be unwieldy to list all publications here; they are detailed in CVs on our website www.holobooks.co.uk. Derek published in all 50 monographs, often with other authors, as well as innumerable articles.

war, on 22 January 1942, aged 30.[20] And there was more than a tangential connection between her and American journalist, writer and China hand Agnes Smedley through their lives and writing. Only once, in January 1993, because it was impractical for Derek to accompany me, did I go to China alone, to attend a symposium in Shanghai in honour of the centenary of Agnes Smedley's birth the previous year. It was attended by many who had known her, and whom Derek and I had come to know. Afterwards we watched the plaque unveiled on the house in which she had lived. And once, in September 1995, when Derek was convalescing from a serious illness, he stayed mostly in our room at the Friendship Hotel, Beijing, while I attended the UN's Fourth World Conference on Women – a most extraordinary experience where, among 17,000 delegates, I bumped into two women, an English woman attending from Pakistan who had been one of the four of us starting a new course at the LSE, the other one-time Minister for Justice in Papua New Guinea.

Just as living in Papua New Guinea for five years had enabled us to visit other countries in the Pacific, so 10 years in Hong Kong did the same regarding Asia. Thus we went to India, Singapore, Sri Lanka, Thailand,[21] Vietnam, Cambodia, Laos, Xinjiang, and Tibet. The Sri Lanka visit, organised by a Sri Lankan colleague of Derek's, was for him to play in a series of cricket matches. When those were over, a minibus was hired to take me to visit places where European women had lived or travelled. However much trips abroad were organised round Derek's work, I either researched or wrote about women as a result.

And, while these visits were often part of Derek's work – conferences, lectures or diplomatic visits to law ministries – our extraordinary visit to Tibet was my venture, as a member of a party of journalist members of the Hong Kong Foreign Correspondents Club (FCC). We were ostensibly to cover the first beauty contest there, the first time that foreign journalists were allowed to report from Tibet for some years.[22] We were also able, supervised, of course, to see out and about around Lhasa, experiences seared on our memories, as well as captured on photographs now, with those from other places, adorning one of our Oxford walls. There was

20. The Beida symposium paper and other writing about Xiao Hong and Agnes Smedley were published in Susanna Hoe, *Chinese Footprints: Exploring Women's History in China, Hong Kong and Macao* (Hong Kong: Roundhouse Publications (Asia), 1996).
21. During a visit to Thailand, Derek gave evidence in a commercial case that required knowledge of Thai law. Because he was co-author (with Mary Hiscock and David Allan) of a pertinent account of it, the judge, knowing of that work, accepted and appreciated the intervention of a foreign scholar, in spite of the other party's attempt to rubbish it.
22. I wrote up the account of that Tibet visit, including what was more of a fashion show than a beauty contest, and it, too, will form a chapter, together with photographs, in a future book. It will also contain pieces on the Agnes Smedley Symposium and the UN World Conference on Women, and about women in other places outside Hong Kong that we visited.

one problem: Derek found the 12,000 feet difficult to cope with, while I, having been at school at 7,000, had no trouble.

How had we come to be members of that FCC party? The journalist, Margaret Kitchen, who had commissioned my 'International Bookshelf' in Papua New Guinea, had by that time moved back to England, where she edited the women's page of the *Liverpool Post and Echo*. She had long since been a friend, rather than a work contact, so I naturally wrote her a newsy letter soon after our arrival in Hong Kong. That led to being commissioned to write a monthly 'Letter from Hong Kong'.[23] This, in turn, qualified me to become an overseas member of the FCC, with Derek as a spouse member. The club turned out to be one of the mainstays of our 10 years. We often met there for lunch, Derek taking the tube (Mass Transit Railway or MTR) from City University in Kowloon, me a taxi or minibus from home; fish and chips in newspaper with friends made a jolly supper. All the time there was a tremendous buzz around us in the bar/restaurant, with celebrity foreign correspondents such as Clare Hollingworth holding a court which we joined, always in the same corner.[24]

There was only one problem with the FCC. I was the member but Derek, a mere spouse, was always greeted as Mr Hoe. This amused him; indeed, he enjoyed it, particularly when we visited in later years. But for me it assumed that I was a Mrs Hoe, rather than Ms Hoe married to Professor Roebuck! Hardly a room shared as equals! (Derek always cut out my too many exclamation marks!)

For the first few months of our Hong Kong stay, I felt a little at sea: Papua New Guinea had left its mark on me, and Hong Kong was so different. While Derek knew exactly who he was, and what he was doing, I didn't seem to have my own niche and was, indeed, simply an over-privileged wife. All that changed following our first leave to England where a friend gave me the contact details of Susan Faircloth, then commissioning editor at Oxford University Press, Hong Kong. Within only a week or so following my proposal, Susan had commissioned me to write *The Private Life of Old Hong Kong*.[25] She was also to commission an OUP reprint of Derek's *The Background of the Common Law* (1988), and a second edition (1990).

The research for my book led me to make contacts, many of whom became friends, and some of them sisters. Derek already had a connection

---

23. I continued to write these 'letters' even after the size of the *Post* had to be reduced during the recession of the nineties, and they were in due course published as *Watching the Flag Come Down: An Englishwoman in Hong Kong 1987-1997*, Oxford, HOLO Books: The Women's History Press, 2007. I have sometimes shortened this title elsewhere as 'Flag'.
24. There is a piece about Clare in 'Flag'.
25. Susanna Hoe, *The Private Life of Old Hong Kong: Western Women in the British Colony 1841-1941*, Hong Kong, Oxford University Press, 1st printing of several, 1991.

with the University of Hong Kong, having been invited to be a member of an over-seeing committee of their Law Faculty; now, on the publication of my book in 1991, I could apply, and be accepted, to be a research associate (later an honorary fellow) of the Centre for Asian Studies attached to the University. For both of us the rival university connection was useful, not only for the library and other facilities but also, with our ear to the ground there, we enjoyed the ingenious productions put on there by a local opera company.[26] The rivalry was, perhaps, most manifest when Derek's cricket team played theirs. This time I was able to fully enjoy watching and overhearing useful opposition remarks, rather than scoring. When Derek joined the Hong Kong Cricket Club there was a memorable match when the Law Society team beat the barristers. Playing for a cricket club team gave us the opportunity of a trip on SS *Canberra* – usually the perk of top civil servants returning home – to play in Singapore.

I much appreciated the intellectual connections I established, but it was the sisterhood that came to be the central feature of my life and, to a lesser but important extent, of Derek's. In 1991 a diverse group of seven of us set up AWARE (Association of Women for Action and Research). This, in time, became part of a coalition of women activists campaigning for a Hong Kong Women's Commission, and an extension of CEDAW to Hong Kong.[27] On International Women's Day, 8 March 1992, all those groups coalesced into a day of disparate activities, with all of us attending as many of them as we could. AWARE's contribution was a coalition gathering with one of its features Ethel Smyth's suffragette anthem 'March of the Women', re-titled 'A Coalition Now', with appropriate words and stickers. The day ended with a march on Government House. On such occasions Derek joined us; he was seen as an honorary member of AWARE.

As well as pamphlets, letters to the governor, and members of Legco (the Legislative Council), appearances on the radio and liaison with other women's groups, AWARE had other projects, one of which enabled me to spread my wings in a new direction.

We established a connection with the Women's Centre which catered for the needs and aspirations of Chinese women, most of them housewives living within its neighbourhood in Kowloon. The director of the Women's

26. While in some ways Hong Kong might have seemed a far away place where international culture was concerned, in fact, because it was on the way to touring places such as Australia, we were extraordinarily well provided with the best in the world as they passed through, whether it was Kiri te Kanawa or Pavarotti, Wynton Marsarlis or top pianists or guitarists, the Royal Shakespeare Company, or the English Ballet; and the Hong Kong Academy for Performing Arts was able to hire top notch performers and conductors. In neighbouring Portuguese Macao, where we often spent the weekend, their annual music festival featured not only opera but also recitals by such divas as Christa Ludwig.
27. CEDAW – Convention on the Elimination of All Forms of Discrimination Against Women.

Centre, social worker Linda Wong, when we approached her to ask what help we could give, said perhaps the most immediate need was to provide an English teacher. While most Hong Kong Chinese spoke English to a greater or lesser extent – after all, it had been a British colony since 1842, and teaching was in English – there were many women, particularly housewives, who did not and who suffered disadvantages, including lack of self-esteem, because of it.

The other six members of AWARE held university positions; I was the only one who could use my time as I chose, so I volunteered. To that end, I took a TEFL (Teaching English as a Foreign Language) course. I disliked it almost as much as I had 'Say it with Fingers' in Papua New Guinea. Although it was useful to have the qualification, apart from the laminated pictures from magazines that we were introduced to, I used none of the methods I'd been taught when teaching the Classmates, as we came to call my housewife students. And from the beginning I banned the term housewives: they rejoiced in calling themselves 'household managers'.

My six years of teaching the Classmates, some of whom stayed with me as long as that, while others dropped in and dropped out, were the most important aspects of my multi-tasking AWARE work. It also taught me something about myself: I had always assumed that, unlike Derek, I was a very impatient person who would never have the patience to teach. Instead, I found within myself unexpected reserves of patience, and that teaching became something special. That specialness was to last on later return visits to Hong Kong when the Classmates and I would meet for lunch. As well as my own learning and memories and an obvious rising in self-esteem for the classmates, which learning of rather more than English engendered, I also had an inspiration that was to further facilitate our endeavours.

I recognised the need for a textbook for the Classmates. So I approached educated and often well-known Chinese women (and one English woman long politically active in Hong Kong) and asked each of them to write a story, a chapter, in English. Those varied entries I put into the order of difficulty of comprehension, each followed by a list of questions, and with an introduction, 'Notes on How to Use the Stories for Classwork'. Initially, the stories were photocopies handed out to the classmates one by one; eventually they were published as *Stories for Eva: A Reader for Chinese Women Learning English*.[28] I was a little taken aback in the first lesson after publication and a heart-warming launch, to see that, instead of using

---

28. Susanna Hoe, ed., *Stories for Eva: A Reader for Chinese Women Learning English* (Hong Kong: The Hong Kong Language Fund, 1997). The book was dedicated to the Classmates 'with love and thanks'. The perfect front cover image was donated to the project by the well-known Hong Kong artist Nancy Chu Woo. The back cover features a photograph of the Classmates. The book was accompanied by a tape of the stories.

the book, many of the Classmates were still using their photocopies. I was sternly informed that the book was far too precious to use for the lesson.

Eva was a Classmate for whom, when each told the class about their background, in English, of course, I introduced the word, 'dogsbody', a sobriquet which highly intelligent Eva would roll around her tongue with relish. Sitting next to me at one of our Classmates' end of term lunches, she told me about the university education of her brothers, and what was expected of her. As I was to write in 1993, 'I gently drew from her an ambition: to use the English classes, which she had quite recently joined, to further her education.'[29] She was to stay with the class until I left Hong Kong, and on my later visits, it was she who rounded up the Classmates. One is not supposed to have favourites, but the title of the book was not surprising.

The success in garnering students for the English classes at the Women's Centre spawned other learning and activity groups – Mandarin, in preparation for the 1997 Handover to China, health and nutrition, and even a working party on CEDAW – but most important where Derek's involvement was concerned was the need at the Centre for a Women's Free Legal Advice Clinic. Julie Macfarlane, an AWARE member and colleague of Derek's, was the obvious one of the sisters to volunteer. In less than a year 180 women passed through the clinic, always with a social worker on hand. So popular did it become that Julie had to ask for other volunteers who would give up a Tuesday evening to listen and advise. Not surprisingly, Derek responded immediately.

In October 1992, Lavender Patten was invited to visit the Women's Centre. She came not so much as the Governor's wife but as a family lawyer interested, in particular, in the Legal Clinic. We hoped that her visit would help publicise it, so that more women would know about it, and more lawyers would volunteer to help. We even hoped that her interest might generate funds so that a part-time co-ordinator could be hired. She was always fair with me – even allowing me to quote her on the cover of *Watching the Flag Come Down* – in spite of the stream of pressing letters I wrote to her husband concerning women's demands.

It was another of Derek's fortés to listen and advise. To that end, he also put himself forward as duty lawyer in the magistrates' courts. Thus I came to learn, as I accompanied him, that I was his 'devil'. However clever and silver-tongued he was, I was able to help. My help ranged from retrieving his mislaid briefcase to over-hearing the comments of relatives sitting near me, or making a judgement from their demeanour, a twisted wedding ring,

29. This account, called 'Stories for Eva', was later published in *Flag*, p 99.

say. Based on this Derek might be able to add to his defence or change its direction.[30]

There was one other specific case, unconnected with the Women's Centre, which meant a visit to the Whitehead Detention Centre for so-called 'Vietnamese Boat People'. It would have been improper for me to write it up at the time, but I did so later and that, too, was published in *Watching the Flag Come Down*. Perhaps on Julie Macfarlane's advice, because she was in the process of adopting two young Vietnamese women so that they could go to Canada with her, Derek was approached, along with other lawyers, by 'concerned people'. The lawyers were asked to double-check the screening process, to reassess the case of someone already screened out, and whose appeal had also been turned down. If appropriate, an application would then be made to the United Nations High Commission for Refugees to exercise its Mandate. The internationally empowered body was a last resort. That visit to Whitehead, with its bright silver corrugated-iron 'fence' glinting threateningly in the sun, remained long on our minds, and not in a good way. Ms Thanh (not her real name) in freshly laundered jeans and top, told an overwhelmingly convincing, but hitherto repudiated, story. The notes I took enabled Derek to compile his report. We never knew what happened to Ms Thanh.

In addition, there were the demonstrations we went on together, quite apart from those generated by women's call for a commission. These started in the weeks leading up to the events in Tiananmen Square of 4 June 1989. At the beginning there were 5,000 of us, among whom was a good cohort of students from Derek's university, particularly the Law School, sitting listening to speeches to mark the important 4 May 1919 Movement.[31] The speeches included a call for democracy, freedom and the expression of solidarity with the Beijing students. A few days later it was 50,000 of us doing the 'demonstration shuffle'; the next time it was 500,000. Derek and I were on the plane, flying home on leave, during the night of 4 June, and learned what had happened from the BBC when we got to the flat that morning. We returned to a different but no less determined Hong Kong. Demonstrations thereafter, particularly on the anniversary, grew in size.

The next demos were against the 1991 First Gulf War. Starting in February and continuing for three weeks, 100 or so of us would gather near the War Memorial in Central Hong Kong. It was before the setting up of AWARE, though organised by Maria Jaschok who was to be an AWARE sister. We would place candles at the foot of the memorial until the police ordered the local council to rope it off with appropriate notices to deter us, as well as visiting one of the organisers, a single mother, at her home one

---

30. I wrote up several of these occasions, also published in *Flag*.
31. The May Fourth Movement was an anti-imperialist, cultural and political movement which grew out of student protests in Peking, as it was then, on that date.

evening to try and warn her off. After that, we would lean over the rope to place the candles as near as we could stretch to the memorial. Our anthems were the two Lennon/Ono lines 'All we are saying is give peace a chance' and Lennon's 'Imagine'. The only problem with that was the ending about 'A brotherhood of man'; I forget what we changed it to.

Another demo, in the lead-up to Chinese New Year in February 1993, was in support of the two-week strike of hundreds of Cathay Pacific cabin staff, mostly young women, and from 10 different Asian countries, whose terms and conditions were unacceptable. The first night they slept outside Government House in the freezing cold, knowing that the Pattens were flying out on holiday with the airline. Derek and I, being made of softer stuff, only spent hours there during the length of the strike, together with other members of the Women's Coalition. Eventually it became a tent city. It was so cold at night that in the rather good photograph I took of Derek with three of the strikers, the young women have red noses. In spite of that, they look radiant.[32] That photograph still proudly adorns a wall of our Oxford house.

Inevitably, those 10 years had to end, but before they did, Derek got hooked on the history of arbitration, as well as setting up an Arbitration course at City University, and he and I wrote the bulk of a book together. Arbitration and that joint book presaged our life in our subsequent 23 years in Oxford leading up to Derek's death on 27 April 2020.

In my research for *The Private Life of Old Hong Kong*, I was intrigued by the fact that the man most responsible for the taking of Hong Kong, Captain Charles Elliot, was accompanied from the beginning of his time in China waters, in 1834, by his wife, Clara. I felt sure that there must be more about her than the couple of passing remarks in what had, until then, been written about that period. My hunt was successful when a cache of letters from both husband and wife to his sister in England emerged. It was the purest chance that a bibliographical entry, not even about China, referred to the papers in the National Library of Scotland of the family of which I knew Charles was a member. The letters, of which a forever-appreciated Librarian sent me photocopies, formed the basis of *The Taking of Hong Kong: Charles and Clara Elliot in China Waters*.[33]

Although I did all but one piece of the research and all the writing, apart from the writing up of that piece of research, it was essential to me that we be named as joint authors. There were three reasons: first, it has always rankled with me when male writers end their acknowledgements with an

32. The reasons for the strike, its course and its outcome are told in fuller detail, as are many other Hong Kong events sketched above, in *Flag*.

33. Susanna Hoe and Derek Roebuck, *The Taking of Hong Kong: Charles and Clara Elliot in China Waters* (London: Curzon Press, 1999 (hb)); Hong Kong: Hong Kong University Press, 2009 (pb)).

encomium to their wives for having made the book possible, often when they have done a vast amount of donkey work on the book, hunting down material, typing, indexing, etc. Second, Charles and Clara Elliots' writing was very difficult to read, especially his which was almost illegible, as even his contemporaries noted. I left a lot of blank spaces in my first, second and third transcriptions. Derek, with his long experience of reading students' handwriting, filled in nearly all the blanks; without that, there wouldn't have been a book because extensive quotations from the letters were integral to the story. And last, something in a letter from Charles, hinted at arbitration. Settling down in Hong Kong's public record office, Derek ploughed through reams of copied reports from Charles to the Colonial Office in London. Among them he found a long, fully developed plan by Charles for introducing arbitration into the disputes of the European merchants trading in China waters. Having included a distillation of it in the book, Derek was later able to spin more than one article.[34]

The preface of the book when published was to end:

We are an English wife and husband team writing as the colony of Hong Kong returns to Chinese sovereignty after more than 150 years of British rule. We have our own views on colonialism, the trading in opium, war, looting and other issues of moment. They undoubtedly form a subtext to this account. One of us usually concentrates on the history and contemporary issues of women, including the place of Clara Elliot in the history of Hong Kong; the other is a legal scholar, writing now a general history of arbitration which includes Charles Elliot's initiatives. We have lived in and written about Hong Kong for ten years; like the Elliots we have learnt lessons here about true and false. The Elliots left as the colony was born, we are leaving as it comes to an end.

We left Hong Kong on 8 July 1997, a few days after the Handover. Those last few days were full of extraordinary events, some of them accompanied by non-stop rain. But the most indelible memory is of the farewell party I threw for the Classmates at the FCC. The club had a separate glassed-off veranda attached to the bar/restaurant, suitable for parties, and that is where ours took place. The usually semi-demure Classmates became what I can only call rowdy, bemusing the 'head waiter', Simon, who had looked after us and our well-behaved guests for 10 years. The most joyous part of the event was the Classmates' reaction to Derek's presence, and our relationship about which they had learnt a bit in class. By then our cargo

34. The articles are included in Derek Roebuck, *Disputes and Differences: Comparisons in Law, Language and History* (Oxford: HOLO Books: The Arbitration Press, 2010). Derek left a half-completed manuscript of subsequent articles which I hope to be able to complete as 'More Disputes and Differences'.

had already been shipped to England, so when they presented me with a huge silk painting of peonies rolled up in a long fat carton that had to be carried on the plane, my pleasure was just a little tempered until we hung it on our bedroom wall in Oxford.

We settled in the house in Oxford which we had bought during a sabbatical there in 1993. We turned the so-called 'master bedroom' into the Library in which we established two desks facing each other and separate areas of the room with stands for our computers. Soon the walls were lined with books as, when we had fully unpacked, were the walls of most of the rest of the house. The walls from the front door to the sitting-room were covered with Papua New Guinea and Pacific islands artefacts and books. As well as Chinese books, the sitting-room housed Chinese pictures, furniture and artefacts. Eventually the loft was converted into an attic workroom and repository for accumulating research papers, and thank goodness for a garage which could take not only a car but box files of material and boxes of books. At last we had a proper shared room in which we worked together most of seven days a week.

The only house rules were that long telephone calls should be made and taken elsewhere, and it made sense to alert the other when 'creating' was about to take place, so that there should be no disturbance. The disturbance might come from me calling out, 'How do you spell such and such?' Derek's spelling was totally reliable; mine isn't. Or, 'I can't think of the word I want, it means such and such'; or, 'What does this Latin term mean?' Derek's might be a question concerning the function of his computer, or 'What should I get from the shops this morning?' No writing of any length ever left the house without the other reading it and, where necessary, suggesting changes. Even important emails – where tone and content had to be just right – were approved before 'send' was pressed. The approval of the other, always expressed, was good for us.

We had very different styles: when we first met, Derek's sentences were rather Tacitian, mine rather over-extended; over the years subtle changes came about. We were both wedded to the rhythm and music of a sentence; for Derek it came spontaneously; for me it required endless polishing, often helped by his suggestions. We had different ways of writing a book: Derek would immediately write when he came across something interesting or important; then he would piece everything together. I would make myself do all the research first, and draw up a chronology before settling down to write. One aspect we were agreed upon: truth is paramount; you never force a jigsaw piece in where it doesn't fit.

But our first task was to get a publisher for *The Taking of Hong Kong* which proved remarkably and misleadingly easy. The acceptance letter from the editor at Curzon Press was one to treasure. Before we left Hong Kong, Derek had been beguiled into writing a historical introduction to the book on Hong Kong arbitration by a close friend and international arbitrator, Neil Kaplan. Now Derek began to think seriously about writing an extended history of arbitration, perhaps one volume. In the meantime he compiled what became *A Miscellany of Disputes*, and contacted a possible publisher for his proposed history. Also before leaving Hong Kong, I had begun to research and write what became *Women at the Siege, Peking 1900*. All seemed set in our writing world. But, as so often happens, the best laid plans ... First I had a heart-stoppingly negative reader's report about *Siege*, and Curzon Press went stone cold.[35] Then Derek heard nothing back about his arbitration history plans.

I can see us quite clearly sitting at the kitchen table early in November 1999 wondering what we could, and should, do. It was urgent that I find a publisher for *Siege* because I'd set my heart on it being published on the centenary of the beginning of the siege a few months away. I had approached other publishers following Curzon's rejection, and received negative responses: the manuscript was, admittedly, rather long and the publishing schedule was unrealistic for a mainstream publisher. What we decided to do was set up our own publishing house, dating it to when we thought appropriate, 5 November. So we did: HOLO Books, with two impressive imprints – The Arbitration Press and The Women's History Press. Our funny name is often queried, disparaged even, but it is the first two letters of the surnames of us both in Chinese (*Lo dap lap* and *Ho siu sam*). The capital letters act as our logo. In retrospect, it is strange that we didn't make any connection with Virginia and Leonard Woolf's setting up of the Hogarth Press in 1917. I'm glad we didn't: it might seem presumptuous.

We were lucky with tips we received on how to establish ourselves and function, and with the responses to our project when we approached the recommendations. As far as I remember, the train of acceptance was sparked by help from a long-standing friend, Mary Jay, who had been running the African Books Collective for some time. Soon, a contact of hers, the late Ray Addicott, became what we always called our Project Manager though he produced books for many other publishers, and our distributors were Central Books under whose umbrella sheltered a host of small, independent publishers. There was a lot to learn and doing so was a distraction from writing. But, looking back over 20 years, it was worth it. We were free: we could publish books exactly the way we wanted them,

---

35. My humiliation over that reader's report was to be tempered by a later letter from a friend who had been connected to the subsequent life of the book. She wrote, ' — confessed that he had written the Curzon "appraisal" and immediately said that he thought it was very rich in source material (this was after publication). He was rather shame-faced and ... I gave him a bad time. I didn't report it all to you because what was done was done AND he had clearly revised his opinion and felt rather bad'.

including length, when we wanted them to appear, and at a price we felt our market for each imprint could afford. I was still a bit traumatised by Heinemann making me cut 10,000 words from my Ernest Bader biography 20 years earlier; that was now erased. First off HOLO Books' stocks was *A Miscellany of Disputes*, and *Women at the Siege*, thanks to Ray, was published on the right June 2000 date. Without Ray, his firmness and patience, we could never have managed to publish any of our books. And we often said to each other, what would we have done if we hadn't set up HOLO Books? We drank to it every Guy Fawkes day.

The freedom we created for ourselves fitted in well with my watchword, that systems are there to be beaten, and Derek's 'Manifesto', as he called the poem of which this is the first of four verses:

Pricks are to be kicked against
Boats are to be rocked
Wind is to be whistled into
God is to be mocked.

I tended to do most of the running of HOLO Books because Derek, as well as writing, also provided, at least for a year or two, legal opinions for a Hong Kong firm, and, for 10 years, from 2000 to 2010, he was Editor of *Arbitration*, the journal of the Chartered Institute of Arbitrators.[36] He also became attached to the Institute of Advanced Legal Studies (IALS) of London University as a Senior Associate Research Fellow; this carried with it responsibilities such as supervising PhD students with topics connected to arbitration and, with his books and articles, adding to the institute's essential profile. These diversions often meant trips to London for Derek, giving me the opportunity to do research in the British Library, and us ending the day at the opera. They had to run in tandem with tending HOLO Books; indeed, some of the London visits were to launch Derek's books at the IALS, and one of mine – *Travels in Tandem* in the chambers of the late and generous international arbitrator Arthur Marriott.

Our demonstrating days were not over: in London we shuffled with an estimated 1.5 million others on 15 February 2003 against the Iraq War; and on 21 January 2017, the eve of Donald Trump's Inauguration, I walked with 100,000 other women from the United States embassy to Trafalgar Square, Derek at a window in Pall Mall waving to me with a red bandana as I passed below. I was active, until Derek became too unwell for me to leave him, in Oxford Labour Women; he often said that I did the politics for us both.

36. When he retired as Editor, Derek became Editor Emeritus and the Roebuck Lecture, with him giving the first, was established. I don't know which of us was more proud.

When 'project manager' Ray died after steering us through many of our publications, Dave Stanford, to whom he had turned for design and typesetting, took over much of Ray's other production roles, but we needed a new editor. Susan Faircloth, who had been our commissioning editor at OUP in Hong Kong had, back in England, set up as a freelance editor. Derek had turned to her with gratitude when the minutiae of editing *Arbitration* was encroaching too much on his writing, and now we turned to her for HOLO Books with even more gratitude. That remains the team, together with the same printers for our publications.

At the beginning we published a couple of books for a legal colleague of Derek's, distributed the book of a woman friend, and distributed left-over copies of my *Chinese Footprints* and the volumes published by Peking University Press of which Derek had been general editor. I was even rash enough to commission a couple of titles in the series I set up, but had very quickly to de-commission them, and had to turn down the manuscript of a friend, the contents of which would have fitted nicely. I had to learn my capacity and the calls on it not only to write, but also to organise publication, publicity, and sales and oversee HOLO Books' website from which we hoped to sell (www.holobooks.co.uk). Because we have been so small and independent, we have never been profit-making; nor even broken even. Derek's volumes have depended for publication on either the generosity of subscribers or that of particular benefactors who had faith in his work. My titles have inevitably often had to borrow from us. At least we learnt quickly to have small print runs, even though that increased unit cost. Storage at Central Books had to be paid for, and our storage capacity at home was limited. Trying to sell remainders is soulless.

Somehow from 2000 to 2019, Derek and I between us managed to write and publish through HOLO Books 20 titles, 11 by Derek, nine by me. It was soon clear to Derek that his history of arbitration and mediation was going to stretch to more than one volume, and so it proved. His last published (5 November 2019), *English Mediation and Arbitration in the Long Eighteenth Century*, was written with two wonderful co-authors, Francis Calvert Boorman and Rhiannon Markless, who hope to continue Derek's work into the nineteenth century. He was not well enough to travel up to London for the launch, nor was he well enough for me to leave him to go, but Rhiannon's husband, Robert, took over the task of book-selling. When Derek died, he left a half-completed manuscript of his relevant articles published in various journals since the publication in 2010 of *Disputes and Differences*, which was based on those until 2009. I hope to complete it for him with the title 'More Disputes and Differences'.

The Women's History Press series I have mentioned is 'Of Islands and Women', in which 'Sardinia: Women, History Books and Places' is to be the fifth, following the publication of *Madeira*, *Crete*, *Tasmania* and

Malta. A bit like Derek, I had planned to write one volume incorporating chapters I had written and would write about various different countries. But one evening, during a recital at the Wigmore Hall, I mused that when people travel it is often to one place, and would they want chapters in one book about many disparate places? But there had to be a limit to the scope of books about one place – why not islands? The title of the series is a riposte to H E Maude's *Of Islands & Men: Studies in Pacific History* (Melbourne: Oxford University Press, 1968). They started off as what I called 'livrets' – pocket-sized volumes for the traveller. But over time, particularly with the development of the internet, and my experience, they have substantially expanded.

It is easy to say that neither Derek nor I could have written our various books without the other, and certainly we made sure that the finished product from the pen of each of us was as good as we could both make it. But in the case of my series, I needed Derek to sacrifice holidays in order to visit all parts of particular islands for my research. In Madeira, where we went following my treatment for breast cancer, Derek literally had to half carry me from the British cemetery to our hotel when I lost all strength. He used to joke about being dragged round cemeteries on various islands. In Crete, he drove us up some hair-raising mountain roads.[37] In later times, when he apologised for my 'having to care for him', I would remind him of how he nursed me through my cancer treatment, and ran the household, earning the sobriquet Woolly Cat (*Chatelaine*).

Islands were not our only travel: once a year, on the anniversary of living together, we went to Paris. This often combined pleasure, such as opera, with work. Derek's second volume, *Roman Arbitration*, was written with the French scholar Bruno de Loynes de Fumichon. Early work meetings turned into friendship meals. Derek's work came to the attention of Charles Jarrosson, editor of *Revue de l'Arbitrage*, who invited him to write an article on English arbitration history. Not only were Derek's books always generously reviewed in the journal, but Charles also became a friend, as is clear from his contribution to this book. In Paris we would trail round the second-hand bookshops and in one we found easily the most expensive present I ever bought Derek.[38]

37. As well as that series, I brought up to date an earlier completed manuscript which I had withdrawn some years before from a difficult publisher. I never liked the old title, but did the new, *Travels in Tandem: the Writing of Women and Men Who Travelled Together* (Oxford: HOLO Books: The Women's History Press, 2012). And I was pleased with the cover image of Florence and Samuel Baker riding camels in tandem with hers in front. The other post-Hong Kong book published by HOLO Books was *Flag*.

38. My present which I think gave him most pleasure was for Christmas 2019 – our last together – the discrete shelf of his arbitration/mediation titles featured on the cover of this book.

It is beside me as I write,[39] and was to form the basis of his volume *The Charitable Arbitrator: How to Mediate and Arbitrate in Louis XIV's France* (2002). It contains a background introduction by Derek, his translation of it from old French, and a facsimile of the first edition of 1666. How Derek managed the translation is a bit of a mystery; I don't remember particularly helping him with it. It always surprised him how he was able to do his own translations from Ancient Greek and Latin; he hadn't been the most assiduous student, at least at Oxford, where sport sometimes took precedence. Language comprehension was another of his fortés: he read a PhD in Catalan for *Roman Arbitration*, and translated from Portuguese to help me with *Madeira*. For *Early English Arbitration*, he took an online course in Anglo-Saxon.

Our second book written together was *Women in Disputes: A History of European Women in Mediation and Arbitration* (2018). Unlike the first, it was very much a joint venture. The preface begins:

> In this book two ways of writing of the past meet and mesh. One of us has written on mediation and arbitration for many years, the other on women's history. Because we have worked in the same room during that time, reading and commenting upon everything the other has written, we have influenced each other's content, so that the dispute resolution histories have included women and the women's history have, where practical, included dispute resolution. Then came the time to take that further. This is the result.

I must credit Derek with the idea; indeed, at first I demurred because it was going to drag me away from 'Sardinia' for which I was deep in research. But I have never regretted giving in. Our history writing was different, not only because Derek dealt with a period, and I with an island from pre-history to 1945. He drew on cases of dispute resolution arising from various courts and drawn from various reports and other sources. I write stories about the lives of individual women, chronologically throughout the centuries, in order to paint a whole picture. I was for ever asking him, when he read out to me some titbit he had found for one of his volumes, 'But what about his wife?' Or, when a woman was involved in a case, 'But what else do you know about her?' I would then go on the internet to prove my point. Now was our chance to incorporate both these aspects. The obvious place to start was with all the women mentioned in Derek's histories, and then to build on their stories and finally to add the myriad women involved in all sorts of dispute resolution who then demanded inclusion. We came across the term 'Peaceweavers' which

---

39. *L'Arbitre Charitable*; subtitled in Derek's translation as *To Prevent Suits and Disputes, or at least to Finish them Quickly, without Trouble and Cost*, Paris, 1666.

really took our fancy, and we dedicated the book to them. That book, as it turns out, becomes a monument to our partnership, our room shared, just as HOLO Books is also, in its own way; both imprints published it.[40]

Women in Disputes finished, it was back to 'Sardinia', while Derek tinkered with increasingly less strength with the articles for 'More Disputes and Differences'. He had just enough strength to read my draft chapters 1–12, and waited with apparent eagerness for me to hurry up with 13 and 14. I kept saying to him, 'When I've finished "Sardinia", I'll help you with "More Disputes"'. But neither the reading of my last two chapters, nor me helping him with his articles was to be. I much regret that my chapters have not had his eagle eye and sharp intellect upon them, nor indeed has this piece. Quite apart from anything else, those two chapters are rather up the street of our interests and experience; I think he would have particularly enjoyed them. He had just enough strength, too, and will, to struggle down to have lunch in the garden which he loved so much, on a lovely sunny April Good Friday. It fulfilled his motto, *carpe diem*, as far as possible combined with fun and a glass of champagne. Thank goodness I took a photograph: it shows no sign of the first verse of his poem 'In Old Age', only the spirit of the rest of it:

The buttons get bigger and the holes get smaller.
The step is higher and the stairs are taller.
And I dread the doorbell of the casual caller,
In old age.

But there's fun in every new endeavour;
The cryptic crossword is not too clever;
And a glass of wine tastes as good as ever,
In old age.

So I'll grab my chances while I can see 'em,
Do in a.m. what I did in p.m.
And stick to my motto – *carpe diem*!
In old age.

40. Selling is not easy for a publishing house like HOLO Books; each sale is an achievement. Derek's volumes have tended to sell because of his growing reputation, and the esteem in which he was held as a scholar; it has been more difficult with mine. For *Madeira*, a member of the long-established Blandy family there agreed to be our distributor, and she organised several talks in hotels when we visited to launch the book. For *Tasmania*, I emailed all the bookshops scattered throughout the island and, when we were there, we drove to each one delivering the quantities they had ordered, having sent a supply to the Hobart Bookshop of Chris and Janet Pearce who, during our stay there, ran the bookshop at the University of Papua New Guinea. In Malta, we not only secured an established distributor, but the book was printed there and copies sent over to us and Central Books. HOLO Books was a 'Partnership'; with Derek's death, I have had to become a 'Sole Trader', a transition I am just learning about. I intend to continue for as long as practicable.

As I reach the end of my account of our 'Room Shared', I hope I have shown that there can be a development from Virginia Woolf's call for 'A Room of One's Own'.[41] Towards the end of her essay, she writes of an insight, which she develops, gained from an activity undertaken by a woman and a man apparently unconnected with her thesis:

> ... the sight of the two people getting into the taxi and the satisfaction it gave me made me also ask whether there are two sexes in the mind corresponding to the two sexes in the body, and whether they also require to be united in order to get complete satisfaction and happiness.[42]

After Derek's death, and with the text of 'Sardinia' completed, I came across a poem written by one of my characters, Joyce Lussu, for her husband Emilio to celebrate the anniversary of their marriage in 1944; he died the following year, in 1975. In some recognisable ways, their life together of activism, politics, and writing bore similarities to ours. It seems right to quote it here in my rough translation of a few lines of the Italian[43]:

> For thirty years, partner mine, for thirty years
> our lives have been intertwined
> like the wicker of a basket,
> like the olive and the graft,
> like two stories told
> through the same voice.

41. Virginia Woolf's extended essay, in spite of being a bit diffuse, should be read if one is interested in the history of women writers, and their attempts to overcome the obstacles put before them, usually by the patriarchy. I've decided to adopt for myself one of the intended slurs directed at Lady Winchilsea (b. 1661): 'a blue-stocking with an itch for scribbling' (p 65).

42. Woolf, pp 92–3. You do not need to ask if Derek and I ever disagreed, if we ever argued, if we ever had rows. Of course we did, like any other couple; indeed, we spent quite a lot of time bickering, and even had bets over who was right and who was wrong about particular issues, often trivial, but never for more than a penny. And he was much better at taking criticism of something he had written than I was. But, most of all, we laughed a lot.

43. Joyce Lussu, *L'Olivastro e l'Innesto: L'incotro con un uomo, la sua isola antica e la sua gente* (*The Olive and the Graft: The Meeting with a Man, his Ancient Island and his People*) (Cagliari: *Edizione della Torre*, 2018).

OBITUARY: DEREK ROEBUCK (1935–2020)

Neil Kaplan CBE QC SBS*

[*Editorial note*: The following is a slightly updated version of the obituary published at [2020] *Asian Dispute Review* 134–136. It is reproduced in this volume by kind permission of the publisher. A similar but not identical obituary was published at about the same time at (2020) 86(3) *Arbitration* 231–233.]

With the passing of Derek Roebuck on 27 April 2020, the world of arbitration has lost its current and much-loved chronicler. Although he was a prolific author of legal texts, he will long be remembered for his outstanding volumes on the history of arbitration from earliest times until almost the present.

Derek was born in Stalybridge, United Kingdom. His early talent as a student won him a scholarship to Manchester Grammar School and thence to Hertford College, Oxford, where he took degrees in Classics and Law. Oxford had a profound effect upon Derek, as it was to this city that he and his wife Susanna Hoe returned and remained after his retirement.

Derek qualified as a solicitor and practised for a short time in Stalybridge and Manchester, but could not resist the offer of a teaching post at Victoria University in Wellington, New Zealand. In 1968, he became a Professor of Law and Head and Dean of the University of Tasmania's Law Faculty. During this time, he was active in the anti-Vietnam War campaign, so much so that Australia's Attorney-General issued a writ for sedition against him for exhorting young men to refuse the call to arms. The writ was later dropped. He also monitored a trial in Angola of 13 mercenaries captured toward the end of its civil war. Another observer was Stephen Sedley (later a distinguished Lord Justice of Appeal) who retained a long friendship with Derek and Susanna. Derek's attendance at this trial resulted in the *Whores of War* (1977), co-authored with Wilfred Burchett.

In 1979, Derek was appointed as Amnesty International's head of research. There he met Susanna, who was also working for Amnesty, and

---

* Neil Kaplan CBE QC SBS. Practising international arbitrator, a Past President of the Chartered Institute of Arbitrators and a former judge of the High Court of Hong Kong.

they married in 1981. In the following year, he became a Professor of Law and Dean of the Department at the University of Papua New Guinea. He also practised in PNG as a criminal defence barrister.

In 1987, Derek was appointed to establish a new law school at the City Polytechnic (now City University) of Hong Kong. He was a Professor and sometime Dean and Head of Department. His achievements at City U included setting up one of the world's first postgraduate courses in dispute resolution, the MA Arb & DR. Professor Fu Hualing, a colleague at City U, remembers Derek's kindness and his having introduced Chinese Law as an academic subject at City U and in Hong Kong generally. Derek also practised as a duty lawyer in the magistrates' courts in Hong Kong. From 1994, he was a Visiting Professor at the People's University of China and a Senior Associate Research Fellow at the Institute of Advanced Legal Studies, University of London.

On leaving Hong Kong in 1997, Derek returned to Oxford. Many years thereafter were spent as the Editor of *Arbitration*, the journal of the Chartered Institute of Arbitrators. In recognition of his outstanding service, the CIArb established the annual Roebuck Lecture, the first of which was addressed in 2011 by Derek himself. It is now a major event in its tenth year.

Derek often reminded me that his interest in the history of arbitration was sparked by my having persuaded him in 1990 to write a chapter on the subject for one of my co-authored books on Hong Kong arbitration.[1] I had no idea of the early history of arbitration until I attended a conference in Darwin [Australia] in early 1990, at which Sir Ninian Stephen gave a fascinating lunch address that took his audience back to arbitration in ancient Egyptian and Assyrian times. Derek, of course, accepted the challenge of writing the chapter on arbitration's long history, even though I told him he only had four weeks to complete it! Naturally, he did so with good grace and with days to spare. Arbitration history remained his passion to the end.

Derek wrote fifty books and authored many articles. Some include fascinating insights about Hong Kong's early days, during which arbitration was practised before the establishment of an English-style court system. His *Miscellany of Disputes* is a wonderful treasure trove of quotes and stories about arbitration that help lighten presentations and after dinner speeches. He was an active member of the Selden Society and enjoyed discussing historical topics with the late Lord Mustill.

Derek's discovery and translation of the *Charitable Arbitrator* (published in French in 1666) is not to be missed. It reproduces a long

---

1. *Editorial note*: Kaplan, Spruce and Moser, *Hong Kong and China Arbitration: Cases and Materials* (1994, LexisNexis: Hong Kong).

letter to Louis XIV by an unknown cleric (whom Derek, of course, tracked down) explaining that the courts were being subjected to chicanery and that the King should impose arbitration on warring parties. And who else would have found a passage from Hansard in 1601 in which Francis Bacon, in introducing a Bill on Marine Insurance, told the House of Commons that it recommended disputes to be referred to arbitration. Why? Simply because the courts were too slow and also lacked subject matter expertise. More than four centuries later in some parts of the world, we can say, '*plus ça change*'.

Individual volumes of Derek's historical series (ten in all) have always been reviewed very favourably. The series starts from the earliest of times and ends with *English Arbitration and Mediation in the Long Eighteenth Century*. He was ably assisted on this book by Francis Calvert Boorman and Rhiannon Markless, whom we all (including Derek) hope will take on the nineteenth century and finish the journey that Derek started.

Earlier this year [2020], Derek was enormously affected by the premature death of Johnny Veeder QC, who was a most enthusiastic supporter of Derek's arbitral and historical *exegesis*. Derek also introduced arbitration to his very close friend Professor William Twining, who describes Derek's writing as 'magnificent historical work'. He and Derek commenced a joint project on the preservation of records of international commercial arbitration, but sadly, Derek's health declined before they got very far, and this project remains unfinished.

It is, however, as a teacher that Derek would like to be remembered. He made an impression on so many students and followed their careers with great interest. Former student Wing So recalls Derek's emphatic advice that students 'think for themselves and understand the underlying principles instead of falling into the lazy trap of learning for the sake of passing the exam'. He also mentions that one of the first ever law books that many Hong Kong students read was Derek's *Introduction to the Law of Hong Kong* (1996). Derek was also the general editor of a Hong Kong law textbook series translated into Chinese in the 1990s.

Professor Twining also fondly recalls Derek and Susanna having shared a passion for writing, helping each other on their respective drafts (Susanna was an historian in her own right). In 2018 they co-authored *Women in Disputes*. They also shared many other interests, including cricket and opera.

Derek was a man of principle who stood up against injustice. Never did he allow differences of principle to affect his friendships. It is hard to think of a kinder, more loyal or more caring man. This would be an epitaph enough for most of us, but when you add in Derek's scholarship and dedication to learning and love of family, it is easy to see why he will be so dearly missed. In addition to Susanna, he is mourned by the children of his first marriage – his daughter Lucy, a doctor in Tasmania, his son Derek, a Professor of Radiology in Perth, WA and Paul, a lawyer in Tasmania. He was as intensely proud of their achievements as they were of his.

DEREK ROEBUCK: REFLECTIONS ON HIS TASMANIAN INTERLUDE

*Her Excellency Kate Warner**

In the third year of my law degree at the University of Tasmania in 1968, we had an exciting new lecturer – Derek Roebuck – who joined the Law School from the Victoria University of Wellington following the lead of his colleague David Allan. Derek taught me Mercantile Law that year and was to have a profound influence on my future career. Tall, blonde, charming and outgoing, Derek was a popular teacher who got on well with staff and students alike. His left-wing politics troubled some of the more conservative members of the legal profession and possibly some parents who worried that their children might be indoctrinated with his left-wing views. The students had no such qualms and welcomed a diversity of views in the academic staff. In any event, Derek's lectures on the sale of goods and the requirement for goods to be of 'merchantable quality' and 'fit for purpose' were devoid of political commentary and not seized upon as an opportunity for a rant against capitalism.

In the late 1960s and early 1970s, women had begun to enrol in law degrees in greater numbers. My year was the first to enrol more than one woman and, from then on, the proportion of women law students grew exponentially. This was a trend Derek supported. He strongly encouraged the female students to take leadership roles in the Tasmanian University Law Society (TULS), participate in mooting competitions and embark on academic careers. In my final year, after David Allan left for a Chair at Monash University (in Melbourne), Derek became Dean of the Law School. David Allan and Derek heralded a much more modern, vibrant and active presence in the Law School than – to quote colleague Frank Bates – the 'splendidly anachronistic'[1] previous Dean, who was rarely seen

---

* Her Excellency, Professor the Honourable Kate Warner AC was appointed as the 28th Governor of Tasmania in 2014. Previously she was Professor, Faculty of Law, at the University of Tasmania and Director of the Tasmania Law Reform Institute. Following her appointment as Governor, she was made a professor emeritus.
1. Frank Bates, 'A Hardy and Individual Man: a memoir of George Wilson'. https://125timeline.utas.edu.au/timeline/1970/hardy-and-individual-man/ (accessed 15 December 2020).

after midday because he (reputedly) spent the afternoons either playing his violin or golf.

After I completed my degree, Derek encouraged me to apply for the position of Chief Justice's Associate and acted as a referee. It's hard to remember when he became 'Derek' to me rather than 'Professor Roebuck'. Perhaps it was when I returned to the Law School as a casual tutor in 1972 after my year as an Associate, followed by a year travelling abroad. These were the days before maternity leave or fractional appointments and, when a position in a law firm fell through because I was pregnant, Derek offered me more casual tutoring work. And most significantly, he encouraged me to enrol in a research higher degree. In those days, a higher degree was not an essential prerequisite for a law academic, an honours degree was sufficient and there were no other higher degree candidates in the Law School. Derek helped me to choose a suitable topic, put me in touch with people who could assist my research and was my supervisor. Completing a research masters set me up for an academic career.

The publication of Derek's book with Wilfred Burchett in 1977, *The Whores of War*, raised some eyebrows in the State. This was not because of the book's content – it was an exposure of the activities of mercenaries, their recruiters and paymasters that the authors had explored while observing the trial of 13 British and American mercenaries in Luanda, Angola. It was because his co-author, Wilfred Burchett, was a controversial journalist, accused of being a traitor in Australia, including by Denis Warner, an Australian journalist and war correspondent and, coincidentally, my husband's uncle. As Denis Warner was sued (along with the *Herald*) for defamation by Burchett, Derek's association with him was not a comfortable topic with my in-laws! Interestingly, the Burchett question is still controversial today.

In the final year of my higher degree study, 1978, I was given the responsibility of teaching the Criminology unit, as well as still tutoring in Criminal Law. This was particularly daunting. At first, I often felt completely out of my depth, particularly with some of the mature-aged students whom I perceived to be particularly critical. I can well remember going to see Derek to tell him that I was struggling and that I felt the students were unhappy with the course. He was enormously sympathetic, reassuring and encouraging and gave me the confidence to persist. When Derek left Tasmania at the end of 1978, the Law School was in a strong position; he had made some excellent appointments, including young academics who went on to have stellar international careers such as Muthucumaraswamy Sornarajah and Norman Palmer. The Law School under Derek's leadership was an extremely collegial place to work and as a fledgling academic and the only female, I felt well supported. Derek had also continued the work of David Allan in establishing stronger links with the legal profession. He entertained and befriended its leading members such as Bruce Piggott (who was prominent in groups such as Lawasia and World Peace through Law) and Roger Jennings (the Solicitor-General and later Deputy President of the Administrative Appeals Tribunal). Bruce Piggott, who had helped establish Lawasia, initiated a project on the contract law of the region and persuaded Professor David Allan to lead the project. David then recruited a research team which included Derek Roebuck. Together, the team published *Asian Contract Law: A Survey of Current Problems* (Queensland University Press, 1969), which was to be the first of a series they published over the next decade or so on Asian commercial law. In Bruce Piggott's memoir, he recounts that Derek introduced Bruce to his future wife, Audrey Beresford. She was a teacher at Sandy Infant School which young Derek and Lucy attended and was invited to dinner 'to complete the table'.[2]

Derek left behind many friends in Tasmania. He had a wide circle of friends within the University, the law profession and many parts of Tasmanian society. He had friends in the arts, such as Claudio Alcorso, Chair of the Australian Opera; in the environment movement and in the Lachlan Valley where he and Peggy had a cottage and an interest in Hopgrove, a small hop farm, with Jack Lomax and Johnny Nicholson. His daughter Lucy and son Derek returned to Hobart from London and studied medicine at the University of Tasmania. Lucy married a Tasmanian General Practitioner and joined his practice. Some years later, his younger son, Paul returned to live here too. For many years, Derek and Susanna made an annual visit to Tasmania until Derek's ill-health prevented the long journey. These visits provided an opportunity to catch up with friends as well as family.

For me, it has been a delight to visit Derek and Susanna at their house in Plantation Road in Oxford and to see that Derek spent such a productive retirement enjoying life, cricket, travel and his work on the history of arbitration. It is a pleasure to contribute this tribute to him as a small way of acknowledging his contribution to my career and to the Law School at the University of Tasmania.

---

2. JB Piggott, *Reflections of a Common Attorney* (1996) 142.

DEREK ROEBUCK: 'A MAN FOR ALL SEASONS'

*The Honorable Justice Lautalatoa Pierre Slicer**

Derek Roebuck arrived at the University of Tasmania towards the end of the 1960s. He arrived at a time when Australian society and the methodology of Australian universities were in a stage of transition. Historically, the University of Tasmania had structured the teaching of law in accordance with a long-standing emphasis on the history of the common law and the statutes enacted by the relevant legislative bodies. Tasmania's Law School had existed since the 19th century and its lecturers had followed a historic approach in their teaching. This was restrictive, since Australian society had undergone a number of significant changes independent of its foundation. An example will suffice. By the mid-1960s the law of equity in Australia was more than 10 years in advance of the equivalent law in the United Kingdom as it had adjusted to a more modern form of finance, duties of care and the interdependence of economic relationships. The historic approach had taken the form of an analysis of English history that required a knowledge of the kings and queens of England. Our academics had been schooled within a discipline which did not take into account Australian conditions (that is not intended as a criticism).

Derek's colleague as professor of law, Norman Dunbar, had been one of the prosecuting team at the Nuremberg War Crimes Tribunal in the late 1940s. Other lecturers had also been schooled in the English tradition. Derek brought a new approach to the discipline. Unlike the other academics, Derek's accent did not grate on the Australian ear. The accent was discernible but not pompous or affected; it had a low tone but was comfortable. There were no class taints but a self-contained clarity.

Many think that the teaching of law is based on the accumulation of data. Most students kept their notes for future reference for use when they entered the profession and practice of the law. After some eight to ten years they would realise that they had never had recourse to those notes. Law is

* The Honorable Justice Lautalatoa Pierre Slicer AO QC is a retired Judge of the Supreme Courts of Tasmania and Samoa.

more complicated, it really teaches a way of thinking and an understanding of the dynamics of a society. It is a discipline which requires a capacity to deal with many areas of life which are dealt with by adjudication and application within the legal framework. A second form of transition was the degree to which a respected academic interacted in the wider society which could be described as the ivory tower.

Derek brought a change which included a more public vista. His public face extended the role of a professor to interaction with wider society. In Derek's case, that involved activity which reflected his own family upbringing and values. Dare one say, it took the form of class analysis.

I first met Derek during the preparation for a moratorium march in Hobart, a campaign to oppose the conscription of young men to fight in the Vietnam War and Australia's participation in the conflict. He brought gravitas to the movement. Australian society was deeply divided on those issues. There were other social changes of concern at the time, including contraception and abortion rights for women, public speech censorship and challenges to existing social and religious mores. There were fears of violence against those who were participating. 'No worries', said Derek, who had dined the night before as a guest at the Officers' Mess at the military barracks in Hobart. The officers had treated him with respect because of his lucid and pleasant manner in discourse.

I had become the State Secretary of the Communist Party of Australia (CPA) and member of the National Committee. Derek had his own contacts within and outside the party. In some cases there were members 'off the book', especially groups of activists who had come to Tasmania to enhance their lifestyle. There were many issues to discuss, including apartheid (especially in sport), incipient racism towards migrants, civil liberties, censorship, movements against trade unions, social welfare, freedom of speech and the beginnings of the green movement.

Jack Mundey and the New South Wales Builders Labour Federation (BLF), of which he was Secretary, had led the way through the imposition of bans protecting heritage buildings and blocking their destruction. Their actions raised wider questions about the environment which impacted ordinary citizens. Central to these issues there remained, until the end of 1972 and the election of the Whitlam Government, the use of conscripts aged 18 to fight, yet none related to the issue of conscientious objection.

There were also matters internal to the CPA. The process had begun which led to the party transforming itself into what became Euro Communism. The invasion of Czechoslovakia and the dismantling of the Dubcek Government in Czechoslovakia raised the issue of what form our party should take. Derek was a strong advocate for internal change. The CPA was one of the first parties to condemn the Soviet Union for its actions and its betrayal of Marxism. The CPA played a significant role in the debate which took place in the last convention of the Internationale, held in Moscow in 1969; it was the first party to publicly denounce the actions of the Soviet Union. It had been our insistence that the proceedings of the Internationale be published in *Pravda*. Thus for the first time Russian people learnt that the party line had been opposed by another communist movement. Many other parties followed the Australian position.

Derek and I developed a strong friendship which lasted through our respective lives and continued until his death in his beloved Oxford. His wit, humour and intellect were effective in our political work. Apartheid, social reforms, attacks on the union movement, human rights, and the commencement of the green movement through the work of Jack Mundey and the BLF occupied much of our time. We ran a printing press and when the then Solicitor-General advised me legal proceedings would be taken for publishing without a licence, the printing press, weighing some two tons was soon safely housed in Derek's garage. The Government was not prepared to search the premises of a respected professor of law.

Derek was a close friend of Elliott Johnston, a South Australian, who became the first Communist to be made a Justice of a Supreme Court in Australia. I became the second.

To me, Derek's greatest gift was his involvement in aboriginal issues. In late 1972 or early 1973 he arranged a visit to Cape Barren Island to meet the aboriginal people living there. Cape Barren Island was still then, in law, governed by the Cape Barren Island Reserve Act 1912. This legislation provided for grants of small tracts of land for Half-Castes [*sic*] living at the Reserve. Despite this, one half of the island had been leased by the State to a private company and used for the raising of cattle. Many of the islanders were living in sealers' huts, built in the 19th century. These huts had dirt floors and newspaper-covered walls, and there was no running water or other services. There was an administrator, a nurse and a school teacher paid for by the State. The aboriginal people had little or no say in their governance. Children were removed into State care, for no reason other than that they had a runny nose or small heath afflictions.

Derek, Max Bound (a former Secretary of the Communist Party) and Ros Langford went to the island to assess the aborigines' plight in an attempt to change Government policy. Despite the legislation, the official position of the State Government was that there were no aborigines still extant in Tasmania. I revisited the island on many occasions as a lawyer acting for the community. On one occasion I returned to act for two youths who had been charged with riding horses belonging to the private company. The court was held on a larger island, Flinders Island. During an adjournment of proceedings I accompanied the two youths and their mothers to the one hotel on that island. The mothers and their children were forbidden to enter the dining room. No aborigine had ever been allowed there. Following an intense argument and our threats of the removal of their licence to operate we were admitted. Following the (successful) court case the Mayor wrote to the Government on behalf of the Council requesting that I be refused a permit to revisit. This was Tasmania in 1973. I became Counsel for the Aboriginal Legal Service that year and held this position until 1985. In 1973 Derek and I, together with Ros Langford, attended the first conference held by the Federal Government setting up aboriginal legal services throughout Australia. After many years of struggle and contest the High Court of Australia determined in 1992 that Australia had not been *terra nullius* at the time of settlement and that all unalienated land belonged to the first nation. We still have a long road to travel.

In 1975 Tasmania instituted a Law Reform Commission. Derek was the representative of the University of Tasmania. I was appointed on behalf of the Tasmanian Bar Association which meant that two of the five appointees were members of the Communist Party. This vexed conservative forces who saw the role of the State being taken over by the enemy. There was a call for my removal by the legal fraternity. This failed.

Derek's activities were not confined to the Antipodes, nor his weapons of combat limited to irony. As an invited member of an international commission of inquiry on mercenaries he attended the trial held in Angola of mercenary soldiers who had been employed to overthrow its Government. He joined the 47 other international observers in pressing the new Angolan regime – with only partial success – not to carry out any death sentences the court might pass. Derek also entered into discussions with representatives of the People's Republic of China. He asked why China had supported the apartheid regime of South Africa (support that included the provision of arms). He was told that he did not understand the politics of the People's Republic of China, that it developed its policies with a view to results some forty years hence. His irony was to no effect and history has shown that the actions of that republic belie its claims of ideological purity. I assume that Derek's weapons of combat included cynicism about his beliefs but he remained loyal to his class. The result of the experience in Angola, which Derek shared with the journalist Wilfred Burchett, was their joint publication *Whores of War: Mercenaries Today* (1977).

Our lives remained intertwined. We would meet when he returned to Tasmania to see his family. I visited him during his time as an academic in Hong Kong. He deepened his understanding of the future of China and marvelled about its capacity to build a city near Hong Kong which was almost a mirror image of that former outpost of the British Empire. When we met in Oxford, following his return from Hong Kong, he hosted me at one of my sacred sites (and his), namely the Bodleian Library, and showed me his College student room, as well as a nearby one, the occupant of which had been Evelyn Waugh.

One of Derek's sons, Paul, lives nearby with his partner (the mother of one of my son's early girlfriends) and we see each other from time to time. Some years ago I helped Paul obtain his legal qualifications. Such are the strands that hold our lives and connections in this complex world.

Above all, Derek's knowledge, personality and intelligence, tempered by his regard for the dignity of others, were values of his humanity. He deserves the title 'A Man for all Seasons'.

Ave Atque Vale

DEREK AS LAWYER, TEACHER AND ACTIVIST

*Justice Royale Thompson**

It was the early 1980s when Derek and Susanna came to Port Moresby in the Independent State of Papua New Guinea (PNG). Derek had known my husband from university days in Tasmania, but it was the first time I had met Derek or Susanna. We developed a friendship which continued for more than 35 years.

Derek's fondness for travel and distant locations (at least, those in which cricket was played) had led him to accept a position in the University of Papua New Guinea (UPNG) Law Faculty, in a young country of widely diverse people speaking over 800 distinct languages, none of which is written. His interest in the country and its people, and his lively, inquiring mind made him a favourite of the law students, whom he enjoyed introducing to the glories of the English common law, and who in turn introduced him to the complexities of PNG customary law.

Although Derek was an academic, I had the unusual experience of appearing with him in court.

At the start of the academic year in 1985, students decided to strike in protest about their government allowance, and the protests had escalated to a stage where the campus was barricaded off, and staff and other students were forcibly prevented from attending classes. I was the lawyer engaged by the UPNG to apply to the Court for an injunction against the student council leaders in charge of the strike. I found myself in a large courtroom almost entirely surrounded by over a hundred students who had come to loudly support their leaders who had been named as defendants in the action. Derek was there to give instructions on behalf of the UPNG, although of course his natural inclination was to side with the student protestors. After sensing the volatile mood of the crowd in the courtroom, Derek entered the fray and appeared with me. His polite but skilful cross-examination of the defendants elicited the information necessary to establish that an injunction would be appropriate. He then sought a short adjournment for the purpose of negotiating with the defendants and students. His mediation

* Royale Thompson is a Judge of the National and Supreme Court of Papua New Guinea.

skills were apparent, and he was able to persuade them to accept terms which Derek carefully devised to preserve the dignity of both sides.

We then, with considerable satisfaction, handed up the draft orders to the judge for approval. Imagine our consternation when the judge, after approving the orders, announced that he felt obliged to make further special orders. He proceeded to strip the leaders of their positions, closed the student offices, banned the leaders from campus, banned them from Port Moresby and ordered the government to return them to their provinces, but only after ordering them to first be jailed for five days. There was uproar in the court. This was the very antithesis of the outcome which Derek had carefully negotiated. While acknowledging the injustice of what had occurred, Derek was nevertheless able to convince the students to respect the judicial process, and he then made immediate bail applications on behalf of each of the defendants. The old adage of justice being dispensed in accordance with the length of the Chancellor's foot had been demonstrated in 'the land of the unexpected', as PNG's tourism promotions proclaimed.

It is a measure of Derek's personal attributes and mediation skills that the UPNG retained the confidence of students after this episode. Derek's classes were always popular, and even after he left PNG, students kept in contact with him. A number of his students went on to hold positions of importance in the development of PNG as a newly independent nation, including a Professor of Constitutional Law, Dr John Nonggorr, Minister of Foreign Affairs, Rimbink Pato, and Judge of the National and Supreme Court, Ambeng Kandakasi. Derek co-wrote what was to become the standard text on Pacific Contract Law. It was a loss to the UPNG Law Faculty, but of course to the gain of the Hong Kong City Polytechnic (later University), when Derek eventually left PNG.

A gentleman and a scholar was never a truer description than of Derek.

DEREK ROEBUCK, ESTEEMED COLLEAGUE

Robert Morgan

I come to write this tribute from a perspective a little different from that of other contributors to this volume: that of a former employee and academic colleague.

My professional and personal life changed dramatically when I emigrated to Hong Kong in 1993. It was the first time I had ever left Europe at all, let alone to live and work overseas. I undertook, also for the first time, an academic career, teaching primarily at postgraduate level. I met my wife Suzan, whom I had previously known briefly in 1989, through the Chartered Institute of Arbitrators (CIArb) and on a purely professional basis prior to her departure to Hong Kong that year; we raised a family and established our own consultancy. I met my co-editor, Neil Kaplan (at the time Judge in Charge of the Arbitration List at the then High Court of Hong Kong (now the Court of First Instance) and a close friend of Derek's), who encouraged me to write. I later became Chairman of the CIArb's East Asia Branch (following in Neil's footsteps), the first former member of the London Secretariat to do so. Multiple strands, but all ultimately stemming from one source: Professor Derek Roebuck, at the time Dean of the newly created Faculty of Law at the then City Polytechnic (now University) of Hong Kong (CPHK).

The trail began in London one day in January 1993, when I received a visit from Rod Germaine, a Vancouver-based labour arbitrator, in my office at the CIArb, to which I was Legal Adviser. After chatting at length about teaching and research in dispute resolution, Rod (who was on a fact-finding tour of institutions involved in dispute resolution) invited me to come out to Hong Kong to give a guest lecture to his students on the then Postgraduate Diploma/MA in Arbitration course (PGD/MA Arb) at CPHK, of which he was Course Leader and which Derek had been instrumental in establishing not long before, in 1991.

I spent ten days in Hong Kong in May 1993. It was while I was teaching at CPHK that I first met Derek. His unbounded enthusiasm for arbitration was visible for all to see even then. Though I was unaware of it at the time, he would not long have completed his first foray into the history of arbitration, his introductory chapter in a co-written volume by Neil Kaplan of cases and materials on Hong Kong arbitration to be published in 1994. He would undoubtedly by that time have begun work on his compendium of research sources for *Arbitration International* that would form the cornerstone of his acclaimed volumes on the history of arbitration and mediation. I found Derek both learned and authoritative, a profoundly interesting companion, immensely charming and gentlemanly, almost diffident, and with a calming and reassuring air that would never fail to put one at ease. There was none of the arrogance and aloofness that, in my experience, afflicted so many of my senior academic acquaintances down the years. No doubt these observations will gel with those of my colleagues in this volume.

Within a week or two of departing Hong Kong at the end of May 1993, I received a call from Rod asking if I would be interested in being interviewed with a view to replacing him as Course Leader. Naturally, I jumped at the opportunity, not least because I had never been headhunted for anything before! This would entail a telephone interview with Derek, about which I was understandably a bit nervous in light, not least, of my lack of previous academic experience. Rod assured me that all would be well, and so it was. Derek did his utmost to put me at my ease while gently gauging my suitability with pertinent questions, leavening the seriousness of the occasion with a little of his trademark gentle humour. At the end of the interview, he had no hesitation in offering me the position, which I took up on arrival in Hong Kong on 8 August 1993, an auspicious 'double 8' in Chinese culture.

I was, naturally, very much a stranger in a strange land at the outset, but I need not have worried. Derek's door was literally always open and it was never too much trouble for him to devote time to addressing any questions and concerns I might have had. A good example of this concerned the transitioning of the course from PGD/MA Arb to PGD/MA Arbitration and Dispute Resolution (Arb & DR). Derek and Rod had wished to broaden the scope of the course to include non-judicial dispute resolution, including mediation, expert determination and all points in between (such as dispute boards and mini-trials). I discovered that a small but restive hard core of the students had been complaining for some time prior to my arrival that the transition represented a dilution of the course's content and authority. It was all I could do to convince them that the transition actually represented both a broadening and a deepening of their knowledge and its scope. The fact that I was following the proverbial 'hard act to follow' as Course Leader did not, of course, help matters. Needless to say, Derek came to the rescue with suggestions, sage advice and judicious intervention. Equilibrium was restored and the rest, as they say, is history.

Derek was happy to know that I found my involvement on the course deeply satisfying. One of the weekly highlights was the Thursday evening Arbitration Practice tutorial, which engaged a stellar cast of guest practitioner tutors, one of whom was Neil Kaplan, as indeed was my future wife, Suzan. Derek was at the same time concerned to learn of the students' regular bad habit of buying 'knock off', Mainland-printed reproductions of prescribed texts (such as Mustill & Boyd) and amused to hear of Neil's dire warning to them (through me) that they would bring reproductions of his two cases and materials volumes to the tutorial at their peril! Such things certainly did exist, but were conspicuous by their absence whenever Neil attended.

Today, the PGD/MA Arb & DR course – the first of its kind not only in Hong Kong but also throughout Asia – continues to go from strength to strength and has been widely imitated elsewhere, both within and outside Hong Kong. Derek's proud advocacy of it, his foresight and his deep understanding of the intellectual and practical needs of the dispute resolution community must take the credit for this success.

Derek's departure from Hong Kong in 1997 was, thankfully, not the end of our collaborations. After he was appointed Editor of the CIArb's journal *Arbitration*, he demonstrated once again his confidence in my abilities by appointing me as an Honorary Deputy Editor with responsibility for new dispute resolution rules and guidelines.

It was a privilege for me to work with Derek, a man for whom the academic term 'collegiality' might have been coined. It is said that if you love what you do (to which I would add 'and the people with whom you share your career'), you'll never work again. Words for the wise indeed.

Vale Derek, a fine colleague, leader, boss, intellectual powerhouse – and, most of all, a consummate gentleman.

DEREK ROEBUCK: 'A FAITHFUL FRIEND'

*Bruno de Loynes de Fumichon**

I met Derek Roebuck in 2000 at Heathrow airport. He had come from Oxford with his wife, Susanna Hoe, to meet me. I had changed my reservation on a direct flight from Paris to Tahiti, where I was living at the time, to spend a few hours in London. Jan Paulsson had said: 'You should meet him.'

Among the limousine drivers, there was a man in his sixties, tall and distinguished, a little embarrassed by his big frame, with a smile, lively, timid and mischievous, and a younger woman by his side. He was holding a sign with a name that I didn't try to read, being too busy observing him. This fair-haired man with sparkling eyes, reluctantly pushing himself to the front, accompanied by his partner, could not be a limousine driver. This was Professor Roebuck. Right.

In a coffee shop, at Terminal 3, amid cups of tea and glasses of tonic water, he quickly made his point: a vibrant plea for the history of arbitration. 'I am reading the proofs of a book that I have just finished on arbitration in Ancient Greece. I have gathered hundreds of references of documents about the history of arbitration. An arbitration journal has devoted a special issue to my bibliography.[1] It is fascinating, arbitration in Rome. In particular, the practice of arbitration.' An Englishman!

Generally, it is the *jurisprudentia* that appeals to Romanists, the Roman legal science[2]: the hundred and more *jurisperiti* – legal experts – such as Papinian, Paul, Ulpian,[3] Gaius and so on, whose opinions and names have been saved thanks to the *Digest* of Justinian, that wealth of ideas.[4] It is

* Honorary *Maître de conférences*, Sorbonne law school (Université Paris I) and Honorary Dean of the Faculty of law of the University of French Polynesia at Tahiti.
1. 'Sources for the History of Arbitration: A Bibliographical Introduction', *Arbitration International* (1998) 14(3) (1998), pp 236–343.
2. See, among others, Fritz Schulz, *History of Roman Legal Science* (Oxford: Clarendon Press, 1946); and Hermann Bölhaus, *Geschichte der Römischen Rechtswissenschaft* (Weimar, 1960).
3. See Tony Honoré, *Ulpian – Pioneer of Human Rights* (Oxford: OUP, 2002).
4. Jean Carbonnier, in *Introduction au droit*, 20th edn, (Paris: PUF, 1991), p 64, says that the *Corpus Juris Civilis* is '*un océan d'idées*'.

the fact – unique in its history – of the law being a cultural phenomenon: the fecundation of the avaricious and litigious mind of the Romans as influenced by elements of Greek culture: logic, ethics, politics. It is therefore out of narcissism, the miracle of a law discovered and created by professors,[5] not by the traditional sources of statute, custom, precedent. No, Derek was interested in the practice of arbitration. Even in Rome, 2,000 years ago.

There was no question of destroying a magic moment with untimely objections. This man, in addition to the members of the university's examining board, would read my thesis: *Recherches sur l'arbitrage* ex compromisso *en droit romain classique*. l would catch my flight, land in Tahiti, amaze the customs officers searching for T-shirts to tax with the stacks of photocopies in German, Italian, etc., in my suitcase. I would complete the thesis, invite him to the dissertation defence at the Sorbonne, and, finally, have a correspondent in Oxford, a friend, I hoped. Our collaboration started then. *Roman Arbitration* was published in 2004.[6] Jan was right.

Later on, with Susanna, at dinners in Paris, at their favourite restaurants, at teas in Oxford, we discovered our other common interests: comparative law,[7] ancient and modern languages, South-East Asia and the South-Pacific islands, human rights, etc.

Derek was born in Stalybridge (Greater Manchester), cradle of the Industrial Revolution, flagship of the textile industry, stronghold of the workers' Left. He spent his youth in Stalybridge and Manchester, gaining a scholarship at the well-known Manchester Grammar School, where he started to build intellectual muscle.

At Oxford, he read first Classics – allowing him in his later work to translate from Greek and Latin and understand the context – and then Law.

After a few years as a solicitor, he embarked on an academic career and rose from lecturer to professor and dean, starting in New Zealand (Victoria University of Wellington), then in Australia (Hobart, Tasmania), in Papua New Guinea (Port Moresby) and finally he was appointed to set up a new law school in Hong Kong at the City Polytechnic, which became City University.

In Australia, he joined two co-authors[8] and together they published (between 1973 and 1980) a series of books on the legal regime for

---

5. The Roman law originated in custom and developed, thanks to legal science, via the praetorian edict, then the constitutions of the emperors. The *leges* and *plebiscita* were always secondary sources.

6. Oxford: HOLO Books: The Arbitration Press, 2004.

7. See Derek Roebuck, 'The Past is another Country: Legal History as Comparative Law', 1994 (3) *Asia Pacific Law Review*, pp 9–23.

8. David Allan and Mary Hiscock.

supplying finance[9] to Australia and nine countries of South-East Asia.[10] I liked to remind him of the first sentence of *Credit and Securities in Sri Lanka*: 'Ceylon is a pear-shaped island ... '. Here was a lawyer with a vast general cultural knowledge writing with style.

In 1978, he made a detour from his academic career in Australasia. He left Hobart for London. His appointment as Head of Research at Amnesty International's Secretariat[11] caused a media storm.[12] It was claimed that one of the most famous and respected human rights NGOs had recruited a leading communist for a top job at its head office. The new man would block the investigations into human rights violations, arbitrary imprisonments in jails and camps in the communist East, it was said.

Derek's appointment was seen as being against the rules of the organisation which, in order to preserve its independence from any State, depended for its influence and success on private funding from donors from mainly Western countries, who despised and feared anything wearing the hashtag 'communist'.[13]

Derek responded, saying that he had been a member of the Communist Party of Australia, but was no longer a member on leaving Tasmania. He explained that he had joined the party in reaction to the involvement of Australia in the Vietnam war, alongside the United States and New Zealand. He was active in the campaign against that involvement. The fact is that he never held any responsibility in the organisation of a little band of idealists, a splinter group that had demonstrated its independence from Beijing and Moscow with a straight condemnation of the Soviet invasion of Czechoslovakia in 1968. He was a plain member of Hobart's discreet CPA's cell, which was made up of a handful of members including a social worker, a nurse, a Roman Catholic nun, a free-thinking university professor and dean (Derek himself) and a fellow lawyer. Until Derek's appointment at Amnesty International, the Hobart cell looked like 'a good girl that isn't being talked about' (Voltaire).[14]

9. The 10-volume series, *Law and Development Finance in Asia*, was co-edited and co-authored by Derek Roebuck, David Allan and Mary Hiscock, with a national co-author for each volume. The individual volumes were entitled 'Credit and Security in ...' (Brisbane: University of Queensland Press and Crane, Russak & Co, Inc.)

10. Australia, Indonesia, Japan, Korea, Malaysia, the Philippines, Singapore, Sri Lanka, Taiwan, Thailand.

11. Derek Roebuck, 'The Ratification of the United Nations Covenants on Human Rights', (1970) 3 *Justice* 29–35.

12. 'Amnesty's Odd Man In', *New York Times*, 14 December 1978.

13. The question of the impartiality of Amnesty International's action is discussed in two recent books: Tom Buchanan, *Amnesty International and Human Rights Activism in Post-War Britain (1945–1977)* (Cambridge: Cambridge University Press, 2020); and Christie Miedama, *Not A Movement of Dissidents – Amnesty International Beyond the Iron Curtain* (Wallstein Verlag, 2019).

14. Voltaire was welcomed at the Academy of Amiens by its president, who boasted that

During the 1970s, Derek attended numerous conferences of the Non-Aligned Movement of the newly independent African and Asian States. This included attending, as an observer, the trial of mercenaries in Angola. That resulted in the publication, with his friend the Australian journalist Wilfred Burchett, of *The Whores of War – Mercenaries Today*.[15] These countries were courted by West and East alike.

In 1982, he resumed his academic career at the University of Papua New Guinea, not far from Australia. In Port Moresby, he wrote *The Background of the Common Law*, which even today students find helpful. While in Hong Kong, as well as publishing several monographs on its law, he was general editor of the seven volumes of the Peking University Press Series on Hong Kong law,[16] some in English, some in Chinese.

Throughout his career, he found the time and energy to practise law, to give advice and opinions, to participate in Law Reform commissions, etc.

He left Hong Kong in 1997, the year of the transfer of power from Britain to China. He and Susanna decided to settle in Oxford, his *alma mater*. They chose a house with a garden on a quiet street: Plantation Road, near Walton Street and the headquarters of Oxford University Press, for which they had both been authors; with a ticket for the Bodleian Library, and a large library at home, he was all set to conduct his research.

Together, they created *HOLO Books*, a publishing company with two imprints: The Arbitration Press and The Women's History Press: a testimony to the respect for the interests and causes of the other partner, and a symbol of a close and united couple.

Derek spent his time between Oxford and London. From 2000 to 2010, he was Editor of *Arbitration*, the journal of the Chartered Institute of Arbitrators. He was also Senior Associate Research Fellow of the Institute of Advanced Legal Studies of the University of London, the research centre that hosted him when he retired from a university.

In 2000, Derek published *A Miscellany of Disputes*, *excerpta* and essays about arbitration and mediation from authors ranging from Aesop to Stravinsky, including Chaucer, Shakespeare, and others. Then came *Ancient Greek Arbitration* (2001), *The Charitable Arbitrator–How to Mediate in Louis XIV's France* (2002)[17] and *Roman Arbitration* (2004).

the Amiens Academy was the daughter of the *Académie française* of Paris. Voltaire nodded: '*Oui, une bien bonne fille qui ne fait pas parler d'elle*': 'Yes, a good girl that isn't being talked about.'

15. London: Penguin Books, 1977), translated into seven languages, including French (Paris: Maspero, 1977).

16. It includes books on the law of contracts, of banking and securities, criminal law and procedure, etc.

17. A translation into English, with Introduction, Notes and Commentaries, of a book of moral maxims for lawyers written by an unknown author in the middle of the 17th century.

After '*Greece*' and '*Roman*', as we nicknamed the two books, he set out to write a history of private arbitration and mediation in England which extended into several volumes. He published *Early English Arbitration* (2008), *Mediation and Arbitration in the Middle Ages* (2013), *The Golden Age of Arbitration: Dispute Resolution under Elizabeth I* (2015), *Arbitration and Mediation in Seventeenth-Century England* (2016), and *English Arbitration and Mediation in the Long Eighteenth Century* with Francis Calvert Boorman and Rhiannon Markless (2019).[18]

Meanwhile, Derek and Susanna wrote two history books together: *The Taking of Hong Kong: Charles and Clara Elliot in China Waters* (1999);[19] and *Women in Disputes: A History of European Women in Arbitration and Mediation* (2018).[20]

Derek Roebuck has made a strong impression on the history of private arbitration and mediation. He will be remembered for several discoveries, for intuitions for which his research has provided ample and convincing historical evidence, for England and elsewhere: what he termed the 'myth of judicial jealousy',[21] the fact that, in this long history, the judges would fain have referred the settlement of disputes to arbitrators or mediators. He also drew attention to the importance of the practice of arbitration and mediation at all times: these methods were 'routine'.[22] Moreover, he demonstrated that public judges and private arbitrators and mediators have throughout the centuries worked together to help settle disputes, using various mechanisms.

Moreover, Derek generously contributed to the history of arbitration and mediation by unearthing from the archives a wealth of documents now made available to the public (researchers, lawyers, legislators, social workers and the general and educated public). His ten books include excerpts from and references to arbitration agreements, orders, awards, judgments, legislation, personal opinions expressed in diaries, memoirs, newspapers, etc. These documents will now be used, interpreted and dissected, to refine our knowledge of the past and of the present, and to imagine and build a better future.

Each year, until recently, Susanna and Derek made a romantic journey to France. They met at Nantes (Brittany) in 1979 at an annual general meeting of the French section of Amnesty International. They were married in 1981. In Paris, they had a group of faithful friends that included Charles Jarrosson.

18. All published by HOLO Books: The Arbitration Press.
19. Curzon Press (1999) and Hong Kong University Press (2009).
20. Published by both imprints of HOLO Books.
21. *Disputes and Differences: Comparisons in Law, Language and History*, HOLO Books: The Arbitration Press (2010).
22. *English Arbitration and Mediation in the Long Eighteenth Century*, p 295.

A faithful friend, an eclectic academic, a devoted and happy researcher enjoying the fun of the discovery, a generous human rights activist, an opera lover, a passionate supporter of Manchester City, of City, not United, indeed, and the English cricket team, a kind and sensitive person. Farewell, Derek!

DEREK ROEBUCK: A 'HAPPY SCHOLAR'

*Charles Jarrosson** *

In 1998, when I was sub-editor of the *Revue de l'arbitrage*, I suggested to Professor Philippe Fouchard, the editor of this *Revue*, the idea of publishing a number of articles on the history of arbitration, aiming to cover as many different countries as possible over the longest possible period.

At that time, I had never heard of Derek Roebuck.

A few months later, after I had contacted several historians specialising in various periods (ancient Greece, ancient and Byzantine Rome, the European Middle Ages and so on), I received a copy of *Arbitration International* and discovered the name of Derek Roebuck and the fantastic work he had completed: a 120-page bibliography entitled: 'Sources for the History of Arbitration (a Bibliographical Introduction)'.[1] I was very pleased to see that at the same time, on both sides of the Channel, the same interest could arise among scholars of arbitration law, from a perspective that completely differed from the usual colloquia dealing with more or less interesting technical issues.

I started a correspondence with Derek which quickly grew from being a casual relationship between colleagues to a warm one. I commissioned him to write an article on the history of arbitration in England, which was published in 2002 and was entitled 'Arbitration under English law before 1558'. We were then able to meet and get to know each other on his annual trip to Paris with his wife and fellow writer Susanna.

These meetings between academics immediately led to a lifelong friendship with Derek and Susanna.

During our meetings, our discussions were in English, even though Derek understood and spoke French. Better still, thanks to his research, he had often worked on manuscripts written in Old French and I remember his astonishment when I told him that, as a French person, I found it difficult to read and understand medieval French and even Montaigne's French. Because of his research experience, he was able to do so. In the end he was more comfortable with Old French than I was. It was therefore no

---

* Professor at the Paris II Panthéon-Assas University; Editor of the *Revue de l'arbitrage*.
1. *Arbitration International* (1998) 14(3) pp 237–343.

coincidence that he followed his translation of *The Charitable Arbitrator* (1666; translation 2002)[2] with the original text, which French-speaking readers will be able to verify is quite unlike modern French.

French-speaking, Derek (like Susanna) was a Francophile and more broadly a Europhile. Brexit's perspective saddened this scholar, who was constantly looking towards what was different and therefore interesting. No doubt his long stays in Australia, Papua New Guinea and Hong Kong had something to do with it!

Derek's personality had some remarkable features. First of all, he had a warm smile on his face and didn't take himself seriously. His natural elegance and simplicity, both physically and intellectually, summed up his personality well. He conceived research as a place of freedom in which he used to walk with enthusiasm and for his greatest pleasure. He was what you might call a 'happy scholar'. I remember a telephone conversation in which he was delighted to have discovered in ancient English law a trace of what could be considered one of the first arbitration clauses, even though, before the 20th century, arbitration was based on an agreement between the parties, made when the dispute had already arisen. On another occasion he shared with me that he took as an accurate compliment the remark of an author who, in a review of one of his books published by HOLO Books, had noted that he enjoyed writing. Derek commented with a big smile: 'That's exactly right!' His first book on arbitration, published in 2000, *A Miscellany of Disputes*, is a perfect illustration of this. Even better, because he expresses and claims it himself, the first sentence of the preface to his book *The Golden Age of Arbitration* is: 'This book has been a joy to write'!

I remember how pleased Derek and Susanna were to be able to attend the tribute that was paid in Paris to Professor Fouchard in the *Grand'Chambre* of the *Cour de Cassation* in 2005. I then organised a dinner at my home with some of the foreign colleagues who had travelled to Paris for this event and discovered on that occasion that this scholar also enjoyed French food and wine. It is also noteworthy that *The Charitable Arbitrator* was published thanks to sponsors, some of whom were French wine houses from Bordeaux and the Cognac houses.

For many years I had the pleasure of adding to my library the books that Derek was writing at a rate that amazed me: in addition to the aforementioned *A Miscellany of Disputes*, there were *Ancient Greek Arbitration* (2001), *The Charitable Arbitrator – How to Mediate in Louis XIV's France* (2002), and *Roman Arbitration* (written with his friend and French researcher Bruno de Loynes de Fumichon, 2004), then the impressive series of five books on the history of arbitration in England: *Early English Arbitration* (2008)

---

2. Published by HOLO Books: The Arbitration Press, Oxford, 2002.

'from the earliest times to 1154', *Mediation and Arbitration in the Middle Ages (England 1154 to 1558)* (2013), *The Golden Age of Arbitration, Dispute Resolution Under Elizabeth I (1558–1603)* (2015), *Arbitration and Mediation in Seventeenth-Century England* (2017), *English Arbitration and Mediation in the Long Eighteenth Century* (2019).[3]

It must be pointed out that Derek rightly did not limit himself strictly to the history of arbitration, but has most often extended his research to mediation. Indeed, arbitration and mediation have been mixed and even confused for centuries and their definitive differentiation is fairly recent.

French arbitration specialists have been able to discover all these publications thanks to the reviews in the *Revue de l'arbitrage* by Bruno de Loynes de Fumichon, Claude Reymond, Jan Paulsson, Catherine Kessedjian and myself.

A special place should be reserved for the book written with his wife Susanna Hoe: *Woman in Disputes – A History of European Women in Mediation and Arbitration* (2018). This book 'marries', it is fair to say, Derek and Susanna's two areas of research: arbitration and mediation for him and women's history for her. This book is, by its very existence, a radiant and moving proof of the fusional nature of the couple that Derek and Susanna formed.

I will end this brief tribute to Derek by talking about the last time I saw him. It was at a dinner in Oxford with him and Susanna in December 2016. He was certainly tired, but still warm, with a smile on his face, and always with plans: we talked about *Women in Disputes*, on which they were then working, about Europe and the unfortunate tendency of some countries to turn in on themselves, but also about wine and friendship. In the evening, when I left them, I reflected that arbitration has at least one unquestionable advantage: it permits, beyond borders, the meeting of interesting and cultured people who become friends.

---

3. All published by HOLO Books: The Arbitration Press, Oxford.

PROFESSOR DEREK ROEBUCK: 'A LITERARY AND SCHOLARLY GIANT'

Hew R Dundas[*]

I am greatly honoured to have been invited to make a contribution to Derek's *Liber Amicorum*, first because I had known of Derek since March 2000 when I purchased his book *A Miscellany of Disputes*,[1] in which I immediately recognised both his great powers of scholarship and, hidden between the lines, a dry and captivating wit. I am proud that I have bought a copy of each of his books ever since and I treasured them at the time, more so now after his sad passing away. Second, I was privileged to write for *Arbitration* under Derek's tutelage from 2002 (Vol. 68/2) to 2017 (Vol. 83/4), 101 articles in 63 consecutive issues, a co-operation from which I learned a great deal.

So how did this all start? In late 2001 I resumed a private free-of-charge newsletter service serving friends and colleagues on an as-and-when basis and, although I did not know Derek personally at the time, someone forwarded some of my output to him and he contacted me immediately to invite me to contribute to *Arbitration* so in January 2002 I submitted four articles expecting Derek to select (at most) one of them for publication. The articles were (i) comment on the *Aneco* case in tort in the House of Lords with the interesting outcome that an insurance broker was held liable in damages vastly in excess of the commission it had earned; (ii) the *Bay Hotel* case in the Privy Council in which their Lordships considered what were or were not adequate reasons in an arbitral award; (iii) the *Coslett* construction case, also in the House of Lords, inter alia concerning whether the Employer or the Contractor occupied a construction site; (iv) the case of *Kuwait Airways/Kuwait Insurance № . 2* in which Langley J

---

[*] Hew R Dundas is an International Arbitrator, Mediator and Expert Determiner in Oil & Gas, Energy and general commercial disputes. He is also a Panel Arbitrator covering, for example, South-East Asia, China, USA, India and Slovenia. He was President of the CIArb (2007) and is Chairman, Advisory Board, Chinese European Arbitration Centre and Honorary Vice President of the Scottish Arbitration Centre. He made significant input into the Arbitration (Scotland) Act 2010 and co-authored the definitive book thereon; he publishes internationally on arbitration law and lectures at several universities.
1. Published by HOLO Books: The Arbitration Press, 2000.

gave valuable guidance on the application of the Arbitration Act 1996, section 49.

I recall Derek contacting me to clarify a few points so I did so in the articles and resubmitted them. I never heard anything further until my copy of Volume 68/2 arrived in the mail with all four articles included so you will easily understand my astonishment. Derek later admitted that he had been short of material for that issue so four articles were gratefully received and we immediately struck up a rapport.

Fairly soon afterwards, Derek invited me to join the Editorial Board, an offer which I accepted with his clarifying that one of my responsibilities was to produce material to fill up the pages if so requested. Editorial policy was largely left in his hands (wholly correctly, in my view) although other Board members were on hand to advise if needed, e.g. on the pre-screening of articles submitted.

The steady flow of materials continued and, with Derek's valuable guidance and suggestions, I began to tailor the style and content to what we agreed were the interests of the majority of readers of *Arbitration*. This led to generally positive feedback. Derek dealt robustly with the occasional complaint, I think seeing his primary duty as being to protect his authors. However, there was one exception where an individual complained forcefully that Volume 76/1 had no fewer than five articles by me, a complaint that Derek dealt with without reference to me. Why five articles in a single issue? The truth of the matter was that he had reserved half of the space allocation for a collection of articles from country X which never arrived so he asked some of the Editorial Board to fill the gap and I duly did.

Volume 80/2 in 2014 became the 50th consecutive issue to which I had contributed and Derek asked my permission 'to write a few words' which I granted, expecting a short paragraph or two. When I opened my copy when it arrived I was staggered to see a 2,400-word tribute in glowing and professorial terms, the remembering of which brings on even today 'a Kleenex moment'. Only a literary and scholarly giant could write something like that.

Having trained in the Roebuck School of legal writing I was well equipped for a separate authorship project and the arbitral community in Scotland indirectly owes Derek a substantial debt of gratitude in that regard.

Even after Derek passed on the *Arbitration* baton to Michael O'Reilly we maintained close contact on various matters and it was a great sadness that his failing eyesight and loss of hearing limited that contact.

In April 2020 the world of arbitration lost its greatest scholar and I lost not only a good friend but an invaluable tutor and mentor. I will not meet such a great man again.

PLAYING AND WORKING WITH DEREK ROEBUCK

*William Twining**

Derek was an all-rounder, not only at cricket. We first met in 1977 at the Sydney Opera House where he gave a motley group of legal theorists a guided tour. He looked improbable in that role, but he knew his stuff, being a lifelong opera lover, and having been chair of the Tasmanian Opera Company, which had links to the Opera House. We soon discovered that we were both not only academic lawyers, although of different genres, but when young we had been goalkeepers, although of different abilities. This immediately created a special bond. Derek seamlessly combined theory and practice in his teaching, writing and many other activities connected with law.

Some years later he introduced me to the world of arbitration when I was involved in a project on preservation of legal records. Concerned about the lack of systematic preservation of historically interesting records of arbitration, I was particularly puzzled by the supposed justification that most aspects of arbitration are governed by strict rules regarding privacy and confidentiality, some of which are said to apply in perpetuity. This puzzlement was heightened by the sense that within the arbitration community these rules were not observed in practice and that archives were the main source of Roebuck's magnificent historical work. Derek and I started on a joint project on preservation of records of international commercial arbitration, but his health declined before we had got very far, and this project is still unfinished business. We were both fascinated by archives, but neither of us could have been an archivist – we loved exploring and playing with these relics far too much.

Derek was a person of principle with many ethical and political commitments. His public ones are well known. In private he also lived out his principles with generosity and firmness, supporting many people and causes and sticking by some seemingly puritanical house rules. One

* William Twining is Quain Professor of Jurisprudence Emeritus at UCL. He first met Derek Roebuck in 1977 and they were friends and colleagues ever afterwards.

firm principle was that anything connected with Rupert Murdoch was not welcome in his home. Fortunately, this did not extend to playing away and in recent years it was customary for Derek and Susanna to visit us to watch a day of cricket on television, whatever the channel. For home tests, they arrived promptly at 10.45 a.m. and usually stayed until the close of play. They brought smoked salmon and excellent champagne; we served up cheese and cricket; Susanna provided excited commentary while Derek and I talked about many things, the three of us coming together from time to time to debate issues of selection learnedly and astutely. Derek had another principle: he despised T20 which he called 'rounders' and which he refused to watch, or even discuss.[1] So far as I know he made very few exceptions to this, whereas Susanna and I share a rather more balanced view.

Derek and Susanna lived, travelled and wrote in tandem. Together they observed a disciplined regime for writing. Although they contributed to seemingly different genres, they shared ideas and commented and helped on each other's drafts. In 2018 they co-authored the aptly named *Women in Disputes*, published by their joint venture, HOLO Books. They were a team.

---

1. T20 or Twenty20 cricket is a relatively recently introduced short cricket match limited to 20 overs of play, lasting for about 80 minutes per innings, with a half-hour interval between innings.

PART TWO

SCHOLARLY ARTICLES
BY DEREK ROEBUCK

A SHORT HISTORY OF ARBITRATION*

Derek Roebuck

[*Editorial note:* This contribution was originally published as an introductory chapter to Neil Kaplan, Jill Spruce and Michael J Moser, *Hong Kong and China Arbitration: Cases and Materials* (1994, Hong Kong: Butterworths Asia/LexisNexis Hong Kong) at pp xxxiii-lxv.]

1. WHAT IS ARBITRATION?

Those who have attempted to write about the history of arbitration have seen advantages in collecting specimens of institutions and procedures having some characteristics which can be compared, even equated, with an element of modern arbitration. Imagination can be fruitfully employed even when it stimulates the self-congratulation common in histories of trade and professions written by their members. But it is necessary to have some limits, some definition which, though scarcely scientific, at least lets the reader know what the author is writing about.

In one sense, arbitration may be as old as human society. One person, with a grievance against another, is likely to seek the help of a third. That third person, if wise, will hear the other's story before giving assistance. Having heard both sides, the third person may declare in favour of one or other or suggest a compromise. The third person's power may or may not be such as to make the decision enforceable.

Children make parents arbiters; adults with little authority give the task to elders; sometimes anyone without connections to either party will do. It is scarcely possible to comprehend the history of such informal resolution of disputes. At times and in places where the institution of arbitration has been struggling for recognition, or when the courts have shown hostility, there have been those who have believed that they could give arbitration greater legitimacy by showing its long and glorious history. That has tempted some writers to give arbitration the widest possible definition, to include any story about a reference to a third party to resolve a dispute. But now that arbitration is an established institution, such an approach is unhelpful.

The proper purpose of a history of arbitration is to show its development from recognisable ancestors into contemporary forms, thereby enlightening the study of arbitration as a modern phenomenon. The first question then becomes, where and how are the lines to be drawn which will most usefully circumscribe the subject?

Definitions in modern legislation or case law cannot be relied on to provide the answer. They have different characteristics and intentions. They are specific to a jurisdiction. They speak about the present and future, not the past. They have normative, not scientifically descriptive purposes.

The first element in a definition must be that arbitration is an *alternative* method of adjudicating disputes.[1] Alternative to what? Always the other is litigation. Arbitration may, of course, be a part of litigation, provided that it is distinct. It may even be the most common way of bringing litigation to a conclusion, as it will be shown to have been at times in the development of the common law.

The second element is related to arbitration's function, which is to *decide* a dispute. Other methods of dispute resolution may dispose of the problem in other ways. The parties may be persuaded to forget their differences in ceremonies of mutual friendship. They may be offered a compromise which avoids further investigation of the merits. Conciliation or mediation may produce the same result as arbitration but there can be no arbitration without an award. It is this element of another's decision, relieving an aggrieved party of the responsibility for self-help, which makes arbitration so attractive in societies which allow, if they do not demand, retaliation for injury. If victims can believe, and can assume others believe, that they have been compelled to submit to the decision of an arbitrator, they cannot be accused of cowardice or negligence in their duty to defend by physical combat the interests of themselves or their clan.

It is often suggested that a third element is the parties' voluntary submission of the dispute to the arbitrator. The voluntariness of each party must be something more real than the free association which proponents of the social contract credulously find in human society. But there is no reason why a definition of arbitration should require that the parties have agreed to arbitration of the particular dispute. It is sufficient if they have joined in an

---

1. For accounts of processes of dispute resolution in societies where there is no distinction between litigation and arbitration: Maine HS *Ancient Law* with intro and notes by F Pollock London John Murray 1912 394ff and 417ff; Bohannan Paul ed *Law and Warfare* New York Natural History P 1967; Hamnett Ian *Social Anthropology and Law* London Academic P 1977; Roberts Simon *Order and Dispute* Harmondsworth Penguin 1979; 'Law, Anthropology and Mediation' (1983) 3 *The Windsor Yearbook of Access to Justice* 171–288. Nader Laura and HF Todd Jr eds *The Disputing Process: Law in Ten Societies* New York 1978.

association which requires disputes of that kind to be arbitrated rather than litigated or resolved by self-help or other means. The merchant and craft guilds provide many examples in English arbitration history.

If research into the development of arbitration is to throw light on present practices, another practical limitation must be imposed. There can be little interest in occasional isolated instances, standing apart from any system and handled without accepted procedures, which neither draw on experience of similar disputes nor provide examples for the future. For any enlightenment to be offered by a report of an arbitration, even if it meets the definition in other respects, it must illustrate a procedure for resolving disputes which is of sufficient formality and regularity for some likelihood of replication to be detected or inferred.

For the purposes of fixing the scope of a history of arbitration, therefore, it is appropriate to impose on the sources a fourfold definition: arbitration is the voluntary submission by the parties of a dispute for decision by recognised and regular procedure other than litigation.

Because this book concentrates on arbitration in a common law jurisdiction, this Chapter puts greater emphasis on the development of arbitration in England, the home of the common law. But it begins by considering what is known about other systems from which the modern common law may have drawn concepts and techniques, conscious of the value of comparison but also of the dangers of finding connections merely in the similarity of functions which arbitration serves. Further research will be necessary before the long and fascinating history of arbitration in China can be added.

Arbitration of disputes between states, though it shares many of the qualities of arbitration between private parties, has its own fascinating but separate history. Because of its importance, its records go back even further. But the significant differences prevent useful comparison and justify its exclusion from a historical introduction to private arbitration.

2. MYTH AND ROMANCE

There are mentions of disputes between two gods being submitted to a third for decision in the earliest myths. Stories from Ancient Egypt tell of disputes between Osiris and Seth, and Horus and Seth, being decided in that way.[2]

The earliest Greek arbitration myth is of a mortal arbiter, Paris, deciding between immortal parties, Hera, Athene and Aphrodite, with disastrous consequences, particularly to the arbiter.[3] A mortal woman, Eriphyle,

---

2. Mantica Margit 'Arbitration in Ancient Egypt' (1957) 12 *Arbitration J* 155.
3. Ovid *Heroides* 17, 118.

appointed arbiter by her husband and brother, took a bribe as Paris had done and brought disaster to herself and all her family.[4]

The first reference in Greek to formal dispute resolution is in Homer's description, in a scene depicted on Achilles' shield, of the referral by the parties to a 'man knowledgeable in law' of a dispute arising from homicide.[5] The passage, probably first sung in the eighth century BC, predates any possible antithesis between arbitration and litigation. The referee presided over a public meeting but it was left to the elders to deliver a verdict, after hearing anyone who wished to speak.

Aeschylus,[6] writing about 459BC, describes a similar procedure. The referee, the goddess Athene, swore in her selection of the 'best citizens' of Athens, who gave judgment. The debate was public. Given some poetic licence – and what writer of fiction has not taken liberties with criminal procedure in the cause of enhancing the drama? – Aeschylus is describing contemporary litigation as his audience would recognise it. The cause between Orestes and the Furies is nevertheless of interest as an early form of dispute resolution as a substitute for the feud. The solemn consideration by representatives of the community of a dispute, submitted by the parties apparently voluntarily, dealt with according to well-known and accepted procedure, followed by a decision enforceable not by the parties, allowed the victim or the victim's clan to accept an ordered alternative to violence, without accusation of cowardice or negligence.

It has been suggested that the judgment of Solomon, between the two harlots who disputed parentage of the baby boy, is an early example of arbitration but it was clearly royal justice.[7] Others have been persuaded that the tribunal which heard Daniel's successful defence of Susanna at the suit of the Elders was arbitral, when it was an ordinary ecclesiastical court.[8]

---

4. Homer *Odyssey* XI 326.
5. Homer *Iliad* XVIII 497–508; Hammond NGL 'Arbitration in Ancient Greece' (1985) 1 *Arbitration Int* 188–190; Gagarin Michael *Early Greek Law* U of California P Berkeley 1986 20–50.
6. Aeschylus *Eumenides* 433–753. Podlecki AJ ed *Aeschylus: Eumenides* Warminster, Aris & Phillips 2nd corrected impression 1992, in Appendix I, 203–213 has the best treatment of 'Athenian Judicial Procedure as reflected in the Trial Scene'.
7. Emerson FD 'History of Arbitration Practice and Law' (1970) 19 *Cleveland State LR* 155. The story is told in the Bible, 1 Kings 3: 16–28.
8. *Apocrypha* 'The Story of Susanna'; Jones WC 'History of Commercial Arbitration in England and the United States: a Summary View' in Domke Martin ed *International Trade Arbitration: a Road to World-wide Cooperation* Greenwood P 1958 127–136 at 127. Elon Menachem (see n37) says arbitration was not known in Babylonia, 'where the Jews enjoyed wide judicial autonomy'. NB each party chose an arbitrator to negotiate for him and a third decided between them. There are accounts of other institutions, from the romantic-historical of Odiorne GS 'The Aztecs and Arbitration' (1952) 7 *Arbitration J* 166–168 and Sullivan AM 'The Brehon – Ireland's Ancient Arbitrator' (1956) 11 *Arbitration J* 32–39 to the scholarly Miller WI 'Avoiding Legal Judgment: the Submission of Disputes to Arbitration in Medieval Iceland' (1984) 28 *American J of Legal History* 95–134.

Such a flexible definition allows even Jesus to be enlisted as an arbitrator, on the strength of Luke 12: 13,14.[9]

3. GREECE

Herodotus, writing at much the same time as Aeschylus, mingles myth with the first real attempt at history. He tells an intriguing story of how Deioces became king of the Medes.[10] He started off as an arbitrator, setting himself 'to profess and practise justice (*dikaiosune*)' better than anyone else. Soon he monopolised the work and not only his own townspeople but those from all over Media would submit their disputes to no one else. Then, when he had them in his power, he got them to make him king. He ruled for 53 years and died, it is said, in 656BC, more than a century before Herodotus wrote his story. This may be the only example of popular success as an arbitrator leading to judicial office and ultimately to the highest power.

There is evidence that by Aeschylus's time there was a well-established and identifiable system of arbitration, separate from litigation and that a number of city states appointed public arbitrators.[11] Most of the evidence relates to Athens, where they were used to ease the burden on the courts. They were drawn from citizens who had reached their 60th year and they had jurisdiction over civil claims of more than ten drachmas. Appeals from their awards lay to the courts.[12]

Most civil cases were dealt with, wholly or in part, by arbitrators. There were many of them, they were held in high esteem and organised in a college. A party who believed that an arbitrator had misbehaved could make a complaint to their general body.[13] Cases were submitted to the public arbitrators by the Forty of the archon, officials in charge of the legal system, and appeals from public arbitrators went back to them.[14]

Moreover, at least from the time of Aristotle (384–322BC), there were private arbitrators (*diaitetai*), in regular employment, who were not required to decide according to the strict law and whose award was final. Though the *diaitetes* had in principle to abide by the law, he could prefer a solution based upon *epieikeia*, usually (but dangerously) translated as equity. Neither

9. Cf *Corinthians* 6: 5.
10. Herodotus *Histories* ed AD Godley Heinemann 4 vols 1946 I 96–98.
11. Bonner RJ 'The Institution of Athenian Arbitrators' (1916) 11 *Classical Philology* 191–195, 192. The city states were Sparta, Gortyn, Ephesus and Lampsacus, according to Hammond NGL and HH Scullard *The Oxford Classical Dictionary* 2nd ed Oxford Clarendon P 1970 92.
12. Aristotle *Athenian Constitution* 53.
13. Cohn EJ 'Commercial Arbitration and the Rules of Law: a Comparative Study' (1941) 4 *U of Toronto LJ* 1.
14. Bonner RJ 'The Jurisdiction of Athenian Arbitrators' (1907) 2 *Classical Philology* 407–418, 408.

party could appeal to the court.[15] Demosthenes set out the basic legal rule on private arbitrators:[16]

> It is lawful for parties who have a dispute with one another about their private obligations, and who wish to choose an arbiter, to select whomever they wish. But when they have together chosen an arbitrator they must abide by his decision and cannot in any way appeal from him to another tribunal: let the arbitrator's decision be final!

It is clear that the preliminary hearing was before arbitrators. The regular court, the Heliastic Court, was made up on at least 201 members and could number up to 1001. It is hardly surprising, therefore, that it restricted its consideration of documents to those produced before the arbitrator. Moreover, in Athens, appeals were based almost entirely on the affidavits presented at the arbitration.[17]

Plato, in *The Laws* written about 350BC, mentions arbitration more than once. In Book Five, he writes:[18]

> But any state would be no state at all if no law court were properly set up. A judge who said nothing, or as little as the parties to a preliminary enquiry, as in arbitrations, would not be effective in dispensing justice.

In relation to contracts, he says:[19]

> Whenever someone makes a contract and then fails to carry it out,... an action may be brought in the tribal courts if the parties have been unable to resolve it before arbitrators or neighbours.

Menander, who was born 40 years after Aristotle, wrote a comedy called 'The Arbitrants' (*Epitrepontes*) and the remaining fragments give a lively and comic account of a completely informal submission to a passer-by.[20]

---

15. Demosthenes XXI 86ff; Aristotle *Athenian Constitution* 53 6; Vinogradoff Paul *Outlines of Historical Jurisprudence* 2 Oxford UP 1922 146–147. Aristotle *Rhetoric* I 13.

16. Demosthenes *Against Meidias*; Bekker *Oratores Attici* 546 6. It is likely that this legislation was enacted by the democratic government restored between 403 and 400BC: Lysias 22.2; which also set up the board of arbitrators; Aristotle *Athenian Constitution* 16 4, Bonner 'Institution' 193,4. An excellent comparative introduction is Appendix X of Kennedy CR ed *The Orations of Demosthenes against Leptines, Midias, Androtion and Aristocrates* London Bohn 1856.

17. Aristotle *Athenian Constitution* c53; Vinogradoff 147; Bonner RJ *Evidence in Athenian Courts* 1905 55.

18. Plato *Laws* ed RG Bury, 2 vols Heinemann 1926 II 443.

19. Ibid 413. At II 399 he recommends an arbitration by a panel of doctors.

20. Wilamowitz-Muellendorf Ulrich von *Das Schiedsgericht [Epitrepontes]* 1925; Murray Gilbert *The Arbitration – The Epitrepontes of Menander* London Allen & Unwin 1945.

They may tell us no more of the details of contemporary formal arbitrations than a modern knockabout farce would do of present-day procedure. But they are evidence of the intended audience's appreciation of a joke about the perils of arbitration, and that says something about the place of arbitration in the general knowledge of the time.

It is tempting to speculate that there may have been a difference in the status of Athenian women before the courts and before arbitrators. The normal rule was that an Athenian woman had to appear through her *kurios* or next friend, usually her father or husband. She could neither be party nor witness. But in a report of an arbitration regarding the legitimacy of two sons of Mantias, their mother Plangon used her opportunity to appear before an arbitrator to good, if dishonest, advantage. She agreed with Mantias, in return for a substantial money payment, that if he called her before the arbitrator to swear that the men were his sons, she would decline, thereby allowing him an award that they were not. He did so challenge her but she swore they were. The arbitrator found in her favour, and made Mantias assume the parental responsibilities he had been seeking to avoid.[21]

Though most of the surviving sources come from Athens, they sometimes describe the practice in other cities. The Athenians were fond of contrasting their way of life with that of Sparta. The law in Sparta was in the hands of the ephors, who held trials every day.[22] Resort to arbitration might avoid the rigours of trial by the ephor, but an arbitrator with a Laconic sense of humour could be worse. Plutarch tells of two men appointing the king, Archidamus II, to resolve their dispute. He took them into a remote temple and made them swear they would abide by his award. He then gave it: 'Stay here till you have made up your quarrel.'[23]

There is no direct link between the practices of Ancient Greece and the English common law, neither in matters of arbitration nor in any other aspect of law. Yet it cannot be said that there is no indirect influence until the sources are discovered which shaped arbitration in Rome, which undoubtedly influenced English arbitration practice.[24]

4. ROME

At about the same time as Aeschylus was writing in Athens, there was produced in Rome the earliest code of laws for that city-state, the Twelve

---

21. Demosthenes 39 [Boiotos I] and 40 [Boiotos II]; cf Isaeus 12 [Euphiletus].
22. Macdowell DM *Spartan Law* Scottish Academic P Edinburgh 1986, 135.
23. Plutarch *Ethics* 218d; MacDowell 136.
24. The connection may become clearer from further study of arbitration in Egypt: Modrze-jewski Jozef 'Private Arbitration in the Law of Greco-Roman Egypt' (1952) 6 *J of Juristic Papyrology* 239–256, which shows relationships in Ptolemaic, Roman and Hellenistic periods. Cohen Boaz makes suggestions of connexions between Jewish, Roman and Hellenistic law, see n37 below, at 182ff. Ducos M *L'influence Grècque sur la loi des douze tables* Paris 1978.

Tables. The reference to arbitrators there is, like so many of that code's fragmentary texts, tantalising. It appears to mean something like: 'if a judge or arbitrator or witness is suffering from a serious illness or on that day is on military service then let there be an adjournment for that day'.[25]

The institution was so well known, and so early, that there was an ancient judicial formula with its own acronym: 'P J A V P V D' – '*Praetorem Judicem Arbitrumve Postulo Uti Det*', 'I request that the praetor, judge or arbitrator should give'.[26]

Plautus, writing about 200BC, and Terence, a generation later, put into the mouths of their comic characters references to arbitration. As in Athens, the audiences must have been familiar with the institution to get the jokes.[27]

If the definition of arbitration requires a system of litigation against which it can be contrasted, it is easily satisfied in Roman law from early times, certainly in Republican Rome, before the Christian era.[28]

By the period of classical Roman law – the first two centuries AD – there was a well-established practice of arbitration separate from the procedures of litigation. Cicero, writing before 50BC, knew arbitration as part of the highly developed legal system of which he was the master:[29]

> A court hearing is one thing, the award of an arbitrator quite another. A trial concerns a definite sum, an arbitrator's award an indefinite. When we go to court we know that we are going to win all or lose all. But we go to arbitration with different expectations – that we may not get all we want but we will not lose everything. The very words of the arbitration contract are proof of that. What is a trial like? Exact, clear cut, explicit. And arbitration? Mild, moderate.

25. Watson Alan *Roman Private Law around 200BC* Edinburgh UP, Edinburgh 1971 2. Bruns CG *Fontes Iuris Romani Antiqui* Tubingen Libraria Lauppiana 1872 18, Tabula II 2: '...morbus sonticus... aut status dies cum hoste... quid horum fuit vitium iudici arbitrove reove, eo dies diffensus esto.' Bruns collects fragments of even earlier regal laws (in Greek) but they contain no reference to arbiters. Livy 3 31 says that the Romans sent three delegates to Greece to enquire into the laws and constitutions of the Greek States and particularly Solon's code for Athens, Lee RW *The Elements of Roman Law* 4th ed London Sweet & Maxwell 1956 7; but the better view may be that there is no close relation between Greek and Roman law until much later, Buckland WW *A Text-Book of Roman Law from Augustus to Justinian* 3rd ed Stein Peter Cambridge UP 1963 2.
26. Lewis CT and Short CS *A Latin Dictionary* Oxford Clarendon P 1879 *sub* 'arbiter'. Westrup CW *Introduction to Early Roman Law* Vol IV Bk 1 London Oxford UP 1950, 132 ff, 147 ff.
27. Plautus *Rudens* 4,3,101: '*ibo ad arbitrum.*' Terence *Heautontimorusmenos* 3,1,90: '*vicini nostri his ambigunt de finibus. Me cepere arbitrum.*' Cf Menander, in n18 above.
28. The *arbitrium boni viri*, in the sense of a reference to a dispute, after it had arisen, for decision by a respectable citizen, was discussed by Cato, who wrote about 160BC: Cato *De Agri Cultura* 148,149; Watson 136,137.
29. Cicero *Pro Roscio* 4,5. Cf Seneca *De Amicitia* 2.7.3.

Litigation itself, throughout Republican times, the Classical period and well into the Empire, was not the preserve of professionals. The state appointed its official, the praetor, to take charge only of the first part of litigation. He required the parties to work out exactly what the dispute was. It had to fit one of the accepted formulas. Having settled the issue, the praetor then sent it to be decided by a single layman, an amateur chosen by the parties.

In classical Rome, the arbitrator was free to decide the issue according to his own opinion of what was fair, untrammelled by legal rules. Writing at the beginning of the third century AD, Ulpian describes the law which had obtained since classical times:[30]

> But the awards of an arbitrator should stand, whatever he has said about the matter, whether it is fair or unfair.

Of course, the law must set some limits on the power of the arbitrator. The award will not stand if it exceeds the powers given to the arbitrator by the arbitration contract, or fails to decide all the issues put to the arbitrator, or imposes a duty to do something which is not honourable (*non honestum*).[31]

But it was generally up to the parties to fix the scope of the submission and thereby the powers of the arbitrator. Like other contracts, an agreement to submit a dispute to arbitration, whether the dispute had already arisen or not, was enforceable only if it could be brought within one of the formulas which the praetor would recognise. The formula for an arbitration contract was *compromissum*.

Compromissum was an agreement by the parties to submit their dispute to an *arbiter*, an arbitrator chosen by them. If the arbitrator agreed to accept the reference, the praetor would require him to carry out that promise. But the praetor would not directly compel the parties to carry out their agreement to submit to arbitration or abide by the award. Therefore, the parties usually secured compliance by entering into penal stipulations by which either of them could enforce a penalty if the other withdrew from the arbitration or failed to satisfy the award.[32]

Because the arbitration was the creature of the parties' contract, it was that agreement which fixed the arbitrator's powers and duties. The quality of the award did not interest the authorities. Neither the praetor nor anyone else was concerned to see that the arbitrator gave an award which was just or in conformity with the law, provided it was within the terms of the submission. The intervention of the law would therefore be unlikely except in a narrow range of events. That is borne out by the surviving authorities. Most of the

---

30. *Digest* 4,8,27,2. Cohn EJ 'Commercial Arbitration and the Rules of Law: a Comparative Study' (1941) 4 *U of Toronto LJ* 1–32, 9.
31. *Digest* 4,8,32,15; 4,8,32,16; 4,8,19,1; 4,8,21,7; 4,8,21,11; 4,8,27,2. Cohen 201.
32. Kaser Max *Roman Private Law* Butterworths Durban 1965 197.

primary sources are lawyers. They tell us about the extraordinary problems which had to be dealt with despite the insistence that the authorities left everything to the agreement of the parties.

It was common to appoint more than one arbitrator. If there were two, could both be compelled to act? Ulpian said that the parties would always be better off with an odd number because no two arbitrators were ever likely to agree and you could at least enforce the award of the majority. If there were two who disagreed, the praetor must compel the parties to choose a third, whose decision would bind them. But if three were appointed and only two acted, then the reference was void. All three must be present, because the absent one might have persuaded the other two to arrive at a different result.[33]

The arbitrator was appointed to dispose of the dispute and accepted that responsibility. He could not therefore require the parties to resort to the court or another arbitrator either on a particular point or generally. The award must be so worded as to put an end to the submission or the parties could ignore it.

In the later law, it appears that the emperor Justinian made a *compromissum* directly enforceable in some cases at least, so that a disappointed party need not sue for the penalty but could enforce the arbitration contract itself.[34]

In later centuries, the law of the Church as well as civil law took some of its ideas and procedures from the later Roman Law. But canon law, though it generally purported to follow Roman law, according to the maxim *Ecclesia vivit lege Romana*, restricted the discretion of arbitrators within bounds which seemed proper to the Church. While the parties might relieve the arbitrator from adherence to the letter of the law, he had to be guided by the Church's tradition.[35]

When English sources become available, they show that the development of law and procedure in England was not immune from similar influences.

5. ENGLAND BEFORE THE COMMON LAW

More than 500 years before the birth of the common law, there is evidence of arbitration in England. The Kentish king, Aethelberht, codified custom about 602AD. He had been converted to Christianity by Augustine's mission from Gregory the Great which landed in England in 597AD and he died in 617AD. Bede wrote that the laws followed Roman examples – *iuxta exempla Romanorum* – though it is not easy to see what exemplars he is referring

---

33. Stein Peter 'Arbitration under Roman Law' (1974) 41 *Arbitration* 203–206, 205. Cohen 201.

34. Cohn 10.

35. Cohn 11, quoting Hieronymus Garzonius: *nulla sane aequitas potest esse in his qui innituntur prudentiae et sapientiae suae quam praeponit decretis patrum… et legibus tot vigiliis et laboribus Deo inspirante pro communi omnium utilitate editis.* Cf contemporary Jewish law, Cohen 205.

to.[36] In the middle of a tariff of payments to be made for various physical injuries, it is provided that 'If a thigh becomes broken, 12 shillings shall be paid. If he becomes lame, in that case friends must [may?] settle it.'[37] This is the first sign of a process that is commonly evidenced later. It has been a regular practice of the court to hand over not only the assessment of compensation but the resolution of disputes of many kinds, including some we would now call criminal, to arbitrators, sometimes judges or other officers of the government but often lay persons.

A clearer reference is in the laws attributed to Hlothere and Eadric, dating from some time between 673 and 688AD. Article 10:[38]

If one man brings a charge against another then, within three days after the other has given him surety, they shall get themselves an arbitrator [*saemend*], unless the plaintiff prefers a longer period. Within a week of the settlement by arbitration [*sace gesemed sio*], the defendant shall do right to the plaintiff.... If not, then he shall pay a hundred shillings one day after the arbitration is done [*ofer thaet gesem bie*].

It is important not to read too much into these instances of the use of words from the 'sem-' root. They can mean 'settle' as easily as 'arbitrate'. The purpose of the reference to third parties was to effect a compromise and through it to restore peace. Yet these instances pass the test set in the definition. There is a legal alternative, another procedure from which the method of resolving the dispute can be distinguished. Moreover, there are contemporary accounts of cases which bear this out:[39]

36. Bede *Historia Ecclesiae* 2; 5. He is referring to the Twelve Tables (see section 4, nn 25 and 26 above), not that of his contemporary Post-Justinian Rome, but he is unlikely to have had access to as many fragments as we now have.

37. Aethelberht art 65 in Attenborough FL *The Laws of the Earliest English Kings* Cambridge UP 1922, reprinted 1963 Russell & Russell NY 12, 13: '*Gif theoh gebrocen weordheth, XII scillingum gebete. Gif he healt weordh, thaer motan freond seman.*' '*Seman*' means to settle or conciliate. Cf Icelandic '*saett*', Miller IW *Bloodtaking and Peacemaking: Feud, Law and Society in Saga Iceland* Chicago, U of Chicago P 1990, 96. In this context '*freond*' may mean relatives. The best treatment of this period is Murray DE 'Arbitration in the Anglo-Saxon and Early Norman Periods' (1961) 16 *Arbitration J* 193–208.

38. Attenborough 20, 21; Whitelock Dorothy ed English *Historical Documents c500–1042* Eyre & Spottiswoode London 1955 360. The distinction between compromise or settlement on the one hand and arbitration, the decision of a third party, on the other was not distinctly drawn, cf *pesharah* in Jewish law, Cohen Boaz 'Arbitration in Jewish and Roman Law' (1958) 5 *Revue Internationale des Droits de l'Antiquité* 165–223, 168ff; Elon Menachem in *Encyclopedia Judaica* Jerusalem, Keter 1971 Vol 3 294–300, sub 'Arbitration', and Vol 12 126–127 sub 'Mishpat Ivri'.

39. Adams Henry 'The Anglo-Saxon Courts of Law' in *Essays in Anglo-Saxon Law* 26, 53 (1876); cited in Vinogradoff Paul *Outlines of Historical Jurisprudence* I Oxford UP 1920 345–354. Of course it is not a requirement of the definition that the parties, or any other actor in the proceedings, should be conscious of the distinction between arbitration and litigation.

A very slight examination of the law cases... will show how rarely the parties were allowed to push their differences to a final judgment. A compromise was always effected where compromise was possible. Arbitration was, perhaps, the habitual mode of settling disputes among the Anglo-Saxons.

The arbitration might take the actual forms of legal procedure, without offering any anomaly to the Anglo-Saxon mind...in order to escape the consequences, the delays, or the uncertainties of strict law, arbitration was a more attractive resort, in nine cases out of ten, than the ordinary judgment of a regular tribunal.

Though the laws of the later Anglo-Saxon kings do not show it, arbitration of the kind described, being part of the judicial process, can be assumed to have continued until the Norman Conquest.[40] Its elements are not always clear. It is hard to be sure that the reference of the dispute to 'friends' was more than an attempt to bring it to an end through conciliation, with perhaps no element of adjudication by anyone.

6. ARBITRATION AND THE DEVELOPMENT OF THE COMMON LAW

Recourse to arbitration was common in medieval England. But the courts did not look very favourably on a practice which tended to diminish their jurisdiction.[41]

Holdsworth's view, determined by the nineteenth century opinion which he accepted, is not supported by the sources. It is true that:[42]

When they were asked to enforce the awards made by arbitrators against recalcitrant parties to an arbitration, they got many opportunities of laying down rules as to the conditions of the validity of these awards, as to the

40. Murray op cit 195–196 gives two more references but neither is substantial. Both show how difficult it may be to show an arbitration as distinct from an arranged compromise. There is a clear reference to arbitration in a letter to Edward the Elder (899–924), quoted in Harmer FE *Select English Historical Documents of the Ninth and Tenth Centuries* Cambridge 1914 60–63.
41. Holdsworth WS *A History of English Law* 14 vols plus 1 vol index London Methuen 1903–72, XIV 187. Holdsworth is less concerned with the development of arbitration as an institution – the topic of this chapter – than with the history of the rules of common law relating to arbitration, which are outside the scope of this chapter. Having decided that Kyd Stewart *A Treatise of the Law of Awards* London Crowder 1791 is 'the best book on the subject' (Vol XII 393), Holdsworth relies comprehensively and injudiciously upon Kyd's text and selection and interpretation of Year Book sources. Even the careful Murray op cit 193 opines that the period 1399 to 1799 'has been superbly dealt with' by Kyd.
42. Id 190.

modes of enforcing them, and as to the conduct of arbitrators, which, at the end of the medieval period, were beginning to make the law as to arbitrators a very technical and not very reasonable body of law.

But at the end of the medieval period there was hardly any branch of the law that was not 'very technical and not very reasonable'. Because the land law had become irrationally technical, could it be shown that the courts looked unfavourably on conveyancing? It is not until the medieval period is well over that there is evidence of the courts' distrust of arbitration. Indeed, the evidence is clear that they took advantage of the benefits which arbitration offered, frequently and regularly, to supplement their own inadequacies.

Holdsworth further suggested that the courts 'from the first' controlled arbitrations with a strictness which showed their jealousy, though he admitted that as late as 1743 there was no rule that a submission to arbitration was impermissible as ousting the jurisdiction of the courts. Though from 1746 there is clear authority that an arbitration clause could not oust their jurisdiction, it seems that no court until that time had taken such an extreme view. The rest of this section, therefore, will describe the development of arbitration in England, living comfortably alongside the work of the common law courts for over 450 years.

Bearing in mind that arbitration is defined by contrast to litigation, it is important to remember how diverse were the courts of medieval England.[43] The administration of justice was a privilege. The right to hold a court was a usual appurtenance of property. The lords of land, lay or spiritual, had the right and the obligation to hold courts for their tenants. The king had his court but no monopoly of jurisdiction. From about the middle of the twelfth century there was something recognisable as common law, which the king's courts applied as uniformly as they were able. But it must not be thought that other tribunals, applying other law, were any less courts for that. The courts which belonged to the Church are an obvious example; but there were many other kinds: local courts of shire and hundred, borough and port and city; merchants' courts of fairs and markets; admiralty courts and courts for tin-miners; feudal, seignorial, courts of the manor or larger holding. Those whose conflicts were resolved in such courts did not voluntarily submit their disputes to them, any more than they did to the king's courts of common law. Submission to their jurisdiction arose not from choice but status.

There were, however, at least three categories of arbitration[44] which can be discerned from medieval sources and whose development can be traced

---

43. Harding Alan *The Law Courts of Medieval England* London Allen & Unwin 1973; Roebuck Derek *The Background of the Common Law* Hong Kong Oxford UP 2nd ed 1990 30ff.
44. There was a tripartite classification under the traditional Hindu *panchayet* system: the lowest among kin, higher among the craft or trade, the highest local. Could the hierarchy reveal stages of civilization? Banerjee DC 'Law of Arbitration in India: its Early History 1' (1905) 2 *Allahabad LJ* 203–206, 204.

to modern times. The first is the creature of the parties' own particular agreement, the progenitor of modern arbitration. The second arose from membership of some community, voluntarily joined, which bound both parties as members to submit their dispute to arbitrators appointed by the community, of which the guild merchant is typical. The third is arbitration ordered or sanctioned by the court, either of its own volition or at the request of one or both parties. Though they have much in common, it is illuminating to keep the distinctions in mind in following the development of arbitration from medieval to modern times.

Litigants who agreed to trial by jury were said to 'put themselves upon the country'. In a report of a case heard in 1206,[45] the defendant is said to have 'put himself upon' two named men and, if they would not accept the task, upon two others unnamed. The plaintiff did the same. Then both put themselves on the judgment of all four plus William de Neketon and agreed to abide by their award. This is an example of the third category, arbitration arising in the course of litigation. An example of the first kind, a submission of a dispute to arbitrators before any court action, is reported from the same year. Humphrey wrongly transferred land which by charter he had granted to Andrew and asked Andrew to accept other land instead. They referred their dispute to arbitrators chosen by each of them.[46] It appears that the court enforced the award.[47] Other entries in the Curia Regis Rolls for 1223–1224 may show that references to arbitration were not uncommon at the time.

One of the most frustrating characteristics of cases reported in the Year Books is that so many of them appear to fizzle out with no record of their conclusion. Of course, only a tiny minority of actions begun today ever lead, or are intended to lead, to trial. If the facts are found and all the law is disposed of at preliminary stages, so that all that is to be done is to make a decision, there is nothing of interest left to report.

One explanation of the indeterminate appearance of reports of medieval cases may be that some of them were sent for arbitration:[48]

---

45. *'Posuit se super'*, Murray DE 'Arbitration in the Anglo-Saxon and Early Norman Periods' (1961) 16 *Arbitration J* 193–208, 197, citing Flower CT ed *Introduction to the Curia Regis Rolls* (1944) 62 Selden Society 292. 'The arbitrator exhibited features of both the medieval and modern views of a juror', Rowney I 'Arbitration in Gentry Disputes' (1982) 67 *History* 367–376, 368.

46. Murray 197, Flower 417. *'et concessum fuit ita quod ipsi compromiserunt in legales homines ex utraque parte electos'*. Not only could they choose their own tribunal, they knew it could not be challenged – 'Despairing of knowing before which authority to bring their suits' Bloch Marc *Feudal Society* Chicago, U of Chicago P 1961, 359.

47. Murray 197.

48. Baker JH ed *The Reports of Sir John Spelman* 2 vols 1976 and 1977 93 and 94 Selden Society II 91,92; cited by Powell Edward 'Arbitration and the Law in England in the Late Middle Ages' (1983) 33 *Transactions of the Royal Historical Society* 5th series 49–67, 50. Murray 198, relying on Sayles GO *Select Cases in the Court of King's Bench* (1936) 55 Selden Society xvii, n4.

perhaps foremost was the possibility of a settlement or a submission to arbitration. It appears to be true of all periods, including the present, that the vast majority of cases commenced in the central courts never reach trial; the issue of a writ is as much an inducement to compromise as it is a threat to pursue the law to its conclusion. The temptation to submit a dispute to arbitrators must have been especially insistent when the plaintiff weighed the possible delays and pitfalls which lay ahead in following the course of law. The arbitrators chosen would often be men of law – apprentices, serjeants, or even judges – who would be expected to apply the law.

Studies of the work of various courts in the Middle Ages show that verdicts were taken in very few cases: one per cent of private suits in King's Bench; few in Common Pleas.[49] No doubt delay and inertia and exhaustion of resources of one kind or another together account for much of this inconclusivity. Debtors pay up under varying amounts of pressure. Self-help was not unknown. Informal settlement probably accounted for most. But mediation and arbitration were also common and regular ways of terminating disputes part way through their process through the courts.

This may be true not only of the central courts. In the ecclesiastical courts, too, 'many cases are recorded as adjourned (*continuatur sub spe concordie*)'.[50]

What was usually expected of a law court was not a clear-cut decision, of right or wrong, on an issue on which the parties had failed to agree, but much more something in the nature of an effort to bring about a settlement of the litigation by an acceptable, honourable compromise. This might be brought about by the mediation of the court... or jurors from the neighborhood or arbiters, accepted or even elected by the parties....[51]

49. Powell 51 citing Blatcher Marjorie *The Workings of the Court of King's Bench in the Fifteenth Century* London U PhD thesis 1936; see now Blatcher Marjorie *The Court of King's Bench 1450-1550: a Study in Self-Help* London Athlone P 1978 59: 'Only twelve of the 958 entries on the civil section of the plea-roll of 1488, and four out of 499 on that of 1490, record the judgment of the court.' But it is dangerous to assume that this is evidence for widespread submissions to arbitration. See also Hastings Margaret *The Court of Common Pleas in Fifteenth Century England* New York Cornell UP 1947.

50. Woodcock BL *Medieval Ecclesiastical Courts in the Diocese of Canterbury* London Oxford UP 1952 60 and the sources cited by Powell 52 n27.

51. Van Caenegem RC *Royal Writs in England from the Conquest to Glanvill* I (1959) 77 Selden Society 41–42. 'Arbitration allowed men to break off long-lasting feuds and cut their losses without suffering the stigma of defeat. In arbitration there was no plaintiff and defendant and... those who rendered judgment were unlikely to reach a verdict which was wholly favourable to one side.' Bellamy John *Crime and Public Order in England in the Later Middle Ages* London Routledge 1973, 118.

Arbitration was popular among all the higher classes, that is among all who could afford to go to law. 'The King, the Chancellor and the Council often resorted to it in their efforts to settle disputes which involved leading magnates' or religious or lay corporations.[52]

It was in common use, too, by those at lower levels, not only those who, as will appear below, were bound by membership of communities to use it. Not only guild members but other masters and apprentices, employers and employees, landlords and tenants are regularly found resorting to arbitration.[53]

Where did the preference for arbitration come from, and from where the technology to handle it? The techniques of the lawyers of classical and Imperial Rome had not been lost, though they had been transformed.[54]

The techniques which arbitration offered had been developed in the twelfth century from the Romanist models of the canon lawyers, as can be shown by their terminology.[55] They were familiar with the *compromissum*, the contract by which the parties bound themselves to abide by the award of specified arbitrators and made their contract enforceable by attaching to it a penal bond.[56] *Compromissum* or *compromissio* was a written contract, 'drafted in precise, formulaic terms designed to survive any subsequent challenge to the award in court'.[57]

The popularity of arbitration when the dispute was between religious parties was supported by the requirements of patristic teaching to avoid litigation and to submit conflicts for resolution in Christian charity.[58]

---

52. Powell 52. 'Le compromise avait, en effet, l'avantage de laisser intacte la souveraineté des parties – l'arbitre n'était pas un juge supérieur aux parties' Chaplais Pierre *Essays in Medieval Diplomacy and Administration* London, Hambledon P 1981, Chapter IX 'Conflits Franco-Anglais au XIVe siècle' 269–302 ; 287. Such arbitration was 'intra- rather than inter-call based', Rowney I. 'Arbitration in Gentry Disputes of the Later Middle Ages' (1982) 67 *History* 367–376, 368.

53. Powell 53 n32 citing copious references from Thomas AH and Jones PE *Calendar of Plea and Memoranda Rolls of the City of London* Cambridge UP 1926–61.

54. Cohn 9–12; 'It seems likely that arbitration became part of the common law through the work of the Ecclesiastical courts, since we find authority for arbitration from the seventh century in canon law, and since we know that, in Bracton's time especially, the canon law governed much of the litigation that is now handled by our regular courts', Sayre PL 'Development of Commercial Arbitration Law' (1928) 37 *Yale LJ* 595, 597.

55. Powell 54.

56. Above section 4 at n32. Jewish law forbade contracts with a penalty clause but Cohen 213 shows how this prohibition could be evaded.

57. Powell 54. 'Compromissio' is Late Latin, dating from c1180. The *Compromissum* survives in some Civil Law jurisdictions; for the *Compromiso* in Latin America Grigera Naon 'Arbitration in Latin America: Overcoming Traditional Hostility' (1989) 5 *Arbitration International* 137–172 and 188 especially 142–149, where its future survival is doubted.

58. There is curious learning on the institution known as the 'loveday'. Its history and etymology have been investigated ingeniously by Spargo JW 'Chaucer's Love-days' (1940) 15 *Speculum* 36–56 and convincingly by Bennett JW 'The Medieval Loveday' (1958) 33 *Speculum* 351–370. Once an action was started, it could not be discontinued even by the parties'

Throughout the thirteenth and fourteenth centuries that popularity spread widely among the laity, as the Curia Regis Rolls and Year Books attest.[59]

A careful comparison of the reports of cases heard by the royal courts with those in ecclesiastical courts might well show more than casual or informal connections. Certainly the contract to submit to arbitration conditioned on a penal bond, became commonplace in the royal courts.[60] By the fourteenth century they required a deed to support a writ of covenant. That should have meant that an arbitration agreement had to be under seal if the royal court was to recognise, let alone enforce it. Indeed, in 1312 Bereford CJ was not prepared to let a party swear that the dispute had already gone to arbitration: the submission was 'a matter to be proved by a specialty, and therefore no averment lies'.[61] But a contemporaneous judgment of Staunton J from the 1313–1314 Eyre of Kent appears contrary:[62]

> You are not in Court Christian where the pleadings must be in writing, but you are under the common law, by which an averment of the arbitration is sufficient.

A case from 1345 held that it was an error for a defendant to have to plead against a claim on a covenant to submit to arbitration unless the covenant was produced.[63]

What is of interest is not whether these cases can be distinguished but that there are so many references to arbitration in the fourteenth century. Already by 1312 the question had arisen whether an arbitration agreement was void as ousting the court's jurisdiction; it was held that once a day had been fixed for hearing in the Bench no private agreement could take away the plaintiff's right to it, a somewhat narrower point.[64]

The courts were not prepared, it seems, to allow an action when the dispute had been the subject of a valid award, even where the action was in trespass, and what would now be regarded as criminal.[65]

---

agreement without the court's consent. Lay courts, if not ecclesiastical, required payment to grant a loveday, an adjournment of the case for settlement or, possibly, arbitration, cf *Hardwick v Wood* n64 below; Bracton H *De Legibus et Consuetudinibus Angliae* ed Woodbine GE New Haven Yale UP IV 159. Clanchy MT 'Law and Love in the Middle Ages' in J Bossy (ed) *Disputes and Settlements* Cambridge 1983 47–67 and 'Law, Government and Society in Medieval England' (1974) 59 History 73–78.

59. Powell 54 n41. Hebrew was the fourth language in England (pace Welsh) and the Talmud was not unknown; its rules on arbitration are in Cohen 183.

60. Simpson AWB 'The Penal Bond with Conditional Defeasance' (1966) 82 *Law Quarterly R* 392–422.

61. Murray 200; Bolland WC ed *Year Books 5 Edward Il* (1916) 33 Selden Society 175.

62. Murray 200; Bolland WC ed *The Eyre of Kent* (1912) 27 Selden Society 23.

63. Murray 201; *De Wetenhale v Arden* KB Roll 20 Edw Ill.

64. *Hardwick v Wood* Bolland 33 Selden Society 214. Unless, of course, a loveday had been bought.

65. Murray 204; Year Books (Ames Foundation editions) Il Rich Il 168; 12 Rich Il 159 and

The common law courts came increasingly to accept that a submission or an award could be pleaded as a bar to an action.[66] Exceptions were narrow, for example duress.[67] The court helped to enforce the award by enforcing the penal bond, compelling, by an action in detinue, the neutral bailee of the bond to hand it over to the successful party in the arbitration and then enforcing payment upon it by an action in debt.[68] What is particularly interesting is that the court seems to have awarded not the amount of the bond but only of the award.[69]

Common law courts could not, however, grant decrees of specific performance or require an arbitrator to carry out the duties imposed by the parties and accepted by him. The Court by of Chancery could and in the fourteenth and fifteenth centuries did so regularly. Indeed it has been suggested that the business of that court was then largely made up of cases on uses, commercial disputes and matters arising from arbitrations.[70]

Before the Court of Chancery would hear a petition, the petitioner must show that a sufficient remedy was not available at common law. In relation to arbitration, that would arise when a party or arbitrator had behaved inequitably. A party might deny the arbitration contract, if the submission was oral or the bond lost, or pursue litigation after the matter had been the subject of an award.[71] The arbitrator might be challenged as obstructive or biased. The Chancellor would then interrogate them, having summoned them by subpoena.[72]

More than the judges of the common law courts, the Chancellor promoted arbitration, not only by offering assistance in enforcement but by referring cases to arbitrators.[73] The Chancellor was sometimes prepared to arbitrate himself.[74] The conclusion drawn by Dr Powell, on whose Alexander Prize Essay so much of this section is based, is powerful:[75]

170. Cf much later survivals in Scotland, Wormald Jenny 'Bloodfeud, Kindred and Government in Early Modern Scotland' (1980) 87 *Past and Present* 54–97; 72, 75, 86–87.

66. Powell 63 n89.

67. Powell 63 n90.

68. Simpson 'The Penal Bond' and the dozens of Calendar Rolls entries cited by Powell 63 n91.

69. Powell 64. The courts also followed the ecclesiastical courts in avoiding usury, which was as much against the common as the canon law.

70. Pronay Nicholas 'The Chancellor, the Chancery and the Council at the End of the Fifteenth Century' in Hearder BH and Loyn HR *British Government and Administration* Cardiff U of Wales P 1974 87–103, who points out that the Chancellors and most of their Senior Officials were trained in Canon Law, 90–92.

71. Powell 65 citing manuscript sources in the Public Record Office: PRO C1/9 no68 and PRO C1/10 no311; and PRO C1/10 no243, C1/33 nos191, 332.

72. Roebuck *Background* 64,66; Baker JH *An Introduction to English Legal History* London Butterworths 3rd ed 1990 119,120.

73. Powell 65. In one bundle of 210 Chancery cases, for 1474 to 1483, 'ten request enforcement of awards made by an arbitrator' compared with eleven on uses and eleven on trusts, Pronay 92.

74. *Borlas v Tregoys* (1436) Powell 66 n108.

75. Powell 66. Dr Powell has developed his work on this topic in *Kingship, Law and Society*

The emerging equitable jurisdictions of late-medieval England reveal the interdependence of litigation and arbitration in its most refined form. The two became part of a single process of dispute settlement, as the fluidity of equitable procedure allowed them to be used almost interchangeably. Common-law procedure did not provide such flexibility but... this did not deter disputants from combining law and arbitration in a general strategy to achieve an advantageous settlement.

Moreover, the courts made use of expert arbitrators when the matter became too technical for the judges. As early as 1290 the Exchequer sought the assistance of arbitrators in a dispute involving complex accounts.[76] In *Costace v Forteneye*, started in the Mayor's Court of the City of London in 1389,[77] the plaintiff claimed the defendant had failed to take delivery of wine and pay for it, as required by their contract. The parties:

of their own pure and spontaneous wish, in open court, put themselves upon the Arbitration of four honest men of the craft of Vintners, to be chosen by Robert Herry, Vintner, ... to inquire and tell the truth... and so that whatever they, so chosen and sworn, shall say or decree..., the parties consent fully to perform and to stand by their award and judgment...

The arbitrators made their award, which was given to the Mayor and Aldermen in the court to enforce. The Mayor's Court was, of course, just as much a court as any. In the fourteenth century it occasionally sent a dispute to arbitration, two arbitrators being chosen by each side, with provision for an umpire.[78] But in the early fifteenth century the Mayor and Aldermen:[79]

probably as a natural development of the equitable jurisdiction of their court, began to assume the function of arbitrators, acting either as a whole

Criminal Justice in the Reign of Henry V Oxford Clarendon P 1989 especially at 93–107, 122–123, 226–228 and 240–246. 'Closer analysis has revealed, however, that throughout the middle ages and beyond modes of compromise complemented legal procedures, and that "love" often prevailed over "law". Arbitration was, indeed, as characteristic of the disputing process as litigation, violence, or corruption.' (p98) 'Perhaps the most important feature of arbitration in late medieval England is the frequency with which it occurred in conjunction with litigation.' (p 100).

76. Murray 205; *Honesti v Chartres* in Hall H *Select Cases on the Law Merchant* II (1930) 46 Selden Society 53, 148.

77. Murray 206.

78. The awards were usually presented to the court in French at that time, Thomas AH ed *Calendar of Plea and Memoranda Rolls etc of the City of London etc 1413–17* Cambridge UP 1943 viii.

79. Thomas vii, ix. Their awards are recorded in Latin. The earliest English awards were from non-officials acting as arbitrators in 1414, ibid.

or as a committee of the mayor and twelve aldermen or delegating the duty to one, two or four aldermen.

It is not surprising that the line between courts and arbitrators is sometimes blurred. There were other tribunals, which were not courts, which dealt with the same kind of disputes, perhaps involving the same people. They were those established by the merchant guilds.

7. THE MERCHANT GUILDS

The guilds or gilds of merchants and crafts in medieval England have fascinating histories.[80] A characteristic of the guild was that members were required to submit disputes between them to the arbitration of arbitrators appointed by the guild. Typically, no craftsman was allowed to take legal action against a fellow-guildsman without leave of the master and wardens, who would attempt to mediate and, if unsuccessful, would appoint arbitrators from among their own number.[81] The sanction which ensured that the award would be enforced was exclusion from the guild and thereby loss of livelihood.[82]

The arbitration might well take place at one of the feasts which the guild regularly held, with much eating and drinking. Perhaps the compromise, whether from mediation or arbitration, was made all the easier to swallow with:[83]

frometye, rost byffe, grene gese, weale, ... capon, pyggys, lambe, costard... spyce cake, good bere and ale... not sparing any dainty fare which might be had for money.

At such a feast 'all private quarrels and emulations were heard and ended to the glory of God and mutual love amongst neighbours'. The argument went: it is good for all people to mend their quarrels; how much better for

80. The great general history is Gross Charles *The Gild Merchant: a Contribution to British Municipal History* 2 vols Oxford Clarendon P 1890, which describes exhaustively all the literature up to that time. For craft guilds see Lipson E *The Economic History of England* vol I 'The Middle Ages' 12th ed London Black 1959 272, 345–346, 391, 398, 406. Histories of particular guilds are numerous. In the context of arbitration the distinction between craft and merchant guild seems unimportant. For our purposes Gross's bibliography is brought forward by Jones SA 'Historical Development of Commercial Arbitration in the United States' (1928) 12 *Minnesota LR* 240–262, 244 n24.
81. Lipson 345. The procedure was not confined to guilds, Rowney 367 gives an example of a similar agreement between magnates going to Henry VI's French coronation.
82. Jones 244 n23. Gross I 32: For very serious offences the guildsmen of Andover fulminated a decree of excommunication against the erring brother – commanding 'that no one receive him, nor buy and sell with him, nor give him fire or water, nor hold communication with him, under penalty of the loss of one's freedom.'
83. The guild merchant at Yarmouth; Gross I 33, II 278.

Christians; better still for Christians of the same fraternity 'bound and linked together by solemn oath for performance'.[84]

Moreover, a lawsuit, like any other dispute, threatened the peace and prosperity of the guild:[85]

> Therefore, if any grudge of a private quarrel should be amongst them, the same will incense and provoke enmity, to the prejudice of the commonwealth where they govern; for most certain it is where anger beareth sway, there can be nothing rightly and considerately advised; therefore, the better to prevent all such unkindness, was this feast held.

The purpose of this high-principled group, however, was to monopolise trade. Not everyone saw that as beneficent. Such privileges could not be created without royal approval and appropriate payment. The king regularly enquired into their extent and justification. In 1330 the king's attorney, in an enquiry into the privileges claimed by the burgesses of Derby, reported:[86]

> the Gild Merchant is granted to the burgesses... as is evident from the charter of Henry III.... And under cover of this Gild Merchant they have been accustomed to oppress the people coming to the said town with vendible wares... and the profit arising therefrom does not accrue to the advantage of the community... which usages redound to the injury, oppression and pauperization of the people.

The guild allowed only its members to trade freely. Others were forbidden or charged tolls for permission. It set prices, too, which all members must charge and pay. Its management of disputes without lawyers, who were barred from the guilds' mediation and arbitration processes, may also have been perceived as a restrictive practice. It would not have been surprising if the lawyers, whose corporate strength was considerable by the end of the fifteenth century,[87] had not responded to their exclusion from such lucrative business.

Though rules requiring members to bring their disputes for arbitration by the guild continued to be drafted and promulgated – and no doubt enforced – a change can be noticed from the latter part of the fifteenth century. Implied[88] and then explicit reference is made to what is to happen if the efforts of the

---

84. Gross Il 278 citing Manship Henry, Palmer CJ ed *The History of Great Yarmouth* Great Yarmouth 1854 52–54.
85. Ibid.
86. Gross I 40.
87. Baker JH 'The English Legal Profession 1450–1550' in Baker JH *The Legal Profession and the Common Law: Historical Essays* London Hambledon P 1986 75–98.
88. Lipson 345, on the rules of London Shearmen (145): 'no man of the said craft shall take action by the law upon another *where the matter may be ended by treaty or compromise*' without leave of the wardens.

guild fail to resolve the dispute. In 1495, the Merchant Adventurers of York ordained that a member might go to law:[89]

> if he that finds himself grieved, have no remedy of the master and constables within fourteen days next after the grievance to the master and constables declared...

In 1504 the government's antipathy to the power of the guilds, perhaps with the connivance of the lawyers, produced legislation presumably intended to break their exclusivity. The statute allowed any guild member to bring an action in the courts against another member without the guild's permission.[90] But no sanctions seem to have been applied for its breach and no prosecution was brought under it, though at the time it was considered to be a serious and even malicious intrusion into the freedom of the guilds, arising from the efforts of the Recorder of London to foster the interests of the lawyers 'by his great labour, subtle wit and crafty means'.[91] The requirement that disputes should be settled by compromise or arbitration within the guild continued to be included in the new ordinances of guilds throughout the sixteenth century[92] and in 1563 a Newcastle merchant had to pay a penalty of six and eightpence for bringing a legal action against a fellow member.[93] The Elizabethan Guild of the City of Exeter, however, did provide that 'it shall be lawful to proceed in wager and trial of law' if the Governor and Consultes of the Company cannot give redress.[94]

8. ARBITRATION BEFORE COKE

During the Tudor period, English merchants took over foreign trade from aliens. England became an exporter of finished goods. Merchants organised themselves into companies and ceased to travel themselves. Tudor governments established new, more intrusive organs of control. The courts of staple and fair and port fell into desuetude. They were replaced by old courts with new ambitions, such as the Admiralty Court, the established courts of common law and equity (including the Court of Requests), with burgeoning machinery and competence, and new courts specially created or developed to do the government's business better and more predictably in the government's interest, the Council and Star Chamber.[95]

89. Ibid.
90. 19 Henry VII c7.
91. Lipson 346, citing Clode *Early History of the Merchant Taylors* I 39.
92. Barber Surgeons London 1530, Merchant Ventures Essex 1560, Lipson 346.
93. Lipson 346.
94. Jones SA 244.
95. Jones WC 'An Inquiry into the History of the Adjudication of Mercantile Disputes in Great Britain and the United States' (1958) 25 *U of Chicago LR* 445–464, 450.

The Council extended its supervision into all kinds of activity in its determination to control and organise. The disputes of merchants were not exempted. As a court of equity, the Council could sidestep the intricacies of the common law. It could call on the expertise of merchants themselves and insist that they gave their time to the resolution of disputes. Moreover, in the many cases which arose from trade with foreign merchants, arbitration allowed some escape from the technicalities of the common law which few English merchants, let alone aliens, could comprehend. The Council readily and often directed the parties to arbitration, organised and supervised the process and enforced the award.[96]

> The desire apparently was to secure a summary procedure, a more competent and informed tribunal, and emancipation from technical rules of the common law.

There were some new topics, too, for which the common law provided no answers, such as insurance, and for these the Council was ready to provide its arbitration services.[97]

One of the worst problems to beset the Council was caused by the growth of trade and the inadequate technology of the common law. The usual way to ensure performance of a contract, not only to pay money but to do an act, was for the parties to enter into a bond.[98] The amount was penal and bore no necessary relation to economic loss:[99]

> the system itself produced ruin out of all proportion to the default. The chain of forfeitures, once begun, brought bonds and counterbonds into suit, brought sale of assets at knock-down prices, brought arrest of the debtor and disaster to his sureties. Any body of responsible men who conceived their duties to society in the widest sense and who had the power to act must have wished to avert results so contradictory to good sense and so harmful to the interests of the creditors themselves.

The Council found ways out of this labyrinth of debt by appointing as arbitrators merchants of standing, sometimes holding elected office; occasionally noblemen or high officials; more often local gentry. They were just the people to do what was needed – to enquire into the failure and

---

96. Dawson JP 'The Privy Council and Private Law in the Tudor and Stuart Periods: I' (1950) 48 *Michigan LR* 393–428, 409ff. This article, on which much of this section is based, draws on the records of the Privy Council, which are ample evidence of its interest in arbitration for disputes of foreign and English merchants alike.
97. Dawson 409.
98. Simpson AWB op cit.
99. Dawson 411.

extend time for payment if that seemed commercially sensible. Creditors usually consented. If they did not, the Council had means of persuasion, as delicately worded as any threat of arrest could be:[100]

> The Council addressed letters to the creditor advising him to follow 'a milder course', since otherwise their Lordships 'shuld be constrained to take that course against him as otherwise they would be lothe to doe'.

An order for arbitration would be coupled with a mandatory stay of process in debt. Moreover the letters appointing arbitrators would 'usually include appeals to human compassion not common in other cases', asking creditors to release imprisoned debtors.[101] It was also common for the Council to order arbitration by local officials or country gentry even when it was admitted that the common law courts had procedures appropriate to the cause but out of the financial reach of a poor complainant.[102]

The Council appointed arbitrators not only to protect debtors – or rearrange the payment of debts in the interest of business efficacy – or to provide an avenue to justice for poor litigants. There was a wide range and a large number of referrals of disputes arising in matters more commonly considered the preserve of equity, including trusts, claims against executors, and even 'fairly common orders for arbitration of disputes as to legal title to land'.[103]

Very common were referrals of disputes relating to married women's property and maintenance of children. Provision for a wife might be awarded by an arbitral commission and enforced by the Council. The Council could revoke a husband's licence to travel abroad until he made adequate provision. It even ordered the Earl of Derby to sell land to pay his wife's debts.[104]

The Council used arbitration, as a regular stage in its ordinary procedure, to save its time by having disputed issues of fact tried elsewhere:[105]

> The Council's lack of leisure is often invoked as a specific reason for requesting assistance from the arbitrators appointed. In the eighty years for which the record is published, the number of cases referred to arbitration by the Council must have reached into thousands.

100. Dawson 412 citing Dasent ed *Acts of the Privy Council* XX 90 (1590). Holdsworth knew of the process but missed its significance. 'In the numerous mercantile and maritime cases which came before the council there is usually a direction that they were to be settled by arbitration' V 130.
101. Dawson 415.
102. Dawson 417.
103. Dawson 423 n101, citing many instances but adding 'No final order after full hearing has been found in which the Council adjudicated legal title to land, but final orders after full hearing were in any case comparatively rare.'
104. Dawson 422.
105. Dawson 424.

Once referred, the case then usually disappears from the register. The letter of appointment required the arbitrators to report back if they were unable to settle the matter. If a party refused to appear, the Council could arrest for contempt. A party who did not comply with an award was brought before the Council to explain. Moreover, the Council, even without such a hearing, might execute the award. The Council could even remove a cause from a court, explaining that that showed no mistrust of the court but was done to take advantage of the consent of the parties to find an amicable resolution.[106]

However surprising it may seem to those educated to assume a struggle for business between common law and equity, or between the King's Council and the Common Lawyers, Professor Dawson has shown from the sources that the Council worked with the lawyers and merchants to provide a more efficient system for resolving disputes by the application of commonsense by arbitrators. The Council's members were not lawyers, except for the Chancellor – not a Common Lawyer among them. But they used Common Lawyers as a matter of course. They appointed them in the same way as laymen were appointed, instructed 'oyer et terminer', to listen and conclude, according to 'equity' and to bring the parties to a friendly end or charitable composition.[107]

The greatest names in the common law were appointed – the Chief Justices of King's Bench and Common Pleas, the other judges of the common law courts, the Attorney-General and Solicitor-General. The Chancellor sat with them or on his own. At that time, common law judges regularly sat in Chancery. Even Coke, whose battles with the representatives of the equity jurisdiction, Bacon and then Ellesmere, were to force the differences between the systems into sharper contrast, sat many times as arbitrator for the Council, required like his fellows to apply those same principles of equity and commonsense rather than the common law.[108]

It must be remembered that, on the restoration of the monarchy, the courts went back to using Law French and, for their records, Latin. As Fifoot says:[109]

> Such gestures were not calculated to reassure the merchants who sought a speedy and sympathetic settlement of their disputes... businessmen preferred to withdraw from the ambit of the courts... the bulk of mercantile litigation was, under the Stuarts, committed to private arbitration.

9. FROM COKE TO THE FIRST ARBITRATION ACT 1697

106. Dawson 425.
107. Dawson 426. Holdsworth V 134,150.
108. Dawson 427.
109. Fifoot CHS *Lord Mansfield* Oxford Clarendon P 1936,6.

Coke it was who in 1612 'reported' the case which has been of greatest influence in determining the assumptions of later generations of lawyers about the attitudes of earlier courts to arbitration agreements. It is significant that *Vynior's Case* (1609) 8 Co Rep 80a to 83a appears in Part 8 of Coke's Reports, Part 1 of which was published in 1600. The first seven parts had been drawn from Coke's large store of manuscripts and covered cases going back as far as 1572, the great mass being from 1581 onwards. But Part 8 was made up predominantly of recent decisions.[110]

Coke's scarcely resemble modern reports, being – as Coke himself sometimes called them – commentaries on the decisions of the courts. Wherever it suited him, or he thought it would please his royal master, they are enriched with free and ample comment and Coke's own uninhibited political slant. By 1612, when he published Part 8, Coke was Chief Justice of the Common Pleas. He became Chief Justice of the King's Bench in the following year. He was then at the height of his power and influence, though he fell from favour and office in 1616, defending the privileges of the common law against the changes which the king wished to introduce on the authority of the royal prerogative.

It is against this background and in the context of recent developments in the law of contract that *Vynior's Case* must be understood. Robert Vynior brought an action of debt against William Wilde on a bond of 20 pounds dated 15 July 1608. The bond was to secure performance of a promise to submit to the arbitration of William Rugge a dispute over 22 pence for parish tax. Vynior claimed not the 20 pounds of the bond but 10 pounds only, which he said was the damage he had suffered. Wilde asked for the bond to be read. He then said that it showed that its purpose was to secure the arbitration but that had not been possible because he had revoked the arbitrator's authority. Vynior then claimed the amount of the bond. Wilde demurred that Vynior was left without an action. Vynior said he had done enough to prove the debt. Coke reports the outcome thus:

> although ... the defendant was bound in a bond to... observe &c the... arbitrament yet he might countermand it; for a man cannot by his act make such authority ... not countermandable, which is by the law and of its own nature countermandable; as if I make a letter of attorney ... so if I make my testament and last will irrevocable. And therefore [even though a distinction has been drawn between a promise supported by a bond and one which is not] ... in both cases the authority of the arbitrator may be revoked; but then in the one case he shall forfeit his bond and in the other he shall lose nothing.

---

110. Plucknett TFT 'The Genesis of Coke's Reports' (1942) 27 *Cornell LQ* 190–213, reprinted in Plucknett TFT *Studies in Legal History* London Hambledon P 1983 XV.

Coke cites plentiful authority for his rule that the contract to submit to arbitration is not binding without a bond but it all predates the then recent law reforms, in which Coke had been centrally involved, reported as *Slade's Case* (1602) 4 Co Rep 91a. That decision, uniquely argued and made the law for all courts, held that an action in assumpsit would lie to enforce – by an award of damages – a promise supported by the consideration of a counter promise.[111] Indeed, later editors of Coke's Reports point out in a note here the later authority that an action would lie in assumpsit for revoking a submission not under seal.

Whether Coke intentionally put the twist in his report, and his false analogy with a promise not to revoke a will is almost enough to show his bias, *Vynior's Case* for 300 years had 'such extraordinary vitality that its doctrine alone has limited the development of arbitration in commercial disputes in all common law countries'.[112] The vitality was greater in the United States than in England, where evidence of judicial animosity against arbitration is slight until the middle of the eighteenth century.

Some glimmer of the public's and perhaps the court's uneasiness in the obligor being required to pay 20 pounds in a dispute over 22 pence may be seen in Vynior's claim for 10 pounds. It was the sort of coercion that might well have roused the interest of the Council and engendered a submission to arbitration. In response to such concerns the Statute of Fines and Penalties was passed in 1687, which disallowed recovery of the penalty and restricted obligees of bonds to the amount they could prove they had suffered as a result of the failure to comply with the terms of the bond.

Moreover, the courts held that the damages recoverable by the obligee of an arbitration bond were nominal, on the ground – manifestly specious and self-serving – that you could not lose by having to go to law.[113]

We have seen that the Council was more than ready to refer cases to arbitration and use Common lawyers as arbitrators. In the 1620s the House of Lords spent much of its time arbitrating simple disputes over property or debts, and getting involved in major and complex commercial matters such as the failure of the Muscovy Company.[114] 'Those who petitioned the

111. Roebuck *Background* 96; Holdsworth III 447; *Freeman v Bernard* (1698)1 Ld Raymond 248.
112. Sayre 601.
113. *Doleman v Ossett Corpn* [1912] 3 KB 268. Much new light has been thrown on arbitration in this period by the very recently published article by Horwitz H and Oldham J 'John Locke, Lord Mansfield and Arbitration during the Eighteenth Century' (1993) 36 I *The Historical Journal* 137–159. Not only does it show the hand of Locke in the creation of the first Arbitration Act, it amply illustrates, with some telling statistics, the prevalence of arbitration and its natural symbiosis with the courts of Common Pleas and King's Bench in this period.
114. Hart JS *Justice upon Petition: the House of Lords and the Reformation of Justice 1621–1675* London Harper Collins 1991 52. 'The Lords handled at least a dozen such conflicts in the early years of the Long Parliament.' Ibid 132.

House directly did so, in the main, because they had been unable to proceed elsewhere.'[115] There were also many domestic disputes, of first instance, most often between husband and wife. It seems no other court could help. 'The Lords proved to be more than willing to entertain cases of this kind, despite the seemingly inconsequential nature of the complaints.'[116] They took advice from their colleagues learned in the law but, as laymen, applying rules of law and equity if they could, they decided as they thought best, paternally for the good of the parties and the nation. They were, however, unlike arbitrators in that they acted on the petition of one party rather than by the agreement of both. Legal advisers also found a way of using the common law courts to ensure that a submission was effective. They began an action and then asked the court to refer the matter to arbitration. Any refusal to proceed with the arbitration or to abide by an award was then a contempt of court.[117]

After some reluctance, the procedure can be seen to be well established by 1670[118] and in 1698 it was given statutory recognition so that no action needed to be brought to start it. The preamble to 9 and 10 Wm III c15 states its objects to be:[119]

for promoting trade, and rendering the awards of arbitrators the more effectual in all cases, for the final determination of controversies referred to them by merchants and traders, or others, concerning matters of account or trade, or other matters....

The parties to a dispute falling within the Act could by agreement make their submission 'a rule of any of His Majesty's Courts of Record' with the consequence that process would issue for default. What was required was an affidavit entered of record and the court would then issue a Rule 'that

115. Ibid 132.
116. Ibid 134.
117. Holdsworth 189, citing Kyd 11.
118. *Hide v Petit* (1670) 1 Ch Cas 185. Horwitz and Oldham show that 'In early modern England, both chancery and the courts of common law seem to have been prepared to encourage the resolution of suits by approving the parties' resort to arbitrators or referees. Furthermore ...the making of "references" in civil cases being tried at nisi prius (both in the metropolis and on assize) seems to have been a frequent occurrence.' (139–140) Moreover 'arbitration in lieu of or at least prior to litigation was even more common.' (140) The attitudes of the courts differed somewhat: in the 1650s and 1660s 'Common Pleas was prepared ... to back up references ... by threatening recalcitrant parties with attachment of the body' (141), but King's Bench was not. By the 1690s, however, both courts would issue writs of attachment and 'allow, as a matter of routine, the entry of references to arbitration in pending suits as rules of court.' (142) For a referral by the Court of Exchequer, see Price JM '*Sheffeild v Starke*' (1986) 28 *Business History* 19–39.
119. The Chancellor was charged with powers and duties of supervision.

the parties shall submit to, and finally be concluded by the arbitration and umpirage'.

Power was, however, given to the courts to set aside an award if it: 'be made to appear, on oath,... that the arbitrators or umpire misbehaved themselves, and that such award, arbitration, or umpirage was procured by corruption or other undue means'.

As Fifoot put it: 'The Statute of William III introduced a tolerable business in arbitration awards, and Westminster Hall echoed, at a chaste distance, the speculative orgy which culminated in the collapse of the South Sea Company.'[120]

Blackstone, in Book 3 of his *Commentaries on the Laws of England* published in 1765, described contemporary arbitration, elegantly and without a hint of judicial antipathy (at p 17):

For though originally the submission to arbitration used to be by word, or by deed, yet both of these being revocable in their nature, it is now become the practice to enter into mutual bonds, with condition to stand to the award or arbitration of the arbitrators or umpire therein named. And experience having shewn the great use of these peaceable and domestic tribunals, especially in settling matters of account, and other mercantile transactions which are difficult and almost impossible to be adjusted on a trial at law; the legislature has now established the use of them, as well in controversies where causes are depending, as in those where no action is brought, and which still depend upon the rules of the common law: enacting, by statute 9 & 10 W. III, c. 15, that all merchants and others, who desire to end any controversy (for which there is no other remedy but by personal action or suit in equity), may agree that their submission of the suit to arbitration or umpirage shall be made a rule of any of the king's courts of record, and may insert such agreement in their submission or promise, or condition of the arbitration-bond: which agreement being proved upon oath, by one of the witnesses thereto, the court shall make a rule that such submission and award shall be conclusive: and, after such rule made, the parties disobeying the award shall be liable to be punished, as for contempt of the court; unless such award shall be set aside, for corruption or other misbehavior in the arbitrators or umpire, proved on oath to the court, within one term after the award is made. And, in consequence of this statute it is now become a considerable part of the business of the superior courts to set aside such awards when partially or illegally made; or to enforce their execution, when legal, by the same process of contempt, as is awarded for disobedience to those rules and orders which are issued by the courts themselves.

120. Fifoot 13.

When the submission complied with the Act's requirements, the courts enforced the award. If it did not, it remained revocable at common law. Holdsworth believed:[121]

> This rule of the common law which allowed a party to an arbitration to put an end to it at any time before an award was given, even though his action involved a breach of covenant, was probably one of the rules which helped, in the middle of the eighteenth century, to give rise to the doctrine that any contract to oust the jurisdiction of the courts was void because it was against public policy.

10. THE MODERN LAW

Holdsworth detected jealousy in the courts for centuries, but that is not borne out by the evidence. And he states unequivocally: 'However that may be, the rule was not heard of till the middle of the eighteenth century.'[122] It was firmly denied by Lord Hardwicke in *Wellington v Mackintosh* (1743) 2 Atkin 570; held to be settled law three years later, with no authority to support it, in what became the leading case, *Kill v Hollister* (1746) 1 Wilson 129; and still disputed into the nineteenth century.[123]

Perhaps the cause of the misunderstanding is the tendency, ever present among legal historians, to concentrate on the courts of common law. A more balanced and comprehensive view is offered by Professor Cornish:[124]

> If the reason why a court could not offer the same advantages was inherent in its structure, it might welcome the spread of arbitration. In the sixteenth century Chancery, the Star Chamber and the Council had all referred disputes to arbitrators as a means of expanding slender resources. But the common law courts of the early modern period, in their hunger for jurisdiction, seem to have taken a more antagonistic view... they might

121. Holdsworth 190.
122. Ibid.
123. *Halfhide v Fenning* (1788) 2 Bro CC 337 per Lord Kenyon; *Michell v Harris* (1793) 4 Bro CC 311; *Thompson v Charnock* (1799) 8 TR 139; *Waters v Taylor* (1808) 15 Ves 23. The most fascinating new evidence (in an article full of new minted ideas) presented by Horwitz and Oldham is serendipitous support for the unorthodox views expressed in the text here. 'Campbell's reading of these cases were based on defective printed reports. Thus Sergeant Hill's unprinted report of *Wellington* indicates that the chancellor dismissed counsel's contention that the arbitration arrangement ... should be construed as "tending to oust the jurisdiction of the court"; Hardwicke thought this "an objection of no weight for most certainly men may submit their differences to the arbitration of persons chose by them without applying to the courts of public justice".'(146) 'Holdsworth's analysis [of judicial jealousy inhibiting use of the 1698 Act] appears well off the mark... the Rule Books of King's Bench demonstrate the contrary.'(155).
124. Cornish WR and Clark GdeN *Law and Society in England 1750–1950* Sweet & Maxwell 1989 36.

insist that a dispute be removed into their court... by allowing one party who had submitted to arbitration nonetheless to bring a common law suit at any time before the arbitrator made his award.

The courts of common law used different techniques to deal with those disputes which could best be disposed of by arbitral, or at least more relaxed and less technical, procedures. Lord Mansfield, with Holt CJ and others, injected the common law with transfusions of new principles, practices and procedures from the law merchant. In ways quite similar to those used at the beginning of the thirteenth century, the jury was given an arbitral role.[125] As Professor Cornish describes Lord Mansfield's reforms:[126]

> His jury comprised special jurors from the City of London, many of them sitting regularly to determine crucial cases on the import of financial, insurance and trading customs. By this approximation many of the most obvious differences between common law rules and commercial arbitration disappeared.

The rule in *Kill v Hollister* was the basis of the decision in the case which marks the beginning of the modern law of arbitration in England, *Scott v Avery* (1856) 5 HLC 811, which held valid an agreement that no right of action could arise until after the award (and in which Lord Campbell gave authority to the myth of 'judicial jealousy' that may have misled Holdsworth).

Lord Mansfield was Chief Justice of King's Bench from 1756 to 1788. In the later years he was in danger of being overwhelmed by the length of the list and the pressure of his work in Parliament, where he was a busy spokesman for the government. He had a shrewd knowledge of what the merchant class required and made much use of arbitration, often appointing the same solicitor, Thomas Lowten, as arbitrator. The strength of Mansfield's approval of arbitration can be seen in his own words in *Nash v Lindgren*: 'I tried all I could to have the whole [case] referred and settled, but the Plaintiff would agree to nothing.'[127]

By the 1780s it became standard practice for the court to include in its reference an authorisation for the arbitrator to take sworn statements from the parties (which gave arbitration a procedural advantage over common law courts, though not equity) and from witnesses.[128]

125. Above n45.
126. Cornish 37, 198–9; Burdick FM 'Contributions of the Law Merchant to the Common Law' (1902) 2 *Columbia LR* 470–485, reprinted *Select Essays in Anglo-American Legal History* (1909) reprint Wildy London 1968; Fifoot Prologue and 82ff.
127. Horwitz and Oldham 150. Oldham James *The Mansfield Manuscripts and the Growth of English Law in the Eighteenth Century* 2 vols Chapel Hill U of Carolina P 1992.
128. Ibid 151 and 155: '[Holdsworth's] account of the legislative reforms of the first half of the nineteenth century exaggerated their novelty since some of the procedural changes they translated into statute had long since been incorporated in rules of court.'

Further legislation in the nineteenth century gave the arbitrator further powers. In 1833, 3 and 4 William IV c 42 provided that an arbitration agreement that had been made a rule of court was not revocable without the court's leave. But its most important contribution was, for the first time, to facilitate the conduct of arbitrations, by providing for the compulsion of witnesses to attend and to produce evidence. The Common Law Procedure Act 1854, s 7 provided:

> Every agreement of submission to arbitration by consent whether by deed or instrument in writing not under seal may be made a rule of any one of the superior courts of law or equity at Westminster on the application of any party thereto unless such agreement or submission contain words purporting that the parties intend that it should not be made a rule of court.

The Act also gave power to the court to grant a stay of proceedings at the request of a party to a written submission; to appoint and substitute arbitrators and umpires; and to remit the award to the consideration of the arbitrator. It gave the arbitrator power to state the award in the form of a case for the court's decision.

Lord Brougham tried to empower the new County Courts to conduct arbitration and mediation but had to omit these powers in his Compromise Act of 1846, though a County Court judge could refer a matter to arbitration.[129] Certainly, by the time of *Scott v Avery*, the higher courts had lost their commercial work. Special courts – the Courts of Requests and later the County Courts – together with new administrative tribunals took work away and 'arbitration attracted increasing attention from both businessmen and lawyers after 1850 while commercial litigation was, by contemporary accounts, conspicuous by its absence from the courts'.[130]

The 1880s were a period of unusual activity in England in the advancement of new ideas in law reform. Even more extraordinary was their success in producing actual changes in the law through legislation. The 1870s had seen the Judicature Acts recast the system of courts. In the next decade, in a fashion never seen before or since, Parliament was persuaded that there was some advantage in codification – at least in the attenuated English sense of that term. The Bills of Sale and the Bills of Exchange Act 1882 were followed by similar partial codifications of the law on mercantile agents (or factors) (1889 and 1890), partnership (1890) and sale of goods (1893).

The conditions seemed to provide an opportunity for a code of arbitration law which would have modernised and simplified the law and brought it

---

129. Arthurs HW *Without the Law* Toronto U of Toronto P 1985, 43. Chapter 3 'Commercial Relationships and Disputes: the Persistence of Pluralism' is valuable on this period, and 101ff on statutory arbitration 'available across a broad spectrum of social and economic concerns'.
130. Arthurs 168.

into line with the expectations of those who made use of arbitration. And indeed, between 1884 and 1889, there was introduced into Parliament an Arbitration Code drafted under the auspices of Lord Bramwell, a judge of the highest eminence among lawyers and merchants.[131] After the fashion of other English codes of the time, it was not intended to be comprehensive of all the law. It gave scope for natural development, dealing more with principle than the details of practice.

Unfortunately, the draft code, which could have provided a model law which would have added to Britain's prestige and the already substantial advantage it had as an arbitration centre, failed to become law. It was a casualty of a change of government. Moreover, even as distinguished, influential and experienced a judge as Lord Bramwell found he could not escape the fate of all those well intentioned law reformers who have underestimated the reactionary prowess of the scorned draftsman.[132]

So it was that, instead of a modern code, Parliament introduced the Arbitration Act 1889, by which the old system of making submissions into rules of court was superseded and a private agreement to arbitrate, without an application to the court, became irrevocable. The 1889 Act provided that a submission, unless it expressed a contrary intention, was irrevocable and had the same effect as if made by court order. Moreover, it would include the provisions set out in the First Schedule, which assumed a single arbitrator, provided for umpires, gave arbitrators powers to summon witnesses and examine them on oath, made the award final and gave the arbitrators power to award costs.

The attitude of the courts at the turn of the century was certainly not hostile to arbitration. On the contrary, the House of Lords enforced arbitration agreements strictly, in accordance with the prevailing notion of 'sanctity of contracts'.[133]

During the early part of the twentieth century the emphasis was on ensuring that the process of arbitration operated fairly. Even when the arbitration was once under way, there was also a distinctly greater willingness to supervise the activities of the arbitrators. By overseeing the arbitral procedure in this way, the House was able to ensure the reliability of arbitration without unnecessarily interfering with its efficiency.

---

131. Veeder VV and Dye Brian 'Lord Bramwell's Arbitration Code 1884–1889' (1992) 8 *Arbitration International* 329–352.
132. The fascinating story is told in Veeder and Dye 340ff, where the code is set out in full.
133. Stevens Robert *Law and Politics: the House of Lords as a Judicial Body, 1800–1976* London Weidenfeld and Nicolson 1979 146.

Acts of 1924 and 1930 allowed a stay of proceedings in breach of an arbitration agreement between citizens of the countries named in the Protocol and for the enforcement of foreign awards.

The Arbitration Act 1934 made comprehensive provision for arbitrations and the supervisory powers of the court where there was fraud or bias.

The Arbitration Act 1979 got rid of the 'case stated' procedure, which lawyers had abused, and provided instead a voluntary system of appeals on points of law.

The story of the development of arbitration is not ended or endable but an account of its history, in relation to the development of English law, must end with the contemporary decades in which the system of arbitration still defined by being alternative to litigation, has grown greatly in popularity and come to share its work with new alternative systems of resolving disputes.

There is much in that history that is still unknown and perhaps even more that is known but wrong. This chapter is no more than a sketch of the topic, attempting to fill some gaps in the former and subtract from the latter.[134]

The difficulty lies not in the new ideas but in escaping from the old ones, which ramify, for those brought up as most of us have been, into every corner of our minds.

---

134. Keynes JM 'The End of Laissez-Faire' *Collected Works* London 1972 IX 277.

CAPTAIN CHARLES ELLIOT RN, ARBITRATOR: DISPUTE RESOLUTION IN CHINA WATERS 1834–1836

Derek Roebuck

[*Author's note*: My first attempt to write about the history of dispute resolution in Hong Kong was published as 'Arbitration in Early Hong Kong 1835–67' (1997) 63 *Arbitration* 263–269. That article was soon superseded when I discovered Charles Elliot's own arbitration scheme. I then rewrote the part dealing with the earlier period, which became this piece and was published in (1998) 14 *Arbitration International* 89–116. The later years have now been covered in a paper written with my friend Christopher Munn 'Something So Unenglish'.[1] He, Susanna Hoe (whose discovery of Charles and Clara Elliot's letters has illuminated Elliot's career) and the late Carl Smith have had a hand in all my efforts to write about Hong Kong.]

[*Editorial note*: This contribution was originally published in (1998) 14 *Arbitration International* 89–116 and is reproduced in this volume by kind permission of the publisher. It was later published in Derek Roebuck, *Disputes and Differences. Comparisons in Law, Language and History* (Oxford: HOLO Books: The Arbitration Press, 2010).]

INTRODUCTION

Captain Charles Elliot of the Royal Navy was more than anyone responsible for establishing the colony of Hong Kong in 1841.[2] But he first sailed for China Waters in 1834 in the lowly position of Master Attendant to Lord Napier, Chief of a Commission of three Superintendents of British Trade

---

1. Derek Roebuck and Christopher Munn 'Something So Unenglish' [Roebuck and Munn].
2. December 1833 Master Attendant; July 1834 arrived in China; October 1834 promoted Secretary of the Commission; January 1835 Third Superintendent; April 1835 Second Superintendent; June 1836 Chief Superintendent; December 1836 takes over from Robinson. Clagette Blake *Charles Elliot RN 1801-1875* has been largely superseded by Susanna Hoe and Derek Roebuck *The Taking of Hong Kong: Charles and Clara Elliot in China Waters* [Hoe].

in China, which had just been appointed to take the place of the East India Company as representatives of British interests.

In all his work, Elliot was a committed and active administrator. He had a clear sense of duty, which drove him to find solutions when others were content to take shelter behind the bureaucrat's excuse of leaving ill alone. In the end, he was brought down by the failure of his superiors in England to back him, perhaps even to understand the problems which he had quite successfully begun to solve.

One of those problems was how to ensure the orderly transaction of business in such a lawless place as Canton, where the Chinese had no system of commercial law, no tradition of international trade and every inclination and opportunity for corruption. The foreigners, on the other hand, mainly British, were for the most part opium traders, what Second Superintendent and future Governor of Hong Kong, Sir John Davis, called 'a vulgar rabble of free traders'.[3] Each community enjoyed a nonchalant assumption of racial superiority over the other, which made communication hazardous even when there were reliable interpreters. Neither could imagine another empire as prestigious as its own; neither was averse to circumventing its emperor's will to make a little money on the side.

The first requirement was some way of resolving disputes and enforcing the payment of debts. But the British Government had carefully subtracted from the Superintendents' authority any civil jurisdiction.[4] Elliot set out to remedy this lack, not only by sorting out disputes himself, as far as he was allowed, but by devising and advocating a novel scheme of arbitration, voluntary if possible, compulsory if necessary.

CAPTAIN ELLIOT'S ARBITRATION SCHEME

On 1 April 1835, Elliot was promoted to Second Superintendent. By 17 April he had presented a proposal to the Chief Superintendent, Sir George Best Robinson,[5] which Robinson sent on with his approval to Lord Palmerston, Foreign Secretary. Elliot's Minute set out a comprehensive scheme for the arbitration of commercial disputes. Because of its inaccessibility and precocious interest, coming at the same time as quite different proposals for law reform in England, the text is edited and published here

3. See Appendix. Sir John Francis Davis, last President of the Select Committee of the East India Company, had been in its service since 1813, studying Chinese language and customs. Became second Governor of Hong Kong in 1844. The first Chief Superintendent was Lord Napier.
4. Derek Roebuck 'Arbitration in Early Hong Kong 1835-67' [Roebuck] deals with the problems caused by this lack of civil jurisdiction.
5. Sir George Best Robinson, Baronet, had been a servant of the Company since c1819.

for the first time in full,[6] with commentary setting it in its context and examples showing how Elliot tried to put his ideas into practice.[7]

The following is a Minute by Captain Elliot, proposing a mode for the adjustment[8] of any commercial disputes which may take place between His Majesty's Subjects at Canton.

Amongst the earliest subjects which engaged my attention after my connexion with this Commission, was the necessity of devising some simple but systematic mode for the adjustment of any commercial disputes which might arise between the King's subjects in the prosecution of their business at Canton. This great commerce is to be conducted under a new and entirely different set of circumstances.[9] Ships will repair to China for a season and perhaps never return, having on board, in many cases, Agents charged with the disposal and purchase of their cargoes, whose transactions with the resident British merchants will probably be very extensive; and in some instances it may be extremely needful to possess such means of constraining such parties to submit disputed points to investigation, *upon the spot*. New mercantile establishments must be looked for, bringing principles for their guidance in the pursuit of business, which may be difficult or highly inconvenient of application in our peculiar position in this country, and... 'the custom of the trade', has [yet] to be formed... the expectation of pretty frequent disputes is not likely to prove ill-founded. In... a commercial difference between a resident merchant and a transient trader, to leave the former to seek his remedy entirely in... consent to arbitration before he left the country, is to rely with more confidence on... moral sense

6. The Minute is in a despatch of 1 July 1835 from Robinson to Palmerston, who received it on 28 January 1836. The despatch enclosed a voluminous bundle of documents relating to a number of disputes (including one between Robinson and Elliot). An extract from Robinson's letter, in *British Parliamentary Papers 40: China: Opium War and Opium Trade* 40 refers to Elliot's Minute but it survives only deeply buried in Robinson's despatches, unindexed and unchronological, in manuscript and on microfilm, where I found it. Robinson's despatch starts *Foreign Office Papers* FO17/10 folios 1-13. The reference to Elliot's Minute is at FO17/10 f13. The documents relating to the various disputes run from FO17/11 ff80-197A. The Minute itself is at FO17/10 ff145-155.
7. All the added emphasis is in the original. The style of the day lent itself to periphrasis. One marvels at the euphuistic facility of written expression of the merchants, administrators and military men of this period but, for economy rather than aesthetics, cuts have had to be made in many of the quotations, shown by dots.... No attempt has been made to ensure that what remains is grammatical, let alone elegant. Additions to help the sense are in square brackets. Because all the documents are manuscript copies, oddities of spelling, punctuation and capitalisation may well have been the copyist's. I have often removed them.
8. The word is most commonly used at this time and this context in its primary dictionary sense of 'settle', but sometimes as a synonym for 'resolve by arbitration'.
9. After the abolition of the East India Company's monopoly and the control the Company had exercised over British merchants and shipping.

than... our nature can sufficiently warrant. On the other hand, to tell the British merchant that he has his remedy by recourse to the courts in England is... effectually to leave him without one. Persons engaged in the engrossing business of an anxious commerce in this remote part of the world, are not in a condition to proceed to England without immense sacrifice... and to confide these matters to other hands is not always practicable.... The advantages... against an absent complainant are striking... inconvenience with respect to the adjustment of disputed points must obtain, in the nature of things, in this country. If both parties, however, *consent* to defer the adjustment of a dispute, there can be no reasonable ground of complaint... but in all cases of difference between British subjects involving pecuniary considerations, *when the one side seeks to be heard*, it is of the very essence of a safe pursuit of this distant and expensive commerce to make adequate provision for the fulfilment of that demand.... the practical problem... is to shape the process... [to] secure *substantial justice* between disputants, with the least possible... delay,... expense, and... interference upon the part of this Commission.... The most succinct and perspicuous course... will be to suppose a case by way of illustration.[10]

A and B have a difference of opinion arising out of a commercial transaction originating at Canton.... [A offers to B] to submit the points in dispute to arbitration. The respective appointment of arbitrators and the joint execution of a deed of agreement to adhere to their decision or (failing their concurrence) to the decision of an umpire, provision for whose nomination should be made *pari passu* with that of the arbitrators in the following manner.

[If] B shall agree to go to arbitration, but shall not coincide in the choice of the person A has named as his umpire, A and B shall each deliver into the hands of a third person the name of the gentleman either shall desire to perform the task of umpire between the arbitrators, written on a slip of paper and sealed up. If the arbitrators shall not be able to agree in a decision, this third person shall be called upon to draw, in their presence, from a box, one of the two slips of paper previously delivered into his keeping, and the person so drawn on by name shall perform the office of umpire between the arbitrators, and his decision shall be final....

It would be convenient to involve... a saving clause... that, if... it should appear to either A or B that there had been some violation of the true spirit

10. Here he excluded cases falling within the Admiralty jurisdiction, which was in any case criminal only, Roebuck p263.

and intent of this mode of adjusting a dispute, either by reason of gross error or partiality, or other obvious ground for disturbing the decision, it should be competent to either... to decline to conform to the decision until the sense of the Superintendents had been taken thereupon. If A and B did not agree by previous concert... in the deed of agreement, of course this last principle of further reference to the Superintendents would not obtain.

The next case... is... a dispute between C and D, C being willing and proposing to arbitrate and D either declining... or evading the... necessary preliminary arrangements. C writes to D a formal letter requiring him to adjust their difference by this process, the delivery of which letter to D, or at his usual place of dwelling, must be proved, if need be, on oath.

Receiving a direct negative or failing to receive a satisfactory... answer, within... five days... C will enclose an attested copy of it to the Secretary of the Superintendents, together with the names of the persons he has chosen as his arbitrator and umpire. The Superintendents call upon D to name an arbitrator within... one week... and failing... a satisfactory reply... proceed to name an arbitrator on his behalf in the following manner.

The names of six British merchants resident at Canton, each written on a slip of paper, shall be placed in a box, and the Secretary, in the presence of the Superintendents, will draw the names of one... and the first drawn... shall... perform the business of arbitrator in the behalf of D. If D can give sufficient cause to the satisfaction of the Superintendents why the person so drawn... should not perform... on his behalf, another name shall be added to the five remaining in the box, and the Secretary shall again draw, and *so on*, until he shall have drawn a name to which it shall appear, to the satisfaction of the Superintendents, there is no sufficient ground of objection on the part of D.

The arbitrator appointed by C, and the person nominated by the aforesaid process on the behalf of D, shall then... determine the matter in dispute; and if they shall not be able to agree, the name of the umpire C has chosen shall be placed in a box and the Secretary in the presence of the Superintendents shall draw another name from the five remaining merchants' names, and the person so drawn (unless there be some satisfactory ground of objection upon the part of D, in which case proceed as before in the respect of the arbitrator) shall be... umpire on the behalf of D, and his name shall be placed in the Box containing the name of the umpire C has chosen. The Secretary shall then, in the presence of the Superintendents, draw... and the person so drawn... shall be umpire.

If the decision... shall be against D... a bill shall be made out to the satisfaction of the arbitrators or umpire who decided the question... of all expenses incurred in the adjustment of the dispute, and of any fair loss or damage C has sustained from the delay occasioned by D's... refusal to arbitrate, and this bill of costs shall be charged against D....

It would be desirable to report in the newspaper an abstract of the case involving the principles upon which the matter has been determined... to establish a small body of useful precedents in disputed cases connected with the commercial custom of the port; and... there may be examples of unprincipled disinclination to adjust disputes, against... which this check of publicity may incidentally operate in a salutary manner.

Be a man never so obviously mistaken, if he be willing to submit his dispute to the examination of indifferent persons, there can be no ground to ascribe to him any thing wrongful beyond that persuasion of judgment which his condition as an interested person may amply excuse. But he who pertinaciously refuses to consent to the intervention of impartial enquiry, or plausibly evades it, renders himself obnoxious to imputation of a very different complexion, and this... it is for the public benefit to expose.

When a decision shall be obtained by this prescribed process, the party against whom it is formed shall be formally required by the Chief Superintendent to conform to it within some reasonable specified period; and, failing any admissible ground for delay, at the expiration of that time it shall be carried into execution by the Chief Superintendent's order, except only under the following circumstances.

If either... C or D... shall think fit to carry an appeal against the decision before the Judicial Committee of His Majesty's Privy Council, notice... shall be given to the Secretary of the Superintendents within... five days.... No notice... shall be... of any force in suspending the execution of the decision..., unless the party giving such notice shall within the... five days, enter into a bond, binding himself and a sufficient surety (under penalty of five hundred pounds to the Crown) that proceedings of appeal... shall be instituted in England within... fifteen months from the date of the notice.

The subsidiary fabric of rules and regulations which it will be necessary to establish respecting the formal manner of carrying on these processes, and... securing to the arbitrators... means of compelling the attendance of witnesses, and respecting the mode of carrying the decisions into execution, will require great care and attention. *To do the least that is* necessary for the accomplishment of the object in view is the principle that should judge us, and perhaps in the first place the wisest course to pursue would be merely to define the *practice*, and to leave experience to indicate the points which will require more comprehensive provision. A needless burden of regulation is a great evil. I very well know (for I have had considerable experience in these matters in other parts of the world)[11] that a copious supply of legal remedies for anticipated difficulties is the sure precursor of an abundant crop of subterfuge, evasion, and chicane. To establish as sound and as *few principles* as we can, and carefully to adapt our practice and proceedings, in any necessities which arise, to those principles, is the task we have to perform....

I cannot help repeating my own conviction, that the British mercantile community is deeply interested in the establishment of some sure and simple means of constraining an unconsenting party to submit to reasonable means of adjustment on the spot. And I trust the facility of appeal, (which the judicial character of the decree by the Chief Superintendent would leave open) will be thought to furnish a sufficient guarantee against the effect of haste, inexperience, or unsound decision.... the principle upon which this scheme is founded, is to place entirely in the hands of the community fair means of determining any commercial disputes which may arise within itself, and simply to leave to the Commission the task of setting the necessary machinery in operation and giving efficacy to the results produced. I think it would be very desirable to take advantage of the present interval of comparative leisure to shape out such rules as may be indispensably needful, into a regular form, and perhaps it would greatly facilitate this labour if the British mercantile community[12] would name a committee of gentlemen to confer with the Commission on the subject. In the course of my career as a member of a Colonial Government I chanced to be a good deal engaged in business of a nature somewhat analogous to the particular duty which has devolved upon the Superintendents by the Orders in Council, in this respect of establishing and adapting rules of proceeding and practice for the more speedy administration of justice.[13]

He concludes by apologising for the hurried nature of his proposals, which, he says, 'some recent circumstances have induced me to put forward in a less clear and finished shape than I had hoped to have been able to arrange it.' To understand the scheme, those recent circumstances need to be examined.

11. Perhaps as Protector of Slaves in British Guiana, where he wrote: 'I am desperately unpopular, although I am sure I have not intended to do my duty captiously. But the fact is that this Colony is in a state of rebellion; the administration of Justice obstructed or totally defeated', KN Bell and WP Morrell eds *Select Documents on British Colonial Policy 1830-1860* p382 [Bell and Morrell], now more accessible in Hoe.

12. Elliot was no doubt encouraged by the establishment of the British Chamber of Commerce of Canton, see Appendix.

13. The only place where Elliot had been a member of the colonial government was British Guiana, where he was a member of the Court of Policy 1831-32 and concerned with the aftermath of the repeal of an ordinance setting up courts of civil justice, Bell and Morrell p377; Hoe pp92 and 237 n1.

THE NEED FOR THE SCHEME

When in 1833[14] the British Government decided to end the monopoly of the East India Company over British trade with China, it resolved that:

> 'whereas it is expedient for the Objects of Trade and amiable Intercourse with the Dominions of the Emperor of *China* that Provision be made for the Establishment of a *British* Authority... for the Purpose of protecting and promoting such Trade...'

its interests would be best served by a Commission of three Superintendents of British Trade in China. The China Trade Act 1833 provided for Orders in Council and Directions and Regulations:

> over and in respect of the Trade and Commerce of His Majesty's Subjects within any part of the said Dominions; and to impose Penalties, Forfeitures, or Imprisonments [for their breach].... And to create a Court of Justice with Criminal and Admiralty Jurisdiction for the Trial of Offences committed by HM Subjects within the said Dominions, and the Ports and Havens thereof, and on the High Seas within One Hundred Miles of the Coast of *China*.

But it did not give the Superintendents any civil jurisdiction, expressly or by implication.[15] Nor did the three Orders in Council of 9 December 1833.

The first provided that 'all the powers and authorities which, on 21 April 1834 shall by law be vested in the Supra Cargoes of the... Company..., are hereby vested in the Superintendents.' Those powers were to be enforced in the same way the Company's Supercargoes[16] could have enforced them 'or by the sentence and adjudication of the Court of Justice established at Canton.' The second established that court 'with criminal and Admiralty jurisdiction'; its procedures were to be those 'of the Courts of Oyer and Terminer and Gaol delivery in England... so far as it may be practicable to maintain such conformity and correspondence, regard being had to the difference of local circumstances.' The third Order imposed customs duties on the value of goods exported, to be estimated by the current market prices at Canton, and provides the first mention of arbitration (and that compulsory) in China Waters: 'if any difference of opinion should arise as to the market prices... [they] shall be determined and fixed by two indifferent British merchants or subjects residing at the place.' One

---

14. By the Acts of 3 & 4 William IV chapters 85 and 93 (China Trade Act).

15. Roebuck p264.

16. Though this is the more common spelling, 'supracargoes' is used in many of the primary sources, including British legislation.

was to be chosen by the Superintendents, the other by the master of the vessel, and those two were to appoint a third British merchant or subject as umpire. The arbitrators had seven days to fix the value, the umpire three if they disagreed.

Before he set sail from Devonport, Napier received Royal Instructions.[17] Paragraph 17, headed 'Protection and Assistance to be afforded to British Subjects', reads:

> And in the discharge of Your Duties... we do require and enjoin You to watch over and protect the Interests of our Subjects resident at or resorting to the Empire of China for the purposes of Trade, and to afford them all such advice, information, and assistance, as it may be in Your power to give, with a view to the safe and successful conduct of their commercial Transactions, and to the utmost of Your ability to protect them in the peaceable prosecution of all lawful enterprises in which they may be engaged in China, and, by the exertion of Your utmost influence and authority, to adjust by arbitration or persuasion all disputes in which any of our Subjects may be there engaged with each other, or with the Inhabitants of China, or with the Subjects or Citizens of any Foreign state, and to mediate between our said subjects and the Officers of the Chinese Government, in order to protect our Subjects aforesaid from all unlawful exactions or hindrances, in the prosecution of their Commercial undertakings.

So civil disputes between British subjects, and between British and Chinese or other non-British individuals, were to be disposed of by 'arbitration or persuasion'. Between British individuals and the Chinese Government, the Commission was to mediate. To enforce their jurisdiction, the Superintendents might use their 'utmost influence and authority'. They had no legal powers at all.

Lord Napier did not last long enough to have to worry about civil disputes.[18] His unhappy time as Chief Superintendent ended in his death in October 1834. The Second Superintendent Sir John Davis succeeded Napier as Chief, Sir George Best Robinson succeeded Davis as Second and John Harvey Astell[19] succeeded Robinson as Third. They were soon called on to deal with civil disputes.

17. FO17/5 f54.
18. Though he did encourage the creation of a British Chamber of Commerce at Canton, which was to have arbitration functions, see Appendix.
19. Robinson, Davis and Astell had all been East India Company men. Astell returned to work as the Company's Canton agent as soon as he decently could, *Canton Register* 7 April 1835. There is no evidence that he ever took much of a hand in the Commission's work. He left China in December 1839, *Canton Register* 10 December 1839, but returned with the expeditionary force from India in 1840.

GODDARD v PEILE

On 26 October 1834, James Goddard, a British merchant at Canton, complained to the Commission that Captain Peile of the *Standard* had refused to deliver the whole of a cargo of rice to Goddard as required by the bill of lading. Peile's excuse was that he had a claim to demurrage, arising from the 'detention of the ship outside, in consequence of the late stoppage of trade'. Goddard said he was willing 'at proper time to submit to His Majesty's authorities' the demurrage dispute but:

At present and immediately I beg to claim their interference upon the first principle of British maritime law, that a ship having earned her freight has an unquestionable lien upon the cargo for the payment... no consideration will justify the further detention of the cargo.'

Goddard asked the Superintendents to enforce his claim 'by attachment of the ship, by the interdiction of any other cargo being put on board, or by the adoption of any different means that they may judge expedient.'[20]

Two days later, the Superintendents instructed their Secretary to write to Peile 'they are unwilling to take any public steps in this matter till they have earnestly recommended you immediately and completely to execute the terms of any bill of lading...' and pointing out that his claim for demurrage would not be prejudiced. Indeed they would help by formally authenticating any protest. But, assuming that the freight had been paid in full and the cargo not delivered, they declared their concern that further refusal would expose him to heavy penalties.[21]

It is clear that Peile did not respond to this temperate request because Goddard wrote again:

I trust that His Majesty's Superintendents will not consider this second call upon their attention either frivolous or vexatious, but be satisfied that I have caused every adjustment[22] to avoid the necessity of applying to them, and as a doubt seems to exist as to their power to interfere, I trust they will not only find it compatible with their functions but by a prompt exercise of their power dissipate so injurious an impression....

Captain Peile has pertinaciously refused all adjustment and I beg to call upon the attention of His Majesty's Authorities to compel the settlement of his accounts before they permit him to leave the port, in any way their judgment may think fit. As the conduct of the parties has been extremely vexatious and evasion repeatedly resorted to, I trust His Majesty's Superintendents will permit me to claim prompt payment before the ship leaves the port (should they be satisfied of the truth and

20. FO17/7 ff133.
21. FO17/7 f134.
22. I.e. 'made every attempt to settle'.

justice of my demand) having exhausted every means of settling by arbitration.[23]

No evidence is available of who was called on to arbitrate, or whether Peile refused to submit to arbitration or ignored an award. But on 3 December 1834 Elliot, then Secretary, was required to reply on behalf of the Superintendents:[24]

> the case is not of a nature in which they can interfere. It seems that there was an agreement to submit the matter to arbitration (and unless the parties are still willing to recur to that determination) the Superintendents consider that the circumstances under which the attempt to arbitrate is alleged to have failed, render the final adjustment of this question a point for the decision of a Court of Law.

This evasion of responsibility may have irked Elliot, who preferred to dispose of tasks rather than avoid them and was never short of ideas for circumventing a lack of authority. Goddard was certainly quick to let the Superintendents know of his contempt for their inaction and worse, their using against him his efforts to have his dispute arbitrated. He wrote from Canton on 12 December 1834:[25]

> I cannot sufficiently express my astonishment and surprise, at the reply of His Majesty's Superintendents to that request - under the consideration that justice has been denied me and that so little consideration has been evinced to afford it me. I hereby most solemnly protest against their refusal to interfere and to their giving credence to the departure of that vessel, in utter disregard to my prayer. I beg most respectfully to state that there could be little or no doubt of its being a question referable to a court of law, which is applicable to all cases where minor authorities have failed. It was to avoid this vexatious and expensive alternative that I exhausted every means of adjustment before I called for the interference of His Majesty's Superintendents. This earnest endeavour... is most incomprehensibly construed to render the case unfit for their interference and I am referred (for the adjustment of a common mercantile account) to a Court of Law at home, a resort which existed previous to the appointment of His Majesty's Superintendents, to avoid the necessity of which has been, beyond doubt, one of the primary objects of this appointment of His Majesty's Commission in China.... I did not require or expect that His Majesty's Superintendents would enter into and decide upon the

23. FO17/7 ff151-152.
24. FO17/ f153.
25. FO17/7 ff164-166 .

merits of the case, but it was reasonable to expect from the constituted authorities of His Majesty[26] (cause having been shown) that they would insist on the party leaving China settling his accounts, and the other party, had there been any ground to suspect a desire to delay, or that they would use their good offices to induce an equitable adjustment.... But... the Captain of the *Standard* has been sanctioned to escape by the signature of His Majesty's Superintendents... with a considerable sum of my money in his possession, and I the petitioner am referred to a Court of Law for redress, with all its contingent expenses.

Not only contempt but threat!

As such a decision in such a case is extraordinary, as this discretionary power assumed of interference and non-interference in the prayer of a petition involves considerations of the utmost importance both to myself and the mercantile interests of the place, I beg most respectfully to inform... His Majesty's Superintendents that it is my intention to petition His Majesty in Council on the subject.

On 16 December 1834 the Superintendents instructed Elliot to tell Goddard, in the most circumlocutory and respectful way, that he was biased. They were satisfied they could vindicate their decision and 'never have assumed and do not pretend to any discretionary power.'[27]

It is their duty to interpose, if the case shall seem to admit of their interposition, in any disputes... between the King's subjects in Canton. The circumstances under which it may be competent for them, or the extent to which it may be just or expedient to interfere, must necessarily vary in different cases... exercising the utmost possible degree of discretion... there is no doubt in the minds of the Superintendents of the actual validity of their authority in this country, as established by Parliament, and His Majesty's Order in Council, and Instructions under the Sign Manual. Whenever the public interests shall seem... to require... they will always be found ready to perform their duties... in that spirit of circumspection and moderation, by which it becomes all men in the public service to be guided and controlled.

The emphasis on public interests as prerequisite for intervention is intriguing. But that appears to be that, no further documents relating to this claim having been found.

GREENFIELD v GUTHRIE

Some insight into how the discretion to interpose was exercised can be found in despatches relating to another dispute at the same time. Frederic

---

26. By now, the repetition of the full title is clearly sarcastic, not respectful.
27. FO17/7 ff166-168.

Greenfield, ship's surgeon on the *Adelaide,* had been instantly dismissed by the captain, RD Guthrie, in November 1834. The Superintendents received a letter[28] from Greenfield on 1 December 1834, not only asking them to get him a month's wages in lieu of notice but charging Guthrie with unnatural crime committed against a black servant. The letter revealed that Guthrie had submitted the criminal charges to an informal tribunal made up of officers of the *Adelaide* and masters of other ships then lying off Lintin. They had found the accusation groundless and malicious. The Superintendents returned Greenfield's letter, on the ground that it was informal and full of 'highly objectionable language and irrelevant allusions.' But they offered to swear him to any affidavit he might want to make, and forward it to HM Government, so that the matter could be tried in a criminal court.

The Commission was clearly unwilling to accept even criminal jurisdiction over such a charge. But they asked for particulars of the claim for wages. Greenfield replied that it was customary to pay even a menial servant a month's wages on dismissal without notice and quantified his claim against the owners of the *Adelaide.* Elliot wrote to Guthrie with those details. After some correspondence disputing the amount and whether Greenfield had left of his own accord, Guthrie sent Elliot a draft for the full amount of the claim. Elliot wrote to Greenfield to collect it and arranged to take a receipt, which he forwarded to Guthrie - all in the name of the Superintendents. Whatever else, it is clear that there were circumstances in which they would lend their assistance to the 'adjustment' of civil disputes, provided Elliot did all the work.

Elliot must have chafed against the Commission's propensity for inaction. He wrote to his sister Emma, Lady Hislop, on 9 January 1835, that his relations with Davis had been 'very confidential... I have worked very hard, both head and hand.'[29] Davis was preparing to leave on 19 January and Elliot was to become Third Superintendent. Elliot and Davis had respected one another but Elliot had a low opinion of Robinson, Davis's successor as Chief:

The Su[perintendent] is on my shoulders here, dear Emy, but you need not be afraid: I will commit no blunders and strive to perform no wonders.... Send an efficient man and I shall be well content to serve under him, but I hope they will not forward any more experimental men. This business will not bear rough handling.

28. All the correspondence on this matter is at FO17/7 ff170-177.
29. Hoe p41.

Astell resigned soon afterwards and Elliot was promoted to Second Superintendent on 1 April 1835. Robinson's preference for non-intervention and his reliance on Elliot may be detected from a letter he wrote to Palmerston a few days later:[30]

With the exception of some trifling disputes between commanders, officers and seamen of merchant ships, which Captain Elliot's competent knowledge of maritime law and usage has enabled me to settle with little difficulty, nothing worthy of notice has occurred.

The 'enabled *me*' is significant. Robinson, who had been in China for sixteen years, never got used to the idea that he was one of three, *primus inter pares*, and that Elliot, with new ideas and much more able,[31] expected to be consulted on all matters.

A SAILOR, A FOREIGNER AND OTHERS v BULLY

The 'trifling disputes' may have included an arbitration referred to in Robinson's letter to Palmerston of 27 April 1835.[32] One of the Superintendents' responsibilities was to see that no British ship left China Waters until its manifest had been signed by an officer of the Commission. Captain Bully of the *Thomas Lowry* had told Robinson 'with much nonchalance that he had been cleared out by some British merchants at Canton and intended to weigh and sail immediately.' Robinson complained that this removed a 'simple but efficient check to all irregularities... sufficient to ensure the correct and proper deportment of all classes of British subjects.' The irregularities in this case included but were not confined to a matter which had been arbitrated.

Some accounts of the ship in question were unadjusted and... claims (of which the principal was that of a foreigner) against the Commander; also... I had a seaman on board HM Cutter, waiting to prefer a charge of assault and illtreatment against Captain Bully who... had acted improperly in forcibly turning a man out of his ship, withholding his wages and clothes

30. Robinson to Palmerston from Macao 13 April 1835, received 26 September 1835, *Blue Book* p39.
31. Davis wrote to the Foreign Office on 13 March 1835 advising them to: 'leave Captain Elliot of the Navy as a member of the Commission. He is a prudent and able man, well known to our Government, and should have come as Chief Superintendent instead of poor Lord Napier' FO17/12 f172 and Sir Robert Peel spoke of his 'singular terseness [not noticeable in his despatches from China] and ability', FO17/12 ff59-61. And on 26 June 1835 Davis wrote to the Foreign Office: 'the Chinese have given fresh trouble and I shall be uneasy unless Elliot is immediately put in charge. Poor Robinson is quite prepared to fall back on the Company. Both justice and policy seem to require that such a man as Elliot should not have to remain below such a man as Robinson.' FO17/12 ff341-44. Robinson was not petty, though; he did give Elliot credit for his knowledge and, we must assume with some hope that it would be taken seriously, forwarded Elliot's scheme, with his own approval.
32. FO17/14 ff295-297.

and leaving him destitute. Captain Bully however, having complied with my requisitions in respect to the sailor, and finally arranged his affairs to the satisfaction of all parties concerned, I do not wish to draw your Lordship's attention to these points... having ascertained that he had acquiesced in the result of an arbitration and arranged his accounts.

Elliot soon fell out with Robinson[33] and seems to have taken the lead in handling the next dispute.

KEATING v SMITH

On 10 April 1835, the Commission wrote[34] to AS Keating,[35] merchant and former editor of the *Canton Register*, enclosing a two-year-old account from John Smith, printer,[36] for unpaid wages, and a copy of a letter dated 7 February 1835 from James Matheson[37] to Smith, stating that Keating had 'agreed to abide by my award. I have told him he must pay you the amount of balance, unless he adduce better grounds for his refusal than he has yet done.' Keating had not complied with Matheson's award and the Superintendents were prepared to use their influence to support it. But it did no good. As they were to find, Keating did not pay debts without a struggle.

KEATING v TURNER & CO

Robinson wrote home to Palmerston on 1 July 1835, enclosing papers in another dispute with Keating, this time for non-payment of a debt to

33. Robinson complained to Palmerston that Elliot had told him to his face that 'although he appreciated my amiable disposition, he was bound to say he considered me utterly incompetent to fill the duties of my present office, and did me the honour to add that it could hardly be expected from a person who had been all his life measuring tea.' FO17/14 f80; Hoe p48.

34. All the correspondence on this matter, with that on Keating unless otherwise specified, is at FO17/11 ff70-197A.

35. Arthur Saunders Keating, British merchant in Canton before Christmas 1830, *Canton Register* 17 January 1831; member of the British Chamber of Commerce, *Canton Register* 16 December 1834; notice of dealings with his posthumous estate, *Canton Register* 22 May 1838.

36. Born Calcutta 1810, died Macao 1852. Printer, auctioneer, hotelkeeper, ship's chandler, soda water manufacturer and purveyor, billiard saloon keeper, and seller of lottery tickets in Macao. He was printing the official *Boletim* in 1850, according to the *Friend of China* 23 November 1850; and the *Hong Kong Almanac and Directory* for 1851, according to the *Boletim* 7 December 1850.

37. Nicholas James Sutherland Matheson (1796-1878) had made a killing on one big opium deal, which enabled him in 1832 to buy into the firm which became Jardine, Matheson. The story is best told by Austin Coates *Macau and the British 1637-1842*; Maggie Keswick (ed) *The Thistle and the Jade*. Matheson must have been an honourable arbitrator; Keating had hired Smith through H Matheson, a member of the family in Calcutta, and Keating printed on James Matheson's press (which had been printing in China since 1827, *Canton Register* 3 March 1835) but Smith presumably trusted James to be unaffected by those connexions. At this time Smith was residing with Innes, see below.

Turner & Co,[38] and explaining his view of the problems the Commission faced.[39] He reminded Palmerston that the China Trade Act 1833 provided for an Order in Council to give them power over trade and for the direction of the British in China. The Superintendents wanted to keep well within their authority and were anxious to interfere as little as possible until further instructions arrived, but they were obliged to scotch any notion that British subjects could please themselves whether they met their commercial obligations. 'Mutual commercial good faith' was enough for most merchants but that did not include Keating, who had bluntly told the Superintendents they had 'no authority to interpose':

> We have interfered in these claims between Turner & Co... and Mr John Smith against Mr Keating, because we believed that it was within the plain intent of the law that we should intromit, if the need were, for the *protection of HM's subjects in their lawful pursuits*... consistent with the general spirit of British law... the fairest investigation... and an opening for appeal. Mr Keating has however rejected every overture either to adjust the demand preferred against him or to submit to further inquiry upon the spot, or to give reasonable security... that he would... appeal in England, or to pay the money under protest... every effort we have made to induce him to submit these disputes to inquiry and adjustment has been alike fruitless... in spite of the concurrent opinions of several of the most respectable merchants in the place, to whom the case was submitted by his own consent, in spite of the opinions of this Commission, to whom it was afterwards referred by his own desire, and in spite of every proposition and injunction that has been made to him to submit to further inquiry here, or to give security that further inquiry should be had elsewhere.

Robinson suggested that an Order in Council be passed 'granting to the Superintendents authority to promulgate some provisional scheme of arbitration (in cases of need) by the compulsory process, in the manner proposed in Captain Elliot's Minute.' The sanction for non-compliance would be a public announcement to the British and Native commercial bodies that the Superintendents would thenceforth offer them no assistance for the adjustment of disputes with the recalcitrant debtor. Meanwhile he asked permission to do just that to Keating.

38. Richard Turner's firm was a middle sized respectable British opium trader. He was a member of the first committee of the General Chamber of Commerce, see Appendix. When he died in 1839, his executors included James Matheson and William Jardine, *Canton Register* 26 November 1839.
39. The significance of this despatch in relation to the difficulty of disposing of civil disputes is considered in greater depth in Roebuck p264.

On 3 January 1835 Turner & Co wrote to the Commission:

The British ships *Madras* and *Planter*, to our consignment, arrived here with each a cargo of rice for AS Keating Esq for which, by charterparty the ships were to be paid a certain rate of freight per pecul[40] delivered. From the amount so ascertained, Mr Keating retains in his hands and refuses to pay $300... from each ship's freight, upon the plea that he has been called upon to pay an illegal charge to that amount upon his rice - a charge he admits to be illegal on either ship or cargo, but which he insists is more properly payable by the ships than by him as consignee of the rice. We as consignees of the ships had them both secured, with the perfect understanding on the part of the securing hong merchants,[41] that the rice was not ours, and might be sold to any one the consignee of the rice might please. The sum agreed on in both cases was $900, as has hitherto been considered by order of the Viceroy the sole charge for securing a rice laden ship;[42] in confirmation of this we beg to inclose you Mowqua's[43] chop in full of all claims against the *Planter*, and Mingqua's against the *Madras*, the ships they respectively secured. We also beg to inclose a circular stating the case, with the opinions of the leading Houses here, British and American, as also Mr Keating's letters, bearing dates January 10th, 10th and 12th. He therein allows he makes 'no claim upon the *Madras* for additional port charges' and 'that all he asks is that his cargo shall not have to pay the deficiency between what the hong merchant requires and what we pay him.' The hong merchants never demanded more than the customary $900 which we have paid and which Mr Keating in his second letter of the 10th instant himself allows they expressed themselves to be satisfied with, so far as the ships and import cargo are concerned. Still he will not pay us the full amount of freight but keeps back $300 on each, making $600 in all. We have now

40. Or *picul*, a measure of rice equal to 100 catties or about 133 pounds.
41. The hong merchants were a group of about a dozen Chinese merchants in Canton given a monopoly of trade with outsiders, first in 1721, then by Imperial Decree in 1755. The Chinese Government refused to deal with barbarians and insisted that any communication should be through the hong merchants, except when in its great magnanimity it allowed a mandarin to receive a petition. The hong merchants 'secured' a ship or cargo by making impositions on it which would satisfy the Chinese customs duties. This opened many opportunities for 'squeeze', as illegal levies were called.
42. 'Rice ships' were ships which carried rice to take advantage of the bounty granted to importers of that desperately needed foodstuff at a time of famine, and to avoid the squeezes of the Chinese officials at Whampoa, known as 'measurement duties' and '*cumshaw*'. Keating openly advertised in the *Canton Register* his assistance in loading enough rice to circumvent these impositions.
43. The Chinese names are the honorifics usually used by English speakers when referring to hong merchants. It is not easy to discover much about their backgrounds or the details of their careers.

to solicit your interference, on the part of the Owners of these ships at home, to decide whether they are to pay this claim, now for the first time brought forward, and at one time given up by Mr Keating, but resumed as per his letter of the 12th Inst.

PS... the *Britannia* brought rice up for Jardine Matheson & Co and they have made no claim on the plea of their rice being subject to an illegal squeeze which they thought would be better thrown upon the ship than borne by their rice.

THE OPINIONS OF EXPERTS

Turners had written to other merchants seeking their opinion and Robinson enclosed an undated copy of the letter to W Forbes, Lancelot Dent[44] and William Jardine.[45]

The *Madras*, Captain Thornton, rice laden from Java to our consignment, arrived in China on the 19th October last, the cargo being for AS Keating Esq. By the charterparty the ship is entitled to retain a sufficient quantity of rice on board to bring her up to Whampoa with all the privileges of a 'rice ship', part of the cargo was discharged at Macao, and with the remainder the *Madras* came up to Whampoa, it being stipulated in such a case that the port charges should be borne by the ship; these port charges being expressly fixed by an edict of the Viceroy at 620 taels, generally taken as $900. Hitherto this has always been considered the correct amount chargeable. At this sum Mowqua has secured the *Planter*, Kingqua the *Britannia*, and Mingqua, in the present case, the *Madras*, and all three declare that there is no further charge on the ship, and that the rice may be sold to any one the consignee may please. Moreover in the case of the *Madras* the rice was not put into the hong of the security merchant for the ship, but into Samqua's. We shall therefore feel obliged by your saying whether Mr Keating has any claim we can properly be called upon to pay, we having had this ship secured independent of his rice altogether. We trouble you a second time, as Mr Keating says he acts, as he now does, in refusing to pay the freight without deducting $300, 'on the written opinions of Jardine Matheson

44. Lancelot Dent, of Thomas Dent & Co, was the major competitor and often the personal opponent of Jardine and Matheson.
45. William Jardine (1784-1843) had been a surgeon's mate with the East India Company since he was 18. He also traded on his own account in haberdashery and bits and pieces. Later he became surgeon to the Company and like the other Company servants clandestinely traded in opium. In 1817 he left the Company, became a licensed private trader (East India Court Minute 7 December 1818) and went into the opium and textile trade full time, with a Parsee friend from Bombay. In 1825 he joined Magniac Brothers, English clockmakers with a profitable sideline in opium.

& Co, Thos Dent & Co, Wetmore & Co and Russell & Co'[46] and also for transmission if necessary to His Majesty's Superintendents, Mr Keating having declined any reference here.

The replies were not entirely unequivocal, though they supported Turners. From Thomas Dent & Co, 8 January 1835:

> Without entering again into the general question, it is now only necessary to give an opinion on the case in dispute. Turner & Co are bound to have the Ship *Madras* secured to enable Mr Keating to land his rice, they paying all charges, whether these charges are $900 or $1200 can be no concern of Mr Keating's, this being a matter of arrangement between Turner & Co and the Hong Merchant, and where, as in the present instance, the rice is landed at another Hong, there cannot be the shadow of a claim that I can see against the ship for any additional charge than what they have arranged for.

Russell & Co simply concurred and Jardine, Matheson said they had given their opinion more than once and saw no reason to change it. Fox, Rawson & Co, British merchants, wrote: 'We have recently had two rice ships secured, for which the charge made by the hong merchant was $900; in one case the rice was our own, in the other case it was the property of another party.' Wetmore & Co: 'Our opinion has been given, and we see no reason for changing it, that is, there can be no claim, upon either the ship or the rice. The party responsible is clearly the hong merchant that secured the vessel.'

Keating lost no time in responding to Turners on 10 January 1835:

> I observe that the paper circulated by you did not give what I consider the facts of the case, I sent round another which is still going the round of Canton.... I make no claim of $300 against the *Madras* for additional port charges. All that I do ask is that my cargo shall not have to pay the deficiency between what the hong merchant requires and what you pay him. Mowqua told me yesterday that he charged you $1200 for the *Planter*. Linchong told me that you must pay that for the *Britannia*. Why put the question in your circular in the way you do...? When did I call upon you to pay anything? I do not deduct $300 from the freight but I insist that $300 shall not be deducted from my rice. Why prejudice my cause by saying that I refused a reference here? Read my letter of the 3rd and say if I did not invite it? The opinions of the several houses are in

---

46. Wetmores and Russells were both American companies, not the 'British merchants' Elliot had stipulated as arbitrators.

my favor, for all say that if you can get the ship secured for $900 - I deny that you can do this - you may pay the hong merchant $900 and leave it for him to *squeeze* the $300 out of me. This is easy enough and rather than displease you the hong merchant makes this bargain, but without that he puts the burthen on me. The fact is that it is altogether a *squeeze* on the part of the hong merchant, against which you and I should alike complain. Will you join me in a petition against this? Whether the ship or rice is cheated out of the $300... he cares not, but why should we submit to their *arrangements*?

Keating was busy that day. He wrote a further letter to Turners, marked 'January 10th 1835. Evening', with new evidence he had collected:

I enclose you an order on the *Britannia* for the rice ex *Pleiades*. I am beat in a just cause by a thing usually had recourse to by the Chinese - direct falsehood. Mowqua who yesterday and for many days demanded $1200, now asks but $900 for securing a rice ship. He is, he says, afraid of a petition, and is willing to lose the $300. Mingqua says the same.... The *fact* is that these $300, *in future as hitherto, will be paid out of the rice*, but the hong merchant will do it quietly, as my threat of the City Gates[47] has alarmed them.... I think it might have been got over *in toto*, had we petitioned. It is a fair proof of the state of foreigners here and should be an additional reason for our 'pulling together' instead of against each other. My contest has not been with *you* but with *the Chinese*, who are defrauding one or both of us. You have mistaken my object... $300 will be taken as an acknowledged though concealed port charge.... In justice to you and to prove that I have not been playing with you, I hand you the evidence of Mr Cushing, a gentleman living in my house, as to the conversations with the hong merchants on this subject.

And Keating enclosed notes from William Cushing and Daniel Caldwell[48] in corroboration.

Keating was not letting up. His next letter to Turners, dated 12 January 1835, added yet more evidence and argument - and a suggestion of how the dispute might be resolved:

the deliberate falsehoods of Mowqua have in at least one quarter caused an impression that I was *mistaken* in my statement of his having...

47. That is of bypassing the hong merchants and appealing directly to the municipal authorities.
48. Later a well known figure in Hong Kong and arbitrator there, featured in Roebuck and Munn. He had the advantage of understanding the Chinese used by Mowqua. Conversations between Mowqua and Keating may have been in Pidgin or Caldwell may have interpreted.

demanded again $1200 from me for securing a rice ship; and as I do not see how, in the teeth of the evidence... I can give up [the Owners'] rights, I am compelled to ask you to join me in bringing the case before HM Superintendents, or any two or three of the merchants of the place.

After that apparent agreement to submit to arbitration, Keating explained that the owners of the rice would be justified in challenging his obligation to pay the $300 in each case - and he was already involved in seven cases. The cause of the trouble was 'shameless and illegal pillage' by the hong merchants, which some had confessed to him, and he could not 'submit in quietness to be thus plundered'. He enclosed translations of three receipts, each for $900, from Mowqua, Kingqua and Mingqua, all stated to be for port clearance.

ELLIOT ON THE LAW

On 14 February the Superintendents wrote to Keating. They set out the facts and arguments in Turners' letter. They also stated their own opinion on the law:

The liability of the consignee of the cargo for the payment of freight is clear if the terms of the charterparty have been fulfilled, and any illegality of charge upon the rice can by no means admit of remedy by the disturbance of a contract made for the conveyance of the cargo...

To let the illegal charges fall on the ship would give colour to the unlawful exactions. The consignees of the ship have nothing to do with charges on rice. The dispute is simple! And the answer is 'pay over the amount of freight due to the ships, according to the conditions of the charterparty.' If any hong merchant is still detaining rice until the $300 be paid, then send a petition through the hong merchants and, if nothing is done within a few days, get all the mercantile community to send a petition to the City Gates. If that fails, send the papers to the Superintendents.

Keating replied from Macao on 17 February 1835:

Petition... would not avail much. It is a charge on all *ships* at Whampoa, being 'linguists and compradores fees'. In 1833 these were disallowed on rice ships, but they are yet paid, and when ship and cargo are to the same consignee, it does not *appear*, as it is at once deducted from the amount for which the rice is sold... that amount is taken from my rice... on rice there is no duty... there is a large bounty. 'Linguists and compradores fees' are charges on ships not on cargo.

It now becomes clear that Elliot was handling this matter. Robinson's despatch includes Elliot's 'observations' - his answer to the question of who should pay such an illegal charge is short: neither. But that is not the true question, which is: 'on what ground does Keating refuse to pay the freight, as required by the charterparty?' The charge - for linguists' and compradors' fees - is not a port charge. It is an extortion, which was disallowed by the Edict of 1833. Elliot was not taken in by Keating's outrage: 'there is no getting rid of the uncomfortable inference that all his... objections to the extortion of the Chinese might be removed by shifting the charge to the ship.'

It was important to keep two points separate. First was the claim of the owners against Keating for freight earned; that was 'to be decided according to the principles and practice of the law.' The amount of port charges was irrelevant. The freight was reckoned at a certain rate per pecul of rice delivered and that was that. Second was the Chinese merchant's claim for the $300 against Keating's rice, to be determined on its merits. If Keating objected, let him have it out with the hong merchants. 'Keating... detains $300 belonging to A because his rice is subject to an unjust charge by B, A and B being parties utterly unconnected.' Elliot shows his mettle:

> in all these matters of extortion, I shall always recommend strong courses. Let us remonstrate first, temperately but firmly, and if that will not do, let us resist the payment, leaving to the Chinese the responsibility of unjustifiable means of recovering it... the Owners of the ship have nothing to do with it.

Meanwhile, Elliot's advice was that the Superintendents should write to Keating, explaining that they would wait for the further details promised in his last letter, but were of the opinion that his defence to Turners' claim 'was not founded upon any sound or admissible principles.' And Elliot emphasised his preference for arbitration:

> I think it would be judicious to add that the Superintendents would have recommended that this dispute should be adjusted by arbitration, if they had not collected from the papers before them that Mr Keating was averse to that course. If... they were mistaken... they were still willing, with the consent of the parties, to suggest a mode of selecting arbitrators and an umpire by the perfectly unobjectionable process of ballot.

Elliot already seems to be working out the details of his scheme. If Keating refused, he should be told that the Superintendents would interpose.

The Commission sent a letter in those terms to Keating on 19 February 1835. Keating replied on 2 March adding further explanation of the extortion and of the accepted ways of getting round it. It was a charge on the outward loading of the ship. It had nothing to do with the inward cargo. Indeed, an inward cargo of rice, even though only a small part of the total cargo, was not only exempt from tax but exempted the ship from measurement dues and *cumshaw*. Therefore, the squeeze did not fall on the cargo. The dilemma could not arise until the rice was consigned to one party and the ship to another. He enclosed documents which he said showed support from William Jardine, who said the point had not previously arisen; from Dents, Wetmores and Russells, saying that no hong merchant could secure a rice ship for less than $1200. Keating also produced copies of his bills of lading, showing that he was liable only for freight and boat hire to and from the ship, not for any tax on rice or port charges. If he had had a big enough godown, he would not have had to pay the $300 to get his rice out.

Why should my cargo be saddled with any portion of the port charges of a ship, legal or illegal? In this country... custom, or an arrangement between the hong merchants to the detriment of the foreigner, tread so close on the heels of law, or rather, they are so mixed together, that it is impossible to distinguish between them.

If he were not correct in his view, the owners of any ship could saddle the consignee of cargo with all the port charges. Petitions would be useless. The local mandarins would refer the matter to the hong merchants, who would deny the truth of the foreigners' statements. And he flung the Superintendents' powerlessness in their faces:

> There is unfortunately no public authority representing Great Britain in Canton, through whom I might make my complaint of the evasion of the law by the hong merchants... the course by me adopted is the only one by which I can protect my property.

FURTHER EXPERT OPINION

There followed an opinion from Jardine of 23 December 1834, saying that the consignee of the rice 'ought to charge it to the ship'. Lancelot Dent declared it was 'rather a nice question':

> The rice has I fancy hitherto most generally borne it, but I should say improperly where, as is usually the case, the ship has to pay the port charges. Put the case, that you make the Agent secure the ship, and sell the rice to another party. Would he do it for $900? Certainly not. And yet how make a positive charge? The hong merchant would not secure a ship without the rice as he durst not make it.

Wetmore and Co, on 24 December 1834, said that all the charges fell on the owner of the vessel. The securing of the vessel was the business of the consignee and the consignee of the rice had nothing to do with it. Russells agreed on 27 December, adding that they did not see any difference whether the expenses were imposed by 'law or the rapacity of the mandarins'. All these opinions seemed to support Keating but Elliot pointed out that they were all 'dated *previously* to those forwarded by Messrs Turner.'

Keating supplied copies of charterparties, which provided that, if the master went to Whampoa 'to avail of the privileges of a rice cargo... the customary expenses shall fall upon the ship'; and a proclamation, 'Duties on Foreign Rice': foreigners might import rice to Canton without paying duty and take on cargo for export, paying the same duties as ships which had not imported rice; illegal fees on the rice ships were prohibited; any customs officers, military personnel, compradors or others who disobeyed would be banished or degraded. And the hong merchants were to tell this to the barbarians.

Elliot's reply was repetitious but firmer than ever. 'Having regard to the rather uncomfortable character of the local government for good faith', Keating had a right to question the sincerity of the prohibition of the illegal squeeze. But the Viceroy's edict of June 1833 was clear. Keating was wrong to characterise the squeeze as linguists' and compradors' fees. Of course, Turners had to show that they had paid all *fees* due from them. But the squeeze was not; the Chinese Government said so. The hong merchants' receipts showed that they had received every lawful charge. Keating admitted the charge was illegal, so it came to this, why should the cargo be burdened with it? Keating put his rice in a godown of a hong merchant (not the one who secured the ship) who demanded a squeeze. Keating had strong ground for complaint. 'Granting for a moment that, owing to the circumstances of our political position, it is impossible to procure redress... we must not betray ourselves into a confusion.' Let Keating petition the Chinese authorities if he wished. But let him do it on his own. If Turners and others joined him, the Chinese would probably say that proved an 'improper collusion between the foreigners' and ask for proof that the hong merchants had asked for squeeze. He should himself petition the hong merchants, not the Government. If he failed, he could then get up a general petition.

Then Elliot made the practical suggestion that Keating should seek the help of the Canton Chamber of Commerce.[49] If their efforts failed, the Chamber should tell the Superintendents, who would give further advice. Accordingly, on 22 March 1835 the Commission wrote to Keating, making all Elliot's points, but: 'with the utmost possible delicacy to you, because they are sensible of the injustice of the Chinese... they anxiously hope that you will not... persist.' Otherwise 'You will have been unjustly detaining money... in the teeth of the opinions of some of the most respectable

49. see Appendix.

mercantile establishments in China and in disregard of the earnest advice and formal injunction of the public servants of your country.' So, Keating was told to pay the balance of the freight, and petition the Government in the usual manner to instruct the godown owner to deliver up his rice. On the same day the Commission wrote to the Chamber of Commerce asking whether it considered this matter 'a suitable opportunity for the prosecution of more strenuous efforts to secure the efficacious operation of the... Edict.'

THE BATAVIAN SUGGESTION

Keating replied on 31 March 1835 repeating his arguments but making a new suggestion, that the matter be submitted to the arbitration of the 'two British Merchants in Batavia, who framed the charterparties, the one on behalf of the ship, the other on mine... appeal to the framers of the charterparty... [is] the readiest and best means of arriving at what justice requires. More than this, I conceive, no one will ask.'

The Commission replied on 8 April 1835 that their policy was to interfere in commercial disputes only to the extent necessary 'for the ends of needful justice and security... If both parties be willing to settle by arbitration or... to remit... the dispute to another time and place' there would be no need to intervene. But if one side refuses, then, though they recognise that 'authoritative interference' rarely serves any purpose:

> The moral force of a very wakeful opinion is of most powerful effect, and the person who pertinaciously refuses... to submit his dispute to the fairest means of adjustment... available, would... find he had done himself infinitely more injury, than... an adverse decision could... inflict.... The superintendents are aware that you proposed to refer the matter to the judgment of two or three merchants, or their own; but... they were very unwillingly induced to turn aside from the usual course they have adverted to [the recommendation to go to arbitration. The opinions of the merchants which Keating had supplied] led the Commission to infer that you were disposed to think your case had been somewhat prejudiced... and in the note of 12th January... you requested them to join you in bringing the matter before the Superintendents, or two or three merchants of the place.

They reminded Keating he had brought the dispute before them, with Turners' consent, because he considered the judgment of the merchants 'had been somewhat unfairly warped'. They had taken on the matter thinking that 'the disposal of the case by them would be more agreeable to you than the mode of adjustment by arbitration.' They thought their judgment might have been more helpful to Keating in explaining to his correspondents in England. They believed that an award of arbitrators would be against him and that he would be more content with the Commission's advice than an adverse award. They had interfered not because they wanted to but because they thought Keating wanted them to. In any case, no harm had been done because he could still go to arbitration. They appreciated the spirit behind the proposal to remit the dispute to the merchants in Batavia, but saw no reason for preferring that course to the one they now formally and finally proposed: to submit the case to arbitration at Canton.

At this point in the bundle of correspondence, Robinson's despatch refers to Elliot's arbitration scheme and reports that, having received no reply from Keating on John Smith's claim,[50] they had written again to Keating, Smith and Turners.

ARBITRATION OR ELSE!

The letter to Keating called upon him:

> to choose in each case an arbitrator and an umpire on your behalf for their consideration and final disposal.... Failing to receive a satisfactory... answer... the Superintendents will proceed to take further steps for the final adjustment of these demands.

The letters to Smith and Turners asked them likewise to name an arbitrator and umpire. To Turners they added that, if Keating did not comply, they would:

> make the best provision in their power for the just disposal of the question at issue, by nominating impartial persons upon his part, and having procured a decision... they will then take such further steps... as the urgency of the case... requires. PS... you have been called upon to name an umpire at once... to gain time.... one of the two gentlemen chosen as umpires for yourselves and Mr Keating would be drawn for out of a box... and the decision of this person would be taken to be final.

These letters were formally served on 28 April 1835. On that day Elliot wrote home to his sister Emma about his relations with his superiors:[51]

> I have been acting under men... who would have long since broken down completely, if I had not been there to sustain them. I shall very

---

50. This letter is not at this place in the bundle. A marginal note says: 'This letter not entered upon the Records', followed by another 'Yes it is, see p140'. I could not find it. Keating seems to be carefully avoiding any discussion of his debt to Smith.
51. Hoe p44.

soon be able to speak the whole truth in that respect, and I will certainly do it.... Since poor Napier's demise, I have done the *whole business of this Commission.*

Smith replied the same day, saying he agreed but wanted his documents back and would prefer '*your opinion* with reference to my claim'. This called forth a refusal, dated 4 May, to express an opinion but an assurance that 'if the matter be determined in your favor by the course of arbitration... [they promised] the efficacious operation of the decision'. And if Keating refused to go to arbitration - again - that would not 'interrupt your just right to have your demand examined and definitively disposed of.'

On 1 May 1835 Turners replied:

We... hoped to have been able to have named some of the mercantile gentlemen of this place, whose experience would enable them to decide in the matter; but we have already... given all our neighbours so much trouble... we should have much reluctance... but to show our willingness... we agree to abide by the decision of any English gentleman who being down at Macao can consult the documents... deemed competent by the Superintendents.

This applied only to the matter of the *Planter*. In the *Madras* case the captain had restricted Turners' authority to asking 'the Superintendents in hopes they would exercise their *authority* and decide the matter. If not it was Captain Thornton's intention to resort to legal measures at home.' They expressed disappointment that progress had been so slow and indeterminate and set out their case again, adding that they did not believe Keating had actually made a payment of the $300 to anybody.

On 9 May 1835, Keating having made no reply, letters were sent to Turners: 'the Superintendents are of opinion that your claim of $300 against Mr AS Keating as Agent for the ship *Planter* is substantiated, and that they will take early steps to draw the matter to a just and final conclusion.' And to Smith 'your claim of $119.99 against Mr AS Keating is substantiated and... they will take early steps to place you in possession of that sum.'

ENFORCEMENT

Robinson continues his report:

Mr Keating having failed to take any notice of the last three letters addressed to him... the Superintendents embarked on board the Cutter *Louisa* and executed the two following injunctions on the 19th instant within the limits of the port of Canton.

They were sent with a letter telling Keating:

> failing your compliance with the provisions thereof, the Superinten-
> dents will pay the sums claimed by Messrs R Turner & Co and Mr
> John Smith against you; and declare you to be a debtor to the Crown...
> give public notice that any persons thinking fit to have any commercial
> transactions with you (originating subsequent to the date of such notice)
> must conform to the understanding, that the Superintendents will afford
> no facilities for the adjustment of any disputes, which may take place
> with you in the course of such transactions, until further information be
> given that your debts to the Crown are liquidated.

And they enclosed the notice, which recited that:

> this dispute was decided by several merchants at Canton, to whose
> consideration it was referred by the contending parties, in favour of the
> Agents... but Mr Keating having declined... and requesting... Turner
> & Co to bring the case before the Superintendents... he was formally
> enjoined either to submit the case to further arbitration... or forthwith
> to pay the balance.... Mr Keating having taken no notice... they... now
> for the last time require and enjoin him to pay... $300 within... ten
> days... or give notice... within one week... of his intention to appeal...
> and... execute a bond (with sufficient sureties)... that... appeal shall be
> instituted in England within... fifteen months.

A similar notice related to Smith's claim, that had already been 'decided
against Mr Keating by Mr James Matheson, to whose decision it had been
remitted with... Keating's consent... and another communication requiring
him again to submit the matter to arbitration' had been ignored.

Keating replied on 25 May 1835, challenging the Superintendents'
authority and denying they had any jurisdiction over him. He asked for
details of the statute under which they purported to proceed, pointing out
there were no lawyers in China to advise him. They referred him to the
China Trade Act 1833 and the Orders in Council. He sent a further holding
letter, reporting that he had asked the Governor of Macao whether the
Superintendents had jurisdiction over him there and would let them know
his answer. Then on 29 May he asked to borrow a copy of the relevant
Order and declared his intention of sending all the correspondence to the
law officers of the Crown in Bengal and London.

The Superintendents replied the same day asking him to declare without
further loss of time whether he had 'definitively resolved to resist all
reasonable means of adjustment'. If so, they would immediately discharge
the claims of Turners and Smith. They enclosed the Order. On 8 June,

having received no reply, they wrote that they would pay Turners' and Smith's claims on 18 June if they had not received a satisfactory answer.

On 11 June 1835 they received a letter returning the Order and enclosing a copy of the Governor of Macao's reply, which declared that the only judicial authorities in Macao were the Portuguese, but no substantive answer from Keating. That came in a letter of the same date totally denying their jurisdiction and threatening them with retribution, jointly and severally, for the damage which was bound to flow from their threatened action. He reminded them 'without intention of offence' that they knew as little law as he did and accused them of allowing 'feelings of a personal nature, somewhat resembling anger, injured pride or revenge' to affect their judgment.

He said he had asked Turners whether they knew he had offered to have the dispute arbitrated 'by the framers of the charterparty in Batavia'. They had told him not. He protested that the Superintendents had no right to refuse that offer unless Turners objected. '[By the Batavians] I mean to be guided, not by your orders; they can settle the point in ten minutes, with the other parties to the charterparty... and if they.. tell me... I should pay it, I will pay it.' And he ended: 'I protest against... your illegal and malicious acts, alike absurd as tyrannical and uncalled for'.

On 17 June 1835 the Superintendents paid the claims of Smith and Turners and informed Keating. On 1 July the Superintendents wrote to Turners asking whether they considered Keating's offer of arbitration in Batavia a fair one and would have accepted it; expressing regret that Keating had not approached Turners with the offer; and assuring them that they would not have objected to such an agreement; it would have been wrong for them to have put that proposal to Turners, knowing they were happy with arbitration in Canton, where the means were just as good for determining the dispute; and it would have been disrespectful to the British mercantile community. Turners replied on 13 July that it was unlikely that they would have accepted Keating's Batavia proposal. They enclosed a copy of their letter to Keating of 6 June 1835, refusing just such a proposal and pointing out: 'your own refusal to submit the... dispute to... our fellow merchants obliged us to resort to... a reference to the Superintendents.' There, for the time being, the correspondence ends.

YUNWO OR PUNHOYQUA v SOMATCHEE OR HORMUSJEE

On 12 January 1836, Robinson wrote a self-congratulatory letter[52] to Palmerston, enclosing correspondence about a Chinese merchant's claim against a Parsee merchant, 'as proof of the disposition of the Chinese to

52. FO17/14 ff8-17.

avail themselves of my interference in their behalf.'[53] The correspondence gives an insight into how debts were dealt with in East India Company days.

Yunwo, or to give him his honorific Punhoyqua, wrote to Robinson on 26 December 1835, asking for his help in recovering a five-year-old debt owed by a Parsee merchant Hormusjee, for whom Punhoyqua had bought goods on account and never been paid. Punhoyqua said that he had asked the East India Company to help and they had 'decided that in reason the debt should be repaid and directed the Parsee Tsengkeen[54] forcibly to detain Hormusjee and to require him to pay the whole amount before he could be allowed to return home.' Years passed but a year ago Punhoyqua had discovered that another Parsee, Natabhoy, had allowed Hormusjee to escape, with the excuse that he was going home to get the money, leaving another to stand surety for him. Now Natabhoy was intending to go home.

> Considering that you, Sir, are the Chief Authority of your country, and that the regulation of the trade is confided to you[55]... I presume to request that you will grasp hold of justice and will exercise your power to compel Natabhoy and Hormusjee to... speedily repay the whole sum, not suffering them to have recourse to long and frivolous delays. Having already received a decision in my favor, I hope to have the same carried into effect.

Robinson replied with an extraordinary claim of authority and with little consideration for the problems of translating highflown verbiage in one language into comprehensible meaning in another:

> My duty and inclination prompt me to afford you and every native of China who applies to me assistance and redress for wrongs or injuries on the part of my countrymen. I am instructed by my Government so to do, and on no occasion I trust shall I be found unwilling and rarely unable to accomplish the ends of justice. For this purpose I am invested

---

53. Later, he speaks of the disposition of the Chinese to avail themselves of a British Authority, but all the correspondence is to and from Robinson himself, not the Commission, and he seems to have kept the matter from his colleagues.

54. A marginal note says 'This is like an European name [Jenkins?]. There is perhaps a mistake in calling him a Parsee. The captain of the vessel in which Hormusjee was going to leave China is probably intended.'

55. From this sentence it is clear that the appeal was to Robinson in his official capacity and not personal, and should have been handled by the Commission. Perhaps he was getting exasperated by Elliot's tendency to commandeer the Commission's machinery for resolving disputes.

with power and authority over the ships and subjects of Great Britain and her colonies.

But he could promise nothing more than to investigate; too long a time had elapsed and he was no longer acting for the Company. He did write to Natabhoy but nothing seems to have come of it. Robinson's claim to the respect of the Chinese merchants might have influenced Palmerston more if he had shown either a successful conclusion of this matter or further requests for his help from Chinese merchants. It is not supported by a letter of 15 March 1836, from Elliot's wife Clara to his sister Emma:[56]

I cannot help wishing that we could hear something definitive had been settled about this Commission. Charlie leads a sad life with Sir George Robinson, who has not a spark of manly feeling, or of trust or of integrity in him; he is detested by the Chinese and a disgrace to the English. I would not write this strongly, were it not the truth and did I not know he had done his best to injure Charlie. I wish I could tell you distinctly all that has taken place but it would be far too long a task for me and besides I feel convinced that the government will ultimately do Charlie justice.

She was prescient. Though Palmerston received Robinson's letter on 13 May 1836, he recalled Robinson and appointed Elliot in his place in June, though they were not to receive their orders until December.

ANTICLIMAX

On 8 November 1836, Palmerston wrote to Elliot, the new Chief, assuring him that he was fully aware of the 'inconvenience' to the Superintendents caused by their lack of power to enforce their decisions and hoping that 'at no distant period, some effectual remedy may be provided... In the mean time I have to recommend to you to confine your interference, when called for, as much as possible to friendly suggestion and advice.' He added, with ill-disguised relish, that the legislation under which Elliot proposed to act, relying on the supercargoes' powers to send recalcitrant debtors home, had been repealed.[57]

Though the search has not ended, no further papers have yet been found which disclose details of how these disputes were finally resolved, if they ever were.[58]

56. Hoe p46.
57. Roebuck p264.
58. Lack of documentation of the outcome of disputes is exasperatingly common, everywhere and throughout history, whether they are arbitrated or litigated, Derek Roebuck 'The Myth

APPENDIX

The Chambers of Commerce at Canton

On 1 October 1834, William Sprott Boyd, the Secretary, wrote from Canton to the Commission,[59] enclosing the draft rules of the British Chamber of Commerce of Canton, pointing out that membership would be open until 31 December next to all who wished to join and the 'probability of several arriving within the next few months in consequence of the opening of trade.' The names of the first members were: William Jardine, James Matheson, James Innes, Richard Turner, John Macadam Gladstone,[60] Alexander Matheson, Andrew Jardine, A Johnstone, Arthur S Keating, Nicholas Crooke, John Slade, Robert Thorn, John Watson, John Middleton and William Sprott Boyd. James Matheson was interim president.

Rule 3 set out among its objects 'to aid or cooperate with HM Superintendents; to be a channel of communication with the hong merchants... also to arbitrate between disputants willing to refer to and abide by the judgement of the Chamber.'

On 9 October 1834, the Chamber sent a 'statement of objections' to the British Government against the 'continuance in China of a part of the East India Company's factory for the purpose of selling bills on India, and purchasing bills on England, by making advances on goods and merchandize of individuals intended for consignment to England.' It was signed by Jardine, Matheson & Co, James Innes, AS Keating, N Crooke, R Turner & Co, J McA Gladstone, J Watson, William Sprott Boyd and Andrew Johnstone and ended:

In a political view, continuing the existence of an influential body, whom the Chinese have been accustomed to regard as paramount here, and whose readier access to the hong merchants, from habit and old acquaintance, may, at any time, afford the means of counteracting His Majesty's Representative.

Elliot, then Secretary of the Commission, replied on 18 October to Sprott's letter of 1 October, acknowledging its receipt. Napier had encouraged the formation of the Chamber but Davis, then Chief, had quite different opinions of its members. He wrote to Sir John Barrow on 8 November 1834:[61] 'Canton is distracted, with parties headed by Mr Daniell and Mr Whiteman on one side and Mr Innes and Mr Jardine on the other

of Judicial Jealousy' 396-97; 'A Short History of Arbitration' in Kaplan, Spruce and Moser *Hong Kong and China Arbitration Cases and Materials* ppxlvi-xlvii.

59. FO17/7 ff124-130.
60. The future Prime Minister's uncle?
61. FO17/12 f172.

- some beating each other with sticks - it began in the *Canton Register...*'
Barrow later passed Davis's opinion to the Foreign Office:[62]

> He is disgusted with the vulgar rabble of free traders into whose hands
> Lord Napier was indiscreet enough to throw himself... those turbulent
> fellows in Canton, a specimen of which you have in the *Canton Register*.'

On 14 November 1834, Davis wrote to the Foreign Office enclosing a letter
written to the Commission two days before by a group of merchants, *not*
the Chamber of Commerce, but including those who Barrow had said were
on opposite sides.[63] Their letter replied to one from the hong merchants
enclosing an Edict requiring them to appoint a new Taipan to manage
British trade in Canton. It explained that on the cessation of the East India
Company's monopoly the British Government had appointed Napier, now
dead, and that Davis had taken his place, and that the Commission now had
authority for making regulations to control British trade.[64]

On 19 November Davis received a letter declaring the interest of a
faction:

> Having noticed in the *Canton Register...* a letter of 24th October 1834
> addressed to your board by the Chairman of an association styling itself
> 'the British Chamber of Commerce of Canton' and also the board's
> reply... we... do not recognize any such body... the signatures and
> opinions therefore of the few gentlemen who have assumed that title
> can only be received as those of the individuals....

There followed the signatures of Thomas Dent & Co, D & M Rustomjee,
Daniell & Co, JS Mendes, Framjee Muncherjee, Nanabhoy Framjee,
Mucherjee Jamsetjee, Whiteman & Co, JB & Poojee Viccajee, Bomanjee
Maneckjee and Burjorjee Furdoonjee. On 23 November Davis replied that,
as there seemed to be no unanimity, it 'may appear desirable to take some
steps towards its reconstruction.'

The Chamber's secretary replied to a copy of that letter on 1 December.
The signatures supporting the constitution of the Chamber were those of
the majority. Those of the opposing few showed they were a minority
and only three of them were from what the law would hold to be proper
British subjects. The opponents raised no objection of substance; they had

62. Also at FO17/12 f172.
63. FO17/7 f142. They were Whiteman & Co, James Innes, Joseph Cragg, R Turner & Co,
AS Keating, J Gladstone, Daniell & Co, WS Boyd, Jardine, Matheson & Co, Thomas Dent
& Co, Fox, Rawson & Co, Framjee Muncherjee, Bassojee Viccajee, Dadabhoy Rustomjee
and JR Reeves.
64. This letter was signed by the same merchants as signed the covering letter.

originally agreed to form a Chamber; some were members of a committee set up to consider its constitution; they withdrew only when the majority adopted that constitution. Moreover:

> all the proceedings relative to the constitution of the Chamber were from time to time submitted... to HM's late Chief Superintendent, Lord Napier, and... the whole were honored by His Lordship's approbation.... amongst no society or class of men can unanimity be rationally expected... the minority will defer to the opinions of the majority... all parties [may] become members by a mere intimation to myself.

So, they should join and make any changes by 'their arguments and votes'. Apparently the Parsees had withdrawn because of the discriminatory system of representation on the committee. The names for and against the adoption of the constitution were listed.

On 3 December Elliot replied on behalf of the Commission. The Royal Instructions directed them to use their utmost influence to adjust by arbitration or persuasion all disputes. Therefore they suggested 'reconstruction'. But they were happy to accept the assurance that anyone could join. The Superintendents merely wanted the Chamber to be useful and hoped that nothing would be allowed to impair that usefulness. 'The institution is purely commercial and therefore they can have no pretension to insist upon any further interference.'

This was followed on 9 December 1834 by a petition to the British Government, not from the Chamber of Commerce but from 61 merchants at Canton, protesting against the limits the Chinese authorities had placed on trade, the 'arbitrary and indiscriminate exactions', the disadvantages of having to deal with the monopoly of hong merchants, the arrogant assumption of superiority over the monarchs and people of other countries claimed by the Emperor of China, and the necessity for showing him 'the true rank of Your Majesty's Empire in the scale of nations' and:

> the inexpediency of assigning the task [of dealing with the Chinese] to any persons previously known in China, as connected with commerce conducted under the trammels and degradations to which it has hitherto been subjected,[65] or to anyone, in short, who has had the misfortune, either in a public or private capacity, to endure insult or injury from Chinese authorities. Equally inexpedient would it be... to treat with any functionary not especially nominated by the Imperial Cabinet.

---

65. Presumably that meant Company men.

And make sure that any Commissioner is treated with 'the dignity of a Minister of Your Majesty and... honor of an Empire that acknowledges no superior on Earth'!

Perhaps Elliot's suggestion that Keating should enlist the help of the Chamber in his appeal to the Chinese authorities had not been so practical after all.[66]

66. A new General Chamber of Commerce was founded in Canton at the end of 1836, with a committee of 13: 5 had to be English, 3 American, 2 Parsee, 1 Dutch and 1 French; one other member was to be elected without national qualification, *Canton Register* 29 November and 13 December 1836.

THE ENGLISH INHERITANCE
What the First American Colonists Knew of Mediation and Arbitration

Derek Roebuck[1]

[*Editorial note*: This article was first published at (2016) 2 *Journal of Dispute Resolution* 1–26 and is reproduced by kind permission of the publisher.]

> How extensive the practice of arbitration was among private citizens with no involvement of lawyers or the courts we will probably never know, as the only records of such practices will be happenstance.
>
> James Oldham and Su Jin Kim[2]

I. INTRODUCTION

It seems fair to assume that the first American colonists took with them attitudes and practices from home, including the ways in which they routinely resolved disputes. For example, on November 11, 1647 the General Court of the Massachusetts Bay Colony authorized the purchase of Edward Coke's *Reports*, *First and Second Institutes* and *Book of Entries*, "to the end we may have the better light for making and proceedings about laws."[3] But does that mean it was natural then for parties with differences to look to litigation for an answer? This Article provides ample evidence of a preference for other ways of resolving their disputes. Its main purpose is to show what dispute resolution attitudes and practices prevailed in England that could

1. Professor Derek Roebuck, Senior Associate Research Fellow, Institute of Advanced Legal Studies, University of London. This article was presented at the University of Missouri School of Law's Center for the Study of Dispute Resolution and *Journal of Dispute Resolution* Fall 2016 Works-in-Progress Conference, which ran in conjunction with the Fall 2016 Symposium entitled, *Beyond the FAA: Arbitration Procedures, Practices, and Policies in Historical Perspective*. For Symposium articles, see 2016 Journal of Dispute Resolution 1. For a more complete discussion of the points raised in this article, please see DEREK ROEBUCK, ARBITRATION AND MEDIATION IN SEVENTEENTH-CENTURY ENGLAND (Oxford HOLO Books: The Arbitration Press, 2017).
2. James Oldham & Su Jin Kim, *Arbitration in America: The Early History*, 31 LAW & HIST. REV. 241, 245 (2013) hereinafter Oldham & Kim].
3. RECORDS OF THE GOVERNOR AND COMPANY OF THE MASSACHUSETTS BAY IN NEW ENGLAND 212 (Nathaniel Bradstreet Shurtleff, ed., 1853) at 212, *available at* https://archive.org/details/record-sofgoverno01mass.

have been transported to the American colonies. It ends by providing, from English sources, names of one or two individuals, namely Nathaniel Bacon and Francis Bacon, who could have been particular conduits, leaving it for others to find and assess the American evidence.[4]

Throughout the 17th century England expanded its interests in the Americas. The colonists brought to North America the dispute resolution practices they had known in England.[5] These practices included mediation and arbitration. [6] There is something to be learned from the English cases reported in the 17th century, but contemporaries thought little of their law reports. As their most disparaging critic concluded, describing in detail the processes by which those reports came to be published:[7]

As if to avenge the seclusion in which this knowledge had been held, the nation dragged to light every thing [sic] which bore so much as semblance to the aspect of law. 'Then came forth', says a historian of the time (5 Mod viii), 'a flying squadron of thin reports', and past doubt there must be meaning in the sudden and unexampled increase of this sort of publication at the epoch of which we speak.... Most of these reports are *posthumous, were printed from MSS not original; and that even the*

4. Oldham & Kim, *supra* note 1, though concentrating on the adoption of the Arbitration Act 1698 Act, contains much more of relevance to the 17th century, particularly on Maryland and Pennsylvania, and is as authoritative for that century as Henry Horwitz and James Oldham *John Locke, Lord Mansfield and Arbitration During the Eighteenth Century*, 36 THE HISTORICAL J. 137 (1993) are for the 18th century. *See also* Bruce Mann, *The Formalization of Informal Law: Arbitration Before the American Revolution*, 59 N.Y.U. L. REV 443, 446 (1984). Mann features Connecticut. Its reliability can be judged by such generalizations, impliedly of England: "For all practical purposes, arbitration awards were unenforceable." For Massachusetts, *see* DAVID THOMAS KONIG, LAW AND SOCIETY IN PURITAN MASSACHUSETTS: ESSEX COUNTY 1629-1692.

5. MORTON HORWITZ, THE TRANSFORMATION OF AMERICAN LAW: 1780-1860, 145-48 (Harvard University Press, 1977); Mann, *supra* note 3, at 443; Eben Moglen, *Commercial Arbitration in the Eighteenth Century: Searching for the Transformation of American Law*, 93 YALE L.J. 135 (1983); Carli N. Conklin, *Lost Options for Mutual Gain: The Lawyer, the Layperson, and Dispute Resolution in Early America*, 28 OHIO ST. J. ON DISP. RESOL. 581, 583-84 (2013); Carli N. Conklin, *A Variety of State-Level Procedures, Practices, and Policies: Arbitration in Early America*, 2016 J. DISP. RESOL. 55, 60-66; Oldham & Kim, *supra* note 1, at 241, 244-251, 266; James Oldham, *The Historically Shifting Sands of Reasons to Arbitrate*, 2016 J. DISP.RESOL. 41, 41-42.

6. For an overview of mediation and arbitration in early America, see generally JEROLD S. AUERBACH, JUSTICE WITHOUT LAW? (Oxford University Press 1983). See also references *supra* note 5 for works on English-style arbitration in specific British colonies in North America.

7. JOHN WILLIAM WALLACE, THE REPORTERS, CHRONOLOGICALLY ARRANGED: WITH OCCASIONAL REMARKS UPON THEIR RESPECTIVE MERITS (T. & J.W. Johnson, 2nd rev. ed. 1845) (emphasis in the original) *available at* https://archive.org/details/cu31924024518346.

originals were not designed for the press. Ignorance and interest and accident all combined to produce error.

The first writers on arbitration law tried to make the best of what they had, but lawyers turning to them for guidance would find them thin sustenance.[8]

There are, however, ample primary sources in the form of records preserved in national and local archives of the work of practicing mediator-arbitrators. Any account of the period must try to take advantage of all of them. This Article relies on the voluminous collection of just one, Nathaniel Bacon (1546-1622), the son of Sir Nicholas Bacon, Elizabeth I's Lord Keeper and the older half-brother of the more famous Francis.[9] Nathaniel was a busy Justice of the Peace (JP)[10] in Norfolk and, as will be shown below, was often commissioned as arbitrator by the government, but often too by private parties who were happy to rely on his reputation for integrity and expertise in private mediation and arbitration. Each side could appoint a single arbitrator or several arbitrators.[11] It was not uncommon for the sides to appoint a single arbitrator when, like Bacon, both sides trusted him.[12]

After Trinity College Cambridge, Nathaniel Bacon entered Gray's Inn, one of England's Inns of Court, but he was never called to practice as a barrister before the courts.[13] Instead, as soon as he could, he settled into the life of a country squire on the family estate at Stiffkey, Norfolk.[14] In addition to serving as JP, Bacon was a Member of Parliament (MP) for King's Lynn, High Sheriff of Norfolk and Steward of the Duchy of Lancaster's lands in the county.[15] He fulfilled his duties as MP but gave priority to the obligations,

8. Perhaps the best example by the author is REGULA PLACITANDI, ARBITRIUM REDIVIVUM: OR THE LAW OF ARBITRATION; COLLECTED FROM THE LAW-BOOKS BOTH ANCIENT AND MODERN, AND DEDUCED TO THESE TIMES, (Rich. & Edw. Atkins, 1694). Unfortunately, the identity of the author of REGULA PLACITANDI is unknown. *See also* JOHN MARCH, ACTIONS FOR SLANDER AND ARBITREMENTS (1648); JOHN MARCH, THE SECOND PART OF ACTIONS FOR SLANDERS, WITH A SECOND PART OF ARBITREMENTS (William Brown ed., 3rd ed. 1674).

9. Nathaniel Bacon lived from 1546-1622 and served as a member of parliament. *Nathaniel Bacon*, THE HISTORY OF PARLIAMENT, http://www.historyofparliamentonline.org/volume/1604-1629/mem-ber/bacon-nathaniel-1546-1622 (last visited Dec. 10, 2016). His younger half-brother, Francis Bacon, lived from 1561-1626. *Francis Bacon*, THE HISTORY OF PARLIAMENT, http://www.historyofparliamentonline.org/volume/1604-1629/member/bacon-sir-francis-1561-1626 (Last visited Dec. 10, 2016).

10. *Francis Bacon, supra* note 8.

11. For English law on the number of arbitrators required for arbitration, see Carli N. Conklin, *A Variety of State-Level Procedures, Practices, and Policies: Arbitration in Early America,* 2016 J. DISP. RESOL. 55, 60-62.

12. Such an appointment would be a sign of esteem. BACON PAPERS IV, *infra* note 17, at xliii.

13. *Nathaniel Bacon, supra* note 8.

14. *Id.*

15. *Id.*

religious and civil, he considered essential to create an orderly and godly community within his jurisdiction.[16] He devoted much of his time to settling disputes, and he submitted his own disputes to private arbitration.[17]

Bacon's enormous collection of manuscripts, preserved and edited under the title, *The Papers of Nathaniel Bacon of Stiffkey*[18] provides the primary sources for an understanding of routine practices and attitudes to dispute resolution in his country at that time. Indeed, they themselves show that some extrapolation may be justified to the rest of England then. As the following account will demonstrate, most of the documents in the *Papers* refer to his work as a JP, many of them commissions to mediate from a great range of authorities, from the King, Parliament and Privy Council, and the various Courts, to individual authorities.[19] But there is also plenty of evidence of his popularity as a private arbitrator, where with no official interference both parties were content for him to sit alone.[20]

This article draws on edited volumes of the *Papers*, beginning towards the end of Elizabeth I's reign and ending with the latest volume in 1607.[21] The volumes contain two hundred or more documents relating to Bacon's activities as resolver of disputes.[22] As the following discussion will demonstrate, mediation was an essential component of keeping law and order. There was no effective police force; as the editors of volume IV of the *Papers* write, Bacon's brother-in-law was injured in a duel and his son-in-law and later his stepson were to be killed in duels.[23] Mediation and arbitration existed as alternative modes of dispute resolution. Bacon's status in the community was reflected in his selection by community members for assistance in peacefully resolving their disputes:

16. *Id.*
17. BACON PAPERS IV, *infra* note 17, at xlii-xliii.
18. THE PAPERS OF NATHANIEL BACON OF STIFFKEY, of which five volumes have so far appeared: Volume I 1556-1577 (A. Hassell Smith, G.M. Baker and RW Kenny eds., (XLVI 1978/1979)) [hereinafter BACON PAPERS I]; Volume II 1578-1585 (A. Hassell Smith & G.M. Baker eds., (XLIX 1983)) [hereinafter BACON PAPERS II]; Volume III 1586-1595 (A. Hassell Smith & G.M. Baker eds., (LIII 1990)) [hereinafter BACON PAPERS III]; Volume IV 1596-1602 (Victor Morgan, Jane Key, & Barry Taylor eds., (LXIV 2000)) [hereinafter BACON PAPERS IV]; and Volume V 1603-1607 (Victor Morgan, Elizabeth Rutledge & Barry Taylor eds., (LXXIV 2010)) [hereinafter BACON PAPERS V]. Two earlier selections will remain useful until the greatly superior Norfolk Record Society edition is complete: NATHANIEL BACON, THE OFFICIAL PAPERS OF SIR BACON OF STIFFKEY, NOR-FOLK, AS JUSTICE OF THE PEACE 1580-1620 (H.W. Saunders ed., 1915) and SUPPLE-MENTARY STIFFKEY PAPERS (F.W. Brooks ed., 1936)
19. *See generally* BACON PAPERS, Volumes I-V, *supra* note 17 (detailing Nathaniel Bacon's work as a JP and the commissions he received to serve as a mediator or arbitrator from the King, Parliament, Privy Council, various Courts, and individuals).
20. *Id.*
21. *Id.* BACON PAPERS I-V, *supra* note 17.
22. *Id.*
23. BACON PAPERS IV, *supra* note 17, at xlii.

Resolution of minor local disputes may have been tiresome and time-consuming but the seeking out of a local gentleman such as Bacon as an arbiter by individuals in the locality or the referral to him of disputes that had reached the centre did two things. First, it reflected his existing standing in both local society and in the estimation of those at the centre.... Second, every act of mediation or arbitration helped to spin out yet further filaments of obligation.[24]

Social class expected privilege. Obligations were more readily accepted on the understanding they would generate reciprocity. Bacon's selection as an arbitrator or mediator to resolve disputes was integral to this system.

This article explores Bacon's role as a mediator and arbitrator, and the implications of that role for the practice of mediation and arbitration in the American colonies, in three parts. Part II explores Bacon's official commissions to arbitrate, which he received from the King, Parliament, Privy Council, Chancery and the Chancellor, the Court of Requests, in his role as High Steward, and from the pre-eminent English jurist, Sir Edward Coke. Bacon's communications with Coke, in particular, are worth looking at in depth as they demonstrate the high value placed on mediation and arbitration in this period.

Bacon also received private commissions to mediate or arbitrate disputes; these commissions will be discussed in Part III. Bacon's selection to serve as mediator or arbitrator for private dispute resolution most likely stemmed from his reputation in the community and his authority as Justice of the Peace. This Article explores several such commissions, including a dispute over land and debts between the widow Elizabeth Earle and her late husband's son, Robert, and disputes between neighbours over conflicts as varied as the use of well water, the payment of rents and tithes, and the killing of a boar. The variety of private commissions received by Bacon provides evidence not only of the broad use of mediation and arbitration to resolve disputes, but also of the great value community members placed on mediation and arbitration for settling controversies and restoring the peace. Indeed, in a surviving letter describing a dispute that Bacon was selected to help arbitrate, arbitration is described as a "pathway to peace" and the arbitrator is lauded as "blessed peacemaker".

Part IV concludes this article with a discussion of exportation of mediation and arbitration to the British colonies in North America. That exportation included not only the practice of mediation and arbitration to resolve disputes, but also the high value placed on those dispute resolution processes by individuals and entities as varied as individual colonists and the Privy Council. Part IV ends with a call for future research in this area,

---

24. BACON PAPERS IV, *supra* note 17, at xliii.

in hopes that the uncovering and exploration of archival materials, like the papers of Nathaniel Bacon, might provide a more complete and nuanced understanding of how the English forms of dispute resolution played out in the early American colonies.

II. OFFICIAL COMMISSIONS TO MEDIATION
AND ARBITRATION IN 17TH CENTURY ENGLAND

A. *Commissions From The King*

It was not uncommon for Bacon to receive an official commission to arbitrate a dispute. The endorsement at the foot of a commission might reveal the King's own hand.[25] For example, Martin Hambleton had mortgaged his land for one year to John Mingay and his son Henry, for £60 at 10 percent interest.[26] The land was leased to Edward Murton.[27] Murton and the Mingays took possession of the house and evicted the Hambleton family, even though Hambleton had offered them all he owed.[28] Hambleton specifically asked for Bacon and four others, or any two or three to examine his petition for redress.[29] The petition dated 16 May 1604 is endorsed with an order from King James I that, if the case was not being dealt with judicially, the arbitrators, or some of them, with two or more chosen by the other parties, should settle it equitably.[30]

Julius Caesar, one of the two Masters of Requests, was the conduit through which the King's instructions were usually sent.[31] On June 24, 1603 he wrote to Bacon and Sir Christopher Heydon, referring to them the petition of Nicholas Ringold to the new King, who had asked that Ringold's cause be sent to "some indifferent gentlemen" of Norfolk:[32]

His Highness' good pleasure is that you should call both him and his adverse parties before you and examine the differences between them, and thereupon mediate such good end and order between them as you shall find to be agreeable to good conscience and dignity, that His Highness be no further troubled.[33]

The request was expressly to mediate an outcome, not according to law, but according to conscience and dignity.

25. BACON PAPERS IV, *supra* note 17, at 108-109.
26. BACON PAPERS V, *supra* note 17, at 108-109.
27. *Id.*
28. *Id.*
29. *Id.*
30. *Id.*
31. BACON PAPERS V, *supra* note 17, at li-lii, 38, 135, 153.
32. BACON PAPERS V, *supra* note 17, at 37-43.
33. *Id.*

Not all Bacon's efforts to mediate were successful. A matter referred to him and others on a petition to the King "concerning a messuage and 103 acres in Briston" was returned on May 1, 1604 when they were unable to persuade the parties to a settlement.[34]

B. Commissions From Parliament

Parliament, too, might send a matter to arbitration, even when it was the subject of a bill before it. For example, Arthur Penning of Kettleburgh, Suffolk died in 1594.[35] His heir and executor was his elder son Anthony.[36] The will provided for his younger brother Edmund to receive £4,000 from the estate.[37] The intention was that Edmund should have a substantial share of the family lands.[38] As it would be impossible to convey land of exactly £4,000 in value, there would be a balance to be paid in cash.[39] A difference as to valuation might have been expected to be a simple matter. It was not.

A committee of the Commons appointed arbitrators: Bacon and Sir Charles Cornwallis for Edmund and Sir John Higham and Robert Kempe for Anthony.[40] Sir Robert Jermyn was appointed umpire but later replaced Kempe as arbitrator.[41] Their many attempts produced considerable heat, partly because Edmund's wife Anne was a determined woman who took over the conduct of their claim from her husband and stood up to Anthony's appointed arbitrators, who tried to bully her.[42] Bacon was magisterial when they tried to insist on their preferred award.[43]

Whatever the law might say about title not being arbitrable, arbitration or mediation was through the centuries the preferred method of dealing with disputed ownership of land.[44] Once the arbitrators had decided the question of title, they would get the necessary conveyances drawn and, when executed, they were as good as any title any court could give.[45]

Anthony Penning wrote to Bacon on 8 September 1606 that he had received a draft conveyance from Edmund and that he had taken exception to it.[46] He had had his own draft prepared by counsel and submitted both to

---

34. BACON PAPERS V, *supra* note 17, at 107.
35. BACON PAPERS V, *supra* note 17, at 17, at 222, n.612.
36. BACON PAPERS V, *supra* note 17, at 221-22.
37. BACON PAPERS V, *supra* note 17, at 222.
38. *Id.*
39. *Id.* The balance to be paid was 560 pounds. *Id.*
40. BACON PAPERS V, *supra* note 17, at 221-22.
41. BACON PAPERS V, *supra* note 17, at 222.
42. BACON PAPERS V, *supra* note 17, at 240-43, 250-51, 261-63.
43. BACON PAPERS V, *supra* note 17, at 261-63.
44. DEREK ROEBUCK, THE GOLDEN AGE OF ARBITRATION: DISPUTE RESOLUTION UNDER ELIZABETH I, at 244-58 (2015).
45. *Id.*
46. BACON PAPERS V, *supra* note 17, at 255.

Bacon and whatever was acceptable to him, Higham and Jermyn he would willingly perform.[47]

Higham got in first. He wrote to Bacon on 9 September 1606 to say he had perused both drafts and preferred Anthony's: "I hold it not reasonable that the woman, if she survive her husband, should hold the land without impeachment of waste."[48] Nor should Edmund have a life estate that he could dispose of, "for then he may, through his want of experience, be brought to pass away that interest and live full meanly all his life after."[49] Better he should have only the profits from the land.[50] Was Higham worried that the woman would manipulate her husband?

A letter from Higham and Jermyn to Bacon dated 30 October 1606 appears in The Papers of Nathaniel Bacon preserved in the Folger Library.[51] Anne had been to see them at Bury St Edmunds.[52] They had not enjoyed her visit.[53] She had shown "great mislike" of their preference for the land to remain in trust, with discretion in the trustees as to where the profits should go in Edmund's lifetime:

> Her importunity was so great as we sent for Mr Anthony Penning to come to us at Bury, where we laboured him to yield so to assure the lands as his brother might have the very land itself during his life a counsellor-at-law (whom the gentlewoman entertained) did affirm that it might be safely done. Mr Anthony Penning desired to be advised by his own counsel, who fully resolved us that, if the land were assured for life as to the husband as it should be to the wife, with remainder to the issue etc, that then the husband and wife might then by recovery cut off the entail, and so in a short time the husband's estate would quickly be overthrown. The gentlewoman misliked of this and urged us to a certificate, and we perceiving her disposition and that nothing will content her but the sale of the land, we have in a letter set down the whole truth and ascertained my Lord Chancellor thereof, whereof if you like we pray you to subscribe, to prevent the malicious purpose of the woman.[54]

Nothing in all the five volumes of *Papers* shows Bacon's qualities as an arbitrator so well as his reply of 1 November 1606:

> Sirs, I have perused the certificate sent unto me under your hands and have considered also of your letter yet I must entreat you to excuse me though

47. *Id.*
48. *Id.*
49. *Id.*
50. *Id.*
51. *Id.* at 261-62.
52. BACON PAPERS V, *supra* note 17, at 261-62.
53. *Id.*
54. *Id.*

I forbear now to join in the certificate. You have had your judgments satisfied by hearing the parties on both sides to speak before you, and it may be I shall be of your judgment when I hear the like. But I am doubtful at this present how to judge this point, *viz* how far forth Edmund Penning shall be barred during his life. I allow well that he be barred to do no act to overthrow the inheritance, and this seemed on our first meeting to be agreed upon between us, and the other point was left doubtful. Therefore, I think it best that a cause of this importance be at London determined upon, where the best counsel in law may be had, and where you, Sir John Heigham, and I are like shortly to meet, and then upon more advice we may certify Sir Robert Jermyn what there falleth out best to be allowed upon and in the meantime the causes may rest as they be.[55]

A model, even for today.

C. Commissions from Privy Council

James I's Privy Council used arbitration to deal with petitions just as Elizabeth I's had done, and Bacon's *Papers* reveal commissions from Privy Council. In giving instructions to those it commissioned, Privy Council rarely made a distinction between mediation and arbitration, or even between an order to resolve a dispute themselves or just to report back, such as in the commission dated 12 November 1604 to Bacon with Sir Miles Corbett, Thomas Cromwell and Owen Sheppard (or to any three or two).[56] They took extensive evidence of the rights of warren over Castle Rising, which were disputed by the Earl of Northampton's tenant and, among others, Sir Henry Spelman, the antiquary's father.[57] The arbitrators were instructed: "upon examination and perusal of such proofs and matters of evidence as they shall have severally to end the controversy if you can, or otherwise certify us of your whole proceedings."[58]

Sir John Popham often referred to Bacon matters that came before him when he was Chief Justice of the King's Bench (CJKB).[59] For example, in 1601 he directed Bacon, Henry Spelman, and Thomas Layer, or any two, to arrange a settlement between Katherine Barr, widow, and the executors of a foreign merchant, Adam Kindt, whom she accused of cheating her of her trading goods.[60] Kindt had died and his executors would not pay his debt.[61]

---

55. BACON PAPERS V, *supra* note 17, at 262-63.
56. BACON PAPERS V, *supra* note 17, at 137-38.
57. BACON PAPERS V, *supra* note 17, at 137-41.
58. BACON PAPERS V, *supra* note 17, at 137-38.
59. BACON PAPERS IV, *supra* note 17, at 206.
60. *Id.*
61. *Id.*

The *Papers* do not always make it clear whether Popham was acting as CJKB or on behalf of the Privy Council. It made no practical difference to Bacon. Popham appointed Bacon sole arbitrator to determine all the disputes between the Reverend Edward Slynne and Robert Younger, gent, except for a matter between them in the Star Chamber.[62] The parties entered into bonds to abide by his award, which survives.[63] On 3 October 1601 he awarded that Slynne should allow Younger to enter the disputed land, of which some was copyhold in the manor of South Burlingham, and to release all actions other than that in the Star Chamber, to hand over the deeds and pay compensation.[64] Younger must allow Slynne to enter land in South Burlingham and release actions and deliver assurances on request, i.e. to execute the necessary conveyances.[65]

Popham's commissions included one about trespasses to land and a stolen boar "to end if he may"[66] and a petition from the poor inhabitants of Wiveton against John King, a man of great wealth, who had got his hands on funds intended for the poor "now ready to starve," which Popham had himself endorsed to Bacon and Henry Spelman, to "examine this cause and, if you may, take some course that the poor may have their due, otherwise to certify me the true state of the matter at the next assizes."[67]

From the Privy Council Popham sent a dispute between two aldermen of Lynn, Baker and Gurlyn, to Bacon and Sir Miles Corbett, "to mediate matters between them and if you may finally to accord them."[68] In June 1602 John Atkins of King's Lynn wrote to Lord Keeper Egerton, on behalf of himself and his neighbours, complaining of the "unjust malefactions" of Alderman Thomas Baker, and asking him for permission to petition the Privy Council for "letters to be directed to 3 or 4 knights or gents in the county to call all the parties grieved before them... whereby some good order may be had for reformation according to their godly wisdoms agreeing with equity." By letter from Popham the Council appointed "the right worshipful my very loving friends Sir Miles Corbett and Nathaniel Bacon Esq":

> With my very hearty commendations. Where there are certain controversies and suits depending between Mr Baker and Mr Gurlyn, two of the aldermen of the town of Lynn, which occasioneth some division in the town to the hindrance of the good governance of the same, I have thought good thereby to pray you to take the pains at this my entreaty to mediate

62. BACON PAPERS IV, *supra* note 17, at 209.
63. *Id.*
64. *Id.*
65. *Id.*
66. BACON PAPERS IV, *supra* note 17, at 324
67. BACON PAPERS IV, supra note 17, at 269-70.
68. BACON PAPERS IV, supra note 17, at 273.

matters between them and if you may finally to accord them wherein in mine opinion you shall do a very good office not only in making peace between these two in particular but in furthering thereby the continuance of the good government of that town.[69]

D. Commissions from the Chancery and the Chancellor

In addition to receiving commissions from the King, Parliament, and Privy Council, Bacon regularly received appointments resulting from petitions to the Chancery, like the one from Thomas Pearce to Lord Keeper Egerton, which Egerton passed to Bacon to deal with alone in June 1600:

> I pray you take the pains, calling both him and his mother before you to examine the matter and by some quiet order agreeable to equity and justice, to prevent and stop these farther suits which were unfit to be between parties so nearly bound to one another in love and duty, and which the petitioner seems to desire to have by this course prevented.[70]

When he became Lord Chancellor Ellesmere, Egerton continued his habit of commissioning Bacon to mediate an end to matters before the Court of Chancery. Thomas Fairfax was plaintiff in a Chancery suit against John Rust. On 15 February 1605 Rust petitioned the Chancellor expressly to appoint Bacon and by a letter of 18 February he was asked "to make some quiet and friendly end between them according to equity and good conscience."[71] But meanwhile Edward Coke had jumped in and sent Rust to Bacon with a letter dated 17 February, asking him:

> to hear and understand the controversy, and thereupon to do your friendly endeavour to end and determine the same between them . . . if by your good persuasion and means you cannot bring them to accept of such order and agreement as you in your wisdom and conscience shall think fit for them, then I pray you to certify to me the true state of the controversy and in whom you find the default to rest, that such order may be taken as is according to justice and equity.[72]

A memorandum of 5 March explains that the dispute was about mutual bonds and that the parties were brought to a settlement, except that Fairfax would not agree to Bacon's finding that he should bear the costs of the

---

69. *Id.*
70. *Id.*
71. BACON PAPERS V, *supra* note 17, at 152.
72. BACON PAPERS V, *supra* note 17, at 153.

Chancery suit.[73] So Bacon had to certify and return the commission, which he did by a letter of 8 April not to Coke but to Ellesmere LC.[74] He explained that the bonds had arisen out of liability for customs duties on barley exported to the Low Countries.[75] Fairfax had had no cause to start proceedings in Chancery, so he should bear the costs of them, £3 or £4.[76] Fairfax could not be persuaded.[77] And so Bacon was certifying and returning the commission, as instructed, "submitting my judgment to your Lordship's wisdom and grave consideration."[78]

On 22 April 1605 Bacon wrote to Coke enclosing a copy of the certificate he had sent to Ellesmere LC on 8 April 1605, and "referring the poor man [Rust] to your further favour for his relief."[79]

E. Commissions from the Court of Requests

Some commissions to mediate went to Bacon through the Court of Requests. For example, after a detailed memorandum of disputes between Robert Barnard and Thomas Clarke relating to corn, oats, straw, malt, peas and a horse, the settlement is recorded:

It is agreed 6 August 1604 between Robert Barnard gent and Thomas Clarke as followeth *viz* Robert Barnard doth accept in full discharge of a debt of £250 due to him from Thomas Clarke the £239 14s 6d demanded by Thomas Clarke, and in discharge thereof, as also of all other demands, agreeth to seal him a special acquittance. And Thomas Clarke agreeth to seal the like acquittance unto Robert Barnard.[80]

F. Commissions Received by Bacon as High Steward

Among his many other public offices, Bacon was High Steward of the Crown and Duchy of Lancaster in Norfolk.[81] He received commissions to serve as arbitrator in that capacity, as well. For example, in November 1604, Thomas Edwards of Wisbech complained to him as High Steward of the King's manor of Walpole that the brothers Griggs had by a suit in the manor court wrongly taken his copyhold land.[82] On 14 November 1604, Ellesmere LC made an order referring the case to Bacon as High Steward "to decide

---

73. BACON PAPERS V, *supra* note 17, at 156.
74. BACON PAPERS V, *supra* note 17, at 169-170.
75. BACON PAPERS V, *supra* note 17, at 170.
76. *Id.*
77. *Id.*
78. *Id.*
79. BACON PAPERS V, *supra* note 17, at 173-74.
80. BACON PAPERS V, *supra* note 17, at 121-24.
81. *Nathaniel Bacon, supra* note 8.
82. BACON PAPERS V, *supra* note 17, at 136.

in law and conscience," "as the fittest person to decide this controversy" but "to make a quiet and friendly end between them according to law and conscience."[83] This made for a nice little conundrum of categorization for the conceptual purist.

Bacon heard the matter as High Steward and wrote forthwith to both counsel that he had considered the legal title and what could be alleged in equity for Edwards and had asked each of the parties whether either would be prepared to renounce the land to the other and for what price.[84] Edwards was willing but the Griggs were not, insisting on their title.[85] Bacon told counsel that he would therefore certify to the Lord Chancellor that a trial be held at the next assizes.[86] Edwards assented but the Griggs said they needed further advice.[87] So Bacon asked counsel to give him their opinions as soon as possible.[88] But even at this stage he made his preference clear: "I incline rather to have the cause mediated than referred to the law if the Griggs would be ruled by me."[89]

Bacon settled another dispute, referred to him by the Duchy Chamber with the consent of both parties. Musket surrendered his rights in a tenement and orchard to Bretland, who agreed to pay him two instalments of £3 6s 8d "in full satisfaction of money due under any cause now depending in the Chamber."[90]

As Chief Steward of the Duchy Lands, Bacon had jurisdiction to decide disputes in his own court. He also performed other judicial functions. For example, if copyhold land was held by a husband in the right of his wife, the wife's agreement was necessary for any transfer.[91] A memorandum of surrender recites that Alice was examined in the absence of her husband by Sir Nathaniel Bacon, Chief Steward, and then John and Alice surrendered the land to Bacon.[92]

G. Commissions from Sir Edward Coke

Edward Coke dominates the legal world of this period. The *Papers* preserve three documents, trimmed and redacted here, which illustrate his involvement with Bacon in the settlement of disputes.[93]

83. BACON PAPERS V, *supra* note 17, at 136, 141-42.
84. BACON PAPERS V, *supra* note 17, at 175.
85. *Id.*
86. *Id.*
87. *Id.*
88. *Id.*
89. *Id.*
90. BACON PAPERS V, *supra* note 17, at 268.
91. BACON PAPERS V, *supra* note 17, at 292-93.
92. *Id.*
93. BACON PAPERS IV, *supra* note 17, at 284-88.

On 8 September 1602 William Cobbe, whose land adjoined Edward Paston's, wrote to Bacon seeking a private arbitration:

Sir, I must confess my presumption to be far greater than my deserts, so as I cannot challenge that interest in your love I so greatly desire. Yet, knowing that it hath been agreeable with your good disposition not to think that time lost which is spent in so good a work as ending of controversies and dissensions, and making of peace and amity between gentlemen and your neighbours, pardon me if I seem troublesome, that am so wrongfully troubled (as I suppose) being not led thereto with self will, yet willing to defend my poor patrimony to my power, being resolved of my right by them of judgment and learning, as also by divers trials lately passed at the common law to my great trouble, charge and hindrance; which by your good means I hope shall now receive a friendly and quiet end (and the rather for that it hath pleased Mr Attorney General [Coke] so earnestly to move the same).

Sir, the sincerity of my cause is to be censured out of your wisdom to which I do appeal, desiring our cause may be weighed in equal balance. I covet not that which I never had, but what my ancestors time out of mind have quietly enjoyed without interruption of them that had the right Mr Paston now hath. Neither build I upon bare presumptions (as shall plainly appear unto you) but upon divers depositions which will be verified by ancient evidence.

I wish the state of my body were such as I might safely adventure to attend you myself, but my cousin Athow [the barrister Thomas Athow] and my wife will be ready at all times to attend your leisure for the same, and what you and they shall agree I will most willingly perform, and acknowledge myself bound to you in bonds of perpetual friendship. William Cobbe.[94]

His wife Mary took over. She wrote to Bacon on 21 September 1602, referring to a visit she had made to him with a Mr. Mingey, a relative of Coke's, with Coke's "request that you should take pains to hear and end (if it may be) certain causes betwixt Mr. Paston and Mr. Cobbe, my husband."[95] If they could not mediate a settlement, the matter would go back to Coke, "that he by his wisdom and better persuasions may effect that which you cannot."[96] She suggested possible dates.[97] She had spoken to Paston and got his agreement to submit to Bacon and Henry Wyndham, "to perform without

94. BACON PAPERS IV, *supra* note 17, at 284-85.
95. BACON PAPERS IV, *supra* note 17, at 285-86.
96. *Id.*
97. *Id.*

delay what shall be then ordered by you and Mr. Wyndham, and consented to by him, my cousin Athow and myself."[98] So William Cobbe had authorised his wife, with the lawyer Athow, to consent to a binding settlement.

Mary wrote to Bacon four days later.[99] She had received his answering letter (which has not survived) and letters from Coke which she had not read but presumed were attempts to fix a date.[100] She pressed for a date before the start of the legal term.[101] Shortly thereafter Bacon and Wyndham wrote to Coke, responding to his request for them to work for a peace between Cobbe and Paston touching certain land.[102] They reported that they had "had a meeting at Appleton, Mr Paston's house, with the allowance of Mrs Cobbe in the absence of her husband, and there we saw the ground in question and did after see their evidence and hear the depositions read."[103]

Both sides had deeds, which conflicted as to whether rights of common were attached to Babingley manor or Newton manor, "and this we left undetermined, with a consent that the same should be used for the graving of flags and such like as hath of late years been most accustomed."[104] Differences as to who should have rights to feed sheep and rabbits were not a major point of contention.[105] But the arbitrators had to listen to all the complaints of both sides' tenants, and that may have been the scarcely concealed collusive object: to get rid of the bickering between their tenants over rights of common and pasture, then a general source of more contention even than the pews in their churches.[106]

They wrote a similar letter to William Cobbe, to tell him of their judgment, adding though that Athow, "your counsellor in the cause" was at the hearing.[107] Would you call that a private mediation, or arbitration, or did Coke's intervention make it Government-ordered? However it may be classified, it seems to have worked. The Cobbes were recusants, as were the Pastons. Religious differences did not inhibit wealthy neighbours from seeking Protestant Bacon's intervention, or affect his willingness to provide them skilled and experienced services.

Coke wrote fairly often and informally to Bacon.[108] He sat with Bacon as a Commissioner for Sewers in 1605.[109] Because of the leading part he played

98. BACON PAPERS IV, *supra* note 17, at 286.
99. BACON PAPERS IV, *supra* note 17, at 286-87.
100. *Id.*
101. BACON PAPERS IV, *supra* note 17, at 287-88.
102. *Id.*
103. BACON PAPERS IV, *supra* note 17, at 287.
104. *Id.* at 288.
105. *Id.*
106. BACON PAPERS IV, *supra* note 17, at 287-88.
107. BACON PAPERS IV, *supra* note 17, at 288.
108. BACON PAPERS V, *supra* note 17, at 143-44.
109. BACON PAPERS V, *supra* note 17, at 187.

in the creation of the modern law, the *Papers'* evidence of his involvement as a party in mediation and arbitration deserves particular attention.

A letter dated 2 March 1603 from Henry Warner, a friend of both sides, asked Sir Miles Corbett to arbitrate in a land dispute between Edward Coke, then Attorney General, and the same Edward Paston.[110] The disputed land in Flitcham may have adjoined both their properties.[111] Bacon agreed to be the other arbitrator.[112] Coke's confidence in Bacon as a mediator is shown time and again in the commissions he sent him, but this, of course, was a purely private arbitration.[113]

The relevant records begin again with a letter of 1 September 1604 from Coke to Bacon and Sir Miles Corbett, which included:

I being desirous not only of quietness between ourselves (whereof I made no doubt) but also between our posterities afterwards, and that suits (that commonly are mothers of unkindness) might stay, desired you (as likewise my cousin Paston did) to inform yourselves of the true state of the matter in variance; and by your good mediation to end the same. Whereupon (as I am informed) you have taken the pains to view the ground, and to hear the allegations and proof of either party. These are to desire you to proceed in so good a work, and to the end your labours already taken may not be lost, and that either party may receive the better satisfaction, that you would be pleased to meet again at Flitcham some time this next week, and to set down the proof and matters tending to the maintenance of the claims by either party, and to the manifestation of the right touching these matters in variance, wherein as you shall do a charitable and friendly work, so shall you make us much both beholden to you for your pains and indifferency herein. And so I commit you to the blessed protection of the Almighty.[114]

That letter was enclosed with the following, dated the next day:

Sir, you shall perceive by these enclosed what a desire I have of quietness, and how bold I am to require your further travails. Sir Miles sent me word by the messenger that any day after tomorrow he would give meeting about the finishing of your former travails. Whereof I am the more desirous, because I would have it driven to an issue before I depart. What day it please you to appoint, this bearer shall give notice thereof to Sir Miles. It was my cousin Paston's resolute request that the reasons

---

110. BACON PAPERS V, *supra* note 17, at 11-12.
111. *Id.*
112. *Id.*
113. BACON PAPERS V, *supra* note 17, at 11-12, 128-129.
114. BACON PAPERS V, *supra* note 17, at 128-29.

and proofs of either side should be set down or else he would no further proceed. And so with my very hearty commendations to you and your good lady I commit you to the blessed protection of the Almighty and ever rest, your assured friend.

Godwike 2 September 1604 Edw Coke[115]

Sadly, the *Papers* tell us nothing more of how this matter was resolved, so research must continue elsewhere.

Coke took pains to encourage Bacon's mediation of a dispute between Jerome Alexander, a King's Bench attorney and Alexander's brother-in-law Robert Plandon over copyhold land.[116] On 16 February 1604 he wrote to Bacon:

After my very hearty commendations. I have received knowledge that there are very many suits betwixt this bearer my servant and one Plandon, his wife's brother. And that there are commissions awarded to you and others directed to examine witnesses and to end and determine the same suits. And forsomuch as I heartily wish a peace between them, lest the one should consume the estate of the other, and in the end feel the sharpness of their own faults to their great hindrances. Therefore I heartily pray you in the behalf of both their goods to take the more pains at my request to reconcile all questions betwixt them, so shall you do a work of much piety betwixt them, and give me occasion to be heartily thankful to you for your travail therein to be taken . . . .

Your very loving friend [signed] Edward Coke.[117]

Unfortunately, the later correspondence shows no signs of a successful settlement.[118]

In the summer of 1606 Coke referred to Bacon to end or certify a petition he had received as Chief Justice of the Common Pleas about a dispute over money deposited with Thomas Thetford in trust for the two brothers and five sisters of John Moretoft.[119] It asked for "some course to come by their money, being very poor and unable to sue for their rights."[120] Four sisters were married and one was a widow.[121] Bacon's own notes show that he addressed the problem, comparatively trivial in financial terms, with as much care as he had the Pennings' £4,000, with the result that: "Mr Thetford

115. *Id.*
116. BACON PAPERS V, *supra* note 17, at 74.
117. *Id.*
118. BACON PAPERS V, *supra* note 17, at 74-75, 77.
119. BACON PAPERS V, *supra* note 17, at 243-44, 249-50
120. BACON PAPERS V, *supra* note 17, at 244.
121. BACON PAPERS V, *supra* note 17, at 243.

agreed to disburse presently 20s apiece" to the three husbands and the widow, and the rest "their portions out of the said remainder" on Thursday at the house of Bacon.[122] A memorandum dated 21 August 1606 sets out the final settlement in detail.[123] Thetford was also a party to a dispute, this time with no less than Sir Christopher Heydon, Bacon's partner in so many arbitrations. Coke as Chief Justice of Common Pleas (CJCP) similarly referred petitions for wrongful possession of a house and – a grandiloquent effort with many Biblical references, some apposite – from "your poor orator . . . whose cry ascends to God."[124]

On 13 August 1606 Bacon's reply to a Coke commission relates that he had tried to mediate a settlement of a claim against the heir of the debtor, who was answering that he had administered the estate and the claim was too late.[125] Bacon wrote:

In conscience (in my judgment) he ought to pay, both in respect of the poverty of the man, who lent the money to old Lambart, and also of the portion of land which was left to the young man by his father being of the value of £40 by year being copyhold. I would have had him repair unto your Lordship with the bearer but he refused to do it without warrant. I have thought fit to certify thus much unto your Lordship referring the poor man to your considerations.[126]

On 5 November 1606 Bacon reported failure to Coke on a matter Coke had referred to him from the Norfolk Assizes: "Bullen, notwithstanding his consent given to abide my arbitrement, refuseth to enter into a bond to perform my arbitrement as touching the matter passed by verdict for him before you Thus leaving the cause to your Lordship's further consideration, I take my leave."[127]

A year later, on 2 November 1607, Bacon's letter to Coke reveals the work he was prepared to undertake to resolve a dispute, and the limitations he laboured under, even with Coke's authority as Chief Justice behind him.[128] He had tried again but:

Bullen refused and withdrew himself in a froward and obstinate sort ...
I moved Bullen to a most reasonable course (as I thought) for end. But his wilfulness was such as he would not be conformable in any sort,

---

122. BACON PAPERS V, *supra* note 17, at 250.
123. BACON PAPERS V, *supra* note 17, at 253-54.
124. BACON PAPERS V, *supra* note 17, at 244-45.
125. BACON PAPERS V, *supra* note 17, at 251.
126. *Id.*
127. BACON PAPERS V, *supra* note 17, at 263.
128. BACON PAPERS V, *supra* note 17, at 300.

which will breed him great trouble from others of his neighbours as well as Laseby.

Thus, being sorry that my labour hath brought forth so little fruit, I yet hope that the wisdom and consideration of your Lordship and the rest will bridle this Bullen, who spareth not to hazard his own undoing for the trial to have his will.

And so I take my leave.[129]

The closeness of their relationship is shown by a letter from Coke to Bacon asking him to play the detective.[130] Joan Cooke had been remanded in custody, charged with poisoning her husband Thomas, parish officer and overseer.[131] Bacon had examined her.[132] Coke commended his actions, particularly in not allowing bail, for poisoning one's husband was the most damnable crime and therefore petty treason.[133] He made specific suggestions:

> It were in mine opinion necessary to get that black stone that was supposed to be brought out of Iceland and to sift out that matter of the ratsbane . . . and to re-examine the widow, where and when she bought it. The matter of unkindness between her and her husband would be thoroughly examined. Your true and loving friend. Edw Coke

> Item   Whether he chewed any tobacco that morning and whether he had any in the house.

> Item   Who were those that saw the body to know it after he was dead.[134]

H. Between Half-Brothers: Nathaniel Bacon and Francis Bacon

The *Papers* provide little evidence of brotherly relations between Nathaniel and Francis, but arbitration crops up even here. In fact, the only substantial record is of Nathaniel intervening to remind Francis of his obligation to arbitrate impartially in a dispute in which he had acted as counsel for one of the parties.[135]

---

129. *Id.*
130. BACON PAPERS V, *supra* note 17, at 257-58, reply at 269-70.
131. BACON PAPERS V, *supra* note 17, at 257-58.
132. BACON PAPERS V, *supra* note 17, at 257.
133. *Id.*
134. BACON PAPERS V, *supra* note 17, at 257-58.
135. BACON PAPERS V, *supra* note 17, at 256-60.

The inhabitants of Southwold had petitioned the Council against Richard Gooch.[136] The matter came by bill before the Star Chamber, which referred it to Francis for report.[137] It was alleged that Gooch had maintained the unfounded complaints of Margaret Raphe, widow, against named persons and other inhabitants of Southwold, twenty persons in all, by bringing frivolous suits in Star Chamber and Chancery.[138] The petitioners introduced what would today be objected to as irrelevant matter: a third of the town had been destroyed by fire, what was left had been ravaged by plague and pirates (Dunkirkers) and "hostile enemies of Spain" and "hard voyages in fisher fare and bad markets whereon the state of the town wholly dependeth" had taken their livelihoods away.[139] They pointed out that Francis had been Gooch's counsel when bringing the bill in Chancery, and Gooch had worked for Francis and Nathaniel's brother Nicholas.[140] He was hardly likely to be impartial.[141] So they asked Nathaniel to write to Francis, asking him either to recuse himself or, if not, to act judicially rather than as an advocate.[142]

On 21 October 1606, two of the petitioners wrote a note to Nathaniel, asking for an answer to their request and setting out the details of their petition.[143] For two years Gooch had wrongfully occupied town lands worth £50 a year in rent and cut and sold timber, with other wrongs, some of them "continued by reason of an injunction grounded upon a report made by a doctor being one of the Masters of the Chancery."[144]

So, on 25 October Nathaniel wrote to Francis:

Good brother, I understand that there is a reference made unto you out of the Court of Star Chamber, of a bill there exhibited by the township of Southwold in Suffolk against R Gooch, my brother [Nicholas] Bacon's servant and your client. And they of the town being not very rich, by reason of the great pestilence which hath been lately amongst them, and by other occasions of piracy and fire, are loth to hold on a chargeable contention, and therefore have entreated me to be a means unto you in their behalf, that some good course might be taken whereby there might be no continuance of the suits between them.

136. BACON PAPERS V, *supra* note 17, at 256-57.
137. *Id.*
138. *Id.*
139. *Id.*
140. BACON PAPERS V, *supra* note 17, at 257.
141. *Id.*
142. *Id.*
143. BACON PAPERS V, *supra* note 17, at 259-60. Letter is to Nathaniel Bacon's clerk, Martin Man. For Man's designation as Bacon's clerk, see BACON PAPERS V, *supra* note 17, at 350.
144. BACON PAPERS V, *supra* note 17, at 260.

The consideration hereof causeth me hereby to be a suitor unto you, that you will take knowledge of the grievances of both sides and, as a judge, advise and move such a proceeding as a peace may be concluded between them. And in so doing, as well Gooch as the townsmen of Southwold shall have great cause to hold themselves beholden unto you, and will be ready to do you any kindness or service for your travail so bestowed, and I also take it kindly at your hands.

When I was at the last parliament I did hear some of them, and R Gooch also speak touching the differences between them, and I then thought Gooch in fault and did tell him that I would complain to his master for the unquiet carriage of himself.

So I commend you to the grace and favour of God.[145]

While hardly affectionate, it was quite straightforward.

III. PRIVATE COMMISSIONS FOR MEDIATION AND ARBITRATION

Bacon's authority as a JP, and no doubt his reputation for integrity and impartiality, led not only to official commissions but also to many private requests to resolve disputes. Perhaps, too, his special skills as a mediator were recognised at all levels within his community, as well as by the several government authorities.

On 13 November 1601 Bacon mediated an end to a dispute over land and debts.[146] Elizabeth, widow of Robert Earle, agreed to pay £100 in two instalments to John Earle, Robert's son, presumably by a previous marriage, who agreed to release her from all claims and convey to her all his father's lands.[147] She also agreed to pay to Robert's married daughter, Margaret Slye, "besides her legacy 20s after three years."[148]

Richard Foster, rector of Burgh Parva, wrote to Bacon to ask him to resolve a dispute between his former servant, poor but honest, and a John Bacon – no relation – who was accusing him of trespass.[149]

In September 1604, Bacon took detailed and rambling evidence in successfully mediating the settlement of a dispute between John Girdlestone and Ellen Howes, a widow.[150] On 25 September the neat and straightforward agreement is recorded: The parties were to exchange bonds, John and his

---

145. BACON PAPERS V, *supra* note 17, at 260-61.
146. BACON PAPERS IV, *supra* note 17, at 219-20
147. BACON PAPERS IV, *supra* note 17, at 219.
148. BACON PAPERS IV, *supra* note 17, at 220.
149. BACON PAPERS V, *supra* note 17, at 129-30.
150. BACON PAPERS V, *supra* note 17, at 126, 130.

brother were to make payments to her, and she was to allow John to farm her copyhold land until her son was 14 – "and all reckoning clear."[151]

Two settlements were recorded on one day, 25 August 1606.[152] One was a simple exchange of a money payment for the release of a bond.[153] The other was of a dispute over Mundy's liberty to draw water from his neighbour King's well:

> King shall pay 10s unto Mundy towards the making of a well in his own ground. And Mundy to forbear to draw water at King's well hereafter. And the 10s is agreed to be left in Robert Walker's hand, and 5s thereof to be paid to Mundy so soon as he doth begin the well and the rest after it is finished. And each party releaseth the peace taken against one another and against the rest contained in the warrants made and granted by Sir Nathaniel Bacon and Mr Gwynne.[154]

Bacon and Gwynne had referred to themselves and mediated a settlement of a matter, which had come before them as JPs, arising from mutual allegations of breaches of the peace.[155] Has there ever been a legal system, which could have produced a more refined resolution?

But sometimes it was arbitration that was expressly required. As Christmas approached and 1602 came to an end, Bacon was as busy as ever. As sole arbitrator on 9 December 1602 he declared his award in a private arbitration between neighbours, Roger Bulwer (and his sons Edward and George) and John Athill.[156] Athill must pay Roger 30s before 1 February 1603, for a boar he had killed.[157] Disputes between Roger and Athill over rents and tithes were to be decided by John Fountaine and if Mr. Fountaine could not reach a decision that both parties agreed to, the matter would be referred to Bacon.[158] "The demand of tithe hay from Mr George Bulwer by Mr Athill in the right of the vicar is referred to a trial at the Assizes in summer next," and Bacon added: "Memorandum: I have promised that no advantage shall be taken of bonds which have been formerly passed for abiding by this my order."[159]

In December 1594, the *Papers* had recorded a violent tithe dispute with a vicious mastiff and heavies imported from Kent with long pikestaffs which the parties had submitted to local mediation.[160] Bacon's role was

---

151. *Id.*
152. BACON PAPERS V, *supra* note 17, at 254.
153. *Id.*
154. *Id.*
155. *Id.*
156. BACON PAPERS IV, *supra* note 17, at 301.
157. *Id.*
158. *Id.*
159. *Id.*
160. BACON PAPERS III, *supra* note 17, at 285-87. *See also* BACON PAPERS IV, *supra* note 17, at 302-303, nn.638-639.

limited to fixing and allocating costs and acting as umpire if called on.[161] The matter arose again eight years later. On 27 December 1602 Bacon had signed a memorandum of evidence in disputes between Armiger and Franklin, which spilled over into the new year.[162] The land dispute was deferred until the following Whitsuntide, "when a sight shall be had of the survey made in the meantime."[163] Certain trespasses were referred to the judgment of the arbitrators, Mr. Holland and Mr. Warde, "on Monday next . . . and if they do not order it then it shall be decided by Nathaniel Bacon esquire."[164] Franklin's demands for tithes and wool and sheep were also "referred to their examination and ordering."[165] "Costs of suit and for battery with costs of suit, referred to Nathaniel Bacon when the other matters be brought to order."[166] On the same day Bacon signed an order for the hearing the following Monday.[167] On time, an agreement between Armiger and Franklin was mediated and signed by Holland and Warde on 3 January 1603:[168]

First Mr Armiger is to pay unto Mr Franklin for the tithe hay 15s.

Item Mr Armiger is to pay him for the tithe rakings five combes barley.

Item Mr Armiger is to pay him for the tithe of tenscore couples of ewes and lambs sold to Mr Buggin 52s.

Item for grasses occupied by Mr Armiger of the parsonage glebe for every acre 16d.

The day of payment of the said sums of money and barley to be set down by Mr Bacon his worship.[169]

One undated letter must suffice to show in detail how a submission worked and how arbitration was valued then:

Good Sir Nathaniel Bacon, mortal men should not have immortal suits, and suits commenced by fathers and continued by their children in an unchristian and uncharitable succession do often times ravel up and

---

161. BACON PAPERS III, *supra* note 17, at 285-87. *See also* BACON PAPERS IV, *supra* note 17, at 302-303, nn.638-639.
162. BACON PAPERS IV, *supra* note 17, at 302-303.
163. BACON PAPERS IV, *supra* note 17, at 302.
164. PAPERS IV, *supra* note 17, at 303.
165. BACON PAPERS IV, *supra* note 17, at 302-303.
166. BACON PAPERS IV, *supra* note 17, at 303.
167. *Id.*
168. BACON PAPERS V, *supra* note 17, at 1.
169. *Id.*

undermine the fathers' estates before they die, and in the end do utterly undo their heirs by descent, when they be dead, a cross and a curse, that contention by God's wrathful ordinance brings with it, which you in your wisdom and experience hath seen to fall upon divers families. Not far off – *sic obdurit cor Pharaonis* ['so he hardened Pharaoh's heart' *Exodus* 7.13 and 14] through the which, by excessive fees disbursed upon exceeding lawyers, both Mr Bulwer's family and mine, shall hereafter fare the worse, for prevention whereof at the first, before any suit was set on foot between him and me, I for my part made an overture of peace unto him, above 10 years since, to submit all intended controversies to any men of worth and wisdom in all Norfolk to decide and censure the same.

But Mr Bulwer then, before the walking spirit of the lands in question was any wise conjured, utterly refused that my peace offering, saying that he would not put his coat to dyeing, to never a man in England. But now of late (and somewhat too late for us both) he hath changed his mind and out of his own voluntary, (the pleasingest motive that may be), it hath pleased him to come walking unto me in the pathway of peace, protesting to embrace that peace now which long since was offered unto him, before any money was spent, or rather spoiled, at law. Requesting at my hands a submission and a compromise of all matters in difference betwixt us, to some men of worship in the country (lawyers excepted, the minters of other men's coin, out of their true owners' purses into their own). Gladly I condescended to this his motion, as proceeding from God, and did put upon him first to choose one for himself and I would second it, suit and sort another of like quality and condition. He, for him, chose Sir Nathaniel Bacon, a knight in his opinion without exception. And I, purposing to choose one that was *omni exceptione major* [above all objection] and in all respects suitable and sortable that never would dissent in judgment, nor jar in the proceeding, chose for me your worship to be the judge, the justicer and *honorarius arbiter* of all our controversies. At which my seconding choice Mr Bulwer was so well pleased that presently off went our hats, on went our hands and hearts to a pacification, which was the first time that ever we two shook either hands or hearts together, making you by mutual and reciprocal consent our judge, if you please to assume that office upon you, *beati pacifici, exuenda est persona amici, et induenda judicis* [the blessed peacemaker must doff the character of friend and don that of judge] to end as in a moment ten years tedious and costly suits, thereby to give better satisfaction to Mr Bulwer, concerning his supposed right and title to the lands in question by delivering your opinion therein, than either the Lord Chancellor or the high court of the Chancery by decree, injunction and commission could do, or than I can do by paying 200 marks out of the said lands to his sister for her marriage portion, and by spending in suit or otherwise 400 marks more *in toto* paid and spent out of my poor purse, twice as much money as the recovered lands be worth. Thus stand I, *de damno vitando* [for avoidance of loss], a loser at the close, although I got somewhat at the crush. Thus contendeth he, *de irreparabili damno* [in relation to loss which cannot be recovered], for lawyers have irrevocably got his money. *Omnia vestigia antrorsum, nulla retrorsum, opera et impensa periit* [if every track leads forward, none back, then the toils and the costs have vanished]. Fearing tediousness I submit myself to your censure, and you and yours I do recommend to the protection of the Almighty, together with my duty remembered to the good Lady Bacon.[170]

Both parties signed, though it was penned by Dr John Hunt, himself a civil lawyer and Master in Chancery (c1596-1615), a JP in Suffolk and an expert devotee of arbitration.[171] If no other record had survived, that fortuitous product of Nathaniel Bacon's determination to hoard every scrap of evidence of his daily work would stand as colourful proof of how mediation was regarded then. It repays the most careful reading.

Nathaniel Bacon was a busy man. He had to arrange for troops to be mustered, taxes collected, and for the support of unmarried mothers and their children.[172] In a footnote to the Papers of Nathaniel Bacon, the editors reveal that Bacon must have acted as mediator in many more disputes than the *Papers* document: "Entries in Bacon's recognizance books suggest that this procedure was widely used but rarely figures in the formal records." [173] He may well have dealt on average with two or three matters every month, which might require him to ride for a day, stay at least two nights away from home, spend a day to inspect many acres of land and perhaps another to hear dozens of witnesses' inexpert testimony.

Many awards make orders, which apply to non-parties. A good example is that of 28 June 1603, in a tithe dispute between Richard Boulter on the one hand and Gyles Mychell and Thomas Grene on the other, referred to arbitrators from the Consistory Court.[174] The calendar reads: "Concerning covenants in a pair of indentures for land lately bargained and sold to Boulter by Mychell, Boulter may reasonably require Mychell's son Mardocheus, at his comng of age, to release to him all title and interest."[175] No quibbles about whether the son was a party could be allowed, even if they were noticed.

---

170. BACON PAPERS V, *supra* note 17, at 113-114.
171. BACON PAPERS V, *supra* note 17, at 114.
172. *Nathaniel Bacon*, *supra* note 8.
173. BACON PAPERS V, *supra* note 17, at 52, n.137.
174. BACON PAPERS V, *supra* note 17, at 39.
175. *Id.*

There was no bar against women being parties to arbitration, whether they were single or married. The *Papers* are weighty testimony of the routine involvement of women in all kinds of dispute, including the ownership of land. For example, Margaret Bosom had no need to involve her husband Adam in a complex claim on a bond involving her son by a previous marriage.[176] She gave evidence and signed her deposition herself.[177] Anne Penning's determination exasperated Higham and Jermyn, who rudely referred to her as "the woman."[178] The evidence from America is the same. I still search, though, for women who resolved disputes in this period.

IV. EXPORTATION TO THE AMERICAN COLONIES

Just a cursory reading of some of the secondary sources has been enough to show not only that a systematic study is wanted, but that there must be primary sources surviving in the United States which have not yet been discovered or fully exploited. The tasks for new generations of scholars will be pleasurable and satisfying. They will know that their work is worthwhile if only to ensure that future practising mediators and arbitrators will not grow up believing, as many of their forebears have done, that: "Arbitration did not become an integral part of the early social and economic development of the country nor a recognised institution of any consequence."[179] Though they may accept as a challenge: "Arbitration literature of this period is exceedingly sparse and enquirers are therefore handicapped in examining the somewhat vague course taken by arbitration and the causes of its inaction."[180]

There is only one way of combatting such apparently complacent ignorance! The American story must be left to American authors. But Connecticut Colonial Records declare that in 1645 that state's General Assembly suggested that trials could be prevented if arbitrations were held privately.[181] There are examples such as George and Christopher Sanders, two brothers who were partners in a commercial venture to Jamaica and England.[182] "When they could not settle their accounts themselves, they submitted their dispute in 1677 to the arbitration of four men."[183] Oldham and Kim's section on "The Maryland Experience" gives the full text of an award of 1668 and comes to the conclusion: "The Maryland archival records

176. BACON PAPERS V, *supra* note 17, at 121-23.
177. BACON PAPERS V, *supra* note 17, at 121.
178. BACON PAPERS V, *supra* note 17, at 255.
179. FRANCES KELLOR, AMERICAN ARBITRATION: ITS HISTORY, FUNCTIONS AND ACHIEVEMENTS 6 (1948).
180. Frank D. Emerson, *History of Arbitration Practice and Law* 19 CLEV. ST. L. REV. 155, 158 (1970).
181. Mann, *supra* note 3, at 452.
182. Mann, *supra* note 3, at 453, n.41, 454 n.43.
183. Mann, *supra* note 3, at 453..

demonstrate an early American endorsement and continuation of English arbitration practices."[184]

So there is evidence (and there are tantalising clues to more) of arbitration's early start in North America. No doubt there is more work to be done on Dutch influence in New York and perhaps Swedish in Delaware, following the example of John Locke, the architect of the Arbitration Act 1698, whose role Horwitz and Oldham have described so well. Two letters from Benjamin Furly, the English merchant of Rotterdam who promoted the first German emigration to America,[185] show his comparative scholarship and merit further attention.

Some evidence from England can contribute. There are a few references in this period to the Americas in the *Acts of the Privy Council (APC)*.[186] The Privy Council might appoint a committee of its own members to resolve a dispute; although that might not be comprehended in anyone's definition of arbitration, it shows an attitude. The best evidence comes from *APC* entries relating to Virginia.[187] In 1627 Sir George Yeardley, the Governor of Virginia, died leaving by his will to his widow and sole executrix, Dame Temperance, always known through three marriages as Temperance Flowerdew, her maiden name, all the household goods in his house in St. James City, later Jamestown, and all his other estates in Virginia to be sold.[188] The proceeds were to be divided, one-third to Temperance, two-thirds to his three children. She then married Francis West, the next Governor, who left to her Yeardley's estate. Temperance could be trusted. She had left England in 1609 with her new first husband Richard Barrow in the *Falcon*, part of that ill-fated community of whom all but a few perished. She was one of those who survived the terrible "Starving Time." Barrow apparently did not.

Yeardley had been in the same convoy but his ship, the *Sea Venture*, was wrecked on Bermuda. No lives were lost and two ships were built from the wreckage. They made it to Virginia in May 1610. Soon thereafter three ships arrived there from England. Temperance married Yeardley. They had three children, Elizabeth, Argoll and Francis. He became Deputy Governor

184. Oldham & Kim, *supra* note 1, at 262-65, 262 n.109 for references.

185. JULIUS FRIEDRICH SACHSE, BENJAMIN FURLY, AN ENGLISH MERCHANT AT ROTTERDAM, WHO PROMOTED THE FIRST GERMAN EMIGRATION TO AMERICA, PRINTED FROM THE PENNSYLVANIA MAGAZINE OF HISTORY AND BIOGRAPHY (1895), *available at* https://archive.org/details/benjaminfurlyane00insach.

186. ACTS OF PRIVY COUNCIL OF ENGLAND. For the Acts of Privy Council of England, see http://www.british-history.ac.uk/search/series/acts-privy-council [hereinafter ACTS OF PRIVY COUNCIL].

187. On Lady Wyatt's petition against the Virginia Company: "take such effectual course for the petitioner's relief as in justice and equity you shall find cause," see 39 ACTS OF PRIVY COUNCIL 360 (J.V. Lyle ed., 1933). For the petition of Elizabeth Barwick, see 45 ACTS OF PRIVY COUNCIL 104-105 (R.F. Monger & P.A. Penfold eds., 1960).

188. For the following account of Sir George Yeardley, Francis West, and Temperance Flowerdew Yeardley West, see 46 ACTS OF PRIVY COUNCIL 38-39 (P.A. Penfold ed., 1964).

in 1616. In 1618 he and Temperance were in London. He was knighted and appointed Governor and granted 300 acres of land. They returned to Virginia and created the Flowerdew plantation of 1,000 acres, producing tons of tobacco annually. He died in 1627. Forthwith Temperance married his successor as governor, Francis West, but she died the next year.

Temperance had sent the tobacco to Yeardley's brother Raph, apothecary of London. When he knew Temperance was dead, under the pretence of affection for the children, he took possession not only of his brother's but also of Temperance's estates. He refused to account to West or come to any agreement with him. The Council, "considering the difference between them rests chiefly upon matter of account," referred it to four merchants, "persons experienced in business of this nature . . . to mediate and settle such an end (if they can) as shall be indifferent and equitable, or certify in writing in whom the default is."[189] That is good early evidence of a mediation relating to the North American colonies.

Ensign Edmond Rossingham was Temperance's nephew. He had asked the Council for "relief and satisfaction out of the estate of Sir George Yeardley in the possession of Raph Yeardley as his administrator."[190] He claimed he had left cattle and goods in Sir George's hands and had performed services for him there.[191] The Privy Council had referred the matter to "certain persons of judgment and experience in the affairs of that Plantation," who had certified that those services had been beneficial, and the cattle worth £360, and that Raph had confessed that the estate in his hands was worth £1,200.[192] Therefore on 19 February 1630, "rather for that by dissolving the Company (the government thereof being assumed by his Majesty into his own hands) the Petitioner was left without remedy in the ordinary course," the Privy Council ordered Raph to pay Rossingham £200.[193] The order would be a sufficient discharge against any other claimants against the estate, "for that it did not appear there were any debts at all."[194]

Another Governor of Virginia was John Potts.[195] He and his wife Elizabeth sailed from London aboard the *George* in March 1619 and arrived in Jamestown in May. In 1623, he prepared the poison which killed 200 native Americans attending a "peace ceremony" at Jamestown. He became

---

189. *Id. See also, A Tale of Two Houses in Virginia and Kirkcudbright*, 74 TRANSACTIONS OF THE DUMFRIESSHIRE & GALLOWAY, NAT. HIST. & ANTIQUARIAN SOC'Y 120-22 (3rd series, 2000) *available at* http://www.dgnhas.org.uk/transonline.php.
190. 45 ACTS OF PRIVY COUNCIL, *supra* note 186, at 285-86. For the following account of Edmund Rossingham, see *id*.
191. 45 ACTS OF PRIVY COUNCIL, *supra* note 186, at 285-86.
192. *Id*.
193. *Id*.
194. *Id*.
195. For the following discussion of John and Elizabeth Potts, see 46 ACTS OF PRIVY COUNCIL, *supra* note 187, at 85-86.

a member of the Governor's Council in 1625 and Governor in 1629. On 9 July 1630 he was convicted of cattle theft and dismissed. He may have lived until 1645. On 30 September 1630 the Privy Council wrote to the Governor and Council of Virginia:

> Complaint hath been made both to his Majesty and this Board against you in a petition presented by the brother of Dr Pott But we are not apt to give credit to any complants of this kind against a man that is entrusted by his Majesty in a place of government as you are. Therefore we have sent you the Petitions take it into consideration and thereupon proceed according to justice and the orders established in that Government with convenient expedition so that there may be no further just cause for complaint.[196]

Eleven members of the Privy Council signed that letter. The *APC* show no further activity in relation to Dr Potts but later the same day it wrote again to the Governor and Council of Virginia.[197] It had received a complaint from Thomas Grendon that he had spent £1,400 in various parts of Virginia, and learned from him that planters only planted tobacco and this did not help the plantation and planters did not have permission to do so. Grendon had supplied "divers ingenious artificers for the making of artificial mills, useful for sundry commodities, and saws for sawing timber," and "people skilful in making rape oils and soap ashes," all "for the good of the Common Weal."[198] The Council "earnestly recommend his good endeavours" and ask the Governor and Council to help Grendon in getting in his debts.[199]

The last record of Privy Council's interest in the colony is a letter of 30 June 1630.[200] John Woodhall was a speculator in the colony who never left England.[201] He had bought land from the estate of Sir Samuel Argoll, famous among other things for kidnapping Pocahontas and bringing her to England. Lawsuits ensued. Woodhall complained that "the chief detainors of his land and cattle are both parties and judges" in his cause.[202] The Privy Council's response was to tell the Virginian Council:

> As we cannot but marvel at such your neglect of the commands and recommendations from this Board and have just cause not only to blame you for the same but for your partial and dilatory proceedings (if they be

---

196. *Id.* at 85.
197. For the following account of Thomas Grendon, see *id.* at 88.
198. *Id.*
199. *Id.*
200. *Id.*
201. For the following discussion of John Woodhall, see 46 ACTS OF PRIVY COUNCIL, *supra* note 187, at 88.
202. *Id.*

such as informed) in the administration of justice we expressly require you to afford the Petitioner expedite justice.[203]

Another example of early American arbitration occurs with Francis Poythress, who went to Virginia c1633 as agent for the London merchant Lawrence Evans.[204] Evans later charged Poythress with breach of trust.[205] In March 1639 the Governor and Council appointed four merchants in Virginia to arbitrate; they decided in Poythress's favour.[206] The Privy Council's committee for the foreign plantations "directed a further enquiry when Evens was to go to Virginia himself."[207]

There is a Canadian reference to arbitration, as well. In 1628 Charles I himself referred to the Privy Council a complaint by two Frenchmen that another Frenchman had "taken them at sea in a voyage they were making for a Plantation in Canada."[208] The Council formed a committee of three of its members (or any two) to report "that thereupon such final order may be taken . . . consonant to justice and equity."[209]

Another example of 17th century arbitration comes from Barbados. The National Archives preserve the record of an award made on 18 June 1652 in a private arbitration between Sir Anthony Ashley Cooper, and Gerard Hawkaine, (probably Hawkins), about a plantation in Barbados.[210] Cooper became the first Earl of Shaftesbury, a member of Cromwell's Council of State and one of the founders of the Whig party.[211] He was John Locke's patron and collaborated with him on the Fundamental Constitutions of Carolina.[212]

V. CONCLUSION

I shall be happy if this Article, with all its inadequacies and perhaps false starts, does no more than attract the attention of scholars, perhaps especially younger Americans, to fill the blanks and correct the errors in what all must agree is at this stage a patchy and inadequate history of dispute resolution in the early American colonies.

203. *Id.*
204. TRANSACTIONS OF THE DUMFRIESSHIRE & GALLOWAY, *supra* note 188, at 120-22.
205. *Id.*
206. *Id.*
207. William B. Hall, *The Polythress Family: A Study of Francis, Francis, Francis, and Francis*, 14 WM. & MARY Q., 77, 77 (1934).
208. 44 ACTS OF PRIVY COUNCIL 359 (R.F. Monger ed., 1958).
209. *Id.*
210. *PRO 30/24/49/1 Award of the arbitrators between Sir Anthony Ashley Cooper and Gerard Hawkaine*, NAT'L ARCHIVES (June 18, 1652), http://discovery.nationalarchives.gov. uk/details/r/C6757225.
211. See *Anthony Ashley Cooper, 1st Earl of Shaftesbury and successors: Papers*, NAT'L ARCHIVES, http://discovery.nationalarchives.gov.uk/details/r/C11970 (last visited Dec. 10, 2016).
212. *Id.*

PART THREE

CONTRIBUTED SCHOLARLY ARTICLES

DEFENDING THE RULE OF LAW: THE NEXT STEPS

Sir Geoffrey Bindman*

I first met Derek Roebuck when he was Amnesty International's Head of Research and I chaired the British Section's Lawyers' Group. We got on well. Our views and our early career paths were similar and I admired his dedication to the causes we shared. And, of course, Susanna was at Amnesty where they first met. After they left Amnesty and made their home and careers in Papua New Guinea and Hong Kong, we were in touch only infrequently. When they returned to Oxford, we met from time to time. I recall enjoyable dinners at the Athenaeum and book launches – and a memorable wedding anniversary party at Hertford College.

Throughout those years, I followed their prolific literary output. Derek's scholarly productivity was remarkable. His career in the law embraced a wide range of skills – as a practising solicitor, an advocate, a prominent human rights specialist and a pre-eminent legal scholar. As a fellow solicitor, I recognised in Derek the depth of practical understanding and sympathy he brought to his later career from his early training and experience in Manchester. He was a man of principle and conviction.

I know that Derek was alarmed by current threats to the rule of law in many parts of the world. In Britain, the rule of law and the protection of human rights have been weakened by the actions and failures of recent governments. The announced intentions of the present government will, if implemented, reinforce that trend.

The crushing victory of the Conservative Party in the General Election of 2019 meant that it could confidently bring forward legislation to implement whatever legal and constitutional changes it wished to make. Those plans were interrupted by the Covid pandemic, but the intention to pursue them remains.

The party's election strategy astutely placed Brexit first and foremost among its election promises, rightly judging that it would be enough to

---

* Sir Geoffrey Bindman QC (Hon), a human rights lawyer and founder of Bindmans LLP, is a visiting professor at University College London and London South Bank University. He is former Chair of the Board of Trustees at the British Institute of Human Rights.

win majority support without undue reliance on other issues. However, it also promised to protect victims of crime and of domestic abuse, to defend freedom of expression and to strengthen employment law.

The Queen's Speech, delivered on 19 December 2019, promised a fuller legislative programme but important gaps and uncertainties remained, most notably in the absence of any substantive response to the forceful demands of both the Bar Council and the Law Society for urgent government action to repair the gaping holes in the legal system. The underfunding of legal aid was not addressed.

The Bar Council's '2019 manifesto' was entitled 'Urgent Action Required'. Stressing that the rule of law and the independence of the judiciary are fundamental pillars of our democracy, the Chairman of the Bar, Richard Atkins QC, pointed out that 'today's justice system is widely acknowledged to be suffering from years of under-investment ... Too many people are unable to access justice quickly or effectively ... Urgent action is needed to remedy this.'

The day after the election, the Law Society published its views under the heading 'The new government should use mandate to fix a justice system in crisis'. Echoing the Bar, the then Vice-President (now President), David Greene, called for 'an immediate and sustained boost in funding if Britain is to retain its world-wide reputation for justice and fairness'. In making their pleas for new funding, however, neither of our profession's leaders advanced the most powerful argument in their favour – that money spent on access to justice actually saves public expenditure by reducing the financial burden on other public services. The striking lessons of the recent World Bank and International Bar Association report, *A Tool for Justice*,[1] which demonstrates the magnitude of such savings, have been ignored.

One would expect a 'one nation' government to find it expedient to respond positively to the need for greater legal aid funding as a means of rewarding its new-found supporters in former Labour constituencies, many of whom are victims of the failures of the justice system. The blueprint for reform already exists[2] in the study led by the Labour peer Lord Bach and the late Sir Henry Brooke. Their recommendations should not be seen as politically controversial.

The Conservative government programme set out in the Queen's Speech lists more than 30 Bills to be introduced in the new Parliament. Of these,

---

1. *Editorial note:* World Bank, *A Tool for Justice: The Cost Benefit Analysis of Legal Aid* (September 2019), available at http://documents1.worldbank.org/curated/en/592901569218028553/pdf/A-Tool-for-Justice-The-Cost-Benefit-Analysis-of-Legal-Aid.pdf.

2. *Editorial note: Final Report of the Bach Commission: The Right to Justice* (September 2017), available at http://www.fabians.org.uk/wp-content/uploads/2017/09/Bach-Commission_Right-to-Justice-Report-WEB.pdf. Sir Henry Brooke, a retired Lord Justice of Appeal, was Vice-Chair of the Commission.

several are consequential on the planned withdrawal from the European Union. Others are described as 'proposals to invest in and support our public services'. These focus on the National Health Service, mental health and education funding. There is to be an Employment Bill which 'will enhance workers' rights'. There will be greater protection for the security and safety of tenants of housing accommodation. There will be pensions reform and an increase in the National Living Wage. The coronavirus pandemic struck early in 2020, shortly after the General Election, and much of the programme has been put on hold, but has not been abandoned.

The programme reaffirms the government's commitment to strengthening the criminal justice system – including a new Royal Commission – but the emphasis is firmly on enforcement and public safety rather than on practical concerns about the current deficiencies so vigorously condemned by the leaders of the legal profession.

By contrast with its near silence on the mechanics of the justice system, however, the government is already embarking on a programme of constitutional reform, especially the role of the judiciary. The Conservative manifesto, under the heading 'Protect our Democracy', castigates 'the failure of Parliament to deliver Brexit – the way so many MPs have devoted themselves to thwarting the decision of the British people in the 2016 referendum has opened up a destabilising and potentially damaging rift between politicians and people.'

This contentious reference to the Brexit debate is followed by the claim that, by ending the supremacy of European law, 'we will be free to craft legislation and regulations which maintain high standards but which work best for the UK.' Unexceptionable as that sounds, it has a disturbing ring when read with the promise to look at the broader aspects of our constitution, the relationship between the Government, Parliament and the courts, the functioning of the Royal Prerogative, the role of the House of Lords, and access to justice for ordinary people.

It goes on to say:

We will update the Human Rights Act and administrative law to ensure that there is a proper balance between the rights of individuals and vital national security and effective government.

There then follows an undertaking to

ensure that judicial review is available to protect the rights of the individual against an overbearing state, while ensuring that it is not abused to conduct politics by another means ...

The last clause, in particular, has obvious echoes of the constitutional controversies of the previous year, when the government was thwarted by the Supreme Court in two notable cases: *R (Miller) v Secretary of State for Exiting the European Union*[3] and *R (Miller) v Prime Minister*.[4] In the first case, the Court was accused by some commentators of overstepping the boundary between legal and political responsibility when it rightly recognised legal limits on the power of the government to implement Brexit without Parliamentary authority. In the second case, it declared unlawful an attempt by the Prime Minister to prorogue Parliament for several weeks without justification. This was an assertion of the power of the Court to impose limits on the use of the Royal Prerogative by the executive. The Prime Minister openly expressed his anger at what he saw as a usurpation of executive discretion.

Is the Prime Minister now bent on revenge? We face the alarming prospect of a struggle for supremacy between the government, Parliament and the judiciary, the three pillars of our democratic constitution.

The battle has been postponed by Covid-19 but the groundwork is being laid. The government has announced a 'Constitution, Democracy & Rights Commission' that will 'examine these issues in depth, and come up with proposals to restore trust in our institutions and in how our democracy operates'. The Public Administration and Constitutional Affairs Committee of the House of Commons is, at the time of writing, canvassing opinion on the terms of reference of this commission, but its membership has not yet been chosen.

The last such commission – the Commission on a Bill of Rights, which reported in December 2012 – failed to reach a consensus. That was perhaps inevitable because its membership was chosen fairly to represent different viewpoints. The choice of members for the constitution commission must be equally impartial. All who believe in parliamentary supremacy, the rule of law and an independent judiciary must keep a very watchful eye on these fundamentally important developments.

A separate commission has been established by the government to examine judicial review. This is the 'Independent Review of Administrative Law' (IRAL), the members of which have already been appointed. The chairman is Lord Faulks, a former justice minister. The other members are mainly academic lawyers, but there is reason to be concerned. Lord Faulks has already publicly committed himself to the view that the judiciary exceeded its powers in the prorogation case referred to earlier. The heading to an article contributed by him to the 'Conservative Home' website (7

3. [2018] AC 61.
4. [2019] UKSC 41.

February 2020) reads: 'Edward Faulks: the Supreme Court's prorogation judgement unbalanced our constitution. MPs should make a correction.'

However, the overwhelming body of lawyers who have practised and studied judicial review disagree and see no justification for significant reform.[5] There is considerable anxiety among practitioners and scholars that changes will be proposed that will curtail the rights of citizens to challenge the conduct of public authorities. The commission has issued a series of questions inviting suggestions for codification and restrictions on the availability of judicial review.

From a government perspective, the appointment of new investigative bodies has the advantage of giving new people the power to make recommendations for reform which the government can present as impartial and authoritative. The members are chosen by the government and their selection will inevitably be influenced by their known opinions and affiliations.

While the present government is in office, there will be a co-ordinated effort by it and its supporters to achieve constitutional reform that will increase the power of the executive and reduce the ability of the citizen to restrain and secure redress against abuses of power and invasion of fundamental rights. There are a number of strands to this assault. As well as restricting the authority of the judiciary, these include the starvation of legal aid, the underfunding and hence understaffing and closure of courts, the threat to repeal the Human Rights Act 1998 and withdraw from the European Convention on Human Rights. Leaving the European Union facilitates such measures and reduces the pressure to maintain democratic accountability in keeping with international standards.

Many lawyers, and especially judges, find it uncomfortable to enter into what can be perceived as political disputes, but when their professional standards and their very *raison d'être* are at risk and the rule of law itself is under threat, they have a duty to speak out. When the rule of law itself is in danger, lawyers should be its most energetic defenders. I am sure Derek would have been in the forefront of the struggle.

---

5. See Michael Zander, 'Heads you win, tails you lose' (*New Law Journal*, 5 February 2021, p. 9).

WHO WERE THE ARBITRATORS IN EARLY MODERN ENGLAND, c.1500–1800?

Francis Calvert Boorman* and Rhiannon Markless**

INTRODUCTION

It is only worth posing our question of who acted as arbitrators in early modern England because of Derek's work, and though we believe the answer itself is important, it also gives us an opportunity to highlight some aspects of his writing that were particularly compelling. One is the sheer breadth of his great series on arbitration, spanning not just centuries but, quite incredibly, millennia. His great feat of intellectual endurance and continued curiosity allows us to take the long view, albeit a lesser period of time than Derek managed, and identify currents in arbitration that ran through the centuries covered by several of his volumes.

There is also his interest in people. The individual arbitrators Derek uncovered were often remarkable and some of the most compelling are certainly not the 'great men' of history. Take, for instance, Thomas Turner (b 1729) of East Hoathly in Sussex, a merchant (among many other things) who was fond of books, cricket and cards, but over-fond of drink. Derek found in Turner's diary a 'philosophy of dispute resolution'. Turner acted as arbitrator in a bizarre dispute over a swarm of bees taken from an estate, with only the permission of a mendacious messenger.[1]

Derek always emphasised the importance of understanding actual practice as well as the law; the rules of the game often give little clue as to how it was played. His aim was to find out how disputes were ended and he had little time for anachronistically imposed modern concerns about arbitration and mediation as strictly defined abstract categories.

* Dr Francis Boorman is an historian of arbitration, locality and London. He is an Associate Research Fellow at the Institute of Advanced Legal Studies, University of London.

** Dr Rhiannon Markless is an Independent Rearcher and Associate Research Fellow at the Institute of Advanced Legal Studies, University of London.

1. Derek Roebuck, Francis Boorman and Rhiannon Markless, *English Arbitration and Mediation in the Long Eighteenth Century* (2019, Oxford: HOLO Books: The Arbitration Press), pp 154–159.

That allowed him to reveal the early modern methods of moving between mediation and arbitration that should be borne in mind throughout this article.[2] Derek's writing brings both psychological depth and an interest in social and cultural history that is too often lacking in legal historians. All of these concerns led us to ask our present question and, of course, influenced our answers too.

So, who were these arbitrators to whom Derek introduced us? They were, in theory, whoever the parties in dispute chose. There was never any official qualification to be an arbitrator, although they were expected to have 'certain qualities, well understood, but not sharply defined', that might include being respectable, law-abiding, or merely sensible.[3] The legal requirements were so open that the defendant could appoint the plaintiff if he/she thought fit to do so.[4]

The two basic requirements identified by commentators were impartiality (although even this was not always required for party-appointed arbitrators) and sufficient knowledge and expertise to meet the needs of the parties. As the anonymous author of *Arbitrium Redivivum* set out in 1694, 'it is thought fit that such persons be Elected as are sufficient and indifferent … though the Law prescribes no rules herein.'[5] The only groups thought to be totally unsuitable were children, madmen, idiots and anyone lacking senses, so, the deaf, dumb and blind. The third edition of *The Compleat Arbitrator* (published in 1770) gave very similar advice, saying, 'the law presumes that every Man will be so wise as to pitch upon a Person, whose Understanding and Honesty he can rely on'.[6]

Thus, from the 16th century onwards, those who served as arbitrators ran the full gamut of society: 'the yeoman and artisan; the country gentleman (and the occasional lady); the official, from highest to lowest; the judges and law officers; members of the [Privy] Council; the civilian doctors; and even the Queen herself.'[7] Despite there being minimal change in the legal framework up to 1800 (the Arbitration Act 1698 had nothing to say on the matter),[8] we shall be analysing the changes that did emerge in the selection of arbitrators.

One thing that changed was the involvement of government in arbitration. The free choice of arbitrators by the parties to a dispute could

---

2. *Ibid*, pp 24–28.
3. Derek Roebuck, *Mediation and Arbitration in the Middle Ages: England 1154 to 1558* (2013, Oxford: HOLO Books: The Arbitration Press), p 398.
4. Derek Roebuck, *Arbitration and Mediation in Seventeenth-Century England* (2017, Oxford: HOLO Books: The Arbitration Press), pp 394–395.
5. *Ibid*, Appendix 1, p 455.
6. Matthew Bacon, *The Compleat Arbitrator; or the Law of Awards* (London, 1770), p 65.
7. Derek Roebuck, *The Golden Age of Arbitration: Dispute Resolution Under Elizabeth I* (2015, Oxford: HOLO Books: The Arbitration Press), p 116.
8. Arbitration Act, 9 & 10 Wm III *c*15 (1698).

be rendered theoretical when a referral was firmly 'suggested' by a body of sufficient authority, which in the 16th century might mean the monarch or the Privy Council.[9] While Elizabeth I and her Privy Council appointed arbitrators across the country as they thought fit, subsequent Stuart monarchs tended to confine themselves to members of the Council or other officials such as judges or law officers. In 1641, the Privy Council lost its judicial powers and never returned to a position of regularly appointing arbitrators.[10] Several schemes to regularise mediation and arbitration were put forward during the Interregnum but none was adopted, despite some official encouragement.[11] Direct government appointment of arbitrators waned, but in the 18th century, arbitrators or commissioners involved in dividing or valuing land for enclosures and building canals proliferated, with the power of Parliament conferred on them through private Acts.[12]

The courts also referred matters to arbitration, often at the suggestion of the judge, who might recommend the arbitrator(s). The rule of court procedure which emerged in the 17th century allowed awards to be registered by the courts, a device that was legislated for in the Arbitration Act 1698. Registrations in the courts, especially the King's Bench, increased greatly in the final third of the 18th century. The entry as a rule of court could either be of an existing arbitration submitting the award, or of an arbitration referred from the court. Among submissions to the King's Bench, local notables predominated as arbitrators, while more referrals were sent to the arbitration of specialists and, increasingly under Lord Mansfield, a small group of legal professionals.[13] At the local level, for disputes which were never going to be taken to the higher courts or even the assizes, the Justice of the Peace (JP) was ever-present as a *quasi*-state sponsored mediator and arbitrator, both voluntarily selected by parties and actively intervening in their disputes. The role of the JP merits its own section below.

It is difficult to make generalisations about party-appointed arbitrators, who were as various as the parties and their disputes. Reference to an arbitrator or arbitrators of higher status than the parties made it more likely they would submit to the award and thus added a layer of enforcement. It was also hoped that choosing someone of higher status left the arbitrator less open to influence, either by pressure or bribery.[14] Yet people also nominated their peers, from groups based around locality, commerce,

9. Roebuck, *op cit* (note 7), p 89.
10. Roebuck, *op cit* (note 4), p 193.
11. *Ibid*, pp 429–432.
12. Roebuck, Boorman and Markless, *op cit* (note 1), pp171–178.
13. Henry Horwitz and James Oldham, 'John Locke, Lord Mansfield, and Arbitration During the Eighteenth Century' (1993) 36 *The Historical Journal* 137–159 at 149–150.
14. Roebuck, *op cit* (note 4), p 193.

occupation or religion. Parties could appoint any number of arbitrators, but especially earlier in our period, an even number was prevalent and the arbitrators nominated by each party were often expected to act on their behalf, not as an impartial judge.[15] By the early 18th century, the bonds parties entered into to enforce an arbitration were more likely to name three arbitrators, protecting them from ungrateful parties who would never know whose vote went against them.[16] If for any reason an arbitration process failed, a dispute could be referred to a mutually acceptable umpire, chosen by either the parties or the arbitrators.[17]

The changing nature of community in early modern England affected choice of arbitrators and many of these changes were driven by economic factors. Economic growth based on increasing use of credit caused many disputes for which litigation was one form of resolution, although mediation and arbitration were often a precursor or an adjunct to litigation.[18] Some of this dispute settlement could rely on traditional community arbitrators, but adjusting disputes involving increasingly complex and impersonal financial instruments like insurance required new expertise in contracts, accounting and much else besides. The bonds of community were also loosened by economic migration, breaking up traditional ties. If people no longer lived in a single parish their entire life, there was diminished social enforcement of dispute resolution. Mobility coupled with population growth also diminished the reach of authority figures like the parish priest or JP, although both retained a central role in dispute resolution. Enforcement of an award could only be founded on social pressure in a small, stable community. The greater involvement of the legal system in enforcing awards also seemed to bring with it a greater proportion of legally trained arbitrators, whether by accident or design.

What of the arbitrator's experience? The role of the peacemaker was always valued and acting as arbitrator or mediator was a reputational boost throughout the early modern period. The recognition that someone had the qualities of honesty and fairmindedness was seen as honourable in the 16th and 17th centuries, as was the avoidance of vexatious suits or even violence by everyone involved, both the parties and the arbitrator.[19]

15. Derek Roebuck, 'Odds or Evens: How Many Arbitrators?' (2014) 80 *Arbitration* 8–15.
16. Derek Roebuck, 'Party-Appointed What?' (2017) 83 *Arbitration* 313–317.
17. Michael Miles, 'Eminent Practitioners: The New Visage of Country Attorneys c1750–1800', in GR Rubin and D Sugarman (eds), *Law, Economy and Society, 1750-1914: Essays in the History of English Law* (1984, Abingdon: Professional Books Ltd), pp 495–496.
18. Craig Muldrew, 'The Culture of Reconciliation: Community and the Settlement of Economic Disputes in Early Modern England' (1996) 39 *The Historical Journal* 915–942, at 921–922.
19. Courtney Erin Thomas, *If I Lose Mine Honour, I Lose Myself: Honour among the Early Modern English Elite* (2017, Toronto: Toronto University Press), pp 66–73; Linda A Pollock,

Although the language of honour was less widely used as the 18th century wore on, it still surfaced in connection with arbitration, as did analogous terms such as reputation. Arbitration was thought of alongside other public services that the property-owning classes carried out, like being in a jury. It thus became associated by some with political virtues such as manliness and independence.[20]

Many groups, such as small tradesmen, saw acting as arbitrator as an obligation that would be performed for free and repaid in kind when needed. Writing in 1751, the merchant Wyndham Beawes was firm: 'An Arbitration is generally an Effect of Moderation in the contending Parties, who think it more safe to refer the Matter in dispute to the Determination of Friends, than to venture a Trial at Law, more especially as the one is costly, and the other transacted gratis'.[21] These words remained in the 5th edition of the *Lex Mercatoria Rediviva* of 1792, while other phrases around them had been revised.[22] At the same time, the payment of arbitrators became increasingly common. It was billed like any other service by lawyers.

Generosity was strained if anyone, from a JP to a cotton weaver, received so many referrals that these interfered with their business day. At that point charges were often introduced. By the end of the 18th century more and more people made some income either acting as an arbitrator, drawing up documents or providing expert testimony.[23] Merchants in Liverpool were, however, still sufficiently embarrassed by their arbitration fees in the early 19th century that they were donated to charity and the donation advertised in local newspapers.[24] Author John Palmer reflected on his experiences of arbitration around the turn of the 19th century, saying that 'a merchant or a gentleman would have felt himself degraded by an offer of payment for what was considered a voluntary act of kindness'.[25] Opinions on payment offer a mixed picture, with attitudes not entirely reflecting the changing reality.

We will now consider the changes in acting as mediator or arbitrator among specific groups, either because they included the most prolific arbitrators (JPs and merchants) or for whom the changes were most pronounced (experts, lawyers and women).

'Honor, Gender, and Reconciliation in Elite Culture, 1570–1700' (2007) 46 *Journal of British Studies* 3–29, at 28.

20. Roebuck, Boorman and Markless, *op cit* (note 1), pp 283–287.
21. Wyndham Beawes, *Lex Mercatoria Rediviva* (1st Edn, London, 1751), p 308.
22. Wyndham Beawes, *Lex Mercatoria Rediviva* (5th Edn, London, 1792), p 370.
23. Roebuck, Boorman and Markless, *op cit* (note 1), pp 285–287.
24. Francis Calvert Boorman, 'Advertising Arbitration: The Origins of the Profession' (2016) 82 *Arbitration* 118–121, at 121.
25. James Oldham, 'The Historically Shifting Sands of Reasons to Arbitrate' (2016) *Journal of Dispute Resolution* 41–54, at 43.

JUSTICES OF THE PEACE

The office of royal judge or *iusticia* was established during the reign of Edward the Confessor (r.1042–1066).[26] For the following 800 years, justices had an important function as conservators of the peace in the 'healing of differences' between members of a community.[27] Sir Thomas Smith[28] noted an increase in the size of the commission in the second half of the 16th century, while others have observed an even greater increase during the late 17th and the first half of the 18th century.[29] It was the Commission of the Peace, reformed during the reign of Elizabeth I, which set out the powers of justices of the peace (JPs) and formalised the quarterly sittings.

Despite a wide range of discretionary powers exercised by JPs, the extent of their pre-trial jurisdiction was restricted by legal rulings. Magistrates were empowered to arbitrate a dispute; to issue bonds to keep the peace; or bind an accused person by his or her recognisance to ensure his or her appearance in court. The anonymous author of the 16th-century manual, *The Institucion of a Gentleman*, suggested that a gentleman living in the country could help the community by becoming a justice of the peace: 'as a stay for simple men and help of their causes by way of arbitration'.[30] Documents which survive in the Surrey History Centre and the Historical Manuscript Commission relating to the career of Sir William More (1520–1600) include records described by the Surrey archivist as:[31]

Property relating to investigations into an arbitration of disputes over the title to property, in some of which the Mores were acting as justices, in others under special commissions from the central courts and in others as local persons of standing and repute.

26. 1 Edw III (1327). The Justices of the Peace Act created the post of justice of the peace, building on the earlier role of conservators of the peace. The Statute of Northampton, 2 Edw III, c 3 (1328) empowered justices of the peace to hear and determine complaints in trespass.
27. William Blackstone, *Commentaries on the Laws of England: Of the Rights of Persons*, vol 1 (1st Edn, 1765, Oxford: Clarendon Press), p 8.
28. Sir Thomas Smith (1513–1577), *De Republica Anglorum: the Maner of Governement or Policie of the Realme of England*, written between 1562 and 1565, first published in 1583; Sir Thomas Smith, *De Republica Anglorum* (Mary Dewar (Ed), 1982, Cambridge: Cambridge Studies in the History and Theory of Politics).
29. Gwenda Morgan and Peter Rushton, 'The magistrate, the community and the maintenance of an orderly society in eighteenth century England' (2003) 76 *Historical Research* 54–77, at 56–57.
30. Derek Roebuck, *A Miscellany of Disputes* (2000, Oxford, HOLO Books: The Arbitration Press), p 18, referring to Anon Bodleian Library Douce G 59 (London, 1555), and JR Lander, *English Justices of the Peace 1461-1509* (1989, Gloucester: Alan Sutton) pp 84–86, 169–170.
31. Roebuck, *op cit* (note 7), p 90.

It is clear that the role of the justice was adaptable and their involvement in local disputes flexible. In considering trends and inconsistencies in the dispensation of justice at a local level, it needs to be borne in mind that magisterial powers were not standardised until 1848 so that the administration of mediated solutions may not have been consistent across different counties, or within the various minor courts.[32]

There were no restrictions on the private settlement of misdemeanours and the settlement of all manner of non-fatal violent crimes might be mediated outside of the court system. Even though the law prohibited the compounding of a felonious larceny (the theft of goods of the value of one shilling) justices were empowered to exercise other civil powers to determine some apparent larcenies as a trespass to goods and make orders for compensation. A voluntary arbitration process had the benefit of allowing unrestricted access to legal advice and representation, although mediated settlements brokered by a sole magistrate were unlikely to offer the same support. Many defendants (whether guilty or innocent) would have been open to pressure from their families, victims and magistrates to subject themselves to settlements that were not necessarily beneficial to them, rather than stand trial and risk conviction and the sentence of the court. Of course, victims of crime were also open to intimidation from the accused or their family to settle a matter privately, particularly if it avoided bringing 'shame' on the individual and his or her family.[33]

Diaries from the 17th century suggest that justices were content to participate in arbitrated and mediated disputes both in their capacity as JPs and, more often, as a party.[34] Samuel Pepys was appointed Justice of the Peace in 1660 (the same year as his diaries begin) although his appointment was a formality and Pepys never sat as a JP in any proceedings. Nevertheless, various diary entries refer to his involvement in mediated disputes, whether giving his 'verdict against Mr Moore on last Saturday's wager' or the appointment of arbitrators in a dispute concerning a debt owed by Mrs Goldsborough to his late uncle Robert, 'so I appoint Mr Moore and she another against Friday next, to look into our papers and to see what can be done to conclude the matter'.[35]

Landowner and Roman Catholic Richard Cholmeley (c.1550–1623) routinely referred disputes to mediation and arbitration, including those in which he was personally involved. When, in 1605, Cholmeley and

32. J H Baker, *An Introduction to English Legal History* (4th Edn, 2007 (first published 1971), Oxford: Oxford University Press), p 511; 11 & 12 Vict, c 43 (1848), The Summary Jurisdiction Act 1848, which consolidated and improved the holding of Petty Sessions.
33. Rhiannon Markless, *Gender, Crime and Discretion in Yorkshire, 1735–1775* (2014, Riga: Scholars' Press), p 304.
34. Roebuck, *op cit* (note 4), p 300.
35. *Ibid*, pp 314–316: Pepys' diaries (1660–1669).

Francis Taylor fell out over the sale of corn, they referred their dispute to Henry Topham. In 1609, Topham was again appointed arbitrator in a more protracted dispute between Cholmeley and his Protestant tenant Roger Weddell which trundled on for at least another 16 years: the difference in religious views was significant, at least on the part of Weddell. Cholmeley was not eligible for appointment as a JP but his case shows that was not the only office which set people up as local peacemakers; his recusancy did not prevent him from presiding over his own leet court at Brafferton and Brandsby, Yorkshire.[36] Its jurisdiction included a duty to view the frankpledge of freemen to keep the peace, overseeing trade and agricultural practices, the punishment of minor crimes committed within the jurisdiction and possibly authority to 'look in general to the morals of the people, and to find a remedy for each social ill and inconvenience', such as that for the leet court at Alcester, Warwickshire.[37]

Justices' notebooks from the 18th century provide further evidence of the involvement of JPs in arbitrated and mediated settlements, such as those of Henry Norris, a wealthy landowner of Hackney, London (diaries 1730–1741), William Hunt, a member of the Inner Temple and Wiltshire landowner (diaries 1744–1748), Edmund Tew, rector of Boldon, County Durham (diaries 1750–1764), Richard Wyatt, a landowner of Surrey (diaries 1767–1776), Thomas De Veil, who sat in Central London, and Thomas Horner, squire of Mells, Somerset (diaries 1770–1777).[38] The diaries show that during their various terms, Norris arranged the settlement of about 110 matters; of 412 relevant entries for Hunt, many declare that they were 'agreed without a hearing' and 112 appear to have been settled with Hunt's help; and Tew's diaries refer to him hearing about 1,000 matters, of which only 18 went to trial. Ruth Paley, Norris's editor, concludes that 'discouraging litigation in this way was one of the hallmarks of correct magisterial conduct'.[39] In contrast, Wyatt's diaries include only one example of his settling a matter; there is little evidence of De Veil mediating, while Horner's diaries note only a few occasions when he expressly recorded that he mediated a matter to a settlement. The disparity in the number of matters resolved by individual JPs may relate in part to the urban or rural location of individual magistrates. Robert Shoemaker and Norma Landau note that the accessibility of the Middlesex and Westminster courts meant that recognisances to compel individuals to keep the peace, attend court or

---

36. *Ibid*, pp 300–301; Cholmeley's diaries (1602–1620).
37. http://www.alcestercourtleet.co.uk/history/court-leet-history/, accessed 1 September 2020.
38. Roebuck, Boorman and Markless, *op cit* (note 1), pp 63–82.
39. Ruth Paley (Ed), *Justice in Eighteenth-Century Hackney: The Justicing Notebook of Henry Norris and the Hackney Petty Sessions Book* (1991, London: London Record Society), p xxxi.

to commit suspects before trial were a more sensible option than in rural areas, where sessions were less accessible to many people.[40]

A magistrate's authority to settle employment and wage disputes, either solely or in pairs, has not always been clear. The Statute of Artificers 1562 stated that magistrates only had the authority to act in cases involving servants employed in husbandry. This limitation was reasserted in 1747, when De Veil stated that 'Persons are very apt to apply for warrants concerning servants' wages, which justices have nothing to do with; except for those that are labourers in the field',[41] and again by the King's Bench in 1796.[42] Yet there is plenty of evidence that disputes concerning apprenticeships and employment were settled through arbitrated and mediated interventions by JPs during the long 18th century.[43] For obvious reasons, industrial disputes of a more technical nature tended to be referred to a specialist in that field rather than a JP.[44]

In order to deal with problems arising at times of food shortages JPs were empowered to hold an assize of bread, whereby they might fix prices, thus averting potential confrontations between merchants and consumers.[45] The decision to hold an assize of bread and setting the price, size, and quality of a loaf of bread was a discretionary power exercised by local magistrates who, in time of scarcity, had to balance the needs of the general population against those of the grain merchants, millers and bakers. The food riots of 1740 provide a case study of the importance of the JPs' use of the assize of bread to mediate community relations.[46]

Two consecutive harsh winters in 1739 and 1740 resulted in the failure of the following spring harvests, while sheep and cattle were lost through a combination of the harsh elements and starvation.[47] In April/May 1740,

40. Norma Landau, *The Justices of the Peace, 1679-1760* (1984, California, London: University of California Press), pp 185–186; Robert Shoemaker, *Prosecution and Punishment: Petty Crime and the Law in London and Rural Middlesex, c 1660-1725* (1991, Cambridge: Cambridge Studies In Early Modern British History), pp 229–230; Markless, *op cit* (note 33), p 18, pp 71–72.

41. Thomas De Veil, *Observations on the practice of a Justice of the Peace: intended for such gentlemen as design to act for Middlelex [sic] or Westminster* (London, 1747), p 16.

42. *Rex v the inhabitants of Hulcott, KB* (1796) 6 TR 583 (*Editorial note*: see also 101 ER 716), in Edward E Deacon, *A Digest of the Criminal Law of England: As Altered by the Recent Statutes for the Consolidation and Improvement of It*, Volume 2 (London, 1831), p 1173.

43. NEC Darby, *The magistrate and the community: summary proceedings in rural England during the long eighteenth century,* unpublished doctoral thesis, University of Northampton, 2015, pp 94–95.

44. Roebuck, Boorman and Markless, *op cit* (note 1), p 222.

45. 51 Hen III (1266–1267). The Assize of Bread and Ale regulated the price, weight and quality of bread and beer manufactured and sold in England and Wales.

46. See Markless, *op cit* (note 33) pp 282–323.

47. CE Whiting (Ed), *Two Yorkshire diaries: The Diary of Arthur Jessop and Ralph Ward's Journal,* (1952, Harrogate: Yorkshire Archaeological Society, Record Series), vol 117, pp 37, 51.

a series of violent riots took place in the area around Dewsbury, West Yorkshire, in which the greater number of participants were drawn from the textile industry, causing damage to granaries, mills and their contents.[48] JPs had missed an opportunity to hold the assize of bread in order to assure the local populace that grain would be both affordable and available. When negotiations between Sir John Kaye MP and the Dewsbury rioters broke down, the mob went to a mill at Thornhill and took grain by force. The rioters reportedly left a sum of money which represented, in their opinion, a 'fair price' for the grain stolen.[49] It appeared that working people had lost faith in the senior members of the community to carry out their civic duties.

While food riots erupted in both the West Riding and North Riding of Yorkshire, there were no reports of food riots in the East Riding. It may be no coincidence that, by contrast with the neighbouring northern and western parts of the county, quarter session records for Hull in the East Riding state that an assize of bread was held as a matter of course each quarter session throughout the period 1735–1745.[50]

This interpretation of events was widely shared. Mr Frankland Lewis MP, in an address to the House of Commons in 1815, asserted:

It was a fact, that in places where the assize was resorted to – for it was discretionary with the magistrates to act upon the law of assize or not – the public were more favourably circumstanced.[51]

Such discretionary intervention was akin to an act of public mediation and its success depended ultimately on the implicit consent of the populace.

In considering the ways in which magistrates undertook their duties, Morgan and Rushton maintain that:[52]

[some] behaved like investigating detectives and prosecutors, while … others [were] more like peacemakers and mediators, neglecting the formal structures of the courts to underwrite community harmony. Given the number of matters drawn to the Reverend Tew's attention, his diary contains few records of formal resolutions in claims concerning personal assault or disputes between master and apprentice or master

---

48. *York Courant*, 6 May 1740.
49. TNA ASSI 45/21/4 f. 91, 20 June 1740, information of John Furnis, millman.
50. ERY Hull, CCQA/2/2–3.
51. https://api.parliament.uk/historic-hansard/commons/1815/apr/04/assize-of-bread, accessed 31 August 2020, HC Deb, 4 April 1815, vol 30 cc0-342, Mr Frankland Lewis speaking on a motion for the appointment of a committee to consider the existing laws with regard to the regulation of the Assize of Bread, and also whether it is expedient or not to have any established assize.
52. Morgan and Rushton, *op cit* (note 29), p 57.

and servant. Some magistrates may have been influenced by handbooks which encouraged JPs to 'mediate and reconcile the disputing parties and only send the matter to trial if they failed to arrange a settlement satisfactory to both parties'.[53]

MERCHANTS

Merchants developed a separate body of law, the *lex mercatoria*, alongside the common law. Although common law courts had high regard for the *lex mercatoria* in cases involving commerce and shipping, the complexities involved in merchants' disputes were sometimes considered too great for common law courts to decide and, by the 16th century, there was already a long history in England of the courts referring matters of international trade to arbitrators. Merchants, both English and foreign, acted as arbitrators. The obvious advantage of choosing an arbitrator who understood one's business was only enhanced by the requirement that they also spoke your language and understood the conditions of trade in other jurisdictions. Thus the arbitrators in a cause might be one English and one foreign, as in a dispute involving Antonye Mazuelo, a Spaniard. The English parties were not performing the award, so in 1546 the Privy Council told them to pay up or appear in person, clearly showing its approbation for the award.[54] Some foreign merchants rose to prominent positions in English society and became highly sought after as arbitrators. Horatio Palavicino (*c*1520–1600), 'the doyen of the merchants of Italian origin', gained a knighthood and the trust of Elizabeth I.[55]

The government was keen to promote trade, and the Privy Council itself sometimes referred the disputes of merchants to the mayors or aldermen of great trading cities, like Bristol[56] and London.[57] The Lord Mayor of London might be asked to appoint a panel of arbitrators comprising equal numbers of English and foreign merchants to arbitrate a dispute between a Spaniard and a Florentine, or to arbitrate himself along with four aldermen, in a case of debt.[58] Under Elizabeth I, the Privy Council continued to promote trade vigorously, while recognising the preference of the merchant community to avoid the common law and have disputes settled by their peers. The

---

53. *Ibid*, at p 71 referring to JM Beattie, 'Violence and Society in Early Modern England', in AN Doob and EL Grteenspan (Eds), *Perspectives in Criminal Law: Essays in Honor of J Ll J Edwards* (1985, Ontario: Canada Law Book Co).
54. JR Dasent (Ed), *Acts of the Privy Council of England* I (1890, London: HMSO), p 540.
55. Roebuck, *op cit* (note 7), pp 201–2.
56. JR Dasent (Ed), *Acts of the Privy Council of England* IV (1892, London: HMSO), pp 7, 27.
57. Roebuck, *op cit* (note 3), pp 70–71, 79.
58. *Ibid*, p 184.

Council therefore frequently called on English and foreign merchants as arbitrators.[59]

The guilds were powerful regulators of domestic trade and the Privy Council involved itself in many of their disputes.[60] However, the guilds themselves took control of dispute settlement between members. The wardens often arbitrated disputes that did not necessarily relate to their trade. The Mercers' Company wardens interceded in all manner of disputes, including a vicious war of words between brothers John and Thomas Shelley, and a dispute between Richard Hunt and Ann Stathom, the widow and executrix of a deceased member.[61]

Private arbitrations and mediations were also arranged regarding all aspects of commerce, though the surviving evidence is rather more sparse, relying on appearances in the Acts of the Privy Council, court records, or arbitration bonds, which must have been copious, but most of which have presumably been lost to us.[62]

Sir Edward Coke's report of *Vynior's Case* in the early 17th century seemed to weaken the underpinning for arbitration but, as Derek explains, 'Commercial people knew how to ensure performance. Throughout the 17th century they got on with their business, submitting their inevitable disputes to mediation and arbitration, confident that other sanctions, most commonly goodwill and reputation, would be enough to safeguard their interests.'[63] As well as their role compounding disputes concerning all aspects of business, merchants were called upon to serve in arbitration tribunals, set up by treaty with France in 1606. All disputes between French and English merchants in London and several French towns were referred to two English and two French merchants, called Conservators of Commerce.[64]

Early printed guides to trade were unequivocal in their support for the use of arbitration among merchants, Gerard Malynes calling it the 'ordinarie course' to settle disputes. Malynes was born near Antwerp and rose to be a mint master and director of the East India Company in England, first publishing his guide to trade in 1622, with several later editions following.[65] The parties chose 'honest men' as arbitrators to make an award 'observing the Custome of Merchants, and ought to be void of all partialitie or affection more nor lesse to the one, than to the other:

---

59. Roebuck, *op cit* (note 7), pp 201–203.

60. *Ibid*, pp 194–200.

61. Laetitia Lyell and Frank D Watney (Eds) *Acts of Court of the Mercers' Company 1453–1527* (1936, Cambridge: Cambridge University Press), pp xxiii, 663–664.

62. Roebuck, *op cit* (note 7), pp 183, 200. For an early example of a bond in our period, see Archives and Cornish Studies Service, R/3162, 11 August 1506.

63. Roebuck, *op cit* (note 1), pp 426–427.

64. *Ibid*, pp 115–116.

65. *Ibid*, pp 289–291.

having only care that right may take place according to the truth, and that the difference may be ended with brevitie and expedition'.[66] Later in the century, James Vernon wrote a guide entertainingly structured as a Socratic business dialogue, which made clear that merchants should not spend their time on disputes: 'if he doth, he may be more fitly called a Solicitor than a Merchant'. That dig at the legal profession was the precursor to an explanation that 'Men of repute, and them that are good Husbands of their Time and Mony, will be willing to refer any Difference that shall happen unto them, unto Merchants or Tradesmen that understand their Disputes.'[67] Merchants looked to other merchants because, apart from all other considerations, they understood that speed was paramount when settling disputes.

In 1696, John Locke was tasked by his colleagues at the Board of Trade, with producing a 'method of determining differences between merchants by referees that might be decisive without appeal'.[68] Although the scheme was to be open to anyone, it was specifically aimed at commercial disputes. Locke set out to solve the problems of revocability and implementation in arbitration by formally enshrining the existing procedure of entering an arbitration as a rule of court, which resulted in the Arbitration Act 1698.[69] The enthusiasm with which commentators such as Blackstone and Matthew Bacon celebrated the use of Locke's Act among the mercantile and business community belies the fact that there was no significant increase in rules of court entered in the initial two-thirds of the 18th century. Arbitration remained widely used and was provided for in many partnership agreements and contracts, but its popularity remained in spite of greater formal recognition.[70] In the Liverpool business community, those merchants called on to mediate and arbitrate in the disputes of their peers advised that a conciliatory attitude, even if it meant losing some money, could avoid further cost, scandal, and even lead to a happier life.[71]

Arbitrations registered in the courts picked up significantly in the final third of the 18th century, particularly in the Court of King's Bench under Lord Mansfield. Men of business were named as arbitrators in a higher proportion of submissions to the court than references from it. Even so, they were seemingly a popular choice both for parties and chosen as lay experts by judges, though in the latter case lawyers became predominant. Merchants were also chosen as arbitrators among groups of local notables

66. Gerard Malynes, *Consuetudo, vel Lex Mercatoria* (London, 1622), p 447.
67. John Vernon, *The Compleat Comptinghouse* (London, 1678), p 236.
68. Quoted in Horwitz and Oldham, *op cit* (note 13), p 138.
69. *Ibid*, pp 138–144.
70. *Ibid*, pp 144–145.
71. Sheryllynne Haggerty, *'Merely for Money'?: Business Culture in the British Atlantic, 1750-1815* (2012, Liverpool: Liverpool University Press), p 147.

in disputes that were not necessarily related to trade, as trusted members of a community.[72] Mansfield clearly valued the expertise of merchants and called upon Thomas Gorman of New Broad Street in the City of London so many times that he started charging fees and made arbitration a part of his business.[73]

Wyndham Beawes was a merchant who wrote a complete guide to business, with a section on arbitration. As with earlier guides, he set out exemplary forms for bonds, awards and submissions. He continued the tradition of being quietly scathing about the courts, nearly quoting Malynes when saying civilians often refer matters of trade to merchants, 'and sometimes recommend the Decision of a mercantile Point to a Trader, after they have long and curiously debated it, without bringing it to a Conclusion.'[74] The reviser for the 5th edition of Malynes' work, former vice consul at Ostend Thomas Mortimer, was unequivocal in his statement of the importance of merchants as arbitrators. Noting that the French had made arbitration obligatory, 'our Statutes recommend these References to the Subjects, and more particularly to Merchants and Traders, as an useful Expedient to end their Disputes with the greater Ease and Expedition.'[75]

The modes of appointing merchants as arbitrators, either privately or as a referral from the courts, seem to have remained largely sufficient throughout the 18th century. Experiments with chambers of commerce acting as centres of arbitration took place late in the century but were confined to London and Newcastle, and were fairly short-lived.[76] While there were calls for the establishment of specialised merchant courts, these were opposed both on political grounds and by the legal establishment, the latter increasing their sensitivity to commercial needs in response.[77]

EXPERTS

Although we have shown that no formal qualifications were required for appointment as an arbitrator, in many disputes some expertise was preferable and expert knowledge took many forms, from the abstract learning of professionals to the practical understanding of the artisan. Knowledge of the customs and rules of any relevant group might also be counted as a form of expertise, be that local community, religious organisation, guild

72. Horwitz and Oldham, *op cit* (note 13), p 149.
73. Oldham *op cit* (note 25), pp 43 and 49–50.
74. Beawes *op cit* (note 21), p 308.
75. Beawes, *op cit* (note 22), p 370.
76. Roebuck, Boorman and Markless, *op cit* (note 1), pp 196–197.
77. Christian R Burset, 'Merchant Courts, Arbitration, and the Politics of Commercial Litigation in the Eighteenth-Century British Empire' (2016) 34:3 *Law and History Review* 615–647.

or club. From as early as the 13th century, expert arbitrators were referred to by the courts for their ability to assess damages competently.[78] In fact, valuations of any kind might need an expert arbitrator; when cattle sent to a garrison needed valuing in 1575, the arbitrators had to be men of 'judgment and knowledge'.[79] Experts might also be asked to give evidence to the arbitrator, as happened in a case of 1524.[80]

Merchants were used as expert arbitrators, especially in cases involving accounts and often referred both from Chancery and the Privy Council, into the 17th century.[81] Gerard Malynes wrote of the reference of causes 'unto the most ancient and expert Merchants in the matters in question'.[82] From the 15th century, the Court of Admiralty sent maritime disputes to the resolution of experts and expertise in shipping was more generally drawn upon, from Trinity House, for instance.[83] Medical negligence cases were referred to expert arbitrators and disputes between medical professionals were referred to their peers through the Company of Barber-Surgeons. Although that livery company largely settled petty personal quarrels, it also decided some matters relating to fees, for which specialist knowledge was relevant.[84]

Land was the major source of wealth in this period and though many arguments have been put forward about the non-arbitrability of title to land, in practice arbitrators were often called in to decide conflicts or simply to separate estates. In determining title, lawyers were the experts and could be called on to arbitrate.[85] Land disputes could require the skills of a surveyor, who could be appointed arbitrator or employed as a consultant; the importance of local knowledge, of land use, traditional boundaries or the nature of features like rivers and ponds cannot be underestimated.[86] Understanding the personalities of the parties and their standing in a community was also useful to resolving disputes of all kinds. Disputes involving buildings were frequent throughout the period, although they increased as a population boom made for larger, denser settlements. The quality of workmanship and materials might need to be assessed, which in the early period would be a job for craftsmen such as carpenters or masons.[87] The expertise of surveyors was particularly in demand following the Great Fire of London in 1666, and the scientist Robert Hooke made

78. Roebuck, *op cit* (note 3), p 56.
79. Roebuck, *op cit* (note 7), p 15.
80. Roebuck, *op cit* (note 3), p 377.
81. *Ibid*, p 70; Roebuck, *op cit* (note 7) pp15 and 203; Roebuck, *op cit* (note 4) pp 127-129.
82. Malynes, *op cit* (note 66), p 450.
83. Roebuck, *op cit* (note 3), pp 80 and 83; Roebuck, *op cit* (note 7), p 199.
84. Roebuck, *op cit* (note 3), pp 90-94.
85. Roebuck, Boorman and Markless, *op cit* (note 1), p 101.
86. Roebuck, *op cit* (note 5) p 90; Roebuck, *op cit* (note 4), pp 193, 218.
87. Roebuck, *op cit* (note 3), pp 124–129, 175–178.

many on-site inspections and settled disputes as mediator and arbitrator in his role as City Surveyor.[88]

The Elizabethan Privy Council could call upon the most exalted experts in the land. A disputed inheritance was referred to the arbitration of the Comptroller and Chancellor of the Exchequer, while the Lord Mayor of London and his aldermen were often called upon for their expertise in commercial disputes.[89] The Lord Mayor also stepped in to establish an arbitration commission to deal with the new field of insurance disputes after the Council struggled to find enough expertise among government and legal personnel in such a new financial technology. The Council continued to involve experts in matters of average, or the proportion of compensation owed by different insurers.[90]

The complexity of insurance and financial instruments made expertise in these areas increasingly useful in the late 17th and early 18th centuries, when the arbitration of merchants' disputes tended to require the knowledge of the quality of goods and an ever more nimble navigation of figures.[91] The increasing intricacy of many business arrangements, such as partnerships, made referral to an arbitrator (perhaps a Master in Chancery if a case had been brought in that court) quite likely. If a dispute were heard in a court like the King's Bench, an expert arbitrator could be called on if neither jury nor judge could fully understand the technicalities.[92] Arranging compromises with creditors was also a sought-after skill in a society increasingly built around borrowing.[93]

The courts continued to refer disputes to a variety of experts in the 18th century, such as grocers, stationers or a captain to assess damages to a ship.[94] The role of surveyors in deciding boundaries continued for private property, but was also an expanding public function as ever more common land was enclosed. Construction of canals required similar expert input to set compensation.[95] To the army of surveyors, builders and carpenters appointed as arbitrators were the added newer profession of architect, which highlights the importance of specialisation in creating new expert arbitrators.[96] Technological change introduced new fields of expertise. To arbitrate in a dispute involving a steam engine for example, knowledge of cutting-edge technology was required. Engineers or

88. Roebuck, *op cit* (note 4), pp 328–337.
89. Roebuck, *op cit* (note 7), pp 9–10, 50.
90. *Ibid*, pp 230–232, 289.
91. Roebuck, *op cit* (note 4), pp 445–446.
92. Oldham, *op cit* (note 25) pp 51–53.
93. Roebuck, Boorman and Markless, *op cit* (note 1), pp 154, 159.
94. *Ibid*, pp 112 and 130; Oldham, *op cit* (note 25), pp 48–50.
95. Roebuck, Boorman and Markless, *op cit* (note 1), pp 171–176.
96. *Ibid*, p 178.

inventors like the famous James Watt could decide such disputes.[97] We know a market for experts both as arbitrators and consultants flourished in 18th century England because they advertised their services in the newspapers, predominantly in settling accounts, though in the early 19th century a veterinary surgeon advertised his expertise in arbitrations related to horses.[98]

LAWYERS

Lawyers of all levels have been engaged as arbitrators since medieval times, be they 'county lawyers', 'scriveners' or clerks of the peace.[99] From those earliest times onward, parties to a dispute have been prepared to run concurrent claims at common law and arbitration in order to reach a settlement, which goes some way to explaining the close association between arbitration and the legal profession.[100] While the importance and instances of informal conciliatory settlements – mediations and arbitrations through lay persons – should not be underestimated, the qualities, knowledge and standing of members of the legal profession have long since been important factors in the selection of at least one member of a panel of arbitrators, or as umpires.[101] Nonetheless, lawyers were not universally popular as arbitrators and one party specified that their selection of arbitrators were as gentlemen and 'not lawyers in studye or in practice'.[102]

It was not unusual to find eminent judges and lawyers selected: Anthony Musson cites a number of examples of Chief Justices and other members of the judiciary being called upon to arbitrate disputes between the late 14th and early 16th centuries.[103] Continuing in the same tradition, Chief Baron Sir Edward Saunders was appointed sole arbitrator over tithes in 1560 and Chief Baron Sir Roger Manwood in 1583 in a dispute as to the title to land.[104] Julius Caesar (Master of the Rolls (1614–1636)) is described as a 'busy' arbitrator throughout Elizabeth's reign.[105] The decision to grant

97. *Ibid*, pp 206–214.

98. Boorman, *op cit* (note 24), pp 119–120; *Morning Post*, 31 May 1802.

99. Anthony Musson, 'Arbitration and the legal profession in late medieval England', in Matthew Dyson and David Ibbetson (Eds), *Law and legal process: substantive law and procedure in English legal history* (1982, Cambridge: Cambridge University Press), pp 56–76, 60.

100. *Ibid*, pp 56–76, 61; Christopher W Brooks, 'Interpersonal conflict and social tension: civil litigation in England, 1640–1830' in AL Beier, David Cannadine and James M Rosenheim (Eds.), *The First Modern Society: Essays in English History in Honour of Lawrence Stone* (1989, Cambridge: Cambridge University Press), pp 357–399, 381.

101. Musson, *op cit* (note 99), pp 56–76, 61, 65.

102. The Shakespeare Centre DR5/1316.

103. Musson, *op cit* (note 99), p 63.

104. Roebuck, *op cit* (note 7), p 90, fn3.

105. Roebuck, *op cit* (note 4), numerous references.

relief in *Tregonwell v Rees* (1599) was based on the Court being 'rather moved' to follow the decision made by Chancellor Baron Heath in an earlier arbitration. This appears to be the only example of an award made by an Elizabethan judge standing as a precedent in formal legal proceedings.[106]

James I and Charles I tended to delegate the work of arbitrators and mediators to members of the Council or other officials, including judges and law officers (the Attorney-General and the Solicitor-General), serjeants, barristers and JPs, taking advantage of their legal knowledge and availability.[107] In addition to official references from the Council, any number of private arbitrations were referred to judges. A bond from 1671 required Robert Houlden of Aston, gent, to submit to the privately arranged arbitration of Matthew Hale, Oliver Cromwell's Chief Justice, and William Allestrey, concerning the title to land.[108]

It is almost thirty years since Horwitz and Oldham discredited the myth of the development of judicial hostility to arbitration,[109] and additional research by Derek and others highlights the positive attitudes to arbitration by, among others, Lords Eldon, Ellenborough and Kenyon.[110] While the practice of calling upon court officers as arbitrators declined in the early 18th century,[111] there was a period of rapid growth in court-based arbitration during the late 18th century and those appointed as arbitrators were increasingly likely to be legal professionals.[112]

Thomas Lowten, the London solicitor and clerk of *nisi prius* for London and Middlesex, stands out as having spent a substantial part of his time as an arbitrator. He was arbitrator in over 60 cases referred from the King's Bench between 1755 and 1786 and appears to have been particularly favoured by Lord Mansfield in this respect.[113] Of 49 references to arbitration made at the London and Middlesex sittings and entered as rules in King's Bench in 1785, Lowten was arbitrator in 23 of them.[114] Experts with relevant professional understanding of the specific matters in dispute were very often appointed arbitrators and, therefore, lawyers were often referred to in disputes involving title to land.[115] By 1805, legal professionals were

---

106. Roebuck, *op cit* (note 7), p 300, referring to WH Bryson (Ed), *Cases Concerning Equity and the Courts of Equity 1550-1660*, 1, pp 273 no 324 (1599).
107. Roebuck, *op cit* (note 4), pp 193, 203.
108. *Ibid*, p 202, referring to Derbyshire Record Office D3155/7918.
109. *Ibid*, p 155.
110. Roebuck, Boorman and Markless, *op cit* (note 1), pp 109–116.
111. Oldham, *op cit* (note 25), p 49; Horwitz and Oldham, *op cit* (note 13), p 150.
112. Roebuck, Boorman and Markless, *op cit* (note 1), p 277.
113. Oldham, *op cit* (note 25), p 49.
114. Horwitz and Oldham, *op cit* (note 13), p 149.
115. An extensive list of arbitrators and their occupations extracted from the King's Bench rule book can be found at James Oldham, *The Mansfield Manuscripts and the Growth of English Law in the Eighteenth Century* (1992, Chapel Hill, NC: University of North Carolina Press), vol II, Appendix E.

chosen as arbitrators in three-fifths of the 260 references entered as rules in King's Bench and Common Pleas, and in one-quarter of submissions.[116]

While the second half of the 18th century witnessed a rise in court-based arbitration, there had been an overall decline in referrals to common law litigation by the middle of the 18th century, followed by unusually low levels of litigation in the central courts for the remainder of the century. At the same time, a statute of 1725 changed the legal procedures for the recovery of debts, such that creditors attempting to recover less than £10 were reluctant to go to law for fear of the additional costs, while defendants were concerned that a plaintiff's legal costs could be added to their debt.[117] In such conditions, it is possible that parties in dispute for sums falling below the £10 threshold preferred to resolve their differences through arbitration.

Christopher Brooks made the connection between the increase in litigation after 1790 and the late 18th century take-off in agricultural and manufacturing productivity, the 'Industrial Revolution'. However, he missed the relevance of the role of lay arbitrators taken by men such as retail grocers William Stout[118] and Thomas Turner[119] in accounting for the disparity between a massive increase in the number of economic transactions and the limited increase in common law litigation.[120]

As with JPs, attorneys routinely sought a compromise in private disputes so that matters were settled by way of compensation or apology and if unsuccessful, used the threat of litigation to encourage a reference to arbitration. If both parties had engaged an attorney, they first sought to come to an accommodation, or if they chose a reference to arbitration, their attorneys helped prepare and present their evidence. When arbitration failed, a dispute could be referred to a mutually acceptable umpire. Eighteenth-century urbanisation and the growth of metropolitan centres away from London led to an increase in complaints concerning the impossibility of using the royal courts to recover small debts.[121] At the same time, attorneys had begun to move from a system of flat-rate fees to charging for specific tasks, such as consultations, letter writing and travel, all adding to the cost of litigation. However, the fee-based structure meant that attorneys could make as much money out of a dispute by encouraging arbitration.[122] Surviving business records of two attorneys serving

116. Horwitz and Oldham, *op cit* (note 13), p 154.

117. Brooks, *op cit* (note 100), pp 365-366, referring to Richard Boote, *An Historical Treatise of an Action or Suit at Law* (1766), pp xi, xiv.

118. J Harland (Ed), *The Autobiography of William Stout of Lancaster, Wholesale and Retail Grocer and Ironmonger, a Member of the Society of Friends, AD 1665-1752* (1851, London: Simpkin, Marshall).

119. David Vaisey (Ed), *The Diary of Thomas Turner 1754-1765* (1984, Oxford: Oxford University Press).

120. Brooks, *op cit* (note 100), p 368.

121. *Ibid*, p 378.

122. *Ibid*, p 381.

in the area around Halifax and Bradford provide evidence of the type of litigation that occupied attorneys working in the mercantile society of the West Riding during the second half of the 18th century.[123] Although much of their work concerned general civil matters (conveyances, bankruptcy and wills), both men acted as arbitrators in disputes over debt, trespass, assault and the like among neighbours. The Bradford attorney, John Eagle, handled more arbitrations than cases that went through the courts.[124] By the nature of the cases referred for arbitration, it is no surprise to find that the majority of clients of one attorney were men drawn from the upper and middling classes (about 67 per cent) while women made up less than 8 per cent of his client base.[125] Roughly half of the disputes taken up by one of those solicitors were settled out of court, showing that involvement of a lawyer did not mean the involvement of a court.[126]

Michael Miles's study also counts the number of references made to different occupational groups in the West Riding of Yorkshire between 1750 and 1800. The largest number of references are the 70 made to attorneys, with 24 made to counsel, 21 to merchants and lesser numbers to gentlemen, professionals, artisans and yeomen. Although attorney John Howarth's record of acting as arbitrator or umpire at least once a year for 12 years is hardly remarkable, it does reveal a consistent use of his services.[127] Barristers like John Stanhope, also of the West Riding, found that their practice consistently involved arbitration too.[128]

WOMEN

Whereas Morgan and Rushton use the term 'peacemakers' to describe the work of some elements of the magistracy, Hoe and Roebuck write of female 'peaceweavers', women more commonly acting in a less official capacity.[129]

While the Roman Emperor Justinian expressly forbade women to act as arbitrators[130] and Saint Thomas Aquinas judged women 'naturally subject to man, because in man the distinction of reason predominates',[131] there was nothing in English law to prevent the appointment of female arbitra-

123. Miles, *op cit* (note 17), pp 470–503.

124. *Ibid*, pp 495–496

125. *Ibid*, pp 500–501.

126. Michael Miles, 'Eminent Attorneys': some aspects of West Riding attorneyship c1750-1800', unpublished PhD thesis, University of Birmingham 1982, pp 337–340.

127. *Ibid*, pp 340–341.

128. David Lemmings, *Professors of the Law: Barristers and English Legal Culture in the Eighteenth Century* (2000, Oxford: Oxford University Press), p 57.

129. Susanna Hoe and Derek Roebuck, *Women in Disputes: A History of European Women in Mediation and Arbitration* (2018, Oxford: HOLO Books), p 5.

130. AD 534.

131. *Summa Theologica* (written 1265–1274); see Hoe and Roebuck, *op cit* (note 129), pp 1-2.

tors, although social conventions might suggest otherwise. Women were called on to mediate in familial disputes, and this role could be crucial to maintaining the stability and honour of households.[132] However, they were infrequent arbitrators in more formal settings, exhibiting similar rarity to female legal practitioners.[133] Nevertheless, Derek Roebuck and others have uncovered interesting examples to the contrary.

It is neither unexpected nor unusual to find one of the kings and queens of England and Great Britain acting as arbitrators on international disputes. One newspaper even published a favourable history of Queen Elizabeth and her preference for ending quarrels by arbitration.[134] She occasionally became directly involved in mediating and arbitrating disputes among her advisers, as with her intervention in the marital dispute between Bess of Hardwick and the Earl of Shrewsbury.[135] 'Sundry poor women' petitioned Queen Elizabeth I concerning the detrimental effects of enclosure by the aforementioned Sir Richard Cholmeley. The Queen's Council wrote to the Lord President of the North in July 1577:[136]

[T]he poor folks deserve to be pitied and relieved as far as in law might be, he is required to direct a commission ... to such persons as his Lordship shall think meet ... for examining the supplication ... and with both their consents to take such as his Lordship shall think agreeable with justice and equity.

In 1703, Queen Anne expressed a desire for an end to the Lüneburg-Prussia feud, in view of ominous effects this might have on the Prussian Empire. At a conference held on 3 July 1703, Prussia stated that it was willing to submit to Queen Anne's arbitration.[137]

Women were commonly named as adminstratrix or executrix under a will and, as such, made decisions on the interpretation and allocation of bequests. Likewise, a female family member might be called on to arbitrate in the settlement of a family estate. Mary Egerton, a member of the Cheshire landed gentry, was appointed in 1563 as one of three arbitrators in a dispute between local landowners about the dower of her relative

132. Pollock, *op cit* (note 19); Courtney Thomas, '"The Honour and Credite of the Whole House": Family Unity and Honour in Early Modern England (2013) 10(3) *Cultural and Social History* 329–345.

133. Wilfrid Prest, '"One Hawkins, A Female Solicitor": Women Lawyers in Augustan England', 57 *Huntington Library Quarterly* (1994) 353–358.

134. *Country Journal or The Craftsman*, 15 February 1729; see Roebuck, *op cit* (note 7), pp 174-175.

135. Francis Calvert Boorman, 'Arbitration and Elite Honour in Elizabethan England: A Case Study of Bess of Hardwick' (2016) 1 *Journal of Dispute Resolution*, 19–40.

136. Hoe and Roebuck, *op cit* (note 129), pp 148–149.

137. TNA SP 90/2/15, 19 June 1703; SP 90/2/27, 3 July 1703.

Margaret Wilbraham.[138] In 1642, mediators in the matter between Henry Seward and William Chance delegated the decision as to which children should have money left by Edward Seward to Mistress Throckmorton.[139]

More unusually, in 1627 the decision on the appointment of an alnager (inspector) by the Clothiers of Coventry was referred by their Council to Frances, Duchess of Lennox and Richmond.[140] Sources reviewed by Craig Muldrew provide evidence of nonconformist minister Oliver Heywood (1630–1702), saying of his mother, 'she was very useful in reconciling differences and making up breaches, taking much pains yet great delight in that work'.[141] Likewise, he notes that the Countess of Warwickshire is reported to have reconciled Sir Richard Everard and his son, and on other occasions making peace between various female neighbours, reminiscent of the literary character Lady Catherine de Bourgh, the overbearing aunt of Mr Darcy in Jane Austen's *Pride and Prejudice*:

> Elizabeth soon perceived that though this great lady was not in the commission of the peace for the county, she was a most active magistrate in her own parish, the minutest concerns of which carried to her by Mr Collins; and whether any of the cottagers were disposed to be quarrelsome, discontented or too poor, she sallied forth into the village to settle their differences, silence their complaints, and scold them into harmony and plenty.[142]

In Holcroft's play *The Rival Queens* (1794), a dispute concerning the building of Covent Garden and its rival Drury Lane was referred to Mr and Mrs Town for a private settlement. Such references found in contemporary literature to the active participation of women in the settlement of disputes suggests an uncommon but apparently acceptable appointment of a woman arbitrator, albeit acting with her husband.[143]

Before the advent of a national police force and prosecution service, the victim of a crime was able to exercise discretionary powers in the resolution of the crime committed against him or her: deciding whether to take an active role in pursuing a prosecution, to exercise mercy by negotiating a private settlement, or remain passive and fail to respond to the offence. Both men and women acted as mediators within local networks.[144] When Michael Smith was suspected of having murdered his wife Mary Honeyman, a neighbour, reported that following a previous assault, she

---

138. Hoe and Roebuck, *op cit* (note 129), p 156.
139. Roebuck, *op cit* (note 4), p 366; Hoe and Roebuck, *op cit* (note 129), p 157.
140. Roebuck, *op cit* (note 4), pp 365–366.
141. Muldrew, *op cit* (note 18), p 932, fn76.
142. Jane Austen's *Pride and Prejudice* (1813), ch 30 – available at http://www.online-literature.com/austen/prideprejudice/30/, accessed 29 October 2020.
143. Roebuck, Boorman and Markless, *op cit* (note 1), p224.
144. Markless, *op cit* (note 33), p18.

had acted as an intermediary between the couple, persuading the wife to return home in exchange for the husband's promise that he would stop beating her.[145] In such circumstances, the social expectation that a wife would remain with her husband was matched by an acceptance that married women were subject to the exercise of 'reasonable' chastisement by their husbands.[146]

Women most commonly appear as parties to arbitrated and mediated proceedings. In the above-mentioned justices' diaries, of about 110 matters referred to Norris, 60 involved women, like Frances Low's complaint against Thomas Clark. She said that he had hit and kicked her.[147] He said she had hit him first with a fire shovel, but 'on the whole they agreed the matter and she acknowledged to have received satisfaction for the injury and I discharged the warrant'. Some 61 of 112 disputes settled with Hunt's help concerned women. Tew settled 422 cases, of which 190 were brought by female complainants, while in many others a woman was a defendant or on the receiving end of warrants issued for assault, some of which were against other women. More than half of about 280 complaints brought before Wyatt concerned women.

Where disputes could be settled privately, pre-trial arrangements provided an opportunity for clemency. During the 18th century, such arrangements avoided the criminalisation of many people and acted as a counter-balance to the excesses of the 'Bloody Code'. A number of complaints would have been discharged when a defendant 'submitted' to the court and paid a voluntary fine as the result of a private settlement between the parties or where the victim was satisfied by the accused publicly begging his or her pardon. A gendered study of the Yorkshire quarter sessions suggests that a greater number of men than women may have benefited from such opportunities, when men were more likely than women to be financially independent and able to offer financial bonds or financial settlements.[148]

Table: Orders to Keep the Peace: East Riding of Yorkshire[149]

Quarter sessions, Beverley	*1765–1775*	%
Orders to keep the peace	105	
Male	101	96.2
Female	4	3.8
		100.0

145. TNA ASSI 45/31/1/282 (1773), information of Mary Honeyman.
146. Bridget Hill, *Eighteenth Century Women: An Anthology* (1984, London: George Allen & Unwin Ltd), pp 137, 143; Daniel Defoe, *The Great Law of Subordination consider'd* (London, 1724), pp 6–7.
147. Paley, *op cit* (note 39), p 57.
148. Markless, *op cit* (note 39), p 71.
149. *Ibid*, p 27.

East Riding of Yorkshire Quarter Session records provide evidence of the relative absence of orders against women to keep the peace. This may be explained in part because of an interpretation of the law that stated that a man might be released on his own 'surety for the peace', but doubted the ability of a married woman (*femme covert*) or a child under the age of 21 to be legally bound without additional securities provided by their friends or families 'for they are incapable of engaging themselves to answer any debt'.[150] For similar reasons, a man who submitted to an arbitrated award on behalf of himself and his wife was bound by that award. His wife was, however, not bound.[151]

The rarity of female arbitrators reflected women's general exclusion from any number of public positions, which was also apparent in the language surrounding arbitration. In the 18th century, arbitration was associated with manliness. For instance, one newspaper carried a report of a dispute between Edward Topham and C Este, owners of the daily newspaper *The World*, in which Este gave Topham a deadline of two days to act, in which time he renewed his 'just and manly offer of ARBITRA-TION. – If he is not just and manly, I cannot help it. He must take the consequences.'[152]

CONCLUSION

Who, then, were the arbitrators of early modern England? Of course they were as varied as the people and their disputes, but we can at least identify some trends. In 1500, our arbitrator might be a government func-tionary appointed by the Privy Council or a court. Parties from a trade might look to their guild to arbitrate, while merchants would look to their own to arbitrate privately, or call in such as the Lord Mayor of London. Local disputes could end up arbitrated by JPs, gentlemen or aristocracy, depending on the status of the parties. A carpenter might be called on to look over building work and a lawyer to make an award on title to land.

The JPs remained everywhere in England and across the period useful arbitrators and mediators in the community. They were able to use signifi-cant discretion to intervene with greater or lesser forcefulness according to circumstances and disposition. Merchants generally preferred the commercial sensitivity of their peers when appointing arbitrators and even when their disputes ended up in court, a merchant arbitrator might still

---

150. William Blackstone, *Commentaries on the Laws of England: Of Public Wrongs*, vol 4 (1st Edn, 1765, Oxford: Clarendon Press), p 251. See also Richard Burn, *Justice of the Peace and Parish Officer*, vol 2, (London, 1755), p 431.

151. Roebuck, *op cit* (note 4), Appendix 2, 'Arbitration in Sheppard's *Abridgment* 1675: William Sheppard *A Grand Abridgment of the Common and Statute Law of England*'.

152. *Gazetteer and New Daily Advertiser*, 30 September 1790.

be called upon to decide damages or unpick accounts, and this financial expertise became increasingly important.

Experts more generally were always sought after to end disputes, particularly in the fields of building and surveying. Experts became more specialist with new professions such as architects emerging and new technologies like the steam engine requiring technical proficiency. Lawyers were a form of expert throughout the period and were needed for specialist roles such as deciding matters of title to land, but their involvement in arbitration increased, especially in the late 18th century.

The role of attorneys, counsellors, esquires and gentlemen as arbitrators provides evidence of 'paternal responsibility in the community'.[153] At the same time others chose to refer their disputes to one of their own, merchant to merchant and gentlemen to gentlemen.[154] Whether this constituted class bias or a sensible means of selecting experts in a particular field depended on the circumstances. Women were often involved in making peace, but their appointment as arbitrators was rare and became even more so through the period.

By 1800, our arbitrator was therefore almost certainly a man – if not a JP, then quite possibly a lawyer or peer of a party, and might well be appointed by a court. They would not have been appointed directly by government, as the Privy Council used to do. It would be no surprise to find an expert in some increasingly specialised field, very often accountancy, though professionals of all stripes were called upon and it was no longer shocking, though some would disapprove, if they made a bit of money for their troubles.

153. Miles, *op cit* (note 17), pp 495–497.
154. Miles, *op cit* (note 126), pp 341–343.

THE RIGHT TO ARBITRATE: A GENERAL PRINCIPLE OF INTERNATIONAL LAW

*Gary B Born**

[*Editorial note*: This article is based in part on the author's 20th Annual Goff Lecture delivered at the City University of Hong Kong in January 2015. An article based on the lecture and entitled 'The Right to Arbitrate: Historical and Contemporary Perspectives' was published in [2015] *Asian Dispute Review* 56–60 (April 2015).]

Derek Roebuck's contributions to arbitration – both domestic and international – were legion and extraordinary. His work not only entailed the contemporary practice and state of arbitration law, but, more recently, explored the history of arbitration. With striking breadth and depth of vision, his later publications examined the use of arbitration in classical Rome and Greece, medieval Europe and England, and more recent epochs. Those works depict, with exceptional detail and erudition, the universality of arbitration, as a means of dispute resolution, over the past 2,500 years.

This essay[1] seeks to build on one aspect of Professor Roebuck's rich legacy. Building on his study of the historical roots of arbitration, it examines the contemporary use of arbitration, and particularly international arbitration. It argues that, consistent with the historic ubiquity of the arbitral process, international commercial arbitration is also universal in contemporary life and that, as a consequence, obligations to recognise international arbitration agreements and awards have the status of general principles of law, binding on all States.

Building on the historic foundations of arbitration that Professor Roebuck has detailed, Part I of this essay describes the significant, and

---

* Gary Born is the author of G. Born, *International Commercial Arbitration* (3d ed. 2020), G. Born, *International Arbitration: Law and Practice* (2d ed. 2018) and G. Born and P. Rutledge, *International Civil Litigation in United States* (6th ed. 2018), as well as Chair of the International Arbitration and Litigation Group at Wilmer Cutler Pickering Hale and Dorr LLP.
1. Excellent research assistance was provided by Dharshini Prasad and Rashmita Roy Chowdury. All mistakes are the author's own.

progressively increasing, success of international arbitration over the past 50 years. That success is reflected in the continuing growth in caseloads at arbitral institutions, the use of arbitration to resolve new categories of dispute and support for the arbitral process by national legislatures and courts. As also discussed in Part I, the success of both international commercial and investment arbitration reflects the inherent advantages of the arbitral process, particularly in international matters, by comparison with the available alternatives. In particular, international arbitration offers a more expert, expeditious, efficient, even-handed and enforceable means of international dispute resolution than national courts. In so doing, again consistent with earlier eras, international arbitration provides a more effective contemporary means of international dispute resolution, and more effectively advances the rule of law, than do national courts.

International arbitration also reflects more fundamental aspects of the rule of law, as discussed in Part II of this essay. Virtually all contemporary international and national legal systems recognise the central role of individual autonomy in commercial matters – particularly in freedom of contract and association. That respect for individual autonomy extends to the freedom of private parties to choose how to resolve the disputes that arise from their contracts and other forms of association: the autonomy not just to form relationships, but also to mend them. That autonomy is uniquely important in international commercial matters, where the need for predictability and certainty is particularly acute, and where recognition of consensual means of dispute resolution are particularly vital to an effective international legal system and the international rule of law. Consistent with that conclusion, and once more building on the historical use of arbitration, a wide variety of contemporary sources, including national court decisions and arbitral awards, have recognised the right of commercial parties to arbitrate. In turn, that consensus reflects a general principle of international law, mandatorily binding on all States, mandating the presumptive validity of international commercial arbitration agreements and awards.

I. INTERNATIONAL ARBITRATION: THE FIVE Es

It is commonplace to observe that arbitration is a preferred – and, increasingly over the past four decades, *the* preferred – means of resolving commercial disputes.[2] Building on deep historical foundations, explored

---

2. *See, e.g.,* Ali, *Approaching the Global Arbitration Table Comparing the Advantages of Arbitration as Seen by Practitioners in East Asia and the West*, 28 Rev. Litig. 791 (2009); Drahozal, *Why Arbitrate? Substantive Versus Procedural Theories of Private Judging*, 22 Am. Rev. Int'l Arb. 163 (2011); Petrevska *et al., The Advantages of Solving Commercial Disputes by Arbitration*, 7 Int'l. J. Econ. & L. 121 (2017); Stipanowich, *Arbitration and Choice: Taking Charge of the "New Litigation"*, 7 DePaul Bus. & Comm. L.J. 383 (2009); Sussman, *Why Arbitrate: The Benefits and Savings*, 7 Transnat'l Disp. Mgt 2 (2010).

in the works of Professor Roebuck and others,[3] arbitration is used in many domestic legal systems to provide a mechanism for resolving numerous categories of dispute – including commercial, construction, insurance, maritime, securities, labour and commodities disputes.[4]

Internationally, arbitration is used for the resolution of commercial disputes in most of the foregoing categories of dispute, and, in some cases, additional categories.[5] Again building on a long history, international arbitration has become the presumptive means for dispute resolution in cross-border transactions in almost all regions of the world, including regions where arbitration was not always historically favoured (such as Latin America, the Middle East and elsewhere).[6]

In both domestic and international settings, the numbers of international arbitrations commenced annually with leading arbitral institutions have increased, very materially and steadily, over the past 30 years. In particular, annual case filings at many leading international commercial arbitral institutions have increased manifold over that period. The Singapore International Arbitration Centre, for example, had two cases filed in 1990, with its case filings increasing exponentially to more than 1,000 cases in 2020.[7] Between 1990 and 2020, cases have increased substantially across all

---

3. *See* D. Roebuck, *Ancient Greek Arbitration* (2001); D. Roebuck & B. De Fumichon, *Roman Arbitration* (2004); D. Roebuck, *Early English Arbitration* (2008); D. Roebuck, *Mediation and Arbitration in the Middle Ages: England 1154-1558* (2013); D. Roebuck, *The Golden Age of Arbitration: Dispute Resolution under Elizabeth I* (2015). *See also* G. Born, *International Commercial Arbitration* Chapter 1 (3d ed. 2020).

4. G. Born, *International Commercial Arbitration* 189-90 (3d ed. 2020). *See also* 2013 AAA Labor Arbitration Rules (labor disputes); 1988 American Arbitration Association Rules for Impartial Determination of Union Fees (organized labor union fees); 2004 ARIAS Procedures for the Resolution of U.S. Insurance and Reinsurance Disputes (reinsurance); 2014 ARIAS-UK Arbitration Rules; 2017 Court of Arbitration for Sports Code; 2017 Federation of Cocoa Commerce Arbitration and Appeal Rules (selected commodities disputes); 2018 German Maritime Arbitration Association Rules (maritime); 2017 London Maritime Arbitration Association Terms (maritime); 2019 National Grain and Feed Association Arbitration Rules (selected commodities disputes).

5. G. Born, *International Commercial Arbitration* 83-87, 94-96 (3d ed. 2020). *See, e.g.*, C. Ambrose & K. Maxwell, *London Maritime Arbitration* (4th ed. 2017); D. Johnson, *International Commodity Arbitration* (1991); F. Rose, *International Commercial and Maritime Arbitration* (1988); J. Hinchey, *International Construction Arbitration Handbook* (2018); Bernstein, *Private Commercial Law in the Cotton Industry: Creating Cooperation Through Rules, Norms, and Institutions*, 99 Mich. L. Rev. 1724 (2001); Muñoz & Andreotti, *Transnational Securities Disputes: A Role for Arbitration?*, 31 Spanish Arb. Rev. 73, 88 (2018) (discussing use of arbitration for securities disputes).

6. *See, e.g.*, N. Blackaby, D. Lindsey & A. Spinillo (eds.), *International Arbitration in Latin America, Overview of Regional Developments* 3-10 (2003); S. Saleh, *Commercial Arbitration in the Arab Middle East* 393-94 (2d ed. 2012); Naón, *Arbitration and Latin America: Progress and Setbacks*, 21 Arb. Int'l 127, 128-40 (2005).

7. *See* SIAC, Press Release: SIAC Sets a New Record in 2019 (8 Apr. 2020). *See also* SIAC, SIAC: Arbitration in the New Millennium, available at https://v1.lawgazette.com.sg/2000-1/Jan00-23.htm; SIAC, *Annual Report* 4 (2019).

leading arbitral institutions. Those increases are depicted in the following chart, which captures only larger arbitral institutions (and omits *ad hoc* arbitrations):

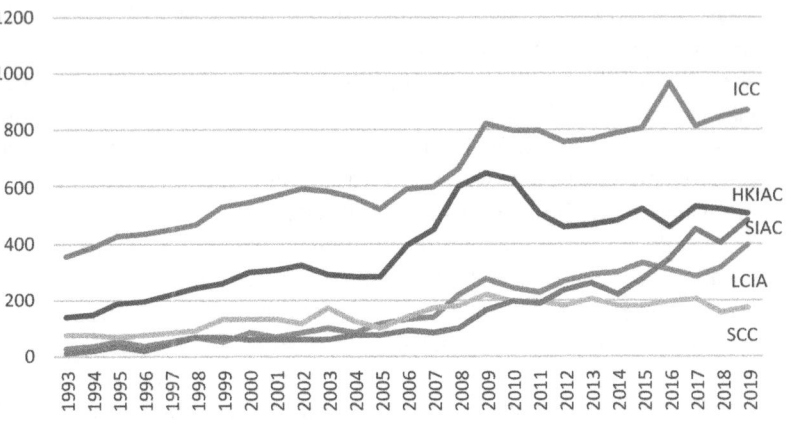

The same conclusions are reached by empirical studies, in which businesses and their advisers consistently regard international arbitration as their most preferred form of international dispute resolution.[8]

During the past four decades, arbitration has also been adopted in a wide and increasing range of new international settings, including for investor-State, sports, intellectual property (IP), double taxation, corporate, trust and financial services disputes.[9] In many of these fields, arbitration was

8. *See, e.g.*, Queen Mary, University of London, *2018 International Arbitration Survey: The Evolution of International Arbitration* 2 (2018) (97% of respondents identified international arbitration as their preferred mechanism for dispute resolution and 99% of respondents recommend international arbitration to resolve cross-border disputes); Queen Mary, University of London, *2013 International Arbitration Survey: International Arbitration: Industry Perspectives* (2013) (52% of respondents across all industries preferred international arbitration and 73% of all respondents found international arbitration suitable to their industry); Queen Mary, University of London, *2010 International Arbitration Survey: Choices in International Arbitration*, 2, 5 (2010) ("corporations ... have strong preferences regarding confidentiality"); Queen Mary, University of London, *2008 International Arbitration Survey: International Arbitration: Corporate Attitudes and Practices* 2, 5 (2008) (88% of corporations surveyed had used international arbitration, and 86% of corporate counsel were satisfied with experience). *See also* Bühring-Uhle, *A Survey on Arbitration and Settlement in International Business Disputes*, in C. Drahozal & R. Naimark (eds.), *Towards A Science of International Arbitration: Collected Empirical Research* 25, 32, 35 (2005); Naimark & Keer, *International Private Commercial Arbitration: Expectations and Perceptions of Attorneys and Business People*, in C. Drahozal & R. Naimark (eds.), *Towards A Science of International Arbitration: Collected Empirical Research* 45 (2005).

9. *See, e.g.*, E. Min & M. Lilleengen, *Collection of WIPO Domain Name Panel Decisions* (2003); L. Reed, J. Paulsson & N. Blackaby, *Guide to ICSID Arbitration* (2d ed. 2010); Ganguly, *Tribunals and Taxation: An Investigation of Arbitration in Recent Tax Conventions*,

not historically utilised and, in some cases, such as IP and trusts, doing so was precluded by national law.[10] In contrast, over the past 30 years, national legislative enactments and judicial decisions have progressively permitted the arbitration of such disputes, while arbitral institutions specialising in handling such disputes have been established.[11] Examples include the Court of Arbitration for Sport (CAS),[12] the International Centre for the Settlement of Investment Disputes (ICSID),[13] the World Intellectual Property Organization (WIPO),[14] and the Panel of Recognized International Market Experts (PRIME).[15]

Arbitration has been chosen in part by businesses, individuals, State entities and others to resolve their international commercial and investment disputes because of its essential characteristics and inherent advantages, when compared with alternative means of resolving disputes. These

29 Wisc. Int'l L.J. 735 (2012); Gildemeister & Koppensteiner, *Arbitration Clauses in Tax Treaties (Conference Report)*, 7(1) Transnat'l Disp. Mgt (2010); Markham, *Mandatory Binding Tax Arbitration: Is This A Pathway to A More Efficient Mutual Agreement Procedure?*, 35 Arb. Int'l 149 (2019) (mandatory arbitration in bilateral tax treaties increasingly accepted); Reilly, *An Introduction to the Court of Arbitration for Sport (CAS) & The Role of National Courts in International Sports Disputes*, 2012 J. Disp. Resol. 63, 64 (2012).

10. G. Born, *International Commercial Arbitration* 1080-83, 1122 (3d ed. 2020). *See, e.g.*, Legler, *Arbitration of Intellectual Property Disputes*, 37 ASA 289 (2019); Strong, *Arbitration of Trust Disputes: Two Bodies of Law Collide*45 Vand. J. Trans. L. 1157 (2012).For proposals for further uses of international arbitration, as a default means of dispute resolution, see Born, *BITs, BATs and Buts*, 10 Rev. Bras. Arb. 138 (2013).

11. The Court of Arbitration for Sport (CAS) was established in Lausanne, Switzerland, in 1984, and is sometimes termed the "Supreme Court of world sport." Established in 2012, the Panel of Recognized International Market Experts in Finance (P.R.I.M.E. Finance) specializes in the resolution of disputes in the financial sector. The Arbitral Centre of the World Intellectual Property Organization (WIPO) was established in Geneva, Switzerland in 1994.

12. *See* D. Mavromati & M. Reeb, *The Code of the Court of Arbitration for Sport: Commentary, Cases and Materials* (2015); Reilly, *An Introduction to the Court of Arbitration for Sport (CAS) & The Role of National Courts in International Sports Disputes*, 2012 J. Disp. Resol. 63, 64 (2012); 2019 CAS Code, available at www.tas-cas.org.

13. *See* A. Newcombe & L. Paradell, *Law and Practice of Investment Treaties: Standards of Treatment* (2009); C. Baltag (ed.), *ICSID Convention After 50 Years: Unsettled Issues* (2017); C. McLachlan, L. Shore & M. Weiniger, *International Investment Arbitration* (2d ed. 2017); D. Bishop, J. Crawford & M. Reisman, *Foreign Investment Disputes: Cases, Materials and Commentary* (2d ed. 2014); M. Kinnear *et al.* (eds.), *Building International Investment Law: The First 50 Years of ICSID* (2015).

14. *See* P. Landolt & A. García, *Commentary on WIPO Arbitration Rules* (2017); Zuberbühler, *World Intellectual Property Organization (WIPO)*, in P. Gola, C. Götz Staehelin & K. Graf (eds.), *Institutional Arbitration: Tasks and Powers of Different Arbitration Institutions* 293 (2009); WIPO, *Guide to WIPO Arbitration* (2004); 2020 WIPO Rules, Arts. 50, 54, 75-78.

15. Meijer & Wit, *P.R.I.M.E. Finance: A New Dispute Resolution Facility for Conflicts Relating to Complex Financial Products*, 14 Bus. L. Int'l 153 (2013); Pusceddu, *P.R.I.M.E. Finance Arbitration – A Lighthouse Safe Harbour in the Mare Magnum of Financial Dispute Resolution*, 3 Indian J. Arb. L. 45 (2014).

advantages might be termed, for convenience and rhetorical effect, the 'Five Es': international arbitration is generally the most expert, efficient, expeditious, even-handed and enforceable means of resolving international disputes available to parties. These various advantages of international arbitration arise from the basic character of the arbitral process and from the legal regime within which contemporary international arbitrations take place. At the same time, these advantages are also reflected in the historic use of arbitration, in the widely diverse historical settings explored by Professor Roebuck and others.[16]

First, international arbitration is generally more expert than litigation in national courts. A defining feature of the arbitral process is the parties' right to select the arbitrators who will resolve their dispute.[17] In practice, this right is almost always exercised after a dispute has arisen, with the parties' choices being based on the subject matter and nature of their dispute: in construction projects, the arbitrators can be construction experts, often with significant experience in the type of project (eg, road works, bridges), geographical region (eg, the Philippines, Brazil) and applicable law(s) involved in the parties' dispute.[18] The choices of both co-arbitrators and presiding and sole arbitrators are usually made by the parties themselves, who have the most knowledge of the needs of the dispute, and the greatest incentive to choose wisely.

The parties' ability to select genuinely expert arbitral tribunals contrasts with national court litigation, where judges are ordinarily generalists, selected randomly, and often have little or no background in the type of

---

16. *See supra* note 3.

17. Queen Mary, University of London, *2018 International Arbitration Survey: The Evolution of International Arbitration* 7 (2018) ("ability of parties to select arbitrators" is fourth most valuable characteristic of international arbitration); Queen Mary, University of London, *2015 International Arbitration Survey: Improvements and Innovations in International Arbitration* 6 (2015) (selection of arbitrators is fourth most valuable characteristic of international arbitration); Queen Mary, University of London, *2010 International Arbitration Survey: Choices in International Arbitration* 2-3 (2010) ("corporations ... have strong preferences regarding confidentiality"). *See also* Bühring-Uhle, *A Survey on Arbitration and Settlement in International Business Disputes*, in C. Drahozal & R. Naimark (eds.), *Towards A Science of International Arbitration: Collected Empirical Research* 25, 33 (2005); Landau, *Composition and Establishment of the Tribunal*, 9 Am. Rev. Int'l Arb. 45 (1998).

18. *Positive Software Solutions, Inc. v. New Century Mortg. Corp.*, 476 F.3d 278, 285 (5th Cir. 2007) (describing expertise as one of arbitration's "most attractive features apart from speed and finality"); *Judgment of 28 April 1999, Attorney Gen. of Kenya v. Bank für Arbeit und Wirtschaft AG*, XXV Y.B. Comm. Arb. 692, 694 (Cyprus S.Ct.) (2000) ("familiarity of arbitrators with their subject matter"); Trebilock & Leng, *The Role of Formal Contract Law and Enforcement in Economic Development*, 92 Va. L. Rev. 1517, 1541 (2006) ("As compared to public courts, the advantages of international commercial arbitration in enforcing contracts include increased flexibility, technical expertise, privacy, and confidentiality, all of which are important in satisfying the needs of private parties for low-cost, expeditious, and effective resolution of contract disputes").

dispute, cultural and commercial setting, or applicable law relevant to the parties' dispute. In many jurisdictions, national courts lack expertise in international commercial matters generally and often have no experience at all in the particular type of transaction that the parties' dispute concerns. Even in specialised courts, which exist in a few jurisdictions, judges are selected randomly, without the consent or input of the parties – generally resulting in decision-makers who are significantly less expert than international arbitral tribunals. Likewise, national court judges are virtually always of a single nationality, and educational and professional background, thus lacking the diversity of expertise and experience provided by three-person arbitral tribunals, which can combine individuals with different legal, commercial and other backgrounds and qualifications.[19]

> National court judges have in numerous circumstances acknowledged the structural advantages of the arbitral process in selecting expert decision-makers, based on information after the parties' dispute has arisen. In the words of the former President of the French Cour de Cassation, '[F]irst, what you do we don't have to do; ... [s]econd, in many fields you are more professional than we are'.[20]

Or, as a US judge put it, in a dispute over agricultural products: arbitrators 'know more about the value of peach orchards, their productivity and earning power than I do.'

Second, international arbitration is generally more expeditious than national court litigation, because of both the inherent character of the arbitral process and the contemporary legal regime which governs it. National court litigation is virtually always a multi-stage process, with two or three levels of appellate review; that process inevitably takes time, often substantial amounts of time. Likewise, in many jurisdictions, first instance proceedings often require substantial periods of time, with delays for interlocutory applications, court holidays, docket congestion and the like. In contrast, even though not all arbitrations are conducted flawlessly, the arbitral process is typically significantly quicker than the litigation process.[21]

---

19. Ashenfelter, Eisenberg & Schwab, *Politics and the Judiciary: The Influence of Judicial Background on Case Outcomes*, 24 J. Legal Studies 257, 266-70 (1995); Drahozal, *Why Arbitrate? Substantive Versus Procedural Theories of Private Judging*, 22 Am. Rev. Int'l Arb. 163, 174 (2011).
20. Lazareff, *International Arbitration: Towards A Common Procedural Approach*, in S. Frommel & B. Rider (eds.), *Conflicting Legal Cultures in Commercial Arbitration: Old Issues and New Trends* 31, 33 (1999).
21. *Stolt-Nielsen SA v. Animalfeeds Int'l*, 559 U.S. 662 685 (U.S. S.Ct. 2010) ("In bilateral arbitration, parties forgo the procedural rigor and appellate review of the courts in order to realize the benefits of private dispute resolution: lower costs, greater efficiency and speed,

International arbitration typically does not involve appellate review of the arbitral tribunal's award: under the UNCITRAL Model Law on International Commercial Arbitration (UNCITRAL Model Law), adopted in more than 100 jurisdictions,[22] awards may be set aside, but based only on limited grounds relating to jurisdiction, serious procedural irregularities or public policy.[23] The annulment procedure is almost always expedited (ordinarily completed in a matter of months) and, in practice, awards are relatively rarely set aside.[24] As a consequence, arbitral proceedings are almost inevitably more expeditious than litigations involving multiple layers of appellate review of trial courts' legal and factual conclusions (even putting aside the possibility that a matter will be remanded to the trial court to commence proceedings anew). That structural advantage of the arbitral process is enhanced by the parties' right to select the arbitrators for their dispute (discussed above), which makes it likely that the tribunal will have expertise in the subject matter of that dispute, in turn enabling proceedings to be conducted more expeditiously.

In recent years, leading international arbitral institutions have also revised their institutional arbitration rules to ensure that proceedings are conducted with maximal efficiency. Among other things, leading institutional rules now typically include provisions for expedited procedures, under which smaller value, less complicated or urgent matters will be heard in a fast-track arbitration (with final awards generally made within

and the ability to choose expert adjudicators to resolve specialized disputes"); *Fradella v. Petricca*, 183 F.3d 17, 19 (1st Cir. 1999) ("The primary purpose served by the arbitration process is expeditious dispute resolution."); *Folkways Music Publ'rs, Inc. v. Weiss*, 989 F.2d 108, 111 (2d Cir. 1993) ("twin goals of arbitration, namely settling disputes efficiently and avoiding long and expensive litigation"). *See also* G. Born, *International Commercial Arbitration* 83-87 (3d ed. 2021).
22. *See* UNCITRAL, Status: 1958 Convention on the Recognition and Enforcement of Foreign ArbitralAwards, available at www.uncitral.org.
23. UNCITRAL Model Law, Art. 34; *Carr v. Gallaway Cook Allan*, [2014] NZSC 75, ¶76 (N.Z. S.Ct.) (Article 34 "sets out an exhaustive list of the grounds on which an award may be set aside."); *Canada (Attorney General) v. S.D. Myers Inc.*, [2004] 3 F.C.R. 368 (Canadian Fed. Ct.); *Methanex Motunui Ltd v. Spellman* [2004] 1 NZLR 95 (Auckland High Ct.); *ABC Co. v. XYZ Co. Ltd*, [2003] 3 SLR 546 (Singapore High Ct.); *D. Frampton & Co. v. Thibeault*, [1988] F.C.J. No. 305 (Canadian Fed. Ct.). *See also* G. Born, *International Commercial Arbitration* 3434-35 (3d ed. 2021).
24. *JVL Agro Indus. Ltd v. Agritrade Int'l Pte Ltd*, [2016] 4 SLR 0768, ¶149 (Singapore High Ct.) ("the grounds on which a court may set aside an award are few in number and narrow in scope"); *AKN v. ALC*, [2015] 3 SLR 488, ¶38 (Singapore Ct. App.) ("the grounds for curial intervention [under the Model Law] are narrowly circumscribed"); *Corporación Transnacional de Inversiones, SA de CV v. STET Int'l SpA*, (1999) 45 OR3d 183, ¶26 (Ontario Super. Ct.) (emphasis added), *aff'd*, (2000) 49 OR3d 414 (Ontario Ct. App.) ("general rule of interpretation ... that the grounds for refusal of enforcement are to be construed narrowly"). *See also* G. Born, *International Commercial Arbitration* 3437-38 (3d ed. 2020).

six months of commencement of the arbitration).[25] Relatedly, many institutional rules also now include mechanisms for early dismissal of frivolous claims or defenses[26] and for emergency arbitrations (conducted prior to constitution of the arbitral tribunal).[27] More generally, many institutions have also instituted case management mechanisms, such as overseeing the progress of proceedings, admonishing arbitral tribunals and providing guidance on conducting proceedings efficiently, to ensure that arbitral proceedings are conducted with maximal expedition.[28]

Third, and relatedly, international arbitration is also generally more efficient and cost-effective than litigation. That is particularly true when litigation involves parallel or multiple proceedings in different national courts – as often occurs where parties from different jurisdictions have not agreed upon an exclusive forum for dispute resolution. Almost inevitably, the cost and other burdens of multiple dispute resolution proceedings will significantly exceed those of a single proceeding.[29]

Even where only a single litigation is concerned, the costs of more lengthy judicial proceedings, with multiple levels of appeal, generally exceed those of arbitral proceedings; the efficiency of the arbitral process is again enhanced by the parties' ability to select expert decision-makers, picked for specific disputes and therefore generally able to conduct proceedings more expeditiously and cost-effectively. The costs of dispute resolution consist in large part of the costs of legal representation and management time, both of which are generally directly dependent on the length of proceedings; the expedition of the arbitral process therefore ordinarily translates into efficiency and cost-effectiveness.

Moreover, the procedures used in international arbitration are those agreed upon by the parties or, absent agreement, directed by the tribunal,

---

25. *See* 2021 ICC Rules, Art. 30(2); 2016 SIAC Rules, Rule 5.1; 2014 ICDR Rules, Art. 1(4); 2018 HKIAC Administered Arbitration Rules, Art. 42(1); 2015 CIETAC Arbitration Rules, Art. 56.1; 2017 SCC Expedited Arbitration Rules. In both institutional and *ad hoc* arbitration, virtually all national laws, including the UNCITRAL Model Law, provide for judicial non-intervention in the arbitral proceedings, further enhancing the efficiency of the arbitral process. Born, *The Principle of Judicial Non-Interference in International Arbitration Proceedings*, 30 U. Pa. J. Int'l L. 999 (2009).
26. *See, e.g.*, 2021 ICC Rules, Art. 22; 2016 SIAC Rules, Rule 29; 2020 LCIA Rules, Art. 22.1; 1966 ICSID Convention (Arbitration Rules), Rule 41(5); 2017 SCC Rules, Art. 39.
27. *See, e.g.*, 2021 ICC Rules, Art. 29; 2016 SIAC Rules, Rule 30.2 and Schedule 1; 2014 ICDR Rules, Art. 6; 2020 LCIA Rules, Art. 9B; 2018 HKIAC Rules, Schedule 4.
28. *See, e.g.*, 2021 ICC Rules, Art 24; 2016 SIAC Rules, Art. 27; 2020 LCIA Rules, Art. 22.
29. UNCITRAL, Explanatory Note by the *UNCITRAL Secretariat on the 1985 Model Law on International Commercial Arbitration as Amended in 2006* ¶15 (2008) ("the parties to an arbitration agreement make a conscious decision to exclude court jurisdiction and prefer the finality and expediency of the arbitral process"). *See also* G. Born, *International Commercial Arbitration* 83-85 (3d ed. 2021); Stipanowich, *Arbitration and Choice: Taking Charge of the "New Litigation"*, 7 DePaul Bus. & Comm. L.J. 383 (2009); Sussman, *Why Arbitrate: The Benefits and Savings*, 7 Transnat'l Disp. Mgt 2 (2010).

based on the circumstances and needs of particular parties and disputes.[30] The resulting flexibility and bespoke character of the arbitral procedures, including the use of site inspections, witness conferencing, fast-track procedures, remote or virtual hearings and the like, again contribute materially to the efficiency of the arbitral process.[31] In contrast, national court litigation almost always uses 'one size fits all' procedures that impose on the parties relatively standardised procedures, designed for all manner of disputes, that necessarily lack the flexibility and efficiency of the arbitral process.[32] As one court summarised these procedural advantages:

> There are myriad reasons why parties may choose to resolve disputes by arbitration rather than litigation ... to choose arbitration by other crucial considerations such as confidentiality, procedural flexibility and the choice of arbitrators with particular technical or legal expertise better suited to grasp the intricacies of the particular dispute or the choice of law. Another crucial factor that cannot be overlooked is the finality of the arbitral process. Arbitration is not viewed by commercial persons as simply the first step on a tiresome ladder of appeals. It is meant to be the first and only step.[33]

Fourth, international arbitration is also more even-handed than litigation in most national courts. As already discussed, arbitral proceedings are conducted by tribunals selected consensually by the parties or, failing mutual agreement, by an arbitral institution which the parties have selected.[34] In both cases, the arbitral tribunal is, as between the parties,

---

30. *See, e.g.*, G. Born, *International Commercial Arbitration* 81-83 (3d ed. 2021); Drahozal, *Business Courts and the Future of Arbitration*, 10 Cardozo J. Conflict Resol. 491 (2008-09) (citing control of parties over decision-maker and procedural flexibility); Rau, *The Culture of American Arbitration and the Lessons of ADR*, 40 Tex. Int'l L.J. 449, 534 (2005) ("parties can experiment with dispute resolution – cutting and tailoring, shaping and adapting different processes to meet their own particular needs").

31. Queen Mary, University of London, *2008 International Arbitration Survey: International Arbitration: Corporate Attitudes and Practices* 2, 5 (2008) ("Flexibility of procedure" cited as prime advantage of international arbitration). *See also* T. Stipanowich & P. Kaskell, *Commercial Arbitration at Its Best: Successful Strategies for Business Users: A Report of the CPR Commission on the Future of Arbitration*, xxiii (2001) ("Ultimately, control over the process – the flexibility to make arbitration what you want it to be – [is] the single most important advantage of binding arbitration.").

32. Stipanowich & Lamare, *Living with ADR: Evolving Perceptions and Use of Mediation, Arbitration and Conflict Management in Fortune 1,000 Corporations*, 19 Harv. Neg. L. Rev. 1, 20 (2014) ("Most respondents believed arbitration to be 'better, faster and cheaper than litigation.'").

33. *Sumito v. Antig Invs. Pte Ltd*, [2009] SGCA 41, ¶29 (Singapore Ct. App.).

34. G. Born, *International Commercial Arbitration* 1764-67 (3d ed. 2021); Queen Mary, University of London, *2018 International Arbitration Survey: The Evolution of International Arbitration* 7 (2018) ("ability of parties to select arbitrators" is fourth most frequently

even-handed and neutral. Those qualities are safeguarded by essentially universal requirements that the arbitrators be independent and impartial,[35] and that the sole or presiding arbitrator have a nationality different from that of either of the parties.[36] Institutional arbitration rules provide fast-track challenge mechanisms which require disclosure by arbitrators of potential conflicts of interest and permit challenges to and removal of arbitrators who lack the required neutrality and even-handedness.

In contrast, national courts almost always lack comparable neutrality and independence as between the parties. Parties frequently litigate international disputes in their own home courts, with, for example, a US party choosing to litigate in Texas state courts, before a Texan jury, in a dispute with a French, Malaysian or Brazilian counter-party; conversely, the French counter-party will also choose to litigate in its own home courts, whether in Paris or elsewhere. In both cases, however, local courts will inevitably lack the even-handedness of a neutral international arbitral proceeding.

Moreover, it is an unfortunate reality that many national courts lack the independence and integrity that is appropriate for international commercial dispute resolution. Numerous empirical studies of corruption in judicial proceedings have documented pervasive corruption in many national court systems.[37] Those findings include numerous jurisdictions in

cited advantage of arbitration). *See also* J. Scott, *The Proceedings of the Hague Peace Conference, Translation of the Official Texts*, II The Conference of 1907, Meetings of the First Commission 698, 704 (1921) (L. Bourgeois) ("[a] judge whom you can choose for yourself, bearing in mind the nature of your case, is humanly a more satisfying decider than one produced, especially in our lower courts, by a political process which has not always been geared to select the best possible man or even a fairly respectable and able man.").

35. *Judgment of 2 June 1989, Gemanco v. Arabe des Engrais Phosphates et Azotes*, 1991 Rev. Arb. 87, 87 (Paris Cour d'Appel) ("[t]he independence of the arbitrator emanates from his judicial function"); Hascher, *Independence and Impartiality of Arbitrators: 3 Issues*, 27 Am. U. Int'l L. Rev. 789, 790-92 (2012); Timmer, *The Quality, Independence and Impartiality of the Arbitrator in International Commercial Arbitration*, 78 Int'l J. Arb. Med. & Disp. Mgt. 348, 349-51 (2012).

36. G. Born, *International Commercial Arbitration* 1868-71 (3d ed. 2021); Lalive, *On the Neutrality of the Arbitrator and of the Place of Arbitration*, in C. Reymond & E. Bucher (eds.), *Swiss Essays on International Arbitration* 23, 24 (1984) (presiding or sole arbitrator's neutrality includes national neutrality: "the fundamental idea of equality of the parties ... appears necessarily to imply and lead to the 'neutral nationality' of the arbitrator"). *See* Art. 20; 2013 UNCITRAL Rules, Art. 6(7); 2021 ICC Rules, Art. 13(5); 2014 ICDR Rules, Art. 12(4) ("At the request of any party or on its own initiative, the Administrator may appoint nationals of a country other than that of any of the parties"); 2020 LCIA Rules, Art. 6(1); 2018 HKIAC Rules, Arts. 11(2)-(3); ICSID Convention, Art. 38; 2017 SCC Rules, Art. 17(6); 2020 WIPO Rules.

37. IBA, *The International Bar Association Judicial Integrity Initiative: Judicial Systems and Corruption* (2016); Transparency International, *Corruption Perceptions Index 2018* (2018); Transparency International, *Corruption Perceptions Index 2011* (2011); Transparency International, *Global Corruption Report 2007: Corruption in Judicial Systems* xxi (2007) ("Corruption is undermining justice in many parts of the world, denying victims and the accused the basic human right to a fair and impartial trial"). *See also* Gloppen, *Courts,*

all geographical regions of the world, including in a number of significant international markets. Even absent findings of outright judicial corruption, national court proceedings lack the neutrality of arbitration: national court judges may be elected, or cases may be decided by lay juries (prone to local bias), and, in any event, local judges inevitably do not possess the national neutrality of arbitral tribunals.

Concerns about even-handedness are particularly acute in cases involving States and State-related entities (which comprise some 15–20 per cent of all international arbitrations). In these circumstances, the neutrality of national courts, involving disputes with local governmental entities, is particularly problematic. In contrast, international arbitration again provides a genuinely independent and impartial decision-maker, rather than one affiliated with and, in varying degrees, dependent upon one of the parties.

Fifth, international arbitration enjoys enforceability premiums, by comparison with litigation in national courts. The 1958 United Nations Convention on the Recognition and Enforcement of Foreign Arbitral Awards (New York Convention) is an essentially universal treaty.[38] Together with other international treaties, including the Inter-American Convention on International Commercial Arbitration[39] and the European Convention on International Commercial Arbitration,[40] the New York Convention ensures that both international arbitration agreements and arbitral awards are readily enforceable, subject to only limited exceptions, around the world.[41] In particular, Article II of the New York Convention

---

Corruption and Judicial Independence in T. Søreide & A. Williams (eds.), *Corruption, Grabbing and Development: Real World Challenges* 68-69 (2014).

38. United Nations Convention on the Recognition and Enforcement of Foreign Arbitral Awards , 330 U.N.T.S., No. 4739 (1958) ("New York Convention"). *See* G. Born, *International Commercial Arbitration* 98-120 (3d ed. 2021). *See also* note 55.

39. Inter-American Convention on International Commercial Arbitration ("Inter-American Convention"), 1438 U.N.T.S 245 (1975). *See* G. Born, *International Commercial Arbitration* 120-21 (3d ed. 2020).

40. European Convention on International Commercial Arbitration ("European Convention"), 484 U.N.T.S. 349 (1961); A. Zeiler & G. Siwy (eds.), *The European Convention on International Commercial Arbitration: A Commentary* (2018); Hascher, *European Convention on International Commercial Arbitration of 1961: Commentary*, XX Y.B. Comm. Arb. 1006 (1995).

41. G. Born, *International Commercial Arbitration* 104-08 (3d ed. 2020). *See, e.g., Comm'n Imp. Exp. SA v. Congo*, 751 F.3d 321, 324 (D.C. Cir. 2014) ("The Convention is a multilateral treaty that, with exceptions, obligates participating countries to honor international commercial arbitration agreements and to recognize and enforce arbitral awards rendered pursuant to such agreements"); *IMC Aviation Solutions Pty Ltd v. Altain Khuder LLC*, [2011] VSCA 248, ¶45 n.16 (Victoria Ct. App.) ("The New York Convention is widely recognised in international arbitration circles as having a 'pro-enforcement' policy"); *Hainan Mach. Imp. & Exp. Corp. v. Donald & McArthy Pte Ltd*, XXII Y.B. Comm. Arb. 771, 778 (Singapore High Ct. 1995) (1997) ("principle of comity of nations requires that the awards of foreign arbitration tribunals be given due deference and be enforced unless exceptional circumstances exist"); *Judgment of*

requires Contracting States to recognise the validity of international arbitration agreements and to refer parties to such agreements to arbitration (rather than permitting litigation in national courts),[42] while Articles III, IV and V require Contracting States to recognise and enforce foreign and non-domestic arbitral awards, subject to only limited and narrow exceptions.[43]

In contrast, there is no equivalent to the New York Convention for either national court judgments or forum selection clauses. The 2005 Convention on Choice of Court Agreements (Hague Convention) would arguably parallel the New York Convention, for forum selection clauses and resulting national court judgments, but most States have declined to ratify the Hague Convention[44] – owing to doubts about the wisdom of undertaking to enforce judgments from jurisdictions where courts may lack independence and impartiality. Moreover, the UNCITRAL Model Law provides an effective and internationally uniform means of implementing

3 June 1988, XV Y.B. Comm. Arb. 498, 499 (Florence Corte di Appello) (1990) ("The New York Convention clearly aimed at making the enforcement of foreign arbitral awards easier").
42. New York Convention, Arts. II(1) & II(3). *See Sabbagh v. Khoury* [2019] EWCA Civ 1219, ¶52 (English Ct. App.) ("Article II(3) requires the court of a contracting state, at the request of a party, to refer the parties to arbitration"); *Midmark Corp. v. Janak Healthcare Pvt Ltd*, 2014 WL 1513009, at *8 (S.D. Ohio) ("[T]here is nothing discretionary about Article II(3) of the Convention. The language of the treaty and its statutory incorporation provide for no exceptions. When any party seeks arbitration, if the agreement falls within the convention, we must compel the arbitration unless the agreement is 'null and void, inoperative, or incapable of being performed.'"); *Judgment of 30 September 2010*, 2011 NJW-RR 569, 570 (German Bundesgerichtshof) ("With the New York Convention, the enforcement of arbitration agreements should be facilitated internationally"); *Hi-Fert Pty Ltd v. Kiukiang Maritime Carriers Inc.*, [1998] 86 FCR 374, 393 (Australian Fed. Ct.) ("Court must stay the proceedings and refer the parties to arbitration").
43. New York Convention, Arts. III, IV & V. *See Ekran OAO v. Magneco Metrel UK Ltd* [2017] EWHC 2208 (Comm) (English High Ct.) ("The grounds on which recognition and/or enforcement may be refused are set out in §103, which implements Art. V of the Convention"); *Judgment of 9 December 2008*, XXXIV Y.B. Comm. Arb. 810, 813 (Swiss Fed. Trib.) (2009) ("New York Convention "aims at facilitating the recognition of foreign arbitral awards"); *Admart AG v. Stephen & Mary Birch Found., Inc.*, 457 F.3d 302, 307 (3d Cir. 2006) ("Under the Convention, a district court's role is limited – it must confirm the award unless one of the grounds for refusal specified in the Convention applies to the underlying award"); *Rosseel NV v. Oriental Commercial & Shipping (U.K.) Ltd* [1991] 2 Lloyd's Rep 625, 628 (Comm) (English High Ct.) ("If none of the grounds for refusal are present, the award 'shall' be enforced"); *Imbar Maratima SA v. Gabon*, XV Y.B. Comm. Arb. 436, 439 (Cayman Islands Grand Ct. 1989) (1990) ("It is plain upon the wording of subsect. (1) that enforcement of a Convention award duly evidenced is mandatory upon this court except in one or other of the circumstances detailed in [the implementing legislation for Article V of the Convention].").
44. Hague Convention on Choice of Courts Agreements. As of April 2020, two states (Montenegro and Singapore) had ratified the Convention; one state (Mexico) had acceded to the Convention; and one state (the EU) had approved the Convention. *See* https://www.hcch.net/en/instruments/conventions/status-table/?cid=98; Garnett, *The Hague Choice of Court Convention: Magnum Opus or Much Ado About Nothing?*, 8(2) Transnat'l Disp. Mgt 7 (2011).

the New York Convention's provisions,[45] while no analogue exists for the Hague Convention.

As a result, at least for the foreseeable future, international arbitration enjoys a significant enforceability premium by comparison with national court proceedings. In turn, that enforceability premium enhances the expedition and efficiency of the arbitral process – ensuring that the parties' agreements to arbitrate their disputes, and arbitral awards resolving them, will be given effect promptly and effectively.

Finally, and most recently, international arbitration appears to have acquired a sixth advantage – making for six Es. The COVID-19 pandemic has forced international arbitration to become more electronic, with filings in arbitration being made entirely online and hearings being conducted remotely. Arbitral institutions and tribunals, as well as counsel, have responded to regulations preventing physical in-person hearings by using on-line platforms such as Web-Ex, Zoom, Teams and the like to conduct remote (or virtual) hearings involving participants from multiple different locations.[46] The flexibility of the arbitral process has permitted such procedural innovations to be developed and applied, ultimately globally, over a very short period of time – contributing significantly to the efficiency of the arbitral process by avoiding the need for travel and accommodation for large numbers of participants.

In contrast, many national court systems have struggled with remote hearings. In some jurisdictions, where lay juries are customary or required, remote hearings are impossible or extremely difficult. In other jurisdictions, mistrust of remote proceedings or lack of infrastructure or judicial training have impeded the use of technology. It also appears likely that

---

45. UNCITRAL, *Note by the Secretary-General*, U.N. Doc. A/CN.9/127, VIII Y.B. UNCITRAL 233 (1977); Sanders, *Unity and Diversity in the Adoption of the Model Law*, 11 Arb. Int'l 1 (1995). *See also* G. Born, *International Commercial Arbitration* 139-46 (3d ed. 2021); *TCL Air Conditioner (Zhongshan) Co. v. Judges of the Federal Court of Australia*, [2013] HCA 5, ¶7 (Australian High Ct.) ("The origin of some of [the Model Law's] key provisions, including Arts 35 and 36, may be traced to provisions of the [New York Convention] ... Those considerations of international origin and international application make imperative that the Model Law be construed without any assumptions that it embodies common law concepts or that it will apply only to arbitral awards or arbitration agreements that are governed by common law principles. The first of those considerations makes equally imperative that so much of the text of the Model Law as has its origin in the New York Convention be construed in the context, and in the light of the object and purpose, of the New York Convention").

46. ICC, Guidance Note on Possible Measures Aimed at Mitigating the Effect of the COVID-19 Pandemic (9 Apr. 2020), para. 23); SIAC, Taking Your Arbitration Remote (31 Aug. 2020);AAA-ICDR, Virtual Hearing Guide for Arbitrators and Parties; Delos, Checklist on Holding Arbitration and Mediation Hearings in Times of COVID-19 (20 Mar. 2020); HKIAC, Precautionary Measures in Response to COVID-19 (26 Mar. 2020); ICSID, A Brief Guide to Online Hearings at ICSID (24 Mar. 2020); Scherer, *Remote Hearings in International Arbitration: An Analytical Framework*, 37 J. Int'l Arb. 407, 433-38 (2020).

national courts will revert to in-person proceedings when health regulations permit, while arbitration seems equally likely to continue to use technological tools to enhance the efficiency and expedition of the dispute resolution process.

For these, as well as other,[47] reasons, international arbitration has been used increasingly in virtually all economic sectors and geographic regions. There have been periodic criticisms of arbitration,[48] particularly in specialised contexts such as consumer,[49] employment[50] and investment[51] disputes, as well as significant procedural and other reforms in some such contexts.[52] Nonetheless, international arbitration has become progressively more widely used, and more popular, over the past four decades.

47. Queen Mary, University of London, *2018 International Arbitration Survey: The Evolution of International Arbitration 7*, 24 (2018) ("87% of respondents believe that confidentiality in international commercial arbitration is of importance"); Queen Mary, University of London, *2013 International Arbitration Survey: Corporate Choices in International Arbitration: Industry Perspectives* 8 (2013) (neutrality ranked second in order of importance among seven perceived benefits of arbitration.); Queen Mary, University of London, *2006 International Arbitration Survey: International Arbitration: Corporate Attitudes and Practices* 6 (2006) ("The ability of parties to select arbitrators with the necessary skills and expertise and who are well suited to the appropriate cultural and legal context was also ranked highly"; 4th among reasons cited by corporations surveyed).

48. *See, e.g.*, Queen Mary, University of London, *2018 International Arbitration Survey: The Evolution of International Arbitration* 7-8, 27 (2018) ("Previous surveys by the School dating as far back as 2006 have shown that users are most discontent with the 'cost' of arbitration. The current survey continues to confirm this trend as 'cost' is yet again the most selected option, and by a significant margin ... A number of respondents and interviewees referred to what the 2015 survey called the 'due process paranoia' of arbitrators as a probable reason for this continued lack of proactiveness"). *See also* Lyons, *Arbitration: The Slower, More Expensive Alternative*, Am. Law. 107 (Jan./Feb. 1985); Silberman, *International Arbitration: Comments from A Critic*, 13 Am. Rev. Int'l Arb. 9 (2002).

49. *See, e.g.*, Cole & Blankley, *Empirical Research on Consumer Arbitration: What the Data Reveals*, 113 Penn. St. L. Rev. 1051 (2009); Bates, *A Consumer's Dream or Pandora's Box: Is Arbitration A Viable Option for Cross-Border Consumer Disputes?*, 27 Fordham Int'l L. J. 823, 845-85 (2003).

50. *See, e.g.*, Schwartz, *Enforcing Small Print to Protect Big Business: Employee and Consumer Rights Claims in an Age of Compelled Arbitration*, 1997 Wis. L. Rev. 33, 36-40, 69-82, 101-04, 106-30 (arguing that clauses requiring pre-dispute arbitration prevent employees from exercising statutory rights and favor employers); Stone, *Mandatory Arbitration of Individual Employment Rights: The Yellow Dog Contract of the 1990s*, 73 Den. U. L. Rev. 1017, 1019-20, 1036-49 (1996) (mandatory employment arbitration clauses in hiring contracts raise due process concerns because employees "lack bargaining power and are needful of employment").

51. Waibel, Kaushal, et. al., *The Backlash Against Investment Arbitration: Perceptions and Reality* in M. Waibel, *et al.* (eds.), *The Backlash Against Investment Arbitration* xxxvii (2010); Faure & Ma, *Investor-State Arbitration: Economic and Empirical Economic and Empirical Perspectives*, 41 Mich. J. Int'l L. 1 (2020); Marceddu & Ortolani, *What Is Wrong with Investment Arbitration? Evidence from a Set of Behavioural Experiments*, 31 EJIL 405 (2020); Nolan, *Challenges To The Credibility Of The Investor-State Arbitration System*, 5 Am. U. Bus. L. Rev. 429, 430-40 (2018).

52. Lyons, *Arbitration: The Slower, More Expensive Alternative*, Am. Law. 107 (Jan./Feb.

II. INTERNATIONAL ARBITRATION: THE RIGHT TO ARBITRATE

As noted above, one of the reasons for the increasing use and popularity of international arbitration is the legal framework within which international arbitral proceedings are conducted. In particular, States from all regions of the world have, over the past five decades, adopted a wide variety of 'pro-arbitration' legal instruments and both national courts and arbitral tribunals have given robust effect to these instruments. At the same time, and consistent with the historic ubiquity of the arbitral process, national courts and other authorities have also increasingly recognised the funda-mental importance of arbitration to the rule of law and basic conceptions of individual autonomy.

The cornerstone of the contemporary international legal framework for international arbitration is the New York Convention, referred to above. Drafted in 1958, the Convention now has 166 Contracting States,[53] making it essentially universal. The Convention imposes mandatory international legal obligations on Contracting States to: (a) recognise the presumptive validity of international arbitration agreements, and refer disputes subject to such agreements to arbitration, subject only to limited exceptions;[54] and (b) recognise the presumptive validity of foreign and non-domestic arbitral awards, again subject only to limited exceptions.[55] Taken together, these

---

1985); Alvarez, *et al., A Response to the Criticism against ISDS by EFILA*, 33 J. Int'l. Arb. 1 (2016); Buehler, *Costs in ICC Arbitration: A Practitioner's View*, 3 Am. Rev. Int'l Arb. 116 (1992); Silva, *An Answer to Criticisms Against the Lack of Efficiency in Arbitration: Measures to Reduce Time and Costs*, 14 Revista Brasileira de Arbitragem 23 (2017); Touzet & Vaublanc, *The Investor-State Dispute Settlement System: The Road To Overcoming Criticism Buehler*, Kluwer Arbitration Blog (6 August 2018).

53. *See* UNCITRAL, Status: 1958 Convention on the Recognition and Enforcement of Foreign Arbitral Awards at https://uncitral.un.org/ (for list of contracting states).

54. New York Convention, Art. II(1). *See also Midmark Corp. v. Janak Healthcare Pvt Ltd*, 2014 WL 1513009, at *8 (S.D. Ohio) ("[T]here is nothing discretionary about Article II(3) of the Convention. The language of the treaty and its statutory incorporation provide for no exceptions. When any party seeks arbitration, if the agreement falls within the convention, we must compel the arbitration unless the agreement is 'null and void, inoperative, or incapable of being performed.'"); *Polimaster Ltd v. RAE Sys.*, Inc., 623 F.3d 832, 841 (9th Cir. 2010) ("the New York Convention was enacted to promote the enforceability of international arbitration agreements"); *Judgment of 30 September 2010*, 2011 NJW-RR 570, 571 (German Bundesgerichtshof) ("[Convention] was intended to facilitate the enforcement of arbitration agreements").

55. New York Convention, Art. V(1). *See also KB v. S*, [2016] 2 HKC 325, ¶48 (H.K. High Ct.) ("The Court's task should be as mechanistic as possible … not entitled to go behind the award by exploring the reasoning of the tribunal or second-guessing its intention"); *Hainan Mach. Imp. & Exp. Corp. v. Donald & McArthy Pte Ltd*, XXII Y.B. Comm. Arb. 771, 778 (Singapore High Ct. 1995) (1997) ("principle of comity of nations requires that the awards of foreign arbitration tribunals be given due deference and be enforced unless exceptional circumstances exist"); Born, *International Commercial Arbitration* 3433-35 (3d ed. 2021).

provisions provide what is effectively a global constitutional charter for international commercial arbitration.[56]

Although the New York Convention is the most important, and most universal, of all international treaties dealing with the arbitral process, other multilateral and bilateral treaties also address the issue. In virtually all cases, these instruments parallel the two basic features of the New York Convention cited above. Thus, the Inter-American Convention on International Commercial Arbitration,[57] the European Convention on International Commercial Arbitration,[58] and the 1972 Convention on the Settlement by Arbitration of Civil Law Disputes Arising out of Economic, Scientific and Technical Co-Operation Relationships (Moscow Convention)[59] all mandate recognition of international arbitration agreements and arbitral awards.

The same is true of bilateral friendship, commerce and navigation treaties, many of which had (and have) comparable, if less extensive, provisions requiring recognition of arbitration agreements and arbitral awards.[60] Although it is unclear how many such treaties are in force, there

---

56. H. Kronke *et al.* (eds.), *Recognition and Enforcement of Foreign Arbitral Awards: A Global Commentary on the New York Convention* (2010); R. Wolff (ed.), *New York Convention: Convention on the Recognition and Enforcement of Foreign Arbitral Awards of 10 June 1958* (2012); Born, *The New York Convention: A Self-Executing Treaty*, 40 Mich. J. Int'l L. 115 (2018) ("the world's most significant legislative instrument relating to international commercial arbitration ... provides a global constitutional charter for the international arbitral process.").

57. Inter-American Convention, Art. 1, 4-5. *See* G. Born, *International Commercial Arbitration* 122-23 (3d ed. 2021); H.R. Rep. No. 501, 101st Cong., 2d Sess. 4 (1990), reprinted in 1990 U.S.C.C.A.N. 675, 678 ("The New York Convention and the Inter-American Convention are intended to achieve the same results, and their key provisions adopt the same standards, phrased in the legal style appropriate for each organization. It is the Committee's expectation, in view of that fact and the parallel legislation under the Federal Arbitration Act that would be applied to the Conventions, that courts in the United States would achieve a general uniformity of results under the two conventions.").

58. European Convention, Arts. II(1), IV and V(1). *See* G. Born, *International Commercial Arbitration* 120-21 (3d ed. 2021); A. van den Berg, *The New York Arbitration Convention of 1958* 93 (1981).

59. 1972 Convention On The Settlement By Arbitration Of Civil Law Disputes Arising Out Of Economic, Scientific And Technical Co-Operation Relationships, May 26 1972, 890 U.N.T.S. 172, Art. II(1) and V(1).

60. *See, e.g.*, Treaty of Friendship, Commerce and Navigation, 29 October 1954, 7 U.S.T. 1839, T.I.A.S. No. 3593 (U.S.–Germany), Art. 6(2) (1954) ("Contracts entered into between nationals or companies of either party and nationals or companies of the other party that provide for settlement by arbitration of controversies shall not be deemed unenforceable within the territories of such other party merely on the grounds that the place designated for arbitration proceedings is outside such territories or that the nationality of one or more of the arbitrators is not that of such other party. Awards duly rendered pursuant to any such contracts which are final and enforceable under the laws of the place where rendered shall be deemed conclusive in enforcement proceedings brought before the courts of competent jurisdiction of either party, and shall be entitled to be declared enforceable by such courts, except where found contrary to public policy"); Convention of Establishment, Protocol,

is clearly a very substantial body of bilateral agreements that also prescribe the same basic rules with respect to arbitration agreements and arbitral awards, as does the New York Convention.

Similarly, in the context of investment arbitration, the Convention on the Settlement of Investment Disputes between States and Nationals of Other States (ICSID Convention) with 155 Contracting States, is also essentially universal.[61] That Convention parallels the provisions of the New York Convention, but with respect to (some) investment arbitration agreements and arbitral awards – again, making both presumptively valid and enforceable.[62] Relatedly, many states have concluded bilateral investment treaties (with some 3,000 currently in force), almost always providing for arbitration of investment disputes with specified foreign investors[63] – with both the resulting arbitration agreements and awards being final and binding on the States.[64] A number of multilateral treaties

and Declaration, Nov. 25, 1959, United States-France, 11 U.S.T. 2398 Treaty of Friendship, Commerce, and Navigation, Oct. 29, 1954, United States-West Germany, 7 U.S.T. 1839; Treaty of Friendship, Commerce and Navigation, Mar. 27, 1956, United States-Netherlands, 8 U.S.T. 2043, T.I.A.S. No. 3942; Treaty of Friendship, Establishment and Navigation, Feb. 12, 1961, United States-Belgium, 14 U.S.T. 1284, T.I.A.S. No. 5432; Treaty of Friendship, Commerce and Navigation, Oct. 1, 1951, United States-Denmark, 12 U.S.T. 908, T.I.A.S. No. 4797; Treaty of Friendship, Commerce and Navigation, Aug. 3, 1951, United States-Greece, 5 U.S.T. 1829, T.I.A.S. No. 3057.

61. *See* Convention on the settlement of investment disputes between States and nationals of other States ("ICSID Convention"), 575 U.N.T.S 159 (1966). *See also* ICSID, *List of Contracting States and Other Signatories of the Convention (as of April 12, 2019)*, available at icsid.worldbank.org. In recent years, a few states have denounced their accession to the ICSID Convention (Bolivia, Ecuador and Venezuela), while a number of other states have ratified the Convention (*e.g.*, Iraq, Mexico, Nauru, San Marino).

62. ICSID Convention, Arts. 25, 53-54; C. Schreuer *et al.*, *The ICSID Convention: A Commentary* Art. 54, ¶¶42-44 (2d ed. 2009).

63. *See, e.g.*, Agreement Concerning the Promotion and Reciprocal Protection of Investments, Denmark- Pakistan, Jul.18, 1996, 2009 U.N.T.S 473, Art.10(2)(" (2) If such a dispute cannot be settled within three months from the beginning of the dispute, it shall, upon the request of either Contracting Party, be submitted to an arbitral tribunal."); Agreement for the promotion and protection of investments, United Kingdom-Paraguay, Jun. 4, 1981, 1694 U.N.T.S 4, Art 9(2) ("If a dispute between the Contracting Parties cannot thus be settled, it shall upon the request of either Contracting Party be submitted to an arbitral tribunal."); Treaty Concerning the Reciprocal Encouragement and Protection of Investments, Germany-Bulgaria, Apr. 12, 1986, 1518 U.N.T.S 22, Art. 7; Agreement for the promotion and protection of investments, United Kingdom-Malaysia, May 21, 1981, 1579 U.N.T.S 12, Art. 7; Agreement for the Promotion and Protection of Investments, UK-Indonesia BIT, Mar. 24, 1977, UKTS 62, Art. 7(1).

64. *See, e.g.*, Broches, *Awards Rendered Pursuant to the ICSID Convention: Binding Force, Finality, Recognition, Enforcement, Execution*, 2 ICSID Rev. 287, 298 (1987); Agreement for the Promotion and Protection of Investments, United Kingdom-Croatia 2038 U.N.T.S97, Mar. 11, 1997, Art. 9(5) ("Such decision shall be binding on both Contracting Parties."); Agreement for the Promotion and Reciprocal Protection of Investments, Argentina-Lithuania, Mar. 14, 1996, 2033 U.N.T.S 260, Art. 9(5) ("The arbitral awards shall be final and binding on the parties to the dispute. Each Contracting Party shall enforce them in accordance with its legislation"); Agreement for the Promotion and Reciprocal Protection

have comparable provisions, including the Energy Charter Treaty, the ASEAN Investment Agreement, the Comprehensive and Progressive Agreement for Trans-Pacific Partnership and the ASEAN-Australia-New Zealand Agreement.[65] Like the New York Convention, and other international commercial arbitration treaties, these various investment arbitration treaties both prescribe, and rest on, the rule that international arbitration agreements and awards are presumptively valid and binding, subject only to limited and defined exceptions.

At the same time, States from all parts of the world have also enacted national arbitration legislation, often derived from the UNCITRAL Model Law. The Model Law is nearly as universal as the New York and ICSID conventions, having thus far been adopted in some form in more than 100 jurisdictions.[66] Like the New York Convention, the Model Law mandates the same two basic rules that international commercial arbitration agreements[67] and arbitral awards[68] are presumptively valid and enforceable, subject to specified and narrow exceptions. Even in jurisdictions where the Model Law has not been adopted (like the United States, France,

of Investments, Argentina-Mexico, Nov. 13, 1996, 2033 U.N.T.S 309, Art. 10(7); Agreement for the Promotion and Protection of Investments, United Kingdom-Paraguay, Jun. 4, 1981, 1694 U.N.T.S 4, Art 9(5).

65. The 1994 Energy Charter Treaty (signed 17 December 1994, entered into force 16 April 1998) 2080 U.N.T.S 100 Art. 26(1); ASEAN Comprehensive Investment Agreement (signed 26 February 2009, entered into force 29 Marcg 2013) Art. 29; Comprehensive and Progressive Agreement for Trans-Pacific Partnership (CPTPP) (signed by 11 countries on 8 March 2018 and entered into force on 30 December 2018) Chap. 28; Agreement Establishing the ASEAN-Australia-New Zealand Free Trade Area (AANZFTA) entered into force in January 2010 for Australia, Chap. 11.

66. UNCITRAL, Status: UNCITRAL Model Law on International Commercial Arbitration (1985), with amendments as adopted in 2006, at https://uncitral.un.org/ (for list of jurisdictions that adopted the Model Law). *See also* UNCITRAL, *Note by the Secretary-General*, U.N. Doc. A/CN.9/127, VIII Y.B. UNCITRAL 233 (1977); Sanders, *Unity and Diversity in the Adoption of the Model Law*, 11 Arb. Int'l 1 (1995). *See also* G. Born, *International Commercial Arbitration* 139-46 (3d ed. 2021). *See also* H. Holtzmann & J. Neuhaus, *A Guide to the UNCITRAL Model Law on International Commercial Arbitration: Legislative History and Commentary* (1989).

67. UNCITRAL Model Law, Art. 8(1). *See also* I. Bantekas, *Article 8: Arbitration Agreement and Substantive Claim Before Court*, in I. Bantekas *et al.* (eds.), *UNCITRAL Model Law on International Commercial Arbitration: A Commentary* 547 (2020); G. Born, *International Commercial Arbitration* 1352, 1359-66, 1367-68 (3d ed. 2020).

68. UNCITRAL Model Law, Art. 35(1). *See also KB v. S*, [2016] 2 HKC 325, ¶48 (H.K. High Ct.) ("The Court's task should be as mechanistic as possible ... not entitled to go behind the award by exploring the reasoning of the tribunal or second-guessing its intention"); *Carr v. Gallaway Cook Allan*, [2014] NZSC 75, ¶76 (N.Z. S.Ct.) (Article 34 "sets out an exhaustive list of the grounds on which an award may be set aside."); *Bayview Irrigation Dist. #11 v. United Mexican States*, [2008] CanLII 22120 (Ontario Super. Ct.) (grounds for setting aside awards are exhaustively enumerated in Article 34); G. Born, *International Commercial Arbitration* 3437-38 (3d ed. 2021).

Switzerland and China), those two basic rules are nonetheless codified in much the same manner.[69]

National courts have fairly consistently adopted robust, 'pro-enforcement' interpretations of both the New York Convention and other international arbitration legislation, and the Model Law. In particular, courts in a wide range of jurisdictions have recognised and enforced international commercial arbitration agreements, holding that such provisions are presumptively valid and enforceable and applying both separability and choice of law principles designed to facilitate that result.[70] National courts have reached similar conclusions with respect to foreign and non-domestic arbitral awards, recognising and enforcing them subject only to limited exceptions.[71]

In contrast, there are virtually no examples of either international treaties or national legislation that deny effect to international arbitration agreements or awards. Historic examples of such prohibitions existed in specialised fields, such as the Calvo Doctrine in the context of foreign investment in several Latin American States,[72] but those prohibitions have been almost

---

69. *See* G. Born, *International Commercial Arbitration* 259-62, 3440-47 (3d ed. 2021). *See, e.g.*, U.S. FAA, 9 U.S.C. §9; *Diapulse Corp. of Am. v. Carba, Ltd*, 626 F.2d 1108, 1110 (2d Cir. 1980); French Code of Civil Procedure, Art. 1484 ("As soon as it is made, an arbitral award shall be res judicata with regard to the claims adjudicated in that award ..."); *Judgment of 9 October 2008*, 2009 Rev. Arb. 360, 362 (French Cour de Cassation Civ. 1) ("challenge [against arbitral awards] is only available on the grounds exhaustively listed in Article 1502 of the Code of Civil Procedure"); Swiss Law on Private International Law. Art. 190; Berti & Schnyder, in S. Berti et al. (eds.), *International Arbitration in Switzerland* Art. 190, ¶1, 18 (2000) (Swiss Law on Private International Law contains an "exclusive list of grounds for the setting aside" of award).

70. *See* G. Born, *International Commercial Arbitration* 386-29, 514-20 (3d ed. 2020). *See, e.g.*, *Judgment of 20 December 1993, Municipalité de Khoms El Mergeb v. Dalico*, 1994 Rev. Arb. 116 (French Cour de Cassation Civ. 1); *Judgment of 17 December 1991, Gatoil v. Nat'l Iranian Oil Co.*, 1993 Rev. Arb. 281, 284 (Paris Cour d'Appel) ("in the field of international arbitration, the principle of the autonomy of the arbitration agreement is of general application, as an international substantive rule upholding the legality of the arbitration agreement"); *Ashville Inv. Ltd v. Elmer Contractors Ltd* [1988] 3 WLR 867 (English Ct. App.); *BG Group plc v. Argentina*, 572 U.S. 25 (U.S. 2014); *Judgment of 31 October 2018, I ZB 17/18 (German Bundesgerichtshof); Judgment of 11 May 2017*, I ZB 63/16, ¶21 (German Bundesgerichtshof) (grounds for invalidity and avoidance of underlying commercial contract do not, in principle, affect validity of arbitration agreement); *Judgment of 29 October 2008*, XII ZR 165/06, 24 (German Bundesgerichtshof) ("In case of doubt, an arbitration clause has to be interpreted widely, to the effect, that it also covers the question of the invalidity of the main contract").

71. *Pharmaniaga Berhad v. E*HealthLine.com*, Inc., 344 F.Supp.3d 1136, 1141 (E.D. Cal. 2018) ("general pro-enforcement bias"); *AO Techsnabexport v. Globe Nuclear Servs. & Supply, Ltd*, 656 F.Supp.2d 550, 554 (D. Md. 2009) ("general pro-enforcement bias"), *aff'd*, 404 F.App'x 793 (4th Cir. 2010); *Omnium de Traitement et de Valorisation SA v. Hilmarton Ltd* [1999] 2 Lloyd's Rep. 222 (Comm) (English High Ct.).

72. C. Calvo, *Derecho Internacional Teorico y Practico de Europa y America* (1868); C. Calvo, *Le Droit International Théorique et Pratique* (4th ed. 1870-72). *See* Baker & Yoder, *ICSID and the Calvo Clause: Hindrance to Foreign Direct Investment in LDCs*, 5 Ohio St. J. Disp. Resol. 75, 91 (1989); F. Garcia-Amador, 2 *The Changing Law of International Claims*

entirely revoked.[73] It is almost impossible to identify any national law or regulation, or national court decision, that rejects the presumptive validity and enforceability of international arbitration agreements and awards. This parallels the essentially universal acceptance of the parties' autonomy to select the law applicable to their international commercial contracts – which is also properly regarded as a general principle of law.[74]

Given this consensus, it is appropriate to recognise that the presumptive validity of international commercial arbitration agreements and awards, subject only to limited exceptions, has attained the status of a general principle of law. Both of those rules of presumptive validity constitute an 'obvious maxim of jurisprudence of a general and fundamental character'[75] and, together, those rules qualify as 'principles that constitute that unformulated reservoir of basic legal concepts universal in application, which exist independently of the institutions of any particular country and form the irreducible essence of all legal systems'.[76] The proper analytical basis for treating general principles of law, in domestic legal systems, as rules of international law is controversial,[77] but the status of such principles as international law, confirmed by the Statute of the International Court of Justice and otherwise, is not.[78]

481-82 (1984); Naón, *Arbitration and Latin America: Progress and Setbacks*, 21 Arb. Int'l 127, 134-37 (2005).

73. Hamilton, *International Litigation and Arbitration: Three Decades of Latin American Commercial Arbitration*, 30 U. Pa. J. Int'l L. 1099 (2009); Naón, *Arbitration in Latin America: Overcoming Traditional Hostility (An Update)*, 22 U. Miami Inter-Am. L. Rev. 203, 231-34 (1991); Preziosi, *The Andean Pact's Foreign Investment Code Decision 220: An Agreement to Disagree*, 20 U. Miami Inter-Am. L. Rev. 649, 662 (1989) ("Significantly, D220 removed the 'Calvo Clause' restriction of D24.... This is an important concession. Formerly, it was not possible to remove a dispute from the jurisdiction of the host country. Now, however, if domestic law permits, the location and the law of dispute resolution can be negotiated.").

74. Born, *Choice-of-Law-Agreements in International Contracts* (2020) (forthcoming).

75. E. Lauterpacht (ed.), *International Law* 74 (1970) (general principles of law are "principles of law, private and public, which contemplation of the legal experience of civilized nations leads one to regard as obvious maxims of jurisprudence of a general and fundamental character").

76. Friedmann, *The Uses of "General Principles" in the Development of International Law*, 57 Am. J. Int'l L. 279, 280-81, 284 (1963); Jalet, *The Quest for the General Principles of Law Recognized by Civilized Nations*, 10 U.C.L.A. L. Rev. 1041, 1044 (1963) (general principles are "principles that constitute that unformulated reservoir of basic legal concepts universal in application, which exist independently of the institutions of any particular country and form the irreducible essence of all legal systems").

77. *See* Jonathan I. Charney, *Universal International Law*, 87 Am. J. Int'l L. 529, 535-36 (1993); Cheng, *General Principles of Law as Applied by International Courts and Tribunals* 1-6 (1953).

78. *See* Lassa Oppenheim, *International Law: A Treatise* 20–25 (2d ed. 1912); *Restatement (Third) Foreign Relations Law of the United States* §102(1)(c) & comment 1 (1987) ("general principles common to the major legal systems of the world"); James Crawford, *Brownlie's Principles of Public International Law* 31-34 (9th ed. 2012).

A classic formulation of the criteria for establishing general principles of law, by the US Military Tribunal, provides:

> In determining whether a fundamental principle of justice is entitled to be declared a principle of international law, an examination of the municipal laws of States in the family of nations will reveal the answer. If it is found to have been accepted generally as a fundamental rule of justice by most nations in their municipal law, its declaration as a rule of international law would seem to be fully justified.[79]

As detailed above, the rule that international commercial arbitration agreements and awards are presumptively valid readily meets this criterion. The consensus accepting that rule is evidenced by the universal character of the New York Convention, by the wide range of related international instruments uniformly codifying and reflecting the same principles, by the uniform treatment of these issues by national law in virtually all jurisdictions and by the expectations of private parties that this rule will be respected.

There is a further, equally fundamental, reason why the presumptive validity and enforceability of international commercial arbitration agreements and awards constitute general principles of law. Both rules rest upon basic concepts of individual autonomy that are fundamental to contemporary legal systems around the world, and recognised in countless historic settings. Equally important, the presumptive validity of international arbitration agreements and awards is fundamental to the peaceful, amicable resolution of international disputes. It is peculiarly appropriate, and equally important, that these rules therefore be recognised as general principles of law.

Virtually all modern legal systems guarantee the autonomy of individuals to contract and to associate with other private parties. That autonomy is at the heart of most contemporary legal systems and is constitutionally protected in most States:[80] individuals are free to choose who they

---

79. *List and Others (Hostages Trial), United States Military Tribunal Decision of 19 February 1948,* 15 I.L.R. 632, 633 (1948). *See also* Michael Akehurst, *Equity and General Principles of Law,* 25 Int'l & Comp. L.Q. 801,813-17 (1976) ('there is only one reliable way in which a general principle of law can be proved, and that is by examining the laws of different States').

80. P.S. Atiyah, *The Rise and Fall of Freedom of Contract,* 36 (2003) ("a contract is a thing under the control of the contracting parties, and subordinate to their will."); Ely, *The Protection Of Contractual Rights: A Tale Of Two Constitutional Provisions,* 1 NYU J. L. & Lib. 370, 383 (2005) ("[T]he capacity of private parties to make economic bargains for themselves. In the late nineteenth century, courts began to constitutionalize this right to enter contracts in a free market"). *See also Printing & Numerical Registering Co. v. Sampson,* 19 L. R.-EQ. 462, 465 (M.R. 1875) ("It must not be forgotten that you are not to extend arbitrarily those rules which say that a given contract is void as being against public policy, because

will contract with, and how, and who they will associate with, and how.[81] Equally fundamental is the right of the parties to such contracts, associations and other types of relationship to choose how to mend and preserve those relationships through amicable resolution of the disputes that inevitably arise from free association. That right to mend relationships is no less important than the right to decide whether and how to enter into and structure those relationships.

Put simply, at the heart of individual autonomy is the right to arbitrate. That right ensures private parties the freedom to choose, voluntarily and consensually, to resolve disputes by way of a decision-maker chosen by the parties themselves – which, as noted above, is the essential characteristic of the arbitral process.[82]

The fundamental importance of this right to arbitrate has been recognised, in widely diverse settings, by courts and legislatures around the world. One of the earliest academic discussions of arbitration was by Gerard Malynes, in his 1622 treatise entitled *Consuetudo, vel, Lex Mercatoria*, where he described arbitration of commercial matters as follows:

> The second meane or rather ordinarie course to end the questions and controversies arising between Merchants, is by way of Arbitrement, when both parties do make choice of honest men to end their causes, which is voluntarie and in their own power, and therefore called Arbitrium, or free will, whence the name Arbitrator is derived: and these men (by some called Good men) give their judgments by Awards, according to Equitie and Conscience, observing the Custome of Merchants, and ought to be void of all partialitie or affection more nor lesse to the one, than to the other, having onely care that right may

if there is one thing which more than another public policy requires it is that men of full age and competent understanding shall have the utmost liberty of contracting, and that their contracts when freely and voluntarily entered into shall be held sacred and shall be enforced by Courts of justice. Therefore, you have this paramount public policy to consider – that you are not to lightly interfere with this freedom of contract. Classical contract theory's emphasis on unrestricted freedom of contract had its roots in nineteenth century political philosophy, which declared 'the end of man is freedom.'").

81. Born, *Arbitration and the Freedom to Associate*, 38 Ga. J. Int'l & Comp. L. 7 (2009); Carolyn, *Freedom of Contract and Fundamental Fairness for Individual Parties: The Tug of War Continues* 77 UMKC L. Rev. 647 (2009); Cohen, *The Basis of Contract*, 46 Harv. L. Rev. 553 (1933); Pound, *Liberty of Contract*, 18 Yale L. J. 454 (1909); Pound, *The End of Law as Developed in Juristic Thought II*, 30 Harv. L. Rev. 201, 204 (1917); Zhaohua, *Party Autonomy, Private Autonomy, and Freedom of Contract*, 10(6) Can. Soc. Sci. 212 (2014).

82. J. Delvolvé, J. Rouche and G. Pointon, *French Arbitration Law and Practice: A Dynamic Civil Law Approach to International Arbitration*, ¶26 (2009) ("recognizes that parties have the right to refer their disputes for resolution by a third party who is called an arbitrator"); Zhaohua, *Party Autonomy, Private Autonomy, and Freedom of Contract*, 10(6) Canadian Social Science 212, 212 (2014).

take place according the truth, and that the difference may be ended with brevitie and expedition.[83]

In addition to expressing an early version of the Five Es (expertise in 'observing the Custome of Merchants'; absence of 'all partialitie or affection'; 'brevitie and expedition'), Malynes' description emphasised the basic character of arbitration as a means of dispute resolution 'which is voluntary and in their own power, and therefore called Arbitrium, or free will'.

The Constitution of Year One[84] in 18th-century Revolutionary France recognised that same conception of arbitration, along with liberty, equality and fraternity, in Article 86: '[n]o encroachment can be made upon the right of citizens to have their matters in dispute decided upon by an arbitrator of their own choice'.[85] That Article gave constitutional status to the right of individual citizens to resolve their disputes by arbitration, with arbitrators selected by the citizens themselves.

It was no coincidence that the Constitution of Year One accorded constitutional status to the right to arbitrate. The monarchy of the *Ancien* Régime had, like other similar regimes, used the judiciary as a means to oppress the French citizenry;[86] arbitration provided a bulwark against continued royal or aristocratic oppression by ensuring that disputes between private parties could be resolved by arbitrators chosen by those parties, rather than imposed by the State.[87] Again unsurprisingly, arbitration was historically

---

83. G. Malynes, *Consuetudo, vel, Lex Mercatoria, or The Ancient Law Merchant: Divided into Three Parts: According to the Essentials Parts of Trafficke: Necessarie for All Statesmen, Judges, Magistrates, Temporal and Civil Lawyers, Mint-men, Merchants, Mariners, and All Others Negotiating in All Places of the World* Chp. XV (1622). *See also id.* at Chp. XV (3d ed. 1685) ("when Merchants by their Letters or Commissions use these or the like words, Let All things be done as shall be thought most expedient or convenient, that the said Commissions or Directions are to be left to the interpretation of Arbitrators when any question ariseth, which is also in many more questions concerning Merchants").

84. Year One of the Revolutionary calendar ran from 22 September 1792 to 21 September 1793, but was in fact so designated retrospectively, the calendar having been introduced in Year Two. The calendar was abolished by Emperor Napoleon I in 1806.

85. French Constitution of Year I, 1793, Art. 86; French Constitution of Year III, 1795, Art. 210 ("The right to choose arbitrators in any dispute shall not be violated in any way whatsoever"). *See* Clère, *L'Arbitrage Révolutionnaire: Apogée et Déclin d'Une Institution (1790-1806),* 1981 Rev. Arb. 3, 5-6; Hilaire, *L'Arbitrage Dans la Période Moderne (XVIe-XVIIIe siècle),* 2000 Rev. Arb. 187. I have copied verbatim from the treatise (fn. 269) "Clère, L'Arbitrage Révolutionnaire: Apogée et Déclin d'Une Institution (1790-1806), 1981 Rev. Arb. 3, 5-6; Hilaire, L'Arbitrage Dans la Période Moderne (XVIe-XVIIIe siècle), 2000 Rev. Arb. 187.

86. Clère, *L'Arbitrage Révolutionnaire: Apogée et Déclin d'Une Institution (1790-1806),* 1981 Rev. Arb. 3, 5-6; Hilaire, *L'Arbitrage Dans la Période Moderne (XVIe-XVIIIe siècle),* 2000 Rev. Arb. 187.

87. Articles 1003 to 1028 of the 1806 Code of Civil Procedure introduced an extremely unfavourable legal regime for arbitration. *See* Clére, *L'Arbitrage Révolutionnaire: Apogée et*

used in other similar circumstances as a protection of the people against potential oppression by the State – including the Beth Din during the Roman era in the Middle East[88] and Europe.[89] Similar rationales underlay the use of jury systems, specialised courts and similar types of dispute resolution mechanism in other historical settings.[90]

The same recognition of a right to arbitrate, and its fundamental importance to individual rights, occurred elsewhere in Europe. The 1877 German Code of Civil Procedure prescribed a liberal, pro-arbitration regime, while 19th century and early 20th century German courts issued decisions embracing the separability of arbitration agreements with a similar pro-arbitration orientation.[91] Despite these authorities, the German National Socialist regime, with its totalitarian bent and mistrust of individual autonomy, issued in 1933, the so-called *Guidelines of the Reich Regarding Arbitral Tribunals*, which forbade the use of arbitration in a wide range of commercial settings. The *Guidelines* declared that 'from a state-political point of view a further spread of arbitration would shatter confidence in state jurisdiction and the State itself'[92] – reflecting a totalitarian view that both feared and denied individual autonomy.

Subsequently, however, 20th-century Germany renounced the Nazis' mistrust of arbitration and instead affirmed the fundamental importance of arbitration to concepts of individual autonomy. Thus, in 1963, the German Federal Labour Court cited Article 2(1) of the German Basic Law, which guarantees 'the right to free development of [a citizen's] personality', as the foundation for the validity of arbitration agreements.In the Court's words:

> The right to agree upon submitting a matter to arbitration is contained in the fundamental right to freedom of contract under Article 2. The

---

Déclin d'Une Institution (1790-1806), 1981 Rev. Arb. 3; M. de Boisséson, *Le Droit Français de l'Arbitrage Interne et International* ¶¶8-11 (2d ed. 1990).

88. II *Encyclopaedia Judaica* 365 (2d ed. 2007); H. Lapin, *Rabbis as Romans: The Rabbinic Movement in Palestine, 100-400 C.E.* 99 (2012) (describing increasing scope of rabbinic arbitration in 3d and 4th century); Warhaftig, *Studies in Jewish Law* 25-26 (1985) (arbitration "gradually established its prominence in Jewish adjudication, until finally it became the sole adjudicative institution that was recognized by the Romans, pursuant to the Emperor's order in the year 398 of the Common era").

89. Hecht *et al.* (eds.), *An Introduction to the History and Sources of Jewish Law* 326 (1996); Kirshner, *Introduction*, 16 Jewish History 1, 10 (2002).

90. *See, e.g.*, D. Rautray, *Master Guide to Arbitration in India* ¶¶1-010 *et seq.* (2008); D. Roebuck, *Ancient Greek Arbitration* 46-47 (2001); M. Bohacek, *Arbitration and State-Organized Tribunals in the Ancient Procedure of the Greeks and Romans* 197-203 (1952); P. Huang, *Chinese Civil Justice, Past and Present* 4, 29 (2010).

91. G. Born, *International Commercial Arbitration* 49-50 (3d ed. 2021).

92. *Richtlinien des Reiches über Schiedsgerichte*, 95 Deutsche Justiz 52, 821 (1933).

restriction of state jurisdiction occurring as a result of the agreement to arbitrate is a result of parties' exercise of freedom to contract.[93]

The German Federal Tribunal later adopted the same analysis, resting the validity of arbitration agreements on basic constitutional protections for individual liberties. The Federal Tribunal held that:

Article 2(1) of the Basic Law guarantees personal freedom and private autonomy. This fundamental right requires that the arbitrability of the matter and the resulting waiver of the right of access to national courts must be based on the parties' voluntary agreement.[94]

Other jurisdictions have recognised a constitutional right to arbitrate, rooted in the principles of individual liberty and private autonomy, in the same terms. In the United States, some 19th-century courts and commentators refused to enforce arbitration agreements in what the country's leading appellate court later termed 'one of the dark chapters in American legal history.'[95] That chapter was emphatically closed, and its contents reversed, with the enactment of the 1925 Federal Arbitration Act (FAA) and, later, ratification of the New York and Inter-American Conventions – which codified the presumptive validity of the arbitration agreements and arbitral awards.[96] These enactments rested on respect for individual autonomy and the right to arbitrate. A 20th-century decision from Hawaii declared: 'The recognized autonomy of parties to enter into an arbitration agreement ... is directly correlated to and stems from the constitutionally protected right of freedom of contract.'[97] In so doing, the Hawaii court gave a constitutional foundation to the FAA's pro-arbitration treatment of arbitration agreements and awards.

Likewise, a recent Quebec decision in Canada applying the UNCITRAL Model Law reasoned:

Arbitration is a fundamental right of citizens and an expression of their contractual freedom. It should not be considered as an infringement upon the monopoly of state justice.Rather, arbitration should be perceived as a means of alternative dispute resolution that, depending

---

93. *Judgment of 23 August 1963*, 1 AZR 469/61, ¶ 2 (German Federal Labor Court).
94. *Judgment of 3 April 2000*, II ZR 373/98 (German Federal Tribunal).
95. *Robert Lawrence Co. v. Devonshire Fabrics, Inc.*, 271 F.2d 402, 406 (2d Cir. 1959).
96. U.S. FAA, 9 U.S.C. §§1-16 (domestic and non-New York or Inter-American Convention international arbitrations), §§201-208 (New York Convention), §§301-307 (Inter-American Convention); Born, *The New York Convention: A Self-Executing Treaty*, 40 Mich. J. Int'l L. 115 (2018); Drahozal, *The New York Convention and the American Federal System*, 2012 J. Disp. Resol. 101, 102–04 (2012).
97. *Kona Village Realty, Inc v Sunstone Realty Partners XIV, LLC*, 123 Haw 476, 478 (2010).

on the circumstances, achieves certain goals pursued by the parties – eg, speed, decision by peers, cost efficiency, etc.[98]

Again, like Malynes, the Quebec court cited considerations of expedition, efficiency and expertise (the Five Es) and, more fundamentally, arbitration's character as 'an expression of their [ie, the parties'] contractual freedom'. That observation, like those of French, German, US and other courts, linked the presumptive validity of arbitration agreements to fundamental concepts of individual liberty and the rule of law.

Most recently, Panama's Constitution was amended to provide, that '[t]he administration of justice may also be exercised by the arbitral jurisdictions as determined by the law'.[99] A recent Panamanian Supreme Court decision cited the new provision in holding:

Arbitrators are judges by the sole application of the Law, and their decisions have coercive force towards the rest of the judicial administrative community, thus giving the parties greater security that their claims, are recognized through arbitral awards, shall be honored [*sic*]. This legal certainty in society will promote the choice of alternative dispute resolution mechanisms, to the benefit of all: faster and expeditious justice; decongestion of courts; increased access to justice.[100]

Other decisions by national courts from diverse jurisdictions in all parts of the world are to the same effect in recognising the constitutional stature of a right to arbitrate – rooted in guarantees of individual autonomy and freedom of contract and association.[101]

---

98. *Laurentienne-vie, compagnie d'assurances inc v Empire, compagnie d'assurance-vie* [2000] CanLII 9001 (Quebec Court of Appeal).

99. Constitution of the Republic of Panama (1972 as amended), Art 202.

100. *Greenhow Associates Ltd v Refineria Panama SA*, 14 February 2005 (Supreme Court of Panama).

101. *Judgment of 9 April 2008, TMC Terminal Multimodal de Coroa Grande SPE SA v. Ministro de Estado da*

Ciência e Tecnologia, Case No. 11.308 (2005/0212763-0), ¶16 (Brazilian Superior Tribunal de Justiça) ("It is well recognized that arbitration does not subtract any constitutional guarantees from domestic proceedings, on the contrary, it implies fulfilling these [constitution rights and guarantees]"); *Judgment of 3 November 2010, Astivenca Astilleros de Venezuela, CA v Oceanlink Offshore III AS*, XXXVI YB Comm Arb'n (2011) 496, ¶ 5 (Venezuelan Tribunal Supremo de Justicia) ("Hence, the principles of competence-competence and autonomy of the arbitration agreement are essential elements in the statutory regime of arbitration, guaranteeing the 'fundamental right to use alternative means of dispute resolution, including, obviously, arbitration.'"); *Judgment of 5 May 2009*, 2010 SchiedsVZ 173, 176 (Schiedsgericht Hamburg) ("On the one hand the interest of the arbitral parties in upholding the arbitration agreement is protected as an element of the freedom of contract and private autonomy pursuant to §2(1) of the German constitution. In the same way as having the right to be judged by one's competent state court pursuant to §101(1)(2) of the German constitution there also

The right to arbitrate has special importance in international matters, as distinguished from domestic matters. As discussed above, dispute resolution in international settings is inherently problematic – with national courts facing inevitable jurisdictional disputes, choice of law uncertainties, national biases of decision-makers, lack of expertise and difficulties in enforcing judgments.[102] Whatever the circumstances in domestic matters, international dispute resolution presents particular challenges for the rule of law and the effective resolution of disputes.

Those challenges have particular importance in international matters, where the need for peaceful dispute resolution is especially acute. Differences in the cultural, legal, linguistic and other circumstances of the parties in international matters make the risk of disputes, and the costs of disputes, particularly significant.[103] Numerous international instruments underscore the vital importance, and mandatory character, of obligations to resolve international disputes peacefully including the UN Charter, the 1982 Convention on the Law of the Sea (UNCLOS), the 1958 European Convention for the Peaceful Settlement of Disputes and the 1976 Treaty of Amity and Cooperation in Southeast Asia.[104] Those obligations give special force to the general recognition of the right to arbitrate in national (and international) legal systems – as an essential element of the international legal system and the rule of law.

International dispute resolution, among both States and private parties, is grounded in consent. That is reflected in the requirement of consent to international courts (like the International Court of Justice)[105] and tribunals

---

exists a right to waive this right by choosing an arbitral court."); *Judgment of 23 August 1963*, 1 AZR 469/62, ¶14 (German Bundesarbeitsgericht) ("The decision of the parties to enter into arbitral proceedings arises from their constitutional right of party autonomy as stated in Article 2 of the [German constitution]. If the scope of application of the State courts' jurisdiction is narrowed by the parties' submission of their dispute to arbitration, this is due to the parties' voluntary agreement, which is in turn guaranteed by the constitutional right to free development of personality under Article [2.1] of the [German Constitution].").

102. Casella, *Arbitration in International Trade*, NBER Working Paper Series, Working paper No. 4136, 1-11; Moses, *Arbitration in International Disputes*, 4 St. John's L. Rev. 36, 38-44 (1929); (1992); G. Born, *International Commercial Arbitration* 29-60 (3d ed. 2021).

103. *See* G. Born, *International Commercial Arbitration* 67-95 (3d ed. 2021); Mattli, *Private Justice in a Global Economy: From Litigation to Arbitration*, 55 MIT Press 919, 932-44 (2001); Nelson, *Alternatives to Litigation of International Disputes*, 23 Int'l L. 187, 188-91 (1989).

104. United Nations, Charter of the United Nations, 24 October 1945, 1 U.N.T.S XVI, Arts. 33-38 of Chapter VI and Articles 11, 99; Convention on the Law of the Sea, Dec. 10, 1982, 1833 UNTS. 397, Arts. 279-96 of Part XV; European Convention for the Peaceful Settlement of Disputes, 30 April 1958, ETS No.023, Chapter I-IV; The Treaty of Amity and Cooperation in Southeast Asia, Feb. 24, 1976, 1025 UNTS. 15, 316, Arts. 13-17 of Chapter IV.

105. Statute of the International Court of Justice, Arts. 36(1), (2), 59 Stat 1055 (1945); S. Rosenne, *The Law and Practice of the International Court, 1920-2005* 9-42, 97-116 (4th ed. 2006); Lister, *The Legitimating Role of Consent in International Law,* 11 U. Chi. J. Int'l L. 663, 681-684(2011).

(like *ad hoc* arbitral tribunals in State-to-State arbitrations);[106] unless such agreements to arbitrate (or litigate) international disputes are given effect, then international disputes will not be resolved and the role of adjudication in the international legal system will not function. Thus, in international matters, the vital importance of a right to arbitrate as an aspect of individual autonomy and protection against governmental oppression is paralleled by the importance of the right to arbitrate as a foundation of the international legal system.

Again unsurprisingly, international tribunals, as well as national courts and legislatures, have affirmed the fundamental importance of the right to arbitrate. Among other things, several investor-State tribunals have held that refusals by States to give effect to valid arbitration agreements and arbitral awards amount to 'denials of justice' or violations of similar internationally protected rights.

In *Saipem v Bangladesh*, for example, an ICSID tribunal held that the purported revocation of an ICC arbitral tribunal's mandate (and related annulment of the tribunal's award) by the Supreme Court of Bangladesh was a wrongful denial of justice, notwithstanding the fact that the tribunal was seated in Bangladesh and was subject to the supervisory authority of the Bangladeshi courts.[107] The tribunal relied on Article II of the New York Convention in holding that the Bangladeshi court's decision had been abusive and arbitrary. Other decisions by investment tribunals have reached similar conclusions,[108] as has the European Court of Human Rights, which held that refusals to enforce an arbitration agreement or award amounted to denials of access to justice under Article 6 of the European Convention on Human Rights.[109]

---

106. *BG Group, plc v. Argentina*, 572 U.S. 25, 46 (2014) (Sotomayor, J., concurring) ("Consent is especially salient in the context of a bilateral investment treaty, where the treaty is not an already agreed-upon arbitration provision between known parties, but rather a nation state's standing offer to arbitrate with an amorphous class of private investors"); *Générale de Surveillance SA v. Paraguay, Decision on Jurisdiction in ICSID Case No. ARB/07/29 of 12 February 2010*, ¶70 ("The State's consent in a BIT is often described as an 'open invitation' or a 'standing offer' to covered investors to submit such disputes to international arbitration, which the investor 'accepts' by giving its own written consent to resort to such arbitration (whether prior to or in its Request for Arbitration)"); C. Schreuer *et al.*, *The ICSID Convention: A Commentary* Art. 25, ¶448 (2d ed. 2009) ("An investor may accept an offer contained in a BIT simply by instituting ICSID proceedings. Tribunals have accepted this form of expressing consent in numerous cases.").

107. *Saipem SpA v The People's Republic of Bangladesh*, ICSID Case No ARB/05/07, Award of 30 June 2009.

108. *ATA Construction, Industrial and Trading Co. v. The Hashemite Kingdom of Jordan*, ICSID Case No ARB/08/2, Award of 18 May 2010; *White Industries Australia Ltd v. The Republic of India*, UNCITRAL Case, Final Award of 30 November 2011.

109. *Case of Kin-Stib and Majki v Serbia* [2010] ECHR 616 (European Court of Justice); *Case of Stran Greek Refineries and Stratis Andreasdis v. Greece*, [1994] ECHR 48 (European Court of Human Rights).

III. CONCLUSION

Building on the historic pedigree of arbitration that Professor Roebuck has detailed so thoroughly, contemporary courts and tribunals from virtually all jurisdictions, from every region of the globe and every type of political system, have repeatedly given effect to international commercial arbitration agreements and arbitral awards. Virtually no national legislature, nor national court, has in recent memory departed from this view. Likewise, courts and tribunals from around the world have emphatically recognised the central importance of the right to arbitrate to the rule of law. That right has properly been founded on constitutionally-protected liberties – freedom of contract, freedom of association and other individual rights. Denials of the right of citizens to arbitrate their disputes is no less a threat to the rule of law and individual liberties than denials of the freedom to contract, associate, or marry.

Recognition of the right to arbitrate is particularly important in international matters, where consensual means of dispute resolution are both ubiquitous and necessary to the international legal system. Respecting the right of parties to agree to resolve their disputes by arbitration, and the validity of agreements doing so, is essential to the resolution of international disputes and the use of adjudication in international matters.

For all of these reasons, the presumptive validity of international commercial arbitration agreements and awards, subject only to narrow exceptions, is properly regarded as a general principle of international law. That rule is mandatorily binding on all States, regardless whether or not they have ratified the New York Convention (or a similar international treaty) and, where national law permits, is directly applicable in national court proceedings. Even absent direct application, the presumptive validity of international arbitration agreements and awards bears on the interpretation of national law, as a rule of construction and an indication of sound policy.

A number of practical implications, which are beyond the scope of this essay, flow from recognition of the right to arbitrate. These include the lack of any justification for: (1) heightened standards for either the substantive or the formal validity of arbitration agreements,[110] (2) restrictive rules of interpretation of the scope of arbitration agreements,[111] (3) discriminatory rules for the validity of arbitration agreements,[112] and (4) most mandatory procedural requirements (such as those concerning mandatory appellate review, public conduct of arbitral proceedings and governmental selection

---

110. *See* G. Born, *International Commercial Arbitration* 799-11 (3d ed. 2021).
111. *See* G. Born, *International Commercial Arbitration* 1445-48 (3d ed. 2021).
112. *See* G. Born, *International Commercial Arbitration* 2319-20 (3d ed. 2021).

of arbitrators).[113] With regard to each of these issues, it is fundamental that the parties' choice of arbitration as a means of resolving their disputes be given full effect. Doing so does not detract from the rule of law but, on the contrary, ensures its preservation.

It is often said that those who ignore history are condemned to relive it. That is true here, as elsewhere. Those who ignore the right to arbitrate, and its roots in constitutional guarantees of individual autonomy and the rule of law in international matters, are condemned to the denials of justice occasioned by the *Reich Guidelines* and the dark chapters in US legal history. Those denials of justice not only force parties to endure more costly, more protracted, less informed and less effective legal proceedings but, most fundamentally, ignore their rights of individual autonomy and the rule of law.

---

113. *See* G. Born, *International Commercial Arbitration* 1681-86 (3d ed. 2021).

THE *ALABAMA* ARBITRATION: FROM COMPROMISE TO LEGACY[*]

Bruno de Loynes de Fumichon[**]

INTRODUCTION

According to two distinguished international law scholars,[1] Albert de La Pradelle (a Frenchman) and Nicolas Politis (a Greek), 'the *Alabama* case occupies an exceptional position in the history of international arbitration and of international law'. They took this view on account of 'the nature of the *dispute*, the *arbitrators'* powers, the length of the debates, the peculiarities of the *proceedings* and of the *award*' and 'the number and importance of the *questions* at issue and of the legal theories called upon'.[2]

[*] This contribution is an adapted and edited version of an article co-authored with Professor William Park of Boston University, and published in French in the *Revue de l'arbitrage*, no 3, 2019, pp 743–834. It has retained, with his permission, an anecdote providing an excellent example that is personal to Professor Park and his family (see note 17). The author wants to thank him for that.
[**] Honorary *Maître de conferences*, Sorbonne law school (Université Paris I) and Honorary Dean of the Faculty of law of the University of French Polynesia at Tahiti.

1. See also, among a vast corpus of literature, T Bingham, 'The Alabama Claims Arbitration', (2005) 54 *International and Comparative Law Quarterly* 1–25; CH Brower II, entry 'Alabama Arbitration' in *Max Planck Encyclopedia of Public International Law* published under the direction of R Wolfrum (Munich and Oxford, 2012); JL Item, R Bismuth, C Crépet-Daigremont and A de Nanteuil, *Les grandes decisions de la jurisprudence internationale* (Paris, 2018), pp 3 *et seq*; A Ouedraogo, 'La neutralité et l'émergence du concept de due diligence en droit international – L'affaire de l'Alabama revisitée', *Journal of the History of International Law/Journal d'Histoire du Droit International*, XIII no 2, 2011, pp 307 *et seq*; Jan Paulsson, 'The Alabama Claims Arbitration: Statecraft and Stagecraft', in U Franke, A Magnusson and J Dahlquist (eds), *Arbitration for Peace*, (2016), pp 7 *et seq*; VV Veeder, 'The Historical Keystone to International Arbitration: The Party-Appointed Arbitrator', 107 *Proceedings of the American Society of International Law* (2013), pp 387 *et seq*.

2. *Recueil des arbitrages internationaux*, vol. II, Paris (1923), p 902. This opinion concurs with that of JB Moore (in *History and Digest of the International Arbitrations to which the United States has been a Party,* Washington DC 1898, vol 1, pp 652–653) that the *Alabama* arbitration, 'whether measured by the gravity of the questions at issue, or by the magnanimous and enlightened statesmanship which conducted them to a peaceful determination, was justly regarded as the greatest the world had ever seen'. Recently, CH Brower II (note 1 above) endorsed the opinion that this is 'the most notable arbitration in history'.

The dispute between the United Kingdom and the United States arose out of the American Civil War (1861–1865) and British neutrality. The agreement to arbitrate (a compromise[3]), negotiated and concluded by the Treaty of Washington in 1871, defined the arbitrators' powers. The proceedings, with their peculiarities, met with setbacks but were concluded on time after several months of hearings. The award and the dissent of Sir Alexander Cockburn, by their answers to the questions at issue, have nourished debates which, since 1872, have accrued to the legacy of this famous arbitration.

THE AMERICAN CIVIL WAR AND BRITISH NEUTRALITY (1861–1865)

The overall story of British policy during the American Civil War (the Civil War) is very ably and interestingly told by Amanda Foreman in *A World on Fire*.[4] We shall limit ourselves here to the facts in relation to the neutrality of the British authorities regarding the actions of the Confederate Navy.

The actions of the Confederate Navy

In the summer of 1861, the Confederacy dispatched agents[5] to England to conclude contracts for guns and ammunition, and for ships to wage war against the Union Navy and prey on Union merchant shipping in order to cripple Northern commerce and, if possible, stop it altogether.

About 20 ships were built (gunboats and armoured ironclads) or bought (transport vessels converted into gunboats) by the Confederate Navy. We can limit ourselves to the few for which the arbitral tribunal found the British authorities at fault: the CSS *Alabama*, the CSS *Florida* and the CSS *Shenandoah*, together with several others.[6]

The CSS Alabama *(May 1862–June 1864)*

The CSS *Alabama* was built at Birkenhead, near Liverpool. She was first named *Hull 290* (being the 290th ship built by the shipbuilders Laird), then the *Enrica*, to give credence to the assertion that she was meant for the Italian government. She was launched in May 1862 to sail as a gunboat raider. The *Enrica* sailed to Terceira Island (in the Portuguese Azores),

---

3. The compromise (from the Latin *compromissum*) is an arbitration agreement negotiated and concluded once a dispute has arisen.
4. *A World on Fire: Britain's Crucial Role in the American Civil War* (New York, 2010).
5. The Confederate agents had offices in Liverpool at the premises of Fraser and Trenholm, a Charleston trading company, the director of which was also the minister of finance of the Confederacy.
6. As to the other ships, see p. 247 below.

where she met two transport ships purchased by Confederate agents: the *Agrippina*, brought from England with cannons, arms and ammunition, 350 tons of coal, crew and victuals, and the *Bahama*, brought from Nassau with a complement of crew and her captain.

Raphaël Semmes commanded the ship outside Portuguese waters. On 24 August 1862, he read to the crew the commission of war transforming the ship into a Confederate vessel and appointing him as captain. The ship received her new name *Alabama*. Semmes, a man with energy and charisma, strong opinions and few scruples, had a crew of 24 officers and 120 men, most of them of British nationality.[7]

The *Alabama* sailed the Atlantic and Indian oceans and the South China Sea. Captain Semmes would approach his prey flying the British flag, board them by surprise, take their cargo, embark the crew on board the *Alabama* to free them later in a neutral port and, finally, burn the ships. Semmes sometimes kept the ships as tenders. In two years, the *Alabama* sank the USS *Hatteras* through a *ruse de guerre* and preyed on Union commercial shipping, capturing about 60 ships – including transport vessels and whalers – and selling their cargo.

In June 1864, the *Alabama* met her Waterloo when she was sunk by the USS *Kearsarge* off Cherbourg in Normandy, France.[8] The *Alabama,* as the most effective of the Confederate commerce raiders, had the 'dubious privilege' (per Federico Sclopis, president of the arbitral tribunal) of giving her name to the whole affair.

The CSS Florida (March 1862–October 1864)

This ship was built at Liverpool. She was first named the *Oreto*, having originally been ordered for the Italian Navy, according to the shipbuilders.[9] In Liverpool, it was difficult to hide the fact that she was a warship: she had no storage for the transport of goods and was equipped to receive six big guns, though in the event (on legal advice) she received none.[10] She was nevertheless registered as a British dispatch vessel.[11]

7. In 1869, Semmes wrote his interesting *Memoirs of Service Afloat during the War between the States.*
8. Captain Semmes and his crew were rescued by an English yacht, the *Deerhound.* The battle was watched by hundreds of onlookers, who came from Portsmouth on private yachts and from Paris by special train, as depicted by the French Impressionist painter, Édouard Manet, in *La Bataille.* The *Alabama* came to Cherbourg to undergo repairs. The Press in both London and Paris announced the battle in advance.
9. The shipbuilders announced that the ship had been ordered by a British subject, the agent of a company in Palermo, Sicily, acting for the Italian government. The Kingdom of Italy had only recently been established, in 1861.
10. When she arrived at Nassau following a non-stop voyage, her gun mounts had already been fitted (see p 236 below).
11. The construction of the *Florida*, as well as the *Alabama* and others, was supervised by JD

The *Oreto* left Liverpool with a British crew of 50 seamen in March 1862 and went to Nassau (Bahamas), a British colony close to the Confederate ports of Charleston (South Carolina), Wilmington (North Carolina) and Mobile (Alabama). The following day, she anchored at the isolated Cochrane's Bay. Two weeks later, there came from England the *Bahama*, a British transport vessel loaded with arms. The *Oreto* met another British transport ship, the *Prince Alfred*, off Green Cay, a Bahamian desert island 60 miles from Nassau, and received an additional cargo of arms, some crew and her captain, John Maffitt.

After a visit to Mobile,[12] where she received her commission of war and the name *Florida*, she preyed on merchant shipping, taking 25 Northern ships. John Maffitt estimated the value of his prizes at more than US$6 million. In October 1864, the *Florida* was captured and taken away near Bahia, within Brazilian waters and in violation of Brazilian sovereignity and neutrality, by the USS *Wachusett*.

The CSS Shenandoah *(September 1864–November 1865)*

This steamer was built in Scotland, launched under the name of *Sea King* as a transport for the China trade and registered by her owner, a British subject. In September 1864, after returning from her first voyage, she was purchased for a Confederate agent by a front man and registered under his name. Soon after, he gave a proxy to another straw man with power to sell the ship.

The *Sea King* left London for Madeira, a Portuguese island in the Atlantic. Once under way, she was sold on the high seas to the Confederate government and turned into a Confederate cruiser. In Madeira, she received her armaments, crew and captain from the *Laurel*, a small transport ship built in England for the Confederacy. Renamed the *Shenandoah*, she received her new flag and commission.[13]

Between October 1864 and January 1865, the *Shenandoah* seized several US merchant ships in the Atlantic. She reached Melbourne, Australia in January 1865, underwent repairs on a government slipway and recruited several dozen men. After leaving Melbourne in February 1865, she sank

Bulloch, who later published *The Secret Service of the Confederate States in Europe* (London and New York, 1883–1884).

12. The *Oreto* went through the Union blockade as a neutral British ship. At Mobile in September 1862, she received her commission of war from the Confederate Navy and her new name *Florida*. She again put to sea, running the blockade and reaching Nassau again. There she took a full load of coal, in violation of British instructions of neutrality of 31 January 1862 prohibiting the use of a British port as a naval base, a sojourn of more than 24 hours, and the full loading of coal when a ship was less than three days away from a home port.

13. The Confederate agents had concealed from US spies the combined operation of the *Sea King* and the *Laurel*. The US embassy was informed of the departure of the two ships only one month after the event.

several US merchant and whaling vessels in the Pacific, until after the end of the war in April 1865, of which her crew were unaware. Having received news of the Confederacy's defeat from a merchant ship on the high seas, in November 1865 her captain took the *Shenandoah* to Liverpool, where he surrendered to the British authorities, still flying the flag of the by then defunct Confederacy.

British neutrality: municipal law under the British Foreign Enlistment Act 1819

What was the state of English neutrality law at the time? The applicable statute, the Foreign Enlistment Act 1819 (FEA), was applied by the court in the case of another Confederate ship, the *Alexandra*.

The Alexandra *and the British law* of *neutrality with regard to ships and their crews*

The CSS *Alexandra* was built in Liverpool and launched in April 1863. The evidence of her military purpose – the ship was missing only her guns – and her destination was gathered by the US consul in Liverpool, transmitted to Charles Francis Adams Sr, the US ambassador in London. He, in his turn, handed it to Lord Russell, the British Foreign Secretary, at whose request the Attorney-General initiated proceedings before the Court of Exchequer in London.

The Lord Chief Baron presiding, the court held that the FEA authorised the manufacture and sale of arms to a belligerent with which Great Britain was neutral. If British factories could sell arms, why could shipbuilders not build warships for them? Under s VII of the FEA, it was prohibited to 'fit out, equip, furnish, [or] arm' neutral ships in British ports. The mere construction of a ship, however, remained lawful. The ship was not completed: 'Though on water, the *Alexandra* is nothing else than under construction.' The shipbuilders had only met a business order but had not fitted out, equipped, furnished or armed the ship.

In June 1863, the jury at *nisi prius* agreed. An appeal by the Attorney-General was rejected by the Court of Exchequer Chamber as not competent. The House of Lords confirmed this decision.[14] The *Alexandra* left Liverpool, changed her name to *Mary* and sailed as a privateer along the eastern seaboard of the US, from Halifax, Nova Scotia to Bermuda and Nassau, all ports under British jurisdiction. She was seized at Nassau by the British government in December 1864, four months before the end of the war.

---

14. It was a vindication of Lord Russell's management of the *Alabama* affair (which concerned construction and escape).

According to the Court of Exchequer, the construction and sale of warships for a belligerent was lawful under municipal law. We have seen that the *Alabama* and the *Florida* were delivered on ballast: only their armament of guns was missing. The sale of rifles and ammunition was also legal, and both the Union and the Confederacy bought large amounts in Great Britain during the Civil War.

The FEA also prohibited the recruitment in British ports of British subjects to a foreign army or navy, under heavy penalties. British subjects enlisted voluntarily on both sides.[15] Many seamen were recruited by employment companies for the Confederate raiders.[16] If sailors of a belligerent set foot on land outside the limits set by the rules while on short visits, they should be interned for the duration of the war. This was rarely the case, as demonstrated by the crew of the *Alabama*, who were rescued by British yachts off Cherbourg and welcomed enthusiastically in England. Neutrality might have been either strictly enforced or more or less benevolent.[17]

The CSS Alabama

During the construction of the *Enrica*, the US consul in Liverpool enquired of his Italian colleague, who answered that he had no knowledge of the affair. Charles Francis Adams urged Lord Russell to detain the ship. The Foreign Secretary consulted the Treasury, whose local officers answered that they had 'every reason to believe that she is for the Italian government, and not for the Confederates'.[18] Russell informed Adams that he could not initiate proceedings, unless supported by legal evidence in a form acceptable to the

15. See Foreman, *op cit* (note 4).
16. Most of the crew of the *Alabama*, the *Florida* and the *Shenandoah* were recruited in England, mainly in Liverpool.
17. During World War II, Allied military personnel were sometimes interned by neutral powers. In 1943, after his ship had been torpedoed by a German submarine, Commander Oliver Park (father of Professor William Park of Boston University) was rescued by Portuguese fishermen and interned in the Azores (where, it will be recalled, the *Enrica*, eighty years earlier, had been turned into the *Alabama* and received her armaments, commission of war, Captain Semmes, crew and flag in 1862). After a short while, the mayor of the internment village allowed Commander Park to 'escape' on a ship leaving the Azores, which permitted his resumption of service in the US Navy. This incident provides a classic example of 'benevolent' neutrality.
18. *Papers relating to the Treaty of Washington*, IV (the Dissent), at p 370. The report from the customs officers stated that (1) the ship was not ready to receive guns, (2) she was destined for the Italian government, (3) her owner and crew were British and (4) she was registered in Liverpool as a British merchant ship. The customs officers relied on the false information given by the shipbuilders. Part of the customs report was therefore erroneous because the ship was not a mere dispatch vessel, she was prepared to receive guns, her destination was not Italy and her captain was a Confederate officer. The assertions on which the customs officers relied were, in part, intended to deceive, because the owner was not British. They were partly true in giving evidence of a violation of the law (*viz*, as to the recruitment of a British crew).

judiciary. The US consul in Liverpool gathered copies of a letter by Confederate agents, sworn affidavits from sailors already recruited and an opinion by a well-known barrister that these documents were sufficient evidence to seize the ship for violation of the law.[19] Adams forwarded the documents to Russell, who asked the opinion of the Crown's legal advisers.[20]

In the meantime, the Confederate agents and the shipbuilders, having been informed of this development, decided to accelerate the ship's sea trials and so, on 29 July 1862, put her to sea without having registered her, under the pretence of embarking on an inaugural trip with ladies and music. The order from London to seize the ship and initiate proceedings arrived in Liverpool one day late. The *Enrica* had escaped.

The CSS Florida

The US consul in Nassau, worried by the simultaneous arrival from England (previously related) of the *Oreto*, as the ship was then named, and of a transport carrying arms and ammunition – the *Bahama* – requested the authorities to seize the two ships for violation of the British declaration of neutrality of May 1861.

The Governor commissioned an officer of the Royal Navy to inspect the *Oreto*. The officer found that she was unsuitable for mercantile shipping (lacking storage space) and was destined to conduct naval warfare (gun mounts and guns having been installed, along with arms and ammunition and a Confederate flag). The Governor initiated proceedings. The judge of the court of Vice-Admiralty decided that there had been no violation of neutrality: there was no evidence that the *Oreto* had received her guns and arms at Nassau.[21] It was understood that the ship had received her equipment at Liverpool[22] or on the high seas, but the court was not competent to judge this. The fraud was evident,[23] as was the complaisance

---

19. RP Collier. His opinion conflicted with the advice given to the shipbuilders and to JD Bulloch by G Mellish QC (later Chief Justice of England & Wales), that the FEA applied only to ships 'capable of committing hostilities when leaving'.
20. British government practice was to send the file to the most senior of the Law Officers of the Crown. Sir John Harding (Queen's Advocate) was mentally ill at the time. This delayed the decision by one week. The other Crown advisers (Sir William Atherton, Attorney-General, and Sir Roundell Palmer, Solicitor-General) thought that the evidence was sufficient. The affidavits declaring that the ship under construction was a warship were not convincingly contradicted by the vague and ambiguous statement by the shipbuilders.
21. For the Attorney-General, there was no evidence that the *Oreto* had received her guns at Cochrane, Nassau. He agreed that, if she had received her cargo there, it would have been a violation of the FEA. He added that the cargo of the *Bahama* had been regularly imported and that its destination, which was purely conjectural, was not illegal.
22. During the inspection, the captain stated that his ship was in the same state (equipped with guns) as when she left Liverpool. The customs officers there had declared that she was leaving unequipped and unarmed.
23. The *Oreto,* registered in Liverpool as a transport ship, arrived after a non-stop voyage at Nassau as a warship (see p 231 above).

of the judicial authorities in Nassau. The proceedings failed and the two ships left under British colours in August 1862.

The CSS Shenandoah

As mentioned previously, the *Sea King* had been sold by a straw man of the Confederate agent to the Confederate Navy on the high seas (off Terceira, Azores). On his return, the straw man was sued by the Attorney-General. He escaped liability by proving that he had not been involved in any recruitment.

The *Shenandoah*, after seizing several US merchant ships in the Atlantic, reached Melbourne, Australia in January 1865 and recruited several dozen British nationals. The US consul asked the Governor to put an end to the violations of the FEA. The captain refused permission for a port officer to come aboard his ship. Instead, he gave the Governor his word of honour as a gentleman that no recruitment had taken place. The Governor gave way. 'Too polite', Federico Sclopis, the president of the arbitral tribunal, commented later, during the proceedings commenced pursuant to a compromise, the arbitration agreement.

THE TREATY OF WASHINGTON OF 1871 AS A COMPROMISE OR AN ARBITRATION AGREEMENT

The 'Treaty for the amicable settlement of all causes of difference between the United Kingdom and the United States' (the Treaty), which had been negotiated by a Joint High Commission of both countries,[24] established arbitral tribunals and mixed commissions to settle the pending differences, of which the *Alabama* claims were the most controversial,[25] though they were not the only ones.[26]

The Treaty's provisions concerning the *Alabama* claims were twofold. They were, first, an arbitration agreement or compromise, a contract to go to arbitration to settle a dispute that had already come into existence[27] in

24. *Editorial note*: The text of which is available at https://ia600303.us.archive.org/9/items/cihm_27720/cihm_27720.pdf.
25. Articles I–XI. It took six weeks for the High Commissioners to negotiate the arbitration agreement to settle the *Alabama* claims, and only three weeks to agree on the other five heads of dispute.
26. The claims related to the Civil War outside the *Alabama* claims (the 'Civil War claims'), were to be examined by a mixed commission (arts XI–XVII). The North-Eastern fisheries dispute was to be settled by the Halifax Commission (arts XVIII–XXV). The conflicts about freedom of navigation on the Saint Lawrence and the Great Lakes, and the related issue of exemption from customs duties on the transit of goods between US ports and mainland Canada were to be dealt with under arts XXVI–XXXIII. The dispute about the frontier between the US and Canada near Vancouver (at San Juan Island) was to be settled by the arbitration of the Emperor of Germany (arts XXXIV–XLII).
27. Such an agreement is traditionally named a 'compromise' after the Roman *compromissum* (see note 3 above).

accordance with the applicable law stated therein. This applicable law was also the substance of a treaty on the law of naval neutrality, for the parties also undertook to apply these principles between them in the future. In England, criticism of the treaty focused on the retroactivity of the law, for the arbitrators were asked to judge the conduct of Great Britain not by the international law in force during the war but by new rules agreed by negotiation after the fact.

The treaty as an arbitration agreement

The arbitration agreement provided for an arbitral tribunal to be set up to render an award on the liability or otherwise of Great Britain. If the country were held liable, the agreement also gave the tribunal the power (but not the duty) to determine the amount of damages and order its payment.[28] The Treaty provided as summarised below.

Article I defined the scope of the dispute as 'the acts committed by ... several vessels which have given rise to the claims generically known as the "Alabama claims"'. These claims were to be referred to a tribunal of arbitrators (the Tribunal) to be appointed as follows: one by Her Britannic Majesty, one by the President of the US, one by the King of Italy, one by the President of the Swiss Confederation and one by the Emperor of Brazil.[29]

Article II stated procedural generalities. The Tribunal would meet at Geneva. 'All questions considered by the Tribunal, including the final award, shall be decided by a majority of all the arbitrators.'

Article III concerned the written procedure. Each party would deliver its case and evidence within six months of the ratification of the Treaty. The simultaneous exchange seems to have been inspired by diplomacy and politics rather than reality. This was harmful to Great Britain. Unable to anticipate the claims of the US in detail, Great Britain submitted a general and weak case and lost a turn in the debate.

Article IV added that a counter-case 'may' (not 'shall', as for the case) be submitted by each party – again, simultaneously – if both parties decided

28. If the tribunal did not award a sum, the Treaty (at Art. X) provided that a board of assessors should determine what amounts should be paid as to each vessel, in accordance with liability as decided by the arbitrators. This mechanism was influenced by the British Admiralty Court system (in seamanship cases) of dividing a judgment into holdings on liability and quantum, *viz* the assessment of damages.

29. Article I included a paragraph for the appointment by the same head of State of an arbitrator to replace the original nominee in any case of refusal to act, death, absence, incapacity, etc. Another paragraph designated the King of Sweden and Norway 'to fill the original appointment' in case the King of Italy, the President of the Swiss Confederation or the Emperor of Brazil failed to name an original arbitrator or to make a replacement later, where necessary.

to take the opportunity, within four months of delivery of the case. The arbitrators had the power to extend this time limit.

Article V stated that each party shall, within two months after delivery of its case and counter-case, deliver a 'written or printed argument, showing the points and referring to the evidence upon which ... [it] relies'.[30]

Article V also gave the arbitrators the power to, 'if they desire further elucidation, require a written statement or argument, or oral argument by counsel upon it; but in such case, the other Party shall be entitled to reply either orally or in writing, as the case may be'. The oral procedure was therefore incidental and sub-optional: that is, if the arbitrators required both an elucidation and that it should be made orally. The Treaty gave the parties no right to present oral argument.

Article VI, which concerned the applicable law, is discussed in the next section.

Article VII concerned the making of the award:

> The decision of the Tribunal shall ... be made within three months from the close of the argument on both sides.
> It shall be made in writing and dated, and ... signed by the Arbitrators who may assent to it.[31]
> The Tribunal shall first determine as to each vessel separately whether Great Britain has, by any act or omission, failed to fulfil any of the duties set forth in the foregoing three rules, or recognized by the principles of international law not inconsistent with such rules ... In case the Tribunal find that Great Britain has failed to fulfil any duty ..., it may, if it thinks proper, proceed to award a sum in gross to be paid by Great Britain to the United States ...
> Article VIII concerned the remuneration of the arbitrators, agents and counsel, and the allowance of costs.[32]
> Article XI concerned the final effect of the award.[33]

---

30. The *argument showing the points and referring to the evidence* turned out to be a vey useful tool. It compelled the parties to identify clearly their statements of facts, arguments, reasoning and requests, and to refer to the evidence supporting their positions on each of these matters. It accelerated the debates and facilitated the arbitrators' work.

31. Nothing was said of possible dissenting opinions.

32. 'Each Government shall pay its own agent and provide for the proper remuneration of the counsel, and ... of the Arbitrator appointed by it, and for the expenses of preparing and submitting its case to the Tribunal. All other expenses connected with the arbitration shall be defrayed by the two Governments in equal moieties.' Nothing was said of the arbitrators. At the end of the proceedings, the three 'neutral' arbitrators refused to receive any remuneration.

33. 'The High Contracting Parties engage to consider the result of the proceedings of the Tribunal of Arbitration ... as a full, perfect and final settlement of all the claims ..., and further engage that every such claim shall,... after the conclusion of the proceedings, be considered and treated as finally settled, barred, and thenceforth inadmissible.'

The new rules on naval neutrality as the law applicable to the arbitration and as a treaty

Article VI of the Treaty stated:

> In deciding the matters submitted to the Arbitrators, they shall be governed by the following three rules, which are agreed upon by the High Contracting Parties as rules to be taken as applicable to the case, and by such principles of international law not inconsistent therewith as the Arbitrators shall determine to have been applicable to the case.

RULES

A neutral Government is bound–

First[ly], to use *due diligence to prevent the fitting out, arming, or equipping*,[34] within its jurisdiction, of any vessel which it has reasonable ground to believe is intended to cruise or carry on war against a Power with which it is at peace; and also to use like diligence to prevent the *departure* from its jurisdiction of any vessel intended to cruise or carry on war as above, such vessel having been specially *adapted*, in whole or in part, within its jurisdiction, to warlike use.

Secondly, not to permit or suffer either belligerent to make use of its ports or waters as the *base of naval operations* against the other, or for the purpose of the renewal or augmentation of military supplies or arms, or the recruitment of men.

Thirdly, to exercise *due diligence* in its own ports and waters, and as to all persons within its jurisdiction, *to prevent any violation* of the foregoing obligations and duties.

Her Britannic Majesty has commanded her High Commissioners ... to declare that Her Majesty's Government cannot assent to the foregoing rules as a statement of principles of International Law which were in force at the time when the claims ... arose, but Her Majesty's Government, in order to evince its desire of strengthening the friendly relations between the two countries and of making satisfactory provision for *the future*, agrees that in deciding the questions ..., the Arbitrators should assume that Her Majesty's Government had undertaken to act upon the principles set forth in these rules.

And the High Contracting Parties agree to observe these rules as between themselves *in future*, and to bring them to the knowledge of other maritime Powers, and to invite them to accede to them.

---

34. All italicisations in art VI and elsewhere (relating to the award and the dissent) represent emphases added by the author of this contribution.

The reason for the retroactivity of the three Rules, this 'apparent anomaly' (per Sir Alexander Cockburn),[35] is to be found in the diplomatic considerations alluded to in the text itself, that 'of strengthening the friendly relations ... and of making satisfactory provision for the future.' At the time of negotiation of the Treaty (1871), Great Britain was concerned about the balance of power in Continental Europe, which had always been of vital importance to her. Prussia had defeated Denmark in 1864, Austria in 1866 and then France in 1870, and in 1871 founded a new German *Reich* which aspired to compete with Great Britain for economic and naval supremacy. Russia had colonial differences with Great Britain in Asia. It was necessary to remove any cause of conflict with the US and to secure effective American neutrality, not the kind of benevolent neutrality that the British had shown to the Confederacy during the Civil War.

Commentary on the rules

The first Rule in Article VI of the Treaty bound the neutral government to use 'due diligence to prevent the fitting out, arming, or equipping, within its jurisdiction, of any vessel which it has reasonable ground to believe is intended to cruise or carry on war ... or the departure of a vessel specially adapted for war ...'. The basis of this text is the British FEA 1819 and American municipal law. It is, however more precise than this. It is enriched by the requirement of 'due diligence'; the High Commissioners discussed and rejected 'active diligence' as excessive and 'reasonable care' as insufficient. It is also completed by the mention of 'having reasonable ground to believe [that the vessel] is intended ...'. The text does not include 'the construction' of the vessel, as suggested by the American commissioners but rejected by the British, but it does include the prevention of the departure of a vessel adapted in whole or in part for warlike use.

The second Rule bound the neutral government 'not to permit or suffer either belligerent to make use of its ports ... as the *base of* naval operations against the other, or for the purpose of the renewal or augmentation of

---

35. 'Every obligation for the non fulfillment of which redress can be claimed presupposes a prior existing law, by which a right has been created on the one side and a corresponding obligation on the other. But here we have to deal with obligations assumed to have existed prior to the treaty, yet arising out of a supposed law created for the first time by the treaty. For we have one party denying the prior existence of the rules which it now consents to submit as the measure of its past obligations, while the other virtually admits the same thing; for it "agrees to observe the rules as between itself and Great Britain in future, and to bring them to the knowledge of other maritime powers, and invite them to accede to them" – all of which would plainly be superfluous and vain if these rules already formed part of the existing law recognized as obtaining among nations.' Dissent by Sir Alexander Cockburn, *Papers relating to the Treaty of Washington* (*supra*, note 18), pp 231 and 232.

military supplies or arms, or the recruitment of men'. It is an adaptation of a rule of customary international law recognised, for example, by the British instructions of neutrality issued on 31 January 1862,[36] with the addition of the prohibition on the recruitment of crew, taken again from both sets of municipal law.

The third Rule required the neutral government 'to exercise due diligence ["due watchfulness" proposed by the Americans having been rejected] in its own ports or waters, and as to all persons within its jurisdiction, to prevent any violation of the foregoing obligations and duties'. It is an innovation and a safeguard against benevolent neutrality in favour of one or the other belligerent.

The arbitral tribunal

Each of the five heads of State named an arbitrator in due time. Queen Victoria, at the suggestion of the Prime Minister, William Ewart Gladstone, appointed Sir Alexander Cockburn,[37] the Lord Chief Justice of England & Wales.[38] Cockburn was very learned, especially in international law, but also arrogant, outspoken and insulting.[39] According to Bingham, he brought to his (admittedly very difficult) assignment the qualities of an ill-tempered partisan advocate and not the even-tempered objectivity of a judicial arbitrator.

The President of the US, Ulysses S Grant, appointed Charles Francis Adams, son and grandson of US Presidents and an epitome of New England's 'Wasps'. As his father and grandfather had been, he was US ambassador in London. He contributed to the success of the arbitration, notably with regard to the 'indirect claims' controversy.

36. See note 12 above about the *Florida*. These instructions were sent at the beginning of the Civil War.
37. Sir Alexander Cockburn (1802–1880) was the nephew of the general who destroyed Washington DC during the Anglo-American War of 1812–1814. He was famous for his bad character and excited considerable controversy. In his youth, he escaped from bailiffs and fathered two illegitimate sons. There is a suggestion that he was a ladies' man and had made the very bad move of seducing one of the Queen's ladies in waiting. For this reason or another, the Queen refused him a peerage.
38. Cockburn was called to the English Bar in 1829, became an MP in 1847, was appointed Solicitor-General in 1850, Attorney-General in 1851, Chief Justice of the Common Pleas in 1856 and Lord Chief Justice of the Queen's Bench from 1859 until 1880.
39. He made derogatory comments about his fellow arbitrators. The president of the tribunal, Count Sclopis, was 'vapid, pompous, ... un vrai phrasier [in French, today a '*phraseur*']', 'a maker of sentences', and a 'chatterer'. The Swiss arbitrator was 'ignorant as a horse and obstinate as a mule'. The Brazilian arbitrator was 'indolent'. His dissent, 'couched in immoderate and unjudicial language', provoked 'a very insulting riposte' by the US counsel, according to Lord Bingham (note 1 above).

The King of Italy, Victor-Emmanuel II, named Count Sclopis, an Italian politician and jurist,[40] Minister of Justice of the Kingdom of Piedmont[41] and later President of the Italian Senate.

The President of the Swiss Confederation named Jakob Stämpfli, a high-ranking Swiss politician and lawyer. Stämpfli had been a Federal counsellor.[42] He was a three-time President (each time for a one-year term) of the Swiss Confederation. Stämpfli had a methodical mind: his motto was 'Preparation and decision'. He had a strong personality and was not at all impressed with the other arbitrators, especially Sir Alexander Cockburn, whom he opposed on many occasions. With Sclopis, he played a decisive role.

The Emperor of Brazil, Peter II, named Marcos Antonio d'Araujo, then Baron (later Viscount) d'Itajuba, then ambassador of Brazil in Paris. D'Itajuba had been a Professor of Law at the University of Olinda before entering the diplomatic service.

THE ARBITRATION AND THE PROCEEDINGS

The written proceedings

The Treaty provided that the arbitrators should meet at the earliest convenient day after their nomination to constitute the Tribunal of Arbitration (the Tribunal), and that the simultaneous delivery of the case and accompanying evidence should take place no later than six months after the Treaty's ratification, which took place on 17 June 1871. On 15 December 1871, the arbitrators met in Geneva and constituted the tribunal, following which the parties delivered their cases.

The Treaty also provided that the counter-cases would be delivered within four months of delivery of the cases. This happened in timely fashion on 15 April 1872. Finally, within two months of delivery of the counter-cases, each party would submit a written recapitulating argument. This deadline – the third exchange of the written procedure – was met by the US (on 15 June 1872), but not by Great Britain.

The procedural setbacks to the tribunal's jurisdiction and method (June-July 1872)

Instead, the British agent submitted a note expressing the regret that the two Governments were unable to agree upon the tribunal's jurisdiction.

---

40. Sclopis was the author of many written works, including a *Storia della legislazione italiana dalle origini fino al 1847*.
41. Sclopis had written the *Statuto Albertino*, the constitution of the Kingdom of Savoy and Sardinia granted by King Charles-Albert in 1848. He was Minister of Justice of Piedmont, which was at the heart of the new Kingdom of Italy.
42. Stämpfli was a Swiss German from Berne. As a Federal counsellor, he was one of six Cabinet ministers of the Swiss Confederation. Successively, he headed the departments of Justice and Police, of Finance and of the Military.

The American case and counter-case indeed claimed compensation for the direct claims arising out of the depredations of the CS Navy, *viz* destruction of private ships and cargo.

The US also claimed damages for 'indirect claims'. These comprised (inter alia) the costs of the supposed prolongation of the war, of lower exports and of the transfer of commercial shipping to foreign shipping operations, estimated at US$2 billion at the time, several times Great Britain's annual budget. Its agent requested an adjournment of the proceedings for eight months to address the issue by negotiation. If this had been granted, it probably would have meant a breach of the Treaty and the collapse of the arbitration.

Both parties wanted the arbitration to proceed, but were unable to agree on the question of the indirect claims. Great Britain wanted the issue to be left outside the jurisdiction of the Tribunal, while the US government, under the watchful eye of Anglophobe public opinion, would not openly waive these 'national claims'.

For four days, the arbitrators, agents and counsel of the parties held informal meetings and finally reached a compromise. On 19 June 1872, the president of the Tribunal made the following announcement:

> The arbitrators think it right to state that ... they have arrived, individually and collectively, at the conclusion that these [indirect] claims do not constitute, upon the principles of International law applicable to such case, [a] good foundation for an award of compensation or computation of damages between nations, and should upon such principles be wholly excluded from the consideration of the Tribunal in making its award, even if there were no disagreement between the two Goverments as to the competency of the Tribunal to decide thereon ...

The statement that the indirect claims had no legal basis and would be excluded from the arbitrators' minds was made without regard to their jurisdiction, about which the arbitrators refused to express their views. Later, the president took every opportunity to correct any misconception: the statement was 'a declaration, not a judgment'. The US was satisfied that the Tribunal had expressed its judgment on the important question of public law at issue, while Great Britain announced that it would withdraw its request for adjournment and was ready to file its written recapitulating argument. This was accepted and done at the hearing of 27 June 1872. Immediately, however, a new difficulty arose.

At the same hearing, the British agent requested permission to submit a supplementary argument, including a discussion of the legal principles and replies to alleged new inaccuracies and allegations by the US. This would have amounted to a fourth stage in the written procedure and result in a six-week delay. The Tribunal rejected the request, but Sir Alexander Cockburn strived, for one month, to have it accepted. Meanwhile, the Tribunal decided on the proceedings in a way that was contrary to the British arbitrator's view: at the suggestion of the Swiss arbitrator, the Tribunal would 'first determine as to each vessel separately', as the Treaty required (per Article VII), whether Great Britain had been in breach of its neutrality.

The disagreement was settled by the Brazilian arbitrator. At his suggestion, the Tribunal decided on 25 July 1872 to make use of its power to request elucidation from the parties on the three legal questions at the heart of the British arguments: (1) the meaning of 'due diligence', (2) the legal effects of a commission of war, and (3) the issue of the coal provisions taken by the *Alabama* and others. Both parties filed their answers within two weeks.

The hearings (July-September 1872)

The arbitrators agreed, at their first meeting in Geneva on 15 December 1871, that the parties' agents and counsel would be allowed to attend the hearings, unless the Tribunal decided to deliberate in camera. They also decided that (1) each arbitrator would express his opinion about each question in writing, (2) these opinions would be communicated to the agents and counsel, and (3) the opinions would be confidential, temporary and provisional. The arbitrators would, however, remain free to decide the questions before them as they wished at the time of decision. The tribunal held more than 20 hearings between mid-June and mid-September 1872.

The British arbitrator argued that the legal issues be studied first but was unable to convince his colleagues of the soundness of his reasoning. After several hearings, the Tribunal proceeded to examine the case of each vessel. The arbitrators found that Great Britain had breached its obligations of neutrality in the cases of the *Alabama*, the *Florida* and the *Shenandoah*.

The Treaty commissioned the arbitrators to render an award as to liability. It also gave them the power, but not the duty, to assess and award damages.[43] They decided to make use of this power and to determine the entire dispute. From 19 August 1872, they busied themselves with this issue. The US claimed US$21 million, including US$7 million for the costs of pursuit[44] of the Confederate vessels. Great Britain admitted US$8 million, including one for the costs of pursuit. During the discussions, Cockburn agreed to US$10 million.

---

43. See note 28 above.
44. The costs of pursuit belonged to the category of national and direct claims, not to the private or the indirect claims.

THE AWARD AND THE DISSENT (14 SEPTEMBER 1872)

The award

The Treaty provided that the Tribunal should determine, as to each vessel, whether Great Britain had or had not failed to fulfill its duties, and that all questions should be decided by a majority. Unanimity was reached in two instances:[45] (1) on the principle of British liability for the *Alabama*, though Cockburn disagreed on the reasons for liability; and (2) on the exclusion of liability for the escape of the *Shenandoah* (the then *Sea King*), from London.

On the question of indemnification of the costs of the pursuit of Confederate vessels incurred by the US Navy, Sclopis, exceptionally, sided with d'Itajuba and Cockburn in refusing this. On the other issues, the majority included Sclopis, Stämpfli, d'Itajuba, the three arbitrators nominated by third parties, plus Adams – except on the issue of responsibility for the recruitment of crew by the *Shenandoah* at Melbourne, about which d'Itajuba agreed with Cockburn.

The text of the award starts with the Tribunal's interpretation of the applicable law, notably the three Rules of Article VI, proceeds to make decisions about each vessel, and ends with the issue of damages.

The first legal issue was that of the 'due diligence' to which the neutral government is bound. According to the majority, it should 'be exercised in *exact proportion to the risks* to which either of the belligerents may be exposed, from a failure to fulfill the obligations of neutrality on their part'. In the same demanding spirit, the Tribunal added that 'the circumstances out of which the facts constituting the subject-matter of the controversy arose were of [such] a nature [as] to call for the exercise on the part of Her Britannic Majesty's Government of *all possible solicitude* for the observance of the rights and duties involved in the proclamation of neutrality issued by Her Majesty on 13 May 1861'.

The second legal issue was about the effect of the commission of war on the Confederate ships. It was a main plea by Great Britain that her authorities were prevented from seizing the vessels by the sovereign immunity accorded to a State's ships by commissions of war. Sclopis called upon the general principle of Roman law that 'fraud corrupts everything' to deal with the argument.[46]

---

45. This was also relevant to the issue of the other ships and the indemnification of the prospective earnings (see pp 247 and 248 below).

46. 'The effects of a violation of neutrality committed by means of the construction, equipment, and armament of a vessel are not done away with by any commission which the government of the belligerent power, benefited by the violation of neutrality, may afterward have granted to that vessel; and the ultimate step, by which the offense is completed, cannot be admissible as a ground for the absolution of the offender, nor can the consummation of his fraud become the means of establishing his innocence ... The privilege of extraterritoriality

The third legal issue was the limits to the hospitality granted by a neutral. How much coal may a belligerent take? By international custom,[47] a ship could take the quantity required to reach her nearest home port. The second Rule of Article VI prohibited the use by a belligerent of the neutral's ports as a 'base of naval operations'. The arbitrators interpreted this clause with great flexibility:

> In order to impart to any supplies of coal a character inconsistent with the second rule, prohibiting the use of neutral ports or waters, as a base of naval operations for a belligerent, it is necessary that the said supplies should be connected with special circumstances of time, of persons, or of place, which may combine to give them such character.

With regard to the *Alabama*, the arbitrators held that, considering the facts of the construction of the then *Enrica* at Birkenhead, and its equipment and armament at Terceira by the *Agrippina* and the *Bahama*, which had been dispatched from Great Britain, the British government failed, by omission, to fulfill the duties of due diligence prescribed in the first and third Rules of Article VI, *viz* prevention of equipment and prevention of a violation of the law respectively. In particular, Great Britain omitted, notwithstanding the warnings of US diplomatic agents during the ship's construction, to take in due time any effective measures of prevention, so that the orders given at last for the detention of the vessel were issued too late to be executed.

After the escape, the measures taken for the pursuit of the *Alabama* – which were imperfect and led to no result – could not be considered sufficient to release Great Britain from the liability incurred. Despite the violations of the Great Britain's neutrality committed by the *Enrica*, the *Alabama* was freely admitted into the ports of British colonies instead of being proceeded against as it ought to have been in any port within British jurisdiction. Finally, the arbitrators held that the British government could not justify its plea of insufficiency of its legal (municipal) means of action.

With regard to the *Florida*, the four arbitrators judged that Great Britain had not fulfilled its obligations under all three Rules of Article VI, *viz* prevention of equipment, use of a port as a base of naval operations and prevention of a violation of the law. In spite of American warnings, the

---

accorded to vessels of war has been admitted into the law of nations, not as an absolute right, but solely as a proceeding founded on the principle of courtesy and mutual deference between different nations, and therefore can never be appealed to for the protection of acts done in violation of neutrality ...' The first sentence, with its convoluted style, was probably written by the president, Federico Sclopis. During the hearings, Sclopis explained himself thus: 'The offence of which this vessel was guilty ... does not disappear as a result of an indecent ruse ... *Dolus nemini patrocinari debet.*' '*Dolus* must protect no one.'

47. See also note 12 above about the British instructions of neutrality of 31 January 1862.

British government took no action to seize the then *Oreto* under construction in Liverpool and, when she reached Nassau, to prevent her enlistment of men, acquisition of supplies and armament at Green Cay, with the co-operation of the British vessel *Prince Alfred*. The judicial acquittal of the *Oreto* at Nassau could not relieve Great Britain from the liability incurred by her under the principles of international law. In spite of these violations, the former *Oreto* was on several occasions freely admitted into British ports.

With regard to the *Shenandoah*, the skill of Confederate agents had concealed her departure, acquisition, transformation and armament. No liability on the part of Great Britain had therefore been incurred for her escape from the country. However, she augmented her forces during her stay in Melbourne, which the British government itself admitted to have been clandestinely effected, by the enlistment of men. By a majority of three (Sclopis, Stämpfli and Adams) to two (Cockburn and d'Itajuba), the Tribunal decided that Great Britain had failed to fulfill the duties prescribed by the second and third Rules of art VI, *viz* use of a port as a base of naval operations and prevention of a violation of the law, and so was responsible for all acts committed after the ship's departure from Melbourne.

The award then made decisions about 13 other Confederate vessels, including the *Georgia*,[48] but not the ironclads,[49] declaring that the three tenders should follow the lot of their principal, that five did not give rise to liability, and that the last five were excluded from consideration for want of evidence.

As previously mentioned, the Tribunal decided to exercise their power to assess damages. On the heads of indemnification, by a three (Sclopis,

48. The *Georgia*, built in Scotland as the *Japan*, was registered by a British merchant. She embarked her crew, recruited in Liverpool, at a different port and received her armament, the name *Georgia*, flag and commission of war, from a transport ship dispatched from New Haven, off the French coast of Brittany. The procedure for illegal enlistment against directors of the recruiting company led to a symbolic judgment of £50 each.

49. The Confederate Navy also bought a new type of warship: ironclads and rams, which would belong to a superior class of war vessel capable of outclassing the US Navy. Two were built by the same shipbuilders as the *Alabama*. US ambassador Charles Francis Adams handed to Lord Russell the evidence obtained by the US consul. Lord Russell replied that the British government was not prepared to act upon these documents. The ambassador wrote a memorable letter to Russell on 5 September 1863. Having said that these ships would be formidable destroyers, he concluded: 'It would be superfluous in me to point out to your Lordship that, if this decision is maintained, this is war.' Lord Russell decided to have the ships seized and, to avoid a judicial setback, the British government bought the rams for the Royal Navy. For the ambassador, the question was not about the legality, under the Foreign Enlistment Act of 1819, of the construction of warships by private firms in Liverpool or elsewhere; rather, it was about whether Great Britain accepted the role of shipbuilder to a belligerent in violation of customary international law. Adams may also have thought, with good sense, that the construction of formidable weapons for a belligerent was inconsistent with a declaration of neutrality.

d'Itajba, Cockburn) to two (Stämpfli and Adams) vote, the Tribunal refused indemnification for the costs of pursuit[50] of the Confederate vessels by the US Navy, which were not distinguishable from the general expenses of the war. The Tribunal unanimously decided that there was no ground for compensation for prospective earnings, as they depended by their nature upon future and uncertain contingencies. To arrive at an equitable compensation figure, the Tribunal decided to set aside all double claims for the same losses, and all claims for 'gross freights', so far as they exceeded 'net freights'. It was also deemed just to allow interest at a reasonable rate (6%).

The Tribunal, by a majority of four to one, awarded the sum of US$15,500,000 in gold as the indemnity to be paid by Great Britain to the US for the satisfaction of all the claims referred.

The award ended with a reminder of its final effect under Article XI of the Treaty. It was signed by the four arbitrators who had given their assent: Sclopis, Stämpfli, d'Itajuba and Adams.

The dissent of Sir Alexander Cockburn

After the award had been read publicly on the last hearing day open to the public,[51] Cockburn handed over a stack of paper containing his reasons for not agreeing with the award. The president accepted that the document be appended to the protocol of the day, but did not arrange to forward a copy to the US agent. It was published later by the *London Gazette*.[52]

The tone of the dissent was violent and derisive, with attacks *ad hominem* on the American counsel[53] and even on the arbitrators, the Swiss arbitrator[54] and the president in particular.[55] Sir Alexander mentioned

---

50. With regard to the costs of pursuit of Confederate vessels incurred by the US Navy, see note 44.

51. On 14 September 1872, the secretary to the Tribunal read the English version of the award, which was then signed by the four concurring arbitrators. This done, the president handed a copy to both agents.

52. On 24 September 1872.

53. 'There is in this extraordinary series of propositions the most singular confusion of ideas, misrepresentations of facts, and ignorance, both of law and history, which were perhaps ever crowded into the same space, and for my part I cannot help expressing my sense, not only of the gross injustice done to my country, but also of the affront offered to this tribunal by such an attempt to practice on our supposed credulity and ignorance.'

54. 'I cannot concur with M. Staempfli, that, because the practice of nations has at times undergone great changes, and the views of jurists on points of International law have often been and still are conflicting, therefore there is no such thing as International law, and that, consequently, we are to proceed independently of any such law – for such is the effect of his reasoning, if I understand it rightly – according to some intuitive perception of right and wrong, or speculative notions of what the rules as to the duties of neutrals ought to be.'

55. 'This is evidently the meaning of an observation of the British counsel at the close of the fifth section of his argument on "due diligence" which the president of the tribunal appears to have found some difficulty in understanding.'

twice[56] in his opinion that he was 'sitting on this tribunal as in some sense the representative of Great Britain'. Most commentators have agreed with this statement and condemned his state of mind and behaviour as that of an advocate and a partisan, not of a judge.

On the question of the applicable law, Sir Alexander expressed his disapproval of the three Rules of Article VI for their retroactivity and lack of precision,[57] and especially about the 'vague and uncertain'[58] expression 'due diligence'. He also criticised the drafters for not stating which 'principles of International law, not inconsistent with the Rules laid down' were to be applied by the tribunal.[59]

Cockburn's opinion covered some 215 pages,[60] discussing all the details of the case and arguments of the parties and quoting abundantly the opinions of a great number of authors on International Law.

In Cockburn's view, the tribunal should first have determined the applicable principles of law. There were heads of complaint by the US that were not concerned with the three Rules of Article VI of the Treaty: (1) whether it was possible to seize vessels upon their re-entry into British ports, once they had received a commission of war from the Confederacy; (2) whether Confederate vessels were permitted to make British ports a base of naval operations against the US; and (3) whether the accommodation afforded in British ports was a violation of neutrality. These three questions should have been dealt with independently from the three Rules and entirely under International law. In truth, the issue of the commissioning of war (head (1)) was already known to international law. The two other issues – of the base of naval operations (head (2)) and of the accommodation afforded (head (3)) – were treated by the second of the Rules of Article VI.

To Cockburn, the standard of 'due diligence', its extent and meaning, and the degree of diligence required, could be established under international law only, the Treaty giving no definition of the expression. The reference in the Treaty to 'the principles of International law not inconsistent with such Rules' allowed this.[61]

---

56. Dissent, in *Papers relating to the Treaty of Washington* IV (*supra*, note 18), pp 286 and 313.
57. 'I cannot but think, to be regretted that the whole subject-matter of this great contest, in respect of law as well as of fact, was not left open to us, to be decided according to the true principles and rules of International law in force and binding among nations, and the duties and obligations arising out of them, at the time when these alleged causes of complaint are said to have arisen.'
58. *Papers relating to the Treaty of Washington* (the Dissent) (*supra*, note 18), p 232.
59. Ibid, p 232.
60. Ibid, pp 230–544.
61. When Cockburn had the opportunity to express his views, he called upon comparative law instead of citing rules of international law, citing the French Civil Code notion of private law, inherited from Roman law, of *diligens et bonus pater familias*, as interpreted by a

It was therefore, said Cockburn, 'desirable, in the first place, to endeavour to take an accurate survey of the law by which the relative rights of belligerents and neutrals are fixed and determined, as essential to the solution of the questions we are called on to decide.' Cockburn's reluctance to accept the three Rules led him to invert the hierarchy of legal principles stated in Article VI. Whereas the Treaty gave the three Rules pre-eminence over 'the principles of International law', Cockburn looked to the principles of international law to discover the meaning of the three Rules.

The majority of the Tribunal considered, however, that it had been sufficiently informed by the exchange of cases, counter-cases and arguments of points and evidence. The three Rules, complemented by several principles of general law,[62] provided a sufficient legal basis on which to decide Great Britain's liability.

While disapproving of the legal motivation of the award, the decisions on the *Florida* and the *Shenandoah* and the amount of damages, Cockburn invited the British people to accept the award as the 'impartial judgment' of the Tribunal. The US$15.5 million were paid within the one-year time limit laid down by the Treaty.

Since 1872, Cockburn's views about the State's international responsibility have nourished debates among internationalists and enriched the legacy of this arbitration.

THE LEGACY OF THE *ALABAMA* ARBITRATION

The *Alabama* arbitration marked a great watershed in relations between Great Britain and the US. It reversed a long period of confrontation between the two countries. Great Britain and the US had been in open hostilities during the War of Independence (1775–1783), then in the Anglo-American War of 1812–1814, and several times teetered on the verge of military conflict, particularly in 1861 (during the *Trent* affair). After the *Alabama* arbitration, the two countries discovered their common strategic interests, initiated the 'Great Rapprochement'[63] and concluded

German scholar, Zachariae. This did not convince his fellow arbitrators. It is remarkable that Cockburn did not refer to the similar legal concept and standard of 'reasonable man' developed by the common law at the same time in *Vaughan v Menlove* of 1837 (3 Bing. N.C. 468) and *Blyth v Birmingham Waterworks* of 1856 (11 Ex. 781). If made, such a reference would possibly have met the criticism of 'vague and uncertain expression' raised by Cockburn with regard to the 'due diligence'.

62. In particular the Roman principle of general criminal law that *Fraus omnia corrumpit* ('fraud vitiates everything').

63. The convergence of interests between the US and Great Britain was accelerated by several events and phenomena. After the resolution of all disputes by arbitral tribunals (the *Alabama* claims and the San Juan boundary dispute) and mixed commissions (the North-eastern fisheries, the Great Lakes navigation and commerce) set up by the Treaty of Washington, came the demilitarisation of the US–Canada border (initiated by Lord Castlereagh as a

a permanent peace and alliance agreement. This strong alliance was so important to the outcome of the first and second World Wars and remains today as one of most stable relationships in the international relations of an unstable world. The *Alabama* arbitration also had important effects on international arbitration and international law. These are considered below.

The contribution of the *Alabama* arbitration to international arbitration

International arbitration born again

Arbitration has a very ancient origin and a long history, as Derek Roebuck convincingly showed in *Ancient Greek Arbitration* and *Roman Arbitration*.[64] In his five books on England, Derek also demonstrated that the practice of private arbitration had been continuous in that country.[65] The situation was probably similar in many countries. Public arbitration flourished to settle international disputes in the ancient world and during the Middle Ages. In modern times, the rise of the nation State – with its sovereign powers and immunity – has coincided with a decline in international public arbitration.

The *Alabama* arbitration gave a new impetus to international arbitration. The arbitration itself was a great success. The arbitrators solved the two problems created by the imprecise wording of the Treaty about the definition of the claims and about the extent of the 'due diligence' to be performed by the neutral State. Their handling of the issue of jurisdiction when the two parties were unable to agree to admit or reject the Tribunal's competence on the indirect claims and threatened to derail the proceedings, was remarkable. The voluntary exercise by the arbitrators of their power to assess and award damages accelerated the solution of a thorny problem and drew the two governments out of a predicament. The award was accepted by both parties and duly enforced. The Tribunal fulfilled its mission of peacemaker with perfect efficiency. Justice was done and it was done manifestly within the time limit laid down by the Treaty.

disarmament measure following the Anglo-American War of 1812–1814 and implemented by the Rush-Bagot Treaty of 1817), the industrialisation of the Great Lakes region and the contribution of the City of London to US private investments. All risks of war disappeared. No more Fenian raids into Canada were tolerated by the US. No more threats of invading Canada were heard at the Senate. Great Britain discovered the help the US could provide against Russia or Germany, and sided with the US during its 1898 war against Spain; British neutrality was then certainly unfriendly to Spain but friendly to the US.

64. *Editorial note*: See, in this volume, Robert Morgan, *Derek Roebuck, Historian: A Literature Review. Roman Arbitration* was co-authored with the author of the present contribution.

65. Ibid.

The *Alabama* arbitration became a landmark in the history of arbitration under public international law. From 1872 until the end of the 19th century, several dozen such arbitrations were initiated in America and in Europe. According to CH Brower II, 'Systematically, if the Jay treaty breathed life into arbitration, the *Alabama* claims infused it with new vigor, even for claims relating to matters of national honor'.

Several institutions relating to international arbitration were later founded by multilateral treaties. These include the International Law Institute (1875), the Permanent Court of Arbitration (PCA, created by The Hague I peace conference and treaties of 1899 and 1907), the Permanent Court of International Justice (PCIJ, 1920) and its successor, the International Court of Justice (ICJ, 1945).

The new form of neutral tribunal created by the Treaty of Washington

The drafters of the Treaty of Washington took advantage of the lessons learned from the Jay Treaty. In 1794, three mixed commissions had been set up. All of them comprised representatives of each party in equal numbers. The president, elected by both parties or drawn by lot, had no casting vote, and decisions should be unanimous. Two commissions had the task of settling claims similar to those in the *Alabama* case. One had to deal with claims by British businessmen for sums owed by American citizens. After settling some of the claims, the commission was divided and had to adjourn its sittings indefinitely. The other commission had to deal with claims made by US businessmen for the irregular seizure of ships and cargo by British authorities during the War of Independence. In eight years, the commission gave more than five hundred rulings and awarded US\$11 million to American citizens. The dead end met by the first commission and the excessive time spent by the second called for improvements to the mechanism and composition of the decision-making bodies.

The arbitration agreement under the Treaty of Washington provided that the '*Alabama* claims' made by American citizens would be taken over by the US government and that the possible damages paid by Great Britain to the US would then be distributed among the private claimants. The dispute would be treated first from the point of view of the illegal deeds of the Confederate vessels, and secondarily from that of their financial consequences to private American citizens.

The Treaty also provided that the Tribunal would be made up of five arbitrators: two designated by the parties and three nominated by independent authorities. All decisions, including the award, should be made by a majority of *all* arbitrators. The three arbitrators named by the heads of State other than those of the two interested parties formed a majority.

The Treaty provided the *keystone*[66] for international arbitration with the invention of the neutral collegial tribunal, including arbitrators selected by the parties. The Tribunal would be made up of, so to speak, three categories of member: some appointed by the parties, some designated by independent authorities and, among the latter, the president.

This system influenced the composition of the later neutral international public arbitration tribunals of inter-State institutions (such as the PCA, PCIJ and ICJ) and the neutral international private arbitration tribunals of business institutions (such as the International Chamber of Commerce and the London Court of International Arbitration). This has ensured both the independence and neutrality of arbitral tribunals, as well as their efficiency, and replaced the much-criticised previous mechanism of arbitration by heads of State. By comparison with the Jay Treaty commissions, the modern arbitration mechanism has transferred the power of decision from mixed commissions of parties' administrative and diplomatic representatives to independent bodies having an international character and exercising judicial function and power.

The contribution of the *Alabama* arbitration to international law

Finally, the *Alabama* arbitration laid down some of the foundations of modern international law.

Kompetenz-Kompetenz

A general principle of arbitration is that the 'arbitrator may do nothing outside the powers granted by the parties'.[67] What if one of the parties disclaims the jurisdiction of the arbitrators? Who has the power of *Kompetenz-Kompetenz*, as the Germans call it? And when may it be exercised?

The answers given by international tribunals and by States' legislation and judiciaries are numerous. 'Although private, arbitration proceeds in the shadow of public coercion'.[68] Generally, national laws provide for co-operation between private arbitrators and public tribunals. The French Code of Civil Procedure,[69] for example, grants an extensive power to the arbitrators to decide upon their jurisdiction during the arbitral proceedings, and a limited one to the courts, both before and after them. The UNCITRAL

---

66. VV Veeder, see *supra* note 1.

67. '*Arbiter nihil extra compromissum facere potest*', wrote, with Latin laconicism, the Roman jurisconsult Paul, *c*.220 AD/CE (D. 4, 8, 32, 21): 'The arbitrator can do nothing outside the compromise'.

68. WW Park, *Arbitration in International Business Disputes* (2012, Oxford University Press), p 236.

69. Article 1458.

Model Law on International Commercial Arbitration explicitly grants arbitrators the power to decide their jurisdiction in an ancillary award.

The declaration made by president Sclopis about the indirect claims on 19 June 1872 stated that the arbitrators were unanimously of the opinion that these claims had no legal basis and would be excluded from consideration, 'even if there were no disagreement between the two Governments as to the competency of the Tribunal ...'. The British Foreign Secretary, Lord Granville, declared that this was an extra-judicial statement. President Sclopis insisted that it was 'une déclaration, pas un jugement'. The US Secretary of State considered the communication made by the arbitrators as the 'view they have formed upon the question of public law involved'.

The legal nature of this act was controversial. In form, it was a declaration. In substance, it was a statement of the law, and an application of its consequences (exclusion of later consideration of its subject matter by the Tribunal), it was therefore a judgment. In the face of a plea by Great Britain to bar arbitration for lack of competence, the Tribunal's initiative had the effect of a voluntary exercise of jurisdiction. It implied an appreciation of its competence 'even if there had been no disagreement between the two Governments over the tribunal's jurisdiction'. Its effects were radical and positive: it prevented the abortion of the arbitration, to the relief of the parties. Its influence is long-lasting.

Since then, the *Kompetenz-Kompetenz* power of arbitrators has been recognised by arbitral awards,[70] treaties[71] and international institutions,[72] in particular by the Statute of the ICJ.[73]

The relationship between international law and national laws

Great Britain looked to its municipal law – the FEA 1819 – to excuse the escape of the *Alabama* and the *Florida*. The customary unwritten constitution of the United Kingdom protected the rights of private persons to property and prohibited seizures by administrative ruling. The 1819 Act authorised the mere construction of warships. The British government was deprived of legal means of action, as was, incidentally, the US government.

With regard to the *Florida*, the majority of the arbitrators decided that the judicial acquittal of the *Oreto* at Nassau could not relieve Great Britain from the responsibility incurred by it under the principles of international law. With regard to both the *Alabama* and the *Florida*, the

---

70. The *Georges Salem* (1932) and *Radio Orient* (1940) cases. The *Nottebohm* award (1953) made by the ICJ expressly refers to the *Alabama* case. See also the *Corfu Channel* (1949) and *Ambatelios* (1952) cases.
71. The Hague I Conventions of 1899 and 1907.
72. The International Arbitration Rules of the International Law Institute (1872). See also (*inter alia*) the ICC Rules of Arbitration.
73. Article 36 para 6.

Tribunal decided that the British government could not justify itself for their escape by pleading insufficiency of its legal (municipal) means of action. The Tribunal applied the three international Rules under Article VI of the Treaty and considered that, for all three ships (which included for this purpose the *Shenandoah*), there had been occasions on which the 'vigilance' of the British authorities had been wanting.

While the Tribunal never expressed the view that international law would be superior to municipal law, later international arbitrators and scholars of international law did take the plunge and declared that an international treaty had an authority superior to that of a State's constitution. This view, of course, is not shared by many countries, States and national public opinion. In the US, the famous *Charming Betsy* case[74] went so far as to decide that US municipal law should be interpreted as much as possible to be in conformity with international law, though the US Supreme Court never went any further than this.

Due diligence and the State's international responsibility

The *Alabama* case was about the responsibility of Great Britain as a neutral during the Civil War. The first Rule of Article VI of the Treaty stated that 'a neutral is bound to exercise due diligence to prevent the fitting out, arming, or equipping ... of any vessel ... intended to cruise or carry on war ... against a Power with which it is at peace ..., and also to use like diligence to prevent the departure ... of any vessel ... adapted ... to warlike use.' The third rule required the exercise of 'due diligence ... to prevent any violation of the foregoing obligations and duties'.

Cockburn criticised the 'vague and uncertain' expression of 'due diligence'. The wording was truly circular, tautological: *bound* to exercise *due* diligence. Which kind and degree of diligence? As mentioned previously, the High Commissioners discussed and rejected the expressions 'active diligence' and 'due watchfulness' as excessive and 'reasonable care' as insufficient. Mainly diplomats, they were fain to get rid of the question and to pass the difficulty on to the lawyers.

The first use of the expression in this case is to be found after the end of the Civil War, in a communication from Lord Russell to Charles Francis Adams dated 30 August 1865. Russell expressed the view that the whole question was whether the British government had acted with 'due diligence, that is with good faith and honesty in the maintenance of the neutrality they proclaimed'.

As mentioned previously, the majority of the Tribunal took the view that due diligence should 'be exercised in *exact proportion to the risks* to which either of the belligerents may be exposed, from a failure to fulfill the

---

74. *Editorial note*: *Murray v The Charming Betsy*, 6 US 64 (1804).

obligations of neutrality on their part'. In the same demanding spirit, the Tribunal added that 'the circumstances[75] out of which the facts constituting the subject-matter of the controversy arose were of a nature to call for the exercise on the part of Her Britannic Majesty's Government of *all possible solicitude* for the observance of the rights and duties involved in the proclamation of neutrality issued by Her Majesty on 13 May 1861.'

Cockburn was of the opinion that the neutral State should be bound to use the means at its disposal. Its diligence should be similar in degree to the *diligentia* required from a *diligens pater familias* for the preservation of private property (sale, lease, pledge): a reasonable degree of care showing neither too much rigour, nor too much indulgence.[76] Also, only *culpa lata* (grave fault or gross negligence) would be a cause for complaint and liability.

The US claimed that the degree of due diligence should be measured by the importance of the subject matter, the reciprocal position of the parties (belligerents and neutral), the means of action of the neutral and the possible damages incurred by a belligerent. Great Britain answered that there were limits to the use of a government's means of action: the limitations were natural (one hour lost), legal (constant and meticulous spying in a free country) and political (measures that were impossible to take).

Since 1872, there have been lively debates among internationalists about the degree of vigilance and action required to be exercised by a State in order to be freed from international liability. The notion of 'due diligence' is now widely accepted and applied by treaties and awards[77] in different branches of international law, such as human rights, international investment and the environment. A sign of this success is given by the editors of the *Max Planck Encyclopedia of Public International Law*, in which a special entry deals with this new legal concept.

Other legacies

It is not possible in this limited space to deal fully with other legacies left by the *Alabama* arbitration. Two are, however, worth mentioning.

First, the admissibility of dissenting opinions seems to have been acknowledged for the first time in international arbitration, when the president of the Tribunal, Federico Sclopis, accepted that Cockburn's stack of paper containing his dissent be admitted with the documents annexed to the record of the last hearing.

---

75. The circumstances alluded to may have included the vital importance of the Civil War to both Union and ports at home and overseas, the leading role assumed willingly by Great Britain in the proclamation of its neutrality.

76. Article 1137 of the French Civil Code. See *supra* note 61.

77. See, in particular, A. Ouedraogo *supra* at note 1.

Secondly, the *Alabama* arbitration proceedings have been influential on later developments. These include the importance of the written phase (case, counter-case and written argument recapitulating the points and referring to the evidence), case management (applying the famous principle of proportionality between costs and benefits), the active role of the arbitrators in using their power of investigation, and assessing and awarding damages.

For these reasons and others, the *Alabama* arbitration is as rich as the wreck of the Confederate vessel lying unexplored on the seabed a few miles off Cherbourg.

NURTURING PROFESSIONALISM THROUGH CLINICAL LEGAL EDUCATION*

*Mary Gold and Neil Gold***

What can [clinical] legal educators do to instill in law students a sense of moral responsibility toward their [future] clients, the legal system, and society?[1]

THE EXPLICIT PURSUIT OF MORAL DEVELOPMENT

In this contribution we will argue that moral development should be an explicit goal of a legal education, especially (but not only) as part of clinical legal education. After all, moral development, as both a process and a result, is an essential element of professionalism, perhaps its most important element. Lawyers, together with others in the legal system, have a sacred trust to protect truth, pursue justice and avoid injustice. We will show that professionalism comprises a set of moral qualities that should be evidenced in the work of legal professionals, whatever their role in the justice system.

In many places, the calls for a more pervasively honest, client-centred, justice-oriented, less self-interested and more forthright legal professional have led to the teaching of legal ethics and professionalism as a curricular requirement as fundamental as contract or tort. However, such teaching, depending on how it is pursued, may do the opposite of teaching professionalism: it may show through positivist case analysis and the legal explication of applicable principles sited in rules of conduct how to use the law of legal ethics to avoid moral conduct.

A legal education course often studies the law applicable to those with advantage. This is especially true of the civil law, which is mostly about

* This contribution is based on a presentation by professors Mary Gold and Neil Gold at the International Journal of Clinical Legal Education and European Network for Clinical Legal Education Joint Conference, Olomouc, Czech Republic, 17 July 2014.
** Mary Gold and Neil Gold, professors *emeriti*, Faculty of Law, University of Windsor, Canada.
1. Lorie M Graham, 'Aristotle's Ethics and the Virtuous Lawyer: Part One of a Study on Legal Ethics and Clinical Legal Education', (1995–1996) 20 *Legal Prof.* 5.

the activities of those with finances. Criminal and public law, as well as tort and family law, often deal with the behaviour of the less well advantaged in society. The obligation to redress the needs of the marginalised and disadvantaged through law has resonated with those who seek social justice through law. For many, commitment to such service is concomitant with moral development and is an indicator, and requirement, of higher learning in all fields, and especially in the provision of professional legal services.

Critiques of legal decision-making should always be founded in both law and justice. Some would say that professionalism is implicit in a legal education. Here we argue that moral development, an essential element of professionalism, a set of qualities that should be found in legal professionals, should be an explicit goal of a legal education, and especially clinical legal education, and that it should be taught directly. In teaching something directly, one is forced to interrogate, analyse and operationalise key concepts, never taking them for granted. Thus, legal educators may not be aware that they are always teaching *something* besides the apparent content of a lesson, not only what was explicitly intended, in virtually everything they do and say. Some of what is done or taught during the educational experience may or may not have been intended; we do not know because nothing is said about it. As a result, there is a kind of 'hidden curriculum', which perhaps teaches unintentionally. This recalls Maine's statement in referring to Maitland: 'So great is the ascendancy of the Law of Actions in the infancy of Courts of Justice, that substantive law has at first the look of being gradually secreted in the interstices of procedure.'[2] Some might say, we are what we do.

Claims that moral development cannot and should not be taught

Before we continue, let us address some common arguments against attempting to teach moral behaviour and professionalism. It is often said that it is too late to effect ethical commitment and professional responsibility through a legal education, given the age of law students, especially in North America, and increasingly in the Antipodes. While admitting moral character is essential to ethical conduct, it is averred that it is established early in life, in the context of the family and childhood development. Others criticise the teaching of moral development and professionalism as akin to an indoctrination through the inculcation or promotion of ideologies. This is not necessarily the case: when done correctly, such teaching is not about *what* to believe or practise: rather, it seeks to educate *how* to think, *how* to believe (or come to believe) and *how* to feel, as human processes. Such an

---

2. HS Maine, *Early Law and Custom* (1883) https://oll.libertyfund.org/titles/maine-dissertations-on-early-law-and-custom (accessed 10 December 2020).

education is not different in kind from our goal of teaching *how* to think, not *what* to think.

We have heard it said that morality is personal, outside the remit of a formal education, except perhaps in the clergy; that being the case, it is argued that it is wrong and unworkable to try to teach morality. Given the relatively short length of a legal education, it must also be contended that there are more important matters for learning in a university, such as constitutional or criminal law. Finally, some shrug and ask: why bother – people will do what serves them best; however effective teaching may be, its gains will be lost, negated or at least undermined, perhaps even transformed, by amoral real-life (practice) experiences. Given the world we inhabit, it becomes clearer by the day that there can be nothing more important than a moral actor. Compare, if you will, Jacinda Ardern with Donald Trump or Boris Johnson.

DEFINING 'PROFESSIONALISM'

'Professionalism' is not easily defined, nor are the boundaries of professional conduct easily circumscribed. It includes fundamentally the care and concern for human needs, from promoting social justice goals to treating others with respect. In its highest form, professionalism involves, as Aristotle offered, 'complete virtue' or 'excellence' in virtue: knowing how to act at the 'right time', with the 'right motive', in the 'right way', with 'reference to the right objects', and "towards the right people'. Action and habitual use are prerequisites to understanding ethics: virtuous actions must be integrated with practical reason before a person can become completely virtuous, and complete virtue involves listening to the dictates of reason.[3]

Hamilton[4] has suggested that professionalism means behaving with commitment to expert knowledge, accountably and with respect for both the Rule of Law and social justice. Professional behaviour evinces core humanistic values, including client centredness, a commitment to meeting client (that is, others') needs, while promoting autonomy over dependence. The professional self-regulates, is autonomous and not dependent on others' approbation. In a sense, the consummate professional's commitment to ethical practice reflects a fiduciary-like duty to altruism, self-efficacy, self-authorship and perhaps (and ultimately most importantly) self-reflection.

Some descriptors of professionalism are included in the list noted.[5] Professionalism is a matter of character: moral *behaviour* (skills), moral

3. Graham, *supra* note 2.
4. Neil Hamilton, 'Assessing Professionalism: Measuring Progress in the Formation of an Ethical Professional Identity', (2008) 5 *U. St. Thomas LJ* 470.
5. Intelligence, integrity, maturity, thoughtfulness, courage, honesty, dependability, loyalty,

sensitivity (awareness) and, importantly, moral *commitment*, the determination to do what is right.[6]

Moral development

Perhaps critically and obviously, we are not born with moral development: it is a process and an end, both of which are learned and can be influenced by teaching. It is a *staged* developmental process through which we each progress through defined stages at *varying* rates. As with all learning, not all persons proceed to the final stage, at least not completely. There are several studied approaches to development, mostly derived from *empirical* research, derived from *thought, action and observation*. The resulting schemas are descriptive and carry no judgements.

Scholars have developed models to illustrate the hierarchy of moral development in both the cognitive and affective realms. A seminal model was developed by Lawrence Kohlberg who envisioned three stages of psychological development, beginning with what he termed the *pre-conventional*, in which an individual's behaviour is initially motivated by either receiving rewards or avoiding punishment. Next, he describes the *conventional* stage, in which one looks externally for the approval of others, often in order to fit in, and values the importance of trust, loyalty, duty and doing the right thing. Finally, there is the *post-conventional* stage, in which the individual looks internally to his or her personal conscience as the guide to making moral choices.[7] Kohlberg sees ethical behaviour as grounded in impartiality, in equality, in justice and in individual rights. Other scholars, such as Carol Gilligan, believe that an emphasis on impartiality is an insufficient motivator and that caring for and being responsible to others are equally important.[8] Branch maintains that the two approaches are complementary: 'Ethical behavior integrates moral sensitivity (ability to recognize ethical issues), moral commitment (determination to do what is right), with moral reasoning (being able to weigh the rights of others and the principles at stake).'[9]

Within the educational context, David R Krathwohl provides a taxonomy of the *affective* domain to illustrate the outcomes that the instructor intends, and the individual achieves, in the process of becoming a moral actor. It enables the instructor to develop a set of learning outcomes to guide the

conscience, openness, sensitivity to clients, trustworthiness, accountable, humble, respectful, observant of both privacy and confidentiality.
6. William T. Branch, Jr., 'Supporting the Moral Development of Medical Students' (2000) 15 *Journal of General Internal Medicine* 503.
7. Lawrence Kohlberg, *The Psychology of Moral Development: The Nature and Validity of Moral Stages* (Harper & Row, 1984).
8. Carol Gilligan, *In a Different Voice* (Harvard University Press, 1982).
9. William T. Branch, Jr., *supra* note 6, p. 505.

teaching and learning enterprise. Key to being able to do this is knowing the level at which the learners arrive in the instruction.[10] The taxonomy has five stages: first, *receiving* indicates an awareness of, or sensitively to, certain ideas and being open to entertaining them; second, *responding* shows an interest in and some commitment to interacting with the ideas; third, *valuing* is a willingness to be perceived as esteeming certain ideas; fourth, *organisation* involves relating new ideas or values to ones already held, *internalising* them and exhibiting a commitment to them; and fifth, *characterisation* results in acting consistently with these values.

Educators can facilitate the moral development of their students and help them to transition from relying on external forces to internally directed considerations, and to progress from relying on simple distinctions between right and wrong to making a more nuanced personal assessment of moral choices and behaviour.[11]

THE HIDDEN CURRICULUM: INFORMAL LEARNING

Because medical education relies so heavily upon clinical teaching, in which students interact with their instructors, patients and each other on a regular basis, the need to address the importance of professionalism within the context of practice has been a concern of medical schools for some time. Concern had been expressed that the focus of professionalism in the clinical setting had been relegated to the context of making correct diagnoses and prescribing appropriate remedies while avoiding mistakes and malpractice – correct, skilled practice. Furthermore, a great deal of attention has focused on the frequent disconnect between the explicit and more theoretical teaching of professionalism that concentrates on moral and ethical dimensions of medical practice and the informal, and frequently unarticulated, learning that takes place when the behaviour of clinical instructors is observed and later emulated by students. Frequently, the observation of behaviour has less to do with the acquisition of medical knowledge and procedures than with the informal observation of the supervisor's interactions with patients, which may fail to take into account their human and emotional needs. This has led medical educators to study how they can improve the informal education of medical students by providing examples of how they can be motivated by altruistic and humanistic principles.

Informal learning was defined thus by Edward T. Hall: 'The main agent of informal learning is a model used for imitation. Whole clusters are

10. David R. Krathwohl, Benjamin S Bloom and Bertram B Masia, *Taxonomy of Educational Objectives, Book 2: Affective Domain* (David McKay Co. 1964).
11. A Petter, 'A closet within the house: learning objectives and the law school curriculum', in Neil Gold ed., *Essays on Legal Education* (Toronto: Butterworth 1982).

learned at a time, usually without awareness that they are being learned at all or that there are patterns or rules governing them.'[12] Albert Bandura stated that '... most human behavior is learned observationally through modeling: from observing others, one forms an idea of how new behaviors are performed, and on later occasions this coded information serves as a guide for action.'[13]

Thus, effective educators must be able to articulate and practise the traits and behaviours of a good role model so that they complement formal classroom learning and teach what ought to be done. The medical educational literature has identified the qualities that positive role models demonstrate: 'expertise, empathy, and positive communication processes with patients and their families as well as with co-workers', 'equally humanistic ... teaching styles', and attention 'to acting intentionally as a positive role-model(er)'.[14] The hope is that by emulating the behaviour of good (both morally and in accordance with the highest standard of medical practice) role models, students can, with practice, absorb it and make it second nature and integral to their own professional *personae*.

The research conducted in the realm of medical education provides guideposts for improving the teaching of professionalism and supporting moral development, in law and especially in the clinical legal education setting. Often, the law school's use of modelling concentrates on demonstrating and achieving skills development and does not address the hidden curriculum discussed above. Legal education, through its current largely hidden curriculum, tends to emphasise the student's amoral agency. For example, from this perspective, law is a study of, among other things:

1. Rational 'thinking like a lawyer' – an objective, dispassionate purely rational examination of facts and rules without concern for the impact on parties in the case.
2. Law not justice – related to (1) but more specifically, the enunciation and explication of the legal rule taken from the examination of a case (or cases), rather than whether it was fair or reasonable or suited to the justice of the resolution.
3. Objective – related to (1) and (2), observing the situation and its resolution without concern for the decision or the rule's factual impact on the parties.

---

12. Edward T Hall, *Summary – The Grip of Culture*. Available at http://archive.wphna.org/ wp-content/uploads/2014/08/2011_Sergio_Missana_The_grip_of_culture_Edward_Hall. pdf.
13. Albert Bandura, *Social Learning Theory* (Prentice Hall, 1977).
14. HGA Ria Jochemsen-van der Leeuw, Nynke van Dijk, Faridi S van Etten-Jamaludin and Margaret Wieringa-de Waard, 'The Attributes of the Clinical Trainer as a Role Model: A Systematic Review', (2013) 88(1) *Academic Medicine* 26.

4. Dispassionate – related to (1) to (3), uncaring or disconnected from the consequences of the choices made.
5. Mono disciplinarity – strictly about law without accounting for the personal, social, economic or policy implications of the legal propositions in play.
6. Not a healing/helping profession – the law and lawyers are not aimed at bringing about peace or reconciliation, about making things better; rather, law is only about rationally deciding between the parties.
7. Decontextualised – concerned with the legally relevant facts and no others that may affect the case or the parties.
8. Psychologically battering – a process that is difficult to endure and takes no cognisance of the psycho-emotional circumstances of the parties and their friends and relations.
9. Win/lose, competitive – adversarial, concerned with success, usually in absolute rather than relative terms: a party wins all or nothing.
10. *My* client over all else, whatever works.
11. Lawyer-centred/hierarchical – focused on the lawyers and their success and not the client, the legal rules or some artifice of persuasion, not the client's well-being.

These values characterise what the Carnegie Foundation identified as persons with a moral lobotomy: 'smart people without a purpose'. They do not provide a guide to fostering moral and ethical behaviour. Law students are left to their own devices when trying to reconcile the human and emotional complexity posed by clients seeking help with their legal problems. This lack of training can be detrimental to the personal, mental, and possibly physical health and moral development of these students. 'Longitudinal studies suggest that law school has a corrosive effect on the well-being, values, and motivation of students, ostensibly because of its problematic institutional culture.'[15] They may find themselves experiencing painful dissonance because their 'professional' values contradict their personal ones. Research has found that '… the emotional distress of law students appears to significantly exceed that of medical students and at times to approach that of psychiatric populations'.[16]

ROLE-MODELLING PROFESSIONALISM

Law clinic supervisors and law teachers more generally, therefore, face the challenge of improving and frequently initiating the learning of this expanded notion of professionalism – the lawyer's moral development.

15. Kennon M Sheldon and Lawrence S Krieger, 'Understanding the Negative Effects of Legal Education on Law Students: A Longitudinal Test of Self-Determination' (2007) *Theory, Personality and Social Psychology Bulletin* 88.
16. Ibid.

The first step involves law teachers becoming aware of their own inter-actions with students and clients, as well as others, and recognising that their conduct and demeanour have a profound if unintentional influence on their students' behaviour. They must come to appreciate that students learn, first, by consciously observing and emulating good role models and then by being given the opportunity to reflect upon how their interactions with clients, both in the classroom and in practice intersect with their own value system, their knowledge and the professionalism required of them: supervisors have to be able to work with students to aid them in achieving this goal.[17]

Reflection: A key component

The importance of reflection has been widely acknowledged as a key to developing and maintaining professionalism. A range of definitions of 'reflective practice' have been articulated. The clinician and researcher, Michelle Leering, stated that:

> [A] reflective practitioner is somebody who considers who they are, where they are, what they're doing, their position in the community, the purpose of the work they are doing and how they are doing it, and takes it *as an ongoing process of learning* and moving forward ... Emphasizing integration recognizes that reflective practice is actually a developmen-tal path to a higher level of professionalism ... Reflective practice then becomes 'a way of being, an orientation,' supporting a lifelong journey of learning, professional growth, and commitment to action.[18]

As we see it, reflection may be viewed as a continuous cycle composed of the following steps:

1. Description: What was I thinking? What did I do? How did I act? What was the result?
2. Reaction: How do I feel about how I acted and what I did?
3. Evaluation: Did I do the right thing, in the right place, at the right time, in the right context?
4. Analysis: Were the consequences as expected or predicted?
5. Conclusion: What else *could* I have thought and done? What else *should* I have thought and done?
6. Action Plan: If the same situation arose again, what would I think and do?

17. Casey B White, Arnold K Kumagai, Paula T Ross and Joseph C Fantone, 'A Qualitative Exploration of How Conflict Between the Formal and Informal Curriculum Influences Students' Values and Behaviors', (2009) 84(5) *Academic Medicine* 597.
18. Michele Leering, 'Conceptualizing Reflective Practice for Legal Professionals', (2014) 23 *J. Law and Social Policy* 83, at 97–100.

The lawyer/law student learns how to reflect on his or her skills and knowledge within the context of his or her attitudes, beliefs and values. The ultimate goal of professional development is professional competence, achieved by understanding fully the choices made and how or whether these choices were influenced by others, by societal norms or by one's own past experiences. The continual self-analysis can lead to a far more holistic, client-centred and justice-oriented approach to the practice of law.

The process of reflection upon practice is a learned activity that can be incorporated into the student's clinical or law study experience. Participating in a range of activities can hone the student's ability to engage in meaningful self-assessment. Such activities include reading and listening to narratives/stories; engaging in storytelling; participating in small group or learning communities; keeping a journal; participating in clinical rounds; engaging in debriefing exercises after interacting with a client, etc; and engaging in internal, mental communication that asks, probes and delves into the myriad of thoughts, feelings and actions in which a person was involved.

Storytelling is a particularly potent device for self-reflection.

[It] is one way we deal with our own experience and understanding of the world and of ourselves in the world ... We find out who we are as persons ... the way we imagine ourselves, and the way we are able to understand and reflect on the way our lives unfold.[19]

Using the storytelling mode either in a personal journal or in a small group (clinical) setting provides a narrative structure to explore (practise) experience, including sensitivity to a client's needs.

The stories that supervisors tell are particularly powerful. Research conducted on this topic concluded that they had many beneficial effects on students' professional development. This interaction with a narrative helped them deepen their relationship with one another and recognise the educational value of good role models. The stories, in addition to being enjoyable, provided an opportunity for students to develop their own knowledge and skills and reflect on their own values and attitudes, thereby clarifying them for further application. The stories expanded their ideas about professionalism and provided examples on how to resolve future problems successfully. Students' level of commitment to their clients was also positively affected.[20]

---

19. James R. Elkins has written extensively on this subject. Unfortunately, we cannot retrieve the source of this quotation. However see, for example, JR Elkins, 'Thinking Like a Lawyer: Second Thoughts' (1995–1996) 47 *Mercer L. Rev.* 511.

20. Jennifer L Quaintance, Louise Arnold and George S Thompson, 'What Students Learn About Professionalism from Faculty Stories: An "Appreciative Inquiry" Approach', (2010) 85(1) *Academic Medicine* 118.

THE EXPLICIT TEACHING OF PROFESSIONALISM

Law school clinicians, in particular, because they are implicitly regarded as role models, cannot avoid addressing the centrality of professionalism and moral development to a legal education. Students, intentionally or unintentionally, emulate their role models, whether by replicating the skills and behaviour they observe or by absorbing the values on display and reflecting them in their subsequent behaviour. By bringing the attributes of professionalism and translating them into practice to the level of consciousness, clinic supervisors can positively influence student behaviour in their interaction with and responsibility to clients and others.

The first step in improving professionalism in (clinical) legal education is to make supervisors/instructors aware of their role model function as well as their need to be continuously aware of the impact of their behaviour on their students. It is also important for legal educators to develop the key attributes of positive role models and formulate them as a set of criteria for training the clinicians to improve their own positive role modelling. The creation of both a self-reflection tool and a feedback instrument would be useful for measuring an instructor's improvement by facilitating their reflection on the behaviours they modelled, and by assessing how well they exhibited exemplary professional practice for their students.

In order to enhance their interactions with students, supervisors/ instructors require guidance on how to assess their students, specifically on providing detailed constructive feedback to them on how well they modelled their superior's behaviour and attitudes toward their clients or legal problems. The time for teaching the teachers may be long overdue.

LEARNING PROFESSIONALISM

Students need to receive explicit teaching on professionalism. This means they have to be able to observe positive role models who are cognisant of their educational role and also be able to reflect on their own understanding of the role models in tandem with reflections on their own experience, including the experience of observing role models. By providing students with these opportunities, supervisors can ensure that students are able to focus on, be exposed to, and practise positive professionalism.[21]

SUMMARISING THE CASE FOR TEACHING MORAL DEVELOPMENT AND PROFESSIONALISM

Moral development is, of course, relevant to everyone, whatever they may choose to do in life. A moral life is one that demonstrates care and respect for others. It brings together the highest affective and cognitive development

21. Ibid.

so that thought and analysis are always married to values and feelings. We think and feel carefully, placing ourselves in another's shoes while always wearing our own. As morally developed beings, what happens around us, to our neighbours and to our environment, in its broadest terms, matters as we consider and choose our own best way forward.

For legal professionals in all roles, the awareness that pervades both the process and outcomes of moral development matter greatly to the overall efficacy and acceptability of law and to the achievement of its highest aspiration, justice. Explicitly involving legal education in moral development acknowledges its inevitability: if we do not, thoughts and behaviours belie their moral content and will be interpreted as such, whether intended or not. Professionalism is not only a series of intentional thoughts and actions; it is a striving we seek always to achieve, if not exceed.[22]

It is helpful to remember that what the student [ultimately] does is actually more important in determining what is learned than what the teacher does.[23]

22. As we were writing this paper Neil thought often of Derek Roebuck, in whose memory the present volume is written. He knew Derek for thirty years, though they had worked closely together for only three. In those years, Derek showed Neil what it meant to be a caring colleague, without thought to his personal interests. Whatever was needed, whenever it was needed, Derek would offer and provide it. He sought to understand and reflect on the challenges Neil encountered and took every action agreed that he might undertake to support Neil and his work. He gave true meaning to the words 'collegiality' and 'personal moral development'.

23. Thomas J Shuell, 'Cognitive Conceptions of Learning' https://journals.sagepub.com/doi/10.3102/00346543056004411 (1986), as cited in J Biggs, *Teaching for Quality Learning at University – What the Student Does*, 2nd edn (Buckingham: SRHE/Open University Press, 2003) p. v.

THE CREATIVE FORCE IN TRANSNATIONAL COMMERCIAL LAW

*Sir Roy Goode**

I first met Derek Roebuck in Hobart in 1975, during the first of several visits my wife Catherine and I made to Australia. He was then Dean of the University of Tasmania Law Faculty and made us both very welcome. Thus began a friendship, albeit with only intermittent meetings until he and his wife Susanna Hoe came to live in Oxford, that lasted until the time of his death. A prolific writer, Derek was a wide-ranging scholar with interests in contract and commercial law, comparative law and criminal procedure; *inter alia*, he co-authored with Professors David Allan and Mary Hiscock an impressive 10-volume work on credit and security in South-East Asia. The field he made peculiarly his own was, however, the history of arbitration and mediation in ancient Greece and Rome, the Middle Ages and England. His work for the Chartered Institute of Arbitrators over many years led to the establishment of the annual Roebuck Lecture in his honour. Above all, Derek will be remembered for his warmth and comradeship, his sense of fun and his love of debate. He will be greatly missed.

INTRODUCTION

Transnational commercial law has been defined as 'that set of principles and rules, from whatever source, which governs international commercial transactions and is common to legal systems generally or to a significant number of legal systems.'[1] Over the past three decades, the growth of transnational commercial law has been powered by a series of international

---

* Emeritus Professor of Law in the University of Oxford and Emeritus Fellow of St John's College, Oxford.

1. Roy Goode, Herbert Kronke and Ewan McKendrick, *Transnational Commercial Law: Text, Cases and Materials* (2nd edn, 2015, Oxford University Press), paragraph 1.03. The first known academic course on transnational commercial law was introduced into the University of Oxford postgraduate law curriculum by the writer in the mid-1990s. The subject is now taught in law schools around the world and is the focus of the Queen Mary-UNIDROIT Institute of Transnational Commercial Law established within the Centre for Commercial Law Studies, Queen Mary University of London, in 2017 under the presidency of the late Professor Alberto Mazzoni, then President of UNIDROIT.

conventions and protocols, model laws, restatements and contractually incorporated rules of international institutions, all designed to harmonise conflicting laws or business practices so as to ensure that all participants, in whatever country they may be, play by the same rules. The process of harmonisation is not a mechanistic one. On the contrary, at its highest level it involves creativity in confronting legal obstacles to cross-border trade and finance and devising new tools to overcome them. Good scholars do not shirk a seemingly intractable problem; on the contrary, they welcome it as forcing them to raise their game. As in science and mathematics,[2] there is artistry in the making of transnational commercial law, in which academic and practising lawyers join with business interests in finding ways of overcoming the obstacles that impede the efficient conduct of cross-border trade and finance. Problem-solving lies at the heart of this endeavour and to do this successfully involves breaking traditional rules in order to make new ones that work.

Works of art make rules;
Rules do not make works of art.[3]

However, rule-breaking requires discipline, which, as will be seen, has not always been exercised.

Sometimes, national laws, whether applied directly or through the conflict of laws, do not yield a solution to a given problem, whether because of doctrinal problems or the absence of relevant legislation. In such cases, creative techniques are necessary in order to surmount the problem. Instances of this will be provided later in this contribution. This is not to say that the past should be jettisoned, only that it should be the servant, not the master, of legal development. This was well understood by that great scholar Savigny, whose profound knowledge of and respect for Roman law did not blind him to the need to adapt to change:

The historical view of jurisprudence is entirely misunderstood and distorted when it is regarded as setting up the law which has descended to us from the past as supreme, and requiring the maintenance of its unimpaired authority over the present and the future...In its special application to the Roman law, the historical view does not consist, as

2. See, for example, Marcus du Sautoy, *The Creativity Code* (4th Estate, Harper Collins, 2019) at p. 5: 'The creative impulse is a key part of what distinguishes humans from other animals and yet we often let it stagnate inside us, falling into the trap of becoming slaves to our formulaic lives. Being creative requires a jolt to take us out of the smooth paths we carve out each day'.
3. Claude Debussy, often quoted by the French musician Edgar Varèse, who was known, among other things, as the father of electronic music, refusing to accept sounds that had already been heard, and was encouraged by Debussy to compose the way he wanted to.

many assert, in ascribing to it an undue authority over us. Rather, on the other hand, it seeks to discover and ascertain, in the whole body of our existing law, what is in truth of Roman origin, in order that we may not be unconsciously controlled by it; and on the other hand it strives, within the known sphere of the Roman elements of our law, to set aside what is in fact dead, and retains only from our misapprehension a misleading show of life, in order that there may be free space for the development and healthy influence of the still living portions of those Roman elements.[4]

TENSIONS ARISING FROM DIFFERENT LEGAL PHILOSOPHIES

One of the problems arising in any harmonisation project is that different legal systems approach an issue from different starting points. The task then is to find a solution that will provide general satisfaction.

The role of comparative law

In the formulation of the different types of harmonising instrument comparative law has been an essential tool,[5] whether in the field of substantive rules or conflict of laws rules.

Though one of the legitimate purposes of the study of comparative law is knowledge for its own sake, it would be a sterile subject if this were seen as its be-all and end-all.

Modern legal comparison is *critical* in its attitude. The comparatist is not interested in the differences or similarities of various legal orders merely as facts, but in the fitness, the practicability, the justice, and the *why* of legal solutions to given problems. The mere description of a certain legal order might be interesting and illuminating; however, such 'foreign legal data' are not comparative law. True comparative method can put the treasure chest of foreign experience to good use, but this does not get to the essence of legal comparison, which is the

4. Preface to Savigny's outstanding *Systems des heütigen Römischen Rechts*, vol. 8, published as an independent work and later translated into English by William Guthrie, *Private International Law and the Retrospective Operation of Statutes: A Treatise on the Conflict of Laws, and the Limits of their Operation in Respect of Place and Time* (2nd edn, 2003, Law Exchange, Clark, New Jersey), which reproduces the entire preface, including, at p. 13, the passage quoted above. In his fine work *A History of Private Law in Europe* (translated by Tony Weir, Clarendon Press, Oxford, 1995) Franz Wieacker gave an example of a new compound produced by the coalescence of principles of Roman and German law, where old Germanic law had protected the rights of the acquirer of goods wrongfully disposed of by a bailee whether or not the acquirer bought in good faith, while in 1586 the law of Lübeck brought the old and new together by introducing the Roman law requirement of good faith.
5. *Transnational Commercial Law* (above, n. 1), paragraph 4.34. Chapter 4 as a whole is devoted to comparative law and its relevance to transnational commercial law.

critical exploration of the usefulness of foreign solutions for the needs of domestic or international rule-making. Its determinant feature with respect to policy, choices, and critiques is related to Jhering's abhorrence of antiquarianism.[6]

This passage by two distinguished legal comparatists, one of whom is still happily with us, neatly illustrates the functional approach to comparative law, which has influenced numerous projects for the harmonisation of commercial law. That ground-breaking work on the common core of contract, led by Professor Rudolf Schlesinger in the late 1960s[7] and covering a large number of legal systems, showed that a broader approach to comparative law than that traditionally adopted permitted 'the discovery, within each of the legal systems selected, of the functional and systematic relationship among a large number of precepts and concepts.'[8] For example, in formulating Part 1 of the Principles of European Contract Law, prepared by the Commission on European Contract Law under the inspired chairmanship of the late Danish law professor Ole Lando and consisting of one member from each of the then 15 Member States of the European Communities, we decided from the outset not to look for the lowest common denominator of our different legal systems but rather to seek the best solutions to typical issues arising in the field of contract law. However, it was natural that each member of the Commission should take as the starting point his or her own legal system and to test any proposed rule against this. Such an approach guaranteed vigorous debate, each of us being initially convinced of the superiority of the legal system with which he or she was familiar. I well recall the distinguished French jurist Denis Tallon exclaiming from time to time:

'Mais quel est le problème? Comme toujours, le code civil fournit la solution parfaite!'

We all expressed great admiration for the *code civil* but ventured to suggest that very occasionally an even better solution might be found! In

---

6. Konrad Zweigert and Kurt Siehr, 'Jhering's Influence on the Development of Comparative Legal Method' (1971) 19 Am J Comp L 215, 220-222. Jhering, who held a chair of Roman law at Vienna, was a leading jurist who conceived jurisprudence not on the historical basis advocated by the famous Savigny but as a tool to advance the needs of society. He became renowned for his magisterial work *Geist des Römischen Rechts*.

7. *Formation of Contracts: A Study of the Common Core of Legal Systems* (ed Rudolf B. Schlesinger, Oceana Publications and Stevens and Sons, 1968).

8. *Ibid.*, p. 2. This was one of the first works to adopt the approach of comparison through a series of fact situations raising legal issues on which each contributor was asked to set out his or her country's law. For more recent examples see the volumes in the Common Core of European Private Law Series published by Cambridge University Press.

the result, all 15 of us were able to reach full agreement on a text. The best solution might not be found in any of the legal systems examined, it might have to be created. The parallel venture, the UNIDROIT Principles of International Commercial Contracts, prepared under the equally inspired chairmanship of Professor Joachim Bonell, adopted a similar approach and with equal success.

Relatively few scholars are true comparative lawyers; there is simply not enough time to master both one's own legal system and a foreign one. The same is true of other subjects cognate to one's own. As a general commercial law mongrel, I have found it necessary to acquire a knowledge of related subjects – contract, tort, property law, equity and trusts, comparative law and private international law – sufficient for my purposes without the need, or indeed the ability, to acquire a mastery of them. Likewise, benefits can be derived from reference to a foreign legal system without a mastery of that system, to which the scholar can usefully resort for the ideas to be extracted from it to solve a specific problem without having a systematic knowledge of it.[9] In the words of that great comparative lawyer Professor Harry Lawson:

> ... there is much to be said for the view that anyone who wishes to get a real insight into law as a whole must be content to develop qualities exactly the opposite to those of the specialist. Instead of getting to know more and more about less and less he must set himself to know less and less about more and more.[10]

Most of the instruments of harmonisation of laws and practices governing cross-border transactions have been guided by the best-solution approach, which often involves either highly innovative techniques or creative ambiguity.[11]

9. See Alan Watson, *Legal Transplants: An Approach to Comparative Law* (2nd edn, U of Georgia Press, London, 1993) 17. Another leading comparativist, Professor Basil Markesinis, has urged the importance of studying a legal system through its case law rather than through its codes. See Basil Markesinis, 'Comparative Law – A Subject in Search of an Audience' (1990) 53 MLR 1.
10. F.H. Lawson, *Selected Essays* (North Holland Publishing Co., 1977), vol. II, 59.
11. See, for example, the 1980 UN Convention on Contracts for the International Sale of Goods, the product of the work of UNCITRAL, Article 7(1) of which provides: 'In the interpretation of this Convention, regard is to be had to its international character and to the need to promote uniformity in its application and observance of good faith in international trade.' The rule of interpretation in Article 7(1) has become the standard in subsequent commercial law conventions except that in the Convention on International Interests in Mobile Equipment (the Cape Town Convention) 'predictability' has been substituted for 'good faith' to avoid the uncertainties attaching to the concept of good faith in relation to transactions involving high-value equipment.

While a given national law rule may have been the source of inspiration of a provision in an international instrument, that provision has to be interpreted autonomously in the light of other relevant provisions of the instrument, though the rule may provide guidance where it reflects the common understanding of participating States.

Private international law and its attempted exclusion

No set of international rules, however comprehensive, can completely cover the chosen field. Those issues not resolved by the text of the rules or the general principles on which they are based have to be settled by the applicable national law as determined by the rules of private international law of the forum.[12] So, private international law, far from being displaced by uniform law as had at one time been its suggested fate, continues to play a vital role and has itself been subject to harmonisation measures in particular fields through international conventions prepared by the Hague Convention on Private International Law and regulations issued by what is now the European Union. There was once an ill-fated attempt to exclude the conflict of laws altogether from an international convention. Article 2 of the Uniform Rules for International Sales (ULIS) embodied in the 1964 Hague Sales Convention provided as follows:

Rules of private international law shall be excluded for the purposes of the application of the present Law, subject to any provision to the contrary in the said Law.

This remarkable provision, reflecting a lack of self-discipline on the part of the drafting committee, met with such a barrage of criticism and ridicule that no organisation involved in harmonisation has had the courage to repeat it, and it finds no place in the successor to ULIS, the 1980 Convention on Contracts for the International Sale of Goods.

The problem with conflict rules is, of course, that since these are everywhere a matter for the *lex fori*, the applicable law depends on the place where proceedings are brought. While the impact of differences in conflict of laws rules is reduced by the widespread adoption of the principle of party autonomy in the determination of the law applicable to a contract, there are many cases, including those where the parties have not chosen the applicable law, in which it remains necessary to carry out the two-stage process of characterisation and designation of the connecting factor which, under the forum's conflict rules, links the issue in question to a given Contracting State. Studies in comparative conflict of laws[13] – bringing together

---

12. But subject to the internationally mandatory rules of the *lex fori*.
13. A subject which that great conflicts comparativist Professor Kurt Siehr has made particularly his own. See Kathariana Boele-Woelki, Talia Einhorn, Daniel Girsberger and

private international law and comparative law – have revealed not only similarities but also sharp differences in national conflict of laws rules. Thus, private international law too has to be brought within the harmonisation process with a view to ensuring that in every State adopting a conflict of laws convention the determination of the applicable law will be the same as in other Contracting States. Hence the Hague conventions on trusts,[14] choice of court agreements,[15] securities[16] and judgments.[17]

International trade usage

From time immemorial, the rights of trading parties situated in different countries have been governed by international trade usage. The mediaeval *lex mercatoria* was administered primarily, though not exclusively, by the courts of the fairs with all the panoply of a commercial centre: a free pass on routes to the fair, merchant judges, police, currency exchangers, financiers, brokers of various kinds and victuallers, all coming together at international fairs to conduct cross-border business on the basis of usage.[18] The old *lex mercatoria* largely disappeared with the growth of towns and national laws but there has been an intense debate about the new international *lex mercatoria*, which in the view of some constitutes an autonomous legal system governing cross-border commerce but which, correctly analysed, owes its force to the readiness of courts to respect reasonable commercial practices. Many of these have now been codified by international business organisations and given effect by incorporation into contracts,[19] thus changing their status and almost invariably replacing some usages with new rules.[20]

Symeon Symeonides (eds), *Convergence and Divergence in Private International Law: Liber Amicorum Kurt Siehr* (Eleven International Publishing, 2010), especially the graceful tribute paid to him by Professor Peter Mankowski in 'The Principle of Characteristic Performance Revisited Yet Again' at 434. See also in the same volume Herbert Kronke, 'Connecting Factors and Internationality in Conflict of Laws and Transnational Commercial Law' 57 at 59 discussing the assaults by other jurists on the connecting factor as nationalising what is intrinsically international.

14. Convention on the Law Applicable to Trusts and their Recognition 1985.

15. Convention on Choice of Court Agreements 2005.

16. Convention on the law applicable to certain rights in respect of securities held by an intermediary 2006. See Roy Goode, Hideki Kanda and Karl Kreuzer, assisted by Christophe Bernasconi, *Hague Securities Convention Explanatory Report*, 2nd edn, the Hague Conference on Private International Law, 2017.

17. Convention on the recognition and enforcement of judgments in civil or commercial matters 2019.

18. See P. Huvelin, *Essai historique sur le droit des marches & des foires* (Articlehur Roussea, Paris, 1897; André Allix, 'The Geography of Fairs: Illustrated by Old-World Examples' (1922) 12 *Geographical Review* 532, describing with maps the great commodity fairs of the Middle Ages.

19. See below, p 291.

20. See Roy Goode, 'Usage and its Reception in Transnational Commercial Law' (1997)

The true *lex mercatoria*, unwritten trade usage, can be hard to identify and even experienced professionals may differ as to their content. For example, asked what was meant by 'payment under reserve' in a documentary credit transaction, one banker replied that if it transpired that the beneficiary was not entitled to payment, the paying bank could recover it, whereas another answered that if the customer refused to reimburse the bank then whether that refusal was or was not justified, the bank could recover the payment from the beneficiary, which was held by the English Court of Appeal to be the correct answer.[21]

Nemo dat versus possession *vaut titre*

The starting point of the common law is *nemo dat quod non habet* (*nemo plus juris ad alium transferre potest quam ipse habet*); a person cannot transfer a better title than he himself possesses. By contrast, civil law systems focus on protection of the innocent buyer. In the words of Article 2276 of the new French *code civil*: 'La possession vaut titre'. There has been a gradual convergence of the two approaches. The common law has always admitted exceptions to the *nemo dat* rule to facilitate the free flow of goods in the stream of trade,[22] for example, dispositions by an agent acting within his actual or ostensible authority; successive sales by a seller whom the first buyer allows to remain in possession and effect a second sale as apparent owner. In some respect, these exceptions go beyond the *possession vaut titre* principle which, under French law at least, protects only a person holding possession with the intention to do so as owner. Thus, the principle does not protect the grantee of a security interest. Relativity of title in relation to goods also presupposes that there can be two titles to goods at any time, one derived from ownership, the other from possession *animo domini*. Possessory title may be asserted against all third parties except the true owner or one asserting rights with the authority of the true owner. This protection of possession is designed to preserve the peace.

ICLQ 1, 14. See also 'Is the *Lex Mercatoria* Autonomous' in Ross Cranston, Jan Ramberg and Jacob Ziegel (eds), *Commercial Law Challenges in the 21ˢᵗ Century: Jan Hellner In Memoriam* (Iustus Förlag, 2007) 73. Both essays are reproduced in Roy Goode, *The Development of Transnational Commercial Law* (Oxford University Press, 2018), Chapters 18 and 21, though the source of the latter is as above and not as shown in the footnote reference.
21. *Banque de l'Indochine et de Suez SA v JH Rayner (Mincing Lane) Ltd* [1983] QB 711.
22. See to similar effect J.-G. Sauveplanne, 'The Protection of the Bona Fide Purchaser of Corporeal Movables in Comparative Law' (1965) 29 *Rabels Z* 651 at 652: 'The rapid circulation of movables makes it difficult, if not impossible, to trace their legal origin. If every purchaser was compelled to investigate his predecessor's title, the circulation of movable property would be seriously hampered. Therefore, as the economic importance of movables increased, the need to protect the purchaser became more urgent, and commercial interests finally outweighed concepts of legal logic.'

These differences in starting point led UNIDROIT to produce in 1968 a draft Uniform Law on the protection of the *bona fide* purchaser of corporeal movables. While this attracted much favourable attention, it was criticised on two main grounds. First, it was tied to ULIS and therefore applied only to dispositions under a contract of sale. Second, it was considered to over-emphasise the protection of the innocent buyer at the expense of the original owner. In 1974, UNIDROIT presented the draft of a Uniform Law on the acquisition in good faith of corporeal movables. This draft detached the Uniform Law from ULIS and its change of title was a response to the demand to move from the protection first and foremost of the transferee in good faith to a balance of the competing interests.[23] Despite these improvements, the new draft Uniform Law fared no better than its predecessor and notwithstanding periodic attempts to restore it to the UNIDROIT work programme, it was finally dropped for want of adequate support.

Absolute title versus relative title

Most legal systems possess the concept of relativity of title in relation both to dispositions of goods and to the assignment of claims. Thus, where the owner of goods sells them first to A and then to B, the question is generally treated as one of priority, not of validity, so that in given conditions a non-owner can pass a good title as described above. A similar rule applies to claims: so, if A assigns a claim first to X and then to Y, priority is usually given to Y if he was unaware of the prior assignment and is the first to give notice of his assignment to the debtor. The underlying policy is that as a means of providing a warning to third parties of the existence of a prior assignment, the giving of notice of assignment to the debtor is the closest approximation to possession, since an intending assignee can enquire of the debtor whether he has received any prior notice of assignment. German law, however, is an exception, taking the position that A, having sold to X, has nothing left to sell. This is in contrast to the rule relating to successive dealings in goods, which German law treats as raising an issue of priority, not of validity, because of the importance attached to possession as an *indicium* of ownership. The reason for the policy difference is unclear.

Privacy of transactions versus publicity

A third source of difference is between those laws which favour publicity of transactions from those which favour privacy. The principal mode of publicity is a public registry, which may be either debtor-based, with searches made against the name of the debtor, or asset-based, searches

---

23. For the text of the Convention, the Annex to which contains the Uniform Law, see 1975 I Unif. L. Rev. 68. The same issue contains the Explanatory Report by Professor J.-G. Sauveplanne at 86 *et seq.*

being made against a uniquely identified asset. Outright sales of goods are rarely the subject of registration, not so much because of privacy concerns but because of the sheer volume of sales and protection of the innocent buyer through exceptions to the *nemo dat* rule. By contrast many legal systems have machinery for registering security interests in goods and receivables. Again, German law contains no provisions for registration, on the basis that most intending financiers will be aware that the debtor may not be the owner of the goods or claim. This may be true but does not assist the financier who is willing to extend credit on the security of a movable but only if it knows that this is unencumbered. The Cape Town Convention here broke new ground in providing for the establishment of an international asset-based registry for each category of equipment, though to date the only registry so far established is the wholly electronic registry for aircraft objects based in Dublin, a highly efficient, modestly-priced system which in January 2020 celebrated its millionth registration, a notable achievement. Further, the system extends to the registration of outright sales, which is both feasible and necessary, given the high value and unique identifiability of aircraft objects.

Self-help versus judicial control

A characteristic of common law systems is that they allow the contracting parties a wide scope to make their own rules governing their relations *inter se*. Thus, in business-to-business transactions a contracting party may, without the need for resort to the court, terminate a contract for breach, rescind it *ab initio* for misrepresentation or exercise default remedies such as peaceable repossession of goods taken as security for a loan or supplied under a title reservation or leasing agreement. By contrast, civil law juris-dictions tend to require leave of the court before any of the above measures may be taken.

The law of trusts

In a common law trust, property rights are divided between trustee and beneficiary. The typical trust is an active trust, where the trustee is given powers to manage the trust fund, which is usually done through fund managers. Beneficiaries under such a trust have a proprietary interest in the trust fund but not in any individual component of the fund. By contrast, beneficiaries under a bare trust, such as that constituted by the opening of a securities account with a custodian or other securities intermediary, are full equitable owners and can give directions to the intermediary for transfer of the interests credited to their accounts.

The law of trusts, which was for a long time focused on the family trust, has acquired much greater significance in relation to commercial transactions, where the trust institution plays a key role in modern finance, partly because of the equitable proprietary interest enjoyed by beneficiaries and partly because the trust has proved an invaluable tool for the co-ordination of fractional interests. For example, where a company issues bonds on the market, the legal title to each bond is vested in the bondholder; the appointment of a trustee for the issue in whose favour parallel covenants are made in favour of the trustee to be held on behalf of bondholders enables the trustee to enforce payment on behalf of all bondholders instead of leaving each bondholder to pursue its own separate claim. The appointment of a trust also facilitates secured lending by a syndicate of lenders who together empower the trustee to act on their behalf.

While civil lawyers undoubtedly appreciate the benefits of the trust institution, they face the problem that the civil law has always set its face against divided property rights, so that the continental trust does not allow division of ownership between trustee and beneficiary but requires ownership to be in one or the other. Where it is in the trustee, the beneficiary has no proprietary rights, only a personal claim against the trustee, which leaves the beneficiary vulnerable if the trustee becomes insolvent.

Functional versus formal approach to characterisation of transactions

When UNIDROIT undertook its initial comparative survey of the law on financial leasing with a view to an international convention, it quickly encountered a problem of characterisation. Under Article 9 of the American Uniform Commercial Code, financial leases were liable to be characterised as conditional sale agreements, which would in turn result in their being classified as security agreements and would do so as a matter of law if containing an option to purchase for no consideration or only a nominal consideration. Under French law, the inclusion of an option to purchase was an essential ingredient of a financial lease. while under English law this would convert the agreement into a hire-purchase agreement, a hybrid halfway between a lease and a sale. Three legal systems therefore characterise one and the same transaction in three different ways.

Commercial law conventions have taken no position on issues of characterisation, alive to the danger of disturbing national sensitivities. The 1988 UNIDROIT Convention on international financial leasing applies to finance leases with or without an option to purchase and in the latter case whether or not for a nominal price or rental, regardless of the characterisation under national law, which in some legal systems will treat the typical finance lease as a security agreement.[24] By contrast, Article 3(1) of the 2008 UNIDROIT Model Law on Leasing provides that the Model Law

---

24. See, for example, the US Uniform Commercial Code, s. 1-203.

does not apply to a lease that functions as a security right, which in effect throws characterisation back to the applicable law. Similarly Article 2(4) of the Cape Town Convention leaves it to the applicable law to determine whether the transactions is a security agreement, a title reservation agreement or a leasing agreement. It had originally been intended to adopt a functional approach to title reservation and leasing agreements in the Cape Town Convention, but this was opposed by several European States on the ground that it was useful to have a variety of instruments, each governed by a distinct legal regime. Again, while laying down conflict rules (Hague Convention) and substantive law rules (Geneva Convention) regarding intermediated securities, the two conventions take no position on the nature of rights credited to an account with a securities intermediary or the persons against whom such rights are enforceable.

THE MOVE TOWARDS CONVERGENCE

The driving force of international trade

The development of transnational commercial law has been powered by the globalisation of commercial transactions and the consequent pressure for uniform substantive law rules to govern cross-border transactions. Without such rules, the rights and obligations of contracting parties will depend on the applicable law, which will itself be determined by the conflict of laws rules of the forum. The problem of differences in conflict of laws rules among different States may be overcome by the harmonisation of conflict rules, through such instruments as Rome I,[25] though this applies only to Member States of the European Union or, at a more general level, the 2015 Hague Principles on Choice of Law in International Commercial Contracts. While this may solve questions of conflicting rules of private international law, however, differences in the substantive laws of different States remain, impeding the efficiency and increasing the cost of cross-border transactions.

There are four international organisations concerned with harmonisation: the International Institute for the Unification of Private Law (UNIDROIT); the United Nations Commission on International Trade Law (UNCITRAL), a specialised agency of the UN; the International Chamber of Commerce (ICC), the world business organisation, an important part of whose work is the harmonisation of trade practice through uniform rules given effect by incorporation into contracts; and, in the field of private international law, the Hague Conference on Private International Law. There are also academic institutions focused on transnational law, such as

---

25. Regulation (EC) No 593/2008 of the European Parliament and of the Council of 17 June 2008 on the law applicable to contractual regulations (Rome I).

the Center for Transnational Law, Cologne which, under the direction of Professor Klaus Peter Berger, has compiled a set of principles based on the concept of the 'creeping codification' of transnational law,[26] and the Queen Mary-UNIDROIT Institute of Transnational Commercial Law within the Centre for Commercial Law Studies, Queen Mary University of London.

First steps

A preliminary to any harmonisation project dealing with a particular type of business transaction is a survey of legal systems drawn from the different legal families, accompanied or followed by a questionnaire addressed to national law experts in selected jurisdictions to determine (a) whether, in view of the differences in national law, there is a need for uniform rules and (b) whether the project is feasible. Good examples are the surveys conducted by the UNIDROIT Secretariat for a proposed project on international factoring[27] and by Professor Ronald CC Cuming on behalf of UNIDROIT in 1989 as to the need for and feasibility of an international regime governing the registration and priority of security interests in mobile equipment of high value, such as ships and aircraft.[28] Responses to these surveys showed general agreement that differences in national laws created significant obstacles to cross-border dealings. This was particularly true of transactions involving high value mobile equipment, where it quickly became clear that conflict of laws rules, even if harmonised, would be inadequate to overcome these obstacles and that the development of substantive uniform rules was both desirable and feasible.

It is fair to say that the end product of the mobile equipment project, the Cape Town Convention, so vastly exceeded the scope of the original project, and entailed addressing such a huge range of issues, that if this had been apparent at the start it is unlikely that the project would ever have been undertaken!

Key elements of a successful project

In the harmonisation of the law governing any type of cross-border business transaction, there are at least three essential prerequisites. First, the study group set up to carry the project forward should include representatives from all the established legal families. This was not always done and complaints were regularly made that projects were too focused on Europe, a focus which changed only with the decline in influence of

26. Klaus Peter Berger and the Translex Research Team, *Principles with Commentary* (5th edn, Cologne, 2019).
27. See UNIDROIT Study LVIII, Docs. 1-3, March 1976 and December 1977.
28. 'International Regulation of Aspects of Security Interests in Mobile Equipment', UNIDROIT 1989, Study LXXII – Doc. 1, Rome, December 1989.

European powers and the involvement of North American, African and Asian States.[29] Second, it mut be shown that the proposed harmonisation is both necessary and feasible and may be expected to bring significant economic benefits. To that end UNIDROIT, for example, commissioned economic impact assessments for the Cape Town Convention and Aircraft Protocol[30] and the Pretoria Protocol.[31] Third, it is not only governments that need to be involved but also the relevant industries, without whose support governments will not act and the contribution of whose expertise as members of study groups and working parties is essential in identifying the problems that arise in day-to-day business and the measures needed to overcome them.

Often, behind these, is the driving force of a single individual. For example, without the huge investment of time and resources by the Aviation Working Group under its Secretary General Jeffrey Wool, the project leading to the Cape Town Convention would never have come to fruition.[32] Similarly the impetus for the Hague Convention on the law applicable to intermediated securities was the energy and drive of an Australian lawyer, Richard Potok, who initiated the project at a seminar in Oxford in May 1990 and took it to the Hague Conference on Private International Law in April 2000. The basic concept was that the law governing rights in relation to securities credited to a securities account should be based on the law of the place of the relevant intermediary approach (PRIMA). The sterling work of the Permanent Bureau, in particular Dr Christophe Bernasconi,

29. See Jürgen Basedow, 'Worldwide Harmonisation of Private Law and Regional Economic Integration' 2003-1/2 Unif. L. Rev. 31.

30. Anthony Saunders and Ingo Walter, *Proposed UNIDROIT Convention on International Interests in Mobile Equipment as Applicable to Aircraft Equipment Through the Aircraft Equipment Protocol: Economic Impact Assessment, A Study Prepared Under the Auspices of INSEAD and the New York University Salomon Center* (September 1998), which concluded that increased certainty and consequent reduction of risk could result in savings of several billions of dollars a year. Subsequent studies carried out after the Convention and Aircraft Protocol came into force have reached the same conclusion. See, for example, Ingo Walter, Anthony Saunders and Anand Srinivasan, *Innovation in Law and Global Finance: Estimating the Financial Impact of the Cape Town Convention*, New York University Leonard N Stern School of Business, Department of Economics (2006); Vadim Linetsky, *Economic Benefits of the Cape Town Convention* (2009) and 'Accession to the Cape Town Convention by the UK: An Economic Impact Assessment' (December 2010).

31. Warwick Economics and Asssociates, *MAC Protocol Economic Assessment* (August 2018), which estimated that at the end of the 10-year assessment period, the stock of MAC equipment in developing countries was estimated to be some $90 billion higher than in the absence of reforms associated with the MAC Protocol and that the annualised impact on gross domestic product was estimated at $23 billion for emerging and developing economies and $7 billion for exporting economies.

32. The Aviation Working Group is a not-for-profit legal entity consisting of major aircraft manufacturers, leasing companies and financial institutions devoted to facilitating aviation finance. It played a major role both in the development of the text of the Cape Town Convention and in promoting adoption through meetings and conferences around the world.

and the Herculean labours of the drafting committee led to its approval at a Diplomatic Conference in The Hague in December 2002, a mere 2½ years after it was introduced to the Permanent Bureau – an astonishing achievement. It is unfortunate that a change of direction as regards the applicable law from the place of the relevant intermediary to the law chosen by the parties to the account agreement, though a better solution, led to opposition from European players, which has held up progress for the best part of two decades. Finally, the adoption of an international instrument represents only the halfway point. There has then to be a drive for ratification. The constrained resources of the harmonising agencies limit their capacity for this key post-adoption activity. Again, it is necessary for both the representatives of participating States and the industries benefiting from the harmonising measure to put their shoulders behind the wheel in promoting the instrument.

Securing agreement

In every harmonisation project there are likely to be issues of policy so central to the legal philosophy of a number of participating States that, without compromise, they will simply not support the proposed Convention.[33] There are various ways of resolving this problem. One, of course, is to modify the rule to which objection is made so as to ensure a consensus, and that is the most common solution. There may, however, be other States for whom the rule is seen as central to the objectives of the instrument and who are unwilling to support a modification. A variety of techniques are available to resolve the impasse.

(1) Allow a Contracting State, when ratifying the Convention, to make a reservation, that is, a unilateral statement purporting to exclude or to modify the legal effect of certain provisions of the Convention in their application to that State.[34] Reservations are binding only on those Contracting States that accept them and modern commercial law treaties usually contain an express provision that reservations are not permitted unless expressly authorised by the Convention, which usually they are not.

(2) Provide in the Convention itself that Contracting States may derogate from or modify particular provisions. Most commercial law conventions allow parties, in their relations with each other, to derogate

---

33. 'Convention' is here used to include a Protocol to a Convention or any other form of legally binding instrument, as opposed to a Model Law.
34. Vienna Convention on the Law of Treaties 1969, Article 2(1)(d). For a detailed analysis of what has been described as a subject of baffling complexity see Anthony Aust, *Modern Treaty Law and Practice* (3rd edn, 2013, Cambridge University Press).

from or vary the effect of any of its provisions except those that are designated as mandatory.

(3) Provide variants of the rule so that a State can select from one or more alternatives.

(4) Enable a Contracting State to make a declaration that the rule is not to apply ('opt-out declaration') or make the application of the rule dependent on a declaration to apply it ('opt-in declaration').

All of these techniques except reservations were utilised in the drafting of the Cape Town Convention and Aircraft Protocol and were critical to their success.

KEY HARMONISING COMMERCIAL LAW INSTRUMENTS

Leaving aside the ill-fated Hague Sales Convention, the period between 1980 and 2019 saw the burgeoning of instruments of different kinds providing uniform rules for cross-border trade and finance. Some of these were failures, either because they did not secure enough ratifications to enter into force at all or because, though entering into force, they were not sufficiently supported to attract the number of ratifications sufficient to make them effective on the international scene. However, even the failures provide instructive examples of creative law-making that deserved better success. All of the instruments examined below were the work of one or other of three treaty-making international organisations, UNIDROIT, UNCITRAL and the Hague Conference on Private International Law. Mention will also be made of much earlier and highly effective harmonisation through rules governing documentary credits, followed later by rules on demand guarantees, promulgated by an international organisation which itself has no law-making powers, the International Chamber of Commerce, but which are made effective through incorporation into all relevant contracts. They are described below less for their substantive content than for their creative force.

The 1980 Convention on Contracts for the International Sale of Goods

This Convention, the work of UNCITRAL and adopted by the UN, is one of the most successful conventions ever in the field of international commercial law, with ratifications by 93 States.[35] It regulates the con-

---

35. The leading text is Schlechtriem and Schwenzer, *Commentary on the UN Convention on the International Sale of Goods* (4th edn, ed. Ingeborg Schwenzer, 2016, Oxford University Press). The UNIDROIT Convention on international interests in mobile equipment (see below) with its associated Aircraft Protocol is now not far behind, with ratifications of the Convention by 82 States and the Protocol by 79 States, together in each case with what is now the European Union.

tractual aspects of sales contracts and has an interesting and controversial scope provision under which it applies to contracts for the sale of goods between parties whose places of business are in different States and where either both States are Contracting States or the rules of private international law (ie, of the forum State) lead to the application of the law of a Contracting State. The Convention can therefore apply even where neither party has its place of business in a Contracting State. Apart from this, the Convention's merit lies less in the use of innovative techniques than in the skilful blending of civil law and common law rules. Among the latter is the concept of breach, which under Article 79 of the Convention includes non-performance excused on the ground of *force majeure*, only damages being excluded as a remedy, whereas in common law jurisdictions a failure to perform through an event of frustration does not constitute a breach at all. Many of the Convention's provisions will, however, also be familiar to common lawyers.

Controversial is whether good faith is required not merely in the interpretation of contracts, as indicated in Article 7(1),[36] but also as a general principle underlying other provisions of the Convention. The proponents of the latter view are unfazed by the fact that good faith is not mentioned in any of the other 100 provisions. Influenced by German law they equate unreasonable behaviour, which could include a perceived unreasonable withdrawal from negotiations or unreasonable exercise of contractual remedies, with want of good faith, but this is not generally true of common law jurisdictions or even of all civil law jurisdictions. What is interesting, however, is not so much the division of opinion but the fact that the final text was masterful in satisfying the holders of the two opposing views that each had achieved its objective!

The 1988 UNIDROIT Conventions on International Leasing and International Financial Factoring

The projects leading to these two international conventions were run in parallel and, unusually, the two were adopted at the same Diplomatic Conference. Though neither was very successful, each showed how creative thinking could overcome doctrinal obstacles.[37]

---

36. See above, n. 11.
37. For a recent detailed treatment of the two conventions see Amin Dawwas, 'The 1988 UNIDROIT Convention on International Financial Leasing' (1997) 21 *Journal of Law – Kuwait University* 3; 'The 1988 UNIDROIT Convention on International Factoring' (1999) 23 *Journal of Law – Kuwait University* 11. Professor Dawwas is a professor of law at the recently founded Arab American University formed in collaboration with California State University and Utah State University and based in Jenin and Ramallah on the West Bank of Palestine.

Convention on International Financial Leasing

This convention had a long period of gestation, the project having begun in February 1974 as involving the drawing up of uniform rules on the contract of leasing. At the time, cross-border financial leasing was quite rare and this was thought to be due, at least in part, to major differences in the treatment of finance leases in legal systems. There was early discussion of the form of instrument best suited for this purpose. Was it to be a uniform law, a model law, an international model contract or a set of standard-term clauses?[38] Then the question arose as to what types of leasing agreement should be covered. The element of internationality was identified from the outset as a prerequisite. As previously noted,[39] however, the legal characterisation of the transaction created a threshold problem because of sharp differences in national legal systems.

A financial lease possesses three key characteristics. First, the rentals are based not on the use value of the equipment but on the amount needed to amortise the cost of acquisition to the lessor and the desired return on its outlay. The finance lease is therefore, in essence, a financial transaction, to be distinguished from the operating lease, where the lessor hires out to different lessees in succession equipment it already owns in return for a use-value rental. Second, it is a tripartite transaction in which the equipment is purchased from the manufacturer or other supplier by a financier, who lets it on lease to the lessee. Third, it is the lessee who, relying on its own experience, selects the equipment and negotiates the terms of the lease. However, since it is the lessor who is the buyer and there is no contractual relationship between lessee and supplier, only the lessor can assert claims against the supplier for delivery of equipment that is not in conformity with the contract. The lessor could agree to hold any fruits of the claim on behalf of the lessee, but this faces the difficulty that since the terms of the lease almost always contain a 'hell or high water' clause entitling the lessor to payment of rentals regardless of any defects in the leased equipment, any damages recoverable by the lessor are likely to be purely nominal, as the lessor will have suffered no loss. For the same reason, the assignment to the lessee of the lessor's rights against the supplier will be of little value.

Two techniques were available to overcome the lack of privity of contract. One was to provide, as a number of legal systems did, that the lessee can enforce a contract made for its benefit as if it had been the contracting party. The alternative, and the one adopted by the Convention on International Financial Leasing, was to exempt the lessor from liability to the lessee except to the extent that the lessee has suffered loss in reliance

---

38. Study LIX – Doc. 1, UNIDROIT 1975, paragraph 22.
39. Above, p. 281.

on the lessor's skill and judgment and its intervention in the selection of the supplier or the specifications of the equipment (Article 8(1)), while on the other hand providing that the duties of the supplier under the supply agreement are also owed to the lessee as if the equipment were to be supplied directly to the lessee, but without the supplier being liable to both lessor and lessee in respect of the same damage (Article 10(1)). Thus was the problem of privity overcome in a very effective fashion.

Though the Convention failed to gain general acceptance, possibly because it did not apply to operating leases, it was acknowledged as an important reference for States drafting their first leasing laws and a useful starting point for the UNIDROIT Model Law on Leasing,[40] which is not confined to finance leases.

Convention on International Factoring

This convention, which is confined to factoring arrangements under which notice of assignment is to be given to the debtor, as opposed to non-notification invoice discounting, contains several useful and to some extent innovative provisions. One of these, designed to overcome a rule in a number of legal systems requiring specificity in identifying the subject matter of an assignment and thus precluding the assignment of future receivables, dispenses with the requirement of individual specification of the assigned receivables and provides that, as between parties to the factoring contract, a provision in the contract by which future receivables are assigned operates to transfer them to the factor when they come into existence without the need for any new act of transfer.[41] Another provision is addressed to the practice by suppliers of including a provision in the factoring contract prohibiting assignment. Such a provision constitutes a serious obstacle to the free flow of receivables in the stream of trade. Moreover, the supplier is likely to be able to impose the provision on the factor only when the supplier has the bargaining power. Article 6(2) in effect overrides such a provision as regards rights against the debtor except where, at the time of conclusion of the sale contract, the debtor has its place of business in a Contracting State that has made a declaration under Article 18 that the assignment is not to be effective. That this Convention did not gain much traction is probably due to a subsequent strong movement towards non-notification invoice discounting, which has for some time been the dominant form of receivables financing but is not covered by the Convention. Nevertheless it has been of some influence, particularly in its treatment of prohibitions against assignment, which have influenced domestic legislation.

---

40. UNIDROIT Model Law on Leasing 2010, Preamble, 5th and 6th clauses.
41. Art. 5.

The 1997 UNCITRAL Model Law on Cross-Border Insolvency

The product of collaboration between UNCITRAL and INSOL International, the UNCITRAL Model Law on Cross-Border Insolvency is designed to facilitate collaboration between courts and insolvency administrators in one jurisdiction and those in another. It applies where there are insolvency proceedings in one State and assistance is sought in another State or a creditor in one State seeks to commence or participate in proceedings in another State.[42] The Model Law has enjoyed considerable success, legislation based on it having so far been adopted in 48 States. It is essentially concerned with jurisdiction, recognition and procedure, not with substantive insolvency law, but it is none the worse for that since collaboration between States in such matters is of vital importance in the application of cross-border insolvency regimes.

The Cape Town Convention and its Protocols

Next to attract attention was the law governing security interests in high-value, uniquely identifiable equipment and its proceeds. The focus on secured transactions in movable property was powered by (1) the enormous value of cross-border transactions involving the extension of secured credit; (2) the pressure on less developed countries from organisations such as the World Bank and the European Bank for Reconstruction and Development to reform their legal regimes in order to promote economic development and secure access to credit; and (3) an awareness that differences in legal regimes governing cross-border dealings in equipment of high unit-value created such risk and uncertainty for potential financiers and lessors that the advance of funds, particularly to developing countries, was either not forthcoming at all or made at very high rates. Research conducted for the project estimated that a sound uniform legal regime could result in savings of billions of dollars a year.[43] As regards mobile equipment, UNIDROIT initiated and, together with ICAO, piloted the Convention on International Interests in Mobile Equipment and Aircraft Protocol, followed by the Luxembourg Protocol on railway rolling stock concluded jointly by UNIDROIT and OTIF, the Space Protocol dealing with space assets and the Pretoria Protocol covering mining, agricultural and construction equipment.

Of all the instruments discussed so far, this convention and its protocols are far and away the most complex. Indeed, had we known at the outset the size and scale of the ultimate project, it is doubtful whether we would

---

42. See the UNCITRAL Model Law on Cross-Border Insolvency with Guide to Enactment and Interpretation (United Nations, New York, 2014); *Goode on Principles of Corporate Insolvency Law* (5th edn, ed. Kristin van Zwieten, Sweet & Maxwell, 2018), pp. 910-943.
43. See above, n. 30.

have had the audacity to begin. These instruments lay down substantive uniform rules governing the creation of international interests[44] in the above categories of equipment, remedies for default, registration in an International Registry established by the Convention and priorities determined primarily by the order of registration as well as the availability of strong protections for the creditor in the event of the debtor's insolvency. Provisions were also introduced governing the constitution and priority of assignments of associated rights, that is, rights to payment or other performance under the agreements constituting the international interest, Space does not allow a detailed examination of these instruments.[45] Suffice to say that they broke new ground in a number of respects, reflecting an unusually high degree of creativity. The following in particular stand out.

- The two-instrument approach by which the Convention is supplemented by a Protocol for each category of equipment which not only supplements but, quite exceptionally, controls the Convention, which can only come into force as regards any category of object when the relevant Protocol comes into force and takes effect subject to the terms of the Protocol.[46]
- The incursion into areas of property law previously regarded as taboo because too specific to policies of national law, in particular the establishment of a new property right, the international interest, priority rules governing competing interests and the modification of national insolvency laws.
- The establishment of an international, asset-based electronic registration system to register international interests and assignments and various other items and the supervision of the system and the Registrar by a Supervisory Authority.
- An elaborate system of declarations by which Contracting States are not bound by certain provisions considered sensitive in terms of national policy unless they opt into them and by other somewhat less sensitive provisions from which they can opt out.

Each of the four protocols raised presented challenges that had to be overcome. The Aircraft Protocol is of particular importance as it became the prototype for all subsequent protocols. It is particularly notable for provisions rendering international interests immune from the effects of

---

44. That is, interests granted by a charger under a security agreement or vested in a person who is the conditional seller under a title reservation agreement or a leasing agreement (Convention, Article 2(2)).
45. For a comprehensive treatment see the various Official Commentaries by the writer.
46. This accounts for the fact that, unusually, the Convention and the Aircraft Protocol were adopted at the same Diplomatic Conference.

the debtor's bankruptcy. In the Luxembourg Protocol, it was necessary to introduce provisions to protect users of public service railway rolling stock by restricting the creditor's rights of repossession,[47] while the Space Protocol limited the exercise of remedies that would make the space asset unavailable for the provision of relevant public services,[48] for example, the provision and maintenance of the space asset and related ground services for educational, navigational, military or surveillance purposes. Moreover, the practice of reinforcing collateral through the assignment to the creditor of debtor's rights, that is, rights of the debtor against third parties for rentals, licence fees and the like, raised the problem how to protect the priority of intangible rights by registration in an International Registry designed for physical assets. The solution was to provide for the recording of such assignments against the registration of the international interest to which they relate, with priority of competing assignments being determined by the order of registration.[49] A further difficulty was the establishment of identification criteria. Many satellites already in outer space had no single mode of identification and even where some of them had serial numbers, they were not visible from Earth. This apparently insuperable problem, which was left to be dealt with by registry regulations, was solved by providing for the Registrar to open a file allotting a unique identification number to each space asset before any registrations against that asset on the basis of information provided to the Registrar by the owner of the asset as to the name of the owner, the name of the manufacturer and the manufacturer's contract reference number, which in the case of a contract covering two or more space assets was to include a unique suffix reference number.[50] The contract would provide all the information required.

Finally, inventory financing, for which no special rules were needed in the earlier protocols, raised special considerations in the case of mining, agricultural and construction equipment, where dealers might hold large quantities of stock subject to an international interest, necessitating multiple registrations in the International Registry to protect interests that in most cases were transitory, coming to an end as items of stock were sold, requiring a continuous series of discharge, thus making the system very inefficient. The solution adopted in the Pretoria Protocol was to allow

---

47. Luxembourg Protocol, art. XXV.
48. Space Protocol, art. XXVII.
49. *Ibid.*, arts. XII, XIII.
50. Space Regulations, Section 5.3 bis and Annex 2. See the Summary Report of the 4th session of the Preparatory Commission for the Establishment of the International Registry for Space Assets pursuant to the Space Protocol, Fourth Session (UNIDROIT 2015, Prep. Comm. Space/4/Doc. 7 rev.), Appendix III. The writer was tasked with preparing the draft regulations and the Explanatory Report, which he introduced at the 4th session. See Summary Report, paras 6-15.

Contracting States to make a declaration excluding inventory from most of the Protocol's provisions and rely on their local registration systems.

The UN Convention on the Assignment of Receivables in International Trade

The Cape Town Convention was quickly followed by the 2001 UN Convention on the Assignment of Receivables in International Trade, an ambitious and carefully crafted convention covering both the assignment of international receivables and the international assignment of receivables. It had been expected that this Convention would be adopted prior to the Cape Town Convention, which to avoid doubt would then state that in case of conflict the Cape Town Convention would prevail. However, the reversing of the expected chronology raised the problem of how the Cape Town Convention could qualify a convention not yet made. The ingenious solution, proposed by the head of the US delegation to the Cape Town Diplomatic Conference, was to provide in an Annex approved by the Conference[51] that upon adoption of the UN Convention by the General Assembly of the United Nations, a new Article 45 *bis* was to be inserted into the Cape Town Convention that in case of conflict the latter would prevail, and this is what Article 45 *bis* now provides – another example of creative thinking and one that will be unfamiliar to most international lawyers!

The Hague and Geneva Conventions

As regards intangible movables, interests in intermediated securities[52] came into focus in relation to the harmonisation both of the applicable law (Hague Convention) and later of substantive rules (UNIDROIT Geneva Convention). The first of these has already been discussed.[53] The Geneva Convention lays down substantive rules for intermediated securities. The drafters of this convention deliberately adopted a functional approach which looked to the results to be achieved, regardless of whether a given jurisdiction adopted the transparent approach, by which ultimate investors retain a contractual relationship with the issuer, a non-transparent approach,

---

51. As noted in the Official Commentary on the Cape Town Convention and Aircraft Protocol (4th edn 2019), paragraph 2.295, the Annex does not feature in the published documents, its effect being exhausted when the insertion was made. However, the Conference approved the draft proposed by the US and the UNIDROIT and ICAO Secretariats, contained in DCME Doc No. 70 dated 13 November 2001 and reproduced at p. 294 of the Conference *Acts and Proceedings*.

52. That is, securities credited to an account with a bank or other intermediary.

53. For a detailed analysis see Roy Goode, Herbert Kronke and Hideki Kanda, assisted by Christophe Bernasconi, *Hague Securities Convention Explanatory Report* (2nd edn, The Hague Conference on Private International Law Permanent Bureau, 2017).

in which each account holder's relationship is solely with its own inter-mediary, or a semi-transparent approach, where the account holder is not recorded on the books of the central securities depositary holding on behalf of the issuer but only on the books of an account holder with the central securities depositary. Recognising that there are limits to what can be harmonised with such a diverse set of rules and systems the drafters of the Geneva Convention devised a novel concept, 'non-Convention law'. This is not to be confused with the applicable law. 'Non-Convention law' denotes the domestic law of a Contracting State, whether or not that law is the applicable law under the forum's conflict of laws rules. The virtue of this system is that in a Contracting State all issues not covered by the Convention are governed by the law of that State.[54]

The UCP and URDG

The rise of the abstract payment undertaking

Nothing more vividly illustrates the power of international trade usage than the emergence of the abstract payment undertaking, a banking device which by the customs of merchants is considered enforceable by virtue of its issue without any of the ordinary elements of a valid contract such as offer and acceptance, reliance, *cause* or consideration. Courts everywhere have found it difficult to accommodate the abstract payment undertaking within traditional doctrine but all have sensibly recognised the importance of upholding such a vitally important financing instrument. What should not be overlooked is the important role of the International Chamber of Commerce in unifying trade and finance practice through the formulation of international rules which are given legally binding force by incorporation into all relevant contracts. There are two main forms of abstract payment undertaking, the documentary credit, governed by the Uniform Customs and Practice for Documentary Credits (UCP), and the demand guarantee, governed by the Uniform Rules for Demand Guarantees (URDG).

The UCP

Pride of place belongs to the UCP, first issued in 1933 but derived from a set of regulations issued in 1920 by the New York Bankers Commercial Credit Conference[55] and periodically revised. The UCP are rules governing the issue of documentary credits. These are undertakings, usually by banks, that the issuer (and in the case of a confirmed credit, the confirming bank) will pay, whether at sight or at a later date through acceptance of a draft

---

54. See Hideki Kanda, Charles Mooney, Luc Thévenoz and Stéphanie Béraud, assisted by Thomas Keijser, *Official Commentary on the UNIDROIT Convention on Substantive Rules for Intermediated Securities* (Oxford University Press, 2012, paragraphs 1-55 to 1-60.
55. Regulations Affecting Export Commercial Credits.

or other deferred payment) a given sum to the beneficiary (typically an exporter of goods under a contract of sale) on due presentation of specified transport and other documents. Documentary credits give the export seller the assurance of payment in advance of its manufacture or purchase of the goods. The influence of the UCP was graphically described by Professor Boris Kozolchyk in an address given at the UNCITRAL Forum für Internationales Wirtschaftsrecht in Vienna in November 1991:

> No other set of international customary rules is as universally observed as the *Uniform Customs and Practice for Documentary Credits* (UCP): Banks, applicants and beneficiaries in more than 150 nations adhere to it; carriers, freight forwarders and insurers draft their documents to comply with its specifications; legislatures model their statutes after it, and courts treat it as a source of law whose misinterpretations cause quick reversal.
>
> The reason why the UCP has inspired such widespread observance is not hard to surmise: It is the living law of documentary credits. By 'living law' I mean the law that not only adjudicates disputes but also governs every aspect of the everyday 'healthy' (unlitigated or undisputed) letter of credit transactions. The UCP, then, is a law invoked in the courtroom as well as applied in practice. As is characteristic of living law, the UCP contains didactic principles that instruct bankers on the basics of documentary credit business.[56]

The current version, UCP 600, forms the basis of over US$1 trillion transactions and has been adopted in 175 countries. How many international trade conventions can match that?

The URDG

More recent are the Uniform Rules for Demand Guarantees, first issued by the UCC in 1992[57] to replace the 1978 Uniform Rules of Contract Guarantees[58] and later revised to provide a more comprehensive set of rules governing demand guarantees. Under the URDG, these are payable on presentation of a written demand, a statement of the respect in which the applicant is in breach of its obligations under the underlying relationship and such other documents as may be specified in the guarantee.[59]

---

56. For a detailed history of the evolution of the UCP see Dan Taylor, *The Complete UCP: Text, Rules and Practice for Documentary Credits*, ICC Publication No 683, which reproduces these extracts from Professor Kozolchyk's lecture.
57. ICC 458.
58. ICC 325. These failed because their requirements came close to requiring actual proof of default.
59. ICC 758, art. 15. Demand guarantees are typically issued by banks to underpin non-monetary obligations of the applicant, such as performance under a construction contract.

Scholarly restatements

Of the various forms of soft law one deserves attention, namely the restatement of contract law by scholars of international standing.[60] Two of these,
the Principles of European Contract Law (PECL) previously referred to
and the UNIDROIT Principles of International Commercial Contracts,
have gained particular prominence.[61] Although the former is regional
and covers both commercial and consumer contracts while the latter is
international but is confined to commercial contracts, there is a good deal
of similarity between these two products, which are characterised by the
fact that they are the work of scholars from different countries and have
not involved either governments or business interests. Both of these, and
particularly the UNIDROIT Principles, have influenced legal decisions,
especially by arbitral tribunals, and national legislation. Most of the rules
follow established principles of contract law, even though their application differs from State to State, but there are a few that are new, at least
in some degree. One in particular deals with change of circumstances[62]
or hardship.[63] Also of interest is the provision, common to both sets of
Principles, designating certain provisions as mandatory and thus incapable
of exclusion by the parties. These include the provisions imposing a
duty of good faith and fair dealing[64] and reduction of grossly excessive
sums payable on default.[65] It may be asked how mandatory rules may be
contained in a set of Principles which does not itself have the force of law.
This is not as strange as it appears, however. In the first place, in those
legal systems which recognise the right of parties to choose internationally
established rules as the applicable law, choice of the Principles will trigger
the mandatory provisions as part of that law. Secondly, where this is not

They share the characteristic of letters of credit in that they are purely documentary and in
the absence of fraud are payable against conforming documents whether or not the applicant
party to the underlying contract has committed a breach of that contract.

60. The word 'restatement', a convenient label borrowed from the American *Restatements*,
is a slight misnomer, since restatements not only state existing law or practice, they also seek
to improve it in some degree.

61. Much valuable work in this area has also been carried out under the auspices of the
Academy of European Private Lawyers in Pavia.

62. PECL art. 6:111, where performance of the contract becomes 'excessively onerous'
because of a change of circumstances.

63. UPICC arts. 6.2.1, 6.2.2, applicable where 'the occurrence of events fundamentally alters
the equilibrium of the contract either because the cost of a party's performance has increased
or because the value of the performance a party receives has diminished.' The increase in cost
or diminution in value must be substantial (Comment 2 to art. 6.2.2), given that it must be
one that fundamentally alters the equilibrium of the contract. Most legal systems have rules
of some kind reflecting change of circumstances (*force majeure*, frustration, etc.), but what
is new, at least in most jurisdictions, is the provision for renegotiation of the contract and,
failing agreement, recourse to the court.

64. PECL art. 1:201; UPICC art. 1.7.

65. PECL art. 9:509(2); UPICC art. 7.4.13(2).

the case, the designation of specified rules as mandatory sends a signal to a court or arbitral tribunal of a general acceptance that such rules are indeed to be considered mandatory, Thirdly, such designation may show an intention that such rules, even if not mandatory, are intended to prevail over other, inconsistent rules unless otherwise expressly agreed.

ENVOI

It is hoped that this this *tour d'horizon* has amply illustrated the creative forces that have underpinned the development of transnational commercial law. They are characterised by a willingness to break with established doctrine in searching for best solutions to typical problems confronting international trade and finance, sometimes drawing on national legal systems or international trade usage, sometimes inventing new legal techniques. Transnational commercial law has come of age.

ASIA INCOGNITA – HERE BE DRAGONS

LAW MODERNIZATION IN SOUTH-EAST ASIA: COLONIAL AND POST-COLONIAL LAND TENURES IN INDONESIA AND MALAYSIA

*Mary E Hiscock**

For my contribution as a friend of Derek to a work to honour his memory, I have chosen a piece, jointly written in the 1970s, which draws on the work that was done by Derek, and me, and my late husband, David Allan. Between 1967 and 1981, we three produced 12 books together with a group of individual contributors.[1] This was an enterprise, sponsored and financed by the Asian Development Bank and the Ford Foundation. Our task was to consider and propose improvements to the legal regime for supplying finance to 10 of the developing countries of Asia. I have no doubt that our sponsors thought we would manufacture a silver bullet in the shape of a legislative solution, the existence of which would be a condition of any lending. Their judgment was not correct. Giving this task to a trio of commercial lawyers, who were also comparative lawyers and legal historians, meant that the depth of the inquiry was not only more interesting for the three of us, but the search took much longer than was anticipated, and led us into unexpected fields.

Derek and David knew each other from the time when they both worked in Manchester, Derek as an articled clerk at Slater Heelis and David as a very junior barrister on the Northern Circuit. Then, separately, and over a period of some years, they both made their way to New Zealand to the Victoria University of Wellington. David supervised Derek's higher degree. Then David moved to the University of Tasmania and Derek came a short time later. I met them both when they were still in New Zealand, but our work began when they were in Tasmania and I was at the University of Melbourne. This was a time when Australia was opening up its legal horizons beyond England, and looking particularly into Asia. There

* Emeritus Professor of Law, Bond University, Australia.
1. A list of these is attached as an Appendix.

was little knowledge or experience of Asian commercial law amongst Australian lawyers, so our first task was to discover what was the contract law of those countries that were part of the United Nations Economic and Social Commission for Asia and the Pacific (ESCAP).

The fruits of this task were manifold. In seeking out scholars to lead the research in each country, and to learn from them, we created a structure that still continues to this day. Most of the original group are now dead, but their students and the students of their students entered into a mutually beneficial familial structure, which has become a large and influential network. It would be so much easier today with access to the Internet, but we did it the hard way with reams of paper, and many visits and long hours of discussion. Many sources were not accessible with any ease and certainly not for the most part in English. So it was person to person activity. As Derek said, in his contribution to my Festschrift:

> We are obliged, if we are responsible comparative lawyers, to take every chance to win the co-operation of our colleagues in other jurisdictions, so that we may take full advantage of an opportunity that we do not have as legal historians: to win from the best sources that understanding of another's legal system.[2]

The journey crossed the legal boundaries and we ventured into anthropology, economic history, political history and elusive areas of policy to understand the systems of others. We were led by our fellow scholars. The impact of colonial law and policy on native land title and custom are still contentious matters with uncertain boundaries 40 years later, even in Australian law, although there has been a profound change in our law since then.[3]

Although the triple working relationship ended many years ago, it had given way to a close personal love and friendship, which only death brought to an end. David and I were joint 'best person' when Susanna and Derek married. Derek proposed the toast, and gave the speech, when David and I married. The extract below is based on papers that David and I gave when we were on sabbatical leave in Germany in 1978 at the Max-Planck-Institut of Foreign and Private Law and at the Free University of

2. 'A Return to that Other Country: Legal History as Comparative Law' in *Scholarship, Practice and Education in Comparative Law: A Festschrift in Honour of Mary Hiscock* (Singapore 2019) p 15.
3. *Mabo and Others v State of Queensland* [1992] HCA 69 decided that the colonial concept of Australia as *'terra nullius'* was no longer Australian law, and that native title to land could be recognized; *Akiba v Commonwealth of Australia* recognized native title off-shore fishing rights; In *Thoms v Commonwealth of Australia* [2020] HCA 3, the High Court ruled that an indigenous man cannot be an 'unlawful non-citizen' and therefore liable to deportation because of his connection to country.

Berlin. The result was published in *Rabels Zeitschrift*.[4] The Institut has given permission to reproduce this material.

INTRODUCTION

A study of the legal systems of south-east Asian countries offers many attractions to the comparativist. There is the opportunity to compare European legal systems in colonial settings; to study the interaction of those legal systems with local cultures and customs; to assess their continuing influence after the former colony achieves independence; and to seek conclusions drawn from the transplanting and operations of law and legal institutions.

It is proposed to examine and compare one aspect of this phenomenon in Malaysia[5] and Indonesia. These two countries have been selected because both share '*adat*' culture; both have been exposed to Islamic,[6] Hindu, and Chinese influences and migration; both have been colonized by the Dutch, Portuguese, and British. But, for this present purpose, most of what is now known as Malaysia was once primarily under British government or influence and Indonesia was most effectively colonized by the Dutch. Each was subjected to the legal systems of the colonizer in varying degrees, and each was moulded by the colonial policies of the British or the Dutch. After World War II, each of them attained independence: though not without armed struggle. Each is today a multiracial society and each has faced and overcome communist subversion. But the institutions and organizations of each still show markedly the influence of the colonial power. This is most true of the law and of legal institutions.

The study and comparison of English and Dutch legal systems working in colonial and post-colonial Malaysia and Indonesia is a topic suitable for a very lengthy dissertation.[7] Here, the scope is limited to one aspect of

4. ME Hiscock and DE Allan, 46 *Rabels Zeitschrift fur auslandisches und internationales Privatrecht* (1982), pp 509–529. The footnotes are contemporaneous, but some have been shortened.
5. Modern Malaysia consists of 13 states which formed four distinct law blocks. Each is a product of its own colonial history, so that it is not feasible here to deal with all of them. This chapter will therefore concentrate on the four states which formed the Federated Malay States: Selangor, Pahang, Perak, and Negri Sembilan.
6. An important feature of Islamic influence in the development of both countries has been the doctrine of '*riba*' which prohibits unearned income, and '*z'akat*', the obligation to spread one's wealth throughout the country – representing an attitude preferring communal rights to individual rights.
7. See B Ter Haar, *Adat Law in Indonesia*, ed EA Hoebel and AA Schiller (New York, 1948); S Gautama and RN Hornick, *An Introduction to Indonesian Law* (Bandung, 1974), ch.4; S Gautama, D Allan, M Hiscock and D Roebuck, *Credit and Security in Indonesia* (St Lucia, 1973), pp 83–93, 104–109; Hornick, 'Indonesian Mortgage Law' (1974) 5 *Lawasia* 30; on land transactions generally, see Ter Haar, op cit, ch.3. For modern land law, see Gautama and Hornick, op cit ch 3. For Malaysia, see DSY Wong, *Tenure and Land Dealings in the Malay States* (Singapore, 1975), chs 7, 8 and 9.

the land law. Land was of the greatest importance to both the indigenous population and the European colonist. Since independence, both countries have retained primarily agrarian economies, although there is an increasing importance on extractive industries. It is, however, necessary to distinguish plantation from subsistence agriculture. Plantations were enclaves for European entrepreneurs; but subsistence agriculture was the traditional means of livelihood of the autochthonous population. Both forms of agriculture survived independence in both countries; both remain economically vital to both countries; both need available sources of credit and finance if they are to survive. Plantations need medium to long term finance to carry them through to production and to continue production. The traditional sector has different needs for seasonal finance, perhaps for no more than six months at a time, to carry the farmer from harvest to harvest. In each case traditional banking and moneylending practices require security for finance or credit, and in each case there is little that can be offered as security except the land itself and its yield.

It is a very narrow issue that will be examined in this paper as a vehicle for comparison of the effects of British and Dutch colonial land policy. Does the legal system, whether colonial or post-colonial, enable the land to be used effectively for the purpose of securing credit, particularly in the traditional sector of subsistence agriculture? In this area of land use, will be found the continued use and practices of native tenures alongside modern systems of land tenure. So is it possible to develop a modern system of land tenure while traditional usages continue *sub rosa*; or is it better to acknowledge and legitimate traditional ways or to ignore them and deny them validity?

THE NATURE OF *ADAT*

The common base on which the British and Dutch colonial legal systems built in Malaysia and Indonesia was '*adat*'. [8] Generally, *adat* is the customary way of living of the people who occupy the Malay peninsula, Sumatra, Borneo, Java, and all the islands of Nusantara. There are today probably more than 250 million people occupying in excess of 6,000 islands.

In Arabic, *adat* signifies custom; in Malay it means more than that and carries a connotation of manners and etiquette, of a proper sense of correct behaviour. It is unwritten custom, a way of life based on collective action for communal purposes, where the community is the village or 'kampung'. It is not a legal system in the western sense, having a much

---

8. See Ter Haar, *supra* note 7, especially editorial introduction. Allan et al, *Asian Contract Law* (Melbourne, 1969). C Van Vollenhoven, 'The Study of Indonesian Customary Law' (1918/1919) 13 *Ill L Rev* 200; 'Families of Languages and Families of Law' (1920/21) 15 *Ill L Rev* 417.

wider compass than the European view of law. Nor is it systematic. There are many variations. Van Vollenhoven[9] classified Indonesia into 19 *adat* law areas and he found two further areas in what is now Malaysia. These correspond to separate cultural and geographic areas, but any classification is arbitrary, reflecting gradations of customs from village to village and from area to area.

Adat does, however, perform many of the functions of western legal systems, the most important being the regulation of communal life based on families living in villages, and the regulation of communal land. The dependence of the community on its land transcends a mere economic relationship. There are few western concepts in *adat*. Dichotomies between public and private, real and personal, movable and immovable are unknown; and *adat* is inconsistent with any concept of individual or private rights.

So far as land rights[10] are concerned, the *adat* concept of ownership is dominated by the community ('In-Groupers'). The soil and the communal group are bound to one another. Therefore individual property rights are merged into the collective community's right of use and disposal. Communal and individual rights interact; the community exercises its right by limiting the activities of its members on the land and by taking the profits. If the individual cultivates a piece of land, a legal relation develops between him and that land which diminishes the rights of the community. But if he neglects it, the communal rights are re-established.

Access by outsiders ('Out-Groupers') is regulated by the community. Out-groupers can never own the land, but they may exploit its use for a fee and with the permission of the chief ('*penghulu*').[11]

In western terms, most *adat* transactions are real agreements rather than consensual contracts. Their contemplated results are therefore immediately obtained at the moment of agreement, and there are few executory obligations. The economic tool in an *adat* community is a real agreement affecting land, and not a contract. It is necessary, however, to distinguish land transactions, obligations involving land, and credit transactions.

Land transactions involve a transfer of land to another, permanently or for an agreed time. They are known as '*jual*' transactions. In High Malay, *jual* simply means transfer; but in modern Bahasa Malay it carries more the notion of a sale.

Obligations involving land are agreements concerning the use of land of another. The land itself is not transferred, and therefore they are non-*jual* transactions.

---

9. Ter Haar's classification is largely based on van Vollenhoven, *Het adatrecht van Nederlansche-Indie* (2nd printing Leiden, 1931).
10. To talk even of 'rights' is misleading if the word carries its European connotation.
11. Ter Haar, *supra* note 7, 87: 'A little gift to the chief is a good Indonesian custom'.

In both *jual* and non-*jual* transactions, in all matters affecting land, the community's rights take precedence over individual rights. It is otherwise in the case of credit transactions. Here, one person gives another something or does something for him, and receives in return an expectation of a return service at a proper time. This is the *adat* 'straining towards equilibrium'. A person who gives more than he receives obtains an overbalance, which calls for a counter-giving. This provides therefore a concept of agreement which is adequate for the needs of intercourse in a closed village community.

Rural communities in both Malaysia and Indonesia, therefore, are affected by two legacies. *Adat* places emphasis on barter rather than cash, and displays an antipathy to the futurity of the notion of credit. Islam carries an abhorrence of interest. How then can credit, moneylending, and security be possible in these communities? Certainly, village farmers need credit, and each village has its merchant (often Chinese) who may buy the crops of the villagers and give them credit in the meantime against security.

Adat has a wide variety of concepts of security for credit which are difficult to classify. There are also some semantic problems in finding suitable words in English to express the concepts of *adat*. Both *jual* and non-*jual* types of security are found, depending on whether a transfer of the land is involved. *Jual* is the more common, and its form may be that of sale, pledge or lease.

Adat knows two types of *jual* securities[12]: the '*jual janji*'[13] which is more important in Malaysia, and the '*hak gadai*'[14] which is more prominent in Indonesia. The *jual janji* is a fictitious sale with a condition that the 'seller' shall have the right to repurchase the property during a specified period. The *hak gadai* is more properly a pledge, involving the reservation of a right to recover the property on payment of an equivalent sum. In both, the value of the land as security was reckoned by reference to what it could produce, for most loans were seasonal. Because of Islamic beliefs, both securities were seen as 'transfers', and 'interest' was the 'price of the transfer'. This was no hypocritical sham, but a manifestation of a deep abhorrence and shame for loan transactions. Both transactions were completed before the chief. Under both, the buyer/pledgee was permitted to take the full profits from the land, although frequently he returned the land to the seller/pledger under some form of share-cropping arrangement.

The major difference between the two forms was that under *jual janji* the 'buyer' became the *adat* owner of the land whereas under the *hak gadai*, although it was strictly a transfer (*jual*), the *adat* ownership remained

---

12. This classification is fairly arbitrary; in fact there are many variations, and similar transactions may have different names in different areas.
13. Literally, a promise of a sale/transfer.
14. Literally, a right of security/pledge.

throughout with the debtor/pledgor. The pledgee was entitled to profits of the land, subject to any share-cropping arrangement, but his use of the land was limited by his obligation to maintain a possibility of redemption. Where the sale form (*jual janji*) was used, there could be a possibility of difficulty in deciding whether the transaction was a genuine outright sale depriving the 'seller' of further interest, or a security transfer where the 'rights' of the seller/debtor should be protected, and in particular his right of repurchase.[15] In many ways, however, in an *adat* community this difficulty was unreal. The purpose of the transaction would be common knowledge.[16]

Strictly, neither *jual janji* nor *hak gadai* were security interests or accessory contracts. They were transfers: the one using the sale form and the other a more limited transfer giving merely full rights of use. Accordingly in both cases 'redemption' of the 'security' is a difficult concept because strictly there was no loan. Nevertheless, 'redemption' would normally be by 'repayment', but there was no obligation on the seller or pledgee to repay or redeem. If the land was not redeemed, in the case of *hak gadai*, the pledger might sub-pledge or assign it or, if the agreement specified a fixed time for redemption, he might call for the full *adat* ownership to be transferred to him if the land was not redeemed in time. But, in the case of both *jual janji* and *hak gadai*, the seller/pledger's right could not be automatically extinguished; time might be extended or the creditor/transferee might be required, as a condition of receiving full *adat* ownership, to pay the debtor the excess value of the land to bring the 'price' up from the initial payment to an adequate market price.

Non-*jual* security transactions appear under different names in different places. Being non-*jual*, none of them involve a transfer of the land, and the transaction is accessory to a loan agreement. The borrower 'assigns' his land as security for a loan; and by so doing, he accepts limitations on his right to deal with the land until the loan is repaid. These limitations may be more extensive if the transaction is concluded before the chief. The borrower retains possession. The continuing sanction of the creditor, which makes the security effective, is communal social pressure.

COLONIAL LAND POLICIES

Indonesia and Malaysia had different colonial and administrative histories. Indonesia was colonized by the Dutch East Indies Company in the 17th century; Malaysia was effectively taken over by the British in the 19th

---

15. Analogies with western institutions at this point are tempting but misleading: *adat* cannot be defined in western terms.
16. In Malaysia, borrowers tend to travel to other communities to raise loans. In this case , local knowledge will not help to characterise the transaction.

century. Both colonial regimes, however, were concerned primarily with the preservation of sufficient order to enable profits to be made. In Indonesia, these profits were derived from a wide variety of crops and minerals, whereas in Malaysia they were derived mainly from rubber and tin.

DUTCH POLICY IN INDONESIA[17]

The Dutch East Indies Company, being essentially a trading society, naturally did not concern itself much with the problem of the best law for the population. The policy was to preserve order and to make profits with as little disturbance of the native population as possible. The easiest solution was to leave the natives alone with their original customary law, but to apply the Roman-Dutch law of the mother country in the trading posts themselves. The principle of concordance of the law in the Netherlands and of colonial law differed sharply from the Blackstonian theory of English colonization.[18] This dualism continued when the new Codes, adopted in the Netherlands following the French Code Civile, were introduced into the colony, and it was enshrined in the Indische Staatsregeling, the Constitution of the Netherlands Indies. Article 163 enumerated different population groups among the inhabitants and Article 131 outlined a basic law policy which was aimed at preservation of native *adat* law as much as possible, a policy of 'anti-acculturation'.[19] The population was divided into racial groups in order to determine the application of systems of law. Briefly, 'Europeans' and 'Foreign Oriental Chinese' were subject for the most part to the Dutch Civil and Commercial Codes, whilst 'native Indonesians' were subject to their own *adat*. Dutch law recognized *adat* as the law of the native population from the earliest days and sought to preserve it. Various schemes were advanced for its codification since 1848, the last being a draft Code in 1926 which was never implemented.

This policy of 'diversity and dualism' led to the development of a complex system of interpersonal law to regulate dealings between persons of different racial groups. Law was personal: race determined the system of law that applied to the person; interpersonal law regulated dealings between persons from different systems.

Land was then treated differently. Laws were developed aimed at preserving tenure and facilitating long-term credit to suit the needs of the colonial entrepreneurs, whilst at the same time preserving the native reversion. Up to 1830, land development took place simply through the sale of land to private entrepreneurs, either by the government or by the

---

17. See Hornick, *supra* note 7, 31–34; Gautama and Hornick, *supra* note 7, Ch 1.
18. Blackstone's *Commentaries on the Laws of England*, ed Kerr Vol I (1857) pp 90–97.
19. See Gautama and Hornick, *supra note* 7, ch. 2, 13-14.

Dutch East Indies Company. Large estates were sold in this way to private developers. But from 1830 to 1854, the policy changed to one whereby the peasants cultivated export crops on their land for the government which took the entire crop in lieu of tax. There was, however, still need for the foreign private entrepreneur, and in 1854 the Governor-General was authorized to grant agrarian leases to foreigners for up to twenty years. This proved too short a period for agricultural development.

In 1870 two measures introduced the system which was to last until 1960. The first was the Agrarian Act, which marked a shift from government monopoly back to private enterprise. The Governor-General was authorized to convey land with 'right of *erfpacht*' to private entrepreneurs for up to 75 years. This was the strongest right over someone else's land, and amounted to full ownership but for the reversion. The legal basis for this was provided by the *Domein* Declaration (an Agrarian Decree of the King of the Netherlands). This declared that land not proved to be '*eigendom*' land (in private ownership under the Civil Code as a result of earlier alienation) was the '*domein*' or the absolute property of the state. It was nationalization subject only to those grants of private ownership that could be proved under the Civil Code. All land, including native *adat* land, vested in the state unless individual Civil Code *eigendom* could be proved. Further, until a grant of land was made by the state, the land was the *domein* of the state; *adat* rights continued only on sufferance. In particular, where the land had not been surveyed to make a grant possible, native rights continued unaffected. All land, therefore, including native *adat* land (with some minor exceptions), was vested in the state, and a legal basis was established for the government to transfer it with western legal rights. The implementation of this policy produced the system of 'dualism' in land. Given the geography of Indonesia, with its multitude of islands and impenetrable mountains, the abolition of 'dualism' was scarcely possible.

Land itself became characterized as western, native or Chinese independently of the race of the person claiming rights in it. The purpose of the characterization was to determine the system of law which would define the rights that could exist in the land and which would control and regulate transactions affecting the land. Native land represented the largest proportion of all. This was rural land except for the plantations. The only rights that could exist in it were *adat* rights, and transactions had to be those recognized by *adat*. The only form of registration of rights or transactions occurred at the tax office. On the other hand, western land, which was mainly urban and plantation land, was regulated by Book II of the Civil Code, which defined both rights and transactions. Registration was effected in the Land Registration Office. There was very little Chinese land and its development is not germane to this paper.

Persons of any population group (with some few exceptions) could enjoy rights over any type of land. This gave rise to some problems of conflict of laws, and so interpersonal law regimes developed. For example, westerners (particularly banks and corporations) sought to acquire rights over *adat* land. There was much customary jurisprudence regulating such a transaction, but there was also some significant statutory architecture.

So far as security was concerned, security was taken over western land by '*hypotheek*' according to Book II of the Civil Code. Security was taken over *adat* land by *adat* pledges (*hak gadai* and sometimes *jual janji*) and non-*jual* devices. In the interpersonal sphere, where for example a western bank wished to take security over *adat* land, the '*credietverband*' appeared. This was created by Royal Decree of 1908 as a special right for some western banks to take security over *adat* land. It was an adaptation of the *hypotheek* giving a real right by way of security subject to registration with the local officer.

Then came the Second World War. The only lasting effect that the Japanese occupation had on the legal system was the fusion of the administration of the law. The native courts were abolished, but otherwise there was no change. The systems of personal law, dualism, of racial land systems, and of interpersonal laws were unaffected. *Adat* securities continued to serve *adat* land.

BRITISH POLICY IN THE FEDERATED MALAY STATES

When the British came to the Federated Malay States,[20] there was an *adat* system of land tenure including *adat* securities in land. As far as the law can be the same, it was the same as the *adat* systems in Indonesia. The state of Negri Sembilan had a peculiar system of matrilineal clan ownership, but rights enjoyed by the clan and by individuals in other states were typically *adat*. There were rights to occupy and to use the land for agriculture in various ways, depending on the type of land and agriculture, either for a period of years before it lapsed back into jungle or more or less permanently for growing rice and vegetables.

This led the British colonial power, from Raffles on, to describe Malay legal rights as proprietary usufructs, with the balance of ownership rights vested in the political chiefs. This was a convenient theory for a colonial power, but it did not accord with local understanding. However, it paved the way for the British to succeed to the rights of the political chiefs,

20. On British colonial policy generally, see R von Albertini, *Decolonization* (Garden City, NY, 1971), pp 33–48, 78–115. For the Federated Malay States, see D McIntyre, 'Political History 1896–1946', in *Malaysia* ed Wang Gungwu (London, 1964) pp 138–148; E Sadka, in *The Colonial Office and the Federated Malay States*, ed J Bastin and R Roolvink (London, 1964), p 184.

thereby having absolute ownership of the land, giving the natives mere lesser rights of use and occupation as if they had been granted to them.

The colonial administration sought a land law that would further its own interests and which would be easy to administer. For this reason English law with its complicated structure of law, equity, statutory and other rights was rejected. Instead the Torrens system of land transfer and registration was introduced by statute. In the ideal Torrens system, all land is measured and recorded, all interests capable of being recognized by law are registrable, and any change in those interests is recorded. Unlike Australia whence the system came, the substance of English land law, both common law and equity, was not received as part of the law of the Federated Malay States.[21] All rights were created and defined by statute only. This led to gaps and to difficult questions of interpretation. Although the statutes were similar, Australian law was not a reliable analogy.[22]

In the Federated Malay States, the Torrens system only applied to land granted by the British in the name of the Sultan. All grants were in the form of leases. Leases were granted of whatever land was wanted for tin mines and later rubber plantations. This was similar to the *erfpacht* policy of the Dutch.

Land left in the occupation of natives was registered on a separate register, which was in effect a rent roll. The land was deemed to have been leased to its occupants. This separate system of land holding was administered by a separate department of government and a simplified system of registration and transfer was introduced.[23]

In stark contrast to the situation in Indonesia, neither in land registered on the Torrens register, nor in land registered as customary land, were native rights and tenures recognized. In each state of the Federated Malay States and in identical terms it was stated that all land was subject to law, that interests in land could only be created and transferred according to the Regulations, and that any attempt to do otherwise would be null, void, and of no effect.[24]

The policy of colonial convenience and ease of administration created two legal problems which might have been anticipated and dealt with by the legislature. But they were not. The first of these problems was the consequences of non-recognition of native rights and tenures in land, especially of securities. These consequences were the more serious because many

21. Wong, *supra* note 7, Ch 3.

22. EA Francis, *Law and Practice Relating to Torrens Title in Australasia*, 2 vols, (1972/3); L Voumard and PN Wikrama, *The Law Relating to Sale of Land in Victoria* (1978).

23. For a discussion of the Makim register, see Wong, *supra* note 7, Chs 3 and 6.

24. Selangor Registration of Titles Regulation 1891; Perak Registration of Titles Enactment 1897; Pahang Registration of Titles Enactment 1897; Negri Sembilan Registration of Titles Enactment 1898.

rural communities continued to use, occupy, and transfer land as they had done for generations, without any regard to their new colonial masters or their law; the second problem was the place of equity, both as to the recognition of equitable interests in land and of equitable doctrines concerning land, and the extent to which these had been taken into Malaysian law by way of statute.

The land legislation expressed a policy of non-recognition of native institutions. Judges tried to give effect to that policy conscientiously. It has been suggested that there was a common policy of non-recognition of native tenures subscribed to by all the judges in the colonial service, and that they would have adhered to this policy even in the absence of the specific words in the statute.[25]

But the real problem was caused by legislation which was so drafted that shrewd lenders could take advantage of the registration provisions to register a *jual janji* security transfer as if it were a sale, thus giving themselves the rights of buyers rather than lenders. The courts could have dealt with this by allowing a borrower to prove the true nature of the transaction as a customary security, as they did in Indonesia, and allowing him to register his interest. But borrowers were reluctant to admit that they were borrowing money, because of their religious beliefs. And courts were reluctant to admit this evidence because they thought that it would undermine the certainty of the register and the policy of the legislation.

The only step taken by the authorities to counteract the side effects of the legislation was to introduce by statute the device of Malay Reservation land. This was land that could only be owned by Malays. The administration believed that no Malay would lend money and so this land could not be lost through the security transfer. As security for a loan, it could only be given to the Resident or to an agricultural co-operative.[26] But the rural Malay still prefers to go to the moneylender in the next town, rather than face up to local publicity or the demands of a far-off city bank.

The Privy Council in *Haji Abdul Rahman v Mohamed Hasan*[27] stated that the statutory system of registration of rights was exclusive and that there was no place for dealings in land not provided for by the legislation or not carried out in the prescribed manner. It then went on to say that there was a total prohibition on the creation of any real right outside the statutory systems. The Privy Council appeared to think that these two statements meant the same thing.

This decision had a considerable effect on the second question, the place of equity in Malaysian land law. Because the natives continued to behave

---

25. Wong, *supra* note 7, pp 12–13.
26. This list of exceptions has been extended by regulation to include several development financing institutions.
27. [1917] AC 209.

as they always had done, entering into transactions not registrable under the law, problems continually arose as to whether equity would recognize any rights in the land created by these contracts. In England, such contracts would have given rise to equitable interests in the land.[28] In Australia, the answer would have been the same because of the interaction of the Torrens legislation and the received English land law.[29] But in Malaysia, with only the local legislation at hand and with no English land law or equity received except through statute, the answer of the Privy Council was in the negative. The decision of the Privy Council has been steadily eroded in relation to its statement as to the place of equity. The questioning of the authority has finally led to a reconsideration of the other question, the policy question on the place of customary securities in Malaysia today.

Since the decision of the Privy Council two major pieces of legislation have been passed. The Federated Malay States Land Code was enacted in 1926, and the National Land Code in 1965. Neither statute embodied a change in the policy of recognition of customary rights. Neither dealt with the consequence of failure to recognize native institutions. The 1926 legislation abolished the separate register of land occupied by natives and the administration of that land. Each statute changed the words of the law slightly without, it is clear, intending any change in substance. The result was an increasing number of diverging decisions concerning *jual* securities, with recognition being given or denied depending on particular facts and the particular judge's policy views. This has been and is a most unsatisfactory and unprincipled way of developing the law. Policy issues of this magnitude are better handled by the legislature than by the judges.

THE MODERN LAND CODES

The Federated Malay States

Beginning in the 1890s, in each of the Federated Malay States an ordinance was passed introducing the Torrens system of conveyancing. Section 4 of the Selangor Registration of Titles Regulation of 1891 was typical.

> After the coming into operation of this regulation, all land which is comprised in any grant, whether issued prior or subsequent to the coming into operation of this regulation shall be subject to this regulation, and shall not be capable of being transferred, transmitted, mortgaged, charged or otherwise dealt with, except in accordance with the provisions of this regulation, and every attempt to ... deal with the same, except as aforesaid, shall be null and void and of no effect, and, in

28. *Walsh v Lonsdale* (1882) 21 Ch D 9.
29. *Barry v Heider* (1914) 19 CLR 197.

particular, the provisions of Part VII relating to enforcement of charges shall extend and apply to mortgages of land which have been made before the coming into operation of this regulation, so that the powers in such mortgages mentioned shall only be exercisable in accordance with the provisions of Part VII or as near thereto as circumstances permit.

In *Haji Abdul Rahman v Mahomed Hasan*,[30] Lord Dunedin struck down a *jual janji* transaction saying that it was a non-registrable transaction and therefore conferred no real rights in the land, but that this finding did not invalidate any personal right that might have been created by contract. Here the seeds of the problem lay because the Privy Council could have given effect simply to legislative policy by refusing to recognize customary transactions in any way. Their validity as contractual transactions having been conceded, the question then becomes what relief would be available either in law or equity. It was clear that the rule in *Walsh v Lonsdale*[31] would not apply to create an equitable interest. But it was also clear from other legislation that the equitable remedy of specific performance was available in Malaysia.[32] If the availability of this remedy could not create an equitable interest in land, what then was its effect?

The next development was the enactment of the Federated Malay States Land Code in 1926 which replaced the provisions in the individual Malay States. Section 55 provided that an equivalent section to the former section 4 of those provisions would apply to land on the Makim register, that is, native land. Section 96 provided, in slightly different words and in a shorter form, the effect of the previous section 4 of the earlier provisions.

So the legislation repeated the policy, although in the slightly different words, that land could be dealt with only in accordance with the provisions of the Code. Only the registration of an instrument is effective to pass or create any interest in land. Other transactions were not declared to be null and void and of no effect, but 'shall not be capable ...'. The law itself therefore is the source of rights or interests in land; and a personal or contractual claim cannot be used as the basis of a claim. But there may be an 'equity' arising out of the contract, and the court may grant such equitable relief as it sees fit, including specific performance.[33] The refusal of the courts to import the equitable doctrine of *Walsh v Lonsdale* in the face of the new legislation made the consideration of the place of equity in the land law, whilst continuing a policy of non-recognition of customary transactions, rather difficult. Perpetuating these distinctions led Malaysian

30. [1917] AC 209.
31. (1882) 21 Ch D 9.
32. Now Specific Relief Ordinance 1950.
33. Ibid, ch 2.

judges into a jurisprudential wilderness, in which they themselves have been lost.

In *Bachan Singh v Mahinder Kaur*,[34] they characterized the rights as rights ad rem which are personal legal rights, and not equitable rights, created when a valid contract relating to land has been made. On the registration of such a contract, real rights, or rights in rem are created. Furthermore the rights can run with the land. In *Chin Cheng Hong v Hameed*,[35] A, B, C, and D bought land which was registered in the name of A. A then sold the land to the appellant, and B and C lodged a caveat. Who had the better claim? Could a contractual claim by B and C take priority over a registrable interest in A and the appellant? The court purported to follow the Privy Council, but it gave priority to the unregistrable interest of B and C, thus converting it into an equitable interest. This is scarcely consistent with the Privy Council's statement that only registration could confer a real right in the land.

In 1965, after independence and pursuant to Article 76(4) of the Constitution, the National Land Code was passed for the purpose of 'insuring uniformity of law and policy'. All land not alienated is state land. The status of Malay reservation land is preserved. The definition of land is taken from English law but the concept of fixtures is varied to include things regarded by customary law as being separate.

The Code provides for two securities: a charge, which takes effect as security only when registered[36] and a statutory lien created by the deposit of issued documents of title and the entry of a lienholder's caveat.[37] The problem continues as to how far the law will recognize interests, particularly customary securities, arising other than in strict compliance with the National Land Code.

The courts have frequently dealt with these problems since the enactment of the National Land Code, usually in the context of priorities, and by resorting to equitable principles. It is interesting to consider how far the necessity to consider equitable interests outside the register has influenced their attitude to customary transactions which are unregistrable in themselves, but which may exploit registration provisions designed to enable other transactions.

In sections 205 and 206, the National Land Code specified the 'dealings capable of being effected under this Act with respect to alienated lands' and 'no others'. In section 206 two stages of any transaction are established: the making of an instrument whose components are specified by statute, and the registration of that interest. But it also provides that nothing in

34. 22 *Malayan LJ* 97 (1956).
35. 20 *Malayan LJ* 169 (1954).
36. Section 241.
37. Section 281.

the section will affect the contractual validity of transactions relating to interests in land. Section 5 defines a dealing as a transaction with respect to alienated land effected under powers conferred by Division IV and any previous land law but does not include any caveat or prohibitory order. In 1971, the problem of the relationship of the register and equity arose squarely for the Malaysian courts to decide. Since the National Land Code is in identical terms to Australian law, following accepted common law reasoning, they took the Australian cases as an analogy.[38] In *Karuppiah Chettiar v Subramaniam*,[39] X owned two-sixths undivided share of a deposited issue document of title. The balance was held by Y who had lodged no caveat. X sold to Z who lodged a caveat. X subsequently transferred the land to Y. The court rejected the earlier reasoning and gave the land to Y, the registered owner. The unregistered sale to Z conferred no rights in the land.

The courts subsequently considered the equitable consequences of refusing recognition to customary institutions. In *Halijah v Morad*,[40] A lent 250$ to R. R gave A possession of the land in dispute. A agreed to return it if E repaid the 250$ plus the expenses of developing the land for three years. If he failed to repay, then R agreed to execute a transfer to A. R sued A for trespass and A counter-claimed for specific performance of the agreement. The Federal Court refused specific performance stating that there was nothing more than a contract for repayment of money lent. The defendant had possession of land as a creditor and not as a purchaser. Here the courts went behind the transaction.

There had been many attempts to get away from the Privy Council decision in *Hadji Abdul Rahman v Mohamed Hasan*. The coincidence that the National Land Code and the New South Wales Torrens legislation were identical helped to bring in subsequent decisions of the Privy Council and of Australian courts. But the issue of native land rights is quite separate from the reliability of the analogy between Australian and Malaysian land law. The link is only that the Court had upheld the validity of contractual rights.

Furthermore, *Halijah v Morad* is an atypical transaction. Usually in a *jual janji* transaction, a transfer of the land is registered. It is then a question of what rights the borrower/transferor has and whether he can lodge a caveat under the National Land Code. What is needed now is a system which protects the borrower during the agreement, preserves his rights to a retransfer, and recognizes a continuing interest in the land, and institution similar to an equity of redemption. Such a right of retransfer

38. *Barry v Heider* (1914) CLR 197; *Abigail v Lapin* [1934] AC 491; *Butler v Fairclough* (1917) CLR 78.
39. *Malayan LJ* 1971-I 116.
40. *Malayan LJ* 1972-II 116.

can be either a conditional right on discharge of the debt or an option to purchase. Neither is recognized by the National Land Code.

Under the National Land Code a caveat can be lodged only by a person claiming title to or an interest in alienated land. Under the present law, a borrower/transferor has no right before discharge. The lender is protected because he has a registrable interest in land, even without registration or a document of title. Since the National Land Code recognized only a charge and not a mortgage, it is difficult to introduce the concept of an equity of redemption. But a caveat might be a simpler solution.

The security transfer has caused great problems. Many Malays still lend on the security of the *jual janji*. This is a reflection of the breakdown of traditional mores. The usual rate of interest on such transactions is an attractive 40% or more. The device of Malay Reservation land will not be effective in this situation. But a *jual janji* is recognized as a sale under the law. Its security aspects are not recognized and therefore the borrower is without any legal rights.

Furthermore, under Muslim law, land is divided amongst the family in varying shares on death. The register may rarely be changed. If one child wants a loan and gives a *jual janji*, he must transfer all land on the title, including that of the rest of the family. The price is still reckoned on the loan amount, so the lender gets a bargain.

A survey was carried out in Malacca in connection with the census of 1960 and 1967. Between those dates, one-third of landowners lost their land through the *jual janji*. This demonstrates the seriousness of the social and economic problem. It is undermining the excellently conceived plans for the development of the rural Malay sector, and adding a new element to interracial conflicts, that of the split between the rural and the urban Malay.

INDONESIA

After Indonesia proclaimed its independence on 17 August 1945,[41] the major thrust of policy was towards national development rather than the procuring and protection of private profit. In a newly independent state, there was objection to large-scale foreign ownership and to systems of law that were seen as designed to protect foreign interests. There was therefore opposition to dualism as being inconsistent with nationalism and sovereign autonomy in the newly emerged nation. A need was perceived for a National Agrarian Law with one scheme of rights for all Indonesian land and capable of being enjoyed by all Indonesian citizens.

This objective is understandable, but it is pertinent to ask what kind of community the Indonesian leaders had in mind. Was it to be urban or

---

41. Official recognition by the Netherlands and the formal transfer of sovereignty were delayed until 27 December 1949.

adat? Or both? Could one law be designed that would serve the needs of both types of community? Was there to be any place in the system for the foreign entrepreneur?

The professed answer to all those questions was that land could be held only by Indonesian citizens; that there was to be one system of rights and one law; and that law was to be *adat*. After 12 years of gestation, the Basic Agrarian Law was passed in 1960.

The Law achieved a number of things. It repealed the Agrarian Act and the *Domein* Declaration. Henceforth the state was to act not as owner of Indonesian land but as a representative of the Indonesian people. Agrarian *eigendom* was abolished. Book II of the Civil Code was repealed except for the articles dealing with *hypotheek*. There was also an implied repeal of any legislation that was contrary to the spirit and intent of the Basic Agrarian Law. For example, the prohibition on the sale of *adat* land to non-natives was impliedly repealed. All racial groups can, in theory, acquire any of the new rights in any land, provided that they are Indonesian nationals and provided also that they are natural rather than juridical persons. All existing rights in land were abolished and converted to a new scheme established under the Basic Agrarian Law.

A uniform system was by this means established, which should have marked the end of dualism. However the reality was somewhat different. The Basic Agrarian Law has been described as 'hortatory and symbolic'. It is alleged that it pays only lip service to *adat*.[42] It declares the *adat* principle of community rights over land to be the fundamental principle; but it modifies it in favour of individual ownership by declaring that the exercise of the community's rights must not be contrary to the national interest or to the policy of the National Agrarian Law – which is concerned to define private rights. It declares rights in *adat* terms, but this does not disguise the fact that, whatever they are called, they are closer to western land rights and they have few counterparts as individual rights in *adat*. There are restrictions on non-Indonesian nationals and on corporations (whether domestic or foreign) owning land, but these have proved inconvenient, and evasive devices have developed. Reconsideration is being given to this policy.

Furthermore, the implementation of the Basic Agrarian Law proved impracticable.[43] The law was predicated on an infrastructure that does not exist. It presupposed cadastral surveys and a system of registration, which through most of Indonesia are neither available nor feasible. For this reason it has not been possible to implement the law fully. It applies to

---

42. Hornick, supra note 7, 31–34.
43. The conversion of western rights was scheduled to take place in September 1980. But, other than changing their names, it is not clear precisely how they were affected.

little more than the former western land and there are no immediate plans for its extension through cadastral surveys because of the cost.

Most former native land, therefore, is not under the Basic Agrarian Law at all, but remains under the old system, and dualism has not been effectively abolished. What effect has this had on the use of land as security for credit?

The Basic Agrarian Law proposed one new security – '*hak tanggunan*' – which is comparable with the civil law *hypotheek*. It is, however, dependent on registration, and therefore is not presently available and its introduction has been deferred. The Basic Agrarian Law therefore preserves the *hypotheek* for western land and also *credietverband* which is now made available over western land. *Hak gadai* is also retained, by the combined effects of Articles 16 and 35 for a limited time until it is abolished. It is seen by some as containing elements of extortion and by others as inconsistent with the principle enunciated in Article 10 that the owner should cultivate the land. However, it is clearly retained because it is a valuable and, so far, the only effective means of securing credit by using the land of the village smallholder.

However, *hak gadai* is preserved only for lenders who are Indonesian nationals, and therefore *credietverband* is retained for non-nationals. Nevertheless, this contrasts with the position in Malaysia, described above, where *adat* securities now struggle for any recognition.

Not only is *hak gadai* retained, but it is strengthened by a Regulation of 1960 which provides that in respect of agricultural land, the pledgee's right expires automatically after seven years, without any obligation on the pledger to repay the money advanced to him. It is thought that the lender should have recouped the amount of loan and interest out of the profits of the land during those seven years. A further Regulation in 1961 proposed to require registered deeds for the creation of *hak gadai* but this has not been implemented.

Accordingly, *hak gadai*, *credietverband*, and *hypotheek* continue today very much as they did before independence. Western land may serve as security through *hypotheek* or, today, through *credietverband*. The traditional and subsistence agriculture of former native land may still use *hak gadai* or *credietverband* to secure credit.

And the system works: urban and productive land, needing long-term credit with security adequate for foreign investors, is created uniformly under one code acceptable to all parties, whether the security is *hypotheek* or *hak tanggunan*. Meanwhile, rural traditional land, requiring seasonal credit only, continues in the old traditional ways, strengthened by some legislation, and supported by the legal system.

CONCLUSIONS

It is dangerous to generalize or to try to draw conclusions from such a narrow enquiry in just two countries. All this paper may have achieved is to provide some data and comparisons that will contribute to an understanding of the broader issues concerning the place of native legal institutions in modern states.

In Indonesia, from the point of view of the colonial powers, the existence of native tenures gave rise to only minor problems, and their deficiencies as securities were fairly easily remedied, for example, by the legislation introducing *credietverband* in Indonesia. Both colonial powers adopted land theories which gave ultimate rights to the colonial powers, and the moral question of the effect of colonial law on native subjects was not regarded as a matter of pressing concern.

Both powers tried to protect the natives by policies of non-interference so far as was convenient; but, whilst the Dutch were prepared to leave the natives with their own institutions outside the towns and plantations, the British were concerned to offer more positive benefits of the protection of English law, and sought to define native rights in English terms. This was not successful,

Both the moral and the legal questions became more pressing to the newly independent states. Their governments were well aware of the problems caused by absentee landlords and by racial tensions. But each country sought a 'modern' sophisticated land law as a mark of independence, almost as a political philosophy. Each pays lip service to *adat*.

In Indonesia, the supremacy of *adat* law is enunciated as an achievement of policy, but is subservient to a statutory scheme of rights which is based on Dutch law. Institutions formerly known by Dutch names now have newly coined Indonesian names. On paper, the Indonesian government achieved what the Dutch never attempted, namely a uniform Dutch system of land law for the whole country. It has so far failed to be implemented, probably for the very reason the Dutch never attempted it: the geography of the country.

In Malaysia, the National Land Code was the first statute to be published in the Malay language, but it continued the policy of the colonial power. Within the formal system, native legal institutions have no place; but they continue, as in Indonesia, in the daily lives of the people.

Given the developmental aims and policies of each country, both the National Land Code and the efficacy of law as a tool of social and economic policy, the experience of colonial and post-colonial land law particularly casts doubt on the merits of codification as a legal tool. It is admittedly administratively attractive. It was widely used by the British in the colonial situation, but after some flirtations was rejected by the Dutch as impracticable for non-Europeans. It is doubtful whether the Dutch principle of concordance of law in the Netherlands and in the colonies was any wiser in view of the disparity of the situation in Indonesia and the Netherlands.

The real problem encountered in Malaysia was twofold: the exploitation of the law by shrewd lenders to obtain an advantage that the framers of the law never intended; and the leaving of the problem of the consequences of non-recognition of native institutions to be settled piecemeal by the judges. Judges should not in any system be called upon to take decisions that are primarily political. The problems in Malaysia were heightened by the fact that the geography of the country, unlike Indonesia, made a cadastral survey possible so that a misguided policy was made effective. Urbanization of large sections of the Malay population then undermined the only protective device that was available to them – Malay Reservation land.

Paradoxically, the situation in Indonesia was better because of the inability to implement the Basic Agrarian Law. Whether this *locus poenitentiae* to rethink the place of native tenures and institutions will be taken is doubtful.

Recognition of native land law is an example of a critical problem affecting much larger areas of the legal system in both countries: the problem of balancing the lessons from other systems with the inescapable legacies of the old system. Each country should rethink the needs of its land users, and consider what kinds of law implemented in what way will satisfy those needs. Both countries need to recognize that laws are simply words written on paper, and legislation alone does not change centuries of custom and practice. No law, especially land law, should develop in a haphazard, unprincipled and unscientific way.

APPENDIX

Asian Contract Law: A Survey of Current Problems, with DE Allan and Derek Roebuck (co-editors and co-authors). Melbourne University Press (1969).

The *Law and Development Finance in Asia* series, with DE Allan and Derek Roebuck (co-editors and co-authors) and a national co-author for each volume was published by the University of Queensland Press and Crane, Russak & Co., Inc. The series comprises the following volumes:

Credit and Security in Indonesia (with Sudargo Gautama) (1973).

Credit and Security in Singapore (with Koh Kheng Lian) (1973).

Credit and Security in Japan (with Hisashi Tanikawa) (1973).

Credit and Security in Korea (with Kwack Yoon Chick (1973).

Credit and Security in Ceylon (Sri Lanka) (with Wickrema Weerasooria) (1973).

Credit and Security in the Republic of China (with Loh Jen Kong) (1973).

Credit and Security in the Philippines (with Sixto de Guzman) (1973).

Credit and Security in Thailand (with Thavorn Tantraporn) (1974).

Credit and Security – The Legal Problems of Development Financing (1974).

Credit and Security in Australia (with Leigh Masel) (1977).

Credit and Security in West Malaysia (with Jaginder Singh) (1980).

REMBRANDT AND ARBITRATION

Neil Kaplan CBE, QC, SBS[*]

Derek Roebuck was a special man. You knew this as soon as you met him. In my case, it was shortly after he arrived in Hong Kong in the mid-1980s. I remember him walking into what were then the newish premises of the recently founded Hong Kong International Arbitration Centre. He was introduced to me by Mr Justice David Hunter and it was not long before we became friends and colleagues. I was sad when Derek and Susanna left Hong Kong but was pleased that we kept in touch, as Oxford was halfway from London to our Cotswold cottage, which allowed us regular visits. Depending on the time of day, champagne or coffee was always in plentiful supply. We kept in touch right to the end.

In 1990 I was co-writing with Jill Spruce and Teresa Cheng the first book on Hong Kong arbitration. In very early 1990, I attended an arbitration conference in Darwin (Australia). The lunchtime speaker was Sir Ninian Stephen, a former Governor General of Australia and a member of Australia's High Court. I did not know at the time that we went to the same school in London – St Pauls. He gave a fascinating talk on the history of arbitration going back to Egyptian, Greek and Roman times. I was fascinated, as I had no idea about arbitration's venerable history. I asked Sir Ninian for a copy of his notes, which he kindly gave me.

On my return to Hong Kong I showed them to Derek and asked him if he would convert them into a chapter on the history of arbitration for our book. Derek of course agreed and even accepted a rather accelerated timescale. However, he delivered a superb chapter, which was the beginning of his fascination for the subject and the rest is truly history.[1]

History and art have always been my main non-legal interests. I was always interested in history and did reasonably well in exams. My interest in art was sparked by my uncle Eddie Kaplan in the late 1950s. He had an

* Neil Kaplan is a practising international arbitrator, a Past President of the Chartered Institute of Arbitrators and a former judge of the High Court (now Court of First Instance) of Hong Kong.

1. See Robert Morgan's article in the present volume (pp 329-373), 'Derek Roebuck, Historian: A Literature Review', for further background. Derek's work appeared a little later, as an introductory chapter in my next co-authored book, Neil Kaplan, Jill Spruce and Michael J Moser, *Hong Kong and China Arbitration: Cases and Materials* (Hong Kong: Butterworths Asia/LexisNexis Hong Kong, 1994).

art gallery in Church Street, Kensington in London and I remember at the time he employed someone called Tom Keating. Unfortunately, Keating turned out to be one of the greatest art forgers of the century! He was, however, acquitted at his trial at the Old Bailey.

My uncle soon moved upmarket and opened the Kaplan Gallery in Duke Street, St James', just off Piccadilly in London, where he specialised in French Impressionist paintings. During holidays from school and university, I worked at the gallery and learned a lot from him, especially when he took me to the National Gallery and introduced me to its many wonderful Rembrandt paintings.

While working at the gallery, I sold several fine paintings that were on sale for around £5,000. I chide myself for not buying one, but then I remind myself that £5,000 was an awful lot of money in the late 1950s or early 1960s and you could in fact buy a house for that sum of money. The first house I bought was just over £8,000, but that was in 1969. Today that £5,000 painting would be worth well over £1 million, which is also what the house would now be worth.

I came across Rembrandt again in about 1971, when I was visiting some people who had a study full of his etchings on the wall. My then wife said to me, perhaps light-heartedly, that she hoped that one day we might be able to afford one ourselves. About 15 years later, when I was practising at the Bar in Hong Kong, I was briefed in a big arbitration matter by a well-known local builder called John Lok. He had built Harbour City for Sir YK Pau's company and disputes had unfortunately arisen.

One evening he invited the whole team to a Charity Ball at the Regent Hotel on Kowloon side in aid of the Hong Kong Ballet Group. As a good host, he bought a number of raffle tickets and handed one to each of his guests around the table. There was one left over and he gave that to my wife Barbara. A little later in the evening the Governor's wife, Lady Pamela Youde, drew out the winning tickets and, much to our surprise and delight, that final ticket given to Barbara won the star prize – a car!

We did not need another car, so we sold the winning car and, as I often put it, with the proceeds of the front offside wing, we went to London to fulfil that ambition of owning a Rembrandt etching. We had no idea where to look, but a friend of mine directed me to a well-known print shop called Craddock & Barnard, which was then, but is no more, opposite the British Museum. I walked in and asked whether they had any Rembrandt etchings and was shown a number to look at. We chose the famous etching of Jan Lutma, the goldsmith and silversmith. The price was not inconsequential, but not excessive.

I started reading about Rembrandt etchings and soon discovered that the etching which we had bought was in fact a posthumous version. I had no idea that, after Rembrandt's death in 1669, a number of his copper plates were still in existence and that for a long time thereafter prints were pulled from these plates. As each print is taken from a copper plate, the image becomes less clear and later engravers, well after Rembrandt's death, re-etched the plate and sometimes added in a few lines of their own. This discovery sparked my lifelong interest in Rembrandt etchings and I learned there was a distinction between those which were printed in his lifetime, as opposed to those after his death. Rembrandt was one of the first etchers to print his trial proofs. It is therefore possible to find early proofs which are particularly collectable. When you then throw in the question of rarity, condition and provenance, you find yourself embroiled in a detective story to ensure that the print you are buying is the genuine article.

I cannot be sure whether my love for and interest in Rembrandt were engendered solely by the quality of his art or whether it was also because he lived between 1606 and 1669, as this period covered my special period in history, namely the first part of the 17th century leading up to the end of the Civil War.

Rembrandt was born the year after the Gunpowder Plot and at a time when Shakespeare was still writing. He lived in Amsterdam, which was a city where religious freedom prevailed. Jews went about their business in Amsterdam and practised their religion without hindrance.

By contrast, Edward I had expelled the Jews from England in 1290 and they were not allowed back until 1656, during the Protectorate of Oliver Cromwell. A Whitehall Conference of 1655 paved the way for their re-admission. A leading proponent of their return was the Dutch Rabbi Menasseh ben Israel. Rembrandt's etching of him is most desirable, but not one that I have yet been able to buy at an acceptable price.

Rembrandt was surrounded by Jews in Amsterdam. He lived near the Synagogue and there is a wonderful etching of Jews at worship there. Yet it was only 10 years before he died, and thanks in part to the efforts of Menasseh ben Israel, that Jews were allowed to return to England.

While England was torn by civil war, Holland went about its business both in Europe and in Asia. Nine years before Rembrandt died, Charles II returned to the throne and a new era began in England. Holland and England had been at war before the Restoration, in the First Dutch War which ended in 1653. In 1665, however, just four years before Rembrandt's death, Charles II declared war against the Dutch yet again, but was forced to sue for peace in 1667. When I study Rembrandt's etchings and paintings, I am struck by the fact that what I am looking at has been created by a contemporary of James I and Shakespeare. Rembrandt's ability to capture feelings and expressions, particularly his own, seems remarkably modern. I recall many years ago visiting the old Getty Museum in Los Angeles and being amazed at Rembrandt's painting of St Bartholomew. It seemed such a 19th-century face and without his wig he looked to me rather like

Clement Attlee, the British Prime Minister from 1945. It all seemed very different from the rather stylised portraits of the Elizabethan and Stuart periods and yet, while Rembrandt was capturing emotion in painting and etching, Shakespeare was capturing it in language.

I have never been able to tie in Rembrandt with arbitration, but when I embarked on writing this article I came across the fact that he had been involved in a substantial amount of dispute resolution. Rembrandt seems to have been somewhat litigious and so I started to dig a little further with the help of Professor Gary Schwartz, a leading Rembrandt scholar. What I discovered somewhat saddened me because it appears that Rembrandt was not good at honouring his contracts and may have been an early example of a guerilla party.

Rembrandt was involved in a number of actions on behalf of or in conflict with his in-laws relating to properties in Friesland. He also had many disputes with colleagues, collectors and patrons. Many of his disputes concerned his personal finances and of course, as we all know, he was made bankrupt. He also had a dispute with a Sephardi about a party wall. Then there was the Geertje Dircx affair, in which Rembrandt was sued for damages for breach of promise to marry.

In 1649 Geertje Dircx sued Rembrandt, declaring that he had made an oral promise of marriage and given her a ring, and furthermore that he had slept with her on several occasions and she had demanded that he marry her or else support her. Rembrandt responded in the following terms:

> Defendant denies having made promises of marriage to the Plaintiff, and furthermore that he is not obliged to admit having slept with her. The Plaintiff is the one who claims this will have to prove it.

After the parties had presented their cases, the Commissioners rendered their verdict 'As good men [to the effect] that the Defendant shall pay to the Plaintiff instead of 160 Guilders the sum of 200 Carolos Guilders annually during her lifetime …'[2]

It is thought that the term 'good men' is a reference to arbitrators,[3] which may have been the formal role of the Chamber of Marital Affairs to whom this dispute had been presented.

Unfortunately, Rembrandt refused to honour this award and in fact went to very great extremes to avoid having to pay the annual support. It appears that he colluded with the lady's brother to prepare insinuating testimony

---

2. I am grateful to Professor Schwartz, for his help with materials about Rembrandt.

3. *Editorial note*: This nomenclature probably derived from arbitration *bonus vir* under Roman law: see Derek Roebuck and Bruno de Loynes de Fumichon, *Roman Arbitration* (2004, Oxford: HOLO Books: The Arbitration Press) and Morgan, *supra*, note 1.

from the neighbourhood about her way of life and eventually had her put away in a penal institution

There was a document of September 1667 which concerned an arbitrated claim of 180 Guilders against Rembrandt by a collector called Harmen Becker. It appears that the dispute had been referred to arbitration by Willem Blaeu, who was a magistrate, and Jacob Lamine and Paulus Buijs, Councillors at Law. Interestingly, they made an order for disclosure of documents against Rembrandt with which he failed to comply. However, about nine months later he appears to have submitted the papers and the finding went against him. He was ordered to 'pay two thirds in cash without any time limit or other specifications and one third in art works or paintings to be executed by the deponent on commission of Harmen Becker and to complete these within a period of six months'. The precise outcome of this is unknown because Rembrandt died in October 1669, but when Becker himself died in 1678, he did own several paintings by Rembrandt.

It does seem that Rembrandt's negotiating style was somewhat unfortunate. He ignored summonses when he thought he could get away with it; he refused to pay fines and debts; he denied that he slept with Geertje Dircx, which was an obvious lie for which the Commissioner increased his annual payment; he claimed to have lost the papers in an agreement with a man who had been his best patron; he delayed proceedings against him whenever it was possible. He often made offers to settle by providing paintings in lieu of funds and very frequently failed to deliver them.

An interesting example can be found in a letter which Rembrandt penned to his Sicilian patron, Don Antonio Roffo, who had complained that an expensive painting delivered by Rembrandt 'was painted on four pieces of canvass sewn together. These four seem so horribly beyond words. Besides, in time, they will crack and consequently the canvas as a whole will be ruined.'

Although he had subsequent commissions for Roffo in the works and stood to gain more, Rembrandt's reply to an agent was somewhat insulting. What was said on his behalf was as follows:

> I am very amazed by what they write about the 'Alexander' which is so well done. I have the feeling that there are not many amateurs in Messina ... as for the canvas I did not have enough of it whilst I was painting and I therefore needed to lengthen it. However if the painting is hung well in daylight one will not notice anything.

The latter comment is reminiscent of the Gilbert and Sullivan line referring to the rich attorney's daughter: 'She may very well pass for forty-three in the dusk, with a light behind her.'

I suppose we ask too much of those whose talents we admire to expect them to behave as if they were angels! They are mere mortals who have been given a gift. They are not all desirable dinner companions!

Derek, however, was a most desirable companion and it was always a joy to share his scholarship, judgment and friendship at any time of the day. His works may not be seen in any national galleries, but his learning and scholarship are there for all to read. I am sure future generations will benefit from his scholarship, especially on the history of arbitration.

POSTSCRIPT

I like to think that I shared a social conscience with Derek. We may have disagreed about how to address inequalities in society, but we did agree that they needed redressing.

I have always thought how nice it would be to trace one's family back to an ancestor who had made a great difference for good in society - a Wilberforce, a Pankhurst, a Fleming or a Salk. Those of us with immigrant forebears, however, understand that, at least to begin with, their efforts were dedicated to survival.

For so long as I can recall, there was one social conscience story in my family that fascinated me. My maternal great-grandfather, Simon Cohen, was born in 1849 in Plotzk – then in Russia, now in Poland. He became a naturalised citizen in the UK in 1891. He lived in the East End of London and was a baker. At this time, there had been an influx of refugees, mainly Jewish, from Eastern and Central Europe.

Simon was appalled at the conditions in which these refugees lived. This was long before the social security system that we have known for the last 73 years came into being. I had always been told (though all efforts to validate the story have led nowhere) that he was so disgusted at the trivial issues being debated in the House of Commons that one day he threw some flour over the balcony of the Public Gallery on to the MPs below.

However, recent research has disclosed a different story. Apparently, Simon was indeed appalled at the conditions in which the refugees were forced to live. He took some of them in and gave them basic refuge on the floor of his bakery. Their living conditions were so basic that the more affluent members of the Jewish community, such as Samuel Montagu and other members of Anglo-Jewry, decided that these arrangements could not be allowed to continue, and so they set up the Poor Jews Temporary Shelter. At least Simon pricked the right consciences!

In 1913, Simon was arrested for obstructing a police officer in the execution of his duty. What he had done was to break through a police cordon in an attempt to serve a letter on King George V, who was riding in his carriage from Parliament to Buckingham Palace. He managed to hand it to one of the horsemen, who promptly dropped it on the ground. When arrested, Simon said that he was not doing this for himself 'but for the people'. In mitigation, he said that he had previously written to the King asking for the appointment of deputies who would see him and discuss the plight of the poor and destitute. He received a reply telling him to contact the relevant minister. Accordingly, he wrote to David Lloyd George (at the time Chancellor of the Exchequer), but received no reply. He sought an interview with the Prime Minister, Herbert Henry Asquith, but this was declined. Simon was bound over for 6 months on his own recognisances in the sum of £50.

Simon appears to have been a frequent letter writer to ministers over his concerns for the plight of poor Jews in England and around the world. He tried to persuade ministers to convene a world conference on this issue. He suggested that if the government had fed and clothed the poor the army would have been boosted with healthier and fitter men.

Simon also campaigned for women's rights, so it was no wonder that with this and his other campaigns, he was regarded as something of a folk hero. I am proud that my great-grandfather tried to do something to help others less fortunate than himself.

Derek would have approved!

DEREK ROEBUCK, HISTORIAN: A LITERATURE REVIEW

Robert Morgan[*]

Lector, si monumentum requiris, circumspice.[1]

PART ONE: INTRODUCTION

As an historian, Professor Derek Roebuck holds a special place in the pantheon of international dispute resolution in general and arbitration in particular, as well as earning the admiration of leading practitioners in the field. He addressed, for the first time and in detail, one of two areas in which there had previously been a dearth of writings (the philosophy of arbitration being the other). He came comparatively late in his career both to arbitration (primarily through the introduction of and his unstinting support for the MA course in Arbitration offered by the then City Polytechnic (later City University) of Hong Kong – the first such course in the territory[2]) and to the role of its chronicler.

As his close friend Neil Kaplan QC succinctly tells it in his obituary,[3] the writing of Derek's prolific and learned accounts of the international history of arbitration originated from an epiphany in 1990, when Neil asked him to contribute a chapter on the history of arbitration to a co-authored volume of cases and materials on arbitration in Hong Kong and China that was published in 1994.[4] Neil's interest had been piqued after

---

* JP, Barrister (England & Wales, Queensland). A Past Chairman of the Chartered Institute of Arbitrators (CIArb) (East Asia Branch), a Past Vice-President of CIArb Australia and a former Legal Adviser to the CIArb in London. Consulting and Technical Editor, Asian Dispute Review, Hong Kong.
1. Epitaph to Sir Christopher Wren (1632–1723), St Paul's Cathedral, London.
2. The course was first offered in 1991. Its scope and content were expanded when it became the MA in Arbitration & Dispute Resolution in 1993, when Derek appointed the author as its second Course Leader.
3. (2020) 86(3) *Arbitration: The International Journal of Arbitration, Mediation and Dispute Management* 231–233; [2020] *Asian Dispute Review* 134-136. The Obituary is reproduced in this volume at pp 31-34.
4. Neil Kaplan, Jill Spruce & Michael J Moser, *Hong Kong and China Arbitration Cases and Materials* (1994, Hong Kong: Butterworths Asia/LexisNexis Hong Kong) (hereinafter 'Kaplan *et al*'). The chapter, entitled 'A Short History of Arbitration', which is reviewed below at pp 332-338, appears at pp xxxiii-lxv of Kaplan *et al* and is replicated in this volume at pp 63-96.

hearing a luncheon address on the history of arbitration delivered at a conference in Darwin, Australia by the late Sir Ninian Stephen (1923–2017), a former Governor-General of Australia and a judge of the High Court, that country's court of final appeal. Once shared, Derek's trademark infectious and relentless enthusiasm for the subject would both dominate the rest of his life and create a monument to his crowning achievement. To quote his wife Susanna, 'Derek was hooked'.[5] To put it in his own words, Derek 'relied on Neil Kaplan's [encouragement] since, fourteen years ago, he first put the words "arbitration" and "history" together for me and challenged me to do something about it.'[6]

It was therefore inevitable that Derek's prodigious talents and energies would not be wasted after he and Susanna left Hong Kong for Oxford in 1997. Having written his inaugural chapter, he embarked upon researching and gathering together an impressive bibliography of sources on the history of arbitration. Published in 1998, it was a sign of things to come.[7]

Indeed – to adopt a geographical term denoting a large chain of islands – Derek devoted the rest of his life to casting his net of historical inquiry far and wide, engaging an 'archipelagic imagination'.[8] The result was a labour of love, certainly: but what Herculean labour, while greater love had no other man for his subject.

This article seeks to encapsulate, modestly and within the confines of a necessarily brief *tour d'horizon*, Derek's detailed writings on the history of arbitration and mediation. It is hoped that it will do all due justice to both the breadth and depth of his *oeuvres*, to his gentle humour in the recording of events, incidents and *dramatis personae*, and to his achievements, not only as a researcher and analyst, but also as a chronicler and storyteller of the ages.

5. Susanna Hoe, 'Derek Roebuck Obituary', *The Guardian*, 26 May 2020.

6. *Early English Arbitration* (2008, Oxford: HOLO Books: The Arbitration Press), Preface, p xiii. In his Foreword to Derek's *A Miscellany of Disputes* (2000, Oxford: HOLO Books: The Arbitration Press), p 7 – see 'Epilogue', below – Neil wrote that 'little did I know what interest the subject would provoke in his ever-enquiring mind. ... [I]n due course I am sure he will give us the *locus classicus*.' As, indeed, Derek did. In his Preface to the same volume at p 13, Derek wrote of Neil's 'priceless gift' of marrying the two words.

7. 'Sources for the History of Arbitration: A Bibliographical Introduction' (1998) 24 *Arbitration International* 235-344, with a Foreword by the late Lord Mustill. So far as the present author is aware, this exercise has not been replicated elsewhere.

8. Édouard Glissant (1928-2011), French Caribbean poet and philosopher, in *Traité du Tout monde* (1998). Closer to home and to physical subject matter, Sir Stephen Sedley states in his article (pp 425-429) that '[u]ntil Derek Roebuck set about it, nobody had attempted a panoptic history of arbitration' (p 427). Further, at p 428, he speaks of Derek's method as 'an engaging series of polymathic raids into the territory of geographers, ethnographers, linguists, lawyers, historians and archaeologists'.

PART TWO: IN THE BEGINNING ...

Introduction

As any historian would readily attest, writing an authoritative historical account is no mean task. Historical method of inquiry requires painstaking research and the dispassionate analysis of primary sources, wherever they may be found, in whatever form and in whatever language. It also requires the researcher not to reach facile conclusions based upon broad and sweeping assumptions and (a concept well known to arbitrators) confirmation bias, but to assess and critique, with a sense of detachment, whatever evidence may exist in the primary sources to support an hypothesis and express it as part of a credible narrative. Likewise, secondary sources should not be read selectively in support of a preferred conclusion but chosen and assessed critically. Furthermore, events, technical processes (such as dispute resolution methodologies), theories and the conduct and writings of *dramatis personae* must be considered not simplistically or automatically through the prism of present mores or through the application of stereotypes. Rather, they must be considered in accordance with the prevailing standards of the time, with balanced comparisons made and supportable conclusions drawn. To quote one leading modern historian,

> ... [T]here can only be one truth, even if it can sometimes be very hard to ascertain. Discovering what really happened in history is difficult. It requires a great deal of hard work, it demands direct examination of the evidence, it presupposes a willingness to change one's mind, and it involves the suspension of one's prejudices and preconceptions. But it can be done.[9]

The following passages from Kaplan *et al* make clear that Derek was fully aware of the uses and abuses of history, had these requirements firmly at the forefront of his mind in embarking on his very first foray into the history of arbitration, and that he would start as he meant to go on.

> Those who have attempted to write about the history of arbitration have seen advantages in collecting specimens of institutions and procedures having some characteristic which can be compared, even equated, with an element of modern arbitration. ...

> The proper purpose of a history of arbitration is to show its development from recognisable ancestors into contemporary forms, thereby enlightening the study of arbitration as a modern phenomenon. The first

---

9. Professor Richard J Evans of the University of Cambridge, 'ThinkPiece: The spectre of conspiracies', *BBC History Magazine* (November 2020), pp 59–64 at 64. This journal was, incidentally, a favourite general history 'read' of Derek's, as indeed it is mine today.

question then becomes, where and how are the lines to be drawn which will most usefully circumscribe the subject?[10]

Thus:

> For the purposes of fixing the scope of the history of arbitration, ... it is appropriate to impose on the sources a fourfold definition: arbitration is the voluntary submission by the parties of a dispute for decision by [a] recognised and regular procedure other than litigation.[11]

Subject to these *caveats* and conformity with the definition of 'arbitration' given above, Derek's chapter in Kaplan *et al* engages in both a ground-breaking and culturally wide-ranging discussion of the history of arbitration, one that would spawn the prolific output of jurisdiction- and era-specific volumes authored and co-authored by Derek and published between 2001 and 2019.

The Ancient World

Derek's credentials and expertise as a classicist are evident in his treatment of arbitration – or something broadly akin to it – both in the myths of ancient Egypt and Greece and in the literature of antiquity, such as the works of Homer and Aeschylus. Facile historical comparisons are studiously avoided: the biblical judgment of Solomon, for example, was not arbitration but 'royal justice', while Plato's reference to arbitrators in *The Laws* (*c*.350 BC/BCE) was wide of the mark in modern terms, parties being free to litigate if arbitration failed to resolve a dispute.[12]

It was with ancient Rome, however, that arbitration began to develop a discernible pattern of comparisons with the present. For example, Derek alludes in his chapter to arbitration having begun to develop as a separate strand of civil procedure during the era of the Republic and having become well established by the first two centuries AD/CE, during the classical (or imperial) era.[13] He also mentions Cicero's contrasts between litigation and arbitration, particularly that in the latter, the parties would not win all but would not lose all either, and that the process was '[m]ild, moderate' by comparison with the '[e]xact [and] clear cut' nature of the former.[14] One is tempted to conclude that Cicero may have identified the origins of arbitration *ex aequo et bono* so well known to modern times. Indeed, Derek goes on to state that 'the arbitrator was free to decide the issue according to his own opinion of what was fair, untrammelled by legal rules.'[15]

10. Kaplan *et al* (*supra*, note 4), p xxxiii (pp 63-64 in this volume). See also Derek Roebuck, *Ancient Greek Arbitration* (2011, Oxford: HOLO Books: The Arbitration Press), pp 3–4.
11. *Ibid*, p xxxv (p 65 in this volume).
12. *Ibid*, p xxxviii (p 68 in this volume).
13. *Ibid*, pp xl-xlii (pp 70-72 in this volume).
14. Marcus Tullius Cicero (106–43 BC/BCE), *Pro Sexto Roscio Amerino* (c.50 BC/BCE).
15. Kaplan *et al* (*supra*, note 4), p xli (p 71 in this volume).

The chapter draws attention to a number of further features of arbitration in ancient Rome that also have a very modern resonance. First, a state official, the *praetor* or magistrate, was responsible under the so-called 'formulary' system for settling with parties at the outset of litigation a precise *formula* or instruction based upon their causes of action, claims and defences and then referring the case to a lay arbitrator (*arbiter*[16]) appointed by them for a decision on the merits. There is a passing resemblance here, at least in principle, to modern court-referred mediation systems, such as those under Lord Woolf's Civil Justice Review of 1999 in England & Wales and the Civil Justice Reform of 2009 in Hong Kong. A comparison may similarly be broadly drawn with the role of an administering institution in international arbitration, such as that played by the International Court of Arbitration of the International Chamber of Commerce in supervising the parties' Terms of Reference for submission to the arbitral tribunal. Ancient Rome also saw the introduction of an agreement to refer an existing dispute to an agreed *arbiter* and, in so doing, fixed his powers, duties and jurisdiction. This form of agreement, a *compromissum,* is known today as a *compromis*, both in arbitration governed by Continental European civil law and in dispute settlement under public international law. In common law jurisdictions it is known as an *ad hoc* arbitration agreement and may be contrasted with agreements to submit future disputes. Finally, and again reflecting modern practice, Rome saw the introduction of multi-*arbiter* tribunals, with an odd number ensuring that majority decisions would be made, and limitation of grounds of challenge to *arbitri* and awards to 'a narrow range of events', which did not, however, include 'conformity with the law'.[17]

England

Perhaps inevitably, given the time constraints for writing the chapter and Derek's roots in the common law (both as an academic and as a practitioner), the bulk of the chapter is devoted to England, covering in a grand sweep the period between the seventh century AD/CE and the amendment of England's previous (pre-1996) arbitration legislation, the Arbitration Act 1950, by the Arbitration Act 1979.[18] This material is undoubtedly of great relevance also in considering the history of arbitration in common law jurisdictions worldwide.[19]

Derek's position as to the irrefutable existence of arbitration in England from very early times was most categorically expressed not in the chapter but in a seminar paper presented in 2017, in which he stated:

16. A Roman law term which now denotes, for example, an arbitrator under Scots law.
17. Kaplan *et al* (*supra*, note 4), p xli (p 71 in this volume).
18. Pages xlii-lxv (pp 72-96 in this volume).
19. For a detailed example, see Derek Roebuck, *Disputes and Differences: Comparisons in Law, Language and History* (2010, Oxford: HOLO Books: The Arbitration Press), pp 378–393. See also Robert Morgan, *infra*, note 28.

A process which included mediation and arbitration [M/A] has been generally practised in England and Wales from time immemorial. Litigation came later, with the state, as a particular alternative. There is ample evidence to show that, at least until the end of the 18th century, the state, as well as other communities, relied on M/A to deal routinely with most kinds of disputes, e.g. in the 16th century Elizabeth I's legal aid schemes, especially for widows; in the 17th Nathaniel Bacon, who accepted all kinds of referrals from the Government and the courts; in the 18th JPs' notebooks.[20]

Clearly, Derek's thoughts had advanced somewhat since writing his 1994 chapter and in light of his subsequent writings.[21] His opening comments in this part of the chapter opined that writings from the early Anglo-Saxon (ie, pre-common law) period were replete with references to 'arbitration', though it was unclear whether required elements of adjudication were present or the system (such as it was) was more akin to conciliation. Furthermore, the Venerable Bede wrote of Roman 'exemplars' appearing in Anglo-Saxon laws via the medium of canon law, though he did not specify whether they included arbitration. Derek's innate historian's caution in avoiding generalised and facile comparisons, combined with his interest in language, also led him to draw attention to the fact that particular Anglo-Saxon words could denote both 'settle' and 'arbitrate'. Whatever form Anglo-Saxon 'arbitration' (so called) took, it would have continued until some time after the Norman Conquest in 1066 and the advent of the common law. In any event, Derek made an important connection: that the development of arbitration into a form that was more recognisable in contemporary perspective would be influenced by that of the common law and the exercise of power over it by common law courts. In so doing, he took issue with leading English legal historian Sir William Holdsworth (1871–1944), who wrote from what was (at the time) a widely accepted 19th century perspective, that ' ... the courts [of medieval England] did not look very favourably on a practice which tended to diminish their jurisdiction.'[22]

20. *Comments on Archives by a User* (2nd Legal Records at Risk seminar, 'The use of unpublished legal documents in socio-legal research', Centre for Socio-Legal Studies, University of Oxford, 22 February 2017), para 2. Available at https://cdn.ymaws.com/irms. org.uk/resource/resmgr/lrar/seminars/centre_for_socio-legal_studies_2nd_lrar_seminar/ handout_thoughts_on_archives.pdf (accessed 31 October 2020).
21. Derek Roebuck, *Early English Arbitration*, *supra*, note 6 and Derek Roebuck, *Mediation and Arbitration in the Middle Ages: England 1154–1558* (2013, Oxford: HOLO Books: The Arbitration Press). These volumes are discussed at, respectively, pp 345-349 and 349-354 below.
22. Page xliv of the chapter (pp 74-75 in this volume), citing WS Holdsworth, *A History of English Law* (HL & HG Goodhart (Eds), 1903-1972), vol xiv, p 187. See, for example, Lord Campbell's memorable comment that the courts once had a 'horror' of arbitration: *Russell v Pelegrini* (1856) 6 E & B 1020, 1026.

From Holdsworth's perspective, this was the so-called 'judicial jealousy' of arbitration, though there appeared to be inconsistency as to whether it emerged during the medieval period or from sometime in the mid-18th century. Derek was of the view that the sources provided no evidence for this, and that Holdsworth was mistaken.[23] Even Holdsworth himself stated that the courts, when called upon to enforce awards, 'got many opportunities of laying down rules as to the conditions of the validity of these awards, as to the modes of enforcing them, and as to the conduct of arbitrators'.[24]

From a contemporary perspective, this is precisely what English courts have done ever since the days of Lord Mansfield, culminating in the English Arbitration Act 1889 (a consolidation but not codifying Act that was an early foundation of modern English arbitration law). Rather than demonstrating judicial jealousy, the actions of the courts reflected an acceptance and encouragement of arbitration, subject to arbitration agreements not purporting to oust their jurisdiction but recognising that the courts had a residual jurisdiction to intervene in arbitrations as a matter of public policy, justice and good order.

Further evidence of the acceptance and co-existence of arbitration by the late Middle Ages lay, in Derek's opinion, in the fact at least three categories of arbitration had come into existence by that time, all of them having a modern resonance. They were (1) arbitration by agreement of the parties; (2) arbitration arising from voluntary membership of a trading community, such as a merchant guild, and accepted pursuant to its rules; and (3) arbitration ordered by a court, either of its own volition or at the request of one or both parties to litigation (arbitration by rule of court, *viz* an order or ruling of the court). Derek concluded firmly from these categorisations that arbitration 'liv[ed] comfortably alongside the work of the common law courts for over 450 years.'[25] He concluded further, in a separate but contemporaneous work, that judicial jealousy was a 'myth'.[26] His commentary in the chapter on the Arbitration Acts 1698–1979 is, accordingly, based upon these premises: the 1698 Act, in particular, marked the first statutory recognition of the right of parties to refer their disputes directly to arbitration without first having to bring proceedings in the courts.

The Roads Not Taken in 1994

1. *Hong Kong*

Given Derek's close academic interest in Hong Kong and the fact that his inaugural historical treatise appeared in a Hong Kong-related cases and

---

23. Pages xliv-xlv and lxii–lxiii of the chapter (respectively, pp 74-75 and 93 in this volume).
24. Page xlv of the chapter (pp 74-75 in this volume); Holdsworth, *op cit* (note 22), p 190.
25. Page xlv of the chapter (p 75 in this volume).
26. Derek Roebuck, 'The Myth of Judicial Jealousy' (1994) 10 *Arbitration International* 395-406. See also Derek Roebuck, in Neil Kaplan *et al* (*supra*, note 4), lxii-lxiii (p 93 in this volume); Henry Horwitz and James Oldham, 'John Locke, Lord Mansfield and Arbitration During the Eighteenth Century' (1993) 36(1) *The Historical Journal* 137-159, at 146-148.

materials volume, it is perhaps surprising that he did not actually discuss arbitration in Hong Kong from 1841, when the territory came under British rule, separating the 'Fragrant Harbour' from Canton (Guangdong).[27] As a colony, arbitration was thenceforth governed both by English common law principles and, incrementally, statute, broadly following mid-19th century legislative developments in England & Wales. The present author attempted to make up for the deficit with a summary history in 1997 which discussed legislative developments affecting both arbitration and the courts between 1844 and 1901,[28] though in the same year Derek published a more detailed article entitled 'Arbitration in Early Hong Kong 1835–67'.[29] This article was later revised and published as two chapters in his 2010 volume, *Disputes and Differences: Comparisons in Law, Language and History*,[30] which dealt separately with the periods 1834–1836[31] and 1841–1865.[32]

2. *China*

With regard to arbitration in Mainland China generally, which was also not covered in the chapter, Derek ended his introduction to it with the following contextually appropriate admonition: 'Further research will be necessary before the long and fascinating history of arbitration in China can be added.'[33]

27. In fairness, however, it should be mentioned that Neil Kaplan stated in his obituary of Derek that Derek was given a short timeframe in which to write his contribution.

28. Robert Morgan, 'Arbitration in Hong Kong – An Introductory Survey', in Morgan, *The Arbitration Ordinance of Hong Kong: A Commentary* (1997, Butterworths Asia/LexisNexis Hong Kong), at pp 2–3. This commentary discusses the genesis not only of Hong Kong's arbitration legislation but also of its superior court legislation during the period 1844–1901. The latter was based on the English Judicature Act 1873 and rules of court, which together provided a structured system for the review of arbitral awards.

29. (1997) 63 *Arbitration* 263–269, which discusses, in particular, the passage of arbitration legislation based on the English model.

30. *Supra*, note 19.

31. See 'Captain Charles Elliot RN, Arbitrator: Dispute Resolution in China Waters 1834-1836' (pp 348-377, reproduced at pp 97-131 of this volume). This discusses arbitration by the Superintendents of British Trade in China (who replaced the East India Company in representing British State interests after the First Opium War of 1839-1842) pursuant to an arbitration scheme devised by Elliot. The scheme was devised to resolve disputes between Chinese and foreign (predominantly British) traders in Canton. Elliot it was who, as Plenipotentiary, claimed Hong Kong on behalf of the British Crown in 1841, later becoming the new colony's first Governor.

32. See '"Something So Unenglish": Mediation and Arbitration in Hong Kong 1841–1865' (pp 378–393). This chapter started life as a co-authored article by Derek and Christopher Munn, at (2010) 26(1) *Arbitration International* 87–102. The quote in the title refers to an observation made about the arbitration arrangements in an editorial in a local journal and gazetteer entitled 'Friend of China', dated 24 February 1844. The chapter discusses the influence of the mid-19th century law of England & Wales on the development both of arbitration and the court system, as well as the not always positive influence of several personalities involved in early Hong Kong arbitration, including governors and arbitrators.

33. Kaplan *et al* (*supra*, note 4), p xxxv (p 65 in this volume).

It is notable that, so far as the author is aware, nobody has yet risen to Derek's challenge to write a detailed and comprehensive history of arbitration in China. Rather, the historical treatments that exist (at least in the English language) remain within the realm of summaries by way of general background in textbooks and cases and materials volumes on arbitration law and practice in modern China. The same may be said of mediation, which is of a more ancient pedigree in China, reflecting as it does the country's underlying Confucian traditions of harmony (both between parties and between them and wider society), compromise and emphasis on informal and non-adversarial forms of dispute resolution based upon discussion and negotiation, ameliorating the effects of disputes by reaching equitable solutions, thereby preserving social order.[34] It therefore reflects also the view of Chinese jurists and legal scholars who reject 'overly litigious' mechanisms such as those prevalent in the Western legal tradition, with its 'singular focus on the vindication of individual rights' rather than the pursuit of social harmony,[35] and which 'trivialise' and 'commercialise' fundamental values such as human dignity into commodities having a market price.[36] Such criticisms may be levelled as much at arbitration as at litigation.

3. *Mediation*

The international history of mediation also merited only a very brief mention in the chapter. Derek likewise remedied this omission, both in *Disputes and Differences: Comparisons in Law, Language and History*,[37] in which he not only made clear that mediation had a venerable ancient history of its own that needed to be told, but also challenged the myth that mediation 'sprang to life in mid-twentieth century USA, either for the first time or after a long slumber,'[38] and in all of his individual volumes. To take but one example, a feature of the relationship between mediation and arbitration in Ptolemaic Egypt having a very modern resonance was that mediation was often attempted before arbitration and that mediated settlements could, for ease of enforcement, be expressed as arbitral awards by

---

34. See, for example, William B Devoe, 'Comment: Commercial Dispute Resolution Between the United States and the People's Republic of China: Problems and Prospects', (1983) 7 *Suffolk Transnational Law Journal* 329–359 at 346.
35. Anne Judith Farina, 'Talking Disputes Into Harmony: China Approaches International Commercial Arbitration', (1989) 4(1) *American University International Law Review* 137–171, at 139.
36. Robert F Utter, 'Dispute Resolution in China', (1987) 62 *Washington Law Review* 383–396 at 392.
37. *Supra*, note 19. See 'The Myth of Modern Mediation' (pp 394-406). This chapter originally appeared at (2007) 63 *Arbitration* 105–116.
38. *Ibid*, p 394.

agreement of the parties,[39] and that it was regularly ordered by the courts.[40] As with arbitration, however, it was left to others to write a comprehensive history of international mediation – not least in China[41] – in the fullness of time.

PART THREE: THE MAJOR TEXTS

Introduction

And so it was that Derek's initial chapter of 1994 spawned a series of 11 detailed volumes between 2001 and 2019, three of which were co-written, one of them with Susanna. In his obituary, Neil Kaplan expressed the hope (one shared by the present author), that two of the other three co-authors will one day fulfil Derek's lifetime ambition of completing the story up to the late 19th century. This would be a fitting final tribute.

There now follows a select review of particularly salient aspects of the history of arbitration and mediation covered in each of the specialised texts.

1. *Ancient Greece*

What immediately strikes the reader of Derek's first detailed study, *Ancient Greek Arbitration*,[42] is an informative setting of the scene (which is adopted also in the volume on Ancient Rome[43]) prior to the substantive discussion on Ancient Greece.[44] As with any modern treatise on arbitration, therefore, he commenced this volume with discussion of several themes. These included (1) identifying recognisable categories of process (such as mediation and arbitration or at least something broadly akin to them); (2) the criteria for such recognition (such as whether they were adjudicatory or conciliatory in nature, or involved some mixture of the two, akin to the modern concept of 'Med-Arb'); (3) the application of processes within the social order; and, reflecting another of his interests, (4) the effects of language and translation (in particular with regard to the limitations of the

---

39. *Ibid*, p 395.
40. *Ibid*, p 405.
41. Also as with arbitration, however, histories of mediation in China remain introductory. See, for example, Peter CH Chan, *Mediation in Contemporary Chinese Civil Justice* (Leiden: Brill Nijhoff, 2017), ch 2, 'Legal History of Civil Mediation in China'; Zeng Xangyi, 'Mediation in China – Past and Present' (2020) 17 *Asia Pacific Law Review* 1–29; Cao Pei, 'The Origins of Mediation in Traditional China,' (May 1999) 54(2) *Dispute Resolution Journal* 32–35.
42. 2001, Oxford: HOLO Books: The Arbitration Press.
43. See pp 340-345 below.
44. For the purposes of *Ancient Greek Arbitration*, 'Greece' included all polities in both mainland and island Greece (usually city-states) and in Ptolemaic Egypt. The primary focus of the volume with regard to exemplars was Athens.

latter and the resultant misunderstandings arising from literal approaches) on the understanding of processes within particular times and contexts.

Applying all of these considerations within the context of Ancient Greece during the period 700–730 BC/BCE meant working from sources that did not (surprisingly, from a contemporary perspective) include juristic writings. Surviving works about the laws and legal systems therefore stemmed primarily from enquiry by philosophers and orators, and, in any event, addressed separate systems of dispute resolution within a multiplicity of polities, there never having been a unified system of law, at least until the Roman era. What was also remarkable was that there was no system of 'litigation', strictly so called, as formally constituted courts did not generally appear in Greece until Roman times. Thus, arbitration (which could include mediation as a precursor process) was not in fact 'alternative' to anything else in juridical terms, save for either self-help (through direct negotiation or violence) or the imposition by the community of a payment or fine for a wrong done or even some *ad hoc* form of adjudicatory process by committees of the citizenry called the *dikasteria*.

The function of mediation (or conciliation) in achieving a consensual settlement was recognised at that time and given primacy for this purpose. Derek also concluded, with regard to arbitration, that parties were generally free from community interference in deciding to refer disputes to arbitration (in other words, they had what is nowadays referred to as 'party autonomy'). One important exception found by Derek – certainly in Athens – was that parties were required to plead their own cases and that there may even have been legislation to prevent professional advocacy; there was, in any event, no such thing as a legal profession.

Arbitration agreements in Greece (which were not universally made in writing (city-states such as Athens being one exception) enabled parties to dictate (1) the subject matter of the dispute; (2) who their arbitrators should be (invariably male and commonly sole); (3) the jurisdiction of the tribunal; (4) the applicable substantive law, which could be either the law of the polity concerned, or rules of equity, which were considered to be 'just', went further than written legal rules and were thought to be particularly suited for arbitration;[45] (5) the rules of procedure, which required the tribunal first to attempt to 'reconcile' the parties (ie, mediate or conciliate the dispute); and (6) recourse against and enforcement of the award by order of the *dikasteria* (though in Ptolemaic Egypt, a more sophisticated and indeed modern-sounding approach was adopted, whereby the parties themselves could provide in their arbitration agreement that the award would have the same force as a judgment).

---

45. *Ibid*, p 36, citing Aristotle, *The Art of Rhetoric* (4th century BC/BCE).

Derek made clear, however, that (with the exceptions of Athens, Egypt and Chios), evidence of the existence of legislation governing a polity's arbitration law was not empirical but, at best, anecdotal, though at the same time there was little evidence of interference with party autonomy: indeed, he described parties as having had 'almost unlimited freedom of choice'.[46]

The position of women in arbitration was not, however, an entirely favourable one. While the sources did not reveal any legislative bar to their appointment as arbitrators, clearly they were never so appointed.[47] They were, however, generally free to represent themselves in arbitrations, by contrast with their position before the *dikasteria* and in litigation during the Roman era, whereby they had to be accompanied by a 'citizen guardian', a notion broadly echoed in the modern 'next friend' in family litigation in common law jurisdictions, though in Ancient Greece such a person had to be male.

Derek's findings and conclusions about private arbitration and mediation in ancient Greece[48] go much further than those in his necessarily brief 1994 chapter and attract some comparison with modern arbitration and mediation, while at the same time cautioning against over-simplification. Significantly, settlement was paramount, so that the mediation rather than the adjudicatory element was in fact both the primary and preferred process. Furthermore, parties could agree that a settlement could be converted into an award for ease of enforcement. This blending of processes, among other factors, led him to conclude that 'in the debates about, and experiments in, new forms of dispute resolution, there may be lessons to be learned, or at least hints to be found, in Ancient Greek arbitration.'[49]

2. *Ancient Rome*

Derek's next foray into arbitration in the ancient world was *Roman Arbitration*,[50] which was co-authored with Bruno de Loynes de Fumichon, himself an acclaimed historian of arbitration in the civil law tradition and a contributor to the present volume.

To begin with, it may be noted that, in addition to detailed historical discussion of the development of Rome's legal system and the sources, as well as arbitration *per se*, this volume has a structure well known to readers of modern arbitration texts, both common law- and civil law-oriented.[51]

---

46. *Ibid*, pp 347–348.
47. *Ibid*, p 349.
48. *Ibid*, pp 347–359.
49. *Ibid*, p 360.
50. 2004, Oxford: HOLO Books: The Arbitration Press. See also Leanne Bablitz, 'Roman Courts and Private Arbitration', in Paul du Plessis, Clifford Ando and Kaius Tuori (ed), *The Oxford Handbook of Roman Law and Society* (2016, Oxford: Oxford University Press), ch 18, which draws widely on this volume.
51. Roebuck and De Fumichon, *op cit*, Chapters 5–11 (pp 46–192).

Discussion by reference to types of arbitration, arbitration agreements, the appointment of arbitrators (hereinafter arbiters or *arbitri*), the hearing, the award, and challenges to and enforcement of awards was, by contrast with Ancient Greece, facilitated by the existence of a broadly unitary system of laws that applied across the Empire (the *ius gentium*).[52] Furthermore, this methodology both permits a comparative law approach and – fulfilling Derek's aim – enables the reader to look beyond simple comparisons with modern arbitration law and practice and to identify areas not only of commonality but also, more importantly, of differences and equivalencies. A significant example of this is the authors' identification of the contractual nature of the relationship between parties and *arbitri* – the *receptum arbitri* (*receptum*) – by reference to Book 4 of the *Digest* of Justinian (c 533 AD/CE).

The authors relate how arbitration was effectively a 'two-tier' and contrasting system of adjudication, utilised according to whether parties were ordinary citizens (and also slaves) or richer and/or high-ranking citizens. Such a bifurcated system therefore reflected both procedurally expedient processes and the structure of Ancient Roman society.

First Tier: Arbitration *Bonus Vir* and Arbitration by *Judex*

The first and earliest tier was arbitration by *bonus vir* (literally, a 'just and honest man'), an entirely private and informal process that did not involve the state (in the person of the *praetor*). Parties would ask the *arbiter*, a trusted third party of their own choice, to adjudicate their dispute, the adjudication being made not solely on legal grounds but also in accordance with ideas of fairness and trust (*fides*) as he saw them. Herein lay the ancient origins of *bona fides* and of arbitration *ex aequo et bono*. The *arbiter bonus vir* exercised multiple roles, including as assessor and expert, according to the nature of the case. The categories of case with which such *arbitri* dealt included agricultural leases, land boundaries, dowry disputes and commercial disputes, and in specialised cases might involve *arbitri* who practised as, for example, architects and surveyors. Awards were neither legally binding nor enforceable *per se*: like settlement agreements, their binding effect depended on party acceptance, while enforcement required an aggrieved party to 'go to Rome', *viz* to seek to enforce his rights by bringing his case anew, either in arbitration *ex compromisso* (discussed below) or in litigation. This also meant that there could be no equivalent to estoppel *per rem judicatam*. Arbitration *bonus vir* also contrasted with arbitration *ex compromisso* in that there was a greater level of what nowadays would be called party autonomy.

An alternative to arbitration *bonus vir* within the first tier was arbitration by *judex arbiterve*, who was selected by the state (the *praetor*, a magistrate

52. *Ibid*, p 199.

or administrator appointed by the Republic or the Emperor) from an approved list. This was an early manifestation of the modern concept of a panel of arbitrators. Arbitration by *judex* was therefore a form of 'public arbitration'. The parties could, however, opt for arbitration *bonus vir* if they did not like the *praetor*'s choice of *arbiter* or wanted to fix their own procedure, thus reverting to private arbitration and a fuller degree of party autonomy). From the third century BC/BCE onward, a formulary system developed whereby, in addition to appointing the *judex*, the *praetor* also set out the claims and the rights on which they were based (the *intentio*) and an order to the *judex* (the *condemnatio*) either to require payment of a sum of money or to hold a party not liable. Arbitration by *judex* had been known since the pre-imperial legal code known as the Twelve Tables (*Leges Duodecim Tabularum* or *Duodecim Tabulae*, c. 451 BC/BCE). As with arbitration *bonus vir*, the *judex* could also act as an expert, assessor or valuer in such cases as actions to partition an estate and boundary actions. Another factor in common was a requirement imposed on *arbitri* to apply the law in a reasonable way and in accordance with good faith. By contrast with arbitration *bonus vir*, however, parties could opt for supervision of the arbitration by the *praetor* and the award would be binding and enforceable by the state through the exercise of powers of *imperium* by the *praetor*.

Second Tier: Arbitration *Ex Compromisso*

The other tier – which effectively developed from arbitration by *judex* – was arbitration *ex compromisso*, which was the system generally described by Derek in his 1994 chapter. This system was predicated on a greater – mandatory – level of involvement by the state through the office of the *praetor*, whose principal functions were to assist the parties in formulating a case for submission to an *arbiter* (sometimes referred to as a *judex*, though this nomenclature could equally have applied to a judge, the terms appearing to have been used interchangeably, both under the Twelve Tables and Justinian's *Digest*[53]), to appoint the *arbiter*, to supervise arbitrations to the extent necessary and to enforce awards. It was developed at some time in the second century BC/BCE and applied throughout Rome, Italy and Mediterranean colonial possessions as a mechanism for applying the *ius gentium*. Its significance lay in the recognition of the status and importance of a formal written agreement between the parties, a set of mutual obligations constituting a contract that the state was prepared to enforce – a feature with a very modern resonance. Tribunals had subject-matter jurisdiction regarding (*inter alia*) disputes over personal status, guardianship, debts and breaches of contract.

---

53. *Ibid*, p 193. In *Early English Arbitration*, *supra*, note 6, Derek stated at p 79 that the expression *judices* actually meant nothing more specific than 'decision-makers'.

The authors comment on what one might term a 'mixed view' by Rome with regard to its interest in arbitration – at the same time both 'hands on' and 'hands off', so to speak. On the one hand, disputes should not disrupt smooth and efficient public administration. On the other, it was not the function of state officers to resolve them directly; parties were therefore left to work out their differences by entering into a formal submission agreement, with the state having only a residual role in dispute resolution to a necessary and appropriate extent, primarily with regard to enforcement of the obligation to arbitrate and of the award itself.

The Position of Women

Although generally disadvantaged as to their substantive rights, women in Ancient Rome had greater rights in arbitration than their counterparts in Ancient Greece with regard to the pursuit of claims. By the classical period, a woman of full age, whether married or single, had capacity to enter into a *compromissum* and therefore to be a party to arbitration in her own right. The same could not, however, be said for women acting as arbitrators or mediators. It was not clear from early sources whether a woman could act in either capacity. The *Digest* of Emperor Justinian (r.527–565 AD/CE), however, put the matter beyond peradventure by expressly prohibiting women from accepting such appointments on the ground that nature did not allow this.[54] While parties were generally entitled to be represented at hearings by an attorney (*procurator*), it may be noted (though not mentioned by the authors) that women were also barred from acting in this capacity.[55]

Conclusions

The authors' conclusions, particularly in chapter 12, are of particular interest for their discussion of the degree to which comparisons may be drawn with contemporary arbitration. They start with the historian's customary caution against 'imposing anachronistic criteria on the raw material of the sources'.[56] With this in mind, they note that arbitration *bonus vir* survived the introduction of both arbitration by *judex* and arbitration *ex compromisso*, which suggests that then, as now, parties wanted suitable choices of procedure and hankered after both improvements and greater choice. They suggest, by reference to 'tangential' sources, that Justinian himself preferred settlement over litigation.[57]

54. Roebuck and De Fumichon, *op cit* (note 50), p 138; Susanna Hoe and Derek Roebuck, *Women in Disputes: A History of European Women in Mediation and Arbitration* (2018, Oxford: HOLO Books), p 1.
55. Richard A Bauman, *Women and Politics in Ancient Rome* (1992 (rev ed 1994), London: Routledge), pp 50–51.
56. *Roman Arbitration*, p 194.
57. *Ibid*, p 197.

The authors suggest the following similarities (though not necessarily equivalencies) between arbitration *ex compromisso* (including mediation) and modern mediation and arbitration:[58]

(1) a certain lack of general willingness to accept mediation, except in relation to family matters;

(2) suggestions by philosophers that it would be better for a *judex* to postpone decision-making for a while and act as a 'friend' or 'peacemaker' to the parties – which accorded with Justinian's view of settlement and reflects contemporary Mainland Chinese- and Hong Kong Chinese-style med-arb; and

(3) potential problems that could arise, said philosophers, from *arbitri* or *judices* (i) using their own specialist knowledge without reference to the parties, (ii) asking questions which neither party had raised, and (iii) giving the parties an advance impression of how their minds were working. All of these are also contemporary, while the proper use of specialist knowledge in particular has been considered regularly by the courts.

Problems apart, the authors drew attention to several interesting parallels in arbitration practice between Ancient Rome and the modern world. These include (1) the appointment of multi-*arbiter* tribunals; (2) that an *arbiter* could not act beyond the scope of the *compromisso* (in other words, beyond his jurisdiction or *ultra vires* in modern terms); (3) that both parties should be present at the hearing, which in turn gave rise to a further requirement to hear both of them (*audi alteram partem*); (4) substantive requirements of finality, certainty and completeness of awards, which are among the requirements for validity recognised today; and (5) release of the *arbiter* from his duties under the *receptum* after making a valid award, which is reflected in the modern principle of *functus officio*.

The authors also suggested, in particular, what they regarded as two 'striking difference[s]' between Roman and modern arbitration:[59]

(1) a bar on the making of arbitration agreements to refer *future* disputes, a problem which has, in some Roman law-based jurisdictions, only been addressed in recent years; and

(2) a bar on parties asking *arbitri* and *judices* from incorporating settlement terms into their awards to facilitate enforcement.

---

58. *Ibid*, pp 199–200.
59. *Ibid*, pp 200–201.

Some may consider it surprising that Derek did not comment on the influence of Ancient Roman arbitration in the way he did on its ancient Greek counterpart. Perhaps this does not matter: there is ample evidence, as related in later writings, of the influence of Roman law on arbitration in other jurisdictions (whether directly or through the Church) over the succeeding centuries.

3. Early England

Derek's first volume on arbitration in England, *Early English Arbitration*,[60] covered the period from the Romans to the Normans and the kingdoms in between. The achievement is impressive for revealing the development of arbitration and mediation during a period of transition of the country from Britannia, a Roman province applying colonial Roman law, to multiple early English polities and legal systems, and ultimately into 'England' proper, a unitary state governed by the common law. The achievement is all the more impressive for the very varied and contrasting sources written in a number of languages and existing across different cultures. Whereas the two previous volumes derived from sources in ancient Greek and Latin, this volume considered sources written in Latin, British Celtic, Anglo-Saxon (or Old English), Norse and Norman French (or Anglo-Norman).

For reasons of space, this section does not discuss in any detail the legal systems of each of the constituent areas of early England and their history. Discussion is limited to the nature of arbitration and mediation as Derek found them on the evidence and how they fitted in to each legal system.

The Roman Province: Britannia

Derek said that it was wrong to assume – though it could be argued – that Roman law applied in Britannia *mutatis mutandis* as it did in other provinces. Only Roman citizens would be required to transact private business – including the resolution of disputes – in accordance with Roman law. Those who were not Roman citizens would, at the private level, continue to resolve disputes through local assemblies and in accordance with customary law, a situation both tolerated and imposed by the Roman authorities. This also meant that, as a matter of public administration, those authorities would have been willing to enforce adjudications made under customary law, not least to maintain social stability and good order.

There is, however, little or no evidence of how arbitration itself developed both prior to the Roman invasion and during the period of Roman occupation, or whether and, if so how, it changed over 400 years of occupation. It could only be assumed that arbitration was conducted

60. 2008, Oxford: HOLO Books: The Arbitration Press. See also Sir Stephen Sedley's contribution of the same name at pp 425-429 in the present volume.

much in the manner of the Roman model by means of arbitration *ex compromisso* (discussed in the preceding section) and may have extended to trade disputes between Roman-British merchants both within Britannia and with their counterparts in Continental Europe. For this purpose, instead of *praetores*, magistrates would have been appointed by provincial governors to perform the tasks of formulating the *receptum* and appointing *arbitri*. There seems to have been no evidence of arbitration *bonus vir*. Derek was unable to find evidence of bishops having acted as *arbitri* in the late imperial era, following the legalisation of Christianity throughout the Roman Empire by the Edict of Milan in 313 AD/CE (though Britannia appears to have been slow at first in accepting the authority of the Church).

Following the collapse of imperial administration in Britain, the Romano-British seem to have attempted to maintain the *status quo ante* in dispute resolution by reference to what could be remembered of Roman law. The fact that Roman law courts were dissolved suggests, but does not prove, that Roman citizens would have turned to an alternative to the courts with which they were familiar. The most that Derek could safely say in this regard was that '[i]t would be surprising if the Roman-Britons did not handle their disputes among themselves in the ways they had inherited, according to Roman law, ...'[61]

Outside of the Romano-British community, the resolution of disputes largely reverted to decision-making under the customary law of the British Celts, though the Germanic customary law of the newly arrived Anglo-Saxons (see below) and the unwritten law of the Church would also be applied over time. One theme which united all of these in Derek's mind, however, was the absence of hard evidence of mediation and arbitration in the conventionally understood sense.[62]

The Anglo-Saxons

The territories of the Anglo-Saxons comprised the Angle kingdoms of Kent and East Anglia and the Saxon kingdoms of Essex, Sussex, Wessex, Mercia and Northumbria (together, the Anglo-Saxon Heptarchy), which were formed following the Germanic settlement of England in the fifth century AD/CE. Each kingdom had its own customary law, which was applied to the resolution of disputes by the edicts of the kings. The early Anglo-Saxon kings, said Derek, were not interested in disputes between Britons and, unlike the Romans, showed no inclination to respect the locals' customary laws. The kings (or their delegates) 'presumably'[63] applied their

61. *Ibid*, p 77.
62. *Ibid*, p 89.
63. *Ibid*, p 88.

own customary law to disputes between Anglo-Saxons and Britons and did so through the expedient of oral adjudications.

> In seeking evidence of mediation and arbitration in England at the beginning of the seventh century, two things can be assumed and must be kept in mind: all disputes which were not settled informally were dealt with publicly by some system of mediation and arbitration provided by the community: ...[64]

While Derek believed that there may have been informal arbitrations, perhaps between merchants, along the lines of the Romans' *bonus vir*, he could find no evidence of them. But there was evidence of public arbitration in the form of traditional assemblies (moots), where men, and women of high status, would meet to discuss and resolve or settle disputes with a view to restoring the community to harmony. Settlement rather than decision was the preferred result. Failing resolution by an assembly, the dispute would be referred to the king or a delegate or even an arbitrator chosen by the parties. Kings did not ordinarily involve themselves in enforcement unless they had an overarching interest, usually the preservation of order; they could rely on clan and kin groups who took responsibility for providing a system for the resolution of conflicts.

Relatively little is known about how the assemblies went about their business, though Derek discovered the first instance of procedural rules for mediation and arbitration in the dooms (legal codes) of the Kentish kings Hlothhere (r.615–685) and Eadric (r.662–668). Significantly, they appeared to illustrate a move from general assemblies of the hundreds, shires and boroughs at which disputes were discussed as part of general business towards meetings specially convened for the purpose. In Wessex, dispute resolution by assembly was also the norm. Although the dooms on the administration of justice of King Alfred (the Great, r.871–899) were silent on mediation and arbitration, the king was emphatic about the importance of such matters as giving testimony under oath and pledges to guarantee performance of obligations before assemblies. The second set of dooms of King Edgar (r.959–975) laid down further procedural rules for assemblies (the *witan*), prefaced with a clause that nobody could seek justice from the king unless he had been unable to get justice 'at home', *viz* before an assembly. Moreover, King Aethelred II ('the Unready') (r.978–1013, 1014–1016) decreed that while it was his responsibility to legislate, that of the *witan* was to declare the general principles of justice which would prevail and of which everyone would have the benefit.

64. *Ibid*, p 91.

There is no mention in Derek's text about Ancient Greek- or Roman-style reasonableness and *bona fides* in applying the law; rather, the emphasis in Anglo-Saxon dispute resolution appeared to be on applying the letter of the law (both royal ordinances and customary law) and, in so doing, reaching the correct decision.

A Norse interlude: the Danes

A Danish invasion of England led by the former's King Guthrum overran the Anglo-Saxon kingdoms of Mercia and East Anglia as well as large parts of northern England but was held at bay by the kingdom of Wessex, which at the time controlled all of southern England. As Wessex had been weakened by the conflict, King Alfred agreed by treaty in *c*.886 to grant the Danes autonomy over the territories they had conquered in an attempt to bring peace to neighbouring Anglo-Saxon and Viking communities. This resulted in the Danelaw, which reflected the boundaries of the territories under Danish rule. Peace did not last, however: full-scale invasions and regular raids and incursions into Wessex began again from 993, continuing into the 11th century.

Derek's discussion focuses on the reign of King Cnut (or Canute, r.1016–1035), who had defeated Aethelred's son Edmund Ironside in battle. The battle was followed by the division of England between Edmund, who would rule the kingdom of Wessex, while Cnut would rule the remainder of England. Cnut's significance lay in his being an Anglophile who respected the Anglo-Saxon kings while, in Derek's view, the Germanic and Scandinavian approaches to law and governance may have been fundamentally similar. This meant that Cnut did not bring about wholesale changes in the laws but, by virtue of decrees of 1018 and 1020, based them largely on dooms of King Edgar and applied them to Danes and Anglo-Saxons alike. King Edward the Confessor (r.1042–1066) left the laws undisturbed. Derek believed that the 1018–1020 decrees may have been the first expression of English customary laws in writing.

This meant that the system of civil dispute resolution was also left largely untouched, with the traditional assemblies continuing to hold sway as the first port of call for disputants, with negotiated or mediated settlement being preferred to arbitration. Given the exponential growth in cross-North Sea trade by the end of Cnut's reign and the existence of trading privileges for Scandinavian merchants in London, special assemblies, known by the Viking name husthing, were established in London to resolve mercantile disputes – perhaps the earliest known instance of London as a mercantile dispute resolution centre. In all cases, however, parties would look to the king to enforce settlements and arbitral awards, whether or not the latter had an interest in them.

The Norman Conquest and After

The volume concludes with discussion of England between 1066 and 1154, from the reign of King William I (the Conqueror, r.1066–1087) to the end of that of King Stephen (r.1135–1154). Its immediate significance for Derek's writings was the emergence of written sources from which conclusions could more reliably be drawn. As the *Domesday Book* graphically illustrates, the Normans were concerned with centralised public administration, the necessarily evidence-based nature of which, along with royal officials' accountability to the king, promoted a culture of written record-keeping.

The Normans needed to consolidate their power over a subjugated and restive community. Perhaps counter-intuitively, this did not entail the reception and imposition of the laws of Normandy in England but, provided that the latter's customary laws did not detract from the king's authority, the king had an interest in retaining the Anglo-Saxon laws and legal system. The hundred, shire and borough assemblies therefore continued to function much as they had before, with settlement of disputes (including ecclesiastical disputes, as in Anglo-Saxon days) being the preferred outcome and with proceedings being conducted in the Anglo-Saxon language rather than the Anglo-Norman of the emerging courts. The king could, however, intervene in the business of the assemblies, including delegating matters to other jurisdictions, though Derek noted that this could give rise to forum shopping by parties in search of the greatest chances of success and reliable enforcement[65] – a very modern concept. Meanwhile, waiting in the wings was the common law, which by 1154 was still in gestation.

4. *Medieval England*

The next volume of Derek's writings covered mediation and arbitration in the period between 1154 and 1558.[66] This period ran from the reign of the Angevin King Henry II and through the Plantagenet era to the eve of that of the Tudor Queen Elizabeth I, from the Middle Ages to the start of the early modern period.

By contrast with early England, the period under discussion was not marked by regime changes resulting from successful foreign invasions and giving rise to the imposition and reception of foreign laws. The legal system (through the development of the common law), administration of justice (with the creation of (*inter alia*) courts of common law and equity) and the 'alternative' processes of mediation and arbitration therefore

---

65. *Ibid*, p 203.
66. *Mediation and Arbitration in the Middle Ages: England 1154 to 1558* (2013, Oxford, HOLO Books: The Arbitration Press).

continued to derive substantially from Anglo-Saxon influences. At the same time, this period also saw the beginnings of a 'drift' toward types of process, procedures and features that are recognisable to modern eyes. Norman influences, meanwhile, continued to lead to inexorable growth in the prevalence of reliable written primary and secondary sources – so much so that Derek confessed to feeling the threat of being overwhelmed by their sheer volume.[67] These sources included the Curia Regis Rolls of the courts of Common Pleas and King's Bench (1189–1243); law reports in the form of the Year Books (1268–1535) and thereafter private reports published by law reporters ('nominate reports'); abridgments (an early form of practice guide); and a small number of scholarly treatises in Latin and French (though not in English until the 17th century).

In sum, therefore, this volume differs radically from its predecessors, as Derek was enabled to speak in far greater detail and with the support of reliable written evidence about the development and content of mediation and arbitration processes within an increasingly more integrated social order. Accordingly, the present discussion will focus on a number of salient matters identified by Derek.

Mediation

Derek showed that he was keen to debunk the idea that mediation really began in the United States in the 1960s – an idea that was even held by people who ought to have known better, such as a retired judge of the English High Court.[68]

Mediation was, by the time of King Henry II (r.1154–1189), well known from several standpoints.

(1) As related previously, the preference was, and remained, for settlement – either by private negotiation or by third party mediation – both *per se* and over arbitration. The king was interested in it to secure communal peace. This attitude was also true of the Church, which discouraged litigation, as it was of the secular authorities.

(2) Secondly, it was, for private disputes, part of the dispute resolution armoury of the traditional assemblies. These were, however, gradually on the wane by this time.

(3) The newly emerged king's courts – usually in the form of the justices in eyre (the itinerant or 'circuit' justices) – were showing themselves willing to accommodate attempts at settlement possibilities in litigation, as did the shire assemblies and the earlier local bishops' courts. Attempting settlement was a precondition to litigation

---

67. *Ibid*, p 4.
68. *Ibid*, p 6.

and arbitration, in the sense that a binding decision would only be made by a third party adjudicator if mediation failed. One particular example of this is the charmingly named 'loveday', by which parties were permitted by the court to arrange, or the court directed, attempts at voluntary or mediated settlement of their dispute at a specific time in proceedings. In this context, the word 'love' signified concord or settlement,[69] reflecting a 12th-century maxim that agreement prevails over law.[70] A settlement was therefore as good as a judgment. Another was a process which was evidenced in the Year Books and which Derek considered akin to modern med-arb, whereby parties would expressly agree to the appointment of arbitrators who would initially act as mediators but then assume their arbitral functions if mediation failed. Such processes were obviously untrammelled by a modern objection to med-arb, *viz* that the tribunal in its arbitral function would have been made aware of privileged information in exercising its mediation function.

(4) Private parties had, for a long time, also been free, as a matter of party autonomy, to appoint their own mediators and arbitrators. The fact that such mediation and arbitration increased during the period under discussion was concomitant to the waning of the assemblies (see (2) above). Processes that were recognisable to modern eyes slowly began to take shape.

(5) Other actors also came into play in providing or promoting both mediation and arbitration, principally the trade guilds for disputes between merchants. For its part, the Church encouraged the use of lovedays by private parties (see (3) above) during Christian festivals, while senior clergy were known to mediate disputes between religious institutions or, in one case of 1383, between the University of Oxford and a local convent in which the Archbishop of Canterbury and the bishops of London, Winchester, Ely and Hereford were appointed by the Pope as mediators.

(6) Finally, Derek also drew attention to a form of dispute resolution deliberately omitted as being beyond the scope of his 1994 chapter, *viz* the mediation of disputes between sovereigns or other persons of high rank asserting sovereign-type rights (an early but not rules-based forerunner of State-to-State mediation under public international law). Such 'sovereign' mediation was often conducted either by high ranking

---

69. JW Bennett, 'The Medieval Loveday' (1958) 30(3) *Speculum* 351-370, at 352.
70. Michael T Clanchy, 'Law and Love in the Middle Ages', in J Bossy, *Disputes and Settlements: Law and Human Relations in the West* (1983, Cambridge: Cambridge University Press), pp 47-48. Lovedays could not, however, always guarantee peace and non-violence: see David J Seipp, 'Don't Bring an Army to an Arbitration (England, 1411)', at pp 431-439 of this volume.

churchmen as delegates of the Pope or, in the most high-profile cases, by the Pope himself as a disinterested sovereign, reflecting the binding universal authority of the pre-Reformation Catholic Church.

The Norman and later Angevin realms stretched from the borders of Scotland to the Pyrenees and across the Mediterranean. There had been a long tradition of mediation in, *inter alia*, the Norman kingdom of Sicily, and both mediation and arbitration were known in Jerusalem following its conquest by the Normans in 1099. It cannot come as a surprise, therefore, that a variety of influences came to bear on mediation in England.

Arbitration

The period under discussion may be characterised in modern terms as one of consolidation, in which little changed in practice, though it witnessed the tentative beginnings of gradual moves toward recognisable forms of arbitration. As with mediation, the courts were prepared both to adjourn litigation proceedings in favour of arbitration and to accept the freedom of parties to refer their disputes to arbitration, pursuant to a bond, and appoint their own arbitrators. They were also prepared to enforce awards – though other actors, such as mercantile guilds, also had mechanisms of their own for enforcing awards in disputes between their members. Contracts containing arbitration clauses referring future disputes were at first unknown, with parties agreeing by bond to refer existing disputes – what in the present day would be called *ad hoc* arbitration agreements or submissions to arbitration.

Derek remarked that there was ample evidence in the sources of the existence and function of written bonds to arbitrate, the English equivalent of the Roman *compromissum*. They revealed a widespread acceptance of arbitration, both *per se* and as a matter of the range of subject-matter arbitrability, which, by comparison with arbitration under Roman law, was extremely wide. It embraced 'all manner of dispute' [sic], including land ownership, feudal incidents of status (such as wardship, marriage and dowry), debt recovery, employment, mercantile disputes (often through the merchant guilds) and maritime disputes (in which arbitration was a matter of custom and usage). From a particularly interesting historical standpoint, Derek noted that the bonds revealed the medieval origin of a common, uniquely English and still prevalent approach to breaking deadlock in a commercial tribunal comprising an even number of arbitrators, *viz* the umpire. An umpire (often someone of higher rank than the arbitrators) could be appointed both where arbitrators failed to agree on the terms of a proposed compromise or on an award determining the dispute.

Derek concluded that the period 1154–1558 was not known for reform, new ideas or procedural innovations in dispute resolution. Things therefore proceeded very much as they had before, though in some areas growth was apparent, such as in dispute resolution by mercantile guilds. Despite such conservatism, the available systems showed resilience in the face of severely adverse external factors, such as pestilence (the Black Death of 1348–1349) and civil wars, such as the Barons' Wars against kings John (r.1199–1216) and Henry III (r.1216–1272) and the Wars of the Roses (1455–1487), together with the longer-term changes they wrought in terms of social and economic dislocations. Similarly, private dispute resolution late in the period covered by the previous volume, *Early English Arbitration*, had been left largely unaffected by the upheavals of the civil war of 1135–1153 between King Henry I's daughter Matilda and his nephew Stephen of Blois (later King Stephen, r.1135–1154), known to history as 'the Anarchy'.

The Position of Women in Dispute Resolution

As a feminist, Derek had always been particularly interested in the role, status and position of women in dispute resolution. He referred to this matter both in his 1994 chapter and in his first three books, which gave some brief cross-cultural comparisons. He continued with a more detailed exploration of the subject in the 1154–1558 volume.

What Derek found was (*inter alia*) a continuing contrast between women's civil rights (for example, to hold land, to engage in trade, to sue, to agree to mediate or arbitrate and to be parties to settlement concords) and their position as mediators and arbitrators. There was no express legal bar at common law to or disqualification of women from being appointed in either of these capacities, and women at the 'sharp end' of dispute resolution were often of high social standing (such as a royal), yet they were not often appointed. There are few records of appointments in mediation, so much so that Derek turned to Geoffrey Chaucer for 'evidence', albeit in a literary context (*The Canterbury Tales*), not only of a female mediator but also of how she successfully went about her work as a mediator – for example, by explaining the purpose of reconciliation to the parties, caucusing with them and doing other things which, he commented, had a surprisingly modern resonance.

With regard to arbitration, Derek noted that there were few records of the appointment of women as arbitrators. As with mediators, they were women of high rank but, by contrast with mediation, the Church showed an antipathy toward the appointment of women which could only ever be overcome following strong political pressure. They were also rarely appointed for mercantile disputes, even if they had expertise in a particular trade. Female appointments were therefore exceptional and invariably reserved for high-profile disputes.

As an aside, and quite apart from gender issues, Derek also credits Chaucer generally for his early contribution toward the vocabulary of dispute resolution. In particular, he noted how the latter's use of the terms 'mediation' and 'arbitration' merited entries in the *Oxford English Dictionary*.[71]

5. Elizabethan Dispute Resolution

The next volume to emerge was *The Golden Age of Arbitration: Dispute Resolution Under Elizabeth I*.[72] The title of the book was perhaps not surprising, given that it celebrated the age of 'Gloriana'. In spite of the main title, the book deals, like its predecessors, with both mediation and arbitration during the reign of Queen Elizabeth I (r.1558-1603). Derek tells us that the processes were known collectively, in Elizabethan parlance, as *arbitrement*, though this word appears to suggest an emphasis on arbitration.[73]

What becomes immediately apparent from this work is how far dispute resolution advances during the period under discussion, so much so that there is an unmistakable modern resonance that even Derek's historian's caution of comparisons could not quite overcome. Like the title that preceded it, this one is also replete with reliable written sources in late Tudor (and therefore closer to modern) English.

Introduction

The opening pages immediately show how far dispute resolution in England had come, even before discussing procedural innovations. 'Arbitration was everywhere, as it had been in the past.'[74] Equally, as in the past, the preference among parties was to attempt mediation first, and this was the invariable first step taken by arbitrators. One thing that did change during the period under discussion was that it became by no means unknown for arbitration clauses to be inserted in substantive contracts, enabling any future disputes that might arise to be referred to arbitration.

In any event, discussion of mediation in the Elizabethan title is conspicuous by its relative absence, while arbitration is considered in detail. Given the amount of innovation in the latter by comparison with the 1154-1558 time period, this is perhaps not surprising. This section discusses a number of salient points raised by Derek.

Another feature of the time was that there were two systems of arbitration: private, which was entirely at the instance of the parties, and public,

---

71. *Historical Thesaurus of the Oxford English Dictionary* (2009, Oxford: Oxford University Press).

72. 2015, Oxford: HOLO Books: The Arbitration Press.

73. For a detailed explanation of the term, see Derek Roebuck, *Arbitration and Mediation in Seventeenth-Century England* (2017, Oxford: HOLO Books: The Arbitration Press), pp 28-42.

74. Roebuck, *op cit* (note 72), p 3.

which was no longer the province of shire assemblies but was the responsibility of the Privy Council. The Council appointed arbitrators pursuant to a request by one party (though it might in exceptional cases not bar both parties from 'going private' by agreement).

Arbitration Procedure

While records of private arbitrations were sparse, Privy Council records were replete with evidence of procedures. Derek assumed, no doubt correctly, that parties expected an identical level of adherence to procedural requirements and standards by arbitrators, whether party-appointed or Privy Council-appointed (or, per Derek, 'commissioned'). These would have included mediation at the outset of the reference, though private parties could agree, while the Privy Council could direct, that it be dispensed with.

One enduring procedural innovation noted by Derek that originated in Elizabethan times – and has very recently been given a new impetus by social distancing in response to COVID-19 – was documents-only arbitration. Although the norm was for oral hearings to be held, arbitrators could in appropriate cases dispense with hearings and decide cases entirely on the basis of the parties' written cases and supporting evidence.[75] Incidental reference was also made to the separate matter of there having been no rules of evidence limiting the tribunal's search for the facts in documents-only arbitrations.[76] Did this imply a right for the tribunal also to act inquisitorially, subject to the observance of natural justice? The text is not clear on this.

Mercantile Arbitration and Disputes with a Foreign Element

The late 16th century in particular saw the increasing projection of England's status as a maritime power, both militarily and in mercantile terms. Trade and competition with Continental Europe had grown exponentially since the 1154–1558 period and government policy was to encourage overseas trade. This was reflected in part by the incidence of disputes having a foreign element, such as those which involved both English and privileged Continental merchants resident in England (known as 'strangers' or 'friendly strangers'). Arbitrations concerned (*inter alia*) marine insurance or incidents that occurred on English soil or in its territorial waters, such as the interception and conversion of a foreign merchant's goods, and delivery and accounting disputes.

One of the more sophisticated and, indeed, recognisably modern aspects of arbitrations with a foreign element carried out in London was the qualifi-

75. *Ibid*, p 10.
76. *Ibid*.

cations of arbitrators and what qualifications were appropriate in particular types of case. High-profile commercial cases having a foreign element, might, in particular, have raised questions of the application and content of the unwritten law merchant (*lex mercatoria*), a civil law construct which foreign merchants preferred to the common law in resolving disputes. The Privy Council, having appointed arbitrators, wished to keep a watching brief on the proceedings. In addition to arbitrators with trade qualifications and doctors of common law, therefore, doctors of civil law from prominent Continental universities, such as those of Paris, Orléans and Padua, would also be appointed as arbitrators in mixed-expertise tribunals.

The Position of Women

Under the common law as it had developed, the substantive civil rights possessed by women tended to focus on whether they were single, married or widowed. Regardless, however, they were generally entitled to petition the Privy Council and so could refer disputes to mediation or arbitration, particularly if they were involved in business. These alternative processes could be of special benefit to poor or widowed women, as the Privy Council was concerned to enable them to obtain redress. It had in fact been prioritising this for the poor since 1491, during the reign of King Henry VII (r.1485–1509), no doubt as a contribution toward the maintenance of peace and social order in the wake of the Wars of the Roses.

The position of female mediators (*mediatrices*) and arbitrators (*arbitratrices*) remained much as it had before, with nothing in law that could inhibit appointments. Likewise, social attitudes operated to prevent appointments on any regular basis. The one exception to this was the Queen herself, who between 1582 and 1586 successfully mediated a reconciliation in an acrimonious dispute between two courtiers, Countess Bess of Hardwick and her husband George Talbot, sixth Earl of Shrewsbury. Their marriage had been put under severe strain following their appointment as jailers to Mary, Queen of Scots – not least amid rumours of an affair between Mary and the earl. Elizabeth considered her honour enhanced through her efforts to restore that of the parties. A good outcome for mediation and its occasional royal practitioner. Elizabeth considered her honour enhanced through her efforts to restore that of the parties – a good outcome both for mediation and for its occasional royal arbitratrix, and what might be termed a 'win-win' in modern dispute resolution parlance.

6. *Seventeenth-Century England*

The next of Derek's works was *Arbitration and Mediation in Seventeenth-Century England*,[77] his largest book, written in swift succession

---

77. 2017, Oxford: HOLO Books: The Arbitration Press.

to the Elizabethan volume – within a little under two years. He thought that it would be his final book on the history of arbitration and mediation; certainly, it was the final book that was written by him alone.[78] Thankfully, owing to collaborations with Susanna (published in 2018) and with Francis Calvert Boorman and Rhiannon Markless (published in 2019), his swansong as a chronicler would be postponed.

This volume covers dispute resolution within the context of a turbulent century that witnessed a battle for supremacy between the ruling House of Stuart and Parliament, a civil war and the abolition and restoration of the monarchy, bookended by the overthrow of two kings. Perhaps surprisingly, however, this turbulence appears to have had little effect on the progress of dispute resolution, just as had been the case during the periods covered by *Early English Arbitration* and *Mediation and Arbitration in the Middle Ages*.

Introduction

Derek's commentary demonstrates that, far from merely following the dispute resolution policies, processes and practices begun under the Tudors, the Stuarts actively sought to make them more efficient and to broaden the system's reach. That they largely succeeded in doing so and in attracting users is demonstrated, in turn, by the following quotation.

> The most striking feature of dispute resolution in the 17th century was its flexibility. Each process was tailor-made to suit the parties' needs, whether established by the state or privately. ... [A]rbitrators could accomplish all that any judge could and much more. ... The range of remedies was limited only by the imaginations of the parties and arbitrators. Even private arbitrators could award damages for delay in payment.

The accolade accorded by the opening words would not go amiss – indeed, would be welcome – in 21st-century dispute resolution.

Encouraging Arbitration and Mediation

It is submitted that the perennial preference on the part of the authorities for private dispute resolution in general and mediation in particular was motivated, at least in part, by a desire to maintain peace and stability and to avoid strife at a particularly restive time, both politically and socially. Schemes were therefore introduced and institutions equipped to support this objective.

First, the early Stuart kings (James I, r.1603–1625 and Charles I, r.1625–1649) continued to apply a state-sponsored dispute resolution scheme

---

78. *Ibid*, p 447.

originally introduced by Elizabeth I, whereby services were provided at no charge to resolve all kinds of controversies involving people from all walks of life, both English and foreign, but particularly the poor and (as discussed in the Elizabethan volume) women.

Secondly, the Privy Council, in the further exercise of its existing public arbitration functions, began to assume powers from 1614 onward to arbitrate, or to delegate to arbitrators, cases brought in the assize and Chancery courts and in the colonies. Derek was informed by another scholar that arbitrator commissions by the Privy Council must have numbered into the thousands over an 80-year period, though it was not clear to which period(s) of time this assertion applied. Derek was himself unable to glean precise figures from the Privy Council records. Regardless, what was clear was that the routine manner in which the Privy Council previously dealt with requests for arbitration had changed from 'hands off' (with exceptions) to 'hands on'. In spite of this, however, the incidence of arbitrations and mediations ordered by the Council had markedly declined by 1629. From 1641, the Privy Council as then constituted was no more, a victim of the struggle for supremacy between king and Parliament; its public arbitration jurisdiction, and indeed public arbitration itself, disappeared with it.

Finally, local archives, court records and the law reports revealed that all common law courts (King's Bench, Common Pleas and Exchequer) regularly referred litigation cases before them to arbitration, as did the Court of Chancery, which exercised equitable jurisdiction. What had begun as an occasional practice of the courts in the 15th century became standard practice in the 17th, with the courts referring cases to arbitration as a rule of court at the request of a party and appointing arbitrators, who could include merchants and other lay (non-lawyer) experts. Even pre-rogative courts, such as the Star Chamber, not only exercised mediation and arbitral functions themselves but also took responsibility for super-vising the conduct of arbitrations ordered by other courts. None of this could remotely be considered to have smacked of the 'judicial jealousy' of arbitration later asserted by Holdsworth. As previously discussed, this was debunked by Derek in his article of 1994,[79] his 1994 chapter having asserted, in turn, that arbitration had happily co-existed with the courts for nearly half a millennium.[80]

The Position of Women

In the 17th century, as in earlier times, there was nothing to prevent women from submitting disputes to arbitration or mediation by agreement with their opponents. Before 1641, they could petition for public arbitration

79. *Supra*, note 26.
80. *Supra*, note 25.

through the Privy Council and appear in proceedings before it, both as petitioners and as defendants.

As in Elizabethan times, there was no law that inhibited women from acting as arbitrators, whereas in practice such appointments were rare. Likewise, no law inhibited them from accepting appointments as mediators. The sources reveal, however, that they often mediated disputes within familial contexts, both their own and those of others, and might even educate their male offspring in mediation skills.

The Development of Arbitration Law – Or, Modest Beginnings to the Shape of Things to Come

Before the late 17th century, arbitration law had evolved slowly and incrementally through precedents of the courts. For an ancient and venerable process, statute law – which today is standard in this field – came relatively late, in England at least, and marked the beginning of the end of arbitration at common law (though not its complete demise). An unsuccessful attempt had previously been made to draft arbitration legislation in the later years of the Interregnum (1649–1660). In August 1696, the newly created Board of Trade gave instructions for the drafting of what became the first English statute, the Arbitration Act 1698.[81] The manner of creation of this Act may be said – tongue in cheek – to have had an 'Ancient Greek' origin, for its draftsman, John Locke (a member of the Board), was not a lawyer but a philosopher.

The 1698 Act was brief and narrow in its ambit, but endured without substantive amendment until the 1830s and enacted rules that would form part of the consolidated English Arbitration Act 1889. In essence, it made submissions to arbitration in writing by the parties (whether by bond or other instrument) irrevocable by making them rules of the court, thereby making submissions enforceable and attempts to revoke them punishable for contempt of court. Submissions to arbitration could concern either existing or future disputes and it was no longer necessary for parties first to bring proceedings in court in order to have disputes referred to arbitration. The Act also provided that an arbitration or 'umpirage' procured by means of corruption or other undue means (such as fraud) would be null and void and of no effect. The Act did not, however, deal with other fundamental matters, which would be left to another day. These included provisions as to the conduct of arbitration, as well as powers of the court to assist and supervise arbitrations and to determine questions of law.[82]

---

81. An Act for Determining Differences by Arbitration, 9 Will III, Cap XV.
82. Paul L Sayre, 'Development of Commercial Arbitration Law', (1928) 37 *Yale Law Journal* 595-617, at 596.

Derek was clear about what he thought of the scope and importance of the 1698 Act.[83] First, it reduced litigation because parties became empowered to refer disputes to arbitration directly, subject only to making them rules of court to ensure their enforceability. Secondly, the rules of court procedure provided an incentive to recalcitrant parties to comply with their obligations to arbitrate. Finally, the Act helped arbitration to become routine in important areas of commerce, notably insurance, construction, partnership and standard forms of contract – much as it is today.

7. The Long Eighteenth Century

The last of Derek's books, co-written on this occasion with Francis Calvert Boorman and Rhiannon Markless (together, the 'co-authors'), was published under the title *English Arbitration and Mediation in the Long Eighteenth Century*.[84] The use of the word 'long' denotes an historian's device for discussing 'a century in which events occurred before its beginning and after its end, but not neatly within it: subject matter, not time, is therefore the governing factor'.[85] Practical examples of this usage by historians include the various Anglo-French conflicts of 1702–1815, which some historians have called the 'Second Hundred Years War' and which were fought during the Long 18th century, and the 125-year period of wars, revolutions and political and social upheavals between 1789 and 1918, dubbed the 'Long 19th century' by socialist historians.

Introduction

In this volume, the 'Long 18th century' was bookended by the years 1698–1708 (involving the creation of the East India Company by a merger of two rivals) and 1794–1815 (with the restoration of trading relations between Great Britain and the newly formed United States of America following the end of the American War of Independence, or Revolutionary War and 'round 2', the later Anglo-American War). What was common to these dates and events was what the co-authors referred to as 'arbitration', though it was arguably more something akin to it than the beast itself.

83. Roebuck, *op cit* (note 77), pp 436–437.
84. 2019, Oxford: HOLO Books: The Arbitration Press.
85. 'Periodization … is one of the key ways we manage the world history enterprise. Increasingly — though probably less uniformly than one might wish – it has replaced the random juxtaposition of civilizations as part of the … ways we really think about world history overall. As in any historical endeavour, periodization is an attempt to manage change, and present it coherently, by noting points where key breaks in framework occur. In world history, periodization has come to convey, particularly, shifts in the pattern of interactions and contacts among many, though not always all, major societies.' (Peter N Stearns, 'Long 19th Century? Long 20th? Retooling That Last Chunk of World History Periodization' (February 2009) 42(2) *The History Teacher* 223–228, at 223).

In the earlier instance, the merger of the constituent East India companies had been agreed in 1702, but with separation of stock and debts maintained for a transitional period of seven years. This expedient but inefficient means of corporate governance was resolved by the arbitration of Sidney, 1st Earl Godolphin, the Lord High Treasurer,[86] who had been appointed by Act of Parliament with jurisdiction to determine the companies' credits and debts, thus creating a single set of accounts. The rest is history: the East India Company went on to govern India and parts of China until its ignominious dissolution following the Indian Mutiny and the Chinese Opium Wars.

The essential seeds of modern arbitration in public international law were sown in 18th century Anglo-US diplomacy. It first emerged with the Jay Treaty (or Jay's Treaty 1794),[87] which was made in an attempt to de-escalate long-running tensions in the aftermath of the American War of Independence (or Revolutionary War) of 1775-1783. This treaty provided for the appointment of 'mixed commissions' to resolve legal disputes between the two countries (such as US-Canada boundary disputes), 'mixed' in this context referring to a commission comprising members from both countries, but without any disinterested members. There was, however, another element of 'mixing', in that the commissions also resolved claims for compensation between US and British merchants that had arisen out of the conflict.

The Jay Treaty system was generally considered to have worked very well, so much so that the system of US-Canada boundary and claims commissions provided for thereunder was revived, with modifications, by the Treaty of Ghent (1814),[88] which ended the Anglo-American War of 1812–1814. The principal difference between the Jay and the Ghent systems was that, under the latter, disputes were referred to disinterested third party umpires if the party-appointed commissioners disagreed.

The co-authors did not hesitate to describe the Godolphin adjudication and the Jay/Ghent processes as 'arbitration'. However, while it may have been tempting to do this, the precise nature of the processes did not entirely attract that characterisation. Godolphin did not arbitrate a 'dispute', as such but sought to resolve a political controversy following a legislative appointment. The result of the 'arbitration' was not 'dispute resolution' as such but what might be characterised today as dispute management or prevention. In essence, the Jay/Ghent commissions were, certainly with regard to the State to State disputes, formalised extensions of diplomacy. According to

---

86. The predecessor office to the present UK Chancellor of the Exchequer.
87. The Treaty of Amity, Commerce, and Navigation 1794.
88. The Treaty of Peace and Amity between His Britannic Majesty and the United States of America 1814.

an anonymous early 20th century US commentator, describing the original Jay system:

> Such commissions, while not strictly courts of arbitration, because they lack the element of an impartial umpire, embody the fundamental principle in arbitration, the substitution of law for force in international relations.[89]

The co-authors preferred, however, the view of a contemporary US commentator, Professor Roger P Alford, who described the commissions as 'the beginning of the modern era of international arbitration.'[90] While Professor Alford and his anonymous counterpart of 1902 may have disagreed as to the precise characterisation of the Jay/Ghent processes in dispute resolution under public international law, both clearly saw significant elements of arbitration in them that would reach its *apotheosis* in the Hague Conventions on the Pacific Settlement of International Disputes (Hague I) 1899–1907.[91]

The Background of Dispute Resolution

While the co-authors recognised the impact of international dispute resolution, they also saw arbitration as a powerful tool for merchants and manufacturers at the domestic level. Arbitration adapted to new types of dispute that arose from the construction of canals and of stationary steam engines to power the factories, mines and construction activities of the nascent Industrial Revolution. The new technologies required specialist knowledge of their design and operation, not least where it was necessary to decide such matters as where liability lay, intellectual property (IP) rights and valuation when disputes arose, and means of imparting this knowledge to arbitral tribunals. The sources revealed that parties to arbitrations regularly appointed architects and surveyors both as arbitrators and as technical advisers or assessors to arbitral tribunals. As technologies advanced, members of the new profession of civil engineer made their names not only as inventors (for example, by pursuing IP right claims in arbitration) but also as expert advisers, both to parties and to arbitrators. The authors also unearthed a source showing that James Watt, the Scots-born inventor of the stationary steam engine, had acted as co-arbitrator in determining a claim for non-payment of the price of a cutting engine and a counterclaim based on allegations of poor workmanship in

---

89. 'Progress of International Arbitration', *New York Times*, 1 June 1902.
90. Roger P Alford, 'The American Influence on International Arbitration', (2002) 19(1) *Ohio State Journal On Dispute Resolution* 69-88 at 72.
91. See, in this regard, the contribution by Bruno de Loynes de Fumichon in the present volume, 'The *Alabama* Arbitration: From Compromise to Legacy' (pp 229-257).

its construction. This was only the beginning of over two hundred years of involvement of civil engineers in decision-making capacities, as arbitrators, independent experts or construction adjudicators. The Institution of Civil Engineers, which would later facilitate dispute resolution by promulgating model arbitration clauses and procedural rules and by appointing arbitrators, was founded in 1818, shortly outside the period covered by the Long 18th century volume. Other professional institutions exercising similar responsibilities would follow as the 19th century progressed (eg, the Royal Institute of British Architects (1834) and the Royal Institution of Chartered Surveyors (1868)).

In any event, the authors remarked that entering into private arbitration and mediation in the 18th century was an ordinary incident in people's lives. The fact that it was habitual tended to make it unremarkable, though the co-authors remarked at the same time that the 18th century saw the beginnings of greater formalism and legalism in the arbitral process, a trend begun in the 17th. The types of dispute most frequently arbitrated concerned ownership of land, boundaries, enclosure of common land, trade, manufacture, insurance, shipping, building, canal construction and mining.

On an interpersonal level, quite apart from cases involving breaches of contract and torts, arbitration was well known in the 18th century in cases involving family and other personal relationships, such as inheritance on intestacy, wills and trusts, as well as feuds between parents and offspring and between offspring themselves. The process could be used as much to avoid disputes as to resolve them. The co-authors even found an instance of arbitration of a claim for breach of promise of marriage. They concluded that arbitration had an important social role to play in resolving, minimising and avoiding disputes as well as keeping the peace, a theme that has run through the previous volumes.

As was previously the case, mediation of disputes was also favoured, particularly between individuals.

The Position of Women

As before, women regularly brought claims in arbitration, in respect both of personal and business disputes. So far as arbitral appointments were concerned, the co-authors found that, whereas appointments of women in the 17th century had been irregular, in the 18th century they were non-existent. The only exception to this trend was Queen Anne (r.1702-1714), who in 1707 arbitrated a dispute between two foreign dignitaries. The co-authors do not mention women having mediated in disputes generally, though they do state that, by contrast with the 16th and 17th centuries, women only infrequently acted in this capacity in family disputes.

8. *Louis XIV's France*

The next book considered here was published in 2002, thus post-dating Derek's 1994 chapter but preceding all of his other books. Entitled *The Charitable Arbitrator: How to Mediate and Arbitrate in Louis XIV's France*,[92] it comprises the text of a long letter to French clerics, provincial governors and 'Lords of Great Fiefs' written by Alexandre de la Roche, Sieur de la Rivière, Prior of St Pierre. The first edition was published in 1666 and presented in 1668 to King Louis XIV (r.1643–1715) under the title (in translation) of *The Charitable Arbitrator: TO PREVENT SUITS AND DISPUTES, Or, at least to finish them quickly, without trouble and cost*. The text is presented both in the original French and in a translation by Derek himself, along with a substantial and detailed 93-page commentary, also by him. The letter in fact takes the form of a manual (the manual) on the resolution of all disputes by mediation and arbitration.

As Neil Kaplan wrote in his obituary of Derek,[93] La Roche was 'an unknown cleric (whom Derek, of course, tracked down) explaining that the courts were being subjected to chicanery and that the King should impose arbitration on warring parties.'

The context within which the letter was written was the disuse into which arbitration in 17th century France had fallen, despite the existence of arbitration laws. As one commentator explained, by way of example, ' … King Francis II (r 1559-1560) permitted arbitration and trade with the Germans, Swiss and Italians under the Edict on Arbitrators of August 1560. However, French *Parlements* later stifled arbitration.'[94]

The *Parlements*, some 13 of them, were the highest royal law courts and courts of appeal at the provincial level in France under the *Ancien Régime*, the most powerful of them being that of Paris. The pendulum did not swing back in arbitration's favour in France until after the Revolution of 1789.

We are indebted to Derek for reinvigorating and more widely disseminating a work both of polemic and of persuasion and practical utility. By providing doctrinal as well as practical reasons for mediating and arbitrating and guidance on how the processes should be implemented, the manual resonates down the centuries and provides invaluable comparative and historical lessons.

Introduction to the manual

Derek emphasises three things in particular. First, that all disputes should be mediated and, if necessary, arbitrated. The manual is on all fours with the policy of dispute resolution down the centuries, as reported by him, that

---

92. 2002, Oxford: HOLO Books: The Arbitration Press.
93. Kaplan, *op cit* (note 3).
94. The Rt Hon Beverley McLachlin, 'A Judicial Perspective on Arbitration: Where Are We Headed? The Kaplan Lecture 2019' [2020] *Asian Dispute Review* 59-69 at 60.

mediation should be tried first. Secondly, that La Roche does not propose anything radical but calls on the highest authorities, both spiritual and temporal, in support of his case, from the gospels of the New Testament to edicts and ordinances laid down by French monarchs from Charlemagne to Louis XIV. Thirdly, he invokes the force of precedent by mentioning a host of practitioners in France, both religious and lay, and overseas, such as in the republic of Venice and in the Eastern Church.

History of Arbitration in *Ancien Régime* France

As part of setting out the context to the manual, Derek discusses extensively the history of arbitration, arbitration law and its reform in France. From the earliest times, French kings claimed the roles of mediator and arbitrator when requested to resolve disputes, both civil and religious. As Derek put it, the kings did not claim a monopoly for the royal courts but were prepared to allow people the freedom to resolve their disputes privately. No doubt, as in other jurisdictions discussed in Derek's books, there was an agenda of preserving peace and social order in the attitude of the authorities.

The years between 1363 and 1629 saw a number of pieces of legislation, edicts and a decree concerning, in particular, arbitration. Derek mentions the following.

(1) An ordinance (*ordonnance*) of King John II (r.1350–1364), dated 1363, which provided (*inter alia*) that an appeal against an arbitral award could only be made to a 'good man' (*bonus vir*), which process should not be bypassed by an appeal to the royal courts.

(2) Two edicts (*édits*) of King Francis II (r.1559–1560), dated 1560. The first, on the execution of arbitral awards, sought to cut down the number of appeals in litigation by promoting direct negotiation and settlement by parties or resolution by arbitrators. The second, on merchants' disputes, was aimed at fostering trade by cutting down on litigation and its harmful effects, particularly by forcing merchants who resorted to chicanery after breaking commercial agreements to go instead to arbitration and to appoint arbitrators (failing which the court would make default appointments). Derek commented that the second edict was in some ways a precursor of the *tribunaux de commerce*, which suggests that the authorities well understood the benefits of mercantile specialists resolving disputes.

(3) An ordinance of King Charles IX (r.1560–1574), dated 1566. This preserved previous legislation on the arbitration of disputes between near relatives regarding distributions and other differences and required the same to be observed without impediment.

(4)   An ordinance of Henry III (r.1574–1589), dated 1579. This also concerned the legislation referred to in (3) above and required it to be observed according to its form and tenor.

(5)   A decree (*arrest* – later *arrêt*) of King Henry IV (r.1589–1610), dated 1610. This sought to provide for the appointment of 'charitable arbitrators' who would determine the disputes of the poor ('widows, orphans, ... gentlefolk, merchants, workers and other unhappy people') – both as plaintiffs and as defendants – for no fee. The proposal was not taken forward as the king was assassinated the same year and later attempts to implement it failed. The proposal had little to say about arbitration *per se*, though the king's confidant and adviser, Maximilien de Béthune, Duc de Sully, stated in his memoirs (published in English translation in 1756) that he had drafted a scheme for arbitration law reform. Notably, arbitrators would be 'a small number of grave and reverend old men', La Roche's equivalent of King John II's *bonus vir*. Clearly, there would have been no place for women as dispute resolvers in this scheme.

(6)   An ordinance of King Louis XIII (r.1610-1643), dated 1629 (the *Code Michaud*). This also insisted on the full observance of the instruments referred to in (2) and (3) above.

In 1657, during the reign of Louis XIV (r.1643-1715), the *Parlement* of Paris confirmed that the king remained the natural arbitrator for religious disputes. The *Parlement* itself, meanwhile, arbitrated disputes in the civil sphere between merchants' guilds, workers and employers, and French and foreign merchants.

Louis XIV himself, advised by his chief minister Jean-Baptiste Colbert, engaged in a programme of law reform from 1664 onward, culminating in the *Ordonnance Civile* of 1667. This period coincided with that in which La Roche was putting together his manual and his epistle to the king. The king declared his opposition to chicanery (*chican*) in the courts, his determination to replace contradictory decrees made by his Council over legal procedure (including the assertion of 'sovereignty' by the *Parlement* of Paris to block appeals to the king against its judgments) and to rationalise the system. While recognising in its preamble the ills of tampering with or non-observance of previous ordinances, the existence of chicanery and of multiple and conflicting interpretations of laws and the need to expedite litigation business more promptly, nevertheless the 1667 *Ordonnance* showed no sign of incorporating arbitration or mediation. As Derek commented:

La Roche must have been disappointed that, despite the king's apparent approval of his manual and the widespread support he [La Roche] insists the first edition [of 1666] received, there is nothing in the *Ordonnance* which directly promotes arbitration or mediation. Perhaps La Roche's disappointment explains the impatience occasionally revealed in [the second] ... edition of 1668, and the persistence with which he is determined to drive his message home.[95]

Frustrated aspirations on the part of reformers of dispute resolution laws and processes have clearly been a perennial theme down the ages.

Also of great interest in further establishing the context of arbitration was Derek's discovery of a legal encyclopaedia which summarised the law as it stood at the time of La Roche's efforts, the *Répertoire Universelle et Raisonné de Jurisprudence*. With regard to arbitration, he noted its statement that while women had been barred from acting as arbitrators since the time of the Emperor Justinian,[96] canon law mitigated this for 'women of eminent rank', who included queens and princesses. With regard to arbitrators, the *Répertoire* stated that their 'powers' (in reality, jurisdiction in modern parlance) were limited to what parties had agreed in their *compromise*. With regard to 'functions' (ie, powers properly so called), it was noted that these were the same as those of judges. Thus, arbitrators could require evidence of disputed facts, hear party testimony, accept oaths and make interlocutory decisions.

The Manual: Salient Chapters

A select number of chapters are summarised below on the basis of their particular interest, relevance and qualities as points of comparison with what went before (see Derek's 2004–2019 commentaries) and with contemporary standards and practice. They are based upon Derek's English translation at pp 131–239 of his book.

(1) *Chapter III*: 'General peace could be established throughout the kingdom' and the evils of chicanery, 'the most lamentable plague on the State could be ameliorated if the clergy (in particular the *Curé*) were prepared to 'lend a hand'.

(2) *Chapter V*: The primary quality of the good *Curé* is to be able to win the confidence of the parties. In addressing parties' animosities, enmities and estrangements, he must hear their complaints very patiently, sympathise with their weakness and share their grief. 'Everybody else' (presumably members of the laity) can also do this.

95. Roebuck, *op cit* (note 90).
96. See Roebuck and De Fumichon, *op cit* (note 50), p 138; Hoe and Roebuck, *op cit* (note 54), p 1. Further, in the 13th century, Saint Thomas Aquinas had added the alleged inability of women to reason as a bar to appointment: *ibid*, p 2.

Neither ability nor eloquence is required, only zeal and good will: see also Chapter X, which not only reiterated this point but also was dismissive of any idea that a charitable arbitrator should have 'the grand manner'.

(3) *Chapter VII*: Bishops can and should settle lawsuits and differences in their dioceses. This is ordained by the New Testament and as a means of assisting the king's justice and, in the words of Charlemagne, maintaining 'equity, peace and concord'.

(4) *Chapter XV*: In the same vein, provincial governors should mediate settlement of disputes. Applying another message that appears throughout the manual, this can be done 'without difficulty, without trouble and without cost'. Chapters XVI and XVII contained similar injunctions to the 'Lords of great Fiefs' to mediate the settlement of their vassals' disputes, the 'Noblemen and ordinary *Bourgeois*' to require their tenants to settle differences, and the 'Great Lords' to settle their lawsuits.

(5) *Chapter XIX*: The 'Lower Classes and the Weak' can and should settle lawsuits with those more powerful than them.

(6) *Chapter XXI*: This chapter gives advice on selecting arbitrators. Parties but not mediators should nominate them. Where a three-arbitrator tribunal is required, each party should nominate one and agree on a third. Failing such agreement, the mediator should make a list from which the parties may strike out the names of those about which they have doubts. Arbitrators should be persons of probity and recognised ability.

(7) *Chapter XXII*: The duty of a good mediator is to persuade the parties, which requires patience, common sense, an appropriate manner, good will and the wisdom and discretion not to offend a party.

(8) *Chapter XXIII*: Like a mediator, an arbitrator should be patient, prudent and, above all, charitable. He should also be a good listener, knowledgeable, skilful and held in high esteem. Parties should not treat their opponents' nominees in the same manner as their opponents and should particularly avoid dislike, hatred and abuse.

(9) *Chapter XXX*: This chapter contains a suggested precedent for a 'compromise' – that is to say, an arbitration agreement or *compromis*, not terms settling a dispute – which the parties may amend by agreement. The precedent is limited to declaring the intention to arbitrate and nominating the parties' arbitrators and the third arbitrator. '[T]he shorter and simpler the compromise [*sic*] [,] the better.'

In spite of the manual having been inspired by the King Henry IV's charitable arbitrator proposals and containing a number of chapters directed to them, its contents clearly sought to have wider application to mediation and arbitration. This makes the manual worthy of comparative historical and processual study for both common and civil lawyers.

9. *Women in Dispute Resolution*

Clearly, on the grounds of time and space constraints alone and despite his deep interest in and support for feminism and gender equality, Derek's 1994–2019 commentaries could do no more than scratch the surface of a very wide subject: the place of women in dispute resolution down the ages. A more detailed treatment of this subject was therefore required. It duly arrived in 2018 with the publication of another co-authored volume, this time with Susanna, *Women in Disputes: A History of European Women in Mediation and Arbitration*.[97]

Like Derek's other works, this volume covered European jurisdictions and time periods from Ancient Greece to England and Continental Europe in the 18th century. It goes further, however, by also discussing the early American colonies. Of particular interest at the outset, however, is the discussion of a female figure from the Biblical Holy Land. This was Deborah, 'one of the very few judging prophets, the only person functioning as a resolver of disputes at that time',[98] who was the only female to hold the position of an Israelite judge and to be recorded in the Old Testament's *Book of Judges*. She settled disputes among members of her community by mediation and adjudication while sitting under a palm tree in the Ephraim hills - possibly the first instance of what is called 'palm tree justice' today, albeit in a pejorative sense.[99]

Women in Disputes is a fascinating account of women's place in and treatment by the dispute resolution process and those who have administered (or, perhaps more accurately, dominated) it down the ages. Also in common with Derek's solo and other co-authored works, *Women in Disputes* draws extensively from events, disputes and their female resolvers both in myth and in literature, ancient and more modern, as well as those in real life. As Derek demonstrated both in his 1994 chapter and in *Ancient Greek Arbitration*, these sources also have lessons to teach us about human (and, indeed, divine) behaviour in disputes. This approach helps to give the book the added cachet of a volume that is as readily readable for personal interest as it is a work of historical reference.

Whatever office and respect may have been accorded to Deborah in the Old Testament, however, it obviously did not permeate through to the

---

97. Susanna Hoe and Derek Roebuck , *op cit* (note 54). The genesis of this book (and others) is discussed in Susanna's chapter in the present volume, 'A Room Shared: My Late Husband as Feminist' (pp 3-30).
98. Hoe and Roebuck, *op cit* (note 54), pp 6–7.
99. Cf Jan Paulsson, 'Omnipotence Fantasies: The Kaplan Lecture 2020' [2021] *Asian Dispute Review* 10–17, at 11.

treatment of women in later centuries, both under Continental European civil law and (to a lesser but still unacceptable extent) the English common law. Under the Roman law-based civil law, in particular, the assumptions made by the Emperor Justinian in the sixth century AD/CE and St Thomas Aquinas in the 13th about the suitability and appropriateness of women for private judicial and even mediatory office[100] continued to hold sway. The authors summed up the position perfectly in the following passage, the final line of which is taken from Justinian:[101]

> Such assumptions were not restricted to the Middle Ages nor to those whose concern was to retain power to themselves in a society ordered to give men power and privilege. From that time to the present, it has been quite natural for otherwise careful scholars to take it for granted that 'women should remember their modesty and do what nature has allowed and abstain from what it has prohibited'.

With respect to Justinian, however, 'what nature has allowed' comes across as a logical fallacy. Other than through physical and environmental limitations and evolution, nature itself (defined by the *Cambridge English Dictionary* as 'the force that is responsible for physical life and that is sometimes spoken of as a person') does not engage in 'prohibition': this is entirely the province of humankind (usually male dominated) and its doctrines, hence its role in creating gender conflict.

The main focus of *Women in Disputes* is not, however, a straightforward recitation or reportage of history, for history is nothing without people, from the highest ranks of the social order to the lowest, with all their qualities, flaws and foibles. The authors continue the approach that Derek adopted throughout his earlier books of finding out why people fell into disputes, what their interests and agendas were, what motivated the actions they took, why they chose particular mechanisms, how the dispute resolution systems responded and, where records are available, ascertaining outcomes.

To this end, the book is a fascinating collection of profiles of the great, the good, the not so great and the relatively lowly, discussing the position of women not only as parties to disputes and users of dispute resolution systems, but also as arbitrators and mediators in their own right. In this latter regard, high profile figures, such as queens and titled women abounded. Among the best known were Eleanor of Aquitaine (wife of King Henry II of England); Jeanne of Valois (mother of Philippa of Hainault, wife of King Edward III of England), a 'peaceweaver' between disputing communities;

---

100. See *supra* note 94.
101. Hoe and Roebuck, *op cit* (note 54), p 2.

Margaret of Anjou (wife of King Henry VI of England), who negotiated truces during the Wars of the Roses; Queen Elizabeth I of England, who arbitrated between two courtiers (see section (5), *Elizabethan Dispute Resolution*, above); and Queen Anne of England, who in 1707 arbitrated one of the first inter-State disputes under what later came to be known as the law of nations (and, later still, public international law): see section (7), *The 'Long' Eighteenth Century*. Titled women were also known to arbitrate: a well-known example was Margaret Beaufort, mother of King Henry VII of England, who arbitrated disputes on her son's behalf when he was absent.

In conclusion, it is worthy of note that, in the Middle Ages, as now, there were a variety of differently named processes that, one way or another, stemmed from or were related to mediation or arbitration. This has a very modern resonance, as today's 'alternative (or 'appropriate') dispute resolution' (ADR) is constantly marked by ever-emerging binding and non-binding processes adapted to different 'markets' of users (ie, particular trades, industries and professions), their needs and the types of dispute that arise in their *milieux*. Susanna and Derek demonstrate that, over and above formal and informal arbitration processes, this has always been so, and women have been a common factor in all of them:

> ... involv[ing] every sort of dispute resolved by any means. What do emerge are the myriad ways, sometimes ingenious, of doing so, and the terms used to describe them. Beyond arbitration and mediation, other terms stand out: decisive conciliator; reconciler; intercession; participant of mercy; ... beneficent interference; intermeddling in political matters; negotiator; peacemaker and our favourite, 'peaceweaver'.[102]

There is nothing that is new under the sun.[103]

Epilogue

Reference has previously been made to Derek's gentle humour, which extended as much to the foibles of dispute resolution and its exponents (of both of which there are many) as to anything else. It is therefore appropriate that this commemoration of his work should end with a mention of *A Miscellany of Disputes*,[104] a humorous but scholastically curated collection of fables and stories about dispute resolution from myth and reality, many of them from the Classical era and from Confucian China.

It is sufficient unto the purpose to highlight one story involving the writer of *The Charitable Arbitrator* under the title 'Resolution',[105] which no doubt would have particularly appealed to Derek:

102. *Ibid*, p 101.
103. Ecclesiastes 1:9.
104. 2000, Oxford: HOLO Books: The Arbitration Press.
105. *Ibid*, p 117.

Perhaps the best known story about mediation was told by Alexandre de la Roche, Prior of St Pierre in 1665. An incompetent but likeable mediator had no idea how to bring the parties to a settlement. After every adjournment, he wined and dined with the parties until he became their friend. No nearer a resolution of their dispute, but increasingly unwilling to offend him, they decided to drop it. Or, as John Milton puts it [in *Paradise Lost*]:

'What reinforcement we may gain from hope;
If not, what resolution from despair.'

And so this review of Derek's *oeuvres* comes to a close. As is so often the case, William Shakespeare comes to the aid of the party with an appropriate conclusion:

The end crowns all;
And that old common arbitrator, Time,
Will one day end it.[106]

It is hoped that Derek's baton will also 'one day' be picked up, so that the story may be taken further into the 19th century – perhaps even the 'long' 19th century, up to the eve of World War I,[107] and with an emphasis on the then developing areas of mediation and arbitration under what would later become rules-based public international law and international relations[108] and their role in furthering Derek's most deeply held passion: peace.[109]

In addition to calling for a detailed history of arbitration in China in his 1994 chapter (see Part Two, section 2),[110] Derek prevailed elsewhere upon scholars to do the same for the history of mediation and arbitration in the United States.[111] His reading of secondary sources suggested

---

106. *Troilus and Cressida*, Act IV, scene 5.
107. Stearns, *op cit* (note 85). Or, alternatively and more ambitiously, a 'very long' 19th century up to 1945, given developments in international dispute resolution, private and public, during the interwar years in particular.
108. The significance of which is highlighted by De Fumichon (*supra*, note 91). See also WL Westermann, 'Interstate Arbitration in Antiquity' (March 1902) 2(3) *The Classical Journal*, 197–211, which draws some direct lines between Ancient Greece and modernity, describing inter-State mediation and arbitration in both as 'an experiment' (at p 211). See further Henry S Fraser, 'Sketch of the History of International Arbitration' (1926) 11 *Cornell Law Quarterly* 179–208. Both articles reflect the growing importance of dispute resolution under public international law following the adoption of the Hague I Conventions.
109. Derek had been very active in opposing the Vietnam War and was a past Head of Research for Amnesty International: see Susanna's obituary, *supra* (note 5). His *Disputes and Differences* volume (*supra*, note 19) was dedicated to 'all who work for peace'.
110. Reproduced in this volume at pp 63-96.
111. Derek Roebuck, 'The English Inheritance – What the First American Colonists Knew of Mediation and Arbitration' (2016) 2(5) *Journal of Dispute Resolution* 325–350. This article

that there may be a wealth of undiscovered primary sources in the US but 'complacent ignorance' as to its existence. His conclusion was that this field of investigation was ripe for exploitation by new generations of scholars, but that '[t]he American story must be left to American authors'.

Furthermore, if Derek's *oeuvres* were to mark the beginnings of even wider and more extensive historical, multi-disciplinary, processual, cross-cultural and gender investigation and discourse at the comparative level, then so much the better. Mission accomplished!

is replicated in the current volume at pp 113-162. See also Frank D Emerson, 'History of Arbitration Practice and Law' (1970) 19 *Cleveland State Law Review* 155–164, at 158–159. The colonists were familiar with both good and bad arbitration 'imports', such as, respectively, the English Arbitration Act 1698 and judicial jealousy of arbitration: see Henry Horwitz and James Oldham, 'John Locke, Lord Mansfield and Arbitration During the Eighteenth Century' (1993) 36(1) *The Historical Journal* 137-159; James Oldham and Su Jin Kim, 'Arbitration in America: The Early History', *Law & History Review* 31(1), 241-266 (2013).

BOOK REVIEW: ENGLISH ARBITRATION AND MEDIATION IN THE LONG 18TH CENTURY

By Derek Roebuck, Francis Boorman and Rhiannon Markless
Reviewed by: Karyl Nairn QC*

[*Editorial note*: Originally published in Vol 13 No 1 of the *NY Dispute Resolution Lawyer*, (Spring 2020), a publication of the Dispute Resolution Section of the New York State Bar Association.]

'In the eighteenth century, arbitration was a more fashionable and civilised way to show manliness than resorting to a duel.'

'Some modern arbitrators assume they are "God's gift" – this evidence suggests that they might be right after all.'

English Arbitration and Mediation in the Long 18th Century is the latest instalment in an important series of books by Professor Derek Roebuck charting the development of arbitration in England. Readers will already be familiar with *Early English Arbitration*,[1] *Mediation and Arbitration in the Middle Ages*,[2] *The Golden Age of Arbitration*[3] (addressing dispute resolution in the reign of Queen Elizabeth I) and *Arbitration and Mediation in Seventeenth Century England*.[4] This latest work is co-written with two colleagues who were researchers for Professor Roebuck on earlier books: Dr Francis Calvert Boorman and Dr Rhiannon Markless. The collaboration has clearly been a happy and fruitful one. This latest volume is rich with detail about the role played by arbitrators and mediators during this most fascinating and tumultuous period in English history.

The authors introduce their book by reference to two arbitrations which framed the century. In 1701, a committee of arbitrators was established to resolve by merger the bitter rivalry between the London Company and the New India Company over their competing trade interests in India. The outcome of the 7-year arbitral process (which included the appointment

---

* Karyl Nairn QC, Partner and global co-head of international arbitration at Skadden Arps Slate Meagher & Flom (UK) LLP London.
1. Derek Roebuck, *Early English Arbitration* HOLO Books: The Arbitration Press, Oxford, 2008.
2. Derek Roebuck, *Mediation and Arbitration in the Middle Ages* HOLO Books: The Arbitration Press, Oxford, 2013.
3. Derek Roebuck, *The Golden Age of Arbitration* HOLO Books: The Arbitration Press, Oxford, 2015.
4. Derek Roebuck, *Arbitration and Mediation in Seventeenth Century England* HOLO Books: The Arbitration Press, Oxford, 2017.

of two leading politicians of the time[5] as arbitrators) consolidated the power and influence of the East India Company (and indeed Britain itself) in India. The arbitral remit encompassed not only matters of empire but 'national debt, party politics, the role of Parliament, trade and monopoly'.[6]

The close of the century witnessed what some consider to be the 'beginning of the modern era of international arbitration'.[7] The Treaty of Amity, Commerce and Navigation made between Britain and the United States in 1794 established commissions of arbitrators to resolve various conflicts arising from the American War of Independence including compensation claims brought by British merchants.

Although the details of these two famous arbitrations are not addressed in this book,[8] they set its tone: arbitration *mattered* in the 18th century. The authors draw on a wealth of source materials, including reported cases, judges' manuscripts and notebooks, personal letters and diaries and newspaper articles, to show that arbitrations and mediations were taking place across the entire breadth of English society in the 18th century over matters as diverse as family inheritance, labour, rights to new inventions, slights to reputation, building and engineering works, sport, gambling, entertainment, religion and even criminal matters. The book also reveals the extent to which judges and officers across the legal system actively promoted arbitration and saw it as an integral part of the usual business of their Courts.

Such material thoroughly debunks the popular misconception of the 19th and 20th centuries that the English Courts were traditionally hostile to arbitration. The case against Lord Campbell as the main culprit peddling that myth is compellingly laid out.[9] Indeed, it never made sense to accept Lord Campbell's mischaracterisations nor Viscount Hailsham LC's later assertion that arbitration was once regarded in England with 'jealousy and aversion'.[10] The 18th century was, after all, a perfect environment for arbitration to flourish. While King and State were dealing with civil unrest, the battle of Culloden, the revolution of 13 American colonies, the fallout from the French revolution, and conflicts with Spain and the Netherlands (to

---

5. Robert Harley, the Speaker of the House of Commons, and Sidney, the First Earl of Godolphin.

6. Roebuck, Boorman and Markless, *English Arbitration and Mediation in the Long 18th Century*, HOLO Books: The Arbitration Press, Oxford, 2019 p 4.

7. Id, citing Roger P Alford, 'The American Influence on International Arbitration' (2002) 19:1 *Ohio State Journal on Dispute Resolution* 69–88.

8. For an account of the East India arbitration see, for example, William Foster, *The East India House, Its History and Associations* (London, 1924), pp 104–105 and Roy A Sandstrom, 'Godolphin, Sidney, first Earl of Godolphin' *ODNB* 2011.

9. Roebuck *et al*, *supra* note 6 pp 261–262 and see also Chapters 7–10.

10. *Id* at p 47. See also Stavros Brekoulakis, 'The Historical Treatment of Arbitration under English Law and the Development of the Policy Favouring Arbitration' (Spring 2019) 39:1 *Oxford Journal of Legal Studies* pp 124–50.

name but a few dramatic events of the time), ordinary citizens were coping with the upheavals of the Industrial Revolution. The cumbersome court system struggled to keep pace with the rapid urbanisation and changing times. For many there was simply no court within physical or economic access.

The research and scholarship underpinning this book is admirable, but the real contribution is the way that the authors draw on existing specialised research on 18th century subjects and weld them with perspectives gleaned from additional materials to shed new light on how arbitration formed part of daily commercial and domestic life at this time.

Keepers of the Peace

One area in which existing research is given a fresh perspective is the fascinating role of the Justices of the Peace. As well as discharging their official duties addressing criminal and other formal complaints, these officers of the State regularly assisted parties across the country to resolve their disputes informally. A few surviving diaries and notebooks, such as those of the clergyman Edmund Tew of County Durham and Thomas Horner, the squire of Mells in Somerset, reveal skilled dispute resolvers, moving seamlessly from a role of judge to mediator to settle private grievances. Tew's notebooks from 1750 to 1764 show him patiently considering all manner of disputes including reputational skirmishes, unpaid wages claims and marital differences. A particular favourite is his entry from 23 April 1751: 'Refused a warrant against widow Raby, publican, for opprobrious words etc against Alexander Knox's wife, 2 very touchy people.'[11]

Horner's meticulous entries from 1770–1777 include a noteworthy reference to Rev John Wesley. The Methodist preacher brought a claim of forcible entry against certain individuals who had paid him an unwelcome 'visit' at his lodgings (they objected to his preaching to the mining communities of Somerset). After proposing that the defendants make restitution, Horner recused himself from further consideration of the matter. He happened to own the freehold of the premises and was afraid of 'incurring the censure of partiality'.[12]

Arbitration-Friendly Courts

It was not just at the informal level of the Justices of the Peace and at the assizes, however, that arbitrations and mediations were prevalent. The authors present substantial evidence that matters were referred to arbitration by judges across the rest of the legal system of the time. Judges sitting in the four High Courts: Chancery, King's (or Queen's) Bench,

---

11. Roebuck *et al*, *supra* note 6, p 74.
12. *Id* at p 82.

Common Pleas and Exchequer as well as the High Court of Admiralty, actively *encouraged* arbitration. Drawing on unpublished reports and previous research undertaken by others such as Henry Horwitz and James Oldham,[13] the book places rightful emphasis on Lord Mansfield's role as the great friend to commerce during his 32-year reign as Chief Justice of the King's Bench. That famous fashioner of the common law supported the developing capitalist economy and the growing arbitration community by dispatching hundreds of business disputes to expert arbitrators – artisans, engineers, surveyors, sea captains, builders – as well as to lawyers and jurymen. His successors, Lord Kenyon and Lord Ellenborough, were similarly supportive. In the case of *Wilkinson v Wilkinson*, brothers John and William fell out with each other after having invested nearly half a million pounds in ironworks around the country. When the matter came before Lord Kenyon in 1795, he advised placing all the disputes before an arbitrator, 'the most unfettered Judge in the world'.[14]

The authors provide ample evidence that many arbitrators appointed through court referrals were nominated by the parties themselves, especially in shipping disputes.[15] Lawyers too were appointed by the Courts and some were much admired. Lawyers of today looking for 18th century arbitrator role models need go no further than the polymath property lawyer, Charles Fearne (1742–1794) of Bream's Buildings, Chancery Lane, whom Lord Campbell later extravagantly praised as 'a man of as acute understanding as Pascal or Sir Isaac Newton'.[16]

Private Arbitrations in Every Sphere of Life
Perhaps the most revelatory part of the book lies in the many and varied accounts of the *ad hoc* arbitrations taking place in all walks of life through the initiative of the parties directly, often with the encouragement of their religious, family or trade community. Almost anything could be the subject of an arbitration at that time, including activities which were illegal such as gambling. Members of the working classes and the aristocracy were keen gamblers, betting on cards, dice and even matters such as which members of a gentlemen's club would die first and whether ' … Buonaparte succeeds in his views upon Spain within 2 years'.[17] Bets often included an arbitra-

---

13. Henry Horwitz and James Oldham , 'John Locke, Lord Mansfield and Arbitration During the Eighteenth Century' (1993) 36:1 *Historical Journal* 137 and other publications cited at Roebuck *et al*, *supra* note 6 at pp 30–38. The authors also acknowledge the generous assistance of Sir John Baker regarding legal manuscripts.
14. *Telegraph*, 22 June 1795.
15. Sea captains or salvage experts appointed by the Courts were typically nominated by the parties in shipping disputes – see Roebuck *et al*, *supra* note 6, Chapter 10, especially p 139.
16. *Id* at p 114 n 54.
17. *Id* at p 235 citing *The Betting Book of White's from 1743 to 1878* (London, 1892) p 38.

tion clause. Although not legally binding, awards rendered were generally honoured for reputational reasons.

The sport arbitrations entertainingly described in the book readily demonstrate why this was not a field particularly suited to the courts – disputes typically concerned the outcome of matches on which substantial wagers were made. The cover of the book is a scene of bare-knuckle fighters in an amphitheatre owned by the boxing impresario, Jack Broughton. In 1743, he promulgated a code for fighting contests which was used for the following 100 years. It included an arbitration process of two umpires chosen by the principals with a third to be selected by the first two, in the event there was no agreement as to the result. Cricket was another sport attracting the gambling public, with matches leading sometimes to riots and calls to make the sport illegal. An arbitration held to determine the outcome of a cricket match between Hadleigh and Ipswich in 1788 was a big news story of the day.[18]

At the other extreme, arbitration was strongly encouraged within many religious communities. The authors proclaim the Quakers as 'the greatest advocates of arbitration in eighteenth century English society'.[19] A rich selection of material supports this thesis, including extracts and advices of the Yearly Meetings of Friends and the diary of one Isaac Fletcher of Underwood in Cumberland who sat regularly as an arbitrator within the Quaker community and even referred his own disputes to arbitration (although apparently not with much success).[20] Also of particular interest is the establishment by a group of Quakers of the Newcastle Upon Tyne Association for general arbitration in 1793 (initially opposed by local lawyers), which must be one of the earliest examples of a general arbitral institution. Referrals of disputes to arbitration by Quakers were often justified by reference to quotes from scripture. Arbitration, it seems, is divinely endorsed.[21] (Some modern arbitrators assume they are 'God's gift' – this material suggests that they might be right after all.)

A chapter is devoted to showing the prevalence of *ad hoc* references to arbitration in many areas of business and commerce. Disputes between business partners were well suited to rapid resolution by industry peers, with many including arbitration clauses in their agreements.[22] The financial stakes were often high. This century marked the birth of mass consumerism. Disputes over scientific inventions and new industrial techniques required specialist knowledge to resolve effectively. Patent disputes were

18. *Id* at p 237.
19. *Id* at p 247.
20. *Id* at pp 250-252.
21. *Id* at p 248.
22. James Watt and his factory owner business partner Matthew Boulton included an arbitration clause in their partnership agreement – *id* at p 209.

frequent but were complex, slow and costly to resolve through the courts or Parliamentary system.

The book provides a fresh perspective on well-known 18th century figures of the Industrial Revolution such as James Watt, Thomas Telford, Matthew Boulton, Samuel Crompton and Richard Arkwright. Private letters show Watt and Telford lending their technical expertise to help others resolve disputes while others appear in records as regular users of arbitration. One of Watt's arbitral awards, which was unearthed in the City of Birmingham archives, is enthusiastically reproduced and speaks across the centuries of his practical and fair-minded approach.[23]

Private Arbitration: Fashionable and 'Manly'

Reassuring for arbitration practitioners today who feel undervalued is the evidence presented of the high regard for the arbitral process and those taking part in it. According to the *British Evening Post* in 1792, arbitration represented 'common sense and common honesty'.[24]

Submitting to arbitration in the 18th century was seen as a way to end a quarrel, while preserving the honour and reputation of the parties. Arbitration was a more fashionable and civilised way to show manliness than resorting to a duel.[25] A letter written to a newspaper by 'Arcadius' in 1773 called duelling a 'Gothic custom' and proposed arbitration as one means of addressing 'many affronts and other intricate matters not cognizable by law'.[26] The owner of a daily newspaper *The World* challenged in the press his fellow disputant to accept his 'just and manly offer of ARBI-TRATION. – If he is not just and manly, I cannot help it. He must take the consequences'.[27]

The status of lawyers in the 18th century was not particularly high but the lawyers who arbitrated disputes enjoyed a welcome boost to their reputations. Particularly in the first part of the century, arbitrators did not traditionally charge for their services so arbitration was community service rather than a remunerative activity.[28] Bishop Gilbert Burnet's

23. *Id* at p 210.
24. *Id* at p 42, n 36.
25. Robert Shoemaker, 'Male Honour and the Decline of Public Violence in Eighteenth-Century London', *Social History* (2001) and 'The Taming of the Duel: Masculinity, Honour and Ritual Violence in London, 1660–1800', *Historical Journal* (2002).
26. *London Chronicle or Universal Evening Post*, 14–16 September 1773.
27. *Gazetteer and New Daily Advertiser*, 30 September 1790.
28. The authors cite the observations of the Radical tailor and diarist, Francis Place: 'I gained much knowledge in many ways and on many subjects by these interferences, for which I never made any charge, unless, the matter related to an association or large body of men, in some such cases I have accepted a sum of money equal to that which the other arbitrators were paid, in three or four instances where the parties were found to be rogues, or where the trouble was occasi[on]ed by bad feelings on both sides I have made charges, as I did not think that rogues and evil disposed persons had any claim on my time because they had misbehaved themselves. See Roebuck *et al*, *supra* note 6 at p 285,

posthumously published history of his lifetime, cited several times in the book, includes advice on the importance of being competent in the law in order that one could aspire to become an arbitrator: It 'makes a Man very useful in his Country, both in conducting his own Affairs, and in giving good Advice to those about him: It will enable him to be a good Justice of Peace, and to settle Matters by Arbitration'.[29]

The accounts of the many arbitrations across daily life bring to mind the memorable observation of the art historian Kenneth Clark that 'eighteenth century amateurism ran through everything: chemistry, philosophy, botany and natural history'. He noted 'a freshness and freedom of mind in these men that is sometimes lost in the rigidly controlled classification of the professional'.[30] These words appear equally apposite to 18th-century arbitration[31] as revealed in this book. There are other occasional echoes of Clark in the bold conclusions of those confident in their command of the subject – in the chapter on theatre, for instance, the authors proclaim, 'there can hardly ever have been at any time or place a more disputatious lot than those involved in the English theatre in the 18th and early 19th centuries'.

The authors do not claim to have written the definitive work on arbitration in this period – they suggest that even their wide-ranging research has only just begun to reveal the importance of arbitration in daily 18th century life. They describe their book as a 'call to action' for other researchers to follow them.[32] But they are too modest about their achievements. Like the earlier works in the series, this is a book to which readers will happily return for inspiration.

29. Gilbert Burnet, *Bishop Burnet's History of his Own Time. From the Revolution to the Conclusion of the Treaty of Peace at Utrecht, in the Reign of Queen Anne* (Dublin, 1734) p 390.
30. Kenneth Clark, *Civilisation* (British Broadcasting Corporation and John Murray, 1969) p 249.
31. Chapter 21 is devoted to the move towards greater professionalisation of arbitration, largely due to the rise of the lawyer arbitrator. For merchants, at least, there remained a reluctance to charge fees.
32. The publication of this book was made possible by the Access to Justice research project on the Development of Arbitration in England and Wales. Contributors to the project included the author of this review.

THE SIMILARITIES AND DISTINCTIONS BETWEEN THE JUDICIAL ROLE AND THE ARBITRAL ROLE

Lord Neuberger[*]

Derek Roebuck was an exceptionally warm and principled human being, as well as being a fine legal scholar who made unique, valuable and lasting contributions to legal research, and in particular to the history of arbitration and alternative dispute resolution (ADR).

I had the pleasure of getting to know Derek and Susanna over many years; they had a remarkably and touchingly close and happy marriage, working and playing together. They even managed to collaborate in writing a book which covered an area which overlapped each of their rather different spheres of academic and social interest, *Women in Disputes: A History of European Women in Mediation and Arbitration*, which was published in 2018.

Derek was a man of great generosity of spirit, who had a very relaxed and courteous manner. These admirable characteristics masked some very strongly held and equally admirable principles, passionately held interests, and an impressive ability to carry out extensive research and then to write up the results. Those interests most notably included arbitration and ADR – not merely in the modern world, but also in history.

To me at least, his most lasting and outstanding contribution was his five volumes on arbitration and mediation in England, covering early English history, the Middle Ages, the reign of Elizabeth I, the 17th century and what he called 'the long eighteenth century'. They are a treasure trove for anybody who is interested in how disputes were settled in England over the thousand years up to 200 years ago. Over and above that, like all good writing which focuses on a limited aspect of life in the past, his books cast a fascinating shaft of light on to the way people lived over the period which he covered.

---

[*] The Rt Hon Lord Neuberger of Abbotsbury is a Crossbench Life Peer (judicial). He is a former President of the United Kingdom Supreme Court and a former Master of the Rolls.

Among very many interesting features, I was particularly struck by two features of the rule of law in UK history. The first was the amount of time and effort which the monarch and the members of his/her Council would give over to resolving specific disputes between individuals, as opposed to dealing with policy matters. I am sorry to say that the present and recent UK governments could learn some lessons from the commitment of central government during many periods in the past to ensure that the rule of law was a reality in terms of having an effective dispute resolution system. The second feature which I found striking was the way in which arbitration, mediation and litigation were so closely connected: indeed, mediation and arbitration were treated as part of the judiciary's armoury in addition to resolving disputes in court.

Unlike Derek, I have no great knowledge of or expertise in legal history, and I cannot claim to have legal academic credentials. So, if I am to write about a subject with which I am familiar, it would have to be a contemporary topic related to my experiences as, successively, a barrister, a judge and an arbitrator. In light of the second feature I have mentioned, it seems to me that, when writing in honour of Derek, it would be appropriate to compare the judicial and arbitral functions in the early 21st century.

Both judges and arbitrators have the same fundamental duty to the parties to a dispute, namely to resolve the dispute honestly, dispassionately and according to the law. However, a judge trying a case is a public figure with a public law duty owed to society (or, more specifically, to the rule of law), and his or her duty to the parties is a secondary duty in the sense that, if it clashes with his or her duty to society, the duty to the parties must yield. By contrast, an arbitrator has a purely private law duty to the parties, arising out of contract. It is true that in almost all jurisdictions an arbitrator's duty is made subject to some statutory (and, in some places, also common law) rules, which are in the public interest, but those rules do not alter the essentially exclusively private law nature of an arbitrator's duty.

The difference is clear from the very outset of any dispute. It is of the essence of litigation that the parties cannot select their judge. In one English case, Mostyn J emphasised that, when it comes to getting judges to recuse themselves for apparent bias, 'the bar is set high because otherwise litigants might be tempted to engage in preliminary exercises of "judge picking"'.[1] However, parties to an arbitration can of course select their arbitrators. Indeed, that is one of the perceived attractions of arbitration over litigation. This is particularly so if they would otherwise have to litigate in a foreign court. People are often uncomfortable about having to accept whichever judge the court system of the country concerned selects,

---

1. *R (on the application of ZAI Corporate Finance Ltd) v AIM Disciplinary Committee of the London Stock Exchange PLC* [2017] EWHC 778 (Admin), at [26], per Mostyn J.

without having the opportunity to stipulate the expertise or characteristics they are (often perfectly reasonably) looking for in their tribunal. As a matter of principle, the difference between the way the tribunal is selected epitomises the point that arbitration is a consensual private arrangement.

Another difference, at least on the conventional view, is that arbitrators are unlike judges in that they have no duty to ensure that an arbitration is conducted without unnecessary delays, without unnecessarily long hearings and without unnecessary expense. There is considerable force in this view. Public interest concerns which judges have to bear in mind, such as the appropriate use of courts, the availability of judges for other cases and more generally the efficient use of public resources, have no part to play when it comes to arbitrations. Equally, if both parties are content to drag the proceedings out and to incur very substantial costs, on what ground can the arbitrators disapprove or seek to stop them, given that one of the founding principles of arbitration is that it is a consensual exercise?

However, it can be said that this discussion throws an indirect light on two connected and slightly uncomfortable aspects of arbitration. First, arbitrators often have a positive financial interest in not objecting to proceedings being dragged out or to a proliferation of hearings. Unnecessary or elongated hearings mean more money for the lawyers, but they also often mean more money for the arbitrators, as they are normally paid by the hour. Secondly, if arbitrators start criticising lawyers' charges and working practices in an arbitration, or penalising a party in costs, they are likely to find that they are nominated as arbitrators in the future rather less frequently than they might hope.

Now I am far from saying that many arbitrators are consciously influenced by such factors, but self-interest has a nasty habit of subconsciously influencing one's decisions. I suspect, and I certainly hope, that the great majority of arbitrators would simply not be influenced by their own potential level of fees out of the particular arbitration, or their future appointment prospects. Nonetheless, given the importance of justice being seen to be done, there must still be some concern that a perception of self-interest could nonetheless be invoked in such a case.

Quite apart from this, there are grounds for challenging the conventional view that arbitrators have no sort of public duty. That challenge is based on the fact that arbitration has become such a significant means of dispute resolution, in terms of both the number of arbitrations and the types of dispute which are arbitrated, as well on the more specific fact that arbitrations not infrequently have significant ramifications for people across the world. Bearing in mind these factors, there is a case for saying that it is no longer realistic to treat arbitration as a purely private consensual exercise. Thus, when deciding investor-State disputes (ISDS) arbitrators are often making decisions which 'include awards which significantly impact on national economies and on regulatory systems within nation states', as the former Chief Justice of Australia explained in a 2014 lecture,[2] and such decisions sometimes also involve effectively overruling national courts, even supreme courts. Indeed, Robert French went on to say that arbitral decisions in ISDS cases 'have general implications for national sovereignty, democratic governance and the rule of law within domestic legal systems'.[3] At a rather different end of the arbitration spectrum, there is growing concern in some quarters in the United States about the fact that employees are required to sign away their rights to go to court in return for the right (and obligation) to arbitrate.[4]

The substantially increased public and global importance of arbitration can fairly be said to call into question the conventional view of the arbitrator simply as one of the parties to a private consensual arrangement who happens to have the responsibility of resolving a dispute, and to cast on an arbitrator a new, more public-interest-oriented judicial role compared with that which he or she has hitherto been assumed to enjoy. It can be argued that such a new aspect of arbitration is reflected by the requirements imposed on arbitrators by many States through domestic statutes and by the procedural rules of many of the arbitral institutions to proceed promptly[5] with any arbitration and not to delay their awards unduly.[6] However, I suspect that such requirements are imposed more because of contemporary expectations of parties to arbitrations and to ensure that arbitration remains a popular form of dispute resolution, rather than for public policy reasons.

While there is undoubtedly force in the contention that arbitration is now such a common way of dispute resolution and so frequently far reaching in its effect that there is a public interest in arbitrators having more judge-like duties, it seems to me that it would be dangerous to run too far with that view. As a matter of principle, any attempt to impose public law duties on arbitrators, at least in normal commercial cases, whether intranational or international, would represent an interference with freedom of contract and the right of self-determination. I strongly suspect that it would also

---

2. Chief Justice RS French AC, *Investor-State Dispute Settlement - A Cut Above the Courts?* (Darwin, 9 July 2014), https://tobacco.ucsf.edu/sites/tobacco.ucsf.edu/files/u9/frenchcj09jul14.pdf (accessed 10 December 2020).
3. Ibid.
4. See, for example, http://prospect.org/article/signing-away-our-rights-0 and http://www.newsweek.com/can-companies-force-workers-go-arbitration-667623 (both accessed 10 December 2020).
5. Most sets of rules are peppered with expressions such as 'as soon as practicable'.
6. Ditto, and some are quite prescriptive – eg Article 31 of the ICC Rules provides that, subject to the ICC Court's power of extension, 'The time limit within which the arbitral tribunal must render its final award is six months from the date on which the Terms of Reference are agreed', although it is normally very easy to get an extension.

risk depriving commercial arbitration of some of its attraction. A more realistic approach might be to identify certain types of arbitration in which some judge-like responsibilities would be placed on the arbitrators. ISDS arbitrations are an obvious example, but there are other disputes, such as those relating to large public procurement contracts, which may give rise to public interest concerns,[7] Indeed, some countries recognise the special nature of awards in such disputes: the French courts have concluded that such awards must be reviewable by the administrative courts[8] and Brazilian statute law requires such awards to be subject to public scrutiny.[9] Otherwise, I think that we have to let the market work, which should lead to maintaining and improving the performance of arbitrators, as I shall discuss a little later.

There are two other significant features of the difference between judging and arbitrating which I have not so far mentioned. Arbitration hearings are almost always private and arbitration awards are almost always private and virtually unappealable, whereas court hearings are almost always held in public, and result in judgments which are almost always both published and appealable. It is often said, and rightly said, that it is fundamental to the rule of law that court hearings take place in public and judgments are given in public. That is because it is the public who should be able to see justice being dispensed and public oversight helps ensure that judges behave themselves: sunlight, it was famously said by US Supreme Court Justice Brandeis,[10] is the best disinfectant. Judges in the UK are and have been keen to support open justice: the UK Supreme Court led the way in ensuring that all its hearings were streamed so that they could be watched anywhere in the world.

Arbitration is very different, and, as in relation to the arbitrator's duties, save in relation to ISDS and some similar types of dispute, there is a case, which I think is very difficult to challenge both in terms of principle and in terms of practice, that parties should be entitled to agree that their dispute resolution arrangements outside court, whether through arbitration or otherwise, are conducted in, and subject to, complete privacy. As to ISDS arbitrations, a 2005 OECD report referred to:

---

7. The *e-Borders* case discussed by Stavros Brekoulakis in 'The Protection of the Public Interest in Public Private Arbitrations' http://arbitrationblog.kluwerarbitration.com/2017/05/08/the-protection-of-the-public-interest-in-public-private-arbitrations/ (accessed 10 December 2020).
8. Decision of the Tribunal des conflits in *INSERN v Fondation Letten F. Saugstad* (2010) and the 9 November 2016 decision of the Conseil d'Etat in Nr 388806, ECLI: FR: CEASS: 2016: 388806.20161109.
9. Law No 13,129 of 26 May 2015.
10. Quoted by Lord Steyn in *Turkington v Times Newspapers Ltd* [2001] 2 AC 277.

a general understanding among the Members of [its] Investment Committee that additional transparency, in particular in relation to the publication of arbitral awards, subject to necessary safeguards for the protection of confidential business and governmental information, is desirable to enhance effectiveness and public acceptance of international investment arbitration, as well as contributing to the further development of a public body of jurisprudence.[11]

Further, the 2014 UNCITRAL Rules require most Treaty-based ISDS awards to be published.[12] In the following year, the UN decided that all Treaty-based ISDS awards should be published.[13] Most International Centre for Settlement of Investment Disputes (ICSID) awards are published by consent and details of ICSID arbitrations are required[14] to be published. As I say, however, it is hard to justify denying strict privacy to all, or at least the great majority of, what might be called purely commercial arbitrations, whether international or not.

However, the consequence of the arbitral proceedings and awards being entirely private can, at least in theory, operate as an incentive to discourage arbitrators from being fair or from applying the law, particularly if the application of legal principles would cause them to reach an outcome or decision which seems to them to be unfair or uncommercial. Judges not infrequently find themselves making decisions that are in accordance with the law but which they personally find unattractive in the light of the moral or commercial 'merits' of the case as they see them. That is because it is inevitable that the law sometimes favours a party who has behaved badly, even dishonestly or dishonourably, over a party who has behaved well, and sometimes proper application of the law produces an unattractive result, particularly on unusual facts. However, knowing not only that they are sitting and giving their decision in private, but also that any decision is likely to be unappealable, an arbitrator must often be tempted to 'cheat' when application of the law produces an unpalatable result.

The strict legal view, at least in the common law world, is of course that an arbitrator should apply the law in the same way as a judge. The common law is not static, so (at least in my view) that means that an arbitrator can develop the law to a limited extent, in the same way as, but certainly no more than, a first instance trial judge. However, subject to that sig-

---

11. Transparency and Third Party Participation in Investor-State Dispute Settlement Procedures: Statement by the OECD Investment Committee. See https://www.oecd.org/daf/inv/investment-policy/WP-2005_1.pdf (accessed 10 December 2020).
12. UNCITRAL Rules on Transparency in Treaty-based Investor-State Arbitrations, Article 3.
13. The Mauritius Convention: – The United Nations Convention on Transparency in Treaty-based Investor-State Arbitration.
14. ICSID Administrative and Financial Regulation 22.

nificant qualification, the traditional view is clear: an arbitrator is strictly required to apply the law. That is, I should say, a view to which I myself subscribe, and I would suggest that an arbitrator who consciously gives a decision or makes an award which does not comply with the law would be acting unprofessionally, indeed improperly. I acknowledge that there is some attraction in the notion that arbitrators should be entitled to be more flexible and commercial than judges in their approach, and that an arbitrator, faced with a very unpalatable conclusion as a result of applying the law, could refuse to apply the law on the basis that arbitration should be more business-minded than litigation. In my view, however, that is a temptation which should be resisted. If the parties have agreed that their dispute should be resolved by, say, English law, then it surely must be wrong for the arbitrator knowingly not to apply that law.

Indeed, I think that there are two other, connected, reasons for arbitrators to adhere to the contractually agreed law. First, if they depart from that law, it will almost inevitably lead to serious abuses, because, once arbitrators decide that they are above the law, the habit of ignoring the law is likely to become pretty quickly ingrained. Secondly, while departing from the law in the odd case may do little harm to the reputation of arbitration, I believe that that reputation will become badly dented if people start to think that arbitrators do not apply the law. As the Chinese have realised, it is essential for a country to have an impartial dispute resolution system and the rule of law in order for business to thrive, and business people will be reluctant to enter into transactions without knowing that they will be interpreted and enforced according to the law – and that is as true of arbitration as it is of litigation.

A paradoxical feature of arbitration is the conflict between the privacy of the arbitral process and the ability to choose your arbitrator. For many individuals and companies, it is a very attractive feature of arbitration as against litigation that parties can choose their own arbitrators, but it is not that easy to discover who is actually a good arbitrator because arbitrations are subject to such stringent privacy rules. In this context, it is interesting to note that, in a pretty comprehensive survey carried out every year by Queen Mary University of London,[15] while arbitration was generally rated a pretty good way of resolving international commercial disputes, the complaints about arbitration included the existence of a 'lack of insight into arbitrators' efficiency', and concern about a lack of 'transparency regarding arbitrator performance to allow for informed appointments by parties'. Indeed, the survey also reported that a 'recurring theme throughout the interviews was users' discontent with the lack of insight provided into

---

15. *Editorial note*: Queen Mary University of London and White & Case, *2015 International Survey: Improvements and Innovations in International Arbitration* (London, 2015).

institutions' efficiency and arbitrator performance, and the lack of transparency in institutional decision-making in relation to the appointment of, and challenges to, arbitrators'. The survey has also reported that the publication of redacted awards or summaries of awards was 'not only favoured for its academic value and usefulness when arguing a case, but [was] also often named as a method to gain more insight into arbitrator performance and to encourage arbitrators to write high-quality awards'.

Another significant difference between judicial and arbitral decisions to which I have briefly referred is in the ability to appeal. In almost any country, one can appeal a judge's decision virtually as a matter of course if it appears that he or she may have gone wrong on a point of law. However, in many countries, one simply cannot appeal an arbitrator's decision on such a ground, and in most other countries it is very difficult to do so. This is an important difference, both in principle and in practice, and while it clearly has advantages in terms of certainty, speed and cost, it not only inherently increases the risk of a wrong answer, but it can also serve to encourage arbitrators to refuse to apply the law, as they know that they cannot be appealed.

So far as principle is concerned, the difference is attributable to two features I have already mentioned. First, judges perform a public function in public. There is a public interest in a public servant being required to get the law right, and being corrected when he or she does not do so. Secondly, as a judge's decision is publicly available, people will assume that the law is as he or she has decided and may make their personal and business decisions on that assumption. So, if the judge got the law wrong, it is important that people should know that the law is not as the judge has declared. (That is especially important in a common law system, such as in the United Kingdom where judges can make and develop the law.) No such principles apply to arbitrators, who, as I have said, have no public duties and whose decisions are given in private. Further, although arbitrators' decisions used to be freely appealable (for instance, in England and Wales until 1979[16]), the current philosophy is that the parties have agreed that their dispute should be determined by arbitration and, in the absence of good reason, it would be an interference with their agreement for a judge's view of the law to be substituted for that of the arbitral tribunal. There is an additional practical reason, namely that parties to disputes want finality – they do not want the delay and uncertainty of appeals.

When I started practising law 45 years ago, arbitration was seen as a quick, cheap and informal way of resolving disputes, which avoided many of the more formal procedural requirements involved in court proceedings. On returning to the world of arbitration following my retiring as a judge

---

16. Compare the Arbitration Act 1950 with the Arbitration Act 1979.

after 21 years, I discovered that those involved in arbitration have become much more concerned with procedural issues. Indeed, it appears to me that arbitrators are more concerned with procedural matters than judges. I think that this development is partly due to the difficulty of appealing on a point of substantive law. It makes a party who is disappointed with an arbitral decision focus on other issues, such as arbitrators being procedurally unfair, not sticking to the procedure which they laid down, not giving a party a fair chance to present its case, being in some way unfair in the way they deal with an issue, or not dealing with a point in their award.

This means that parties to arbitrations, and indeed arbitrators themselves, have become almost obsessed with procedural issues – 'due process paranoia', as it has been called in some quarters.[17] It is a tendency which has been reinforced by two types of problem that are sometimes encountered after an arbitral award has been made. The first problem is that of the occasional unduly harsh overruling by a judge of an arbitrator's procedural ruling. Some national courts seem, at least to a UK judge's view of things, to appear to adopt an inappropriately exacting approach when it comes to assessing arbitrators' procedural decisions. Secondly, and more frequently, successful parties sometimes encounter difficulties when seeking to enforce awards. One of the attractions of arbitration over litigation arises from the New York Convention, which enables arbitral awards to be enforced easily through the courts of countries which have signed up to the Convention, and very many countries have done so. However, judges in some of those countries sometimes appear to be reluctant to enforce awards and can be relatively easily persuaded to refuse enforcement because of some procedural defect that is often insignificant or even illusory.

At any rate to a lawyer brought up in the common law tradition, such an exacting concern about procedural issues appears not merely undesirable, but positively inconsistent with what commercial people would expect. I fear, however, that the concern is exacerbated by the involvement of some institutions in arbitrations. It is not so much the rules that are made by those institutions: it is more their attitude to the drafting of the awards. When considering draft awards, their concern with procedural issues appears at times to verge on the obsessive. Again from my perspective, it is in surprising and stark contrast to the relative lack of interest on the part of many institutions when considering whether there are sufficient, or indeed any, reasons in the award as drafted to support the conclusions of substantive law reached by the tribunal. (I think that it is only fair to the institutions to add that there have been several occasions in which their corrections to my drafts have been very welcome.)

---

17. See Queen Mary University of London and White & Case, *Improvements and Innovations in International Arbitration* (2016).

Despite these downsides, very many companies and their lawyers prefer arbitration to litigation. Why is this? At a recent conference I attended in London, I mentioned in my introductory speech the perceived advantages of arbitration over litigation as they are understood by most independent lawyers and judges. Those advantages were: private hearing, private award, the ability to choose one's tribunal, greater informality, international enforceability and no right of appeal. I was interested that, later in the conference, a panel of general counsel from various substantial multinational companies in different countries all agreed that, unless the litigation would be in the courts of a country whose judges could not be trusted, the only one of those factors which really mattered to them was international enforceability.

I sometimes think that, at least in some legal circles, lawyers prefer arbitration to litigation because, as I have explained, arbitrators, unlike judges, do not exercise much control over unnecessarily expensive or time-consuming activities undertaken in the course of the arbitration, and so, to put it bluntly, lawyers can often make more money out of arbitration than out of litigation. Again, this is not a suggestion that anything dishonest is going on, but it is a suggestion that self-interest will inevitably influence any decision subconsciously – in this case, a decision whether to advise a client to arbitrate rather than litigate. I think that lawyers have to be careful in this connection. The costs of arbitration are in general getting very substantial, sometimes prohibitive, and there is a danger that it could eventually price itself out of the market. The combination of increasing expense and due process paranoia is not a good one. Arbitration currently remains a popular way of resolving disputes, and it deserves to be so – provided that it is properly and proportionately conducted both by lawyers and by arbitrators. However, just as it is true that it is best if lawyers stop their clients getting into difficulties rather than helping them once they get into difficulties, it seems to me that if problems with an arbitration start to develop, those involved should try and head them off before they become very serious, rather than waiting for the problems to appear and only then trying to cope with them.

Even now, then, it is the case that arbitration has developed, at least in some quarters, a reputation for slowness, due process paranoia and excessive cost. This means that arbitration is at risk of becoming less attractive, and, unless something is done, that state of affairs will continue. This inevitably means, in turn, that those who might otherwise arbitrate will be more open than before to suggestions that they consider other, cheaper, quicker and less procedurally sclerotic means of resolving their disputes. Mediation is an obvious alternative, some would say the obvious alternative.

THE TRANSIENT AND THE PERMANENT IN ARBITRATION

William W Park[*]

He who would confine his thought to present time will not understand present reality. (Jules Michelet, 1798–1874)[1]

Several years ago, Jan Paulsson observed that Derek Roebuck might substitute for a time machine, providing a way for us to voyage backward with a guide to put everything in context.[2] Indeed, the great Derek Roebuck, to whom we dedicate this set of essays, gave much of his professional life to making sure that by receiving a glimpse of dispute resolution in earlier times, we might have an opportunity better to understand the reality of present-day arbitration.[3]

Arbitration's history reminds many observers of the primordial Greek sea god Proteus, who could alter his shape at will, notwithstanding that his divine substance remained the same. Proteus reinvented himself by

[*] Professor of Law, Boston University. General Editor, *Arbitration International*. Honorary Fellow, Selwyn College, Cambridge.
1. 'Celui qui veut s'en tenir au présent, à l'actuel, ne comprendra pas l'actuel'. Introduction to Jules Michelet, *Le Peuple* (1846), at xvii. In his study of the French working class on the eve of the 1848 Revolution, Michelet recounts his own origins, assisting at his father's printing press. According to the author, his origins of 'The People' led to a deeper understanding of their present condition. On that personal note, Michelet continues with the general observations about our need to go beyond present time in order to understand present reality.
2. Jan Paulsson, Book Review of Derek Roebuck, 'The Golden Age of Arbitration: Dispute Resolution under Elizabeth I', (2015) 31 *Arbitration International* 519. Paulsson wrote, 'We do not have a time-traveling machine, but those of us who take an interest in the antecedents of modern arbitration have Derek Roebuck, and that is even better: not only a way to voyage back in time, but a guide who puts everything brilliantly in context.'
3. His studies include *The Charitable Arbitrator: How to Mediate and Arbitrate in Louis XIV's France* (2002); *Roman Arbitration*, with Bruno de Loynes de Fumichon (2004); *Early English Arbitration* (2008); *Ancient Greek Arbitration* (2010); *Disputes and Differences* (2010); *Mediation and Arbitration in the Middle Ages: England 1154 to 1558* (2013); *The Golden Age of Arbitration: Dispute Resolution Under Elizabeth I* (2015); *Arbitration and Mediation in Seventeenth-Century England*; *English Arbitration and Mediation in the Long Eighteenth Century*, with Francis Calvert Boorman and Rhiannon Markless (2019). (All published Oxford: HOLO Books: The Arbitration Press.)

adapting to new circumstances, while remaining unchanged in essence. Likewise arbitration's outward shape undergoes alterations when examined through the lens of the trappings of legal culture in each age.

The essence of arbitration has remained remarkably unchanged over the years. Parties consent to binding dispute resolution pursuant to agreements that waive jurisdiction of otherwise competent courts, in favour of adjudication by decision-makers chosen, directly or indirectly, by protagonists of the relevant controversy. National judicial power may be invoked to recognise an arbitral award, or in some instances, to annul an award for gross procedural defects. The merits of the parties' dispute, however, remain in the hands of the arbitrators.

This protean nature gives arbitration elements both transient and permanent,[4] as illustrated by a long-standing problem: how to treat arbitration awards annulled under national statutes, but presented for enforcement in another country. The difficulty arises in the context of the proverbial 'regretted choice' for merchants who agree to arbitrate but later (having lost their case) give way to second thoughts.

Decades of divergent reactions to this conundrum provide a miniature time machine that might have delighted Derek. To illustrate, one might take a cross-border sales agreement subject to an arbitration clause, with an award made in England but presented for enforcement in Paris or New York. Most agree that freely accepted obligations generally deserve respect. If a buyer in the United States promises to pay $100 for goods imported from France, the purchaser should make payment absent some good reason. Who is to determine whether a 'good reason' does in fact exist? The American buyer might say the merchandise was defective. The French seller maintains the product was perfect. Does the matter go to courts of the United States or to courts of France? Or to some transnational body, such as an arbitral tribunal in London?

In the search for a fair and certain forum, a common solution would be arbitration, at least for international transactions like the one above. To pursue matters further, let us assume the controversy goes to arbitration in London, as agreed to by both sides. The arbitral tribunal decides in favour of the French seller/exporter: the goods were indeed up to the contractually stipulated quality and the American buyer owes money for failing to pay. Let us posit further that, rightly or wrongly, an English court at the seat

---

4. The phrase 'transient and permanent' seems first to have appeared in a sermon by the New England preacher Theodore Parker, delivered at the ordination of Charles Shackford in the Hawes Place Church in Boston in May 1841. Theodore Parker, 'The Transient and Permanent in Christianity', in *The Transient and Permanent in Christianity* 447 (George Willis Cooke ed., 1908), 447. An early Unitarian, Parker unsettled much of his community by suggesting that the message of Jesus was valuable solely because of the truth it revealed, not due to any divine credentials of the one who delivered the revelation.

of the arbitration vacates the award due to violation of a provision of the English Arbitration Act.[5]

When the French winner under the award (now annulled) seeks to have the award enforced by attaching the American company's assets in New York and in Paris, those enforcement courts will need to decide whether to give effect to the arbitral award itself, which says that damages must be paid, or to the English court judgment setting aside the award, thus relieving the American buyer of its obligations pursuant to the arbitration.

What is to be done? Award enforcement implicates one of the most successful instruments of international law: the 1958 United Nations (or 'New York') Convention,[6] now signed by 166 States ranging from Afghanistan to Zimbabwe. The Convention provides for recognition of foreign arbitral awards, but with some significant caveats, in particular concerning awards annulled in their country of origin. These caveats have been applied differently by courts in France, the United Kingdom and the United States. Indeed, the Convention's language has been applied differently even within the United States, with divergence derived not from any perversity of judges but from good faith variants in perspectives on how to construe the treaty.

The battle plays itself out, in part, through Article V(1)(e) of the Convention, the application of which triggers different results depending on whether the word 'may' is read as conveying (a) permission, or (b) expectation, a matter that sometimes depends on the context of the case, or on which of the five official language versions gets consulted.[7]

The English version of that provision reads:

> Recognition and enforcement of the award *may* be refused [emphasis added], at the request of the party against whom it is invoked, only if that party furnishes proof that ... the award has been set aside or suspended by a competent authority of the country in which, or under the law of which, that award was made.[8]

5. The 1996 Arbitration Act might permit annulment, for example, due to a perceived procedural irregularity as enumerated in section 68 of that Act. Or, an award in some instances may be set aside following an appeal under section 69 on a point of law, in this context defined by section 82 to include the law of England and Wales.
6. Convention on the Recognition and Enforcement of Foreign Arbitral Awards, New York, 10 June 1958, United Nations Treaty Series, vol. 330, no. 4739.
7. Convention Art XVI(1) says that the treaty's Chinese, English, French, Russian, and Spanish texts are 'equally authentic'. On the comparison of treaty texts with different meanings, see Art 33(4) of the Vienna Convention on the Law of Treaties, 23 May 1969, United Nations Treaty Series, vol. 1155, no. 18232, at 331, which provides for adoption of the 'meaning which best reconciles the texts, having regard to the object and purposes of the treaty'.
8. The careful reader will note that the permissive 'may' in the English text of the Convention ('recognition ... may be refused') leaves open more than one meaning. The verb 'may' could

By contrast, the French text lends itself to a more forceful interpretation that could mandate deference to the annulment court decision:

La reconnaissance et l'exécution de la sentence ne seront refusées, sur requête de la partie contre laquelle elle est invoquée *que si* [unless] cette partie fournit la preuve que la sentence ... a été annulée ou suspendue par une autorité compétente du pays dans lequel ou d'après la loi duquel la sentence a été rendu.

The direct English translation of that French text would read as follows: 'Recognition and enforcement will not be refused ... *unless* [*que si*] ... the award was annulled or suspended by a competent authority of the country in which, or under the law of which, that award was made.'

Absent from the French text is a notion of discretion in the recognition forum, conveyed by 'may' in English. Rather, the 'unless' [*que si*] combined with the future indicative tense (recognition will not be refused) normally compels an expectation of non-recognition of the annulled award.[9]

Judges in the United States have taken a mixed approach, sometimes deferring to the judiciary at the arbitral seat, enforcing an annulled award,[10] while in other instances enforcing an award notwithstanding *vacatur* in

---

contemplate equally viable options, as in 'For dessert, you may choose vanilla ice cream or apple pie'. In the context of the Convention, however, the verb 'may' might hold a more forceful sense of expectation, as in 'You may worship according to your own conscience.' Indeed, the treaty context suggests an expectation of non-recognition if one considers the other listed items for which enforcement 'may' be refused as outlined in that Art V(1): refusal to recognise an award when there is no valid arbitration agreement, absent proper notice, if one side's right to present its case has been denied, when an award goes beyond the scope of the arbitration clause, or when the parties' agreement has been ignored in the composition of the arbitral tribunal. Would or should courts enforce awards not based on an agreement to arbitrate, or when one side was denied an opportunity to present its case? Reference to annulled awards sits squarely in the same coterie of grounds for non-recognition.

9. The mandatory (or expectation) tone in such a future indicative construction might be illustrated in a sentence such as, 'The scholarships will not be revoked unless ('la bourse ne sera révoquée que si...') the student is found guilty of cheating.' On the 'may' versus 'must' debate in relation to New York Convention Art. V, see, for example, Georgios Petrochilos, 'On the Mechanics and Rationale of Enforcing Awards Annulled in their State of Origin Under the New York Convention', (1999) 48 *Int'l & Comp. Law Q.* 858; Richard W Hulbert, 'Further Observations on Chromalloy: A Contract Misconstrued, a Law Misapplied, and an Opportunity Foregone', 13 *ICSID Rev.* 124, 144 (Spring 1998); Jan Paulsson, 'May or Must Under the New York Convention: An Exercise in Syntax and Linguistics', (1998) 14 *Arb. Int'l* 227.

10. See, for example, the US federal court decisions in the following cases: *TermoRio S.A. v Electranta*, 487 F.3d 928 (D.C. Cir. 2007) (deferring to the annulment in Colombia of an award made in Bogotá); *Baker Marine v Chevron*, 191 F.3d 194 (2d Cir. 1999) (deferring to the Nigerian court *vacatur* of an arbitral award made in Lagos); *Thai-Lao Lignite (Thailand) Co. v Gov't of Lao People's Democratic Republic*, 864 F. 3d 172 (2d Cir.) (deferring to a Malaysian court judgment annulling an arbitral award made in Malaysia); *Bechtel v Dubai*, 300 F.Supp.2d 112 (D.D.C. 2004) and 360 F.Supp.2d 136 (D.D.C. 2005) (refusing to enforce an award annulled for failure to administer an oath invoking God Almighty as required by UAE law, at a time when the UAE had not signed the New York Convention).

its country of origin.[11] Much debate has focused on whether annulment should trigger universal effect, making an award unenforceable anywhere when presented for enforcement abroad where the losing side has assets, thus permitting a court at the place of arbitration to uproot an award once and for all.[12]

Notwithstanding the more forceful text in the French version of the New York Convention, jurists in France generally see the Convention as providing more leeway and discretion, with recognition of an annulled award proving the rule rather than the exception. French courts look to its Article VII, which provides that the treaty shall not deprive any interested party of a right to avail itself of an arbitral award in the manner allowed by the law where the award has been relied upon. The French judiciary thus gives effect to vacated awards under the national law of France, as enforcement forum.

Shifts of emphasis to notions of 'a-national' arbitration and 'international *lex mercatoria*' enter international disputes through national legal theory, espoused by French scholars such as Emmanuel Gaillard, Philippe Fouchard and Berthold Goldman.[13] The Gallic view received its most classic expression in the *Hilmarton* case.[14]

11. See *Corporación Mexicana De Mantenimiento Integral v Pemex–Exploración Y Producción*, 832 F.3d 92 (2d Cir. 2016). This *Pemex* decision recognised an award annulled at the seat in Mexico, pursuant to provisions of Mexican procedural law that had changed since the parties' initial agreement to arbitrate. In *Chromalloy v Egypt*, 939 F.Supp. 907 (D.D.C. 1996), an arbitral tribunal in Cairo gave damages to an American company for breach of a helicopter maintenance contract, in an award later vacated in Egypt for the tribunal's alleged failure to apply the correct law. In the United States, where the losing side had assets, the American court reasoned that error of law did not constitute a ground for *vacatur* in the United States, thus permitting award enforcement.

12. For some scholars, the New York Convention has been interpreted as containing an implicit understanding that the arbitral *situs* will monitor an arbitration's procedural integrity, in exchange for which other countries will recognise awards that pass muster where rendered. See W. Michael Reisman, *Systems of Control in International Adjudication and Arbitration* 113–120 (1992). See also Albert Jan van den Berg, 'Annulment of Awards in International Arbitration', in R Lillich and C Brower, eds, *International Arbitration in the 21st Century* 133 (1994); W Laurence Craig, 'Some Trends and Developments in the Laws and Practice of International Commercial Arbitration' (1995) 30 *Tex. Int'l Law J*. 1.

13. See Philippe Fouchard, 'La Portée internationale de l'annulation de la sentence arbitrale dans son pays d'origine', 1997 *Rev. Arb.* 329; Philippe Fouchard, Emmanuel Gaillard and Berthold Goldman, *Traité de l'arbitrage commercial international* (Paris: Editions LITEC, 1996) ss. 270, 1595, 168789. For contrasting perspectives, see, for example, William W Park, 'Duty and Discretion in International Arbitration' (1999) 93 *Am. J. Int'l Law* 805; William W Park, 'Lex Loci Arbitri and International Commercial Arbitration', (1983) 32 *Int'l & Comp. LQ* 21; Jan Paulsson, 'Delocalisation of International Commercial Arbitration: When and Why It Matters,' (1983) 32 *Int'l & Comp. LQ* 53; Jan Paulsson, 'Arbitration Unbound: Award Detached from the Law of its Country of Origin', (1981) 30 *Int'l & Comp. LQ* 358; Emmanuel Gaillard, 'Enforcement of Awards Set Aside in the Country of Origin', (1999) 14 *ICSID Review (Foreign Investment Law J* 16.

14. *Hilmarton v OTV*, 1997 *Rev. Arb.* 376, note Ph. Fouchard; see, for example, Philippe

In the *Hilmarton* case, an arbitrator in Geneva had denied a claim for consulting fees to a consultant who had helped obtain a concession for drainage in Algiers, erroneously believing that the consultancy violated Switzerland's public policy. While there was no allegation of bribery, the consultant's activity purportedly offended an Algerian statute on commercial intermediaries. After a Swiss cantonal court vacated the award that had denied consultant's fees, on the basis that the arbitrator made a mistake in understanding that statute,[15] a new arbitral tribunal awarded damages to the consultant.

In France, both awards were recognised, each in a separate proceeding: first, the annulled award in favour of the defendant which resisted payment of the fees,[16] and then the award in the second arbitration in favour of the claimant consultant who won his fees.[17] Ultimately, the French *Cour de Cassation* held that the *res judicata* effect of the first judgment, recognising the annulled arbitral award, prevented recognition of the second award.[18] Given the different interpretations of the Convention, and the intricacies of national law, an arbitral award annulled in its country of origin could be presented for enforcement against assets in other countries with dramatically different results. Courts purporting to apply the very same treaty to the very same facts may come to diametrically opposed conclusions.[19]

Fouchard, 'La Portée internationale de l'annulation de la sentence arbitrale dans son pays d'origine', 1997 *Rev. Arb.* 329; Jean-François Poudret, 'Quelle Solution Pour en Finir avec L'Affaire Hilmarton?' 1998 *Rev. Arb.* 7 (1998); Eric Schwartz, 'French Supreme Court Renders Final Judgment in the Hilmarton Case', 1997 *Int'l Arb. LR* 45; Georges Delaume, 'Enforcement Against a Foreign State of an Arbitral Award Annulled in the Foreign State', 1997 (No. 2) *Rev. droit des affaires int./Int'l Bus. LJ* 253; Jan Paulsson, 'Enforcing Arbitral Awards Notwithstanding a Local Standard Annulment', 9 *ICC Bull.* (May 1998), at 14. For an earlier decision along these lines, see *Pabalk v Norsolor*, Cour de Cassation, 9 Oct. 1984, 1985 *Rev. Arb.* 431, note B. Goldman; (1985) 112 *J. Dr. Int'l* 679, note Ph. Kahn (award vacated in Austria enforceable in France).

15. The award was rendered in August 1988 and thus subject to challenge for 'arbitrariness' under Art 36 of the Intercantonal Arbitration Concordat. Upheld by the Swiss Tribunal fédéral, the Geneva court found that conflict with Algerian legislation did not constitute a violation of Swiss public policy. See 1993 *Rev. Arb.* 315 (Court de Justice du Canton de Genève, 17 Nov. 1989), 322 (Tribunal fédéral, 17 Apr. 1990). For awards rendered from 1989 onward, a different result would probably obtain under the Loi fédérale sur le droit internationale privé (LDIP).

16. Cour d'Appel de Paris, 1993 *Rev. Arb.* 300, relying on NCPC arts 1498, 1502, which do not include annulment where rendered as grounds for award non-recognition. The appellate court's judgment was upheld by the Cour de cassation, 1994 *Rev. Arb.* 327, with commentary by Charles Jarrosson; English translation in 9 *Mealey's Int'l Arb. Rep.*, E-3 (May 1994); 20 *Y.B. Com. Arb.* 663. See, for example, Vincent Heuzé, 'La Morale, L'Arbitre et Le Juge', 1993 *Rev. Arb.* 179.

17. The Nanterre Tribunal de Grande Instance recognised the second award in a decision confirmed by the Versailles Cour d'Appel, 29 June 1995, 1995 *Rev. Arb.* 639.

18. 10 June 1997, 1997 *Rev. Arb.* 376.

19. For an interesting twist on competing views about the effect of arbitral awards rendered abroad, see *Dallah Real Estate & Tourism Holding Co v Ministry of Religious Affairs, Gov.*

Some observers might roll their eyes at the different results derived from nuances in wording and legal framework, including various connotations given to the verb 'may' in the English version of the New York Convention. Does justice and equity depend on such 'technicalities'? For better or for worse, it seems so, at least at present. For those in the thick of the action, the buyer and the seller in a commercial transaction, justice and equity depend on precisely such parsing of language. The seller who wins the arbitration will say, 'Where is the justice in denying the arbitrators' clear decision?' The buyer who has obtained annulment of the award will retort, 'Where is the equity in disregarding a ruling of the court?' Each seeks justification in a treaty which may allow more than one response.

General discussions of law take meaning only in concrete cases, some of which prove quite mundane, except to those whose welfare and fortunes remain in jeopardy. In the narrative set forth above, human rights include an entitlement to be paid (for the seller), just as State sovereignty (for the seller) implicates respect for the judicial decisions at the place of arbitration.

Looking forward, the transient aspects of arbitration can be expected to continue their evolution. Different parts of the world provide divergent legal frameworks for cross-border dispute resolution, whether in respect of statutory grounds for award *vacatur*, or for recognition of awards annulled pursuant to those statutes. The substance of arbitration, however, retains its core of permanence, resting on agreements that the merits of a dispute will be adjudicated by decision-makers chosen by the parties. This interaction of the permanent and the transient will enrich scholars and practitioners with challenges that Derek would have delighted to share.

of Pakistan [2011] 1 AC 763. The UK Supreme Court refused to enforce an ICC award made in Paris, in favour of a Saudi company, reasoning that under French law the Pakistani government was not bound by an arbitration agreement signed by a trust established by that government. A year later, however, a French court came to the opposite conclusion in rejecting an application to vacate the award in favour of the Saudi creditor, reasoning that the intervention in contract negotiations by officials of the Pakistani government meant that the State (not the trust) was in fact the true contracting party ('la véritable partie pakistanaise lors de l'opération économique'). See *Gouvernement du Pakistan contre Société Dallah*, Cour d'appel de Paris, 1ère Chambre, 17 février 2011, no. d'inscription 09/28533.

THE POWER OF STATES TO MAKE MEANINGFUL PROMISES TO FOREIGNERS

Jan Paulsson[*]

[*Editorial note*: This contribution is a slightly amended version of an article that originally appeared at (2010) 1(2) *Journal of International Dispute Settlement* 341–352 and is reproduced by kind permission of the publisher.][**]

Derek Roebuck was a wonderfully singular man; somehow, every conversation with him left one with the equable sense that the world was a pleasanter and friendlier place than what one might have been thinking. He found many things interesting and most things humorous, and rejoiced in his discoveries – and just as much, it seemed, in those of others. This, of course, spilled over to his scholarship. It helped very much that he had a knack for breathing life into his unparalleled forays into the history of arbitration, and for reducing complex and arcane historical developments to their significant contextual essence. I am no legal historian, but once thought it would be useful to emulate him as I set out to describe the antecedents and emergence of a new feature of international arbitration, and to do so as best I could in the straightforward way which I perceived and appreciated in Derek's work. This is what came of it.

This article examines fundamental principles and objectives of relevance to States that enter into treaties for the protection of foreign investment. Leaving aside matters of idealism and principled governance, the author suggests that the obvious policy objective is access to interna-

[*] Professor of Law, University of Miami; Centennial Professor, London School of Economics. This article is adapted from 'El poder de los Estados para hacer promesas significativas a los extranjeros', (Spring 2009) 6(21) *Revista de Economia y Derecho* 79, itself developed from the author's inaugural lecture as honorary professor of the Faculty of Law of the Universidad Peruana de Ciencias Aplicadas on 29 August 2008 and from his contribution to the United Nations Lecture Series on International Law. The author has acted as advocate with roughly equal frequency on behalf of States and investors in disputes under investment treaties.

tional capital at the lowest possible cost. Investors are rational: to insist that those who act in the name of governments have an unfettered right to alter the terms of investment in the alleged public interest would lead to tragic disempowerment and dependence. If States were incapable of giving reliable promises—because their misconceived 'sovereignty' renders them powerless to do so—the policy objective of attracting foreign investment would be illusory.

States tend to be annoyed when a foreigner claims that they have violated legal obligations. States are even more irritated when they are required to defend themselves before an international court or tribunal, perceiving it as an affront to their sovereignty.

Let us then explore three broad questions. First, is a voluntary restriction on sovereignty a violation of sovereignty? Secondly, if restrictions on sovereignty are a matter of sovereign choice, what are the reasons for accepting such limitations? Thirdly, what are good State practices in circumstances when a State has made a commitment of this nature?

We need to begin by considering the meaning of the word 'sovereignty', which is not that 'I do what I want.' It certainly does not mean 'all powerful'. Children dream of omnipotence, and long for the day when they no longer have to seek their parents' permission for anything. But adults know that we confront the daily reality of a thousand reasons why we cannot do whatever we want.

A more interesting question is whether sovereignty, even if it does not give us the power to overcome the forces of nature, or even the effects of accidents and miscalculations, at least means that no one else can tell us what to do. This merits some reflection. If all men are equal, then in this sense every person would be sovereign. No one could tell anyone else how to behave. But the fact is that individual human beings *do not really want to be sovereign in this extreme sense*. We are willing to give up some of our freedom, indeed we insist on the opportunity of making a bargain:

- we accept that criminal laws apply to us so that we can be protected by those same laws;
- we accept that we have to pay for our reckless behaviour so that we can live in greater tranquillity because that rule has the consequence that our fellow citizens will also tend to behave less recklessly;
- and we accept that we are held to a bad bargain because if our contracts are not binding we will be stuck in the poverty of a primitive economic system where every transaction is instant—cash and carry—and we are thus left incapable of creating wealth by shared enterprise, by investment in reliance upon long-term commitments, or by the use of capital from willing lenders.

States have similar motives for accepting legal limitations on their future conduct. And just as individuals must accept that it would be calamitous if every individual had the 'sovereign' right to decide whether he is guilty of criminal conduct, recklessness or breach of contract, so too a State must accept that it cannot be the judge of a controversy as to whether it has transgressed legal limits. No one, even a State, can be a judge in his own cause. These concepts are simple, but they demand mature reflection. Dictatorships seek to abuse law, and seek to disguise this abuse by pretensions of sovereignty.

This is an immense danger, and needs to be exposed for what it is. But let us first recall some basic principles, illustrated by a famous example.

On 21 March 1921, a British steamship named the *SS Wimbledon*, operating under charter by a French transporter, was informed by the German authorities that it would not be allowed transit through the Kiel Canal, which runs through northern Germany, connecting the Atlantic and the Baltic. The French Government espoused the claim of its national, stating that Germany had violated international law and should be ordered to pay reparations. The ship was carrying munitions loaded in Greece and destined for the Polish naval base at Danzig. As a result of the German refusal of transit, the *Wimbledon* was immobilized for 11 days and then had to seek longer passage north of Denmark. Germany contended that it was in the right, pursuant to its own national Neutrality Orders—concerning Germany's neutrality in the Russo–Polish war—which prohibited the transit of such cargo. France, joined by Britain, Italy and Japan, brought suit before the Permanent Court of International Justice (PCIJ—the predecessor of today's International Court of Justice), asserting that the German refusal breached the Treaty of Versailles, under which the Kiel Canal was to 'be maintained free and open to the vessels of commerce and war of all nations at peace with Germany on terms of entire equality'. Germany was entitled under the Treaty to impose charges and regulations, but only so long as they did 'not unnecessarily impede traffic'.

The PCIJ recognized that Germany had 'sovereign rights which no one disputes that she possesses over the Kiel Canal'. But those rights were subject to a limitation, namely that established in the Versailles Treaty. Germany insisted that its right as a neutral power to decide whether munitions destined for a country at war were 'an essential part of its sovereignty' which could not be waived by agreement. The PCIJ disagreed, and ordered Germany to pay compensation to France on account of its national, the transport company.

The most famous passage from the Court's judgment, rendered in 1923, reads as follows:

The court declines to see in the conclusion of any Treaty, by which a State undertakes to perform, or refrain from performing, a particular act, an abandonment of its sovereignty. No doubt any convention creating an obligation of this kind places a restriction upon the exercise of the sovereign rights of the State, in the sense that it requires them to be exercised in a certain way. But the right of entering into international engagements is an attribute of State sovereignty.

'*But the right of entering into international engagements is an attribute of State sovereignty.*' This is a simple sentence, but it has great weight. The ability to make a binding commitment is part of what makes a State a State. We are talking about the power to make a meaningful promise. If States did not have that power, they would be handicapped. The act of limiting possible conduct tomorrow is an exercise of authority today. And if that act is to be internationally meaningful, it must first of all create binding obligations—and secondly be evaluated by an impartial court or tribunal. It is really no different than what we see in relations among ordinary individuals—a man whose promises mean nothing will have great difficulties in life. He will have to work alone, and he will always have to pay cash.

So let us move to our second theme. Now that we know that the capacity to agree to binding limitations on sovereignty is an *attribute* of that same sovereignty, why should any State do so?

There are many possible reasons. Some have to do with a wish to exercise leadership. A State is unlikely to project international influence, and to convince other States to cooperate in certain ways, unless it shows that it abides by its own commitments. The impulse to make international commitments may also be an expression of popular will, as political candidates identify a public desire for the expansion of certain values (such as human rights or environmental protection), are elected on such a platform, and once in office are prepared to join leaders of other countries to pursue a common goal to secure those values.

But perhaps it is easiest for the purposes of analysis to focus on a type of limitation on future government conduct which is accepted predominantly *as a matter of self-interest*—through the mechanism of treaties for the promotion and protection of foreign investment. There are over 2,000 bilateral treaties of this kind. They are commonly referred to as bilateral investment treaties (BITs). Although not identical in every detail, they almost invariably contain four commitments. First, each State promises that it will not nationalize the investments made by nationals of the other State, or take steps equivalent to nationalization, without requisite compensation. Second, each State promises that it will not discriminate against the nationals of the other State. Third, each State promises that it will treat investors from the other State in accordance with international law, and therefore notably in accordance with the concept of fair and equitable treatment. Finally, these three broad substantive commitments are given force by a fourth promise, which is that each State accepts that any claim for breach of the substantive promises may be brought by the complaining investor to international arbitration.

There have over the past 20 years been many arbitrations under these BITs. In all of those arbitrations, a State has been the defendant. Sometimes the State has prevailed, sometimes it has lost and sometimes the result was not wholly favourable to either side.

But States never enjoy having to defend themselves before an external body. Some of these cases have been politically controversial. It has been pointed out that the arbitrators are private persons, and the question has been asked whether their decisions violate sovereignty. We have already seen that this is a bad question. It is not a violation of sovereignty for a State to be held to its own commitments. The good question is rather whether it is in a State's interest to give the promises contained in these BITs in the first place. Some wonder if it is not against a State's interest to agree to BITs. So let us examine possible objections.

Are BITs inherently unfair? Some critics have suggested that BITs may be the handiwork of powerful investors, who convince their home States to put pressure on capital-importing States to sign them, or—rather insultingly to the negotiators—that they are signed in ignorance of their consequences.

This is not a valid objection. It is easy to test it, by examining the contents of the many BITs which have been entered into by developing States *among themselves*. We might call them 'South-South BITs'. These are obviously not the handicraft of capital-exporters. So it is interesting to consider what they contain: precisely the same four promises found in other BITs. Indeed, the first of the modern investor-State arbitrations, 25 years ago, in the case *SPP v Egypt* brought under the ICSID Convention,[1] arose out of the famous Egyptian Law No 43 of 1974—not from a BIT at all.[2] This Law No 43, which initiated a successful Open Door Policy for foreign investment, was conceived by the Egyptian Parliament, not by Western countries or corporations. And yet Law No 43 contained the same protections. More recently, in February 2008, in another ICSID case brought under the Oman–Yemen BIT, a treaty whose only official version is in Arabic, an Omani investor's claim was resolved, and the outcome

---

1. International Centre for Settlement of Investment Disputes (ICSID), established by the Convention on the Settlement of Investment Disputes between States and Nationals of Other States of 18 March 1965 (ICSID Convention).
2. 14 April 1988, 3 ICSID Rep 131 (1995).

accepted by both sides.[3] The treaty contained the usual undertakings. We must conclude that these protections are ones which developing countries themselves consider fair and appropriate.

Is it possible that arbitrators who decide BIT cases render unfair decisions? Many losing parties will say so, and in some they may even be right in the eyes of impartial observers. Justice is not perfect in every case. Still, advocates who represent States as often as they represent investors are unlikely to say that there is a general bias against respondent States. There are certainly numerous examples of successful defences against investor claims—and examples of furious protests by investors who considered the rejection of their claims to be miscarriages of justice.[4] Better, from the States' point of view, unsuccessful investors have on occasion been ordered to pay significant costs. (Hungary, Ukraine, Mexico, Pakistan and Turkey, for example, have been beneficiaries of such orders.)

Investment tribunals have, moreover, shown that corruption and other illegality is not tolerated. Kenya, El Salvador and the Philippines have, for example, obtained the dismissal of claims without even considering whether they may have been well founded in principle due to the fact that the original investment involved bribery, misrepresentations or other breaches of national law.

And where the investor has prevailed, international tribunals have often reduced lost-profit claims by considerable margins, leaving many investors with the feeling that their recovery was undeservedly reduced.

It is understandable that in notorious cases the public perception tends to be simplistic: any international tribunal is good if we win, bad if we lose. But we are not discussing sporting competitions like the World Cup. Resolving disputes properly is essential to the successful management of relations with investors. A State may be happy to win, but what counts for its long-term reputation is that it confronts the inevitable occasions of disagreements in a loyal, businesslike and efficient way—and that it respects the outcome of international legal proceedings. Mexico is an outstanding example. When it became a party to the North American Free Trade

---

3. *Desert Line Projects v Yemen*, ICSID Case No ARB/05/17, 6 February 2008.

4. When an affiliate of the US corporation Thunderbird Resorts lost its claim under NAFTA against Mexico following closure of its gaming facilities (and was moreover ordered to pay Mexico $1,250,000 in legal costs), (*International Thunderbird Gaming Corporation v The United Mexican States*, 26 January 2006), its Board of Directors issued a press release in which the General Counsel was quoted as saying that 'the Company believed that NAFTA would level the playing field in Mexico ... clearly it did not as this same government... has given permits for hundreds of new locations'. The President and CEO, for his part, was quoted as speculating: 'It is not coincidental that the 'permits' were issued to the most powerful interests in the country while [the relevant Minister] was seeking to become the next President of Mexico.' Press release dated 27 January 2006, published the same day on the OGEMID mailing list http://www.transnational-dispute-management.com/ogemid accessed 30 June 2010, or ogemid@jiscmail.ac.uk.

Agreement (NAFTA), Mexico opened the door to international claims against it by US and Canadian investors. There have been a number of such claims. Mexico has won some of them, and lost others. What the international community has observed is (i) that Mexico defended itself competently, (ii) that its losses have been moderate and (iii) that it has paid the amounts ordered. Its reputation has been enhanced.[5] And compared to the vast benefits of NAFTA, in the magnitude of billions, former Mexican observers have pointed out that incidental payments to wrongfully treated investors, in the magnitude of millions, is a small price to pay.[6]

In highly controversial cases it may indeed be very attractive for States to have the problem resolved once and for all on the international level rather than to fester on the local scene, creating tensions, disruption and adverse reputational consequences for a very long time. A case like *World Duty Free v Kenya* might have led to disaster if it had not been solved internationally. The claim was for US$500 million, the investor had shown himself willing and able to corrupt national officials at the very highest level, and an official inquiry at the time showed that the Kenyan judiciary itself was severely compromised.[7]

Should we not consider, one might ask, whether acceptance of BITs in fact leads to more foreign investment? This might—just possibly—be an interesting question in particular circumstances. As a general proposition, however, the premise is dubious; it seems to be wrong; it seems most unlikely that the signature of BITs leads directly to an increase in foreign investment. Foreign investments would flow massively into Switzerland even if Switzerland had never signed any BITs. Anyone can understand why. A solvent State with stable good governance attracts investments without BITs. On the other hand, a State with a record of financial crises, repudiation of debts and arbitrary policy changes will not suddenly look attractive just by signing BITs. For a State to demonstrate enduring reliability is a matter of much greater complexity. It requires mature institutions: a tradition of efficient and reliable governance. The rule of law is a part of such an environment, and the network of BITs contributes to the rule of law.

The insight is not complicated: a country governed in accordance with the rule of law has little to fear from BITs, or from international tribunals. (Switzerland, although it hardly needs to prove its institutional bona fides,

---

5. For instance, NAFTA trade in goods in 2009 totalled $735 billion and regional trade in services during 2008 was $69.8 billion <http://www.ustr.gov/trade-agreements/free-trade-agreements/north-american-free-trade- agreement-nafta> accessed 24 June 2010.
6. Guillermo Aguilar-Alvarez, *NAFTA @ 15: Lessons Learned, Moving Forward*, lecture delivered at the University of Miami School of Law on 23 March 2010 (to be published). Mr Aguilar-Alvarez, a senior member of Mexico's NAFTA negotiating team, also pointed out that NAFTA has become a remarkable instrument of self-discipline and dispute avoidance.
7. ICSID Case No ARB/00/7, 4 October 2004.

has signed a range of BITs; they are unlikely to be of concern to the Swiss government as a potential source of international liability.)

Equally, a failure to accept the concept of investor protection will certainly discourage investors, including *present* investors who should be the first target of capital-importing States: to persuade them to expand their investments in magnitude and duration.

Let us then consider the fundamental purpose of investor protection. It is certainly not to protect multinational corporations. It is nonsense to speak of the interests or rights of corporations in the abstract. We have no *a priori* stake in the survival of corporations as a way of doing business. If they did not serve society, they could be abolished without regret. But of course they have proved unsurpassed as levers for the mobilization of capital and the use of technology. So when we protect the 'rights' of corporations, which of course means the rights of the people behind them, we do so because that is the price of sustaining a valuable system, explicitly embraced by both capitalist and social-democratic theory—and implicitly by the central planners of State capitalism.

When we look at the world in this light, we discover that *the objective of investment protection is to convince investors to invest for the longest time possible and for the lowest possible return.*[8] That is how the capital-importing country maximizes its benefits. In a lawless country, someone will always be prepared to speculate, but only if there is a spectacular rate of return—after which both the investment and the profits vanish. This is not desirable investment.

So let us conclude with respect to this second theme.

The idea that States may be held accountable under international law by arbitral tribunals created by treaty is neither new nor radical. There were hundreds of such cases in the 19th century. The defendant States were of all types: rich and powerful, European or ex-colonial. International tribunals held the United States responsible for actions which its Supreme Court had declared not to be breaches of international law. Those awards were nevertheless respected by the United States.[9] When one of the most illustrious of all awards was handed down against Great Britain in the *Alabama Claims* (1872), the British arbitrator issued a harsh dissent, calling the award of some US$15 million gold 'unjust', but his government—far more powerful at the time than the United States—nevertheless paid the awarded amount.[10]

---

8. I am indebted to important insights found in an early contribution to this field, Jürgen Voss, 'The Protection and Promotion of Foreign Direct Investment in Developing Countries: Interests, Interdependencies, Intricacies' (1982) 31 ICLQ 686.
9. Jan Paulsson, *Denial of Justice under International Law* (2005) 257.
10. Ibid 261.

This tradition of respect for international law as applied by international tribunals should be kept in mind by critics of investment protection. Such critics sometimes imagine that international tribunals can be paralysed by declarations of municipal courts that the treaties creating international jurisdiction are contrary to national constitutions. But to suggest that the alleged requirements of a nation's own constitution may neutralize the international undertakings of its government flies in the face of international law itself. It may happen that such undertakings are an excess of power under national law, or may run afoul of national law in other ways. But they do not (provided of course that the appearance of authority is sufficient for the purposes of international law) prevent anyone from relying on those undertakings internationally. Whatever their force as a matter of national law is, such arguments evaporate on the international plane.

Judge Keba Mbaye (once the Vice-President of the International Court of Justice, and before that the First President of the Supreme Court of Senegal) put it as follows: 'A state must not be allowed to cite the provisions of its law in order to escape from an arbitration that it has already accepted.'[11] Lord Mustill suggested that: 'Perhaps it should be classed as a principle of international *ordre public*.'[12] This concept was firmly endorsed in a landmark arbitration brought by a German private party against Belgium, in a case called *Benteler v Belgium* (1984).[13] It has even been incorporated into the *municipal* law of Switzerland, which provides that a state party to an arbitration agreement 'cannot rely on its own law to contest the arbitrability of a dispute or its own capacity to be a party to an arbitration'.[14]

Criticism of international tribunals on the grounds that they impede democratic policies — whether protection of the environment or the labour market — is misdirected. International tribunals do not establish policy. They give effect to international agreements. To deny the authority of international tribunals is to deprive States of the power to make meaningful promises. The French Professor Pierre Mayer wrote a comprehensive and fundamental article some 20 years ago on 'The neutralisation of the normative power of the State with respect to State contracts', in which he queried: 'Is it not paradoxical that the exaltation of sovereignty over natural resources implied preventing the sovereign State from entrusting their temporary exploitation by a foreign corporation possessed of the

---

11. *60 Years On: A Look at the Future* (ICC Publications No 412, a collection of papers from the 60th Anniversary of the International Chamber of Commerce) 296 (1984).
12. Michael Mustill, 'The New *Lex Mercatoria*: The First Twenty-Five Years' in M Bos and I Brownlie (eds), *Liber Amicorum for Lord Wilberforce* (1987) 149, at 177, n 91.
13. Jan Paulsson, 'May a State Invoke its Internal Law to Repudiate Consent to International Arbitration?' (1986) 2 *Arb Int'l* 90.
14. Federal Act on Private International Law art 177(2).

necessary capital and technology, on the grounds that the State cannot validly accord the guarantees required by the corporation?'[15] He added: 'to allow States to undo their commitments means in practice to forbid them from making undertakings in the future'.[16]

When France wanted to ensure that the Walt Disney Corporation would build Eurodisneyland outside Paris and not in Spain, the Parliament passed a special law to authorize the government to accept the jurisdiction of international arbitration (ICSID) in agreements 'with foreign corporations for the implementation of operations having a national interest'.[17] The US corporation was adamant about a neutral jurisdiction in the event of a dispute with the French government.

Criticism of international tribunals on the grounds that they should operate more efficiently, transparently, coherently and fairly are entirely legitimate. But no human institutions are perfect. International arbitral tribunals have existed for many generations; complaints by those disappointed in their awards have existed for precisely as long. One must be careful to recognize criticism which is only a cover for the disinclination to obey international norms and institutions.

It thus seems that many of those who challenge the legitimacy of international adjudication aim at the wrong target. They criticize the principle of the supremacy of international law when their real complaint has to do with the political choices of their own government in making the bargains reflected in international treaties. The mistake is a dangerous one. For what will happen if they destroy the authority of international law? What then does it matter if they are right about the policy? What will they do once they have prevailed— once they have achieved agreement as to important rules for the protection of the environment, the elimination of child labour, the proper treatment of persons accused of crime, an adjustment of the terms of trade in favour of impoverished producers denied access to markets? What a hollow victory indeed, to stand there empty-handed, deprived of a shattered tool.

To sum up: in the field of international investments, arbitral tribunals are instruments of the rule of law. Their purpose is not to favour the rich, but to enable States to make reliable promises. To undermine that reliability is to deprive the State of a valuable tool, to generate international transactions as favourable terms. Arbitral tribunals are not to be blamed for the contents of treaties. International tribunals tend to irritate respondent States—whether they are rich or poor—in individual cases; yet their

15. Pierre Mayer, 'La neutralisation du pouvoir normatif de l'Etat en matière de contrats d'Etat' (1986) J Droit Int'l 5.
16. Ibid, ('*[P]ermettre aux Etats de se délier, c'est en pratique leur interdire de se lier dans le futur.*')
17. Article 9, Law No 86972 of 19 August 1986, *Journal officiel*, 22 August 1986, 10190.

decisions should be respected in order to achieve the long-term benefits of the rule of law. Respect for settled and legitimate expectations is a precondition for healthy international relations.

And finally, our third and final theme. It will be the shortest. What should a State do once it has accepted certain limitation of its sovereignty by making these promises to foreigners? In very broad terms, what are best practices once a State has signed BITs?

In some countries, international arbitration is viewed in a defeatist and defensive way. There is a failure to perceive that effective use of the arbitral process is an important task in managing international economic relations— indeed, in managing the national debt. Wherever such defeatist views prevail, the attachment of foreign investors to the arbitral process will continue to be viewed as part of a strategy of the rich to take unfair advantage of the poor.

Here are some premises of defensiveness or defeatism that explain negative views of international arbitration:

- States are reluctant to subject themselves to the jurisdiction of tribunals that are not part of their own apparatus. This is generally an especially important consideration with respect to newly independent nations, where the weaknesses of the local private sector are such that foreign investors and international banks demand direct contractual commitments by the State itself. As national economies develop, it becomes increasingly rare that ministries act directly as signatories to private law contracts.
- When developing countries find themselves in international arbitration with foreign investors, they often participate with misgivings or even bitterness. Such feelings tend to intensify over time as new officials—or indeed new regimes—look back critically on the work of their predecessors.
- Many parties from developing countries misunderstand the international arbitral process in a number of ways. They assume that it is a mechanism designed for the protection of the investor, when in fact it is a two-way street with significant advantages to the State as compared even to its domestic courts. It should be obvious that the failure of foreign investors to fulfil contractual undertakings may give rise to important and justified claims or defences. International arbitral awards tend to be vastly more enforceable, as a practical matter, than domestic court judgments, which benefit from very limited recognition abroad.

Many States still believe that international arbitration intrinsically favours the foreign party, when experience over the past two generations has shown that serious governments even in poor countries are able to use the process successfully. Moreover, the leading international arbitral institutions have responded to the vast changes in the identity of their users by making corresponding changes in their governing structure. For example, a majority of the members of the International Court of Arbitration of the International Chamber of Commerce are today neither European nor North American.

It is also a mistake to suspect investors of trying to lure inexperienced States before courts which are biased against them, because serious foreign investors understand that it is in their own interest that host States have enduring confidence in international arbitration.

It serves little purpose to tell host States that they should respect the international arbitral process because it is the right and decent thing to do, and that in the long run foreign investors will think better of them for it. To get anywhere, one must rather understand that the arbitral mechanism is something they can use effectively to their concrete benefit.

It is a serious mistake to focus on the *opposition* between investor and host State. The true dividing line goes *within* the community of investors; there are good investors and bad investors. Good investors are there for the long haul, and want to make a decent return, as is understood by everyone from the beginning. In order to merit that reward, they expect that they will be held to making a real contribution, which they are happy for anyone to evaluate. Their enemy is not the host State, because they have shared interests, but the bad investor, a dubious operator who wants to make a quick buck, getting vast profits for shoddy goods, procuring signatures on all sorts of opaque documents, contracts, amendments and certificates designed as a legal cover for poor performance—or worse. The bad investor creates a climate of suspicion and despair which also harms good investors.

Those who operate transparently, professionally and rigorously, and create an atmosphere of seriousness and reliability, are on the same side, whether they represent investors or governments. They are united in their desire for an environment in which long-term legitimate expectations may be relied upon. If such an environment is brought about, and if bad investors are discouraged or flushed out, many dubious debts will evaporate and Ministers of Finance will sleep better.

How may such a good environment be created and maintained? It seems clear that good practices include rigour and professionalism in monitoring foreign investment—as it enters the country, as it is implemented, and as returns on investments flow back to the investor. It seems equally clear that it is bad practice to sign a BIT and then forget about it. Unfortunately, as my father often said, 'Good examples are admired; bad ones followed.' But this cycle of negligence can surely be broken. There are many capital-importing countries which develop serious and enduring structures to channel investments in positive ways. This does not happen automatically. If the benefits of foreign investment are to be maximized, the hard work for the capital-importing State begins after the BIT has been signed. It is imperative that officials with adequate knowledge and experience review the regulatory framework critically. Is it clear? Is it effective? Are relevant systems of approvals and licences comprehensible to foreigners? Is the decision-making process transparent?

In one Latin American country which has been exceptionally successful in attracting foreign investment, an important inter-Ministerial Commission ensures oversight, coordination and implementation. It has set up a comprehensive website which contains complete and comprehensible information not only in Spanish and English, but also French, German and Italian—that is to say, languages chosen to facilitate relations with major economic partners.

Reducing the obscurity of governance is of benefit not only to the foreign investor, but also to the host State; opaque bureaucratic procedures are breeding grounds for corruption, and corruption obviously leads to pathological decision-making.

BITs should be adjusted to suit the policy desiderata relevant to the particular bilateral relationship. When two countries share a common border, they may wish to achieve substantial integration of their economies, and on that basis provide full investor protection to whatever investment finds its way across the border, even if it has not been specifically approved. Even when the two countries are situated far apart, the attitude may be the same, on the reasoning that medium-volume investments should be encouraged as well, and are less likely to be initiated if formal approvals are required from the central government. But some BITs follow the example of Malaysia and Belgium/Luxembourg, who limited the applicability of their BIT to approved projects. In a case called *Gruslin v Malaysia*,[18] where the claimant was a Belgian national who had done nothing more than to invest in a fund which had made portfolio investments on the Kuala Lumpur Stock Exchange, an ICSID tribunal refused even to consider the complaint on the basis that it was not covered by the treaty because the investment had not been approved as required under that BIT.

In sum, although the purpose of agreeing to limitations on sovereignty is to gain the power of making meaningful promises, these promises go as far as they go—and no further. This too is an essential element of international law.

---

18. ICSID Case No ARB/99/3, 27 November 2000.

MEDIATION

Sir Bernard Rix*

It is a great honour to have been invited to contribute to this *Liber Amicorum* in memory of a delightful and learned colleague and friend, Professor Derek Roebuck.

After some thought, I concluded that I would like to mark the occasion not with something more or less technical, but with something broad, reflecting alternative dispute resolution over the ages and across the oceans and beliefs that can divide humankind.

I have therefore chosen to publish here the slightly edited version of a lecture on Mediation which I gave in October 2019 at the Ismaili Centre in London, on the occasion of World Conflict Resolution Day 2019. I do so with the kind permission of Mr Naushad Jivraj, President of the National Council of the Ismaili Centre of the UK.

Another impetus to the choice of the lecture on Mediation for inclusion in this *Liber Amicorum* is that it was Derek who, back in 2008, was the first to encourage me to publish anything (other than judgments, which in any event are something that lie entirely in the hands of the law reporters). That was another lecture which I gave in an interfaith setting, on that occasion to the Three Faiths Forum.[1] Derek had somehow, such was his mastery of research, found an account of my lecture online, and he rang me up out of the blue, as the then Editor of *Arbitration*, to request my permission to publish the lecture. I demurred, protesting that it said nothing at all about arbitration. However, Derek insisted, and I therefore volunteered, adding a postscript on arbitration.

So this, by way of preface, is a personal note to reciprocate Derek's encouragement to me on that occasion. I like to believe that he would have appreciated the sentiments expressed below. I shall miss him greatly.

****

---

* A former Lord Justice of Appeal (Court of Appeal, England & Wales), arbitrator, mediator and Chairman of Coexist House, London.

1. 'The Jewish contribution to the English legal system' (2008) 74(3) *Arbitration* 21–27.

The theme of my lecture this evening is Mediation.[2] But first, may I begin by expressing my thanks, accompanied by my deep sense of honour, for the invitation to speak to you tonight. I consider it to be a privilege to be associated, however briefly, through my lecture this evening, with this extraordinarily beautiful building, and the important work done here by the Ismaili Community in the United Kingdom, and throughout the world.

I am also conscious that today is World Conflict Resolution Day, and that this lecture marks the occasion of this Day. Ever since 2005, World Conflict Resolution Day has been set for the third Thursday in October, so that people in all lands can celebrate it on the same day. Its purpose is to promote awareness of mediation, arbitration, conciliation and other creative means of resolving conflict, and to promote the use of such means of conflict resolution in schools, families, businesses, communities, governments and legal systems.

Unfortunately, we seem to live in a world marked by conflict. Perhaps, but we should not be resigned to it, conflict is to some extent inevitable in a world of seven billion human beings, of many different ethnicities, nations and faiths; in a world which, increasingly over the millennia, by its very creativity, sets up tensions and conflicts of interest between people and peoples.

Daily we learn of fresh misfortunes which threaten the peace of nations. But grim as those misfortunes are, they do not perhaps threaten those overwhelming losses of the two world wars of the twentieth century. My continent of Europe, which prides itself on many things, has not acquitted itself well in the century of my birth. But perhaps it is learning from its travails. We must all hope to learn from our mistakes. This is perhaps lesson number one of my subject this evening. I will call it the lesson of self-realisation. Mediation could well be described as a process which teaches all sides to a dispute to look into their own hearts, to look at themselves in the mirror, to count their own faults and errors, and in this way to arrive at a resolution of their dispute.

Lesson number two is that, globally speaking, we are discovering a new community of interest in the realisation that our planet is threatened by global warming. This is of concern to peoples of every kind, in every corner of our world. This is of course a matter of the gravest danger, but it is also something which can bring peoples in all their multiple diversities together in their search for solutions to a common threat.

However, I am not here tonight to speak of international relations, or international law, or of global warming, fascinating as those subjects are. I am not a politician, nor a diplomat, nor a scientist. I have spent my life as

---

2. The lecture utilised a range of source material listed under *References* at the end of this article.

a lawyer, sometimes as an advocate, sometimes as a judge, sometimes as a university lecturer, and increasingly now as an arbitrator and mediator. I have therefore had long experience of conflict resolution through litigation, arbitration and mediation. I have also in recent years another aspect to my work, which is as Chairman of an interfaith charity called Coexist House. Coexist House is the birthchild of its parents in the form of Cambridge University, the City of London Corporation, the Inner Temple (one of the four Inns of Court), and the Victoria & Albert Museum. It aims to bring peoples of different faiths into a better understanding of one another, by exploring and learning about their different cultures and ideas at the very same time as celebrating what is common to them in the form of the spiritual heart of their faiths. And it seeks to do so from a physical home which is to bear the name of the charity itself, Coexist House.

So you will understand that the purposes of Coexist House and those of World Conflict Resolution Day are not a million miles apart.

That is by way of introduction. But to my theme, which is in praise of mediation as a form of conflict resolution.

This can perhaps best be understood by contrasting mediation with litigation.

Litigation is a process of trial in a national court. The language and laws will, broadly speaking, be those of the nation in whose courts the claim is brought. The judges will be the judges of those courts. Those judges are chosen by selection processes obtaining within the nation concerned and, having nothing whatsoever to do with the litigants, as judges they will generally be unknown to the litigants, and will be of uncertain expertise. Litigation is a tough and often extremely expensive process. It is essentially adversarial, even if in civil law, as distinct from common law countries, the sparring advocates may play a secondary role to the inquisitorial judge. But I am not sure which is worse: the opposing advocate, or the judge inquisitor. And if a litigant is a foreigner to the national courts concerned, as may readily occur in international trade or in matrimonial and family disputes, I can well understand that the foreign litigant feels uncomfortable, however able his or her lawyer, at dealing with the stress of litigation in a system which is essentially unfamiliar to them.

Of course, every nation must or should provide access to fair and impartial courts where citizens may bring their disputes. But, I have to say, after twenty years as a judge in the High Court and the Court of Appeal of this country, that I am inclined to think that litigation is, for the litigant, a distressing and highly stressful process, with results which, at any rate in the more difficult cases, are uncertain and may ricochet from appeal to appeal. It can also be a ruinously expensive business.

Mediation, however, is a process where the parties choose a neutral and independent mediator, who may be of any nationality or background, and may conduct the mediation in any place or language which the parties have agreed upon. It is, in other words, an entirely consensual process. The role of the mediator is to listen to both parties, to hear about their rights and wrongs, as they see them, to look through those complaints and explanations for a solution to their dispute which might be acceptable to them, and then, by explaining each side to the other, to try to bring them to a place where they can settle their dispute for themselves. A settlement is then written up and signed straightaway. Since the parties are agreed, there is usually little need for the settlement agreement to be enforced.

Who is the mediator? He or she is chosen by the parties. Often the mediator is a lawyer, but he/she need not be. The legal issues may provide the background to the dispute, but, although they often have to be taken into account, they are not determinative. Often psychological and emotional factors are in play; and sometimes those factors have to be laid to rest. At least the parties have a chance to express their emotions, their worries, fears and hopes: and that can be cathartic and thus helpful.

What do lawyers and judges think of mediation? As for lawyers, many of them are suspicious of it, partly because they think, wrongly in my view, that it will take the bread out of their mouths, by undermining litigation; and partly because they feel more comfortable with the familiar processes of the law. As for judges, I think it is on the whole true that they fall into a number of camps. There are those who are alive to, even impressed by, what mediation can achieve. There are those who, having been brought up all their professional lives in litigation, as well as in the ordinary opportunity for settlement negotiations that lies within litigation, are sceptical of what mediation adds to that world. And there are those who float ambivalently in the middle, willing, but needing, to be persuaded of mediation's virtues, if any.

Be that as it may, let us just stand back for a moment and consider some of the advantages and disadvantages of litigation and mediation respectively. Litigation's advantages, as it seems to me, are these. It gives you an answer in accordance with law. It is coercive, because it is backed by the power of the State. It is transparent, because the fundamental principle, even if there are exceptions to it, is open justice. It has a well-developed procedure which is good at defining issues, obtaining documents and exchanging evidence, both factual and expert. Finally, because – at any rate in the common law – there is its doctrine of precedent, it enables you to predict with a reasonable measure of accuracy the outcome of any case. And to assist in that prediction, it has a series of appeals to iron out any mistakes.

Litigation's disadvantages, on the other hand, are that it can be slow and has become increasingly expensive, with potentially ruinous costs implications. It can produce answers which are very black and white, so that you either fall on one side of a line or the other, even if the facts and merits appear to be rather more grey than black and white. Its remedies are limited, to the standard remedies of damages, and a few discretionary remedies in terms of injunctions and declarations and suchlike. Because it is coercive, and the process is owned by the courts, not by the litigants, it can be an extremely divisive and anxiety-ridden experience. Finally, its openness can count as a disadvantage, by making settlement more difficult.

I turn to mediation's advantages and disadvantages. Its advantages are that it is a consensual, not a coercive, process. Because it is consensual, it is owned by the parties, not by the courts. It ends, if it is successful, in agreement, in a shaking of hands, and not in the highs and lows of victory and defeat. If it is successful, then by and large its remedies will be real and immediately available, because parties will generally not agree on matters which they are unable to deliver. Enforcement therefore becomes, generally speaking, unnecessary. The roller-coaster ride of appeals and reversals are eliminated. Its remedies can be much more variable and imaginative than those of the courts: they can include such matters as apologies, the striking of new deals, the preservation of relationships. It can be relatively quick and inexpensive, at any rate as compared with the full-blown version of litigation. It is private and confidential.

Its disadvantages, however, are first of all that it may not work at all. In that case, it is an expense without a result, an expense which may simply have to be added to that of litigation, an additional inconvenience; and it may add to the delay of litigation. Because it is private and confidential, it is lacking in transparency. It does not give a decision according to law, but in accordance with compromise. Although compromise may be considered to be a virtue, it is possible also to think of it as a potential vice, where claimants are wearied into accepting less than their rights, or where defendants are cajoled into buying off claims which would ultimately fail at trial. And then there is also the public interest: a distinguished academic, Professor Hazel Genn, has complained that its successes deprive the courts of the material needed for the development of the law.

There is truth, some truth, in all of these points. However, as someone who has spent nearly fifty years as first an advocate and then a judge and then an arbitrator, I would wish to emphasise the following points. *First*, I do not regard mediation as being in opposition to litigation, as distinct from being allied to it. No doubt you need the coercive forces of litigation to make your litigation opponent listen to you, whether you are a claimant seeking a remedy or a defendant seeking a proper definition of the complaint or proper disclosure of documents. Moreover, the familiar processes of litigation, namely definition of issues, disclosure of documents and exchange of witness statements, are valuable tools towards a solution, and can therefore be a prelude not only to a trial and judgment, but instead to a solution found by the parties themselves in a mediated settlement.

Secondly, we know that most cases settle. A world in which all, or even a majority of cases proceeded to trial would be a world too awful to contemplate. Litigation, after all, is a calamitous process, however necessary it is in a civilised society to avoid even worse, and however fairly and justly it is conducted. Anyone would tell you it is, or ought to be, the last resort of its participants. If, therefore, most cases settle, and we applaud that as a good result, then there is obviously good sense in a professional process which utilises the skilled services of a mediator, an honest broker, who can assist the parties, where they need such assistance, towards a solution to their difficulties. It is not a universal panacea, but it has proven results, and its costs are a fraction of the costs of preparation for and undergoing trial.

Thirdly, I do not think we need be concerned with the courts being deprived of material for their development. There is more than enough litigation around. We are drowning in reported and unreported decisions of the courts. It is not like arbitration, where even the disputes which go to a hearing remain out of sight, because of confidentiality and inadequate reporting of awards, and where in the international commercial arena arbitration is a dominant force.

And *fourthly*, there is something human and democratic about the autonomy of mediation, and in the final prospect of disputing parties leaving their dispute with a handshake rather than the twin perils of victory or defeat, both of which are probably bad for you.

It seems to me, therefore, that mediation is a given good, and deserves to be promoted and encouraged.

The mediation with which I am most familiar is the mediation of commercial disputes, where the bottom line is so often financial. However, mediation is of increasing importance in family, employment, and community contexts, and even of course in the international context, where the issue may well be war or peace. It seems to me that mediation has as great a role, or even a still more significant role to play, in these areas, rather than in the commercial context. That is because the causes of dispute are more varied and more emotional. It is particularly in contexts such as these that some commentators promote the idea of transformative mediation. At this point, many of the writings become more difficult for lawyers and more congenial to sociologists and psychotherapists! But the essence of transformative mediation is, I think, this: that the process encourages the participants towards *change*, in their emotions, in their understandings, in their outlook, in their reciprocal feelings. The concept is for the mediator to be an almost passive centre around which the parties whirl and talk and engage and re-engage, and discover (no doubt with some very careful, shrewd, and almost invisible steering from the mediator) the solution for themselves. It is particularly valuable where what has to be mediated is a community-wide dispute, as for instance where there is a dispute between resource companies and the communities where those companies wish to mine; or between employers and employees.

As a member of a panel of judges awarding prizes for the best in mediation work, I well remember a most moving film I watched about a long-term mediation which brought a South American community and a large foreign mining company into harmony and out of bitter misunderstanding and discord.

In this context, let me tell you also about the great case of the *Alabama*, albeit that it ended in arbitration rather than mediation: in any event, in another, consensual, process of dispute resolution, as distinct from litigation or even open armed conflict. Following the American Civil War, a dispute broke out between the US and Great Britain because of a number of powerful, fast, steel warships built in Britain for the Confederate States, which the Confederate States used to harass the shipping of the Northern States with devastating results. Britain was a neutral state, but after the Civil War was over, the US accused Britain of violating her neutrality by building and supplying these ships to the Confederate States. How was this dispute to be resolved? It began in litigation. Relations between Britain and the US were gravely damaged. The US claim was enormous, at times valued at up to US$2 billion (a modern figure would be countless billions more). At first, there was what might be called a mediation, between commissioners appointed by the two countries: and that led to a treaty, the Treaty of Washington, which provided for an arbitration of the claims before a tribunal of five arbitrators, to be composed of an arbitrator appointed by each of the US, Britain, Italy, Switzerland and Brazil. That arbitration in turn led to the upholding of the US claims, albeit with the British arbitrator dissenting – which only goes to show the importance of the international dimension, ie the dimension which takes you out of your own background. And so there was an enormous award of damages in favour of the US. Gladstone, Britain's Prime Minister at the time, considered the award 'harsh in its extent and punitive in its basis' yet 'as dust in the balance compared with the moral example set' of two proud nations resolving their dispute 'in peace and concord' rather than by the sword. And from that day, the US and Britain, which had been three times at war in the then previous century became the closest of allies. It is an extraordinary story of the success of which mediation, arbitration and conflict resolution are capable.[3]

A more modern success for mediation is the recent signing this year of the Singapore Mediation Convention. Built on the example of the

3. [*Editorial note*: See the article above by Bruno de Loynes de Fumichon for further details of this arbitration.]

enormously successful New York Convention for the enforcement of international arbitration awards, the Singapore Convention aims to promote international enforcement of mediated settlement agreements, provided (a) they are in writing; (b) result from a mediation; (c) are between parties who have their place of business in different states; and (d) those different states are parties to the Convention. As I have said, most mediated settlement agreements are performed for the very reason that they constitute the parties' own settlement: but the Convention will ensure that all such settlement agreements are entered into in good faith, and not for the sake of delay or the avoidance of legal proceedings, and will give, I predict, a significant boost to the mediation of international disputes.

So, I have touched on a famous 19th century case of mediation and arbitration; I have spoken about mediation in general; and I have come right up to date with reference to the Singapore Convention.

But let me end my lecture this evening by going back, if I may, to the roots of mediation in ancient times, and in the faiths of the Abrahamic tradition.

I would like to stress how very old mediation is. The Hebrew bible speaks of laws, and of the importance of justice, and of judges, but it does not speak of lawyers. It appears that the parties are very much their own advocates. It refers repeatedly to the elders at the gate as those before whom people bring their problems and disputes for resolution, a form of community mediation. We hear of how Jethro advised his son-in-law, Moses, about how to delegate judicial authority, so that only the most important cases came before Moses himself. We have the famous dispute that came before King Solomon, about the two mothers who each claimed the baby as hers. That is an example of regal judgment, not mediation, but again one may note that the mothers speak for themselves, without the advocacy of lawyers.

But above all, one has the three great occasions on which first Abraham, and then Moses, mediates between God and the people. In Abraham's case, he intercedes on behalf of the cities of the plain, which God had threatened to destroy. Like a mediator passing terms of settlement backwards and forwards, Abraham challenges God to relent, if there are 50, 40, 30, 20, or even 10 righteous men in the cities. How brave Abraham was! He challenged God: 'Shall not the judge of all the earth do right?' he asked. So Abraham won on the law, but lost on the facts. Later, Moses interceded on behalf of the children of Israel at Sinai, after the incident of the Golden Calf, and persuaded God to forego the destruction of the people and to create anew the second set of tablets of the Ten Commandments. As part of that intercession, Moses persuaded God to reveal himself in terms of the 13 attributes of God's mercy. And thirdly, later still, Moses interceded again after the people had lost heart after the discouraging report of the spies and wanted to return to Egypt. Moses cited back to God the 13 attributes of God's mercy of which God had spoken at Sinai; and God said: 'I have forgiven, according to your word', thereby treating Moses rather than himself as the originator of the expression of God's mercy. This is transformative mediation at the very highest level.

In the Christian bible, we have the figure of Jesus himself as a mediator between God and man. But we also have Jesus's advice reported in the Gospel of Luke to the effect that 'when you are on the way to court with your accuser, try to settle the matter before you get there'. And we know of Paul, who instructed the church at Philippi to act as the mediator between two of its warring members, Euodia and Syntyche.

And in the Qur'an, we find the suggestion that a husband and wife in trouble should appoint family mediators to help the couple towards reconciliation. We also find the Prophet asking the tribes who were contesting the right to preside at the setting of the Black Stone to select leaders who could together, one at each corner, come together in equal harmony to set the Stone. Moreover, the great Muslim jurist al-Mawardi speaks of the importance of settling disputes by making peace to the mutual satisfaction of both parties as an alternative to the obligations of a legal judgment.

One can conclude, therefore, that mediation goes back far into human history, indeed is likely to be older still than judges and judgment, since those require a more developed form of human society. Nowadays, overwhelmed by the sheer volume of litigation, as Moses once was until Jethro taught him to delegate judgment, we are learning anew the importance of helping people and communities to settle their disputes with the aid of the neutral mediator.

There will always be disputes. But in my book, mediation is the best way of settling them. It is owned by the parties; it is consensual; it enables the rigour of the law to be softened by mutual give and take; it enables litigants to understand each other's concerns; it is flexible in its possible remedies; it avoids the necessity for appeals and mechanisms for enforcement; and it also sets at naught the imposters of victory and defeat. These are, to my mind, good thoughts to be having on World Conflict Resolution Day.

And there is this last thought. The role of the great prophets as mediators, Abraham, Moses, Jesus and Mohammed, shows us that mediation is close to the unimaginably important virtues of repentance and forgiveness. These are virtues that humankind, in communication with God, have taught each other. It is the virtue of mediation that it can teach us that by giving up something we hold dear, by repenting, as it were, our rights and defences, we can achieve a forgiveness of the wrongs which we think we suffer at each other's hands.

References

Robert Baruch Bush and Joseph Folger, *The promise of Mediation: The Transformative Approach to Conflict*, (Jossey-Bass, 2005) 1–287.

Tom Bingham, 'Alabama Arbitration' in *Max Plank Encyclopaedia of Public International Law* (Oxford University Press, 2006) https://opil.ouplaw.com/home/MPIL (accessed 11 December 2020).

Tom Bingham, 'The Alabama Claims Arbitration' (2005) 54(1) *International and Comparative Law Quarterly* 1–25.

Joseph Folger and Robert Baruch Bush, 'Transformative Mediation: A Self-Assessment' (2014) 2(1) *International Journal of Conflict Engagement and Resolution* 20–34.

Mohamed Keshavjee, *Islam, Sharia and Alternative Dispute Resolution: Mechanisms for Legal Redress in the Muslim Community* (IB Tauris, 2013) 1–237.

Carrie Menkel-Meadow, 'Mediation: Merging the Old and the New' (2018) *Asian Journal on Mediation* 1–20.

Bernard Rix, *The Interface of Mediation and Litigation*, (2014) 80(1) *Arbitration* 21–27

Derek Roebuck, 'A Pinch of Reality: Private Dispute Resolution in Eighteenth Century England', in Hong Kong International Arbitration Centre (Ed), *International Arbitration: Issues, Perspectives and Practice: Liber Amicorum Neil Kaplan* (Kluwer Law International, 2018) 581–590.

Derek Roebuck, 'The Myth of Modern Mediation' (2007) 73(1) *Arbitration* 105–116.

EARLY ENGLISH ARBITRATION

*Sir Stephen Sedley**

[*Editorial note*: This article was first published in the *London Review of Books* (vol 31, no 3, February 2009) as a review. Hence the parenthetic indication that the reviewer knew the writer. A slight update indicates that the series has reached the 18th century. The article is reproduced in this volume by kind permission of the publisher.]

When the Archbishop of Canterbury suggested in a lecture in 2008[1] that there was room within national legal systems for some degree of religious law for members of particular faiths, the country shook with indignation – not at what the prelate had actually said, but at the menacing story the broadcast and print media extracted from it. *The Sun*'s uniquely helpful contribution was a 'Bash the Bishop' campaign, corroborating Martin Amis's suggestion in *Yellow Dog* (2003) about the way the red-tops view their readers.

All Dr Rowan Williams was trying to argue was that a universalist doctrine of human rights does not demand what he called 'an unqualified secular legal monopoly' but leaves space for religious inputs. He was clear that these could not include a licence to undercut fundamental rights or general laws. He was not endorsing or advocating the dualist systems of places like Iran, Afghanistan, Pakistan and northern Nigeria, where *shari'a* courts are permitted to administer sometimes appalling forms of sectarian justice within or alongside a formal constitutional system of law. What he was describing was actually our system as it has been for many years.

One of the least remarked ways in which particular communities, not only religious ones, have for centuries been able to apply their own law to their own members is by arbitration. This has not happened by stealth or accident. Legal systems, our own included, positively welcome consensual

---

* A Lord Justice of Appeal for England and Wales, 1999–2011; Visiting Professor Of Law, University of Oxford, 2011–2014.

1. [*Editorial note*: Dr Rowan Williams, *Civil and Religious Law in England: a religious perspective*, Temple Festival foundation lecture, Royal Courts of Justice, London (8 February 2008), available at http://aoc2013.brix.fatbeehive.com/articles.php/1137/archbishops-lecture-civil-and-religious-law-in-england-a-religious-perspective.]

private forms of dispute settlement, and traders commonly find them cheaper, quicker and more alive to practical realities. The courts, in consequence, will abdicate in favour of a binding arbitration agreement, and the law will lend the winning party the State's power to enforce the award. What is more, the parties can choose the law by which the arbitrator is to determine the dispute. In commercial arbitration agreements this usually means stipulating which country's laws are to apply. But there is nothing to stop the parties to a dispute agreeing that it is to be privately determined by some other code of law, which may be a religious one. A good many religious organisations and sects require this of their members, and a good many more permit or encourage it.

This is not to say that private arbitration within religious communities is without problems, as the archbishop might have done well to recognise. It may be entered into less by free will than by moral coercion. It may well subject some members, often women, to disadvantage or indignity. Further, disputes not infrequently arise between the priests and scholars of a religious community as to what its law actually is. For these and other reasons, the legal system of the host society needs to be ready to step in. The likelihood is, however, that arbitration and mediation in one form or another are a great deal older than the legal systems of the States in which they now exist.

The reason is simple enough. A court before which the wronged and the indignant can haul their antagonists requires an organised State with ascertainable laws and an adequate apparatus of adjudication and enforcement. Simple societies and small communities, lacking this, need other ways of preventing resort to self-help and violence each time a dispute arises. Communal pressure on the parties to find a compromise is one way, akin to modern methods of mediation. Another is to encourage or permit parties to find their own judge or judges and to agree to abide by their decisions: that is, to go to arbitration. The later Romans recognised both methods: the State's adjudicative power was exercised by a *judex*, consensual adjudicative power by an *arbiter*, though the two were not always clearly distinguished.[2]

It is easy to overlook the chronological overlap between Roman and early British society. The *AngloSaxon Chronicle*, begun toward the middle of the fifth century AD/CE, antedates Justinian's code by about ninety years. Indeed, Justinian's code, still taught as a primary source of Roman law, is the law of a nascent feudal society that had long since been driven eastwards out of Rome and Italy. There is, however, very little evidence

2. [*Editorial note*: See Derek Roebuck and Bruno de Loynes de Fumichon, *Roman Arbitration* (2004, Oxford: HOLO Books: The Arbitration Press) and, in the present volume, Robert Morgan, 'Derek Roebuck, Historian: A Literature Review'.]

in Britain of cultural overlap. The institutions and practices exported by the Romans to their colonies were almost certainly confined to imperial enclaves and do not appear to have outlived Roman hegemony. The Latin element of the English language entered with the Normans, while William the Conqueror, far from imposing a new legal order as an aspect of regime change, took pains to assert that the laws of England were to remain those of Edward the Confessor. It is with Henry II and the first foundations of a modern legal system in the mid-12th century, as a regular court begins to sit in London and the king's justices ride out on circuit carrying the common law with them, that Derek Roebuck's *Early English Arbitration*[3] ends.

We possess the texts of a good many Anglo-Saxon laws, translated here by Professor Roebuck into readable modern English; though there are some words that will not translate – for example, *domas*, which means both a law and a judgment, becomes 'doom', leaving him no escape from 'deeming a doom'. However, until Edgar, in the 10th century, ordered his laws to be copied and distributed, royal dooms were little more than instructions to local arbitrators, telling them such things as how much they should exact for a stabbing (knife crime seems to have been a problem in early English society), depending on the injury. For the rest, customary law prevailed: in cases of adultery, the Domesday Book reveals that, in Kent at least, the king took the fine paid by the man and the archbishop the fine paid by the woman. (This actually seems quite rational at a time when the Treasury wants judges to be paid out of court fees.) The typical arbitral proceeding, not only here but throughout early society, seems to have been a communal assembly at which priests or elders would attempt to mediate a settlement or, failing that, make an adjudication. In either case, the characteristic penalty for non-compliance was not enforcement or incarceration but (as in some parts of the world it still is) expulsion or ostracism.

Until Derek Roebuck set about it, nobody had attempted a panoptic history of arbitration. Since his retirement from a succession of chairs of law – in Australia (where he was teaching when I first met him), Papua New Guinea and Hong Kong – he has produced volumes on arbitration in ancient Greece and in the Roman Empire, and on English arbitration down to the 18th century. The ancient societies are far better documented than early and medieval England (the only evidence we have that the Romans invaded Britain in 55 BC/BCE, for example, is that Caesar says they did), to the extent that much of Professor Roebuck's material about Britannia comes from Roman sources. Thus, some evidence for an early legal profession in these islands comes from Juvenal in the second century AD/CE: 'Gallia causidicos docuit facunda Britannos', rendered here as 'Fluent

---

3. 2008, Oxford: HOLO Books: The Arbitration Press.

Gaul has taught the British advocates', though it could also be 'France has taught British advocates eloquence'. Neither translation means much until one adds to it the fact, noted by Professor Roebuck, that there were Roman schools of rhetoric in Marseille, Toulouse, Bordeaux and Trèves, and the further fact, noted by Juvenal, that these schools had Athenian origins.

There is, however, no evidence that the Greco-Roman tradition of advocacy, or indeed any recognisable legal system at all, survived the departure of the Romans. There is only one hard piece of evidence of the way law might have worked in practice, and that is the much studied Fonthill Letter. This was written in about 920 AD/CE by an arbitrator, Ordlaf, who was not chosen by the parties but appointed by the king and so was more nearly an ad hoc judge than a consensual arbitrator (Professor Roebuck characterises this method as public, as opposed to private, arbitration). The letter reports to the king that Ordlaf, in return for a piece of the action, secured settlement of a long-running land dispute by establishing which of the hard-swearing parties was 'nearer the oath' – that is to say, which of them held a document of title to corroborate his oath. While Professor Roebuck reserves the possibility that this was an atypical procedure, it is likelier that the Fonthill dispute was an example of a monarch lending his authority to a respected individual to procure or impose a resolution of a potentially explosive quarrel – a precursor, arguably, not of arbitration but of litigation.

In the unsurprising absence of much other hard evidence of earlier dispute resolution, at least before the 11th century, Professor Roebuck's method is an engaging series of polymathic raids into the territory of geographers, ethnographers, linguists, lawyers, historians and archaeologists, fetching back the kind of data that reminds one there is no such thing as useless information, and assembling it into tentative shapes. He had, however, to accept the fuzzy character of the shapes:

> First, the definition [of arbitration] by distinction from litigation is irrelevant when there is no litigation, properly defined, with which to contrast it. Secondly, the requirement that arbitration be consensual ... is anachronistic when applied to societies where such emphasis on individuality was unknown.[4]

> ...

> There is no evidence of professional arbitration in England as there is in contemporary Ireland, where the *brithem* was a legal expert who regularly heard disputes. Nor is there any sign of the *bonus homo*, the

4. Ibid, p 226.

single private arbitrator of Roman law, even in Roman Britannia ...
When the Anglo-Saxon for *boni homines*, *god man*, is found, they are
acting as 'witnesses', a role which there included representing the whole
assembly.[5]

Some scholars might have been daunted by such incertitudes. If *Early
English Arbitration* is consequently a history less of arbitration than of
dispute resolution, and one mapped less by landmarks than by intersect-
ing lines, it is nevertheless an engaging rattlebag of facts and notions. Of
course, speculation, as Professor Roebuck reminded himself, has its limits,
though they did not stop him having a shot – not necessarily any wilder
than the standard druidic and human sacrifice explanations – at appropri-
ating the standing stones of Avebury as a site of early dispute resolution.

More relevantly, Professor Roebuck was fascinated by a polished flint
object, a stylised human head with open mouth, found not in England but
in Ireland and dating from the fourth millennium BC/BCE. Archaeologists have decided it was the head of a warrior's mace. It is, however, too
small and light to have been the business end of a weapon, and Professor
Roebuck suggests that it was more probably the head of a speaking-staff,
an analogue of the mace of the Speaker of the House of Commons, an
object described in the *Iliad* ('one after another took the *skeptron* ... in
their hand and adjudicated') and still used today by, among others, some
Australian aboriginal communities. It may not add much to the history of
arbitration, but it is reassuring to reflect that preventing everyone talking
at once has been an art form for so long as there have been arguments, and
that human communities have recognised for a long time that facilitating
argument is a better use for a mace than breaking heads.

---

5. Ibid, p 227.

DON'T BRING AN ARMY TO AN ARBITRATION (ENGLAND, 1411)

*David J Seipp**

The name of our friend Derek Roebuck will always be linked to the long history of arbitration and mediation which he has chronicled so thoroughly in a dozen volumes by my count and many articles and chapters. On a spectrum of dispute resolution methods from formal courtroom litigation to savage brute force, arbitration stands at an interesting intermediate point. In tribute to Derek's memory, I offer this glimpse of a curious episode at the intersection of due process of law, armed violence and principled arbitration. It reminds us that these three alternatives were not always as widely differentiated as we suppose.

This episode took place in England in 1411. A justice of the Court of King's Bench, one Robert Tyrwhit, had agreed to arbitrate a land dispute. He showed up to the arbitration with some 500 armed men. Parliament condemned and punished Tyrwhit for this outrage. I did not learn of this episode in 2013 from Derek Roebuck's masterful *Mediation and Arbitration in the Middle Ages: England 1154–1558*, though he recounts it there. His brief account takes up most of page 151 in that volume. The king's justice who brought an army to an arbitration had long before earned the attention of and condemnation by legal historians, however. Tyrwhit's betrayal of the rule of law was taken as emblematic of the lawlessness of late medieval England. Even a principal officer responsible for upholding the law had, it seemed, utterly abandoned the rule of law.

In volume 2 of his *History of English Law*, written in 1903, William Holdsworth summarised thus:

> In 1411 Sir Robert Tirwhit, a justice of the bench, confessed that he had arrayed a small army of five hundred men and set an ambush for Lord Roos, who had arranged to meet to compromise a dispute as to a common of pasture; and he actually put forward in extenuation of his

---

* David Seipp, a historian of medieval English common law, is Professor of Law at Boston University. He holds law degrees from Oxford, Cambridge, and Harvard Universities and has compiled an index and paraphrase of reported English cases, 1268 to 1535.

offence the wonderful plea that he, a royal judge, did not know that he had broken the law.

'If these things were done by the lawyers', Holdsworth asked, 'what could be expected from the laymen?'[1] Holdsworth was preceded in this judgment by Charles Plummer, whose 1885 introduction to Fortescue's *Governance of England* called this same Robert Tyrwhit a 'turbulent justice' and 'guilty of the grossest turbulence and breach of the peace'.[2] Foss's *Judges of England* likewise gave him a 'violent disposition'.[3]

Writing well over a century ago, Holdsworth and Plummer had made Robert Tyrwhit a villain, an exemplar of 15th century lawlessness, a royal justice who betrayed the law and sided instead with the worst sort of violent interference with orderly dispute resolution. Derek Roebuck could only spare a bit less than 400 words for Tyrwhit's story. He chose his selection of facts well, commented only that even in those troubled times, Tyrwhit's behaviour 'was unseemly for a judge in the eyes of his contemporaries', and concluded with a wistful observation that the full historical record includes 'much more detail' of this episode. I think he wanted to say more, so I take this as his invitation for us to take a closer look at the episode and its main protagonist. One might call my inquiry 'Who Framed Robert Tyrwhit?'

Tyrwhit was the son of a knight from Kettleby in Lincolnshire. He had been a serjeant at law since 1398. He was appointed king's serjeant by Henry IV in 1399. From 1398 until 1411 he acted as justice of assize on the Midland circuit. In 1403 he was required to lend the king £100 to fight Welsh and Scottish campaigns. He could afford it, because as a serjeant he held annual retainers to counsel a duke, an earl, a couple of towns, a cathedral and an abbey. In 1408 he was appointed one of three Justices of King's Bench and was knighted. He was one of two justices permitted by royal patent to take recognisances wherever he might happen to be. Beginning in 1410, he acted as a trier of petitions in Parliament. By the time he died, Tyrwhit held 14 manors in Lincolnshire, several manors in other counties and an inn in London.[4]

In 1411, Sir Robert Tyrwhit brought a writ of trespass in King's Bench, his own court, against various defendants associated with William, Lord

---

1. WS Holdsworth, *A History of English Law*, 2, 415 (citing Rotuli Parliamentorum 3, 649). I adopt the spelling of Tyrwhit's name in JH Baker, *The Order of Serjeants at Law* (1984), based on wills or royal patents.

2. J Fortescue, *The Governance of England*, ed. C Plummer (1885), 22 n.2, 385.

3. E Foss, *The Judges of England*, 4, 368 (1851).

4. Biographical details are taken from the entry by AF Pollard, revised by Edward Powell in the *Oxford Dictionary of National Biography* (2004, Oxford: Oxford University Press) and entries in Baker and Foss, cited *supra* notes 1 and 3, supplemented by RP Tyrwhitt, *Notices and Remains of the Family of Tyrwhitt* (1858).

Ros of Helmsley: first, John Rate, who was the steward of the courts of Lord Ros, on his manor of Melton Ros; second, Lord Ros's bailiff of the same manor; and third, 11 named tenants at will and villeins of Lord Ros. It was not forbidden for Justices to be litigants in their own court, and in fact they and other officers of their court had a privilege to sue and be sued only in their own court. The writ was for digging turf, cutting trees and underwood and taking away the turf, wood, grass and ferns from a piece of Tyrwhit's land near Wrawby, in northern Lincolnshire, damaging Justice Tyrwhit to the amount of £40.[5] This was, thus far, a perfectly ordinary writ of trespass like thousands of others.

Lord Ros's steward, bailiff and tenants pleaded that Lord Ros had rights of common to pasture cattle, take turf (right of turbary) and take wood (right of estovers) on that piece of land. Again, this was a perfectly ordinary pleading in defence. While this writ of trespass was pending, Lord Ros and Justice Tyrwhit submitted themselves with this lawsuit and all its corollaries to the arbitration and ordinance of William Gascoigne, Chief Justice of Tyrwhit's Court of King's Bench. No arbitrators other than Gascoigne were mentioned. Tyrwhit's opponent Lord Ros of Helmsley was a Knight of the Garter and a Privy Councillor, and had been Henry IV's Lord Treasurer of England six years before. Gascoigne, with the agreement of Justice Tyrwhit and Lord Ros, ordered them to be before him at the place of the alleged trespass, Wrawby in Lincolnshire, on Saturday, 3 October 1411, for what was called at the time a 'loveday'.[6] The parties were expected to be there with their documents, in order to explain their titles and rights in this matter.

The arrangements for this arbitration specified who could accompany each party. Lord Ros was allowed to bring 'two barons' related to him, 'or other friends, in a peaceable manner, with as many persons as they customarily used to ride forth with'. Justice Tyrwhit was permitted to come to arbitration with two of his relatives or other friends, in a peaceable manner, with as many people as belonged to their status and degree, the usual retinue of persons of importance. Lord Ros brought with him Henry, Lord Beaumont, who was chamberlain of the Duchy of Lancaster and a second cousin of the king, and Thomas, Lord de la Warr, a son and brother of lords who fought under Edward the Black Prince, with lands in Gloucestershire, Somerset and Sussex. They would have had the usual number of servants, and probably some legal counsel for Lord Ros. Lord Ros came ready to explain his title and right and to abide by the arbitration.

---

5. These details and those that follow are taken primarily from *The Parliament Rolls of Medieval England*, ed. C Given-Wilson (2005), 8, 519–23 and appear also in *Rotuli Parliamentorum* (1767–77) 3, 649–651.

6. On this terminology, see JW Bennett, 'The Medieval Loveday', (1958) 33 *Speculum*, 351–70.

Lord Ros's petition to the king and Parliament told what happened next. 'Robert Tyrwhit, notwithstanding that he was a Justice of Assize and keeper of the peace' for that county of Lincolnshire, 'plotted by scheming and malice aforethought to raise and assemble at Wrawby that Saturday a large number of men, numbering about 500, armed and equipped to make war, against the king's peace, to the great disturbance of all the surrounding lands'. Justice Tyrwhit's little army, Lord Ros told Parliament, 'lay in wait there in several groups, in a warlike manner', close to the place specified by Chief Justice Gascoigne, 'in ambush for Lord Ros and for his kinsmen Lord Beaumont and Lord de la Warr, in order to forcibly overcome and dishonour the agreement to arbitrate, to the great shame of Lord Ros and the two other Lords'. I presume that Justice Tyrwhit's show of force put a halt to arbitration that day, and both sides went back to their manors. Lord Ros petitioned the king and Parliament to redress Tyrwhit's evil trespass and offence. Parliament took up this dispute immediately after the Chancellor opened its session with his customary speech on 4 November 1411. Lord Ros complained that what Justice Tyrwhit had done was an outrage, set out the circumstances in great detail and left the appropriate remedy up to the king.

The Parliament roll mentions that both parties put forward various arguments, responses and replications on the days assigned to them during the Parliament session. On Friday 27 November 1411, Lord Ros and Justice Tyrwhit both came with their counsel before Henry IV and the lords. All that was recorded of their argumentation was that Justice Tyrwhit explained to the king how 'through foolishness and ignorance he had acted in this matter otherwise than as he ought to have done, to the king's displeasure'. Tyrwhit put himself on the king's mercy and prayed for his mercy and pardon. The king asked the justice whether he put himself on the king's mercy for his ignorance, or for the deed he was said to have committed. Justice Tyrwhit told the king that it was for the deed specified in Lord Ros's petition. Justice Tyrwhit did not deny the material allegations against him. He had brought with him to the arbitration a large assembly of armed men.

Parliament's consideration of this dispute ended when Tyrwhit capitulated. He submitted himself to arbitration by any two lords related to Lord Ros, whom Lord Ros would name. Lord Ros readily agreed to this, and in the presence of the king and lords in Parliament he nominated Thomas Arundel, the Archbishop of Canterbury and Lord Grey of Codnor, the king's Chamberlain, to be the arbitrators between them. The king was relieved that he would not himself have to decide between Justice Tyrwhit and Lord Ros, so he told Justice Tyrwhit that Tyrwhit 'would not depart entirely without the king's grace', whatever that meant.

The Archbishop and Lord Grey then proceeded to their arbitration of the entire dispute. Their award was enrolled in Parliamentary records in English. They said that contrary to the 'loveday' arranged by Chief Justice Gascoigne, Justice Tyrwhit had not come to arbitration with the number of men who should have accompanied him according to his degree. They awarded that Tyrwhit and Ros should submit themselves back to Chief Justice Gascoigne for decision of the underlying legal dispute as to Lord Ros's claimed rights of common on Tyrwhit's land. They further awarded that at a time settled by Lord Ros, Justice Tyrwhit had to deliver to Lord Ros's manor of Melton Ros two tuns (500 gallons) of wine from Gascony, two fattened oxen, and 12 fattened sheep, to be eaten at dinner by those present. They awarded that Justice Tyrwhit had to come to Melton Ros with the wine, oxen and sheep, and with the knights, squires and yeomen who had led Tyrwhit's armed force. In front of his own men and those of Lord Ros, Justice Tyrwhit was ordered to repeat the confession that he had made to the king in Parliament, and then was ordered to make a further speech dictated by the Archbishop and Lord Grey:

> My Lord Ros, I know well that you are of such birth, estate, and might that if you had wished you could have come to the … loveday with such a following that I should have been quite unable to challenge you; yet you wished to come [without a large accompanying force of men], having consideration for your position. And through misleading information, I was afraid that I would be harmed, so with the intention of saving myself, I did assemble these persons there, not to cause harm or offence to you, my lord Ros; and I will apologise here in any way you wish. Moreover, since I am a Justice, I should have behaved more wisely and peacefully than any other common man, and I know well that I have failed and have offended you, my Lord Ros, whereof I pray for your grace and mercy and offer you 500 marks [£333 6s 8d, this when a justice's annual salary was £10] to be paid at your will.

The Archbishop and the Chamberlain were not finished. They ordered further that Lord Ros should politely refuse the 500 marks, taking only the wine, oxen and sheep from Justice Tyrwhit for the dinner, and that Lord Ros should publicly forgive Justice Tyrwhit and all those he led in his armed company of all their offence and trespasses, with the exception of four named knights who could not be forgiven with the rest. Justice Tyrwhit had to bring these four to Lord Ros's castle at Belvoir to ask his grace and mercy. Lord Ros was further ordered to act toward these four knights in such a manner that they should consider themselves well and mercifully treated.[7]

In brief, Justice Tyrwhit was allowed to say by way of apology that he led an army of 500 men in an act of self-defence, because he was led to believe that Lord Ros would come to their arbitration with an even larger and stronger army. This may have been what Tyrwhit had been arguing to the king and to these arbitrators all along. What interests me particularly is what happened to Justice Tyrwhit next. Tyrwhit did not lose his job. He remained on the Court of King's Bench, was reappointed at the accession of Henry V in 1413 and at the accession of Henry VI in 1422, serving for another 16 years, until shortly before his death in January 1428. He continued in active participation in Year Book cases. The only effect on Tyrwhit's career stemming from his armed encounter with Lord Ros seems to have been his transfer some time late in 1412 from the Midland circuit (which included Lincolnshire, where this dispute arose) to the Northern circuit. A statute of the same year charged justices of the peace and sheriffs to prosecute any 'riot, assembly, or rout of people' or to pay the king £100 if they did not.[8] Chris Given-Wilson, who edited the Parliament roll for this reign, suggests that this Statute of Riots might have been Parliament's response to the Tyrwhit-Ros affair.[9]

Tyrwhit seems to have reconciled quickly with Lord Ros, as shown by the roles the two men played just a year later in another 'loveday' gone wrong. In 1411, Alexander Meryng and John Tuxford disputed over part of the manor of Little Markham in Nottinghamshire. Tuxford brought in a powerful neighboring landowner, Sir Richard Stanhope, on his side, and in retaliation Meryng enlisted Sir John Zouche and Sir John Leek to help him. The confrontation ended just short of bloodshed. Early in 1412, Meryng then brought an assize of novel disseisin against Tuxford, and this they brought before the assize justices for the Midland circuit, who were still headed by Justice Tyrwhit. In October 1412, while the action was still pending, both sides submitted their dispute to the arbitration of three men. The three arbitrators, just one year after the Wrawby ambush, were Justice Robert Tyrwhit, Chief Justice Gascoigne and William, Lord Ros of Helmsley – that is to say, the two opponents in the October 1411 loveday ambush and their arbitrator. It took four years for these three to complete their arbitration for Meryng and Tuxford, and Meryng had to get a royal order to proceed with the assize. In the end, however, Tyrwhit, Gascoigne

---

7. Archival and manuscript sources include C65/72 m.14; 3 Rot. Parl. 648b–651a; Cottonian Records of Rolls of Parliament, 13 Henry IV, m. 14, Lansdowne MS 207 *a*, dated about 1411–1412; also Lansdowne MS 2076, fol. 593, cited in the Lincoln volume of Proceedings of the Archaeological Society (1850), 66.

8. Statute of 13 Hen. 4, ch. 7 (1411).

9. Parliament Rolls of Medieval England, *supra* at note 5, 558 n.2.

and Lord Ros were sufficiently reconciled to agree that the disputed lands should be divided equally between the two parties.[10]

Robert Tyrwhit's descendants also did not suffer for their ancestor's 'turbulent' behaviour and 'violent disposition'. His son Sir William fought alongside Henry V at Agincourt as part of his bodyguard, and another descendant, Sir Robert, a courtier to Elizabeth I, was married to the Queen's former governess. This Sir Robert renewed the feud with the Ros family, leading to the loss of several lives. Between the two parcels of land, a gallows was erected by order of James I that stood until the 20th century. An 18th century descendant, Thomas Tyrwhitt, was a fellow of Merton College, Oxford, edited Chaucer's *Canterbury Tales* and served as Under-secretary of War and Clerk of the House of Commons.[11]

One reason why Justice Tyrwhit might have thought he did nothing wrong on 3 October 1411 was that, five years earlier, the Chief Baron of the Exchequer, John Cokayn, had ejected Chief Justice William Gascoigne and former Exchequer Baron Laurence Allerthorpe, with two others, from the manor of Baddesley Ensor in Warwickshire. According to Gascoigne and Allerthorpe's petition to the king and Parliament, Chief Baron Cokayn came against them with a force of 200 men arrayed to make war, and this little army had terrorised their tenants.[12] The result of the complaint by these two king's justices against a third royal justice are not recorded, but immediately after this petition Chief Baron Cokayn was also made a Justice of Common Pleas, held both judicial positions and both salaries for six years and remained on the Common Pleas bench for 23 years in all. Cokayn died in possession of this manor of Baddesley Ensor. The response to Cokayn's 200-man show of force seems to have been to give him a second judicial position and salary. Perhaps Tyrwhit can therefore be forgiven, five years later, for thinking that he had done what any landholder, royal justice or not, would do in such a dispute – if he could afford to rally 500 armed men. Even for a king's justice, there seemed nothing particularly unusual or inappropriate about a show of force of this type.

Tyrwhit's ambush became memorable not because of his own show of armed force but because of Lord Ros's brilliant strategy against him. Lord Ros outmanoeuvred Justice Tyrwhit by coming to the arbitration with just the two friends and their usual retinues, as their arbitrator Gascoigne had

10. Edward Powell, 'Arbitration and the Law in England in the Late Middle Ages', *Transactions of the Royal Historical Society*, 33 (1983), 57–58, citing KB 9/204/2, mm. 6, 10; Alan Cameron, 'Meering and the Meryng Family', *Transactions of the Thoroton Society of Nottinghamshire*, 77 (1973), 41–52; also KB 27/64, Rex mm. 9 and 12; *History of Parliament*, see under Meryng, Sir William (d. 1449).
11. *Notices and Remains of the Family of Tyrwhitt, supra* note 4.
12. *Parliament Rolls of Medieval England, supra*, at note 5, 414 no. 15, correctly dates this petition to March 1406 and summarises it briefly. The petition is recorded in full in *Rotuli Parliamentorum, supra* at note 5, vol 3 cols 360–361.

ordained. This gambit allowed Lord Ros to play the victim, to petition the king and Parliament, to decry the hypocrisy of royal justices doing what Cokayn and Tyrwhit had done, to humiliate Justice Tyrwhit, to get a good dinner for his tenants, and almost certainly to gain an advantage in the decision of the underlying dispute about rights of common of pasture, turbary and estovers.

Holdsworth in 1903 and Plummer in 1885 did not need all of these details to condemn Robert Tyrwhit for his betrayal, in their eyes, of the rule of law. The fact that this royal justice admitted bringing a force of several hundred men against an opposing party during litigation was damning enough. They may have considered Tyrwhit suspicious for agreeing to arbitration with Lord Ros in the first place. Legal historians take the view that law is a good thing, and more law is better than less. For those of us trained in the law, how could law be the villain? So if law is the good guy, the winner, the hero of the story, surely the bad guys are crime, violence and disorder. Legal histories often presume a constituency for law, a market for law, a demand within society for more and better law as a way of arranging people's affairs, accomplishing their goals and resolving their disputes. Orderly procedures in the courts are always better than armed gangs in the streets or pitched battles in the fields. Abstract, impersonal principles should determine winners and losers, not brute force or threats of violence.

Arbitration, viewed as an alternative to courtroom litigation, has sometimes incurred the hostility of courts and lawyers. It has sometimes been dismissed by legal historians as 'not law'. The late medieval period was not one of those times. Fifteenth-century judges and lawyers participated actively in arbitration, as the episode described here shows. Courts regularly enforced covenants to ensure compliance with arbitral awards. Edward Powell, in the second of his excellent 1983 and 1984 articles about arbitration in 15th-century England, taught us to stop viewing arbitration as an enemy of the common law. Instead, he wrote, '[t]he two were used in conjunction and often simultaneously, as alternative means to the same end of securing the favorable resolution of a dispute'.[13] Powell added parenthetically after this sentence, '[a] popular third means was of course the use of violence or armed force'. Those inside the legal system as well as outsiders all weighed the costs and benefits of arbitration versus courtroom litigation. The use and threat of violence was, I am suggesting here, a third alternative with its own risks and opportunities, like the other two courses. Still more alternatives would be resort to other tribunals, to the Chancellor, to the king's council or, very late in the century, to the Star Chamber.

13. Edward Powell, 'Settlement of Disputes by Arbitration in Fifteenth-Century England', (1984) 2 *Law and History Review*, 21, 38; also Edward Powell, 'Arbitration and the Law in England in the Late Middle Ages', (1983) 33 *Transactions of the Royal Historical Society*, 49, 64 on resort to Chancery.

Fifteenth-century judges and lawyers co-existed with this third way of settling disputes, by shows of force, alongside their core preoccupation with courtroom litigation and their thriving sideline of arbitration. It is a commonplace nowadays to suppose that settlement negotiations and arbitration take place 'in the shadow of the law', with both sides guessing the likely outcome of potential litigation. Fifteenth-century litigation, I am suggesting, may have taken place in the shadow of the violent world of private warfare among powerful lords. Lawyers and judges were not a besieged, embattled minority defending a pure rule of law against lawless magnates, nor were they prelates and priests of a secular religion of common law observance, non-combatants by choice in the escalating private warfare of ordinary landholders. It is that ancient maxim of the law: If you cannot beat them, join them. And bring an army of 500 with you if you possibly can.

On a personal note, I want to express my appreciation for the friendship of Derek Roebuck, whom I first met more than 25 years ago. He showed me hospitality then and since, and has been for me a model of scholarly generosity. I am proud that some work of mine was of help to him in his research on *Mediation and Arbitration in the Middle Ages*, and I especially treasure his kind words on pages 10 and 351 of that book. I am happy now to be able to contribute this essay in his memory.

TRANSPARENCY AND EFFICIENCY IN INTERNATIONAL COMMERCIAL ARBITRATION[*]

Professor Janet Walker[**]
Professor Doug Jones AO[***]

INTRODUCTION

There are few for whom the tribute that they 'spoke truth to power' could be more apt than Derek Roebuck. Throughout his life, from Manchester to various posts in the Asia-Pacific region and back to Oxford, Derek delighted in speaking out against injustice wherever he found it. We say 'delighted', because no matter how serious the cause, and how seriously he took it, it was always accompanied by an irresistible air of mischief. This invigorating sense of adventure took him from being charged with inciting sedition in Australia (for his acts of protest against the war in Vietnam), to founding what was to become the Faculty of Law of the City University of Hong Kong, to uncovering stories of arbitrators and arbitrations stretching back two millennia into history. It also attracted comrades and co-conspirators, a number of whom have contributed to this volume, but the greatest of whom was Susanna Hoe. Together, Derek and Susanna waged war on the most pernicious of injustices – ignorance – with their many volumes containing stories of arbitration, of women, and generally of things about which we are all better off knowing. Theirs

* This article has been adapted from Professor Walker's public lecture, 'International Commercial Arbitration in an Era of Transparency' (Jean Gabriel Castel Lecture Series, Glendon College, Toronto, 26 February 2019) (Walker (2019a)) and Professor Jones' keynote address at the 8th Asia Pacific ADR Conference on 20 September 2019 (Jones (2019)). The authors gratefully acknowledge the assistance provided in the preparation of this paper by legal assistants, Brendan Ofner and Sara Pacey.
** Janet Walker, Distinguished Research Professor, Osgoode Hall, Toronto. Professor Walker is an international arbitrator with chambers at Toronto Arbitration Chambers; Int-Arb, London; and Sydney Arbitration Chambers.
*** Professor Doug Jones AO holds professorial appointments at Queen Mary College, University of London and Melbourne University Law School. Professor Jones is an international arbitrator and serves as an International Judge of the Singapore International Commercial Court.

was an optimism about the good that comes from being well informed and that stands as an inspiration to all those who love life and learning. It is in this spirit that we offer a critical review of the transparency movement, together with our thoughts of what good might come from knowing more about what really goes on in a commercial arbitration – how it is run by the arbitrators, and how it is managed by the arbitral institutions. Mindful that efficiency has been a more prominent concern for parties to commercial arbitrations, we ask whether increased transparency causes more harm or good to that aspect of the process. As will be seen, we reach a conclusion with which we hope Derek would have concurred: that despite the disruption that it might cause, knowing more about international commercial arbitration (ICA) could serve to improve it and maintain its legitimacy.

Turning to the subject of transparency, much of the debate in recent years on investor-State dispute settlement (ISDS) has been preoccupied with its legitimacy. It is an area of dispute resolution that is inextricably linked with issues of public policy and the rights and obligations placed upon States.[1] Many agree that these matters of public interest should not be decided behind closed doors by mysterious tribunals that are capable of binding governments yet are not subject to review by State courts.[2] What is needed is greater transparency. The calls for transparency have spread to ICA, prompting a range of efforts to increase transparency in all aspects of commercial arbitration, from the process, to the awards, to the arbitrators themselves. This contribution will consider the impact of this trend on ICA and the improvements in efficiency that greater transparency can bring.

The term 'transparency' as used herein is not restricted to the public accessibility of hearings or to the arbitral proceedings themselves. Instead, this contribution will consider transparency in the broader sense of the availability of information about the process and those who participate in it, both before and after the hearing. By increasing access to this information, we argue that the quality, efficiency and legitimacy of the process of ICA can be improved.

Increased transparency has the potential to redress longstanding complaints associated with ICA, including unnecessary costs and delay.[3] Greater access to information increases predictability of outcome and aids the development of law, allowing parties to make informed decisions on a variety of issues. These include selecting arbitration as a form of dispute resolution, appointing proficient arbitrators and deciding which arguments

1. UNCITRAL Working Group III Draft Paper, 'Possible reform of investor-State dispute settlement (ISDS)', 7 September 2018, p. 2.
2. Walker Lecture (2019a).
3. Queen Mary University of London Research Survey 2019, p. 9 ('QMUL Survey 2019').

to run in their submissions. These decisions, made easier by the availability of information, allow parties to dispose efficiently of their dispute, either through a binding dispute process or by settlement.

Further, the importance of ICA as a dispute resolution forum is being challenged by the emergence of new alternative mechanisms.[4] In the Asia-Pacific region, the Singapore International Commercial Court (SICC), established in 2015,[5] and the China International Commercial Court (CICC), established in 2018,[6] are two additions to the dispute resolution system which provide alternative fora for commercial dispute resolution, particularly in relation to infrastructure disputes.[7] The use of ICA is widespread and has been considered for many years as the preferred method of resolving disputes between parties from different jurisdictions undertaking international commercial transactions. However, the continued importance of this mechanism is contingent on its ability to continue to meet commercial expectations by innovating and evolving.

A core component of this evolution requires ICA to adapt to the information age, where access to material about virtually everything is a mere click away. For arbitration, this means its users demand more data on the process, on the arbitrators and on their decisions than ever before. There is uncertainty as to whether the current practices in ICA will remain satisfactory to users as time goes on.[8] Indeed, the 2018 QMUL survey results confirmed that participants would like to 'have access to arbitrators' previous awards, know more about their approach to procedural and substantive issues and have a clear picture of their availability to take on new cases'.[9]

This contribution will discuss the interplay between transparency and efficiency by addressing three key topics: first, the publication of arbitral awards as a mechanism for improving transparency and efficiency; secondly, the areas in need of elucidation with respect to arbitral procedure, which is often known only to the participants of each arbitration; and thirdly, the role of arbitrators themselves, particularly the need for more objective material on their abilities to conduct efficient arbitrations and deliver sound results. The relevant starting point in this analysis requires an understanding of the fundamental difference between ICA, which is generally between two private parties (albeit sometimes between private parties and States) and ISDS.

---

4. Walker, 'International Courts' (2019b).
5. SICC.gov.sg (2020).
6. CICC.court.gov.cn (2020).
7. Walker, 'International Courts' (2019b)
8. Hay (2018), [3.3].
9. Queen Mary University of London Research Survey 2018, p. 9 ('QMUL Survey 2018').

Differences between ISDS and ICA

The process that has been adopted to date in ISDS has followed processes akin to those generally used in ICA. Accordingly, some of the criticisms in the ISDS debate are framed around procedures that are commonly adopted in ICA. However, there are fundamental differences between the purposes of the two forms of dispute resolution and those who are affected by their outcomes. International commercial arbitration arises directly from party autonomy, having its very existence dependent upon the agreement of two or more parties to have their disputes resolved by independent arbitrators. Its purpose is to resolve disputes between private parties arising out of commercial transactions.[10] The private nature of this process remains, even if one of the parties is a State entity.

This form of arbitration differs from the juridical concept of ISDS, although there exist theories which emphasise some commonality of the source of jurisdiction. Investor-State arbitration arises out of an investment treaty existing in public international law. The claimant is an investor while the respondent is a State. ISDS decisions therefore often have significant public interest implications, due to questions of sovereignty, domestic issues, the expenditure of public funds and governmental decision-making processes. These are all features that militate in favour of greater transparency. As a former Chief Justice of the Australian High Court observed, the significant impact of ISDS awards on national economies has 'raised questions about the consistency, openness and impartiality of decisions made in ISDS arbitrations'.[11] This movement has paved the way for key developments, such as the Mauritius Convention and the work undertaken by UNCITRAL Working Group III.[12]

Many argue that different, but equally important, public policy concerns exist in ICA. There is judicial support for the notion that there may be circumstances in which 'the public has a legitimate interest in knowing what has transpired in arbitration',[13] a statement of Mason CJ which was met with criticism at the time.[14] Demands for greater transparency with respect to the arbitrators, procedure and awards have grown, with many believing that greater transparency will increase the legitimacy of the process.[15] Others believe transparency is needed to assist in the development of the law, as arbitral awards have the potential to contribute

---

10. Allsop CJ (2018), [21].
11. French CJ (2014).
12. UNCITRAL, United Nations Convention on Transparency in Treaty-based Investor-State Arbitration (2014).
13. *Esso Australia Resources Ltd v Plowman* (1995) 183 CLR 10, p. 31 (Mason CJ).
14. Bennett (1996), p. 16.
15. Allsop (2018); Neuberger (2015), pp 430–431; Rogers (2006), p. 1312.

to law-making by creating a 'soft' form of precedent.[16] In addition to this, transparency may promote greater efficiency in ICA by addressing existing complaints of cost and delay. A shift toward greater transparency is needed in order to ensure arbitration remains the preferred method of international commercial dispute resolution and continues to enjoy widespread respect.

ARBITRAL AWARDS

An obvious starting point in an analysis of the shift toward transparency is with the end of the arbitral process – the award. The publication of awards is said to be to be a useful mechanism to address the information deficit in ICA. While the publication of awards has obvious benefits with respect to transparency, it can also increase the overall efficiency of arbitration by creating precedents of the decision-making process undertaken by the tribunal. This enables the parties to make choices, based on previous awards, that best suit their dispute and facilitate its efficient disposition. It also holds arbitrators accountable, incentivising them to render well-reasoned and timely awards. This raises two questions: first, what value can be derived from publishing awards; and secondly, what has been achieved in this space to date?

Why publish awards?

Awards are the product of the arbitral process. Their publication is therefore an important means of providing the public with insight into the decision-making process undertaken by the arbitrators, which is usually cloaked in confidentiality. Most awards detail the tribunal's reasons, the facts, the parties' submissions and the evidence considered, thus providing users with a history of the steps taken by the arbitrators to reach their decision. Awards also provide parties with the views of tribunals on matters of law and practice which might inform them in the process of anticipating the outcome of disputes.

An oft-cited criticism of the confidentiality of ICA relates to its impact on the development of the common law. Many areas of law are almost entirely dealt with by arbitration, of which the maritime and construction industries are prime examples. This issue has generated significant controversy in the international arbitration community and has prompted some to question the legitimacy of ICA.[17]

In 2016, the Lord Chief Justice of England and Wales at the time contentiously described arbitration as being a 'serious impediment' to the

---

16. Thomas (2016), p. 2.
17. Allsop (2018); Neuberger (2015); Rogers (2006).

development of English law and called for a reform of award appeal mechanisms to empower English courts to review questions of public importance decided in arbitration.[18] His Lordship expressed his dissatisfaction with the situation in which 'great legal minds ... retired from the bench, are giving awards and setting out principles which are known only to the cognoscenti'.[19]

It is clear that great benefit can be derived from accessing the awards in which arbitrators decide issues of law related in many cases to commercial practices. In addition to contributing to legitimacy, the development of arbitral law could be a useful reference point for arbitrators, potentially reducing the time taken to render an award. Although these would not be binding precedents as they would be if decided by courts, they could assist counsel in developing their case, knowing what has succeeded in previous arbitrations, rather than trying to run a case, the outcome of which is unpredictable and uncertain.

Arbitration is not always as simple as interpreting contracts and applying the facts to reach a conclusion on the dispute. It will often require the development of relevant principles, commercial terms to be fixed for the future and applying those principles to the contract in question, in conjunction with the facts.[20] As a result, arbitrators have decided issues at the forefront of many areas of commercial activity (for example, infrastructure, shipping, commodities, resources, insurance and capital markets), which could inform the way in which parties conduct their commercial activities in the future.

Although awards are not subject to a formal system of common law precedent, the decisions of arbitral tribunals may have persuasive value insofar as they are well reasoned and they usefully contribute to the development of the law. Awards can therefore act as a reference point for lawmakers and parties alike — for instance, the ICC Dow Chemical award, a leading decision that recognised the 'group of companies' doctrine, which was upheld by French courts.[21] While the status of this doctrine at common law remains unsettled, the decision has sparked lively legal and academic discussion of the group of companies doctrine.[22]

---

18. Thomas (2016).
19. Thomas (2016).
20. Jones, 'Lawmakers' (2017a), p. 3.
21. *Dow Chemical France, The Dow Chemical Company and others v Isover Saint Gobain*, Zwischenschiedsspruch v 23.09.1982, ICC Case No. 4131, Y. Comm. Arb. 1984, 131. See decision of Paris Court of Appeal, 21 October 1983, Rev. Arb. 1984, p. 98.
22. Ferrario (2009) p. 669; see *Peterson Farms Inc v C & M Farming Ltd* [2004] 1 Lloyd's Rep 603 for circumstances where a non-signatory party had been bound to proceedings under the 'group of companies doctrine' in a successful appeal to the England & Wales Commercial Court.

Substantive issues may be clarified by the publication of awards, as arbitrators are often tasked with deciding questions of law, ranging from novel questions in particular factual scenarios to substantial issues of law.[23] One industry in which commercial arbitration remains the preferred method of dispute resolution is construction; and arbitrators are therefore well positioned to contribute to the development of law in this area. Awards dealing with topical issues, such as good faith, penalties or liquidated damages, provide guidance for construction law decision-makers. Had these cases been decided by national courts, they could be regarded as major developments in the law.

Arbitrators are also uniquely placed to make decisions on arbitration law issues, such as questions of jurisdiction, choice of law and arbitrability. Accordingly, if these awards were publicly available, greater guidance could be provided to arbitrators, parties and national courts alike.

In the 2019 QMUL Survey, however, 'confidentiality and privacy' was one the top three most frequently chosen characteristics of arbitration that led parties in the construction industry to favour arbitration over court processes.[24] Still, the same survey also identified the need for reform as 35 per cent of respondents chose not to pursue an international construction arbitration because of concerns about its efficiency at least half the time.[25] While arbitration must adapt to allow the development of law, it must also preserve this key feature, which attracts parties to the process.

The award may also provide suggestions for procedural options. The majority of arbitral awards contain a procedural history, giving insight into the procedural issues raised and the arbitrator's decision on these issues. Questions of costs and interest are also decided in the award, which, if published, could give future tribunals guidance on contested questions such as the calculation of post-award interest. These procedural questions arise time and time again in arbitrations and it is therefore in the interests of transparency and efficiency to have them aired in the public arena. This would enable them to be dealt with quickly, assisted by reference to earlier arbitral awards.

The publication of awards could therefore serve as an important step in increasing the legitimacy of ICA. However, there are further questions that this contribution seeks to address concerning whether the publication of awards effectively promotes greater *efficiency* in international commercial arbitration.

The information that can be gleaned from awards could also be used to resolve challenges to the process that increase time and cost. The

23. Jones (2019), p. 1.
24. QMUL Survey 2019, p. 22.
25. QMUL Survey 2019, p. 22.

efficiency of an arbitration is sometimes hindered by diligent advocates who, in seeking to advance their client's case, persist with submissions that are marginally relevant or peripheral to the main issues in dispute. If awards are increasingly made available to the public, this may change. An informed party could rely on previous awards to ascertain which lines of argument have been most successful and deploy those that relevantly address the issues genuinely in dispute. The analysis of previous decisions in awards could allow parties to see what arguments have succeeded and how issues have been dealt with. Not only could this make the party's case more persuasive, but it could also increase the efficiency of the arbitration, reducing cost and time.

Further, access to previous awards could provide parties with insight into an arbitrator's case management skills (including his or her level of proactivity) and an understanding of how he or she has dealt with procedural and substantive issues in previous cases.[26] These insights could assist parties in making informed decisions in selecting their arbitrators – who could ultimately prove critical in enabling efficiency.

Increased transparency in respect of awards provides greater certainty and predictability for parties. This will also increase the efficiency and legitimacy of the process by making information about the manner and quality of an arbitrator's decision-making publicly accessible. The more information available about an arbitrator's capabilities, the better equipped parties are to appoint arbitrators who are well placed to dispose of their disputes fairly and efficiently.

For these reasons, the publication of arbitral awards is one method that could address this issue and contribute to the overall efficiency and legitimacy of the process.

Developments in publication of awards

It is important to pause here to consider developments thus far with respect to the publication of awards that have paved the way for further reform. This is a topic that has generated significant discussion, and while no solution as to the systematic publication of awards has been established, significant consideration has been given to this important topic.

Commentators are divided on how best to increase transparency through publication, with many calling for the organised publication of arbitral awards by institutions, while some go further and say that States should publish awards and enshrine such a principle in their national laws.[27] Irrespective of the school of thought to which one subscribes, institutions are undeniably key players in this discussion. Generally, arbitral institutions

26. QMUL Survey 2019, p. 21.
27. Comrie-Thomson (2017), p. 284.

have taken up the important role of promoting efficiency and transparency in ICA. The legitimacy of the arbitral process is aided by developments pioneered by these institutions, particularly in relation to the publication of awards.

It is necessary to consider some of the various responses of institutions to the legitimacy 'crisis'. The movement to publish awards has been implemented most comprehensively by the International Chamber of Commerce (ICC). In addition to articles and statistical reports, the ICC has published extracts of 800 awards and a number of procedural decisions in its Dispute Resolution Library.[28] The institution introduced changes in December 2018 providing for the publication of awards on an opt-out basis, in the hope that this will increase the dissemination of information on ICA over time.[29] Although these decisions are published several years after the arbitration and are only available to ICC Digital Library subscribers, they serve as an important reference point for users seeking to understand the process undertaken by arbitrators. While the London Court of International Arbitration (LCIA) does not publish awards, even in redacted form, it may publish abstracts of decisions by the LCIA Court on challenges to arbitrators and caseload statistics.[30] In a similar vein, anonymised decisions on arbitrator challenges are also published by the Arbitration Institute of the Stockholm Chamber of Commerce (SCC). The Korean Commercial Arbitration Board (KCAB) has taken steps to promote efficiency and transparency by implementing provisions in the 2016 KCAB Rules that allow the KCAB Secretariat to publish redacted arbitral awards if the parties do not explicitly object to such disclosure.[31] The Singapore International Arbitration Centre (SIAC) has, for some time, indicated to newly appointed arbitrators that it intends to publish awards and has asked them to indicate whether they consent to having their name noted in the awards published.

The award scrutiny process undertaken by leading institutions, including the ICC, SIAC, KCAB, and Hong Kong International Arbitration Centre (HKIAC) deserves mention. This process increases the legitimacy and efficiency of the arbitral process. The confidential review undertaken by the institutions ensures that arbitrators conduct arbitrations and render awards to a certain standard, knowing that they will be rigorously reviewed by their peers at leading arbitral institutions.[32]

The publication of arbitral awards is commonplace in investor-State arbitration. The parties to an ICSID arbitration may agree to publish the

---

28. 800 awards as at July 2020, ICCWBO.org (2020).
29. ICCWBO.org (2020).
30. LCIA.org (2020).
31. KCAB Rules 2016 Art 57(3).
32. Walker Lecture, p. 9 (2019a).

entire award and other case material on the ICSID website. If they do not agree, then ICSID will publish excerpts of the legal reasoning contained in the award. Evidently, even absent party agreement to publish the award, information can be accessed that gives interested third parties access to important legal reasoning. The UNCITRAL Rules on Transparency[33] enhance legitimacy by requiring the publication of documents,[34] open hearings[35] and allowing third parties to file and make submissions.[36]

Confidentiality (not to be confused with privacy) varies across jurisdictions. In many, including the US and Sweden, the presumption that confidentiality in ICA applies as a blanket rule has come under fire.[37] Regardless of the outcome of this continuing debate, it is clear that confidentiality remains important to users. This is reflected in the results of the 2018 QMUL survey on international arbitration, with the majority of respondents saying confidentiality should apply on an opt-out basis.[38] It follows that arbitration, in responding to calls for greater transparency, must also preserve the features that make it a desirable form of dispute resolution.

It is open for similar transparency practices to be adopted in ICA, with necessary changes to account for the distinct purposes of ISDS and ICA. It is clear that there is no simple solution to the legitimacy challenges that have flowed from investor-State arbitration into ICA. A careful balance must be struck between the private interests of parties seeking confidentiality and the public interest in seeing increased transparency with respect to the process, arbitral awards and the arbitrators themselves. It should be noted that securing legitimacy does not require a blanket approach to transparency: measures can still be taken to protect the legitimate needs of parties for confidentiality, including keeping it intact where this is agreed, redacting sensitive information, or protecting the identities of the parties where necessary.

Evidently, published awards can offer persuasive value and may address criticisms that arbitration undermines the development of the law. While the trend is gaining momentum, further work is needed to determine the best path forward. For the publication of awards to achieve its desired effect, support from the parties, institutions and arbitrators will be necessary. It remains to be seen whether parties will encourage further transparency by

33. UNCITRAL Rules on Transparency in Treaty-based Investor-State Arbitration (New York, 1 April 2014) (UNCITRAL Rules).
34. (UNCITRAL Rules), Article 3.
35. (UNCITRAL Rules), Article 6.
36. (UNCITRAL Rules), Articles 4–5.
37. Hay (2018).
38. QMUL Survey 2018, p. 3: '87% of respondents believe that confidentiality in international commercial arbitration is of importance. Most respondents think that confidentiality should be an opt-out, rather than an opt-in, feature.'

consenting to the systematic publication of awards. Greater efforts from arbitral institutions will also be required to devise a uniform approach to publication across institutions. If some of the larger institutions engage in regular publication of redacted awards, many of the smaller, regional institutions will likely do so, in order to remain competitive. Finally, the publication of awards poses many challenges in balancing the confidentiality required by the parties and the need to release an award of sufficient value to be a soft form of precedent.[39] Due consideration must therefore be given to the manner in which publication occurs.

By making these decisions publicly available and attaching to the award the names of arbitrators and counsel, efficiency may also be encouraged. These developments may also serve to enhance the quality of arbitral awards, as arbitrators are incentivised to handle the parties' dispute effectively and efficiently, in anticipation that the award will be published. As the database of published awards grows, there will emerge a benchmark or standard against which new awards can be compared, increasing the overall quality of the process.

PROCEDURE

The publication of arbitral awards alone, while important, is not enough to address the challenges of transparency and efficiency. No single document, including the award, provides a roadmap or toolbox for procedure in ICA. This is in stark contrast to domestic court proceedings, in which court procedure is usually clearly defined by a uniform set of rules. The flexibility of procedure in arbitration can, if skilfully handled, ensure that a dispute is resolved both fairly and efficiently, and indeed is a feature of arbitration that parties value highly. In the 2018 QMUL survey, flexibility was ranked the third most valuable characteristic of arbitration.[40] This flexibility provides scope for innovation, as arbitrators can create unique procedures tailored on a case-by-case basis. However, confidentiality is an equally important tenet in arbitration and a similar number of respondents placed confidentiality and privacy as the most valuable characteristic of arbitration.[41] The challenge posed by confidentiality is that the procedural innovations developed for one case are inaccessible to the next. While confidentiality is an important feature of arbitration, it should not operate to prevent the dissemination of procedural innovations that have proved successful in efficiently resolving disputes. Drawing on the framework provided by existing soft law instruments, arbitrators still need to fill in the gaps and tailor the procedure to the dispute. Greater transparency is needed

---

39. Jones (2017b).
40. QMUL Survey 2018, p. 7.
41. QMUL Survey 2018, p. 7.

with respect to this process, as increasingly efficient procedure cannot continue to benefit all users if innovation occurs behind closed doors.

Soft law

It is instructive to consider first the major soft law instruments used by arbitrators as a starting point for setting the procedure. The UNCITRAL Notes on Organising Arbitral Proceedings is an exceptionally useful 'toolbox', providing an array of options for consideration.[42] There is also a growing range of soft law instruments that have, to some degree, elucidated the arbitration process. Soft law guidelines continue to inform the development of best practice and can also aid in the development of a procedural framework. In the interests of brevity, this contribution will discuss two: the International Bar Association (IBA) Rules on the Taking of Evidence in International Arbitration (IBA Rules),[43] and the recently developed Rules on the Efficient Conduct of Proceedings in International Arbitration (Prague Rules).[44] Some of the respective procedural features offered by each will be highlighted, as well as areas requiring further reform.

International commercial arbitration provides a forum for resolving disputes between parties from around the globe. In addition to the physical geography that often separates parties and lawyers, so too are they separated by 'legal geography'. The particular domestic legal history and culture from which participants and practitioners come often inform their procedural approaches to international arbitration. One broad distinction in this field is between the common law system and the civil law system. While the common law traditionally favours an adversarial system, the civil law prefers, generally, an inquisitorial approach. In order to craft a successful arbitral procedure, attempts are often made to form an amalgam of common law and civil law procedural traditions, drawing together the best aspects of both systems.

The IBA Rules 1999, as revised in 2010, are the most commonly adopted benchmark for dealing with evidence in arbitral proceedings. The IBA Rules attempt to strike a balance between the common law and civil law traditions. They affirm the tribunal's broad discretion to decide procedural matters but go some way in providing predictability in the taking of evidence. The IBA Rules provide mechanisms for the presentation of documents and the handling of lay and expert evidence, as well as the conduct of evidentiary hearings.[45] The 2010 revisions have modernised

---

42. UNCITRAL, *Notes on Organising Arbitral Proceedings* (2016).
43. International Bar Association, *IBA Rules on the Taking of Evidence in International Arbitration* (29 May 2010) (IBA Rules).
44. Rules on the Efficient Conduct of Proceedings in International Arbitration (2018) (Prague Rules).
45. Prague Rules, Note from the Working Group, p. 2.

the rules and enhanced the efficiency of procedure, particularly making changes which account for advances in technology.

There has, however, been criticism of the absence of soft law instruments which offer civil law procedural options. Historically, this may have been the result of the tendency for common law practitioners to form the majority of those practising in the field of ICA. However, with the growing use of arbitration in the Asia-Pacific region by participants from both civil law and common law countries, there has been an increasing demand for more arbitral procedural options suited to the traditions of their participants. The civil code, inspired by Roman law principles,[46] has survived since Napoleon's time to become the most widely practised system of law. Indeed, the civil law system operates in countries that represent over 60 per cent of the world's population.[47]

Against this backdrop, a working group of predominantly civil law lawyers conducted a survey on procedural traditions in international arbitration in their respective countries, in order to develop soft law guidelines on arbitral procedure, oriented on the civil law tradition.[48] Following a rigorous review process in which the draft rules were debated at conferences held around the world, the working group released the Prague Rules on 14 December 2018.[49] The Prague Rules provide a procedural system with a range of tools derived from the inquisitorial system adopted in the civil law. The Prague Rules actively encourage the tribunal to adopt a proactive approach to case management.[50] In line with the inquisitorial approach, greater powers of case management are granted. In particular, the Prague Rules provide greater scope for the tribunal to provide preliminary views on the issues in dispute,[51] and greater powers for the tribunal to assist the parties to reach an amicable settlement, subject to objection by either party.[52] The Prague Rules further recommend the use of tribunal-appointed rather than party-appointed experts.[53]

These are just some of the many aspects in which the Prague Rules differ from the IBA Rules. Each arbitration presents its own set of unique procedural problems calling for the adoption of a bespoke approach to address the real issues of the dispute as efficiently as possible. When tailoring procedure, arbitrators should make use of the wide array of procedural tools at their disposal and parties should consider these instru-

46. Bell (2015), 45.
47. University of Ottawa (2019).
48. Prague Rules, Note from the Working Group, p. 2.
49. Prague Rules, Note from the Working Group, p. 2.
50. Prague Rules, Note from the Working Group, Art 3.1.
51. Prague Rules, Note from the Working Group, Art 2.4(e).
52. Prague Rules, Note from the Working Group, Art 9.
53. Prague Rules, Note from the Working Group, Art 6.

ments when drafting arbitration agreements, should they wish to prescribe a particular soft law instrument.[54]

It is without doubt that the present range of soft law instruments have improved academic discourse on arbitral procedure. The arbitrator's toolkit grows with the addition of new materials, which both add to the currently existing range of procedural tools and remove those which are no longer functional. In order to move from a soft law guideline to a functioning procedure, significant work must be done by arbitrators and the parties. Much of this crucial work remains fluid, requiring skilful handling to ensure that the dispute is resolved efficiently, through a process that is often unclear to the uninitiated, and sometimes eschewed by them. Taking document production as a case study, consideration will be given to areas of case management where the need for transparency is at its greatest, demanding a wider dissemination of information to improve the efficiency of arbitration.

Case study: Document production

An example of where greater transparency would result in greater efficiency is in the area of document production. As identified above, arbitration is a key dispute resolution mechanism in international infrastructure projects. The QMUL Survey 2019 shows that the two factors that most differentiate international construction arbitration from international arbitration generally are: (i) factual/technical complexity (chosen by 73 per cent of respondents); and (ii) the large amounts of evidence involved (chosen by 66 per cent of respondents). Improving efficiency in this area, while important to international arbitration more broadly, is of particular importance to the Asia-Pacific region, given the large number of international infrastructure projects in the region.

Document production is a procedure born out of the common law and is not common practice in the civil law system.[55] The distinction between the two legal systems is reflected in the IBA and Prague rules, with the IBA Rules demonstrating a more common law approach and the Prague Rules tending toward civil law practices. The problem is that neither instrument performs adequately in the uniquely hybrid legal environment of arbitration, thus leaving it to arbitrators to develop their own innovations to arbitral procedure.

The IBA Rules, on the one hand, provide that the admissibility of evidence is to be determined with reference to the relevance and material-

---

54. Walker, Janet (2019c) 'The Prague Rules: Options and Opportunities for Asia' (January 2019) 38th Seoul IDRC Lecture Series (Seoul).
55. ALI/UNIDROIT, *Principles of Transnational Civil Procedure* 12–13 (2004) (proposed final draft of 9 March 2004); Reymond (1989), p. 357.

ity of the evidence which a party seeks to produce.[56] While these rules of evidence have attempted to strike a balance between the wider approach to disclosure adopted in the common law and the generally narrower approach in civil law, document production tends to resemble more closely the common law practice.[57] However, if it is not carefully handled, time delays and massive cost expenditure will result. This is perhaps a consequence of document production being of common law origin, and a challenge with which the common law world has attempted to grapple over the years.[58]

It has further become usual practice to prescribe the use of a 'Redfern Schedule', with the aim of concisely summarising document requests to narrow the disputed issues between the parties as to what should be produced and why.[59] However, this approach is often fraught with challenges.

The Prague Rules, on the other hand, in adopting civil law procedural approaches, discourage document production. Under the inquisitorial system, disputes are predominantly controlled by the court. Accordingly, the ability for parties to demand documents from each other or third parties is virtually non-existent.[60] Where document production is necessary, the Prague Rules provide that document production should be addressed at the first Case Management Conference (CMC). In principle, CMCs offer a real opportunity to resolve issues much more expeditiously and at an early stage, preventing the issue from escalating. However, this presents to the tribunal the same temporal issue as that posed by the Redfern Schedule, *viz* that the pleadings to which these documents relate have not yet been ventilated before the tribunal.

Arbitrators, faced with the challenge of having to manage parties and counsel from both civil and common law frameworks, must therefore develop their own innovative document production techniques to ensure efficiency in arbitral procedure. Anecdotal evidence would suggest that, short, focused videoconference hearings seem to be workable mechanisms to enhance existing practice in document production. However, the anecdotal nature of this suggestion is reflective of the lack of open discussion of arbitrator-driven procedural innovations, which hinders the development of arbitral procedure. It follows that the key change to drive efficiency is the greater dissemination of information in relation to procedural techniques.

56. IBA Rules, Art 9.
57. Prague Rules, Working Group Note, p. 2.
58. Ashford (2012), p. 5.
59. Blackaby et al (2009), p.113.
60. Born (2014), p. 2345; Borris (1995), p. 97; Rubino-Sammartano (1986), p. 93; Triebel (1982), p. 227.

Ongoing reform

For arbitral best practice to remain flexible and efficient, close attention should be paid to domestic procedural reforms. One important distinction between common law and civil law traditions is the way in which the two procedures develop. In civil law systems, legal procedure is often debated at the highest academic levels, and it is from this academic level that procedural innovation occurs. In contrast, common law practice tends to favour practitioner-led procedural developments. Arbitrators should learn from both systems; in doing so, they may find valuable techniques to add to their toolbox of procedural options.

The Asia-Pacific region continues to enjoy some of the highest levels of economic growth. Alongside this, there has been a great deal of development in domestic commercial legal practices in these countries. Domestic legal procedures have been forced to develop to meet the challenges of massive growth in economic activity within the region. Arbitrators deciding disputes originating in the region must stay abreast of these developments in order to deploy procedures that accord with the wishes of the parties and are most efficient in the circumstances.

One emerging phenomenon is the establishment of international commercial courts. Many of these courts provide information about their processes by making judgments publicly available online, as well as producing procedural guides and practice notes and, of course, holding open court proceedings. The SICC is demonstrating leadership in this area, as is China with the relatively recent introduction of the CICC. On the SICC website,[61] users have access to extensive information on the procedures adopted by the court, as contained in the court rules, the SICC procedural guide,[62] and court forms which provide information on court fees and services. These features provide users with an understanding of the processes used by the courts in managing a case to its conclusion. The effect of this transparency is that it gives users assurance of the overall quality of international commercial dispute resolution, providing predictability for parties and accountability for judges insofar as their decisions are capable of scrutiny by the public. Although complementary to ICA, the development of international commercial courts presents a challenge for the international arbitration community to learn from these developments and to increase the transparency of its own procedural innovations.[63]

61. SICC.gov.sg (2020).
62. SICC.gov.sg (2020).
63. Walker Lecture (2019a)

ARBITRATORS

Unlike domestic courts or some international tribunals, arbitration does not have a fixed pool of decision-makers to whom disputes are assigned.[64] Instead, arbitration presents the opportunity for parties to have their say on who should constitute the arbitral tribunal. This choice has long formed an essential feature of arbitration. In *The Iliad*, Homer describes an 8th-century BC/BCE dispute regarding a blood debt in which the parties made a mutual choice as to a man 'versed in the law' to preside over a tribunal of elders, to render reasoned oral opinions.[65] The efficiency and legitimacy of arbitration ultimately depends on the performance of arbitrators. The availability of information upon which parties make the decision to appoint a particular individual is therefore of crucial importance. It is certainly true that the degree of transparency in relation to the quality of arbitrators has greatly increased. Indeed, merely purporting to be 'versed in the law' is unlikely to yield a great number of appointments in the contemporary marketplace. Despite these developments, there is still insufficient objective material on arbitrators, particularly on their quality and efficiency. It follows that it is necessary to touch briefly on the information that is currently available and then discuss the challenges that remain within the arbitrator appointment process.

Information on arbitrators

There has been a massive increase in the availability of information on arbitrators, which is a step in the right direction. It takes three forms. First, there is the information provided directly by the arbitrator through publications, presentations delivered at conferences and information made available on the arbitrator's website(s). Secondly, there is information arising from referrals and through word-of-mouth exchanges in the arbitral community. Finally, there are third-party sources, such as commercial directories and arbitral institution panel lists.

There has been a substantial increase in the amount of information provided by third parties, through commercial directories such as *Who's Who Legal Arbitration*[66] and *Best Lawyers*.[67] There are also paid subscription arbitrator tools such as the Kluwer Law International 'Arbitrator Tool' and the GAR 'Arbitrator's Research Tool', which rely to a lesser degree on information provided by arbitrators and provide summaries of information on arbitrators' recent work.

64. Born (2014), p. 1364.
65. Hammond (1985), p. 189 (citing Homer, *The Iliad* XVIII 497–508).
66. WhosWhoLegal.com (2020).
67. BestLawyers.com (2020).

While much has been done to increase the available information, there is a paucity of objective material regarding the performance of arbitrators. Many of the metrics listed do not give a comprehensive guide as to the quality and efficiency of arbitrators. Many have indicated that the available resources are too inconsistent and sparse to provide conclusive positions on a range of issues available.[68]

Additionally, from existing information there is limited scope for gaining an insight into an arbitrator's decision-making process.[69] For instance, it cannot be said, on the information available, whether arbitrators are inclined to decide disputes on a legal model following the black letter of the law, or on the basis of what is commercially sound in the circumstances. While there are obvious reasons why this type of information should, to some degree, be assessed in context, greater transparency in this regard may allow parties to have more meaningful power when selecting arbitrators to decide their disputes.[70]

It may be said that a similar lack of information applies to national judges who may otherwise be adjudicating the dispute. However, such a comparison is misconceived, as, in the first instance, national judges find their authority not on the basis of the consent of the parties but rather by virtue of a mandate of the particular jurisdiction. As arbitrators are selected by the parties, it follows that information must be available to give meaning to that choice. Further, national judges' decisions are generally subject to appeal. However, in most national jurisdictions the grounds for reviewing arbitral decisions are extremely narrow.[71] This adds weight to the importance of publicly available information.

Appointment process

In virtually all jurisdictions, there are obligations on arbitrators to exercise independence and impartiality. This obligation is referred to in both the New York Convention[72] and the UNCITRAL Model Law (the Model Law).[73] One issue bedevilling ISDS is perceived bias in party-appointed arbitrators. There has been debate in the ISDS context, run by both Jan Paulsson and Albert Jan van den Berg, that party-appointed arbitrators almost always

---

68. Brekoulakis (2013), p. 562; Besaiso, Fenn and Emsley (2017), p. 290; Besaiso and Fenn (2020).

69. Besaiso and Fenn 2020.

70. See Besaiso and Fenn (2020), an empirical attempt to do so on the basis of interviews with 28 international arbitrators.

71. The New York Convention, Article V; UNCITRAL Model Law, Article 36; Van den Berg (1981), p. 314.

72. The New York Convention indirectly addresses the subject in Articles II(1), II(3) and V(1)(d); Born (2014), p. 1762.

73. UNCITRAL Model Law on International Commercial Arbitration of the United Nations Commission on International Trade Law, GA Res 40/72, UN GAOR, 40th sess, 112th plen mtg, Supp No 17, UN Doc (A/40/17) (21 June 1985) (amended on 7 July 2006), Art 12.

decide in favour of the party who appointed them. In 2010, Paulsson argued that 'unilateral appointments are inconsistent with the fundamental premise of arbitration: mutual confidence in arbitrators'.[74] These sentiments, as shared by van den Berg,[75] have been reinvigorated by growing levels of data that show the tendency for party-appointed arbitrators to find in favour of their appointer in the context of investor-State arbitration.[76]

This debate does not apply to the distinct nature of ICA, which is born solely out of the agreement of commercial parties. While it is true that partiality remains a real and central concern for ISDS, this issue does not arise to the same degree in ICA. Certainly, doubts regarding the legitimacy of ICA do not exist to the same degree as they do in the ISDS context. Instead, it remains of fundamental importance that parties retain the ability to choose their arbitrators, with the chair selected either by them or by an institution. The centrality of this right to party autonomy with regard to the appointment of arbitrators is demonstrated by Article 11 of the Model Law.[77] Results from the QMUL Survey 2018 provide empirical support for the importance of this choice. The survey identified the 'ability to select arbitrators' as respondents' fourth most valued feature of international arbitration.[78]

In light of the debate surrounding ISDS, discussion of alternative mechanisms for appointing arbitrators has arisen also in ICA. There does exist within the AAA-ICDR an alternative appointment mechanism, in which all the members of the tribunal are proposed by the institution and are appointed following a process of consideration by the parties. While parties retain the right to agree to an alternative mechanism for the appointment of arbitrators as provided by Article 11 of the Model Law,[79] this approach does not seem to have found favour in the larger arbitration community.

Thus, the devising of systems for institutional appointment replacing the party-appointed model does not seem to be a burning issue in the minds of users. The present challenge is to enable parties to choose the best people to serve on their tribunals under the existing system. The best appointees will contribute to the fairness and efficiency of the process, and therefore also to its continuing legitimacy. It is suggested that more objective infor-

74. Paulsson (2010).
75. van den Berg (1981); cf Brower and Rosenberg, 'The Death of the Two-Headed Nightingale: Why the Paulsson — van den Berg Presumption that Party-Appointed Arbitrators are Untrustworthy is Wrongheaded' (2013) 29 *Arbitration International* 7–44)
76. Strezhnev (2016).
77. UNCITRAL, Explanatory Note by the UNCITRAL Secretariat on the 1985 Model Law on International Commercial Arbitration as Amended in 2006, 23 (2008), Art 11.
78. QMUL Survey 2018, p. 9.
79. UNCITRAL, Explanatory Note by the UNCITRAL Secretariat on the 1985 Model Law on International Commercial Arbitration as Amended in 2006 23 (2008), Art 11.

mation must be made available, to increase transparency surrounding the quality and efficiency of arbitrators. This will ensure that disputes are handled by the appropriate decision-makers. Further transparency will also act as a catalyst for efficiency, as ultimately, the efficiency of an arbitral tribunal turns on the quality of its arbitrators.

CONCLUSION

The legitimacy challenge presents a unique opportunity for ICA to achieve greater efficiency. This has been the trend in recent times, with increasing levels of transparency in relation to arbitral awards, arbitral procedure and the arbitrators themselves. Parties, equipped with more information than ever before, can then make informed decisions on the seat, institution or arbitrator(s), allowing them to resolve their dispute efficiently. Although steps have been taken, further work must be done to maximise efficiency and legitimacy.

Transparency must be balanced against the confidentiality of arbitral proceedings. As Paulsson comments, 'arbitration is not a spectator sport'[80] and many users select arbitration as a form of dispute resolution owing to its privacy and confidentiality. However, these important tenets may still be preserved, notwithstanding the movement towards transparency. Transparency and confidentiality are not at odds with one another. They are two distinct concepts that operate in different ways.[81] It is therefore critical that they be pursued in ways that preserve the critical concerns of both, to increase the attractiveness of arbitration and address the current legitimacy crisis.

Ultimately, improving transparency is contingent upon the elucidation of information where it is appropriate to do so and with the consent of the parties. There are important developments that should be encouraged, including: (a) the publication of arbitral awards, (b) illuminating arbitral procedure and (c) improving access to objective information on arbitrator performance. Transparency will prove to be useful in improving the legitimacy and efficiency of ICA, ensuring that it remains among the preferred methods of international dispute resolution in the future.

REFERENCES

Allsop, James, Chief Justice 'Commercial and investor-state arbitration: The importance of recognising their differences'. Presented at the ICCA Congress in Sydney, Australia, 16 April 2018. *Note:* Chief Justice Allsop presides over the Federal Court of Australia.

80. Editorial (1995), p. 235.
81. Jones (2017b). p. 16.

Ashford, Peter 'Document Production in International Arbitration: A Critique from "Across the Pond"' (2012) 10 *Loyola University of Chicago International Law Review* 1.

Bell, David (2015) *Napoleon: A Concise Biography*. Oxford: Oxford University Press.

Bennett, David, QC 'Public Interest, Private Arbitration and Disclosure' (1996) 49 *Australian Construction Law Newsletter Issue*, available at http://classic.austlii.edu.au/au/journals/AUConstrLawNlr/1996/54.pdf. (Accessed 8 December 2020).

Besaiso, Haytham, Fenn, Peter and Emsley, Margaret 'International construction arbitration: a need for decoding the black box of decision making' [2017] ICLR 288.

Besaiso, Haytham and Fenn, Peter 'How Do International Construction Arbitrators Make Their Decisions? The Status of Substantive Law' [2020] 37 ICLR 199–226 at 200.

BestLawyers.com (2020) https://www.bestlawyers.com/canada/international-arbitration (accessed 15 July 2020).

Blackaby *et al* (eds) (2009) *Redfern and Hunter on International Arbitration* Oxford: Oxford University Press, 5th ed.

Born, Gary (2014) *International Commercial Arbitration*. New York: Wolters Kluwer, 2nd ed.

Borris, Christian 'Common Law and Civil Law: Fundamental Differences and Their Impact on Arbitration' (1995) 2 *Arbitration & Dispute Resolution Law Journal* 92.

Brekoulakis, Stavros 'Systemic bias and the institution of international arbitration: a new approach to arbitral decision-making' [2013] 4(3) *Journal of International Dispute Settlement* 553–85.

Brower, Charles and Rosenberg, Charles 'The Death of the Two-Headed Nightingale: Why the Paulsson–van den Berg Presumption that Party-Appointed Arbitrators are Untrustworthy is Wrongheaded' (2013) 29 *Arbitration International* 7–44.

CICC.court.gov.cn (2020) http://cicc.court.gov.cn/html/1/219/193/195/index.html (accessed 15 July 2020).

Comrie-Thomson, Paul 'A Statement of Arbitral Jurisprudence: The Case for a National Law Obligation to Publish International Commercial Arbitral Awards' (2017) 34 *Journal of International Arbitration* 275.

Dow Chemical France, The Dow Chemical Company and others v Isover Saint Gobain, Zwischenschiedsspruch v. 23.09.1982, ICC Case No. 4131, Y. Comm. Arb. 1984, 131. See decision of Paris Court of Appeal, 21 October 1983, Rev. Arb. 1984, p. 98.

Editorial (Paulsson), 'The Decision of the High Court of Australia in *Esso/BHP v Plowman*' (1995) 11(3) *Arbitration International* 231.

Ferrario, Pietro 'The Group of Companies Doctrine in International Commercial Arbitration: Is there any Reason for this Doctrine to Exist?' (2009) 26(5) *Journal of International Arbitration* 647.

French, Robert, Chief Justice 'Investor-State Dispute Settlement – A Cut Above the Courts?' Presented at the Supreme and Federal Court Judges' Conference,

Sydney, Australia, 9 July 2014. *Note:* Chief Justice French (as he then was) presided over the High Court, the final court of appeal in Australia.

Gonzalez-Bueno, Carlos (ed) (2018) *40 Under 40: International Arbitration (2018)* Spain: Dykinson S.L.

Hammond, Nicholas 'Arbitration in Ancient Greece' (1985) 1(2) *Arbitration International* 188 (citing Homer, *The Iliad* XVIII 497–508).

Hay, Emily (2018) 'Winds of Chance, Confidentiality and International Commercial Arbitration' in Gonzalez-Bueno (2018).

ICCWBO.org (2020) https://library.iccwbo.org/dr.htm?AGENT=ICC_HQ& AGENT=ICC_HQ (accessed 15 July 2020).

International Bar Association (2010) *Rules on the Taking of Evidence in International Arbitration.*

Jones, Doug (2017a) 'Arbitrators as Law Makers' (2017) 6(2) *Indian Journal of Arbitration Law*, 3.

Jones, Doug (2017b) 'Confidentiality: A Slippery Slope' (Speech, Australian Disputes Centre Presentation 2017).

Jones, Doug (2019) Keynote address at the 8th Asia Pacific ADR Conference on 20 September 2019 (Jones (2019).

Korean Commercial Arbitration Board Rules 2016.

London Court of International Arbitration, 'LCIA Notes for Parties', 19. *Confidentiality and Publication of Awards*, available at: https://www.lcia.org// adr-services/lcia-notes-for-parties.aspx#19 (accessed 15 July 2020).

Neuberger, Lord 'Keynote Speech' (2015) 81 *Arbitration* 427.

Paulsson, Jan 'Moral Hazard in International Dispute Resolution'. Lecture, University of Miami School of Law, 29 April 2010.

Peterson Farms Inc v C & M Farming Ltd [2004] 1 Lloyd's Rep 603.

Queen Mary University of London and Pinsent Masons Research Survey '2019 International Arbitration Survey: Driving Efficiency in International Construction Disputes' (2019). Download available at: https://www.pinsentmasons.com/thinking/special-reports/international-arbitration-survey) (Accessed 8 December 2020).

Queen Mary University of London and White & Case Research Survey '2018 International Arbitration Survey: The Evolution of International Arbitration' (2018). Download available at: http://www.arbitration.qmul.ac.uk/research/2018/ (Accessed 8 December 2020).

Reymond, Claude 'Civil Law and Common Law: Which Is the Most Inquisitorial? A Civil Lawyer's Response' (1989) 5(4) *Arbitration International* 357.

Rogers, Catherine 'Transparency in International Commercial Arbitration' (2006) 54 *Kansas Law Review* 1301.

Rubino-Sammartano, Mauro (1986) 'Rules of Evidence in International Arbitration: A Need for Discipline and Harmonization' 3(2) *Journal of International Arbitration* 87.

Rules on the Efficient Conduct of Proceedings in International Arbitration (2018) (Prague Rules).

SICC.gov.sg (2020a) https://www.sicc.gov.sg/about-the-sicc/establishment-of-the-sicc#:~:text=The%20framework%20for%20the%20establishment,launched%20 on%205%20January%202015 (Accessed 15 July 2020).

SICC.gov.sg (2020b) https://www.sicc.gov.sg/docs/default-source/legislation-rules-pd/sicc-procedural-guide-(20190724)-(pdf).pdf (Accessed 15 July 2020).

SICC.gov.sg (2020c) https://www.sicc.gov.sg/guide-to-the-sicc (Accessed 15 July 2020).

Strezhnev, Anton 'Detecting Bias in International Investment Arbitration'. Speech, 57th Annual Convention of the International Studies Association, Atlanta, Georgia, 16 March 2016.

Thomas, John, Lord Chief Justice, 'Developing commercial law through the courts: rebalancing the relationship between the courts and arbitration'. Bailii Lecture, 9 March 2016) 2, available at: https://www.judiciary.gov.uk/wp-content/uploads/2016/03/lcj-speech-bailli-lecture-20160309.pdf (Accessed 8 December 2020). *Note*: The Lord Chief Justice of England and Wales may be viewed as the second-highest ranking official in the hierarchy of the legal system of England and Wales.

Triebel, Volker 'An Outline of the Swiss/German Rules of Civil Procedure and Practice Relating to Evidence' (1982) 47 *Arbitration* 221.

UNCITRAL, Explanatory Note by the UNCITRAL Secretariat on the 1985 Model Law on International Commercial Arbitration as Amended in 2006, 23 (2008), Art 11.

UNCITRAL, Notes on Organising Arbitral Proceedings (2016).

UNCITRAL, UNCITRAL Rules on Transparency in Treaty-based Investor-State Arbitration (New York, 1 April 2014) (UNCITRAL Rules).

UNCITRAL, United Nations Convention on Transparency in Treaty-based Investor-State Arbitration (2014).

UNCITRAL, Working Group III Draft Paper, 'Possible reform of investor-State dispute settlement (ISDS)', 7 September 2018.

University of Ottawa, *Percentage of the World Population, Civil Law and Common Law Systems*, available at: http://www.juriglobe.ca/eng/syst-demo/tableau-dcivil-claw.php (Accessed 8 December 2020).

van den Berg, Albert Jan (1981) *The New York Arbitration Convention of 1958*. New York: Kluwer Law International.

Walker, Janet (2019a), 'International Commercial Arbitration in an Era of Transparency'. Presented at the annual Jean Gabriel Castel Lecture Series in Toronto, Canada, Glendon College, 26 February 2019.

Walker, Janet (2019b), 'Specialised International Courts: Keeping Arbitration up to its Game' (2019) 85 *Arbitration* 2.

Walker, Janet (2019c) 'The Prague Rules: Options and Opportunities for Asia' 38th Seoul IDRC Lecture Series (Seoul), (January 2019).

WhosWhoLegal.com (2020) http://whoswholegal.com/news/analysis/article/34252/arbitration-2018-analysis/ (Accessed 15 July 2020).

PART FOUR

SELECTED CHARTERED INSTITUTE
OF ARBITRATORS ROEBUCK LECTURES

CHARTERED INSTITUTE OF ARBITRATORS
THE 2011 ROEBUCK LECTURE, 12 MAY 2011

TIME TO THINK: UNDERSTANDING DISPUTE MANAGEMENT
Derek Roebuck

The inaugural Roebuck Lecture, May 12, 2011. This is the first in a series of annual lectures which the Chartered Institute of Arbitrators has instituted in honour of the former editor.

[*Editorial note*: This lecture was published at (2011) 77(3) *Arbitration* 342–350 and is reprinted by kind permission of the publisher.]

> Well, Sir Anthony, since you desire it, we will not anticipate the past, so come, young people, our retrospection will now be all to the future
>
> Mrs Malaprop in Sheridan *The Rivals*

Introduction

Who better than Mrs Malaprop to introduce this lecture? All my research on the management of disputes has been about the past but ten years' experience of editing our journal has meant I have read and discussed, with their authors and peer reviewers, such a wealth of thinking about contemporary problems that I am emboldened to offer some thoughts about the future. I hope thereby to set off a chain of lectures that will concentrate our minds, once a year, on where our research might be directed.

Scientists—scholars of all disciplines—are rarely unanimous about anything but they seem to agree that, in all research, it is the question you ask that matters. I have asked myself: "How can we understand dispute management better and use that understanding in our work?" Having long since retired from practice and now from editing the journal, I have time to think about what we are all up to in our efforts to resolve disputes, to improve the processes and to pass on our skills and understanding to others.

Negotiated settlement is the first and most natural response to most differences and can dispose of them before they become disputes. Recently my hearing aids developed faults. They were out of guarantee. The customer service department agreed that we should not let our difference develop into a dispute. I was offered either a newer better model or three-quarters of my money back. I chose the former and I can hear your mutterings at the back. If a supplier has a contract with a purchaser, by which it has undertaken to supply parts for the purchaser's best-selling machine for three years, and after one year a competitor takes the market, the parties may agree to modify their contractual obligations to require the supplier to make parts for the purchaser's new model, at a different price.

As far as I can discover, such settlements have always and everywhere been normal and natural. They leave few records but I expect you would agree that the great majority of differences end like that. When that happy outcome is not possible, the parties may call in a third party. Again, in all times and places I have studied, the first and most natural step is for that third party to try to mediate. In many places, that has been the first response of arbitrators and even judges. The concern of mediators everywhere at all times is to bring about a resolution which both parties accept. When an authoritative voice is raised, then, which warns against the unquestioning popularity of mediation, it should concern us.

What Is the Norm?

Every word of the Master of the Rolls' recent Bentham Lecture[1] deserves careful study. The only bit that caught the attention of the *Law Society Gazette*[2] was what it called his warning "against mediation being used as a replacement for the courts". The media will ensure, if they can, that differences of opinion about the proper role of mediation will blossom into a dispute. I recognise the dangers of unsolicited interference, but offer to mediate by showing that a better understanding of the role of mediation will reduce the scope of the burgeoning differences and transform them into a healthy debate on the essential points.

First, let us look at what Lord Neuberger said. His concern was to establish the crucial importance of the courts in protecting those rights which are essential to civil society—and access of all to the courts:[3]

> "In our modern consumer, market-based society, with its multiplicity of laws and rights, and its increasing scope for legal disputes, it is more important than ever that we have effective, accessible institutions of law. If not, laws go unenforced. They cease to be rights, but rather become privileges for those select few who can afford them ... the irreducible cost of a genuinely accessible and truly effective legal system has to be paid if we wish to remain a civil society."

The first three-quarters of Lord Neuberger's lecture are a carefully crafted argument for a better system of legal aid. Those of us who have watched his career with close attention are relieved that the responsibility

---

1. "Swindlers (Including the Master of the Rolls?) not Wanted: Bentham and Justice Reform" delivered at University College, London, March 2, 2011 (hereafter "Swindlers not Wanted").
2. March 10, 2011 p.4.
3. "Swindlers not Wanted" pp.7–8 paras 16 and 18.

for civil justice has passed to him from Lord Bingham. I have never shirked the responsibility a law professor has to criticise our judges,[4] but they now need all our support in their mighty battles against those in power who espouse an ideology of short-term expediency over all other principles.

Having established the case for equal access to justice without financial barriers, including a wicked suggestion that legal aid might be financed by fines on those wealthy parties which abuse the processes of litigation, at the very end of his lecture Lord Neuberger says:[5]

> "The development of mediation as a means to resolve disputes amicably has been, and will continue to be important and valuable. But, and this is a big but, ... those alternative mechanisms cannot be the norm, or approach the norm ... in some cases facilitating a mediated settlement will be the right thing to do. But, ultimately, our civil society is not based on a commitment to utility. It is based on the rule of law." I would like to circumscribe the debate by removing one element, which arises from the ambiguity in the word "norm". *Norma* in Latin is a set square. You use it to check right angles. Legislation and the courts develop law which provides norms in that sense. Mediation can play no part in that. The outcome of a successful mediation is a settlement. Norms cannot be established by private contract. Moreover, to establish norms decisions must be regularly recorded and published.[6]

But the word "norm" has another sense in English. It can mean "what is usual". The *OED* gives that meaning first: "what is expected or regarded as normal; customary behaviour". I can show you that mediation is and always has been just that—and, indeed, in most societies more the "norm" than litigation, which it predates. Though mediation can never provide a legal "norm", I hope to persuade you that mediation is more normal than litigation.

Ordinary people do not choose to litigate. They cannot afford it. Even those with wealth and privilege have often preferred mediation. In an article in *Arbitration* four years ago,[7] "The Myth of Modern Mediation", I hoped to scotch the myth that mediation was a modern technique. I failed. For example, the foreword to the CIArb's recent useful booklet *What is Alternative Dispute Resolution (ADR)?*[8] says:

---

4. "The Diplock Report on Mercenaries" *New Statesman* August 13, 1976 reprinted with introduction in Derek Roebuck *Disputes and Differences: Comparisons in Law, Language and History* (Oxford: HOLO Books: The Arbitration Press, 2010) (hereafter *Disputes and Differences*) pp.79–83.
5. Paragraph 41 out of 50 excluding 3 of conclusions.
6. In our society but not all, cf. Confucius's preference for the law to be unknown.,
7. (2007) 73 *Arbitration* 105–16; reprinted in *Disputes and Differences* pp.394–406.
8. (London: Chartered Institute of Arbitrators, 2010) p.ix.

"Beginning in the late 20th century ... powerful societal forces ... began to challenge the notion that courts could or even should be the primary forum for dispute resolution."

Nothing began in the last century, except new forms of dispute resolution crafted to deal with the shortcomings of litigation in the United States.[9]

My article remains unchallenged and I know that you not only read every word of the journal but retain the arguments, so I won't repeat them now. I will just add some new examples.

In the first years of the second century AD, the legal system in Rome provided a simple and cheap process for dealing with civil claims; but Pliny the Younger complained of being beset by the disputes of his tenant farmers.[10] More than seventeen centuries later, Francis Place, the farm labourer who started the first agricultural workers' union in England and became a Liberal MP, expressed the same sentiments:[11]

"I had many matters brought to me for adjudication, arbitration or arrangement. I hardly know the time when for three months together I have been free from this kind of interference."

In the fourteenth century, Geoffrey Chaucer, man of many parts—diplomat, royal adviser, linguist, poet—used the words "arbitration" and "mediation" for the first time in surviving literature. I cannot for the life of me work out why, when it was his turn to tell a story in his *Canterbury Tales*, he chose to switch from verse to prose and produce twenty pages of such aching boredom that Neville Coghill felt justified in leaving it out of his Penguin translation. But it is lucky for us that Chaucer did tell the tale of Melibeus, whose wife Prudence conducted a mediation after the fashion of the time. We can follow every step, as she produces a settlement between her husband and his adversaries, who had broken in, beaten her and wounded their daughter. She caucuses with the parties separately. She even uses the trick which nobody would dream of using now: she lets each side think she has a soft spot for them.[12]

---

9. Even there, informal mediation has a longer history, though it seems, with arbitration, to have fallen into disuse and "discord and dispute ... were complacently accepted phenomena, to be settled by force or litigation": Frances Kellor *American Arbitration: Its History, Functions and Achievements* (New York: Harper, 1948) pp.5–6. That was not the way of the native American, whose culture of mediation has given us the word "caucus".

10. Derek Roebuck *Early English Arbitration* (Oxford: HOLO Books: The Arbitration Press, 2008) pp.56–57.

11. J.A. Jaffe "Industrial Arbitration, Equity, and Authority in England, 1800–1850" (2000) 18 *Law and History R.* 1.

12. L.D. Benson (ed.) *The Riverside Chaucer* 3rd edn (Oxford: OUP, 1988) pp.236–39, particularly lines 1706ff and 1755ff.

In the civil strife of the next century, mediation was the preferred method of resolving even the most bloody disputes. The courts were there, including Parliament, but they preferred to delegate their powers to mediators and arbitrators to find a solution which would stick because it relied not on any legal rules but on a distribution of value which both sides could accept.[13]

For example, when the rules relating to the barring of entails had yet to be established, there were many family disputes over land, which could last for generations. Landowners wanted to ensure that their lands, often spread widely around the country, would stay in the family when they died. So they created a form of ownership, the fee tail, which required the land to pass to their offspring, generation after generation, usually by male primogeniture, with some provision for females and others. The next generation might not see it that way. All the courts could do was come down on one side or the other—would the entail hold or had it been legally barred? A mediation, however, with arbitration if necessary, could produce a much better solution. Why not group landholdings together geographically, then distribute them according to what the parties could be persuaded was fair, with cash payments to take care of any remaining inequalities? That was then the norm.[14]

We need not restrict ourselves to the past or to England. In the special issue of the journal on mediation, Sarah Rainsford, the BBC correspondent, described the work of a professional mediator in today's Turkey:[15]

"The sofas in Sait's office were filled with men, seeking his mediation ... Sait is shuttling between the two families, attempting to negotiate conditions for peace. Instead of the blood maybe some money, maybe a formal apology—maybe both."

In modern Ethiopia, a woman mediator practised regularly and successfully in all kinds of disputes, over land, fighting and matrimonial quarrels:[16]

"The first morning I spent in Chimate's household, people waited for her and served up their disputes with the first coffee of the day. Men and

13. Norman Davis (ed.) *Paston Letters and Papers of the Fifteenth Century* Parts I and II, 2 vols (Oxford: Clarendon Press, 1971–), reprinted with corrections 2004: Richard Beadle and Colin Richmond (eds) Pt III (Oxford: OUP for Early English Text Society, 2005). The 1051 documents tell many stories in detail.
14. A good example is described in S.J. Payling "Arbitration, Perpetual Entails and Collateral Warranties in Late Medieval England: A Case Study" (1992) 13 *J. Legal History* 32–62.
15. Sarah Rainsford "The Turkish Peacemaker" (2007) 73 *Arbitration* 100–104.
16. Judith Olmstead *Woman Between Two Worlds: Portrait of an Ethiopian Rural Leader* (Urbana: University of Illinois Press, 1997), with photographs between pp.108 and 109 of a mediation as it took place.

women stopped her as she walked the paths of Dita and sought her in the marketplace."

I hope someone told her of the first of her predecessors, Arete, in Homer's *Odyssey*:[17]

"The people think she is divine and greet her as she goes through the city, because she has plenty of decent common sense and, if she feels like it, she resolves their disputes—yes, those of the men as well."

In a recent *Observer*, Mariella Frostrup told of present-day reality:[18]

"Men with guns are littering Ivory Coast with corpses while my female companions in P.A's Ribhouse in downtown Monrovia outline inspired, achievable solutions to ending that conflict. In the same gentle voices that cajoled Liberia's bloodstained dictator Charles Taylor into resigning his presidency ... they explain their plans ...

It wasn't the African Union or the UN but Liberian women who brought the warring sides to the peace talks and subsequently, on the back of that success, have played a major part in conflict resolution in Sierra Leone, Sudan and Rwanda ... when it comes to encouraging and facilitating peace they have unique skills."

Not only can I show that mediation is normal. I can show that litigation is abnormal, a pathological aberration in most cultures. In some it produces some of the norms but it is not the process that most people with a difference want or need to submit it to. Let us then agree to drop abnormality as an argument against mediation.

Mediation as a Threat to Legal Development

From his justified and laudable insistence that access to the courts is a fundamental right, Lord Neuberger continues:[19]

"If there is no effective access to the courts, the fundamental underpinning to all forms of dispute resolution ... falls away. The only reason the strong and rich will negotiate, arbitrate or mediate with their weaker and poorer opponents is the knowledge that ultimately there is the authority and power of the justice system standing behind the arbitration and mediation systems. Furthermore, unless there is a healthy justice

---

17. Homer *Odyssey* 7.69–74.
18. "Let Women Lead the Way to Peace in Africa" *Observer*, April 10, 2011 p.38.
19. "Swindlers not Wanted" para.43.

system, with judges developing the law to keep pace with the ever accelerating changes in social, commercial, communicative, technological, scientific and political trends, neither citizens nor lawyers will know what the law is."

There are two points there. First, if parties in the wrong refuse to mediate, the only way in which parties *in the right* can get what they deserve is to go to court. Secondly, to get the law we need, the courts must have enough cases in which to develop it. It would be wise to make some preliminary concessions to both these arguments.

Of course, there is no way a recalcitrant party can be compelled to make a mediated settlement. It is different in some other cultures even today but in ours you can't force anyone to settle. You can require them to try and nobody argues for any more than that. A determined refusal to mediate should not inhibit a party's right to litigate, though there is no reason, if that stubbornness is an abuse of the legal process, why it should not prove costly. So, let's restrict the debate to the merits of *making an attempt* at mediation compulsory.

We have been talking about "the party in the right". Does that mean the party with the better law or the one with the merits?

Merits and Law

All my legal life I have been reminded of the gulf between legal rights and merits. As a lad, just starting my articles, I prepared the brief for Hartley Shawcross in a claim against our client John Summers, the steelworks. We were pouring cyanide into the Dee estuary, which upset the salmon, who were determined to make their way up the river to die in the traditional way on the hooks of the owners of riparian fishing rights. In 1958 Shawcross was the Garfield Sobers of the Bar, so quick and brilliant that I found it hard even to follow what he was doing. On the other side was Charles Russell, appearing to move more at my speed. I could not imagine a more overwhelming case than that which Shawcross presented. Russell hardly raised a point. He just left it to the scientific experts to establish the cyanide spill and to the judge to find the law he wanted. We lost, of course. We never had a chance of persuading the judge that the law should override the merits. Perhaps he liked to do a bit of fishing himself.

Fifty years of experience have taught me that judges are suckers for merits. I have still to come across one who enjoys deciding a case on unmeritorious law. But the John Summers case was unusual. There the merits were plain for all to see. In few of the international commercial disputes I have been involved in since have any merits been discernible, let alone arguable. In my little world of negotiable instruments, it was usually a question of whether a company, which had made a written promise to pay and taken value for it, could wriggle out of liability for what now looked like an inflated price. And it is funny that faults in goods supplied only appear when the market falls. So one should be slow to assume that legal rights necessarily represent some genuine value. As Lord Justice Sedley has written, "precedent provides off-the-shelf solutions where merits don't, simply because most litigation is barren of self-evident merit on either side".[20]

The antithesis between a mediated settlement and a decision on legal rights is not a simple one of greater and less justice. To go back to the Middle Ages, were the distributions of mediator-arbitrators on contested entails more or less just than the corresponding decisions of the courts? To bring us up to date, does the present law on frustration of contracts produce as fair a result in charterparty cases as a properly mediated settlement could do? To quote Stephen Sedley's next sentence: "I thought at one time of suggesting to Lord Woolf that his procedural reforms might include a power in really tedious cases to declare a draw." Or quite firmly suggest mediation?

Litigation and Development of Law

The second point is that we must have litigation for the law to develop.

The problem is not the same the whole world over. There are more than a billion people in China and in India. Not one in a thousand could even think of litigation. Even here in England, very few people with claims have access to the courts, at least not those where judges make new law. The threshold for the High Court will soon be £100,000.[21] That should make sure it is the law of the wealthy which is developed.

Is there evidence that alternative forms of dispute management are reducing the flow of litigation to the level where the development of new law is endangered? That is a suitable research topic.

If parties want to settle, they will, with or without mediators. Can we think of a suitable deterrent? It will have to apply to arbitration as well.[22]

An older problem arises from the very nature of our legal system. Think how long Lord Denning had to wait for an opportunity to "develop the law" on a promise of partial performance as consideration.[23] During the decades when all lawyers knew the law was unsatisfactory, before the modern mediation machine was assembled, we advised clients to settle.

20. Stephen Sedley *Ashes and Sparks: Essays on Law and Justice* (Cambridge: CUP, 2011) p.203.
21. *Law Society Gazette* March 31, 2011 p.2.
22. From which no precedents can flow. ICSID is a world unto itself.
23. *Central London Property Trust v High Trees House* [1947] 1 KB 130.

We did not suggest an expensive and chancy trip all the way to the House of Lords so that the law might be improved for others. And how often have you been involved in a case where the parties had no notion, when they first disagreed, of the point of law that was later litigated? Litigators trim the problem to fit the law. Mediators don't need to; they can keep hold of the reality.

Of course, mediators need to know what the law is. Even if all disputes could be mediated, we would still need a refined and up-to-date set of legal principles to guide settlements. The law may even be a determining factor in the settlement. But it need not be; other factors may prevail. I believe they will increasingly do so. So we may need to find other ways of developing it. Some jurisdictions have effective law reform commissions. Jurisdictions outside the Common Law seem to manage without a doctrine of precedent.

Online Dispute Resolution

Meanwhile, other developments threaten the whole system, for example online dispute resolution (ODR). There are more than a million eBay transactions a day: "eBay today resolves through ODR about sixty million disputes per year". In total, ODR may already be resolving billions of disputes a year. Fewer than one in a million end in litigation. What law applies to those that are settled? Effectively none! All the eBay settlements are determined by eBay's policy. Surely the courts are needed to enforce settlements? Not at all! The sanction on the less than 2 per cent who do not comply consists in the negative "reputation points" that attach to each user's profile.

My source Thomas Schultz must be allowed his own words:[24]

"Square Trade used to offer mainly two dispute resolution processes: computer-assisted negotiation and on-line mediation. Both processes relied heavily on on-line forms produced by Square Trade's system. These forms suggested typical issues that the parties may have, thereby helping them identify and understand their issue, and then recommended typical settlement agreements that statistically were likely to be accepted in the situation described by the parties. It was based on a simple form of artificial intelligence, called an expert system, that learned from prior cases to try to predict what the parties' issues and agreeable solutions were likely to be. The aggregated understandings of the rights and obligations of users were thus reflected in the issues and

24. Thomas Schultz "The Roles of Dispute Settlement and ADR" in Arnold Ingen-Housz *ADR in Business: Practice and Issues Across Countries and Cultures* Vol.II (New York: Wolters Kluwer, 2011 (hereafter *ADR in Business*) pp.135–56.

solutions suggested by the computer. These suggested solutions framed, informally but effectively, the realm of likely outcomes for any given case. The outcomes of prior cases were brought to bear on subsequent cases; they acquired a de facto precedential value, which was soft and relatively diffuse but nonetheless effectively improving predictability by setting guideposts. The expert system's purpose was to bring the dispute resolution system closer to the pursuit of the rule of law."

Rule of law? Our law is found in precedent. Precedent is about legal rules, not the accumulation of decisions on similar facts. Schultz presents a challenge to all of us to think what this means—a billion disputes settled every year by a computer program that doesn't think about the consequences on the rule of law. Once the program is written, with its built-in cybernetic self-corrections, won't errors reduplicate and "injustice" proliferate? Will eBay's policies, which provide the underlying law, prefer consumers, with one-off interests, to suppliers with their repeated custom? How can we know? And what about Amazon—and Chinese virtual banks using their own virtual international currency?

How long before multinationals decide that this is the cheapest and most predictable way to resolve their *big* disputes? Won't it be easier to persuade your directors and shareholders that you were right to settle by shared algorithm rather than risky and costly litigation?

Cooperation and Partnering

The big companies and the influential professional institutions have already left the lawyers behind. Recognising the costs and other drawbacks of fighting legal battles and the advantages of providing in their original contracts for cooperation in managing differences, they have begun to prefer partnering contracts which require them not only to act in good faith but to cooperate in maximising profit for both sides.[25]

Good corporate governance now suggests mediation. There is evidence that the companies which use ADR most adroitly have the best price/ earnings ratio. The ambition to increase value, rather than get the bigger share of a fixed pie, now motivates many top managers, whatever their legal advisers tell them. Do professional ethics already require lawyers to recommend mediation?

Modern contracts increasingly include stepped clauses to deal with disputes. They require the parties first to make serious efforts to resolve

25. There is a growing literature: e.g. most of *ADR in Business* and Stephen Furst "Dispute Avoidance—Good Faith/Partnering/Cooperation Clauses in Contracts" (talk to CIArb East Asia Branch, Hong Kong, October 7, 2010); p.2 of the latter cites the JCT Constructing Excellence Contract 2007 2.1.

differences by negotiation; if that does not work, then to try mediation and only if that fails to go to arbitration. No litigation. They may require parties to act in good faith. How far does that go? Almost all jurisdictions other than those which stick close to the English version of the Common Law require the parties to act in good faith in making and performing their contracts. In England we have come to do so in different ways, mainly through implied terms. Judges do not enjoy encouraging bad faith, however cautious they are about introducing broad principles.

There is nothing airy-fairy about this. Experience has taught me that builders have hard heads. Yet this is what their modern contracts provide:[26]

> "Under the JCT Non-Binding Partnering Charter the parties agree to act in good faith; in an open and trusting manner; in a co-operative way; in a way to avoid disputes by adopting a 'no blame' culture; fairly towards each other; and valuing the skills and respecting the responsibilities of each other. In the ACA Standard Form of Contract for Project Partnering PPC 2000, the parties agree to work together and individually in the spirit of trust, fairness and mutual co-operation."

So we are used to good faith in making and performing. What about a general duty to resolve disputes in good faith? Will that include willingness to mediate?

Two developments of recent years have changed attitudes. Negotiators have always known that it is pointless to deal with anyone who has no authority to settle. Mediators realise they have a greater chance of success if they bypass the lawyers and talk to those concerned with the realities of the dispute. So they now regularly expect to talk to someone near the top.

Moreover, we may wonder what the world has come to when the boss of an airline moves to head a retail chain, then to a bank and at last to advise the Government on the media. Such mobility—unthinkable when experience within an industry was a condition of advancement and there were industries worthy of the name—permeates big business now. Think of those a rung or two below. As they negotiate, they cannot be unaware of potential openings for employment with the other party. *La Ronde* comes to mind.

---

26. Nerys Jefford "'Soft Obigations' in Construction Law: Duties of Good Faith and Co-operation" available at http://keatingchambers.co.uk/resources/publications/2005/nj_soft_obligations_construction_law.aspx [accessed May 4, 2011]. I am grateful to Lorena Carvajal, PhD candidate at Portsmouth University, for this reference and for other fresh ideas on good faith. Stephen Furst "Dispute Avoidance" p.2 cites the JCT Constructing Excellence Contract 2007 2.1, an even more ambitious attempt to provide for cooperation.

The Future: A Call to Action

So what can be said about the future? That will be largely in the hands of our successors. As the people change at the top of our professions, the world views of younger generations will displace ours. It will be their dreams and plans which matter, which they will construct from their own experience. And new problems produce new solutions, as the collapse of Lehman Brothers produced the Hong Kong Scheme.[27] But there are things we can all do and that leaves us with immediate responsibilities.

I am not offering answers. I do not even know what the questions are, other than those I have raised today. They are:

1. How can we ensure the proper development of the law?
2. What is the jurisprudential significance of ODR?
3. Should there be a duty of good faith in resolving a dispute?

There is one thing we should do now. We should accept the responsibility we have always had as an institution but have not discharged. We should justify our claim—one we make to the Charity Commissioners if no one else—to be a learned institution. How can we do that? Simple! We finance research and publish the results. Distance from HQ is no longer a problem.

A start has been made, which should be recognised and applauded. But I challenge all the trustees to go back to their electorates and raise the money to support one or more researchers, PhD students or not, to address the questions which the trustees, properly advised, consider most important. The advisers charged with choosing next year's lecturer may wish to develop the same theme: how can CIArb contribute to the scholarship we all agree is needed to ensure the best possible development of dispute management processes to cope with what the future holds? We are not likely to run out of questions.

27. Investment Products Dispute Resolution Mediation and Arbitration Scheme; see http://www.info.gov.hk/hkma/eng/new/lehman/explanatory_b.htm [accessed May 4, 2011]; Gu Weisha "ADR and Financial Disputes in Hong Kong: The Lehman Brothers Experience and the Way Forward" (2011) *Asian Dispute Review* 20–23.

CHARTERED INSTITUTE OF ARBITRATORS
THE 2013 ROEBUCK LECTURE, 26 MAY 2013

MEDIATION: A SOCIAL ANTIBODY?
Stephen Ruttle QC*

[*Editorial note*: This contribution originally appeared at (2013) 79(3) *Arbitration* 295–308 and is reproduced in this volume by kind permission of the publisher.]

I am delighted, a little bit surprised to be honest, to see so many here at 7 p.m. on a warm May evening with the pubs outside doing a roaring trade! Mediation, whether or not a social antibody, had considerably less lustre, but for those of you who are here – echoing the Fosters ad – "good call"!

Thank you to the Chartered Institute for inviting me to give this year's Roebuck Lecture. It is a real privilege. I feel quite grown-up. I gave a presentation a year or so ago (I think) to the Chartered Institute after its annual conference. I was allowed 45 minutes at the end of the day for a slot called simply "Personal Reflections". Much of what I want to say tonight was pre-figured then; I apologise to those who may have been there on that occasion and who now want to hear something new. I think that my application of the themes has changed and I hoped developed since then. But the essence is unashamedly the same; we commercial mediators need to take more seriously, rather than less seriously, what we do. We need to recognise that we are in a privileged and important position as stewards of this odd process that we call "mediation". The challenge then is at the same time to be bolder about what we have and humbler in the way in which we apply it.

Welcome: thank you: now an apology. What I want to say is very much **a** personal reflection as a mediator. By definition this is necessarily limited by my own experience of mediation over the last 15 years. Many others have much more experience than I and may have very differing views to mine about the role of mediation in our society and its impact. I am not therefore speaking on behalf of the Chartered Institute nor on behalf of the Civil Mediation Council nor on behalf of any other mediator or mediating body. If I am wrong then I alone am wrong and you have only me to blame.

1. Objectives

My first objective is what I call **"challenging division"**. I am not suggesting here that there are not different practices (and the need for

* Stephen Ruttle is a Commercial Mediator at Brick Court Chambers, a community mediator and a mediator in disputes involving faith-based issues.

different training) between different sorts of mediation. What I have in mind is the mindset that sees these practices as quite separate disciplines and not as aspects of a larger whole. Why is this important? First because it emphasises our need (all of us facilitators/mediators) to work together. We cannot afford either to ignore each other or to squabble. What we have is too important to be wasted. There is a mutual inter-responsibility. Secondly, by experiencing different applications of what is essentially the same process, we deepen our own skills as mediators and enrich and broaden our own practices.

My second objective is what I call "broadening the vision". Yes I know; a call to "broaden the vision" immediately connotes the evangelistic if not downright messianic! Doing all I can to guard against that impulse my encouragement is that we should all take more seriously, rather than less seriously, the significance of what we are doing as mediators. Why? Quite simple. What we do does, of course, change the world. Not usually in headline grabbing ways, but in the way in which the having of a difficult conversation, the mending of an impaired relationship, even the ability of erstwhile litigants now to be able to sleep well at night, **always** changes the worlds of those individuals.

In one sense this has always been the case; conversation is the atomic glue that holds most people together. (Although as mediators we are all taught that only 7 per cent of communication is verbal with the balance a mixture of vocal and body language it is still a pretty important 7 per cent: without conversation, there is no structure on which the other non-verbal forms of communication can operate.) My point is different. In a world in which conversation, real conversation and engagement, is increasingly rare those of us whose jobs or calling or pastime is to help others have difficult conversations have an increasingly important role to fulfil.

If our vision is to be broadened we will also need applications within which this broader vision can be applied. I have some suggestions here too—and I hope there will be time for you to share your own insights. Specifically I would like to develop a concept of a community peace service (CPS); a loose network of community peace centres [CPC], which should be one-stop shops in their communities, to which all disputes which affect that community can be referred. These CPCs are in turn backed up by panels of mediators of different practices, many of whom will be acting wholly or part time on a voluntary basis. Different mediators working together. Specifically those who are able to generate funding by mediating particular sorts of dispute make a part at least of that funding available to support and maintain vital mediation work that attracts no funding.

2. My Story

As a mediator I wear three hats. My job is that of **commercial mediator**. For the last 12 years I have worked full time as a mediator. I still practise from Brick Court Chambers. I mediate all types of legal dispute from the very small to the very large. We commercial mediators tend to think that because we mediate cases involving, maybe billions of pounds, we are therefore very, very important! And that everyone else should listen to what we say. That is a bad mistake. In fact commercial mediation is merely the tip of an iceberg; perhaps more visible because it deals with high-profile business disputes and those who practise it accordingly come away with substantial fees. But with privilege comes responsibility. We commercial mediators are privileged indeed—to mediate cases that enable us to make the living we do. We have, I believe, a corresponding responsibility when it comes to the wider profession of mediation (of which more anon).

My second hat is that of **community mediator**. From almost the time I began to do commercial mediation I have been active in the community mediation world. This has been a huge help because it has given me a different lens through which to see commercial mediation. Initially I served as Vice-Chair of Mediation UK, an umbrella community mediation body. Mediation UK, with a reduced grant income and, I fear, riven by internal disputes, went out of business in 2005. In 2003 I was involved with setting up WMS [Wandsworth Mediation Service] which registered soon after as a charity. Against all the odds WMS continues to thrive. We have had a turbulent passage. A generous grant from the DCA [Department for Constitutional Affairs] enabled us to rent premises opposite Wandsworth Town Hall, employ a manager and seek to develop a local dispute resolution service. We ran out of money, our manager threatened to take us to the employment tribunal for constructive dismissal, we ended up mediating with him and when the dust settled we Trustees sat down and we looked at the four lever arch files of email traffic that the last year had generated and decided that enough was enough. There was no obvious source of funding to come; the council though supportive and very sympathetic was not in a position to help us financially.

To some extent this is the story of the community mediation world in England and Wales over the last 10 years. When I began at Mediation UK there were perhaps 200 to 300 local community mediation organisations operating in the UK, some of them with up to 20 years' experience of doing quite remarkable things in their communities. They had built up a wealth of expertise and had forged brilliant links with police, community groups and the like. When I was trained by CEDR [Centre for Effective Dispute Resolution] in 1998 the man in charge of the faculty—Tony Curtis, one of the most brilliant teacher/trainer/communicators I have ever met—commented that the real mediation coal-face, the place where the seriously skilled mediators were—was as volunteers on community mediation panels up and down the country. He was completely right. One of the tragedies of the mediation world over the last 10 years is the demise of many of these organisations. This means that local mediation organisations that have played a key role in their communities are going to the wall and taking all their expertise with them. This is a national tragedy. No one knows quite how many such organisations are now functioning in the UK. There may be 50 to 70 as compared to 250 plus less than 10 years ago.

The most obvious reason for these failures is lack of funding. Ten years ago most community mediation organisations depended on a mixture of local authority funding (often 60 per cent or more) and a combination of grants, gifts and payments from large foundations or funds. Today the money has almost entirely dried up.

The problem is not only a lack of funds. Many mediators (some would say all of them) are prima donnas. We are not always good at working together. I am Neo—the one—not you! I am going to do the **really important case** (and change the world). When making presentations like this I still get push back in the form of suggestions that I am a fat cat lawyer (which I was and maybe still am); and that my vision of mediators—lawyer, non-lawyer, commercial and community working together as part of a national joined-up peace service—is a form of paternalism from a wealthy commercial mediator. I have thought about this carefully. There are points that can be made. We commercial mediators are immensely fortunate in what we are paid, and we typically do work that is less demanding (from a mediation perspective) than than that done by two non-lawyer mediators, on say a WMS panel, mediating a dispute between neighbours on the 11th floor of a tower block on Battersea Park Road who are posting the unmentionable through each other's letter box. I come back to two answers. The first is pragmatic. Unless we work together I fear that the funding problems will mean that community mediation coverage over the UK will be patchy at best and probably non-existent. Secondly, philosophically, I think that mediators from radically different backgrounds and types should be working together. Most of the process that we offer has to do with managing difference. If we mediators cannot do this ourselves then we are not walking the line. If we cannot operate together in a joined-up way then at best we will be a marginalised and disparate group operating on the margins or in particular specialist niches. But if we unite then ... the future is orange!

Let's go back to the story of WMS. It is almost a paradigm situation. We had run out of money. There was no regular funding offered by the council or by any white knight. We had been locked into dispute with our manager. We were tired and fed up. We took a break. WMS was dormant for a while in a broom cupboard in a printing business run by one of our trustees. Then St. Marks Church, the church I attend in the heart of Battersea, which had recently had a significant new re-build offered us a tiny office in which to be based. We then developed a simple funding model (of which more again anon) which began to generate income.

Five years on we are still based at St. Marks. The arrangement has worked incredibly well. Our work complements the social programme of the church, although we remain a non-aligned independent charity. We work with people of all faiths and none. The church has superb facilities and the rooms that we use for our mediations are some of the most congenial I have ever mediated in. We wondered initially whether mediating in a church would cause difficulty for our clients and we always give them the option of electing some other venue. I think, to date, no one has requested some other venue. Our experience does, I think, raise possibilities. There must be many churches, mosques, synagogues, temples and the like in our communities that have excellent facilities and at which other services like WMS could be based. There are obvious potential costs savings here

My third hat is what I call **faith mediation**—where a faith-based issue is important. This may be a dispute within a particular faith group; thus within the Church the theological disputes relating to women's episcopacy, sexuality and the like are extremely well known. There is a Christian denomination near us in Battersea where the police have had to attend morning services to prevent scuffles and violence from breaking out between members of the congregation. My dear friend Zaza El Sheikh has mediated a number of "honour" disputes within her Muslim community. Or it may concern inter-faith issues which may lead to widespread community unrest. I am a member of BIMA [Belief in Mediation and Arbitration], a charity that Zaza set up a year or so ago whose members are mediators from different faith traditions. We did an event last year on the anniversary of 9/11 looking at forgiveness from different faith traditions. We hope to launch a series this summer on the theme of extreme conversations and the need to have them. An article in last week's *Times* on religious radicalisation at student level underlines the huge importance of the subject.

A word about faith in passing. Much of my own thinking about mediation involves my own faith background. I am not being exclusive or dismissive. I am certainly not saying that mediation is somehow the province of those from a faith background; although I note that many who practise as mediators do hold to or incline to such beliefs. I would be surprised if it was otherwise; the virtues of kindness, humility and compassion that faith systems seek to develop (do they in practice?) should encourage many followers to practise those virtues in mediation. One of the deeply disturbing things that I have found over the years—I am encouraged by what is happening at present—is the ambivalence within my own faith group (the Church) both to peacemaking and to the notion that we might somehow just be wrong and somebody else right! The Christian anthropologist Oz Guinness, writing recently, posed this question:

"How do we live with our deepest differences? This is one of the most profound questions of our time".

In this context in particular the appointments of Justin Welby to Canterbury and Francis to Rome are hugely exciting.

3. My Own Journey

Fifteen years ago, if not perfectly contented with my practice at Brick Court Chambers, I found life still to be pretty good. I had taken silk a couple of years previously and had a reasonably busy practice in the insurance/reinsurance and shipping fields. Colleagues in chambers, from Jonathan Sumption downwards, were giving important lectures and making important legal decisions in the High Court, Court of Appeal and the House of Lords. Brick Court was, and remains, an incredibly stimulating and satisfying place from which to work.

Then I got on a bus marked ADR that had no destination on it. Beware! The bus in my case was a five-day CEDR Mediation Training Course. The venue was unpromising; a recently built hotel near Daventry in sad-looking countryside on clay. It rained all week. There were 25 of us, a mixed bunch of lawyers and non-lawyers. I expected an easy ride; we were exploring the oddities of a strange new process called Mediation. Was it meditation or medication or something different again? I found it five of the hardest days' work I had ever been involved with. The faculty members were superb. Their job was to train me to start thinking differently about conflict resolution. That disputes were not wars to be fought and won (as a practising barrister and litigator I functioned primarily as a legal mercenary) but problems to be sorted out and not by me as a lawyer but by the parties themselves. Shock horror! Three out of our group of 25 left (two of them in tears) at the end of the second day. I completed the course, began to mediate a few months later (none of my first five mediations settled) and went full time a couple of years after that.

I was asked once, in an interview in a legal periodical, what was the most important piece of advice that I had been given. I answered by reference to a story my father told at his retirement speech (in about 1978) at Westminster County Court. There was a small group of dignitaries present together with most of the staff of the Court, perhaps 30 in all. He described how on his appointment as a judge a well-known member of the Court of Appeal who knew him well wrote to him suggesting that the way forward for him was "to do his best and not to give a damn about anybody else". Most of the audience nodded approvingly, thinking that this was the point of my father's story. He however paused for a moment and observed, "But that was not the way I have tried to do things". Some scratching of heads, and then my father continued. "Instead I have tried to live in accordance with the guidance of the prophet Micah". Some real consternation now; Micah was not an authority regularly quoted at that particular court. My father continued, quoting from chapter 6:

> "He has shown you O man, O woman, what is good. What is it that the Lord requires of you but to do justice, to love mercy and to walk humbly with your God?"

Over my years at the Bar I had often pondered the application of those two themes, the "doing of justice" and the "loving of mercy". My own experience (a consequence perhaps of being represented by me) was that at the end of the case, win or lose, my clients had gone through a mangle! By contrast the ethos that emerged from my mediation course attracted me. Helping parties talk to each other struck me as essentially "merciful" in the Micah sense; and conversations that led to a different sort of justice, a justice chosen by the parties in the context of relationships, rather than an edict imposed from without by a distant judge or rule maker, had considerable attraction.

I do have mixed emotions looking back. On the one hand gratitude; work became vocation and that is a huge privilege. On the other hand a degree of terror! So far as I am aware, I am still on the bus and I still have no idea where it is taking me!

One of my hobbies is fly fishing at night in remote countryside in central Wales on a river called the Towy. I am a member of an august London club called "The Fly Fishers" whose motto is "There is more to fishing than fishing!" At a recent dinner a club member from Zimbabwe told a story reported the previous week in the press. A bus driver was transporting 40 patients from one mental institution to another. They were loaded on to his double-decker which presumably on its front had the sign "Sorry out of use". The day was hot, the driver and his conductor became thirsty and as evening approached, an hour or so away from his destination in Bulawayo, he pulled into a wayside shebeen for refreshment. One drink followed another and by the time the driver and the conductor made it back to the bus the bus was empty and there was no sign of his passengers. Nothing daunted, he changed the label on the front of the bus to "Bulawayo", drove to the next bus stop and collected the first 30 passengers waiting in the queue. Telephoning ahead to his destination, he warned the orderlies that his charges were particularly excitable and would need extremely firm handling on arrival. Many suffered from acute delusions of normality. On arrival at Bulawayo the orderlies took possession of the furious passengers and wheeled them off to the mental institution. It took a full three days before the consistency of their stories persuaded those in charge that there had indeed been a mistake. As to the missing 30 patients nothing more has been heard of them. They have smoothly and seamlessly blended back into the fabric of society! So beware of buses marked ADR!

4. Reflections on Mediation

At least from my standpoint (as a commercial, community and faith mediator), I think that mediation has become something of a phenomenon. In a remarkably short time commercial mediation has become mainstream. Anecdotally 70 per cent or so of business/commercial cases going through the High Court now mediate at some stage. Two years ago the government published a detailed Dispute Resolution Pledge. There is pressure now on local authorities to make a similar commitment. Academics now talk about the privatisation of civil dispute resolution. There is similar enthusiasm for community and faith mediation and, I am told, for the other sorts of mediation. Most of us can talk anywhere about mediation and at the end of the talk there will be 10 or 15 people saying that they would like to be trained as volunteers. Mediation is "cool". There is, I think, a genuine groundswell of interest and enthusiasm that needs to be harnessed. An article published two weeks ago shows a photo of Ian Duncan Smith at the new office of a gangs mediation organisation in his constituency called Gangs Unite.

I am sometimes asked whether mediation is still a white middle-class *Guardian* readers phenomenon. It probably never was (a large number of communitarian cultures around the world have operated a mediation-type process for some thousands of years) and in the last 10 years it has become still less so. I spoke some years ago about mediation training at a group called "Only Connect" that works with ex-offenders, training them to write a play and then to perform it. I was talking about the impact we had seen at WMS of mediation training – specifically that it might be good to factor it into a rehabilitation programme or to add it on to the NA [Narcotics Anonymous] or AA [Alcoholics Anonymous] 10-step programme. One of the participants—an Elephant & Castle resident—interrupted me and said that he was a peace-maker. I asked him to tell us. He told of a street situation with a group of about 12 young adults, one of whom had pulled out a knife. He told us how he talked the knife down. What did he do?

"Well I talked, then I got everyone to sit down and then we had some spliffs."

Now there is a new way of handling a difficult plenary session! I asked him what he felt like when the knife went down. A big man, 6ft 6in, 16 stone, he levered himself upright from his chair and said:

"Man, I felt wicked. I have never felt so high in my life and I have done everything."

He came up afterwards and said:

"Please train me as a mediator, I want to do this stuff."

I have already made reference to the "tip of the iceberg" phenomenon. The more I reflect on the three mediation hats I wear – commercial, community and faith – the more apt I think this analogy is. But it does not necessarily follow from this metaphor that those at the top of the iceberg should become involved with, still less owe any responsibility towards, those below the waterline; to those much less visible, much less well paid (if at all) who work in communities, prisons, neighbourhoods, faith groups and the like. So why then do I suggest that we commercial mediators do? This leads me into deeper water and to a consideration of whether this wider mediation phenomenon may have an important social role.

5. Social Antibody?

"An antibody, also known as an immunoglobulin, is a large Y-shaped protein ... that is used by the immune system to identify and neutralize foreign objects such as bacteria and viruses."

In ordinary language it is an agent developed by the immune system of a living body, the function of which is to fight disease. The body recognises a threat which, if unchecked and ignored, will threaten its continued life. Societies are made up of groups of individual bodies. Sociologists (so my elder son tells me!) regard societies as following to some extent the practices of human bodies. Societies, if threatened, should therefore, entirely reasonably, develop defence mechanisms to deal with the threat that would otherwise potentially undermine and destroy that very society. Can the mediation phenomenon be seen in this light? Is it, in essence, the emergence of a process or practice designed to deal with a fundamental social malaise?

There are two images or metaphors that I use to illustrate the point. The first I call "Spiralling out of control". The second I call "Bridging the

Gap". Both derive from twentieth-century poems. The Irish poet William Butler Yeats, in a poem published in 1921 called "The Second Coming" described the post-First World War society in the following way:

"Turning and turning in the widening gyre
The falcon cannot hear the falconer;
Things fall apart; the centre cannot hold;
Mere anarchy is loosed upon the world,
The blood-dimmed tide is loosed, and everywhere
The ceremony of innocence is drowned;
The best lack all conviction, while the worst
Are full of passionate intensity."

The poem's ending (that still send shivers down my spine) is:

".And what rough beast, its hour come round at last,
Slouches towards Bethlehem to be born?"

Yeats' own vision was occultic and apocalyptic. He thought that about every 2,000 years society would disintegrate and a new order be formed. This disintegration stemmed from polarisation: "things fall apart; the centre cannot hold". The image with which the poem begins, a falcon spiralling in ever-widening circles (things spiralling out of control), is literally an image of wide application today.

The second poem is by the Welsh priest R.S. Thomas. Published in 1992 in an edition called "Mass for Hard Times" it is called "Tell Us":

"We have had names for you:
The Thunderer, the Almighty/Hunter,
Lord of the snowflake
and the sabre-toothed tiger.
One name we have held back
unable to reconcile it
with the mosquito, the tidal wave,
the black hole into which
time will fall. You have answered
us with the image of yourself
on a hewn tree, suffering
injustice, pardoning it;
pointing as though in either
direction; horrifying us
with the possibility of dislocation.
Ah, love, with your arms out

wide, tell us how much more
they must still be stretched
to embrace a universe drawing
away from us at the speed of light".

Thomas's poem recognises the same polarisation of which Yeats writes. Unlike Yeats however, and drawing on an explicitly Christian image, his vision is of a bridge between polarised extremes; albeit at a cost, a "stretching", so extreme as to raise the horror of "the possibility of dislocation".

Mediation is often defined as "helping people have difficult conversations" and this statement may clarify where I am seeking to go with this metaphor. When conversations stop, whether between individuals, families, family groups, interest groups and nations, two things tend to happen. First, those who need the conversation and who, for whatever reason, are unable to have it effectively tend to move apart from each other. A gap develops, widens and deepens. This separateness tends to cause them to think worse rather than better about the other and demonisation and hostility increase. Secondly, the consequence of this process is disintegration. This may be dramatic or better described as a dropped stitch in a fabric. But a series of dropped stitches in a tapestry threatens an unravelling of the entire unity. And where that tapestry is a society that depends ultimately on peaceful and harmonious engagement between individuals and groups of individuals at grass-roots level, then this disintegration brings with it distance, discord and eventually breakdown.

Of course the point can be overstated but I think it nevertheless applies at many levels.

1. First, at individual level. In the UK we have an increasingly rights-focused culture. The Human Rights Act 1998 is (for most of us) a great good. But it comes with a cost. Mechanisms are needed with which to enforce rights and these mechanisms are court based. The courts now occupy a much more prominent role in communities than they did 30 or even 20 years ago. An increasing awareness of rights tends to lead to increasing conflict; not everyone agrees that the other does have a right, particularly where it impacts on the second person's wishes. Conflict increases and this in itself generates the need for conversations, conversations that are often very difficult. These conversations frequently require a considerable degree of emotional intelligence and ability. Increasingly these conversations are not happening; partly because those involved in the conflict have neither the inclination nor the ability successfully to hold the conversations required. An irony of modern life is that the ability instantly to communicate with each other

in numerous ways has never been higher; and perhaps because of this the quality of the engagement is poor. Where communication is almost entirely verbal those involved in communication at this level will often struggle when faced with the need to engage directly to resolve conflict. The problem is exacerbated in a society where communities, families and relationships are under increasing threat.

2. Secondly, at communal level. The globalisation of culture means that groups of profoundly different people are increasingly being forced to live together and to seek to engage with each other. Diversity for its own sake frequently leads to separateness with a greater, or usually lesser, degree of mutual respect.

3. Thirdly, at a faith level. Jimmy Carter, in his acceptance speech for the Nobel Peace Prize 10 years or so ago, spoke of what he saw as the deeply worrying move towards polarisation and fundamentalism in all the major faith traditions; commenting subsequently that the previous decade had been a deeply disturbing one for all of those from *all the major faith traditions*, who believed in *kindness*.

4. Fourthly, at international and ecological levels. Two world wars and the advent of the nuclear bomb have perhaps convinced us that the traditional method of dealing with international disputes (war) is no longer viable; it is too dangerous. Globalisation means that a local dispute in, say, the Middle East, results in a 9/11 event or a dirty bomb. At the ecological level the increasing problems posed by population growth and climate change mean that the great conflicts of the future will have to do with food and water. (See the observations of Ken Cloke, President of Mediators Beyond Borders, in *Thinking Differently: Making a Difference Using Mediation*.)[1]

Urgent and difficult conversations are needed to resolve these conflicts both at the micro level (between two individuals in a housing complex who believe that their respective pets should have priority in the small shared garden) and at the macro level (between two states in dispute about respective shares of reducing resources). If these conversations are happening at all, progress is usually extremely slow if not non-existent.

6. Mediation and Difficult Conversations

Where does mediation fit in? Although very generalised, and with many exceptions in practice, this Mennonite model of development of conflict may be helpful:

1. (Edinburgh: Core Solutions Group, 2010).

1. *Problem solving*

   Differences have occurred but the parties still understand each other. Conflicting goals mean that they frequently feel uncomfortable in each other's presence. At this stage they are problem orientated not people orientated. The language used is clear, specific and not loaded or blaming. They remain "face to face". Mediation is not needed. Coaching of the parties in the means of engagement is needed.

2. *Disagreement*

   Although the focus may still be on problem solving there is often an increasing tendency to personalise the dispute. "You" statements develop. Language shifts from specific to generalisation; and self-protection becomes an increasingly important objective. An element of shrewdness and calculation appears. Parties call on friends to discuss the problem. Caution rather than hostility prevails. This can prevent people getting close enough to each other to resolve the dispute. With increasing personalisation the original dispute becomes obscured, peripheral disputes emerge and the dispute widens. The parties are still "face to face" but only just. Mediation is often needed.

3. *Contest*

   Win/lose dynamics begin. The objective is no longer self-protection, but winning. Individuals find allies who think the same. Language distorts with over-generalisations, exaggerations, polarisation and assumption. Personal attacks are common, with irrational behaviour also common: building a case, viewing feelings as facts. There is inconsistency. Psychologically the parties turn their backs on each other because of the discomfort of their previous engagement. Effective communication instantly ceases. Mediation is almost always required at this level.

4. *Fight/flight*

   There is a further shift from winning to getting rid of the other person. Neither believes that situations can change. Conversation has now ceased entirely. Triangulation has developed: explaining, complaining, asking for others' opinions, gossip, public criticism. Eventually factions emerge, with groups solidified. It is very difficult to accept or listen to contrary information. Language moves into ideologies, with principles, not issues, now at stake. Mediation is essential.

5. *Warfare*

   The conflict is now unmanageable, having run amok. Personalities have become the issue. Frequently there will be a relentless obsession with accomplishing the objectives at all costs. Vindictive behaviour occurs. The opposition's behaviour is sometimes seen as harmful to society, not simply to the offended group, and the object now is to destroy the other party.

7. Types Of Intervention

Different types of conflict require different types of intervention.

1. In lower-stage conflicts (problem solving and disagreement) individuals should be able to resolve the issues together, without outside assistance, by applying basic principles of relationship and engagement. We all benefit from training and coaching in these areas. Susan Scott's *Fierce Conversations: Achieving success in work and in life, one conversation at a time*[2] and Marshall Rosenburg's *Nonviolent communication: a Language of Life*[3] are invaluable. Where individuals do not have these skills then some form of facilitation or mediation may be needed.

2. Imagine two friends. Face to face they seek to work out the answer to a problem. The solution is elusive and they become frustrated with each other. This frustration leads to them beginning to blame each other. This is a fertile source of further criticism and before long the dispute is personalised with the original difference obscured. Anger builds and tension increases. At last one turns his back on the other and the other follows suit. With their permission a mediator steps between them and lays a hand on both.

- Note the difficulty of either turning around without assistance.
- Note the deficiencies of litigation as a means of restoring the relationship.
- The mediator steps down from a distant position and walks towards the conflict.
- The mediator seeks permission from each party to enter a relationship of some intimacy.
- The mediator acts as a turning agent, a bridge, a buffer between the polarised individuals.
- Note "the possibility of dislocation".
- As the parties re-engage the mediator moves back into the shadows.

8. Success

What is "success"? There is no one definition; all depends on the dispute and the nature of the intervention/remedy.

2. (London: Piatkus, 2003).
3. (Encinitas, CA: Puddle Dancer Press, 2nd edn, 2003).

A helpful image involves a series of concentric circles. Each of these circles represents an outcome that could be regarded as "success".

1. *Ceasefire*

   This can operate on a number of levels. One may be talking about actual war or violent behaviour or violent language. At one level a short-term violence reduction might be negotiated (time to bury the dead, temporary ceasefire, police guards installed, agreement to come no closer than 200 metres). There may be long-term violence reduction or safe isolation or a degree of minimum co-operation. Thus two neighbours may agree not to slag each other off when they meet in the lift or they may agree their protocol for managing noisy music or late night parties. These are successes.

2. *Resolution of the defining issue*

   Thus an individual monetary or property dispute is "settled". The flashpoint that created the dispute is discussed and a resolution achieved. Imagine two children fighting in a sandpit over a ball; resolving the defining issue means reaching agreement about use of the ball.

3. *Resolving the underlying issue*

   The defining issue may be sorted out, but belief systems, emotions and feelings that lie below it remain unresolved. Thus the reason why the boy would not give his sister the ball to use was because she embarrassed him. Dealing with the underlying issues raises deeper issues such as needs, fears and longings.

4. *Apology, reparation, restitution*

   Success at level (3) (dealing with the underlying issues) often brings with it a recognition of one's role in causing the wrong and the desire to put matters straight on a relational basis. An apology, if unconditional (avoid if, but and maybe), can be hugely powerful.

5. *Forgiveness*

   What comes first, forgiveness or apology? This level deals with the remembrance or recollection of the offence: I choose not to think about it or remember it again.

6. *Reconciliation*

   To have travelled through these five concentric circles will almost inevitably bring about reconciliation between estranged individuals or groups. The journey is one which has led to apology, restitution, forgiveness and a resolution of underlying and defining issues. That which had impaired the relationship has been resolved and the relationship is restored.

7. *Transformation*

In one sense this is the "gold standard". Individuals reconciled as a result of the journey they have undergone frequently find their relationship enhanced, sometimes even transformed. Conflict can therefore be a springboard for growth; an opportunity, something that can be "stewarded".

9. Application

These images underline the importance of mediation. In a society that is "back to back" how else will people turn round? If they do not do so what happens? Seeing it in this way should encourage co-operation between mediators and should expand the vision. It may also help the UK mediation world to avoid some of the outcomes of his US mediation experience on which Peter Adler reflected in his recent presentation to the CMC [Civil Mediation Council][4]:

1. The decline and decay of true mediation.
2. The pull of the courts.
3. The domination of lawyers.
4. The profession that isn't.
5. The search for identity.

This last critique is particularly telling. If the having of difficult conversations is a social imperative (and not an optional extra), if our communities and society at large are to remain cohesive and integrated and if we mediators by enabling those conversations thereby discover an identity, will not that go a long way towards dealing with these problems?

10. Towards a Community Peace Service?

All well and good it may be said but how are we income-generating mediators to engage actively with other community-based mediators? Not all of us may have the desire, or energy or time or indeed ability to train in those areas. For a number of years I have pondered the idea of a united mediation service or peace service in which local peace centres—one-stop shops in communities to which all disputes that affect the community can be referred—form a loose association within some form of national structure. "Localness" is vital because these peace centres will be backed by panels of, usually volunteer, mediators competent to mediate whatever dispute is referred. This concept has attracted a degree of interest in the

4. Peter Adler, "Expectation and Regret", paper presented at the Seventh Civil Mediation Council National Conference, London, May 2, 2013.

last year or so and there is no reason why it could not work. It requires some national and regional structure; it also requires efficient local "hubs" which do not need to be over-staffed, but do require efficient managers and administrators and supporters of the volunteer mediators. For this, a level of funding is required and it is this funding requirement (or more accurately lack of funding over the last few years) that has seen many of these mediation organisations go out of business.

The model that we have used at WMS is one that could be applied across the UK. It is a funding model that provides a significant proportion of WMS's budget. WMS is supported by two separate panels of mediators. The **community panel** comprises volunteer community mediators who do the primary charitable work for which WMS was set up; community disputes throughout the LBW [London Borough of Wandsworth]. This work currently generates little significant income. The second panel is a panel of about 15 **trained commercial mediators** some of whom are experienced and some of whom are brand new. They agree to make their services available maybe once a month to mediate smallish legal disputes emanating from the County Court, from local solicitors, or from other users with whom WMS (accredited by the CMC as a mediation service supplier) has formed links, and hopefully in due course from the [Borough] Council. WMS charges the litigants a fee based broadly on a tariff originally set up by the government some years ago to support the National Mediation Helpline. This fee is a small proportion of open-market rates. The selected mediator usually waives this fee, thus enabling WMS to generate income. One case a week may generate, say, £1,000. Extended across the year this amounts to a significant part of the budget.

This model, were it to be extended across the UK, should enable two currently untapped resources to be harnessed:

1. The very large number of individuals across society who would give their time as **trained volunteer community mediators** to help to make their communities a safer and more harmonious place. The amount of interest in mediation is startling and there are hundreds and probably thousands of individuals who would be willing to work as volunteers.
2. The hundreds, probably now thousands of **trained commercial mediators** who are currently deeply frustrated about their lack of ability to do what they dearly wish to do, namely to mediate legal disputes. Commercial panels give these mediators an opportunity to start mediating and to develop their skills.

From a mediation perspective the model is elegant and has a win/win feel to it. (The WMS model is based around the generosity of commercial mediators but the same principle would work with family mediators, workplace mediators and any mediator who could expect to be paid a fee for the mediation).

1. *Clients like it*

   Fees that would otherwise be paid to their solicitors are recycled into the community to support the peace centre.

2. *Solicitors like it*

   They can take on cases that would not otherwise be cost efficient; at the same time as supporting a significant local charity.

3. *Communities like it*

   Peace centres obtain regular funding which helps them train and supervise other local community mediators. This in turn increases the profile of the service thereby generating referrals of more community disputes.

4. *The Court Service/Ministry of Justice should like it*

   It is a means of dealing with some of the blockages at County Court level due to budget cuts, the closure of courts etc.

5. *Government should like it*

   It should really be a vote catcher. "Big Society" may be a will-o-the-wisp but this comes pretty close.

11. The Current State of Play

If this is to work it probably needs the support and backing of those already active in the community mediation world; and to obtain their buy-in to this project.

There seems at present to be real interest in the project from a number of entities.

One way of taking it forward might be to seek to set up, say, 10 commercial panels in various parts of the UK supporting existing or new peace centres.

Research needs to take place to work out what exactly is going on at present in the community mediation world.

There is potential for using the premises of faith groups as places at which these peace centres could be based in order to minimise overheads etc.

With a number of these panels operating an analysis of the results could then be written up by a researcher.

Thought needs to be given to the development of a national structure.

CHARTERED INSTITUTE OF ARBITRATORS
THE 2018 ROEBUCK LECTURE, 14 JUNE 2018

ARBITRATION: THE TERMS THEY ARE A-CHANGIN'
Dame Elizabeth Gloster[*]

[*Editorial note*. This lecture is published here by kind permission of the Chartered Institute of Arbitrators.]

Opening remarks

1. It is a huge honour to have been asked to give the 2018 Roebuck Lecture here at the Chartered Institute of Arbitrators. I am proud to be a patron of the London branch.

2. This year I have delivered lectures to the Employment Law Bar Association, the Modern Studies Property Law Conference and the Singapore Law Society, amongst others, but I am particularly delighted to be speaking on an area with which my commercial experience is closely aligned.

3. It is even more fitting given my recent retirement from the bench after 25 years, with the last five spent at the Court of Appeal. I consider it an appropriate time to hand over the baton on dealing with the challenge of an increasing number of cases before our courts that involve litigants appearing without counsel.[1]

4. Further, as the courts embark on the greatest modernisation effort in their history, I will watch with interest as my former colleagues grapple with these changes. As a judge, I was a committed user of technology and embraced the technological solutions that offered practical benefits to my work. Counsel who appeared before me were accustomed to requests from my clerk for electronic case files prior to a hearing. I can assure you that they saved me time both during the hearing and in the judgment writing process. One thing I have always loved about arbitration is its openness to technology.

5. I have thoroughly enjoyed my time as a judge. I will miss the variety of cases on which I sat: mainly high-profile commercial and Chancery cases, ranging from public international law, capital markets, shipping, insurance, tax, and insolvency to Libor fixing. I

* Former Vice President of the Court of Appeal (Civil Division). I gratefully acknowledge the assistance given by my former judicial assistant, Joel Semakula, barrister, with the preparation for this lecture.
1. The number of permission to appeal applications brought by litigants in person ("LiPs") in the Court of Appeal stood at 42% in the 12 months ended 31 January 2018. This number has risen by 50% in the last 10 years: See https://www.legalfutures.co.uk/latest-news/master-of-the-rolls-more-than-four-in-ten-of-applications-to-court-of-appeal-come-from-litigants-in-person

am forever grateful to the fantastic legal minds I have been fortunate enough to call colleagues and opponents. It has also been a privilege to be a part of shaping the law in this jurisdiction. I did ask the Master of the Rolls if I could take my robes with me – a request that he unfortunately declined.

6.   I look forward to the new challenge of "flogging [my] services" as *The Times* described it,[2] as I join your ranks as an arbitrator working out of my old chambers, One Essex Court. It will definitely be a change to hear cases in conference centres and hotel rooms rather than the grandeur of the Royal Courts of Justice, but it is a change for which I am very excited.

Introduction

7.   As a Court of Appeal judge, I heard a number of arbitration cases, the most recent full appeal being *Sabbagh v Khoury*,[3] which the Court of Appeal handed down in July of last year. The crux of the decision were obiter comments about establishing jurisdiction for bringing a claim against multiple defendants under the Brussels Regulations.

8.   However, one issue we had to determine was whether the relevant claims should be stayed for arbitration. We held that they should not as the appellant would only be bound by the arbitration clauses so far as the claims were based on the contract containing the clause, which in our view, neither of the claims in this case were.[4] I am hoping that arbitration is far less tangential to my talk today.

9.   This brings me to the essential theme of my talk: the key ways in which arbitration is changing. The relevant law on which I will focus will be the Arbitration Act 1996 ("Arbitration Act"). What I intend to examine are the timely debates around ethics and diversity in the field of arbitration, focusing on relevant case law and commentary. I will argue against a binding code of ethics for arbitrators but push for an even greater focus on the key diversity issues; namely with regards to women and ethnic minorities. I will go on to suggest that despite Brexit, there are plenty of reasons to be optimistic. London will retain its position as the best place in the world for international parties to arbitrate and much of that has to do with the ease with which parties can secure enforcement of English arbitral awards.

10.   I will take this in three parts:

   i)   ethics;
   ii)   diversity;
   iii) the triumph of the common law despite Brexit.

2. *The Times*, The Daily Brief, 7/6/2018.
3. [2017] EWCA Civ 1120.
4. [2017] EWCA Civ 1120 at [123] – [131].

Part 1: Ethics

11. In line with my training at Bar School, I will focus on <u>three</u> aspects again. In my view, the three biggest issues in this area are the use of tribunal secretaries, concerns about arbitrator bias and the case for a binding code of ethics.

(1) Tribunal secretaries

12. It is common in complex international arbitration and investor-state arbitration cases for arbitral tribunals to engage tribunal assistants to assist them in carrying out their duties. They are used in the interests of time efficiency and cost. The concern, however, is that arbitrators unlawfully delegate their duties to this third party by involving him or her in the decision-making process. This is contrary to the very ethos of arbitration.

13. In the recent High Court decision of *P v Q*[5] – which was handed down in February of last year – the judgment of Mr Justice Popplewell provides some lessons for parties and arbitrators when considering tribunal secretary appointments. In this case, the court considered a removal application under s24(1)(d)(i) of the Arbitration Act to remove two co-arbitrators from their positions in an ongoing LCIA arbitration.

14. Section 24(1)(d)(i) provides that a party to arbitral proceedings may (upon notice to the other parties, to the arbitrator concerned and to any other arbitrator) apply to the court to remove an arbitrator on grounds that he has refused or failed to conduct the proceedings properly.

15. In the application to the High Court, P had three complaints against the arbitrators, in that they had:

    i)   improperly delegated their role to the tribunal secretary by systematically entrusting the secretary with a number of tasks beyond that permissible under the LCIA Rules and LCIA Policy on the use of tribunal secretaries;

    ii)   breached their mandate as arbitrators and their duty not to delegate by not sufficiently participating in the arbitration proceedings and the decision-making process

    iii)   negligently and/or innocently misrepresented to P the position as to the existence and/or nature and/or extent and/or effect of delegation of their roles to the secretary.

16. The court refused P's disclosure application requesting disclosure from the arbitrators of "instructions, requests, queries or comments

---

5. [2017] EWHC 194 (Comm).

from the Co-Arbitrators (or from [the Chairman] to which the Co-Arbitrators were copied) to the Secretary."[6] P also requested the secretary's responses to those emails as well as all communications sent or received by the co-arbitrators which related to either the role of the secretary or the tasks delegated to the secretary. In my view, the application was too wide and the judge was right to refuse it.

17. Given the refusal of the disclosure application, P's removal application relied largely on the comparable time recorded by the arbitrators and the secretary along with one wrongly sent email, which the original chairman had accidentally sent to a paralegal at P's solicitors' firm instead of the intended tribunal secretary.

18. Popplewell J dismissed the removal application finding that "there [was] no merit in any of the arguments, either singly or cumulatively, that the Co-Arbitrators failed properly to conduct proceedings."[7] He further held that no substantial injustice had been proven even if there had been merit in the claims made.

19. First, in considering his view of the argument that the arbitrators improperly delegated their role, the judge reviewed the time spent by arbitrators on the case and drew on his experience to find they could not properly be criticised for the way in which they carried out their adjudicatory functions. In coming to his decision, Popplewell J rightly emphasised the court's supervisory and non-interventionist role.

20. Second, on the question of substantial injustice, the test was the same as that for an appeal under s68 of the Arbitration Act, namely that the conduct of an arbitrator goes "beyond anything that could reasonably be defended."[8] It is the applicant who has the burden of showing that the arbitrators' failure caused the tribunal to reach decision(s) which, but for the failure it might not have reached.[9] Popplewell J found no grounds for such a finding.

21. The use of tribunal secretaries has been under greater scrutiny since the Russian Federation challenged one of the three arbitral awards handed down by the Permanent Court of Arbitration in The Hague ("PCA") in July 2014 in the arbitration proceedings brought by the former shareholders of OAO Yukos Oil Company ("Yukos"). The arbitral tribunal in the PCA unanimously held in the awards that the Russian Federation had deliberately expropriated Yukos and

6. 2017 EWHC 148 (Comm) at [22].
7. [2017] EWHC 194 (Comm) at [87].
8. (Departmental Advisory Committee Report on the Arbitration Bill 1996).
9. *Maass v Musin Events* [2015[2 Lloyd's Rep. 383; *Terna Bahrain Holding v Al Shamsi* [2012] EWHC (Comm) 3283).

awarded its former shareholders damages of $50 billion. The Russian Federation made an application to set aside the award in January 2015. It argued, among other things, that the arbitral tribunal had not fulfilled its mandate personally given the significant role played by the tribunal assistant in the analysis of the evidence and legal arguments, in the tribunal's deliberations and in the drafting of the awards.

22. On 14 April 2016, the Hague District Court set aside the award on a different ground and did not deal with the contention that the tribunal improperly delegated its duties to the assistant. Given the Yukos former shareholders has lodged an appeal against the Hague District Court's decision, there is the possibility that the superior court of the Netherlands might yet deal with the case. However, it may be some time before that appeal process is completed.

23. Bringing it back to this jurisdiction, in *P&Q*, Popplewell J described the "considerable and understandable anxiety in the international arbitration community that the use of tribunal secretaries risks them becoming the 'fourth arbitrators'."[10] In his judgment, he noted the disparate views among practitioners and commentators as to their appropriate use.

24. He held:

> "the safest way to ensure that the secretary does not become a 'fourth arbitrator' is for the secretary not to be tasked with anything which involves expressing a view on the substantive merits of an application or issue."[11]

25. The key message was that no member of the tribunal should abrogate or delegate his or her personal decision-making function. He clarified, however, that receiving or soliciting views from a tribunal secretary would not automatically demonstrate an arbitrator's failure to discharge his personal duty to perform the decision-making function and responsibility himself.

26. It is obviously a major decision for a party to make an application to remove an arbitrator. *P&Q* demonstrates the high bar for parties when pursuing such an application – both in terms of gathering potential evidence and demonstrating a breach of duty by the tribunal that has caused substantial injustice. The use of tribunal secretaries in arbitration remains a live issue and arbitrators must be on guard about their influence. It is important that both parties and arbitrators consider the rules and guidance on their role and this decision should

---

10. [2017] EWHC 194 (Comm) at [68].
11. *Ibid.*

provide some assistance. As recommended by Popplewell J, I would affirm the view that parties should raise any potential concerns and set out the parameters with the arbitral tribunal at the inception of the appointment of any tribunal secretary.

(2) Arbitrator bias

27. Under section 33(1)(a) of the Arbitration Act 1996, tribunals must act fairly and impartially. Section 24(1)(a) allows a party to make an application to remove an arbitrator if "circumstances exist that give rise to justifiable doubts about his impartiality."[12]

28. In making this determination, the common law test of apparent bias[13] provides a clear, consistent and thorough approach. It examines whether, looking at all of the facts, the fair-minded and informed observer would consider there to be bias.[14]

29. Nonetheless, it is no secret that some parties emerge from arbitral proceedings concerned about an arbitrator's impartiality, even where such concerns are not sufficient for a section 24(1)(a) removal application to succeed. Two recent decisions have demonstrated that actions creating an impression of bias may be insufficient to meet the common law test for apparent bias.

30. The first is *Halliburton Company v Chubb Bermuda Insurance Ltd*[15] in the Court of Appeal, which was handed down earlier this year. This was an appellate ruling which focused on the arbitrator's duty to disclose appointments in overlapping cases, and how the resulting disclosure issues triggered the issue of bias, real or apparent. The case dealt with two questions: first, what is apparent bias and second, should it be disclosed?

31. Halliburton and Transocean had been co-defendants in American proceedings. Halliburton settled the claim and sought to claim on its insurance policy with Chubb. Chubb rejected the claim on the basis that the settlements were unreasonable. Halliburton commenced arbitration. The High Court selected M to be the third arbitrator under the arbitration agreement.

32. M properly disclosed his role in previous arbitrations involving Chubb. There were no objections raised by Halliburton against M's impartiality at that stage. However, following M's appointment, Halliburton became aware of several facts which led to it making a

---

12. Section 24(1)(a), AA 1996
13. *Locabail v Bayfield* [2000] 2 W.L.R. 870
14. *Porter v Magill* [2002] 2 AC 357
15. [2018] EWCA 817. [*Editorial note*: Since affirmed by the UK Supreme Court, [2020] UKSC 48.]

section 24 removal application. Halliburton argued M's conduct gave rise to the appearance of bias due to:

i)   M's acceptance of appointments in arbitrations relating to claims brought against Transocean arising from the same underlying American proceedings;

ii) M's failure to disclose those appointments to Halliburton;

iii) M's response to the challenge to his impartiality.

33. M later accepted that it would have been prudent to disclose the above, and Halliburton accepted that the omission was an innocent oversight.

34. Nonetheless, Popplewell J dismissed Halliburton's application, finding that the fair-minded and informed observer would not have found any grounds to remove M.[16] However, the aforementioned acknowledgment suggests that M's actions did give rise to reasonable concerns as to his impartiality even if they were not sufficient to meet the common law test for apparent bias. Halliburton appealed.

35. While the appeal was pending, the tribunal issued an award in Chubb's favour. The result was unanimous but one arbitrator refused to join the award because of his "profound disquiet about the arbitration's fairness"[17] in the light of the foregoing circumstances.

36. Delivering the Court of Appeal's judgment, Hamblen LJ affirmed Popplewell J's decision that M should not have been removed. An arbitrator is permitted to accept appointments in two proceedings concerning the same subject matter in which only one party is the same. "Something more is required"[18] to give rise to an appearance of bias. The "starting point is that an arbitrator should be trusted to decide the case solely on the evidence or other material adduced in the proceedings in question."[19]

37. Extraneous information arising from the double engagement will put arbitrators on notice of the possibility of even unconscious bias. That said, while a party in Halliburton's position may legitimately be subjectively concerned, that is not enough to ensure the success of a section 24 challenge.

38. Popplewell J determined that since the second appointment did not give rise to an appearance of bias, it followed that M had no duty to disclose it.

16. *H v L and others*[2017] EWHC 137 (Comm).
17. [2018] EWCA 817 at [24].
18. [2018] EWCA 817 at [77].
19. [2018] EWCA 817 at [50].

39. The Court of Appeal disagreed. In doing so, it established that there is a lower threshold for an arbitrator's duty of disclosure than for his removal. The Court of Appeal determined that an arbitrator <u>must</u> disclose circumstances that would or might lead a fair-minded observer to conclude there is a real possibility of bias. The fact that disclosure was required as a matter of international best practice helped persuade the court that it was also a requirement of the law.

40. The court then had to consider the consequence of M's failure to disclose. Quoting Lord Bingham, the court held that the fact of non-disclosure "must inevitably colour the thinking of the observer".[20] The court can use it as a factor in applying the apparent bias test and hence in its consideration of a removal application under section 24(1) (a). However, if the non-disclosed circumstance is insufficient for removal, the failure to disclose alone cannot be sufficient to meet the test, either. The court held, again, that "something more is required."[21] On these facts, the appeal was dismissed as the court could not find that "something more." I consider this analysis to be correct.

41. *Halliburton* is the first English arbitration case to deal seriously with a duty of disclosure as an obligation that is distinct from the duty to be impartial. Given the Court of Appeal's decision that non-disclosure can be a factor in the apparent bias test, and the lower threshold for the duty to disclose, I expect claims of non-disclosure to become more prevalent in arbitration challenges. On a more general note, it is now up to the courts to add some colour to the *Halliburton* test in the context of varying fact patterns.

42. The second relevant case is *Symbion Power LLC v Venco Imtiaz Construction Co*[22] of last year, in which the Technology and Construction Court ("TCC") considered an application under section 68 of the Arbitration Act. In this case, serious concerns were raised by the judge (apparently on her own initiative) regarding the conduct of Symbion's party-nominated arbitrator. The arbitrator had sent an email to Symbion's counsel that expressed negative views about the tribunal chairman but had failed to copy in the other party or arbitrators.

43. Jefford J was right to state that such unilateral contact had been wholly inappropriate because:

> "the ability of each party to appoint an arbitrator is intended to… give the parties confidence in the balance and fairness of the tribunal.

20. [2018] EWCA 817 at [76].
21. *Ibid*.
22. [2017] EWHC 348 (TCC).

The party-appointed arbitrators patently do not represent the party that appointed them and they are under a duty, as individual arbitrators and as a tribunal, to act fairly and impartially."[23]

44. Despite the fact that such unilateral communication "may give rise to concerns that the arbitrator is not acting fairly or impartially,"[24] it was not enough to lead to the conclusion that there were justifiable doubts as to the arbitrator's impartiality, as the English law test requires. I am surprised by this decision, however, as with all of these cases, it turns on the facts of the case as a whole.

45. It is no surprise in both of these cases that one of the parties may have come away with reasonable concerns as to the impartiality of the arbitrators. This may give them the impression that some of the tribunal may be influenced against them. A common reason for these doubts, in part, is the misconception that a party-nominated arbitrator is a representative of the relevant party. While all in this room know this is incorrect, it raises the question as to whether arbitration needs to take steps to address the threat posed to the integrity of the arbitral process by issues of apparent bias.

46. The key question that arises from the literature is whether we should consider an alternative to the system of unilateral appointments. Jan Paulsson[25] and The Hon. Sundaresh Menon SC,[26] among others, have suggested creating a disciplinary body for arbitrators. I consider such an idea would inspire greater confidence in the system as a whole. I expect this Institute would play a central role in any such process.

47. I would also support a further look at their proposals on improving the rules on pre-appointment interviews; in particular limiting the length of pre-nomination interviews and releasing transcripts of such interviews to the other side in order to increase the confidence of parties in the impartiality and fairness of arbitrators.

48. However, this must be approached in a careful manner. The goal should be to strengthen arbitration, which means any proposal must be implemented properly to prevent their use by parties as a tactic used to influence arbitrators' decision-making process or to delay proceedings.

(3) The case for a binding code of ethics

49. As the market for international arbitration has grown, there has been an expansion in the pool of arbitrators as well as counsel involved in

---

23. [2017] EWHC 348 (TCC) at [85].
24. [2017] EWHC 348 (TCC) at [85].
25. Scholar and practitioner in the area of international arbitration; a founding partner of Three Crowns LLP.
26. Chief Justice of Singapore and a former Attorney-General.

international arbitration. Those that participate in these disputes come from a range of cultural and legal traditions. Where a conflict arises between these different traditions, there is the question as to what guidelines or rules, if any, should govern international arbitrations.

50. In 2010, Doak Bishop[27] gave the keynote address at the ICCA Congress in Rio de Janeiro on the topic of ethics in international arbitration advocacy.[28] He posited that there was a current, compelling need for a Code of Ethics in international arbitration to be developed. He further argued for the adaptation of tribunals and institutions to the adoption of such a code.

51. In proposing a Code of Ethics, Mr Bishop suggested that such a Code could accomplish three goals:

    i)   clarify the applicable rules and reducing ambiguity;

    ii)   level the playing field so that conflicting obligations do not unduly benefit one party at the expense of the other; and

    iii) provide greater transparency, which would build confidence in the system.

52. The issue is a difficult one. As Peter Halprin and Stephen Wah point out in a recent article,[29] ethics rules can differ significantly by region. I cannot see how these differences can be resolved through one single code. As we are at the Chartered Institute of Arbitrators, I will focus on this from the position of the arbitrators rather than counsel.

53. Halrpin and Wah encourage arbitrators to take the time to consider pertinent case law that sets out what national law requires of them in terms of impartiality and independence,[30] the lack of which can provide grounds for the challenge of an arbitrator[31] or to an award.[32]

54. I know the Chartered Institute of Arbitrators maintains a Code of Professional and Ethical Conduct ("CPEC") which its members are required to follow. Part 2 of the CPEC relates

> "to the conduct of members when acting or seeking to act as neutrals in alternative dispute resolution processes, wherever conducted,

27. Listed by *Chambers USA* in Tier 1 as a top seven U.S. arbitration counsel, and by *Chambers Global* in Tier 1 of the top 11 international arbitration counsel globally. He is also listed as a top 20 arbitration specialist by *Cross-Border Quarterly,* published in the UK.
28. *See* Doak Bishop, Ethics in International Arbitration INTERNATIONAL COUNCIL FOR COMMERCIAL ARBITRATION, 1 (2010), http://www.arbitration-icca.org/media/0/12763302233510/icca_rio_keynote_speech.pdf.
29. Peter Halprin and Stephen Wah, 'Ethics in International Arbitration', 2018 J. Disp. Resol. (2018)
30. *Ibid* at p. 89.
31. Arbitration Act 1996, s. 24(1)(a).
32. Arbitration Act 1996, s. 68.

whether or not they have been appointed so to act by the Institute or any officer of the Institute and whether or not the process is conducted under the auspices of the Institute."[33]

55. CPEC is described as a "reflection of internationally acceptable guidelines".[34] It rightly recognises that nearly all arbitrators are bound by multiple codes of conduct or practice by which they must abide given their inevitable membership in a number of other professional organisations. Where there is a tension, it seems to be that each member must follow the rules of his primary jurisdiction.

56. It is no secret that London faces stiff competition from a number of other centres of international arbitration, which have their own institutions and jurisdictions all putting forward their own version of ethical rules that should apply when resolving disputes that are governed by those institutions.

57. My reading around this topic has exposed me to the level of uncertainty facing arbitrators on this issue.[35] When carrying out their duties, arbitrators must consider a range of material in order to determine the potentially applicable ethical rules. The most appropriate place to start is with the arbitration clause. I would then consider the institutional rules, the guidelines of local bar associations and any applicable case law. Just as parties expect of those on the bench, early disclosure is the key to preventing difficulties. Following the appointment of the tribunal, it would be of benefit to all involved to have an early discussion as to the applicable ethical codes.

58. On the case for a binding code of ethics for arbitrators, however, I am not persuaded that it is possible to design such a code in a field where participants hail from such a range of jurisdictions. I support the movement in favour of "international principles or guidelines that arbitrators and counsel can look to in a dispute without making compliance with such principles or guidelines mandatory".[36] In my view, an approach that encourages parties and arbitrators to come to an agreement on the applicable code of ethics[37] is much more compatible with party autonomy which lies at the heart of international arbitration.

33. Chartered Institute of Arbitrators, The Chartered Institute of Arbitrators Code of Professional and Ethical Conduct for Members, 1 (2009), http://www.ciarb.org/docs/defaultsource/ciarbdocuments/guidance-and-ethics/practice-guidelines-protocols-and-rules/code-of-professional-and-ethical-conduct-october-2009.pdf?sfvrsn=2.
34. *Ibid.*
35. Peter Halprin and Stephen Wah, 'Ethics in International Arbitration', 2018 J. Disp. Resol. (2018) at p. 23.
36. *Ibid* at p. 108.
37. *Ibid* at pp. 100-101.

Part 2: Diversity

59. I could not come here today and not speak about diversity and inclusion. It is an issue that has been important to me throughout my career as a female practitioner at the Commercial Bar, as the first woman judge at the Commercial Court and as one of eight women of 38 Court of Appeal judges.[38]

60. It is also an issue that often came up in many of cases that I heard, one of the most recent being the case of *Al-Hijrah School*,[39] which the Court of Appeal handed down in October of last year. We were asked to determine whether an Islamic school that segregated girls and boys from the age of nine for religious reasons, was in breach of the Equality Act 2010. We determined the segregation did constitute direct discrimination. Both male and female pupils lost the opportunity to socialise, interact and learn with, or from, the opposite sex. However, the majority held that such segregation did not impose a particular detriment on female pupils, a point on which I dissented. Much more ink has been spilt about my dissenting opinion but that is beyond the scope of this talk.

61. Turning back to arbitration. Diversity and inclusion has rightly been given centre stage over the past year. The 15th Annual American Society for International Law Conference, held in Washington, D.C. on 4 April 2018, was the first major international conference to tackle this issue in the context of international arbitration. The conference examined the lack of diversity in arbitral tribunals, as well as in lead counsel and expert appointments, with respect to gender, race, national origin, and other forms of diversity.

62. As the international arbitration field has grown, the faces of the parties using this alternative route to resolve their disputes have changed. As Louise Barrington[40] and Rashda Rana SC[41] put it in their 2015 article, "Dealing with Diversity in International Arbitration":[42]

> [d]isputes arise between Asians and Africans, South Americans and Europeans, Americans and the Middle East. Women have entered the business world, and the field of law, in droves. Nevertheless, the faces of the counsel leading the legal teams, and of the

38. Prior to my retirement.
39. [2017] EWCA Civ 1426.
40. Chartered arbitrator and accredited mediator, legally qualified in Ontario, New York and England.
41. Heads up RANA IDRS and is a commercial & construction/infrastructure lawyer with over 25 years' experience in the legal profession. She has worked as counsel and arbitrator in a number of international jurisdictions including London, Australia, Hong Kong, Singapore, Malaysia and China.
42. See https://www.transnational-dispute-management.com/article.asp?key=2233.

      arbitral tribunals deciding the disputes, remain – with the exception of a couple of high-profile exceptions – overwhelmingly white, Caucasian and male.[43]

63. The latest data indicates that female arbitrators constitute only about 16% of total appointments.[44] Going further, using the statistics from the International Centre for Settlement of Investment Disputes ("ICSID"), only about 4% of cases are arbitrated by entirely non-Anglo-European tribunals.[45]

(1) Women

64. Let me start with the women. There are many reasons for the low levels of diversity. I took great interest in reading about Professor Lucy Reed's[46] keynote address at the International Law Conference, in which she described it as the likely result of "caution + habit + bias".[47] She argued that parties take a cautious approach to high-stakes disputes. This is understandable given that awards can very rarely be appealed and can be enforced relatively easily. In these circumstances, it leads to parties forming a habit of appointing arbitrators from a limited group of individuals who possess the most experience. It is at this point that bias creeps in. Habit and bias (at least unconscious bias) are divided by a thin boundary, Reed argued – "if habit is knowing and selecting whom you know, bias tends to slide into knowing and selecting people just like you".[48]

65. There is the added challenge that many people consider the 16% proportion to be a "good enough" sign of progress, despite the fact it is far from parity. In reality, "this is far from looking for genuine diversity, based on overall balance and merit, individual tribunal by individual tribunal",[49] Reed said. I found her argument persuasive that "patience, persistence, and inclusion" could replace habit and bias from the equation, which would lead to "better diversity". In my

43. *Ibid.*
44. See http://arbitrationblog.kluwerarbitration.com/2018/05/07/implicit-bias-in-arbitrator-appointments-a-report-from-the-15th-annual-ita-asil-conference-on-diversity-and-inclusion-in-international-arbitration/.
45. See http://arbitrationblog.kluwerarbitration.com/2018/05/07/implicit-bias-in-arbitrator-appointments-a-report-from-the-15th-annual-ita-asil-conference-on-diversity-and-inclusion-in-international-arbitration/.
46. National University of Singapore.
47. See https://globalarbitrationreview.com/article/1167732/reed%E2%80%99s-diversity-equation, pg 2.
48. See https://globalarbitrationreview.com/article/1167732/reed%E2%80%99s-diversity-equation, pg 2.
49. See https://globalarbitrationreview.com/article/1167732/reed%E2%80%99s-diversity-equation, pg 2.

experience, having talented women available is not enough. There has to be a concerted effort to getting and keeping them in the room.

66. I am proud to say that I am one of 2,870 signatories[50] of the Equal Representation in Arbitration Pledge ("the Pledge"), which encourages practitioners to appoint more female arbitrators. The Pledge came into existence on 18 May 2016 in London and was introduced, in recognition of the under-representation of women in international arbitral tribunals. The aim of the Pledge is "to increase, on an equal opportunity basis, the number of women appointed as arbitrators in order to achieve a fair representation as soon as practically possible, with the ultimate goal of full parity".[51]

67. Rather than pushing for quotas or targets, I support the use of a more flexible standard to reach this goal. This is in line with what is described as the standard of 'equal opportunity', which contemplates that arbitral appointments and other opportunities in the field of arbitration should be based on equal qualifications.

68. What I find particularly encouraging is the fact the Pledge sets out some concrete and actionable steps that this community can and must take towards achieving these general objectives and the ultimate goal of full parity. One such example is effectively requiring parties to spend just five minutes longer when drawing up a list of potential arbitrators to think of some suitably experienced women.

69. Finally, it is important to stress that the Pledge does not envision itself as providing the final answer to the issue of diversity in arbitration. There remains a need to increase diversity in all its forms in this field. It is right to view the Pledge as the first step in the direction of achieving representation that is more equal for all under-represented groups who operate in this area.

70. It appears to me that the recent increase in the number of women and minorities appointed by parties[52] is an indication that the Pledge is chipping away at those old habits.

(2) Ethnic minorities

71. Now, ethnic minorities. Turning back to the data. The London Court of International Arbitration ("LCIA") has been transparent about its arbitration caseload on an annual basis. In 2016 it recorded a total of

---

50. Signatories as at 29 May 2018. This number includes both individual signatories signing in their own name and organisation signatories to the ERA Pledge. While most signatories are listed on http://www.arbitrationpledge.com/about-the-pledge, some individual signatories choose to remain anonymous.

51. See http://www.arbitrationpledge.com/about-the-pledge.

52. See https://globalarbitrationreview.com/article/1167732/reed%E2%80%99s-diversity-equation.

303 cases with African and Middle Eastern cases which accounted for 15% of the total (up from 11.5% the previous year). 23% of the cases relate to disputes arising from Energy and Natural Resources transactions.[53] As such, it cannot be fairly posited that as disputants, these regions cannot be seen in any of the recognised international arbitration arenas.

72. However, when one considers this against the participation of counsel and arbitrators from these regions, the figures are disappointing. Of the 496 arbitral appointments made by the LCIA that year, 180 (35.3%) were non-British arbitrators while 321 (64.7%) were British arbitrators.[54] Despite the clear increase in arbitration proceedings originating from the Middle East and Africa, there continues to be little growth in the ethnic diversity of arbitrators being appointed in these disputes.

73. International arbitration cannot be truly international if the arbitrators and practitioners do not reflect the diversity of disputes coming before it. The impression to an observer (and even to many involved with international Arbitration) is that it is the exclusive domain of a selected few.

74. Of the '34 Most in Demand Arbitrators' globally in 2018, as listed by Chambers & Partners, only 3 were women[55] and the majority of the 31 men were white Europeans.[56] This is probably the result of parties' focus on arbitrators having an established practice in international arbitration when choosing how to assign work. There is a tension between this approach and a desire to increase diversity amongst arbitrators.

(3) Does diversity matter?

75. In her first keynote address at the 3rd Annual Conference on Energy Arbitration and Dispute Resolution in the Middle East and Africa in March of this year, Funke Adekoya[57] rightly asked the question, does diversity matter?

76. She noted that arbitration is a private process in which parties have one objective: the speedy resolution of their disputes by the most competent persons. Parties to a dispute have an interest in ensuring

53. 1st Keynote Address presented by Funke Adekoya SAN at the 3rd Annual Conference on Energy Arbitration and Dispute Resolution in the Middle East and Africa on 6th March 2018, pg 3.
54. *Ibid.*
55. Jean E Kalicki, Gabrielle Kaufmann-Kohler and Brigitte Stern.
56. See https://www.chambersandpartners.com/15649/1245/editorial/2/1/global-global-wide-arbitration-international-most-in-demand-arbitrators.
57. Partner and Head of Disputes Resolution Practice Group at AELEX.

they appoint experienced, efficient and capable arbitrator(s) who will determine their dispute in a fair manner. While it may be true that the arbitration field is dominated by Anglo-European males, if they are completely able to effectively carry out their duties as arbitrators, why are proponents of diversity so set on disturbing the status quo? The question she asks is whether "there is any benefit to the international community's clamour for diversity in international arbitration".[58]

77. I found her answer persuasive. Individuals and organisations across the world take part in international arbitration. The inclusion of people from a diverse range of racial, ethnic, gender and social backgrounds provides a public value to the idea that arbitration is truly international as it should be seen to be open to individuals from all over the world.

78. She puts forward three reasons in support of increased diversity. First, the lack of diversity can negatively impact the quality of arbitral awards. Empirical studies are cited as finding that "the deliberative process before the arbitral tribunals is likely to be crucial and, therefore, the diversity of views may be fundamental for a fair process and outcome".[59] Second, increasing the pool of arbitrators through the appointment of younger arbitrators is likely to lead to the sustainability of the arbitration pool. Third, it is likely to lead to continued acceptability and increased legitimacy of the arbitration process.[60]

79. So yes, diversity does matter.

(4) How to increase diversity in international arbitration

80. Given all of this, commentators have suggested a number of ways in which diversity can be increased in international arbitration. Three, in particular, have resonated with me. First, parties and institutions should be encouraged to first list the desired characteristics of an arbitrator prior to brainstorming names. This slight increase in thought in the process means newer and diverse candidates are more likely to make selection lists. Second, all of us should question "the perception that a track record of prior appointment is the best way to evaluate an arbitrator's experience and competence".[61] Third, when arbitral

---

58. 1st Keynote Address presented by Funke Adekoya SAN at the 3rd Annual Conference on Energy Arbitration and Dispute Resolution in the Middle East and Africa on 6th March 2018, pg 3.
59. Carol Mulcahy in Berwin Leighton Paisner's report on International Arbitration Survey: Diversity on Arbitral Tribunals, Are We Getting There?, pg 7.
60. 1st Keynote Address presented by Funke Adekoya SAN at the 3rd Annual Conference on Energy Arbitration and Dispute Resolution in the Middle East and Africa on 6th March 2018, pg 4.
61. Implicit Bias in Arbitrator Appointments: A Report from the 15th Annual ITA-ASIL Conference on Diversity and Inclusion in International Arbitration: http://arbitrationblog.

institutions find themselves in the appointing seat, they should add diversity to their pre-qualification list. They are in the most advantageous position to increase diversity, since their knowledge base of potential arbitrators is generally much wider than that available to the parties or their counsel. It is encouraging that the institutions have taken this responsibility seriously as evidenced by the fact they have generally been better than parties at appointing a diverse range of arbitrators when given the chance.[62]

81. Further, I want to put everyone in this room on notice to the Alliance for Equality in Dispute Resolution, which the campaign for increased diversity in international arbitration launched in January 2018. On its website, the Alliance states that it was formed to "advocate for increased diversity in the international dispute resolution community".[63] It aims to "promote inclusivity in all aspects of the dispute resolution world" and "strive for equality of opportunity regardless of sex, location, nationality, ethnicity or age".[64] In addition to dealing with the under-representation of women, it plans to "focus on addressing the lack of diversity in relation to ethnicity and geography in international arbitration".[65] It is the next step to the Pledge.

82. As I have learned throughout my career, there is no blanket solution to making our institutions and organisations more reflective of those they serve. The challenges that come with securing diversity are spread across gender, race, national origin, and in many other forms. However, as we have learned in the judiciary, increasing diversity and inclusion is central to ensuring the accuracy, legitimacy and acceptability of the process and the outcome. I agree with the closing remarks of Funke Adekoya in her address, "if we want international arbitration to be truly international, it is left to all of us to make it more inclusive for all of us".[66]

Part 3: The triumph of the common law despite Brexit

83. I cannot leave you without bringing up the "B" word. Although Brexit is changing things, I want to assure you that the role of the English supervisory courts in international arbitration is not changing.

kluwerarbitration.com/2018/05/07/implicit-bias-in-arbitrator-appointments-a-report-from-the-15th-annual-ita-asil-conference-on-diversity-and-inclusion-in-international-arbitration/.
62. See London Court of International Arbitration Casework Report, 10 April 2018: http://www.lcia.org/News/lcia-releases-2017-casework-report.aspx.
63. https://www.allianceequality.com/.
64. *Ibid.*
65. *Ibid.*
66. 1st Keynote Address presented by Funke Adekoya SAN at the 3rd Annual Conference on Energy Arbitration and Dispute Resolution in the Middle East and Africa on 6th March 2018, pg 8.

84. There are plenty of other reasons to be optimistic. In a recent survey conducted earlier this year, London retained its place atop the global league table for commercial arbitration, allaying fears that Brexit might drive cases to other centres. Researchers asked 900 arbitrators and lawyers to name the top venue for arbitration work and London came top by 10 percentage points over its historic rival, Paris.[67]

(1) Enforcement

85. In my view, one reason for such a result is the fact that enforcing awards in England & Wales is significantly easier than doing so in other European countries. Unlike our French and Spanish neighbours, the English courts are far less likely to invoke the public policy exception[68] save where it is absolutely necessary.

86. Further, English courts are not afraid to use creative tools such as receivership to enforce judgments. I was the first judge to affirm this was possible in the context of foreign assets in *Masri v Consolidated Contractors International ("Masri")*,[69] when I sat as a High Court judge. In that case, I determined that the English court had jurisdiction to make orders prohibiting the assignment of an interest in a foreign asset and appointing a receiver of the proceeds of the sale of the asset as protective measures in support of substantive English proceedings, and the court made such orders as a matter of discretion. The Court of Appeal (Ward LJ, Lord Neuberger of Abbotsbury and Lawrence Collins LJ) upheld my determination.[70]

87. Seven year later, this was first done in the arbitration context in *Cruz City v Unitech & Ors*.[71] In that case, the High Court heard a dispute over enforcement of an arbitral award between a Mauritian claimant and an Indian defendant. As is common with international commercial contracts, neither of the parties had any operations or any other relationship to England or the United Kingdom but they had chosen English law as controlling, and they had an English arbitration clause in their contract with a London seat.

88. The judge noted "the clear policy of English law that judgments of the English court and English arbitration awards should be complied with and, if necessary, enforced"[72] and applied the principles set out

---

67. See https://www.thetimesbrief.co.uk/users/39175-the-brief-team/posts/32997-paris-fails-to-capitalise-on-brexit-in-battle-for-arbitration-crown?utm_source=newsletter&utm_campaign=newsletter_121&utm_medium=email&utm_content=121_10.05.18%20The%20Brief%20iPhone%20justice%20(1)&CMP=TNLEmail_118918_3304732_121.
68. Arbitration Act 1996, s. 103.
69. [2007] EWHC 3010 (Comm).
70. [2008] EWCA Civ 303.
71. [2014] EWHC 3131 (Comm).
72. [2014] EWHC 3131 (Comm) at [47].

in *Masri*.[73] He held that it was appropriate to appoint receivers over the foreign defendant's assets pursuant to the provisions of s.37 of the Senior Courts Act 1981 in order to enforce the English arbitration award.

89. While this judgment did not reach the Court of Appeal, I considered an earlier connected permission application in that court,[74] in which I exercised my discretion under CPR r.52.9(1)(c) to make an order for a payment to be made into court in the full amount of the judgment debt awarded in arbitration proceedings, as a condition of the grant of permission to Unitech to appeal against a post-judgment order for disclosure of assets. This was in line with the earlier stated clear policy.

(2) Optimism

90. If we look at the London Court of International Arbitration, parties continue to come from all around the world. There remains a broad geographic spread, with over 80% originating from outside the UK.[75] People continue to overwhelmingly choose English law and a London seat because of its proven neutrality and impartiality. They appreciate the responsiveness of English arbitration law and the courts. I do not expect this trend to change.

(3) Diversity

There was a record increase in the number of female arbitrators that were appointed. The LCIA continued to be a leader in gender diversity and its example of publishing detailed information about the gender diversity of its appointees is to be commended. In 2017, its gender diversity figures improved once again, with women being appointed 24% of the time.[76]

91. While in the past, these increases have mostly been attributed to the LCIA selecting a larger proportion of women, some of the 2017 increase can actually be traced to parties showing a demonstrable improvement in the rate at which they chose women: from 4% in 2016 to 17% in 2017. It is the LCIA, however, which continues to lead the charge: selecting women 34% of the time in 2017.[77]

---

73. [2008] EWCA Civ 303.
74. [2013] EWCA Civ 1512
75. London Court of International Arbitration Casework Report, 10 April 2018: http://www.lcia.org/News/lcia-releases-2017-casework-report.aspx.
76. London Court of International Arbitration Casework Report, 10 April 2018: http://www.lcia.org/News/lcia-releases-2017-casework-report.aspx.
77. *Ibid.*

Conclusion

92. Drawing the threads together, I hope to have shown that there is much that is changing in the field of international arbitration. As lawyers, ethics must be at the core of all that we do, even when we are not in operating in a courtroom. The international nature of arbitration means conflicting duties can be challenging for those of us that operate in this sphere. In my view, the solution is not a binding code of ethics but a focus, early on in the appointment process, on parties, counsel and arbitrators agreeing on the applicable rules. With diversity, we all benefit from a wider base of expertise and talent. While there is much work to do, there is some small room for celebration when considering the progress that has been made quite recently. And Brexit. This jurisdiction continues to be the best place for international parties to arbitrate and I do not expect the decision of the 51% to change that.

93. At this point, I would love for Bob Dylan to start playing in the background but perhaps it is more appropriate for me to take some questions.

CHARTERED INSTITUTE OF ARBITRATORS
THE 2019 ROEBUCK LECTURE, 14 JUNE 2019

Professor Stavros Brekoulakis[*]

[*Editorial note*: This contribution originally appeared at (2020) 86(1) *Arbitration* 97–103 and is reproduced in this volume by kind permission of the publisher. This speech won the 2020 *Global Arbitration Review* Award for Best Public Speech.]

I am both delighted and honoured to have been asked to give the Roebuck Lecture this year. I am delighted because, as the Editor of the Institute's Academic Journal, I have witnessed all these years the Institute's remarkable work in educating new generations of arbitration lawyers around the world, as well as the Institute's important contribution to the public discourse and scholarship of international arbitration. I very much hope that the Lecture tonight will further contribute to the educational and academic legacy of the Institute.

And I am honoured because the lecture I was asked to give tonight is named after a man who I deeply admire for his outstanding work as a former Editor of the Institute's Journal and as the single most important legal historian in the field of English arbitration.

It is thus mainly in an homage to Professor Roebuck's work that I have chosen to talk tonight about the historical development of the policy in English law favouring arbitration.

Today, it is generally accepted that English law and courts favour arbitration as a matter of policy. However, the prevailing narrative in legal literature suggests that this pro-arbitration policy of English law only developed as recently as in the last 40 years, and especially after the introduction of the 1996 Act.

It is thus argued that English courts in the 17th, 18th and 19th centuries were generally suspicious of, if not hostile to, arbitration. Relying on a limited number of cases and Lord Campbell's observation in *Scott v Avery* (1856) that English judges traditionally 'had great jealousy of arbitrators', a number of commentators have argued that the rise of the common law during the 17th and the 18th centuries entailed that common law courts felt empowered to curtail the scope and powers of arbitration, which was largely seen as a threat to their authority and an unwarranted substitution of court litigation.

* Stavros Brekoulakis is a Professor in International Arbitration, the Director of the School of International Arbitration at Queen Mary University of London and an arbitrator at 3 Verulam Buildings (Gray's Inn). He is the Editor-in-Chief of *Arbitration*.

Tonight, I will argue, contrary to the common belief, that English judicial attitudes in the 18th and 19th centuries never reflected a hostility, or a broader ideological opposition, to the idea of arbitration. And I will offer, arguably for the first time, an account of English arbitration as a dispute resolution system which originally emerged *as being part of, rather than antagonistic to*, the English courts system. To highlight the unique and privileged treatment of arbitration by English courts and English law, I will conclude by comparing the English approach to contrasting historical experiences from other jurisdictions, notably France, the United States and Germany.

One may ask, why does it matter tonight to look back at the history of arbitration law in England? Well, understanding the history of arbitration's development in England is important not only for historical purposes and to honour Professor Roebuck's work. It is also important because it provides helpful insights into current debates surrounding the legitimacy and potential reform of English arbitration law. More importantly, understanding the unique historical treatment of arbitration can bring about a strong positive message about the future of English arbitration law and practice in the post-Brexit era.

Let me first start by offering the broader historical picture of arbitration practice at the end of 17th century, and at the time that the first arbitration statute was introduced in England. To understand how a statutory policy for arbitration was developed, it is important to first understand how arbitration was perceived and practised by merchants at the time. Indeed, already from the 17th and the 18th centuries, the majority of merchants were typically agreeing both in writing and orally to submit their disputes to arbitration under the common law prior to a court lawsuit. Historical records show that standard forms of contract in certain lines of trade, notably in the field of construction and insurance, included arbitration agreements as the default option. Ninety surviving building agreements between 1720 and 1730 for the Grosvenor Estate in Mayfair required that any dispute between builders be submitted to three arbitrators, who were typically architects, surveyors and craftsmen.

Further, there are numerous historical accounts of individuals working as busy arbitrators and mediators, commissioned not only by private parties but also by the courts, the government and even the Palace, throughout the 17th and 18th centuries. Nathaniel Bacon, for example, the older half-brother of the more famous Francis was a very popular arbitrator, sitting in two or three arbitrations every month (and I am saying that with some degree of envy).

There are several reasons that explain the preference of arbitration to common law courts. First, arbitration was favoured by merchants for being cheaper and quicker than litigation. We all know that and often claim that arbitration is still cheap and quick today, but if we look at the practice of arbitration in the Early Modern Era, we may want to consider what we claim for today. For a start, parties usually dealt with the arbitration without legal counsel, who was required only for complex disputes referred to arbitration by equity courts. Also, arbitrators, at least before the 18th century, were not paid for their services, which were considered akin to public service. Indeed, the role of arbitrator was considered an honourable distinction for prominent men known for their sense of fairness and justice (and they were invariably men, as few historical examples of women acting as arbitrators exist). Popular arbitrators only decided to make arbitration part of their business when the number of arbitration references significantly increased at the end of the 18th century, and even then, they were charging modestly. As regards speed, in an observation that would probably embarrass many arbitrators today, arbitrators generally delivered their decisions on the same day as the hearing, with the longest hearings lasting no more than a few days.

Secondly, arbitration had a broader jurisdictional scope than courts and was therefore more suitable for cross-regional and international disputes. Because of their consensual nature, arbitration tribunals could assume jurisdiction over disputes between merchants from different regions and or even different states, including foreign merchants who were not subject to the jurisdiction of common law courts. The idea of private international law that would allow a national court to assume jurisdiction over a dispute involving a foreigner was alien at the time. Tribunals had no such problem.

Further, and more decisively, arbitration was <u>trusted</u> more than English courts because it operated as a community-based dispute settlement process. Unresolved disagreements were perceived as a threat to the social structure of a community and could potentially lead men to abandon reason and resort to violence. Thus, there was a strong sense of duty within the community, underpinned by ethical Christian values at the time, to assist their members to settle their disputes outside courts in an amicable way. Individuals who were frequently requested to act as arbitrators were prominent members of the local community, often including friends, neighbours and kinsmen, who had the advantage of knowing the disputing parties and often the history of the dispute.

The concept of arbitration as a means to promote peace explains why arbitrators in the 17th and 18th centuries were inclined not to declare a clear winner and leave a demoralised loser, but to arrive at a compromise which would be acceptable to all stakeholders in the dispute. Honour was traditionally of great importance to dispute resolution in England. A compromise would permit the losing party to save face and engage again with the winning party in a commercial relationship. While today arbitrators are often criticised when they reach a compromise decision on the ground that 'splitting the baby' is essentially a questionable attempt on the part of the arbitrators to appease both parties because they are paying their fees, arriving at a compromised decision that could bring about broad consensus was originally considered a distinct advantage of arbitration and a manifestation of justice.

Even further, merchants were keen to have their disputes resolved by arbitrators because they tended to apply the laws and practices of the market, which were familiar to the merchants, rather than to apply the common law which was generally alien to them (remember merchants would typically appear before tribunals without a legal expert or counsel). Relatedly, arbitrators were also willing to consider the broader context of disputes. Unlike courts, which tended to focus on a single legal point of dispute, which might merely be symptomatic of a deeper conflict between the disputing merchants, arbitration allowed parties to ventilate all their grievances. This broader approach to dispute resolution offered better prospects for arbitration to achieve an overall and lasting settlement of disputes compared with court judgments.

Overall, from the 17th century there was a broad realization among English merchants of the time that arbitration could achieve more than the law. This observation can explain why, by the end of the 17th century, Parliament was keen to enact for the first time in the history legislation on arbitration and turn this commercial practice into statutory policy.

I will now turn to discuss this statutory policy in more detail.

Until late in the 17th century, there were two main types of arbitration. First, parties would agree, orally or in writing, to submit an existing dispute to arbitration under the common law before they could bring a lawsuit in court. This type of arbitration was called 'submission' under the common law. Secondly, there were disputes that were referred to arbitration by English courts or other judicial authorities. Often, when a party was bringing a mercantile dispute to common law courts, English courts would issue a rule referring the dispute to arbitration, on the basis that arbitrators were better equipped to decide complex commercial disputes. This type of arbitration was called 'reference'.

However, both submissions and references exhibited important limitations.

Submissions, despite their great popularity, offered weak legal protection in two important respects: first, agreements to submit to arbitration were revocable at will by either party at any time until the issuance of the award. Indeed, there are historical accounts of parties who issued a self-executing deed of revocation of an arbitration agreement after the hearing and just a couple of days before arbitrators were about to render their award.

Second, the decisions of arbitrators were not enforceable. The losing party could simply elect not to comply with them. To address these two problems, parties in the 17th and 18th centuries would usually enter into an arbitration bond, which allowed a party to bring a lawsuit before courts and secure compliance with an arbitration agreement in the event of revocation, and to enforce the decision of arbitrators in the event of non-compliance. These remedies, however, meant that the aggrieved party had to sustain all the expenses and delays associated with litigation to achieve enforcement of arbitration agreements and awards.

By contrast, in references, the compliance of the parties with both the reference to arbitration and the arbitrators' decision was secured through the courts' power to punish for contempt because the final award was eventually filed as a court judgement. However, even with references, parties were wasting considerable time and expense in initially submitting their dispute to the courts hoping that they would end up in a tribunal. Decisively too, the parties could never be certain whether a judge would indeed agree to refer their dispute to arbitration, as such a decision remained at the discretion of the courts.

Overall, at the time, neither submissions nor references were offering commercial parties an effective means to go to arbitration.

In response, Parliament enacted, in 1698, the first Arbitration statute in the world, marking a significant moment of evolution for English arbitration. The Act is often referred to as the Locke Act, because it was single-handedly drafted by John Locke, after the London Board of Trade commissioned him to "draw up a scheme of some method of determining differences between merchants by referees, that might be decisive without appeal". Locke, who was familiar with arbitration, drafted a bill which introduced a policy favouring arbitration by expressly stating that a legal mechanism for the protection of arbitration agreements was necessary "for promoting Trade and rendering the Awards of Arbitrators the more effectual in all Cases". Under the Act, private parties could use the Court's contempt powers to enforce their submissions, without having to commence court litigation in the first place. The Act was a masterstroke which introduced a third type of arbitration (statutory arbitration) which combined the good parts of both references and submissions, without their limitations. The Act lent significant impetus to statutory arbitration, so that the number of cases being conducted under it increased tenfold between 1715 and 1785.

A statutory policy favouring arbitration was thus introduced in English law there and then. A series of subsequent arbitration acts further developed the policy with a number of significant advancements. For example, the 1854 Act set out, for the first time, statutory powers to refer the parties to arbitration for any dispute falling under an arbitration agreement. The 1889 Act made arbitration agreements irrevocable and offered statutory protection to arbitration agreements for both existing and, crucially, future disputes. In the 20th century, the 1950 Act accorded arbitrators the power to grant interim relief, while the 1979 Act gave parties the significant power to agree, if they wished, to exclude arbitration awards from judicial review for errors of law. And, of course, the current 1996 Act made it even harder for parties to challenge an arbitration award before English courts.

Overall, since the 17th century, the Parliament has been consistently enacting legislation that has given effect to a clear policy favouring arbitration as a means of promoting business.

Having discussed the position of English statutory law towards arbitration, I will now turn to discuss the position of the English courts under the common law towards arbitration.

Admittedly here, under the common law, the policy favouring arbitration matured much later than that under statutory law. Even after the introduction of the Locke Act, many merchants continued to submit their disputes to arbitration under the common law rather than under the Act. However, an arbitration agreement that was outside the protective scope of the Act was still revocable at will under the common law because of the legal principle that a private agreement 'could never oust' the jurisdiction of English courts. It was not until 1856 and the House of Lords' decision in *Scott v Avery* that the attitude of English common law courts towards enforceability of arbitration agreements would change.

But while a policy favouring the enforcement of arbitration agreement developed much later under the common law, this does not entail that common law courts in early modern England and until the mid-20th century were collectively and as a matter of general approach antagonistic to arbitration as the prevailing narrative in literature suggests. Claims for judicial hostility of common law courts towards arbitration are exaggerated, if not altogether inaccurate.

Indeed, arbitration, in the 17th and 18th centuries, was not conceived as an extrajudicial mode that was a substitute for English courts, as the prevailing narrative assumes. In fact, arbitration was often operating as part of the English judicial system. Indeed, English courts or other judicial authorities, including the Chancellor and the Council, were habitually referring a great number of disputes, both mercantile and non-mercantile, to arbitration throughout the 17th and 18th centuries. While Lord Mansfield, the Chief Justice at the time, had a strong reputation as a skilled judge of complex commercial disputes, he actively encouraged settlement of disputes by arbitration and typically referred cases to be decided by distinguished commercial lawyers of the time, such as James Burrow and Thomas Lowten. The fact that English courts frequently made use of the commercial expertise of arbitrators suggests that in the eyes of the judiciary, arbitration was not perceived as an outsider or a potential competitor. Rather, arbitration traditionally was seen as an ancillary to the judiciary in England.

So, if claims for judicial hostility are mistaken, what then describes the attitude of English common law courts towards arbitration? To answer this question, I will now turn to the next and final part of the lecture where I will offer a general appraisal of the historical treatment of arbitration in England and compare this with historical experiences from other jurisdictions.

In my view the historical attitude of English courts towards arbitration can be more accurately described as one of cautious trust.

The trust part was informed by two considerations.

First, the traditional respect of English courts and the common law for party autonomy. Valuing the idea that merchants should be presumed to know best how to organise their affairs and resolve their disputes, English courts were historically keen to give effect to private dispute resolution arrangements by commercial parties.

The second consideration is English courts' typical pragmatism which meant that they viewed arbitration as a potentially useful dispute resolution method that could alleviate the burden of their own heavy caseload. It is estimated, for example, that in early modern England an average of about 60,000 lawsuits were brought every year before the central courts of King's Bench, Common Pleas, Chancery and Exchequer. In addition, around 400,000 lawsuits were brought annually in urban courts, and another 500,000 in the small courts in the countryside. This is close to a million of annual lawsuits for a population which at the time was estimated to be between 4 and 5 million. English courts, in the 16th and 17th centuries, found it difficult to cope with the litigious culture of the time, and references to arbitration were seen as a helpful and welcome development.

The cautious part was explained by the fact that arbitration agreements were freely revocable by the parties at will, and this legal principle remained part of the common law until the 19th century. But how can we explain the persisting appeal of the rule of revocability until so late? As I suggested above, for English courts at the time arbitration was seen as a dispute resolution method that was ancillary to but could never be a *substitute* for the courts of law. Thus, an arbitration agreement could never be valid, as a private agreement that purports to substitute English courts and confer judicial powers to a panel of arbitrators. Rather, arbitration agreements at the time were seen more as *agency agreements* conferring powers to arbitrators who were acting as agents for the disputing parties and with a mandate to determine their rights and liabilities. Such agency agreements were valid under the common law, however, and, like any agency agreement, they had to be freely revocable upon notice.

It can be thus understood that the main objection of the English courts to the binding force of arbitration agreements was essentially a doctrinal one

which was eventually addressed by the House of Lords in *Scott v Avery*;
it was not an ideological objection against arbitration or an objection as a
matter of legal policy.

The judicial and legislative treatment of arbitration in England should be
contrasted, for example, with the position in other countries where judicial
attitudes in certain times in the 18th, 19th and (even in) the 20th century
reflected a fundamental, often ideological, opposition to arbitration which
was largely seen as a private, and therefore suspicious, mode of dispute
resolution that was lacking the necessary safeguards for the protection of
the public interest.

In France, for example, after the French Revolution, arbitration was
considered a threat to the rule of law and the authority of the revolutionary
state. Napoleon was also apparently suspicious of the idea of arbitration
and his Procedure Code imposed a number of important restrictions on
arbitration agreements and the arbitration process, which as one commentator notes, "reflected a hatred of arbitration agreements and provided
evidence of a secret desire to eliminate their existence". French courts
often considered arbitration as necessarily inferior, with the French Cour
de cassation (the highest court in France) observing in the mid-19th century
that "one does not find with an arbitrator the same qualities that it is assured
to find with a judge, namely the probity, the impartiality, the skillfulness,
[and] the sensitivity of feelings necessary to render a decision".

A similar opposition to the main idea of arbitration was exhibited by
the US courts during the 18th and 19th centuries. The mistrust of arbitration and arbitrators was summarised by Joseph Story (the celebrated US
Supreme Court Justice) who observed that

"We all know that arbitrators at common law ... are not ordinarily well
enough acquainted with the principles of law or equity to administer complicated cases; At all events courts of justice are presumed to be better
capable of administering and enforcing the rights of the parties and have
superior knowledge than any mere private arbitrators".

Because of this ideological opposition to arbitration, arbitration
agreements for future disputes were considered in the 19th century and at
the beginning of the 20th century as being against US public policy and
arbitrators' authority was largely curtailed.

In one of my favourite quotes, the US Second Circuit as recently as in
the 1960s noted that as "Issues of war and peace are too important to be
vested in the generals ... decisions as to antitrust regulation of business are
too important to be lodged in arbitrators."

Equally, while historically commercial arbitration was commonly used
by merchants in what today is Germany, German courts and commentary
developed an acute mistrust for arbitration after the rise of the National
Socialists in the 1930s, systematically curtailing the use of arbitration as

a matter of policy, so that no municipal authority was allowed to submit to arbitration. As commentators have observed, "to the regime of the time, with its doctrine of the all-encompassing power of the state, arbitration was seen as a suspicious attempt of private individuals to free an important part of their activities from the dominating force of the government".

To a large extent, of course, hostile attitudes to arbitration in these jurisdictions can be explained by some exceptional historical and constitutional circumstances, particularly in France and in Germany, which had a profound effect on the role of the state under Napoleon and the National Socialists.

By contrast, parliamentary sovereignty in England was largely established in the 18th century and, as a result, English courts had fewer reasons to perceive arbitration as a challenge to the authority of the state law and courts. Thus, the largely doctrinal objection of the English courts against arbitration agreements was very different from the broad concern that arbitration, as a private mode of dispute resolution, is a potential threat to the state and the public interest, as is suggested by the French, American and German experience.

So, why does it matter to challenge the prevailing narrative about the traditional hostility of English courts and law to arbitration?

As I mentioned at the outset, it matters for several reasons. First, it matters because it provides helpful insights into current debates surrounding the legitimacy of arbitration and calls for a potential reform of English arbitration law.

A wide range of scholars currently criticise arbitration as being part of a broader project of neoliberalism to serve private interests, and in particular the interests of powerful corporations. It is thus argued that the legal policy favouring arbitration, which means that arbitral awards cannot generally be reviewed by national courts on a question of law, should be curtailed, or altogether abolished, because it is "part of a corporate strategy to enable private parties to operate in the shadow of the law".

To support this view, some commentators argue that historically arbitration was largely curtailed rather than supported by national courts in England. According to this account, it is only recently, when the rise of capitalism in the second part of the 20th century challenged the authority of states to regulate their affairs, that a policy favouring arbitration was developed to further erode the power of the state and state judiciaries.

However, such suggestions are premised on two questionable ideas. First, that arbitration is and has always been antagonistic to national courts and state institutions and, second, that a policy favouring arbitration is a recent development of the 20th century. As this lecture hopefully demonstrated, associating support for arbitration with the rise of capitalism in the second part of the 20th century is historically questionable, at least in England. The preference for arbitration was not the result of a sudden change in the policy of English law and courts that occurred at in the last 50 years. As explained, a clear policy favouring arbitration has been embedded in statutory law from as early as the end of the 17th century, and was subsequently adopted by the common law in the 19th century. Importantly, the pro-arbitration policy in English law was not driven by the ideological forces of capitalism aiming to erode the powers and interests of the state; rather, the policy favouring arbitration was implemented in the 17th century simply to protect a sound commercial practice which was widely shared by merchants for its distinct advantages over litigation.

Further, success of arbitration is not symptomatic of weak state authority and state institutions. Arbitration in England did not historically emerge to challenge the state courts. Rather, as explained, arbitration in England developed as part of the court system and was largely viewed as a trusted supplement, rather than a substitute, for the courts. While some concerns about the boundaries of private justice are sound and must be addressed when it comes to the field of investment treaty arbitration, calls for an indiscriminate abolition of the policy favouring arbitration represent a split from a long tradition in English law and are premised on a crude and historically unsupported account of arbitration as antagonistic to the judiciary and the state. Such views are erroneous and should be challenged.

But an accurate historical account of the legal treatment of arbitration matters today beyond the debate about the legitimacy of private justice. This is because the positive account I offered brings about the realization that the policy favouring arbitration is historically embedded in English law and English courts. And, at least for me, as we are all painfully entering the unknown and possibly uncertain times of the Post-Brexit era, this realization gives me great cause for optimism about the future of arbitration in England.

Thank you for your attention.

CHARTERED INSTITUTE OF ARBITRATORS
THE 2020 ROEBUCK LECTURE, 11 JUNE 2020

GETTING AHEAD OF THE CURVE: HOW ARBITRATION CAN BETTER MEET THE NEEDS OF PARTIES, PEOPLE AND PLANET

Cherie Blair CBE, QC MCIArb[*]

[Editorial note. This lecture is published here by kind permission of the Chartered Institute of Arbitrators.]

Colleagues, friends and fellow members of the arbitration community,

It is a great privilege to have been invited to give today's lecture. It is particularly poignant to give the tenth Roebuck Lecture after Derek sadly passed away in April, and I am grateful to Catherine for her beautiful words in his memory.

When I was asked to pick a title back in February, I could scarcely have anticipated quite how apt my theme would be for today's much-changed world.

Who would have thought that the Roebuck lecture would be live-streamed to an audience of over 1,700 people around the world? Many of you will be listening from the comfort of your homes, hopefully without a tie, jacket or high-heeled shoe in sight, and can ask me questions without having to face international travel or – even more painful – London traffic.

The arbitration community has long reflected on how to adapt to better meet the needs of the parties, and address growing concern about imbalances in the protections given to people and our environment. But we know that lawyers – yes even international arbitration lawyers – are slow to instigate and accept change. That's why COVID-19, for all its appalling devastation, might just spur positive evolution by forcing us to adjust our processes and priorities – necessity being the mother of invention.

Already, we are doing things that before we only spoke about doing. And we are doing them pretty well.

Tonight my message is: we should embrace the opportunity to adapt. We should challenge customary processes and received wisdom, we should re-consecrate our principles and we should put integrity at the heart of our ambitions.

* * *

And after such vaulting rhetoric, where better to begin than the enemy of the air-mile: virtual meetings and hearings.

One of the great advantages of arbitration is the ability to respond to the needs of the parties. In the last few months, we have seen that in action.

* Cherie Blair is a barrister, arbitrator and mediator. She is Founder and Chair of Omnia Strategy LLP and Founder of the international Cherie Blair Foundation for Women.

Today's technology enables us to conference with our clients, attend virtual settlement meetings with counterparties, and conduct entire hearings via the ubiquitous Zoom. To achieve such a dramatic shift would have been unthinkable even three months ago. Of course, we had the technology and we even used it sometimes – but certainly not in such a wholesale manner. Some condemn lawyers as Luddites, but we have been forced to suck it and see, and we have seen that is not too bad.

Showing commendable leadership, CIArb was quick to react and issued its *Guidance Note on Remote Dispute Resolution Proceedings* on 8 April 2020, urging: "business should not be burdened by unresolved disputes due to the inability of parties to meet physically to resolve disputes". The note offers practical advice on how proceedings can continue remotely, but also how to proactively and positively adapt for the long-term.

Similarly, the ICC issued a *Guidance Note on Possible Measures aimed at Mitigating the Effects of the COVID-19 Pandemic*, and the Stockholm Chamber of Commerce together with Thompson Reuters is offering their online SCC Platform for free to ad hoc arbitrations registered by 31 December.

On 16 April, 13 arbitral institutions issued a joint statement in a show of willingness to work together affirming that:

"By jointly enabling international arbitration to deliver some degree of certainty in a volatile economic climate, we seek to jointly contribute to a world better prepared to meet the challenges of the post-corona crisis".

This international co-operation is admirable.

What can we learn from these developments? That the arbitration community can change and adapt quickly, to help protect and enhance the effectiveness and efficiency of the arbitral process. I hope this spirit of co-operation and willingness to change will endure long after lockdown has ended and penetrate other areas of arbitral practice.

Of course, we still need to have in-person meetings, and certain cross-examinations are more effective face-to-face. But we have learned a few things:

1.   *First*, we don't need to travel quite as much. This will allow us to have more quality time for our clients (and our families). Busy arbitrators will be able to finalise awards more quickly.

2.   *Second*, certain parts of the arbitral process can be streamlined and expedited when we put our minds to it. Parties and arbitrators should think more about whether in-person hearings are required. Can it be done via video conferencing? Or can certain parts of the process be done on a doc-ument-only basis? Counsel and parties might even be willing to move to a more continental, less adversarial style of advocacy in some cases. Clients might sometimes forego the brilliant QC performance if it helps secure a speedy decision.

3. *Third*, institutions can work together where it makes sense for them to do so. Collaboration rather than competition can benefit arbitration as a whole.

4. *Fourth*, we can save our clients some expense in the process. The rising cost of arbitration is one of the threats to the system. In many cases, it is now the preserve of the elites – unless you have a case that appeals to litigation funders. Commercial and State parties alike are finding the costs prohibitive.

Omnia Strategy recently provided strategic assistance to the Government of the Gambia in an investor-State arbitration using the International Development Law Organization's Investment Support Programme for Least Developed Countries. Without securing that financial support, one of the poorest countries in Africa would have struggled to fund the expert evidence it needed to defend a claim.

5. *Fifth*, jaw jaw is better than war war, as Churchill once said. In April, the British Institute of International and Comparative Law (BIICL) published a concept note discussing the effects of COVID-19 on commercial contracts, suggesting that encouraging parties to negotiate or conciliate rather than focusing on enforcing strict contractual rights could ensure better long term outcomes for the global economy. There is no clear evidence yet that we have seen more settlements of disputes over the last couple of months, but this would be a logical result. Those facing economic hardship are likely to want to find cheaper and faster ways of resolving their disputes. The note also refers to the need to bring "breathing space" to allow for the continuance of a viable contract rather than bringing it to an abrupt end, and suggests the law should be slow to find such conduct amounts to a waiver of rights.

Let's harness this willingness for change and focus on delivering an efficient process to the users of arbitration, even when the COVID-19 crisis is behind us.

* * *

Having touched on some ways that arbitration can better meet the needs of parties, let's turn to less well-trodden territory: its impact on people and the planet.

Proper consideration of human rights and sustainability was once an esoteric exercise – essentially the preserve of the odd philosopher or lawyer. Sometimes the very odd ones.

Today, these issues are fast-establishing a *lingua franca* for business, investment, sustainable development and policy-making.

For our clients – governments, corporates, investors and beyond – this means that leadership and management at all levels need to be conversant not just in "ROI", "P&L" and "KPIs", but also in "ESG": environmental, social and governance concerns.

And if our clients are becoming fluent in this new values-based terminology, then any lawyer worth their salt needs to be just as familiar. And yet, lawyers – and indeed the system of arbitration itself – have been slower on the uptake.

This is not just semantics or value-signalling. ESG data and rankings are starting to shape States' policies and investors' business decisions.

An upwards trend of shareholder activism, civil society campaigning and public and employee disquiet has reinforced the growing importance of these issues to investors and business leaders.

The international policy and regulatory landscape has also evolved.

The UN-supported *Principles of Responsible Investment* were launched in 2006 and now have almost 2,500 signatories representing some 80 trillion US dollars under management.

The UN *Sustainable Development Goals* helped to galvanise, broaden and organise the movement. Expect to hear even more about the SDGs as we approach the 2030 target for the goals to be achieved.

But it is the *UN Guiding Principles on Business and Human Rights* that are widely regarded as having established a modern authoritative global standard on human rights and, indirectly, environmental protection.

Endorsed unanimously by the UN Human Rights Council in 2011, the "UNGPs" set out a three-pillar framework:

- the *State duty to protect* human rights,

- the *business responsibility to respect* human rights, and

- importantly, the principle that victims of business-related human rights abuse should have *access to effective remedies*.

More and more we are seeing this non-binding guidance crystallising into "hard law".

The UK Modern Slavery Act, with its requirement that business executives sign-off statements on steps taken to combat modern slavery, got boardrooms engaged. Last year, the independent review of the Act recommended that an enforcement body should be empowered to impose sanctions for non-compliance.

The French Duty of Vigilance Law requires companies to map their human rights, health and safety and environmental risks, and to have a plan to address them. The law instantly led to high-profile litigation before the French courts.

Lastly, the EU is proposing by 2021 to require businesses to carry out human rights and environmental due diligence. Justice Commissioner Didier Reynders announced the initiative in April and raised the prospect of sanctions, saying "a regulation without sanctions is not a regulation". Just this week, Commissioner Reynders reaffirmed his strong commitment to this initiative – as did the German Government, which assumes the Presidency of the Council of the EU on the 1st July.

COVID-19 has added further impetus to the EU proposal by highlighting concerns about environmental risks, social inequalities and increased legal risks, with States and employers now bracing themselves for a slew of claims.

* * *

There is a clear role for international arbitration in resolving human rights disputes whether arising out of contracts or under treaties. Arbitrators and counsel will, I am sure, rise to the challenge of grappling with these important questions in the context of changing social expectations.

We see this most clearly in Investor-State Dispute Settlement (ISDS) – once an elite backwater and now the centre of significant debate.

The current pandemic has bolstered calls for ISDS to be reformed or even scrapped. Last month, the Columbia Center for Sustainable Investment called for an immediate moratorium on all investment treaty arbitrations and a permanent restriction on all arbitration claims related to measures taken to address the pandemic. Civil society groups are calling on States to terminate investment agreements that provide for ISDS.

Leaving aside practical difficulties around implementation, this reflects a growing trend of questioning whether the unique privileges given to investors are necessary to facilitate international trade.

Bluntly, ISDS has been suffering bad press for some time. You will probably recall the last major flare-up over the Obama Transatlantic Trade and Investment Partnership (TTIP) plans.

ISDS ensures foreign investors enjoy protection against arbitrary government measures affecting their investment. There are myriad examples of confiscatory, unreasonable and – frankly – corrupt decisions by States whose own judicial systems are not robust enough to withstand direct or indirect interference from those with power.

Leaving foreign investors unprotected would not only affect narrow corporate interests. It would also have crippling effects on global supply chains, the wider economy, and local communities.

At its best, foreign direct investment facilitates access to international markets, infrastructural development, transfers knowledge and skills and contributes to sustainable development, bringing fundamental necessities such as electricity and water to various countries. At its worst, it can encourage predatory exploitation of a country's precious resources and limit States' ability to undertake legitimate policy initiatives.

The ISDS system was not conceived to be one-sided in favour of investors. However, its evolution has been perceived as doing just that: embracing the narrow interests of claimant investors at the expense of people and planet. There is a danger that this perception could lead to

ISDS being swept aside in the stampede to find an elusive better way. We see this most clearly in Europe, in relation to both the Comprehensive and Economic Trade Agreement (CETA) and intra-EU Bilateral investment treaties (BITs).

But the perception ignores the reality of further changes already underway, even if more needs to be done.

ISDS already recognises the State's right to regulate in the public interest. The notorious Philip Morris arbitration provoked an outcry not least in the European Parliament a few years ago.

Ultimately, of course, those claims did not succeed against Australia or Uruguay.

In the *Uruguay* case, for example, the tribunal dismissed all Philip Morris's claims, finding that a State is owed "substantial deference" when addressing major public health problems. Uruguay, it concluded, had acted in a coherent and well-motivated fashion to protect public health.

In the near future, States seeking to justify COVID-19-related measures could also rely on the defences under the law on State responsibility, such as force majeure, state of necessity, and distress. Yes, there are strict requirements for these defences to apply. But the COVID-19 crisis is unprecedented and I expect tribunals will consider such defences seriously as they balance public and investor interests.

We are also seeing more States bringing counterclaims against investors for business activities that have adverse human rights impacts, including environmental harm. In my view, this is entirely appropriate and reflects arbitration's in-built adaptability and its founding principle of reciprocity: finding new ways to establish jurisdiction and balance effectively the objectives and expectations of States and investors.

The ICSID case of *Urbaser v Argentina* (2016) illustrates the evolution in tribunals' approach to human rights. The claimant was a concession holder that in the early 2000s provided water and sewerage services in Buenos Aires. After Argentina's financial crisis in 2002, the State took emergency measures resulting in the termination of the claimant's concession in 2006. The claimant filed for arbitration with ICSID, alleging that Argentina had violated the BIT due to its obstruction and persistent neglect of the investor's interests.

Argentina raised a counterclaim against the claimant, claiming that the investor's failure to provide the necessary level of investment in the concession led to violations of the human right to water. In its defence, the claimant alleged that, as a non-State actor, it was not bound by human rights obligations. The tribunal rejected that argument and a further argument that the BIT conferred no obligations on the investor.

Instead, the tribunal established that, because corporations are subjects of international law, they can also bear obligations in international law. Further, the tribunal explicitly recognised that: "international law accepts corporate social responsibility as a standard of crucial importance for companies operating in the field of international commerce". In other words, the tribunal found that rules of international law, which include human rights, cannot be ignored when adjudicating claims arising from BITs.

While the tribunal ultimately rejected Argentina's counterclaim, this case represents a watershed moment in investor-State arbitration by accepting jurisdiction over a human rights counterclaim.

In recent years, tribunals have also addressed environmental counterclaims. For example, two parallel ICSID cases against Ecuador – *Burlington* and *Perenco* – concerned investments in oil blocks in the Ecuadorian Amazon region. Ecuador's environmental counterclaims were based on domestic environmental and law and contractual obligations. Both tribunals found that the investors were liable for the costs of restoring the environment in the areas where the oil blocks were located. The *Burlington* tribunal awarded Ecuador 41.5 million US dollars, and the *Perenco* tribunal awarded 54.5 million US dollars.

As the world belatedly reacts to the dangers posed by the climate emergency, we can expect new regulations from States taking steps to meet their Paris Agreement commitments. These may clear the path for new claims and counterclaims. At the very least, investors commencing their own investment treaty claims should be advised on the risks of having to defend their human rights and environmental record.

Critics of the ISDS system often point to the large sums awarded by certain tribunals to investors. The 2 billion US dollars awarded to Unión Fenosa Gas, a Spanish company, against Egypt, comes to mind.

Certainly, not all investors prevail and obtain amounts of this magnitude. According to UNCTAD, by the end of 2018, investors prevailed and were awarded damages in 29% of the cases. Nonetheless, tribunals should be cautious when presented with exorbitant claims for compensation.

Dismissing most of the multibillion claims for breaches of the law of the use of force and international humanitarian law during the Eritrean Ethiopian War of 1998 to 2000, the Eritrea-Ethiopia Claims Commission observed that claims of such magnitude raise: "serious questions involving the intersection of the law of State responsibility with fundamental human rights norms". As the Commission noted:

> "Huge awards of compensation by their nature would require large diversions of national resources from the paying country—and its citizens needing health care, education and other public services—to the recipient country".

Of course, the circumstances of that case were different and may not necessarily translate into investor-State arbitration. But still, tribunals should think carefully about whether large monetary awards are justified or not.

Large awards penalise a State for its behaviour – but ultimately it is the taxpayer and citizens who suffer the consequences. It is important for tribunals to consider the implications of awards and be as smart as possible when determining remedies.

Of course, the global pandemic will create new challenges for tribunals and experts, who will have to consider the effects of COVID-19 when developing the "but-for world" to quantify damages. Quantifying damages was a complex exercise even before COVID-19, when conditions were relatively stable. Post-COVID, one cannot assume that the but-for world will ever return to that scenario of stability.

Tribunals already have at their disposal certain tools to reduce damages in certain circumstances.

Tribunals can take into account an investor's failure to mitigate losses, as we saw in *EDF v Argentina*.

And an investor's contributory fault can reduce damages. While this may bring to mind extreme circumstances involving illegal activities by the investor, this principle is broader and encompasses imprudent and negligent conduct – see for example the 30% and 50% reductions in *Copper Mesa v Ecuador* and *MTD v Chile*, respectively.

Perhaps there could be a role for the bifurcation of quantum – a practice not common in investment arbitration but not foreign to international law. In *DRC v Uganda*, the International Court of Justice's 2005 judgment on the merits held both parties liable to make reparation for their breaches of international law and invited them to engage in settlement discussions on damages. Such an approach by investment tribunals could potentially expedite settlement.

Consistency in decision-making is fundamental to the legitimacy of ISDS. I suggest these are areas where coherent guidelines from tribunals could help the parties and the arbitration system generally.

* * *

Similarly, in commercial arbitration, the pressure for accountability and effective dispute resolution will naturally increase.

One can imagine why businesses may prefer to thrash out sensitive human rights arguments with commercial partners or their own people behind the closed doors of an arbitration rather than in open court.

Increasingly, lead companies' supplier agreements require adherence to a code of conduct or specific human rights norms. These might be supported – for example – by rights to inspect documents, audit premises and even terminate the relationship. Within the company itself, contracts with officers and employees might also demand compliance with policies, including – increasingly – the enterprise's human rights policy. Of course, these might be included principally for optics or as new ethical boilerplate, but that will not stop creative lawyers from using those clauses in a dispute scenario if relevant.

We can also expect tribunals to face more novel arguments and claims. Arbitrators will be asked to interpret contracts and assess conduct in the light of soft law and other human rights and sustainability guidance and best practices. Most obviously, the practical consequences of a company recognising its responsibility to respect human rights – or, more broadly, having obligations under international law – could certainly become a point of contention in an arbitral dispute.

Executives' handling of environmental risks will become not only a matter of contractual performance but also evidence of business judgment. Parties may claim that legal duties have expanded to encompass human rights and sustainability. After all, for how long can directors be said to be acting in the best interests of the company while also ignoring existential climate-related risks or enabling human rights violations?

Indeed, we have started to see such issues considered by apex courts. In February, in the case of *Nevsun Resources v Araya*, the Canadian Supreme Court ruled that a private, non-State actor may be held liable in Canada for its alleged breaches of international law abroad.

The US seems to be heading the opposite way over the Alien Tort Statute. Invigorated in 1991, when the Second Circuit allowed ATS claims based on modern human rights law in *Filartiga v Pena-Irala,* more recently in *Jesner* in 2018, the Supreme Court ruled – 5 to 4 – that foreign companies cannot be sued under the Act. After a filing by the US Department of Justice a fortnight ago, in *Cargill v Doe*, it seems likely the Supreme Court will soon reconsider whether corporations *generally* are similarly immune from ATS claims. Watch this space.

Closer to home, last year in *Vedanta*, the UK Supreme Court found that the English courts could hear a tort claim against a UK holding company and its Zambian subsidiary for alleged environmental damage in Zambia. Omnia acted for the interveners in that case. Three of the five justices from *Vedanta* will be in action again in a fortnight when the Supreme Court hears the appeal in *Okpabi v Shell*.

* * *

One of the most interesting developments has been led by the Permanent Court of Arbitration in The Hague, on the back of the so-called "Bangladesh Accord arbitrations" in 2016-2017.

In the aftermath of the collapse of the Rana Plaza building in Bangladesh in 2013, faced with public outcry and outrage, over 200 fashion brands and trade unions who operated in the area decided to sign a binding business and human rights agreement.

In October 2016, two labour unions, IndustriALL Global Union and UNI Global Union commenced arbitration proceedings against two unnamed fashions brands. They sought a declaration that the Respondents breached human rights guaranteed by the Accord, as well as a contribution to remediation costs.

We did not benefit from a new line of jurisprudence, as both cases settled. However, this development again showed the fascinating flexibility of the international arbitration system, and a procedural gateway to human rights claims by nationals against investors in different host States.

In 2017, the UN Working Group on Business and Human Rights proposed that arbitration should be used as a binding mechanism to resolve business and human rights disputes. In response, building on the PCA's experience in these cases, a team led by Judge Bruno Simma drafted the Hague Rules on Business and Human Rights Arbitration, which were launched in the Peace Palace on 12 December 2019. I have some familiarity with the process as Omnia provided input as a member of the drafting team's *Sounding Board* and one of our partners spoke at the launch.

The idea is that these specially designed arbitration rules, modelled on UNCITRAL rules, would then be applied by the existing arbitration institutions. The development is particularly impressive because it shows how the main features of international arbitration may be used to embrace new fields of law, not least bringing international enforceability to the sphere of human rights.

As you would expect, it will take time for the new Rules to become an established tool in the international arbitration toolkit. I suspect that B-to-B disputes and public procurement contracts provide the most likely first uses of the Rules, and it will be fascinating to watch and participate in this development.

You will also appreciate that the Rules themselves cannot overcome every hurdle. Indeed, they do not purport to do so – for example, as with other arbitration Rules, they are consent-based but are silent on how that consent should be established.

Also, notwithstanding careful drafting and consultation, inevitably there remain challenges that the parties and arbitrators will need to deal with. For example, around funding and equality of arms, confidentiality versus transparency, and the participation of victims of human rights abuses.

* * *

We have seen that commercial and legal pressures are starting to build pressure on firms to align their business activities with the human rights commitments they now espouse. This applies to the conduct of arbitration, where lawyers handling disputes will need to be versed in these important values and cultural factors as much as the legal contest in question.

This includes the proper and thoughtful use of technology – not just remote proceedings but also – I suspect – newer tools such as data mining, artificial intelligence and blockchain. These will help us achieve greater efficiencies and limit our environmental harms. But we must also be alive to human rights risks – from access to justice and equality of arms to unintended discriminatory effects.

Undoubtedly, we must also be more inclusive. Our arbitration community must better reflect our clients and society if we are to avoid group-think, benefit from a diversity of talents and perspectives, and foster greater trust in the system. I am certainly not the first person to advocate for diversity in arbitration. Dame Elizabeth Gloster stressed the importance of diversity in the 2018 edition of this lecture.

There are important initiatives to promote women within arbitration – and I am delighted that *ArbitralWomen* and *ERA* are among the sponsors of this lecture. Yet we must acknowledge there is still much for us to do on that front. To be genuinely inclusive we must also set our sights on pulling down other barriers – those concerning race, socio-economic background and age, to name just a handful. Building a more just system requires curiosity and honesty about systemic discrimination, and leadership in dismantling it.

I was pleased to see that yesterday ICCA published its first formal policy on diversity and inclusion, together with an implementation plan. ICCA President Lucy Reed said that "diversity and inclusion are never 'done'", just as CIArb's own Catherine Dixon pledged two days ago to continue to promote diversity, equality and inclusion and to review what more can be done to give practical effect to that commitment. These are words that should ring in our ears as each of us reflects on what more we can do.

And let me challenge you still further. In some instances, our clients might be best served if we depart from the standard "win at any costs" mindset, and embrace a more nuanced approach that reflects and advances the role of businesses as corporate citizens. It is not enough only to pay lip service to respecting human rights. Increasingly our clients recognise the imperative to embed that respect not only through their businesses and their supply chains, but also into the way they conduct their disputes. They will need our help in doing so.

What am I asking the arbitral community to take away from all of this? Let's harness the current energy and use the COVID-19 lockdown experience as a spur for further reform. Let's continue to work as a community to introduce new ways of working that protect the integrity of the arbitral process and make it relevant to future generations. Perhaps, if we lawyers fully embrace the ESG principles in the same way as we have embraced Zoom, we would all be operating in a better world.

Thank you very much.

INDEX

Compiled by Robert Morgan

Notes

Personal names appear in contributions only where they are of particular significance, and generally within subject references. For the same reason, the names of monarchs, presidents and other rulers, both ancient and modern, are generally avoided.

With regard to cases, statutes, treaties, model laws, other state instruments of governance and 'soft' law instruments referred to in the text and listed in the Index, all necessary citations are given in full in the footnotes to each contribution.

1. Court of Appeal's decision affirmed by
the UK Supreme Court, [2020] UKSC 48.

2. Replaced in 2011 by the Arbitration Ordinance (Cap 609).

---

3. Now the 2020 edition.